# HOW TO BE A CHILDREN'S BOOK ILLUSTRATOR

3dtotalPublishing

**3dtotal**Publishing

Correspondence: **publishing@3dtotal.com**
Website: **store.3dtotal.com**





First published in the United Kingdom, 2020, by 3dtotal Publishing.

Reprinted in 2025 by 3dtotal Publishing.

**Address:** 3dtotal.com Ltd, 29 Foregate Street, Worcester, WR1 1DS, United Kingdom.

**Hard cover ISBN:** 978-1-912843-19-0
Printed and bound in Shanghai, China, by KS Printing.

Visit store.3dtotal.com for a complete list of available book titles.

**Managing Director:** Tom Greenway
**Studio Manager:** Simon Morse
**Lead Designer:** Fiona Tarbet
**Lead Editor:** Samantha Rigby
**Editor:** Philippa Barker
**Designer:** Joseph Cartwright

MIX Paper from responsible sources FSC® C151298

**Cover images by individual artists as listed throughout this book**

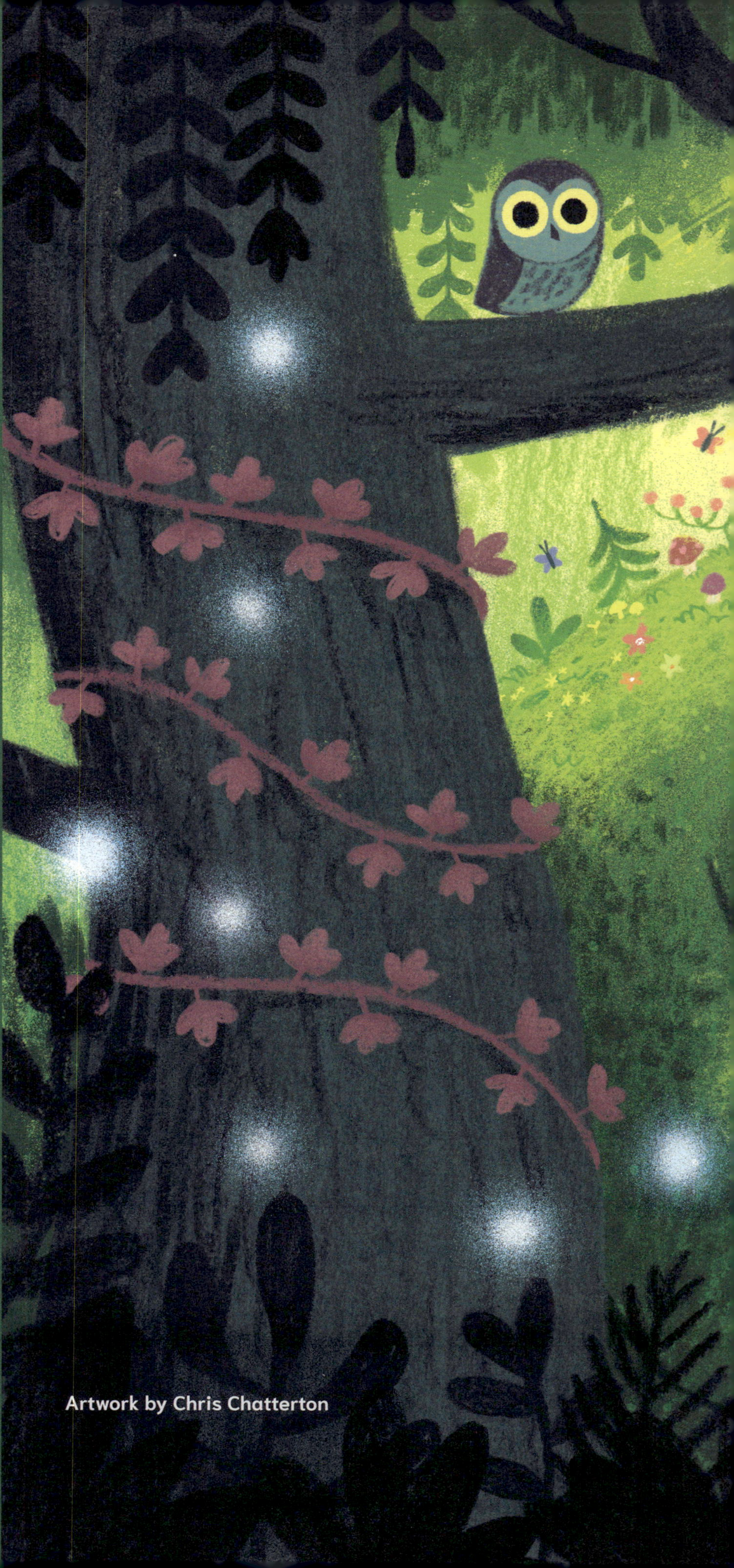

**Artwork by Chris Chatterton**

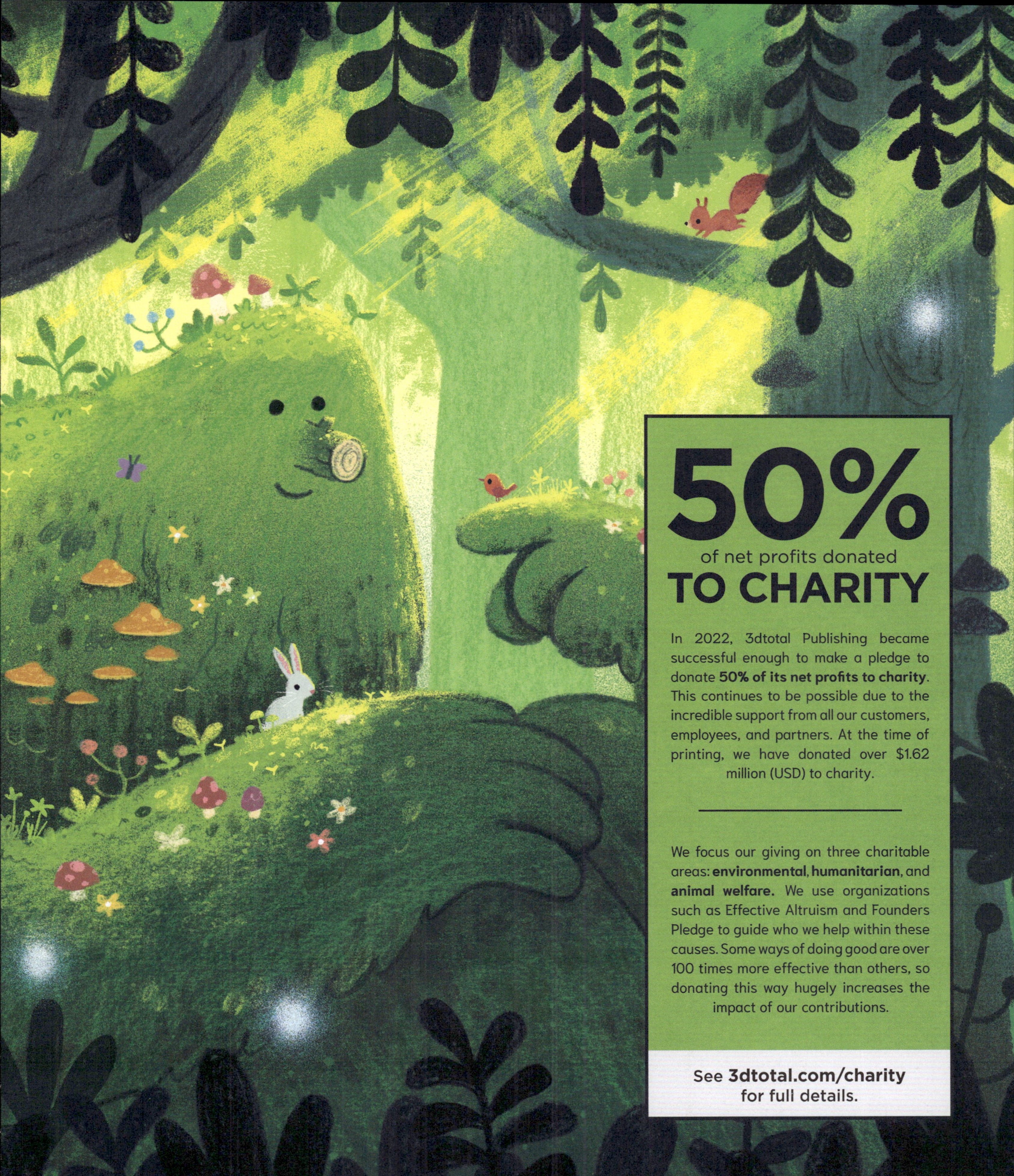
50%
of net profits donated
TO CHARITY
In 2022, 3dtotal Publishing became successful enough to make a pledge to donate **50% of its net profits to charity**. This continues to be possible due to the incredible support from all our customers, employees, and partners. At the time of printing, we have donated over $1.62 million (USD) to charity.
We focus our giving on three charitable areas: **environmental**, **humanitarian**, and **animal welfare.** We use organizations such as Effective Altruism and Founders Pledge to guide who we help within these causes. Some ways of doing good are over 100 times more effective than others, so donating this way hugely increases the impact of our contributions.
See **3dtotal.com/charity**
for full details.

# CONTENTS



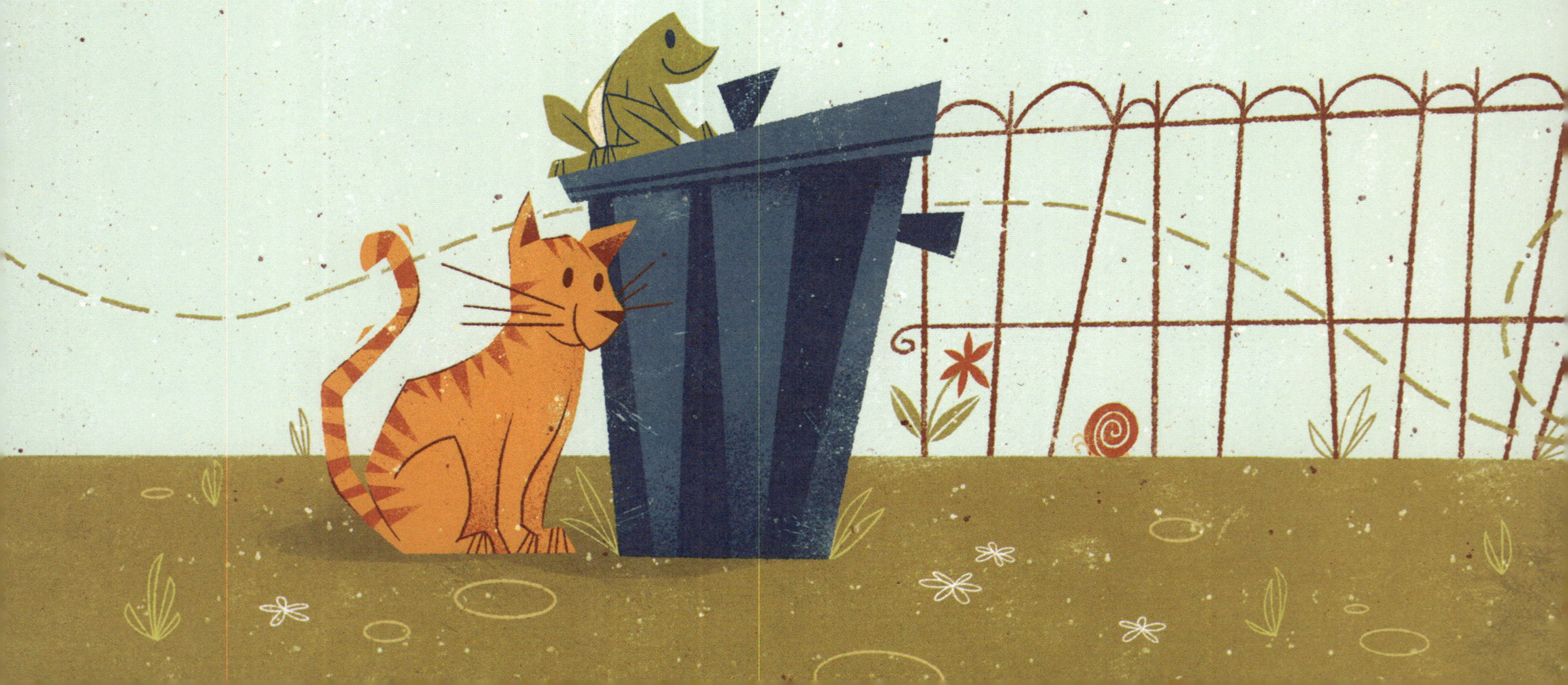

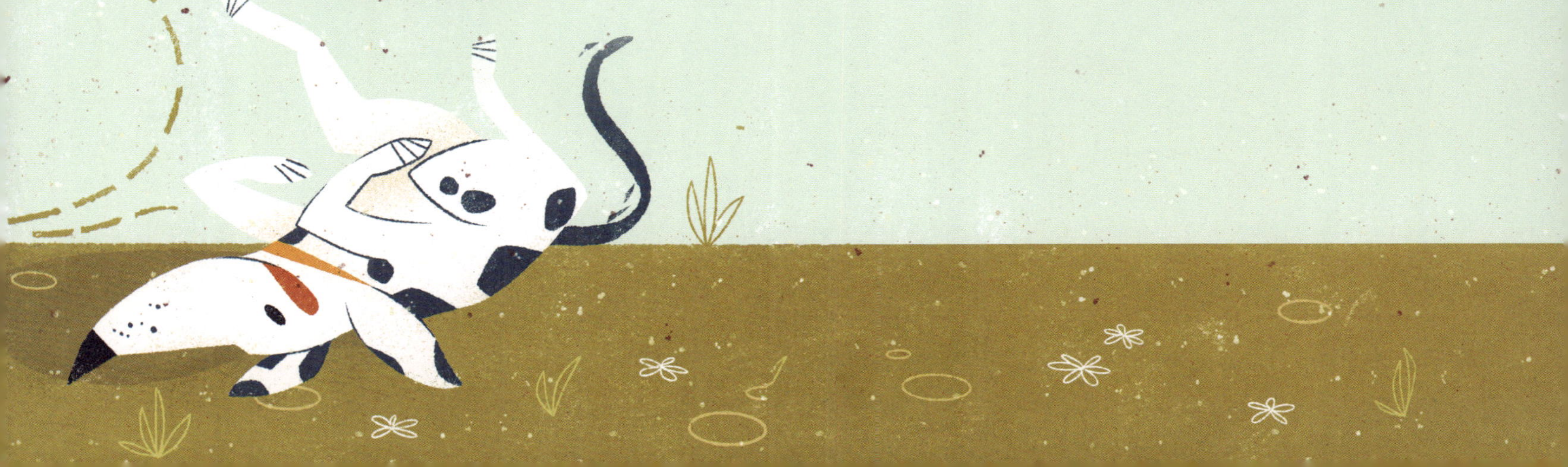

# FOREWORD

After studying graphic design in college, I worked in advertising and graphic design for some time before being reintroduced to picture books on a reference trip to a local bookstore for an animation project I was pitching on. Staring at the packed shelves of books, I was immediately transported back in time and remembered all the picture books I'd read and got lost in as a child. Something sparked inside me that day, prompting me to make the move to working as a freelance children's book illustrator. Several years on, with more than thirty published titles under my belt to date, two of which I also authored, I hope by now I know a thing or two about creating children's books. So please believe me when I honestly say, if you're new to illustrating for children or just want to delve further into this world, I guarantee you will get so much from this book.

When approaching illustrating for children's books, there are many important things you need to consider as an artist. If you're new to this area of publishing, or new to illustrating for children in general, it can be a lot to take on board. There's a lot of technical jargon and you will be required to make a lot of calculated decisions before you even put pencil to paper. These can range from the reader's age, culture, tone, and emotion, right through to character design, thumbnailing, layout, and color palette. But if you're reading this thinking "Oh no, what have I let myself in for?!" please don't be concerned. This book addresses all of these subjects and a lot more. It will guide you through every step and procedure that goes into creating a picture book, with insightful chapters that are easy to follow and understand. Plus, every page overflows with beautiful illustrations to further help you along on your journey of discovery.

It's always fascinating to see a fellow illustrator's process and style. This book includes a comprehensive, behind-the-scenes look at not just one but eight artists' work and techniques in the sample story chapters, which is incredibly useful. You will learn a lot from reading why the artist came to certain decisions and how they take a text and interpret it in their own style.

Once you have worked your way through these creative chapters and are inspired with ideas for your very own first picture book, you will likely want to get it out into the world for everyone to see. This book also covers this side of being a children's illustrator, with chapters on marketing and self-promotion, which in the age of social media and building an online presence is enormously important. Dealing with publishers, contracts, royalties, rejection, and artist's block is all part of the job, and there are further sections on these subjects too. The following pages really do contain everything you need to know to equip and inspire you to succeed in the world of children's illustration.

I'm fortunate enough to have made it as a professional freelance illustrator with no illustration training or prior knowledge of the publishing world and picture-book industry (other than reading them as a child, of course). But let me tell you, the contents of this book would have really come in rather handy back when I was starting out! So please, do yourself a favor and use this book and its insightful chapters as a guide and inspiration as you embark on your own career in children's illustration.

Good luck, don't give up, and above all, have fun!

CHRIS CHATTERTON

**Children's author & illustrator**
**chrischatterton.com**

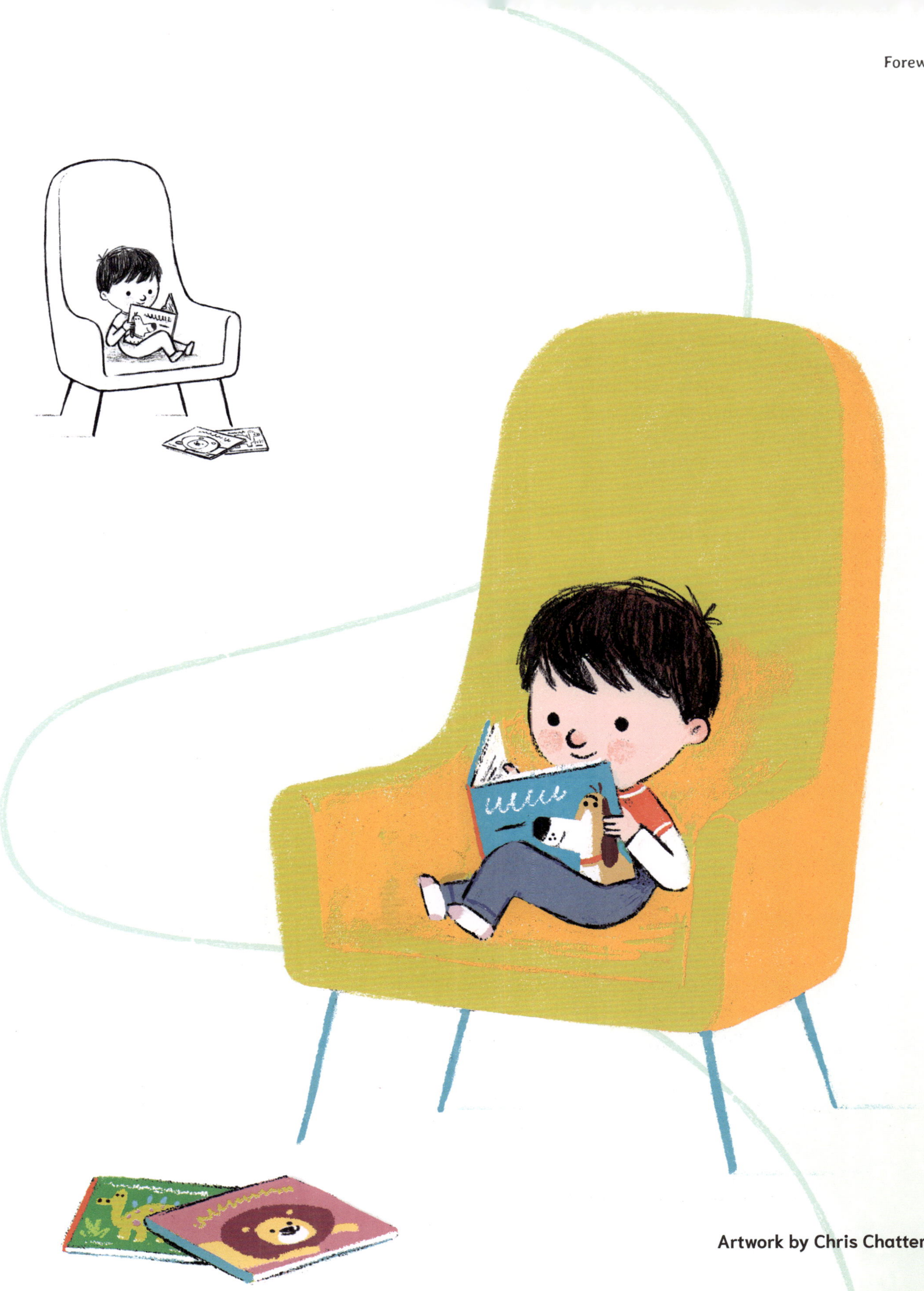

Artwork by Chris Chatterton

# INTRODUCTION

Books began to be mass produced in color in the 1920s, with literacy becoming widespread enough to create an industry for children's books. Over the decades, picture books have evolved and grown into a thriving industry, with a wide variety of beautiful books published each year. Covering a multitude of topics and styles, from educational non-fiction to whimsical tales that deal with real-life issues, the appeal of picture books extends not only to children, but to the adults reading them too. This book delves into how to illustrate a children's book, specifically a picture book for ages 0–8 years. Guiding you through the different stages, it covers the various elements that need to be considered to create a thoughtful and engaging picture book that both children and adults can enjoy.

The following seven chapters will explore what goes into illustrating a children's picture book and the various routes you can take when illustrating books professionally, whether working with a writer, writing your own book, or being hired by a publisher to illustrate an existing story. They will cover important factors to consider and discuss with the writer or publisher, as well as key steps in the process, such as negotiating and signing a contract, discussing important themes and visual ideas for the book, and the format in which you will be required to lay out the artwork. Over the course of the chapters you will learn how these discussions with the writer or publisher can be applied to the book you're illustrating, along with elements to consider to help you create successful and compelling imagery.

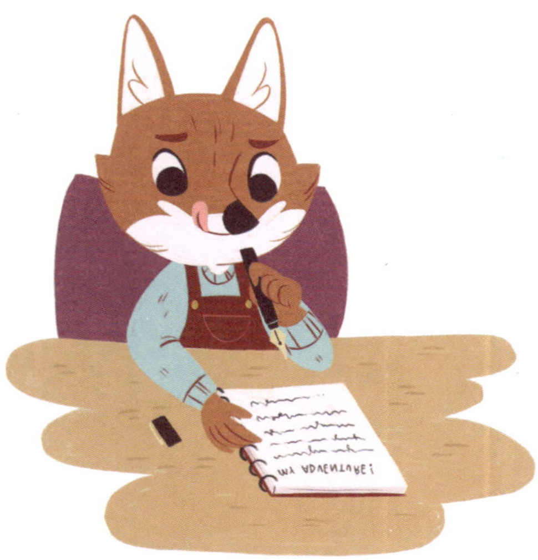

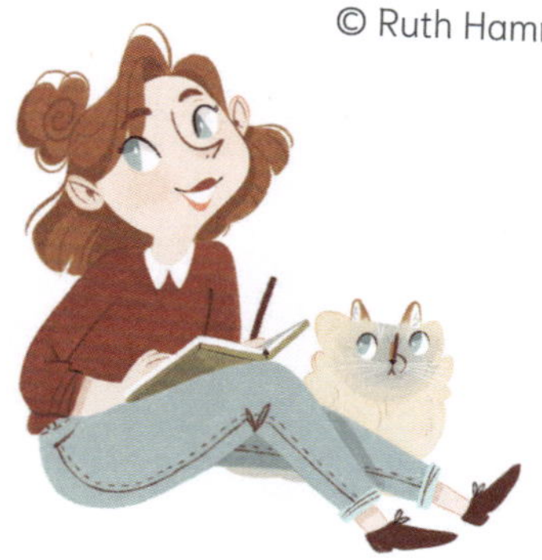

© Ruth Hammond

Written and illustrated by

**RUTH HAMMOND**

Freelance illustrator

**ruthhammondillustration.com**

Ruth loves creating colorful, whimsical pieces for children's illustration and editorial pieces under the supervision of her cat. She is based in York, UK, and in her free time she enjoys working on her own literary pieces.

The book will explore how to illustrate an ongoing narrative, tell the story through your imagery, and utilize key narrative devices to achieve this. It will also cover the importance of considering your audience when creating age-appropriate imagery, how to keep readers engaged through the use of color and relatability in the artwork, and how to lay out the story text around it. Later chapters will walk you through the different routes you can take to pursue a career in illustration, either approaching it academically, following a university or online course, or without any formal educational support. This is followed by advice on working with publishers, plus potential technical or legal issues you could encounter with them. The chapter on troubleshooting will unpack various obstacles you may run into as an illustrator, plus tips to overcome them.

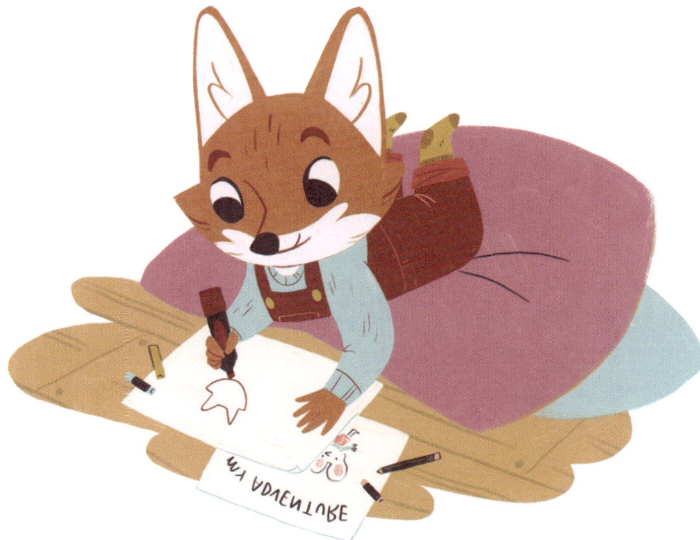


After this come eight sample stories, which have been beautifully illustrated by a selection of leading illustrators. Each story is accompanied by the artist's analysis, providing you with an invaluable behind-the-scenes look as they talk you through how they developed their illustrations from initial ideas to final spreads. Toward the end of the book there is also a useful glossary, containing definitions of key publishing and illustration terminology that you can refer back to as needed.

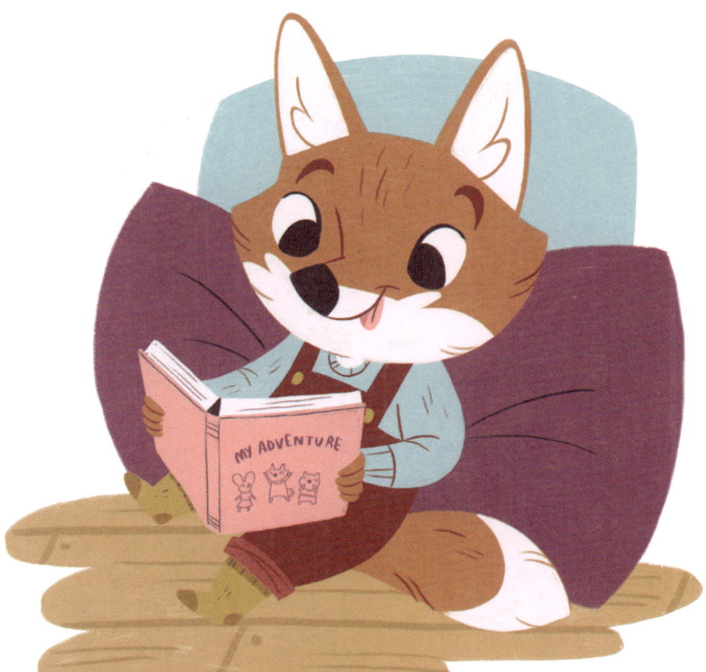


I have always enjoyed telling stories through my illustration and at the age of eighteen I made the decision to pursue a career in children's books. I have spent the years since finishing my degree illustrating picture books and it's still my favorite way to spend my time. Creating fun, colorful, and whimsical imagery for children (and their parents!) to enjoy is incredibly rewarding – I hope the following chapters unlock something of its magic and inspire you on your own journey in children's book illustration.

The following seven chapters will guide you through the process, from determining what the book you have been commissioned to illustrate is about, to developing the illustrations, to seeing the book you created in print.

# CONSIDERING YOUR AUDIENCE

Audience is one of the first things to think about when illustrating a children's book. The imagery you create needs to be compelling and relatable for each child that reads it, but considering the fast rate at which children develop and the different backgrounds children have, the concept of a children's book can become quite broad! Children's books can therefore be split up into a few sub-groups, each with its own factors to consider.

The most crucial and recognized of these is age, as children's books are usually divided into and sold under the following age groups: 0–24 months, 2–4 years, 4–6 years, and 6–8 years. Though these age brackets are only a couple of years apart, there are significant differences in how you illustrate for each one in order to cater to the intellectual development of children at these different ages. For example, board books for babies aged 0–24 months, where imagery is the most important element, will look significantly different to a book aimed at eight-year-olds, who will likely be reading independently.

While keeping age in mind, you also need to consider the different kinds of backgrounds children come from and what each child will find relatable. This means your illustrations should be inclusive of all children, including those of different races, cultures, sizes, and abilities. Taking the target age range along with different backgrounds into account will help you to create a captivating and relatable body of illustrations that all children can enjoy.

"YOUR ILLUSTRATIONS SHOULD BE INCLUSIVE OF ALL CHILDREN, INCLUDING THOSE OF DIFFERENT RACES, CULTURES, SIZES, AND ABILITIES"

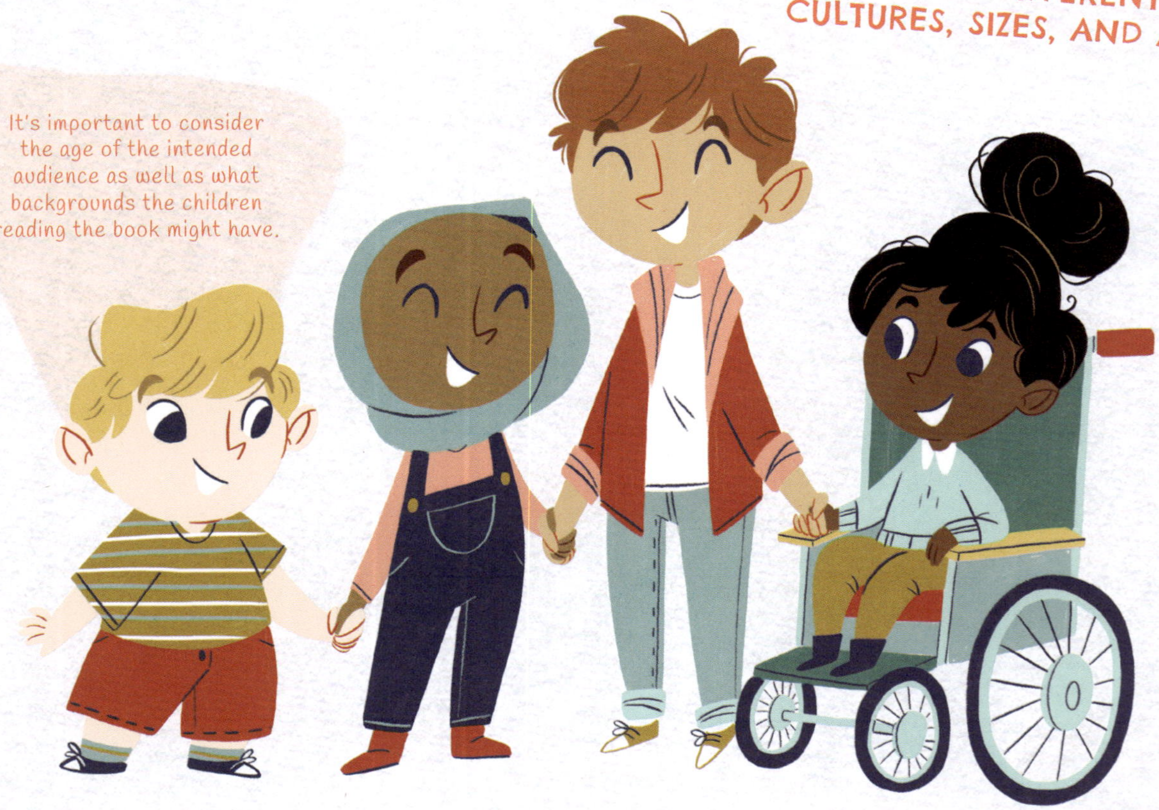

It's important to consider the age of the intended audience as well as what backgrounds the children reading the book might have.

# AGE

Age is the most important sub-group to consider before you start illustrating a children's book. Whether you have been commissioned for a book or are writing one yourself, you must first discern what age the book is aimed at, in order to create interesting and engaging imagery for your target audience.

Due to children's fast intellectual development, books for each age range will differ in a number of ways, including in the amount and level of text, color palette, character design, and overall detail of the illustrations.

## 0–24 MONTHS

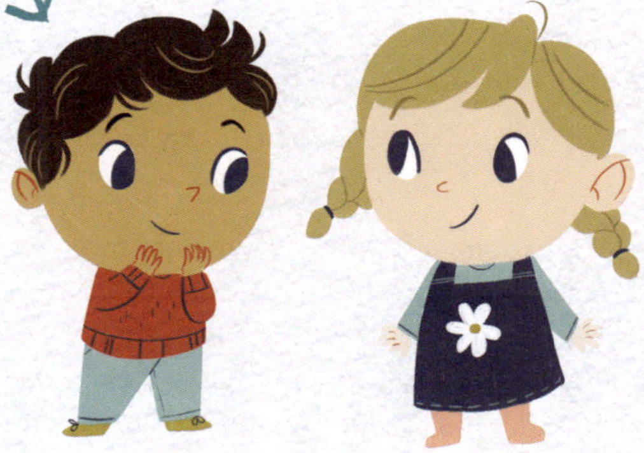

- Board books for babies and toddlers, read aloud by an adult.
- Simple text and illustrations.
- Illustrations are bright and eye-catching, featuring simple shapes and bright, bold colors.
- Characters are made up of simple shapes and small features, and are usually animal characters or very young children.

## 2–4 YEARS

- Picture books for preschool-age children.
- Minimal text, but slightly more complicated narratives.
- Usually read aloud by an adult to a child.
- Illustrations have more detail but are still engaging. Color palettes are often used to depict different moods in the narrative.
- Characters are a mix of children and animals, with children having large heads and small bodies (though bigger than characters in board books), paired with proportionate limbs and facial features.

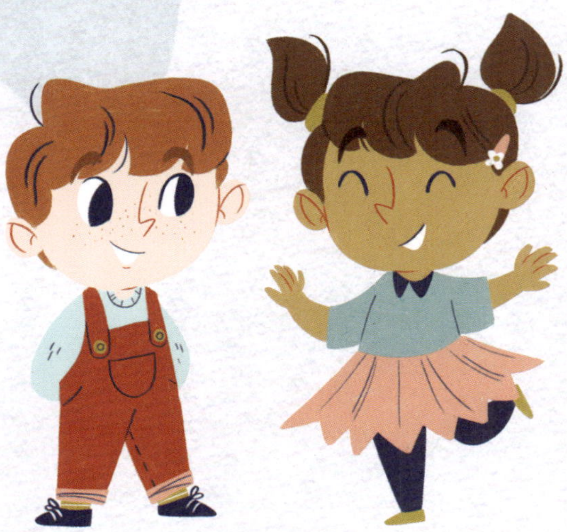

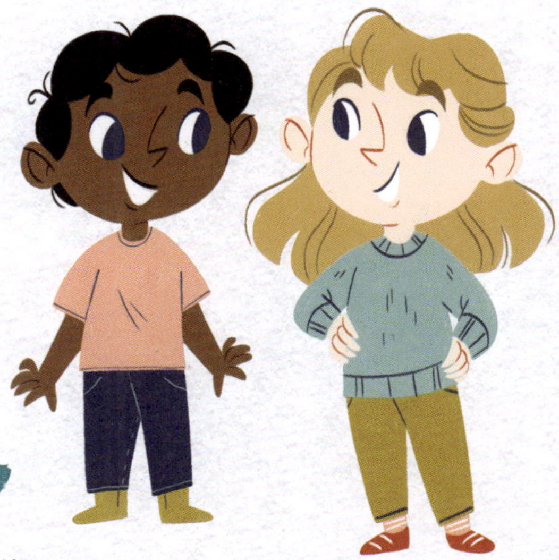

## 4–6 YEARS

- Picture books, but with mid-level text and more interesting narratives.
- Adults and children read together, as the child starts to learn to read.
- Illustrations become a little more complex to match the text.
- Use of bright colors to keep things interesting, though may vary depending on the tone and mood of the text.
- Characters are mostly children and look a little older, with slightly longer bodies and necks.

## 6–8 YEARS

- Books become more dependent on the text than illustrations, resembling mini novels/chapter books.
- Generally independently read by the child without an adult helping.
- Illustrations are still important to keep the reader engaged, but are generally black and white with more vignettes and spot illustrations (see page 22) than full-page artwork. Capturing the mood is also important.
- Characters look a little older, with longer bodies and necks, and with more proportionate heads.

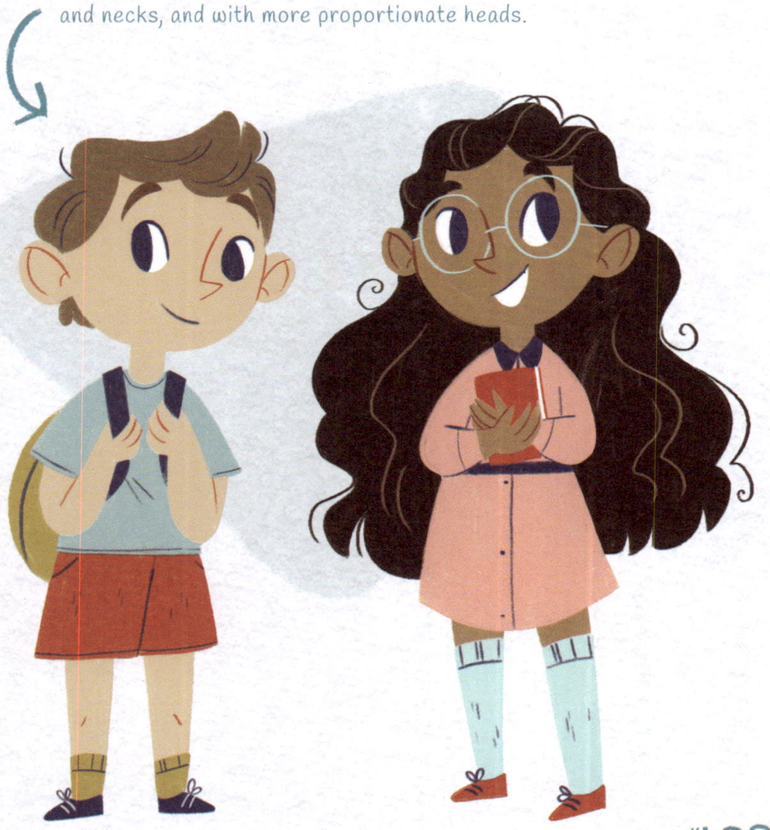

As the target age increases, so does the sophistication of the text, age of the characters, and level of detail in the illustrations, allowing children to continue finding enjoyment and interest in books as they grow older.

There are numerous things to take into account when considering the intended age of your audience, which can make starting work on a children's book a little daunting at times. Here are some useful tips to get you started:

**Carry out visual research:** This can come in many different forms, the most useful of which is looking at children's books that have already been published. This will help you distinguish the visual development of books across the different age groups, which will benefit your illustrations greatly. Most children's book illustrators will have their own mini library of children's books to refer to, regardless of whether or not they have children themselves!

**Talk to young children:** Talking to your target audience will help you work out the sort of things that excite them and pique their interest. You can even show them your illustrations to get some first-hand feedback and see if there's anything you need to change in order to capture and hold their attention.

**Respect your audience:** It's sometimes easy to assume that children's level of understanding is limited and therefore children's books should be overly simple and primitive, but this is not the case. Children are capable of understanding a lot of complex issues and this is something you can reflect in your illustrations. For example, you can convey the seriousness of a situation by using darker color palettes in your illustrations, but remember to keep the style light and appropriate for the age group so it remains appealing and not too scary.

> "LOOKING AT CHILDREN'S BOOKS THAT HAVE ALREADY BEEN PUBLISHED... WILL HELP YOU DISTINGUISH THE VISUAL DEVELOPMENT OF BOOKS ACROSS THE DIFFERENT AGE GROUPS"

# DIVERSITY

Within every age group there will be an abundance of readers from a variety of different backgrounds, upbringings, and ethnicities, all of which need consideration. Children's books are set in different countries around the globe, which means illustrators need to look beyond their own perspective and experiences to discover how different children might experience the world. By doing this you will broaden your audience, as more children will be able to relate to your work. So how can you achieve this?

Start by considering where your book is set and make sure the characters and environment reflect this. If the story is set in an Indian jungle, you will need to research the people groups who live in Indian jungles, as well as the sort of animals and plants found there. This will make the illustrations feel more believable to the reader. If the book is set in a world with no specific location, then it's important to try to include characters from lots of different backgrounds, including different genders, ethnicities, cultures, and abilities. Every child reading your book should feel like they have some form of representation in your work – you don't want anyone to feel left out or like they don't belong.

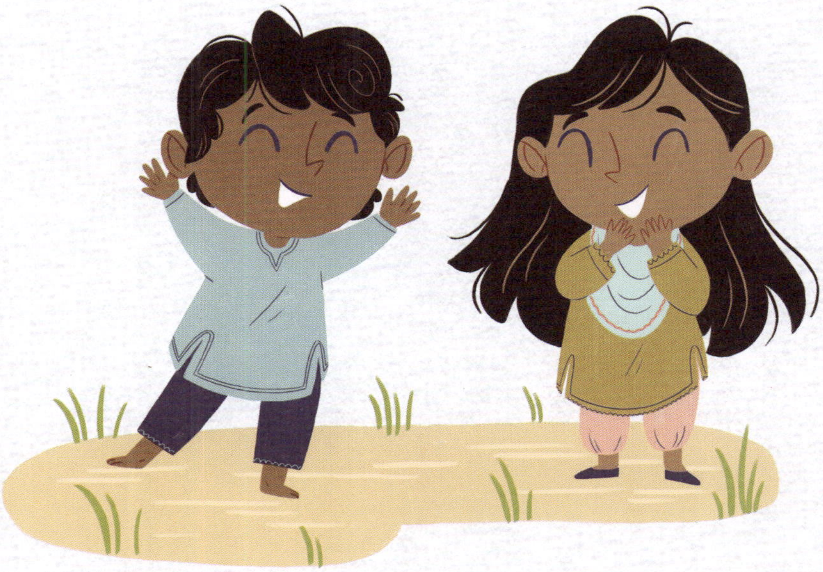

If the book is set in a specific location, such as an Indian jungle, you need to consider the type of clothing people would wear there.

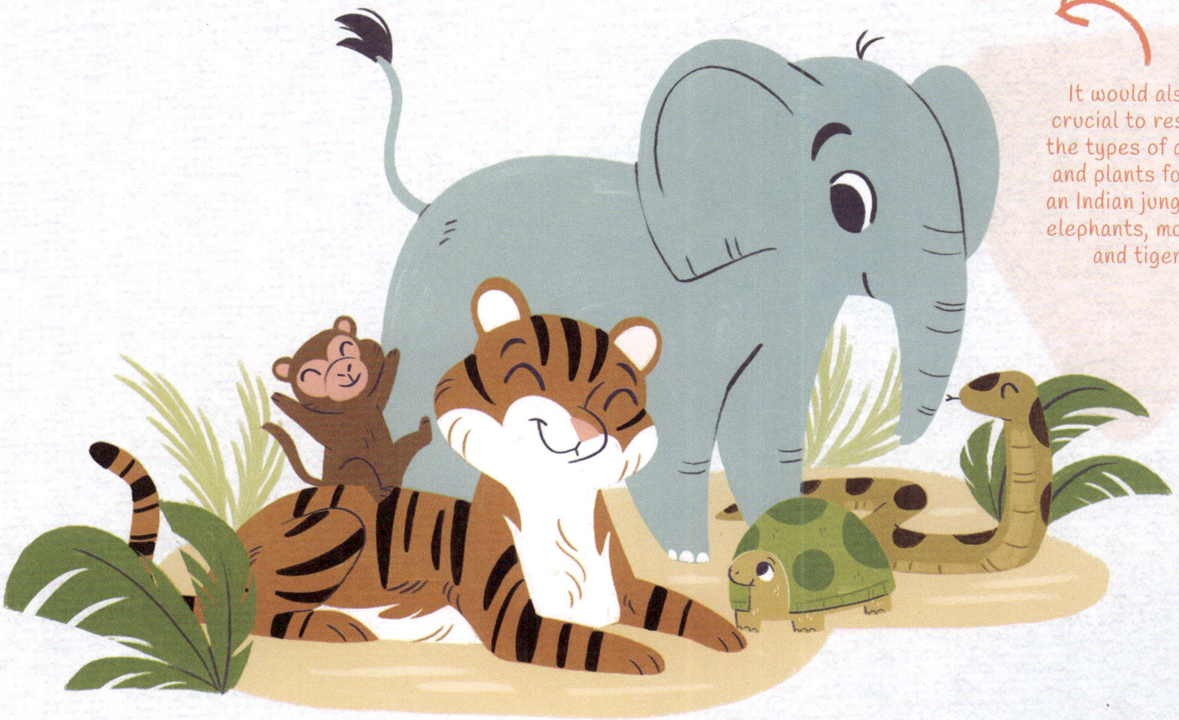

It would also be crucial to research the types of animals and plants found in an Indian jungle, like elephants, monkeys, and tigers!

# TONE

The next factor to explore is the tone of the book. This is particularly something to consider for books for older age groups, as their narratives are usually a little more complex, often teaching children how to cope with situations they will go through in life, such as moving house, bullying, and other fears or worries. As board books for babies and toddlers have much simpler narratives, their tone is generally light and happy, with illustrations that reflect this.

The tone may change throughout the book to reflect certain scenes in the narrative. It's the illustrator's job to convey any change in tone through the artwork. This will help the reader to feel the characters' emotions and better understand the story, keeping them engaged and invested in the book. The tone should always remain grounded, however, so that it doesn't overwhelm or become too much for the reader.

There are a few different ways imagery can be used to convey tone in a story, including perspective, scale, and, most predominantly, color. For example, if the story has a scene where a child character is lost in a crowd, you could emphasize the fear and confusion of such an overwhelming situation by drawing the character very small among a crowd of tall adults. Adding rain and using grays and blues would further emphasize the upsetting situation, though it shouldn't be overly dark or heavy for the reader. A good balance could be achieved by adding a pop of color to the character's outfit, drawing the reader's attention to them, in addition to adding a light source that the character is heading toward, to convey hope that things will get better. Then, when the character finds their way out of the crowd and is no longer lost, you can change the colors so they're lighter, brighter, and more cheerful, reflecting the joyful tone of the scene.

The young child character is shown walking alone down a crowded street in the rain. The use of cool blues and grays emphasizes the worry he feels as well as the coldness of the rain, while the yellow contrasts against the blue and conveys a feeling of hope.

**"THE TONE MAY CHANGE THROUGHOUT THE BOOK TO REFLECT CERTAIN SCENES IN THE NARRATIVE"**

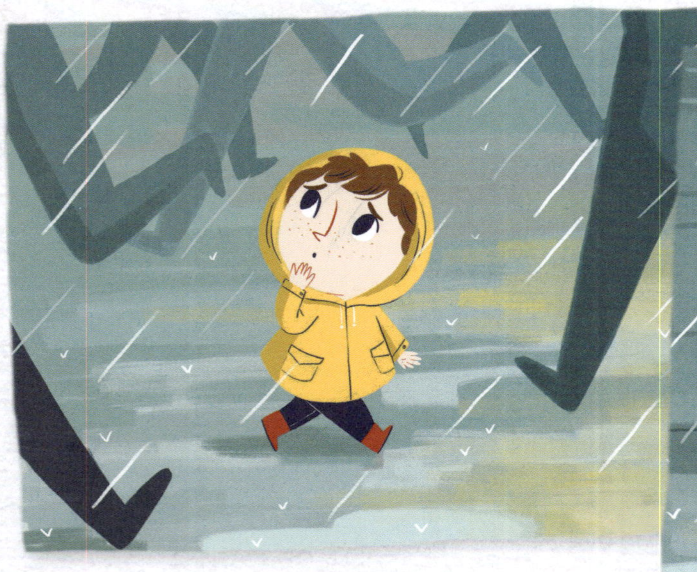

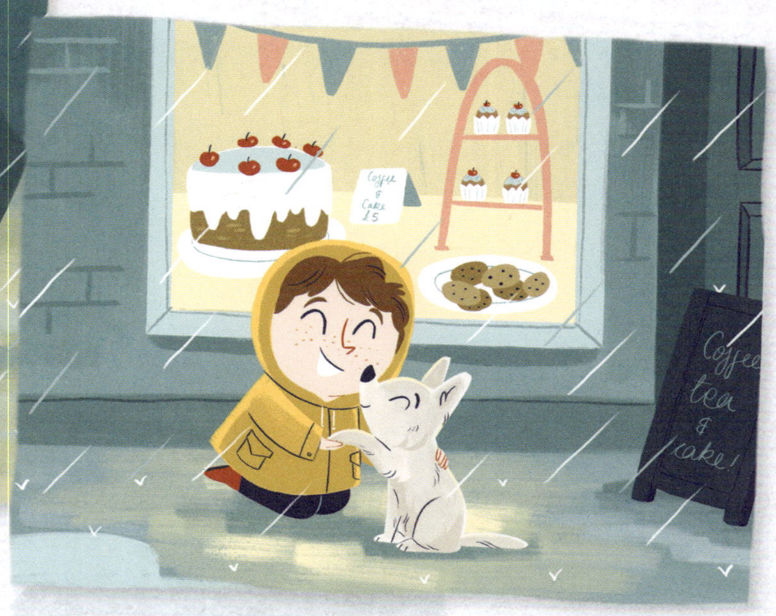


The character has found what they were looking for – their puppy friend! The colors are still blue for continuity, but the backdrop behind them is warm and inviting, reflecting their feelings of happiness.

# DIFFERENT INTERPRETATIONS

After considering your audience's age, background, and the tone of the book, it's important to take some time to consider how an image could come across to different readers. As an illustrator you need to be aware of your own preconceptions and visual understanding in order to recognize when an image is likely to be misunderstood by others. This means carefully making sure the emotions and actions of the characters and scenes are easily discernible to readers.

For example, does your character look obviously happy in the happy scene you're drawing, or could their expression and body language be mistaken for another emotion? Does the playground scene look like a playground, or could it be misinterpreted as a back garden? Does it look like the character is brushing their teeth, or could they be misinterpreted as doing something else?

The best way to avoid misinterpretation is to use references:

### Characters

- Draw from life, studying people around you as well as yourself, or sign up for life-drawing classes.
- Look at other children's books to see how different illustrators convey emotion.
- Watch movies, particularly animated ones, to study expression and body language.
- Look up images of various poses, gestures, and expressions online.

### Backgrounds

- Study the sorts of objects you would find in that environment.
- Watch movies that include a similar setting and draw from them to help make your character's world feel whole.
- Look up different places and environments online.
- Look at other children's books to see how different illustrators have designed similar backgrounds.

However, it's important to ensure your work is entirely original and not copied from any of your reference material. If you're feeling unsure about the clarity of your work, try stepping back and not looking at it for a few days, or ask someone else to look at it (preferably someone in your target audience, as this will provide the most accurate feedback).

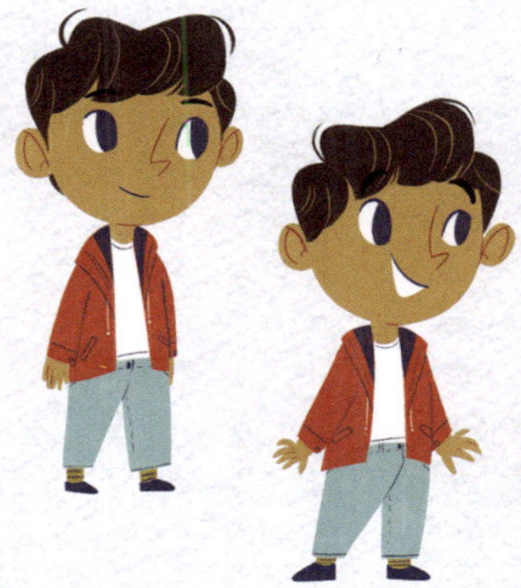

This character is meant to have a happy expression, but in the left image he looks more serious. By shifting the character's weight onto his right foot, opening his mouth in a smile, raising his eyebrows, moving his hands outward, and raising his head, the character is made to look much happier.

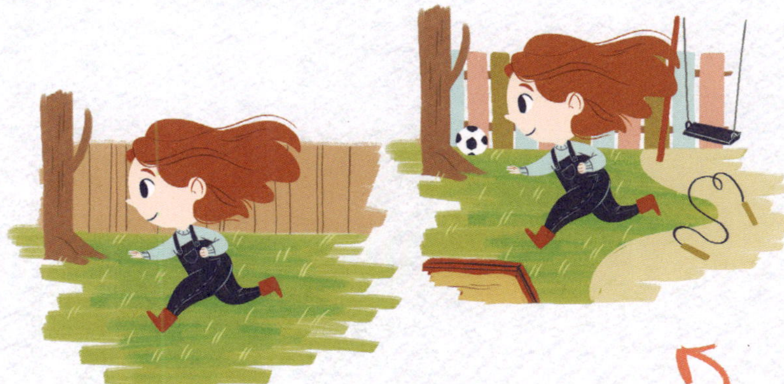

This character is meant to be running through a playground at the park, but there is nothing in the background of the left version that indicates it's a park. In the version on the right, however, there's a skipping rope, sandbox, swings, football, and more colorful fencing in the background, which are all items you might find in a playground.

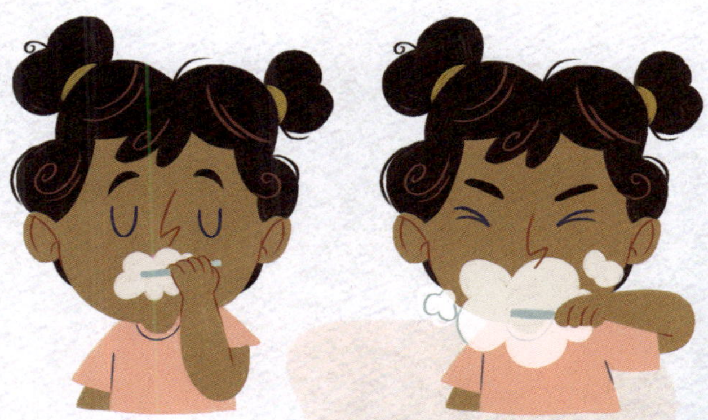

This character is brushing her teeth, but the version on the left looks awkward and unrealistic. The version on the right looks more realistic as her arm is raised horizontally, her expression is more intense, as if she's really scrubbing her teeth, and there is more foam around her mouth.

# ILLUSTRATING AN ONGOING NARRATIVE

Illustrating an ongoing narrative is very different to illustrating a single illustration. Each illustration needs to tie into the next, following the story of the main character or group of characters over the course of the narrative. There are therefore various stages of development you need to work through in order to achieve this.

Before you start, set aside some time to carefully read through the narrative and decide how you are going to interpret it in your illustrations, referring to any guidance the writer or publisher has provided. This will then lead into picture planning, where you create thumbnail sketches to explore ideas for your illustrations and character designs, and produce a page plan (see page 20) to work out the staging and pacing of the story. It's important to keep continuity in mind while working through these stages, considering how you can maintain it throughout your illustrations. To demonstrate these stages, we will be following the story of Arthur the fox as he goes on an adventure.

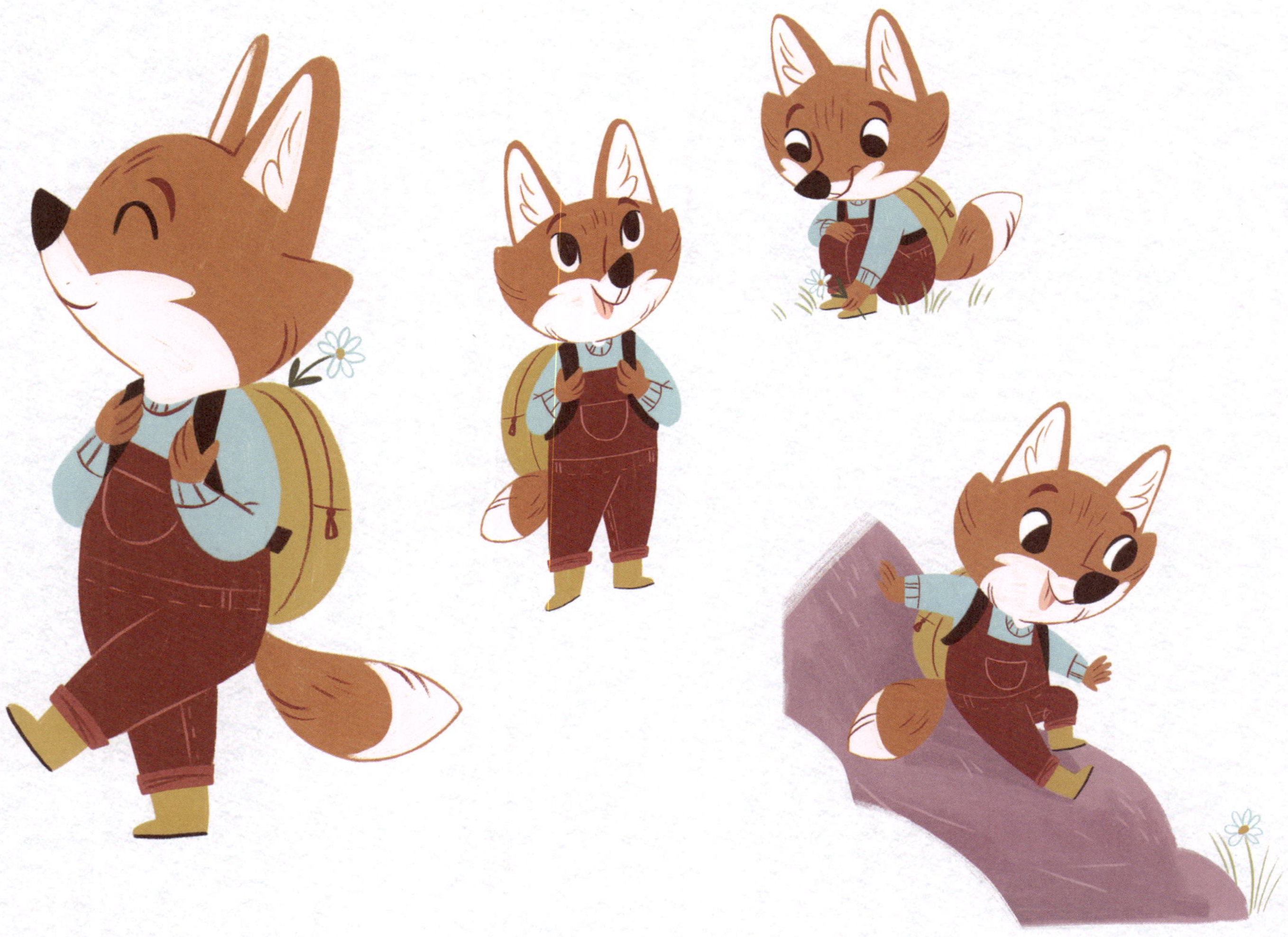

# INTERPRETING A STORY

Start by familiarizing yourself with the story and consider how you are going to interpret it in your artwork. This requires a little more thought when illustrating a story written by someone else, rather than one you have written yourself, so it's essential to spend some time exploring how you will draw out the key message and most important aspects of their story.

If possible, the easiest way to do this is to talk to the writer and find out the message they want you to convey in your illustrations. They will often have a good idea of how they want their characters to look and the sort of message and tone they want the book to have. Plus, they should be able to provide you with great insight into their story. From personal experience, writers are almost always open to the illustrator's input and ideas, and sometimes the illustrator can present an interpretation the writer hadn't initially considered. Conversation with the writer can make this stage much more collaborative.

However, direct contact with the writer isn't always possible and sometimes the only contact you have is with the writer's publisher, meaning you will have to draw out your own interpretation of the story. To do this you will need to think about all the characters and their personalities, and how you can bring them to life through their designs. You also need to unpack what the story is about, the situations the characters experience, and any lessons they subsequently learn. How can you show this flowing narrative and character growth in your work?

The best way to do this is to pick out key moments from the plot to summarize what happens. For example, if you look at the illustration on the right-hand side of this page you will see the key points of Arthur's story.

Read the story through carefully and consider which key story moments you will choose to illustrate.

Arthur embarks on an adventure to his grandfather's house

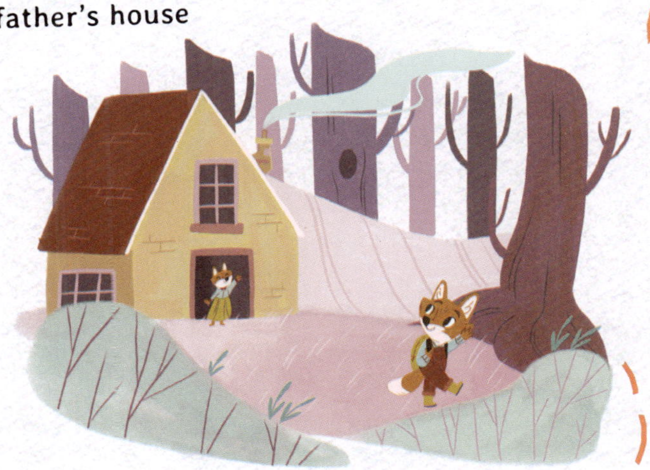

He meets two friends on the way

As night draws in, they see the light coming from his grandfather's house

They notice something is wrong – there's a thief in Arthur's grandfather's house!

They hatch a plan to rescue Arthur's grandfather

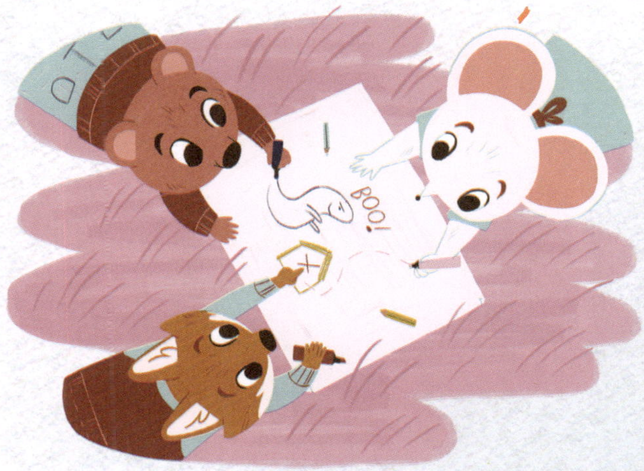


They execute the plan and the thief escapes

Everyone is happy and they finally get some rest

# PICTURE PLANNING

After you have considered how you're going to interpret the story, you can start planning the spreads. This stage lets you dive in and get all the ideas that have been building up inside your mind down on paper and explore where they will go. It's important to work through this stage in order to ascertain which of your ideas will work on paper, and which will not.

This section will follow the story of Arthur the fox, exploring the stages below as we plan his adventure:

- Thumbnailing
- Creating characters
- Considering the page plan
- Staging and pacing
- Continuity

"THUMBNAILS ALLOW YOU TO QUICKLY EXPLORE LOTS OF IDEAS BEFORE NARROWING THESE DOWN TO THE ONES THAT WORK BEST"

## THUMBNAILING

Thumbnailing is a good place to begin when planning a picture book. Start by picking out the key moments in the story, then create lots of small, rough ideas. Thumbnails allow you to quickly explore lots of ideas before narrowing these down to the ones that work best, which you can then explore on a larger scale later on. All illustrations should start with a thumbnail sketch, even if it's just a single illustration.

1.

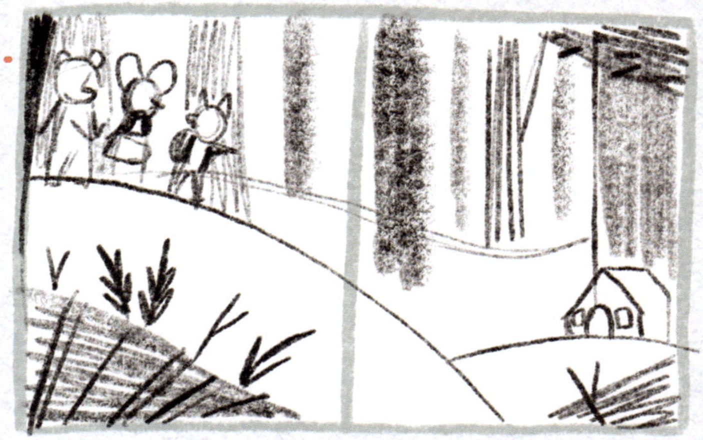

2.

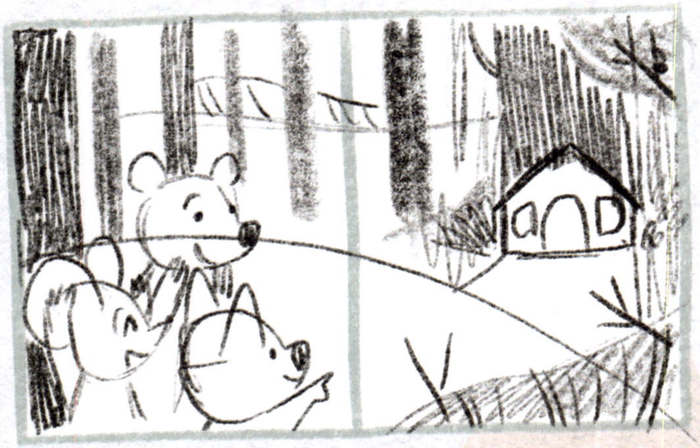

3.

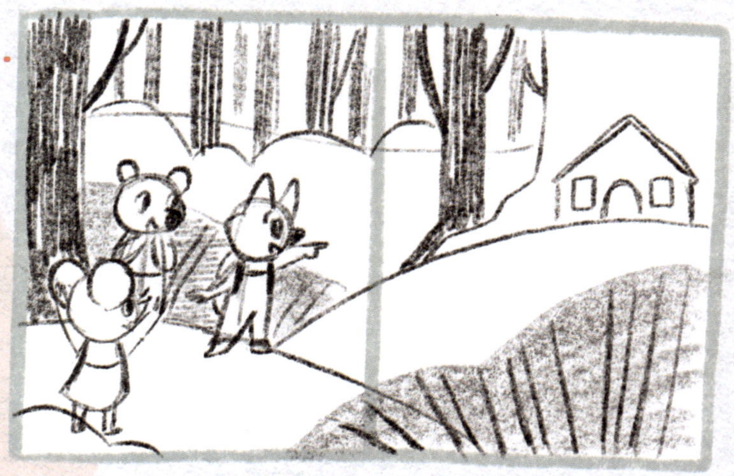

These thumbnails explore different ideas for the spread where the friends see Arthur's grandfather's house in the distance. It's important to experiment with different compositions and character positions to make sure the image is readable. The first and third thumbnails are the most successful.

# CREATING CHARACTERS

While thumbnailing, start to think about the characters and sketch out ideas for how you want them to look. It's important to consider their personalities and how you can reflect them in the characters' designs. For example, Arthur likes to wander around and embark on little adventures, making friends along the way. His outfit and design should therefore help to convey this. Arthur's grandfather, however, is much older and likes sitting cozily by the fire in his favorite armchair, making his character design significantly different to Arthur's. Similarly, the thief who breaks into Arthur's grandfather's house needs to look unfriendly and thief-like.

After trying out different outfit designs, you can then start to explore how the characters will look when they react to different situations and feelings. Consider how their body language will change with different emotions. As the characters in Arthur's story are all animals, think about how their animalistic facial features will move with their mood.

When creating a character, start with a rough sketch or concept, refine the lines and design, choose the colors, and then polish the final design.

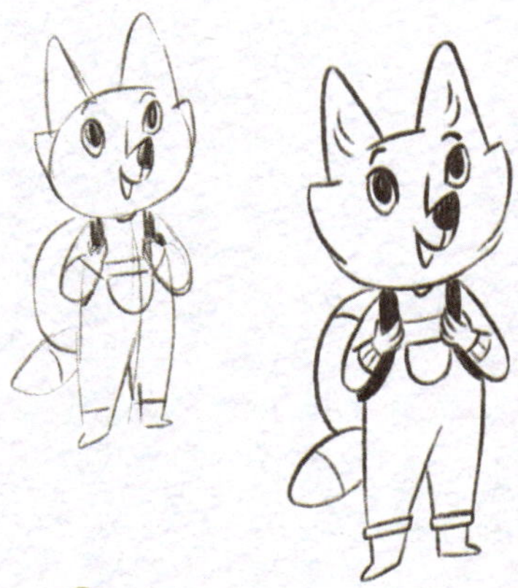

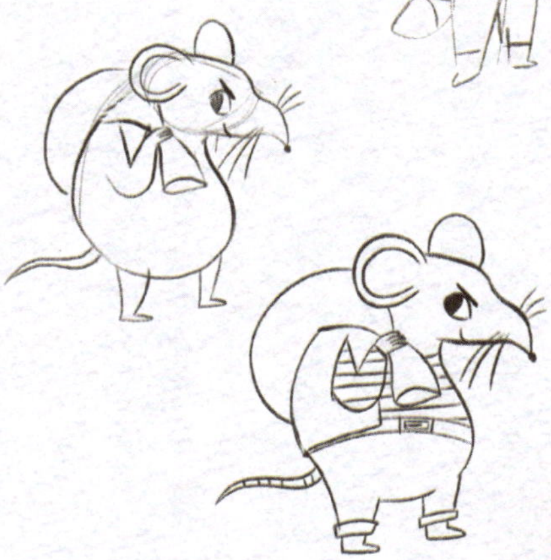

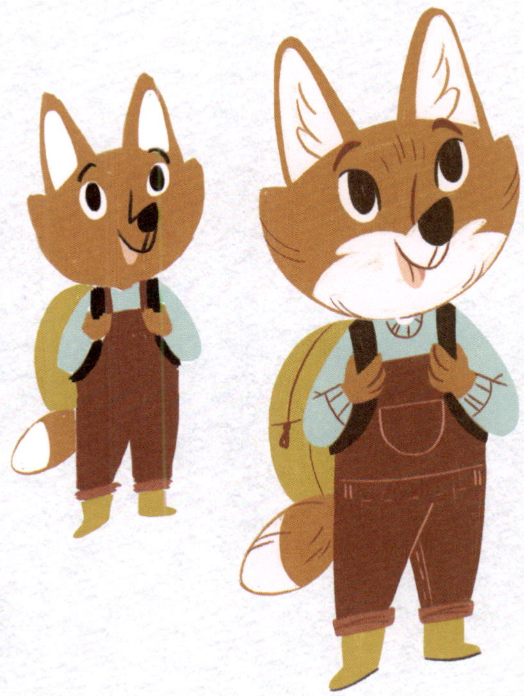

Arthur is wearing dungarees, as these seem most fitting to his playful character. The big backpack he carries is full of supplies to help him on his adventures.

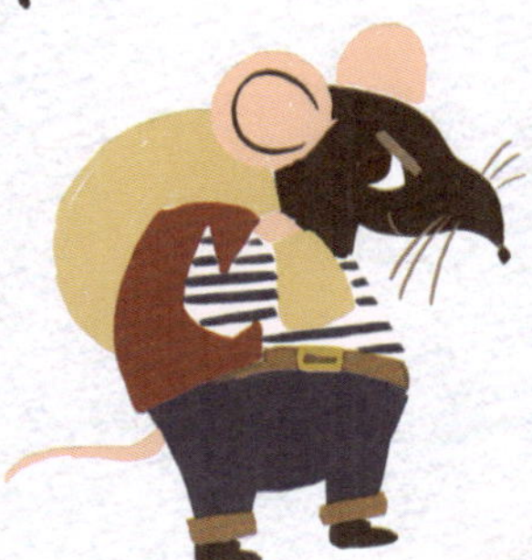

The thief needs to look unfriendly, sly, and thief-like, so he has pointed facial features, rough clothes, and a giant sack on his back. The curved shape of his ears and nose tone down his wicked character, ensuring he's still age-appropriate for the reader.

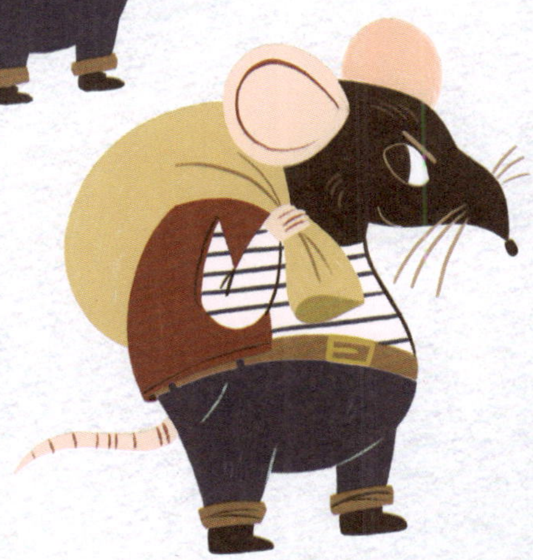

When designing characters, remember that you will have to draw them multiple times over the course of approximately 32 pages (see page 20). Make sure you know their designs and personalities inside out to ensure their designs are consistent throughout. Draw your character as many times as you can, with different poses and expressions, to help you get to know them.

# CONSIDERING THE PAGE PLAN

Creating a sample page plan is a crucial stage in illustrating a picture book, as it allows you to plan out the flow of the narrative and work out where the key moments need to be. The typical paperback picture book is generally 32 pages, but different publishers use different book formats, and different ways of arranging their pages. It's important to ensure you fully understand what is required before you begin. A standard layout might look something like this:

**Page 1**
Half title page – a right-hand page featuring just the story title.

**Page 2**
Imprint page – a left-hand page featuring the publisher's imprint and copyright information.

**Page 3**
Full title page – a right-hand page showing an image from the story, the title, and the publisher's logo.

**Pages 4–32**
The story, ending on a single left-hand page.

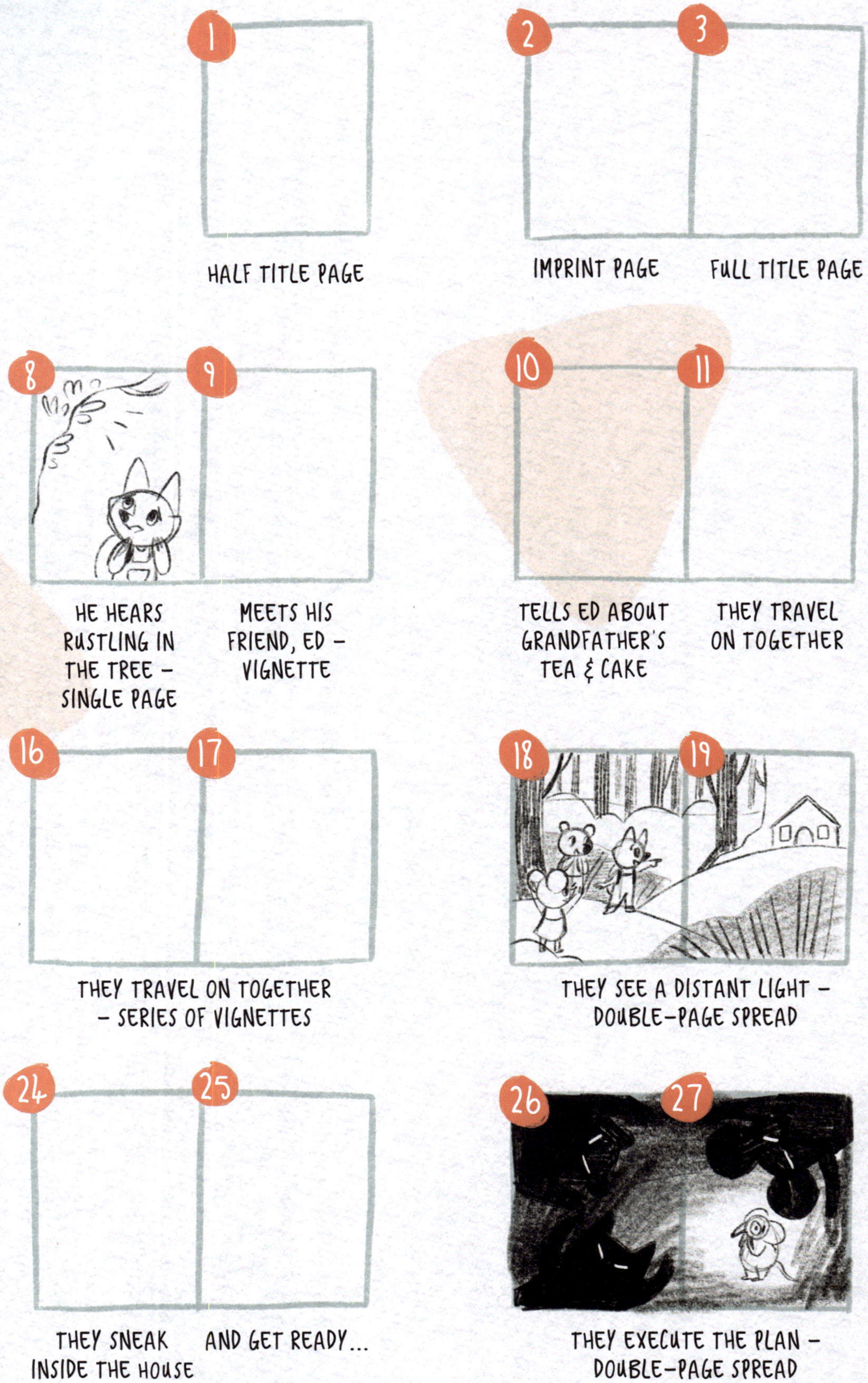

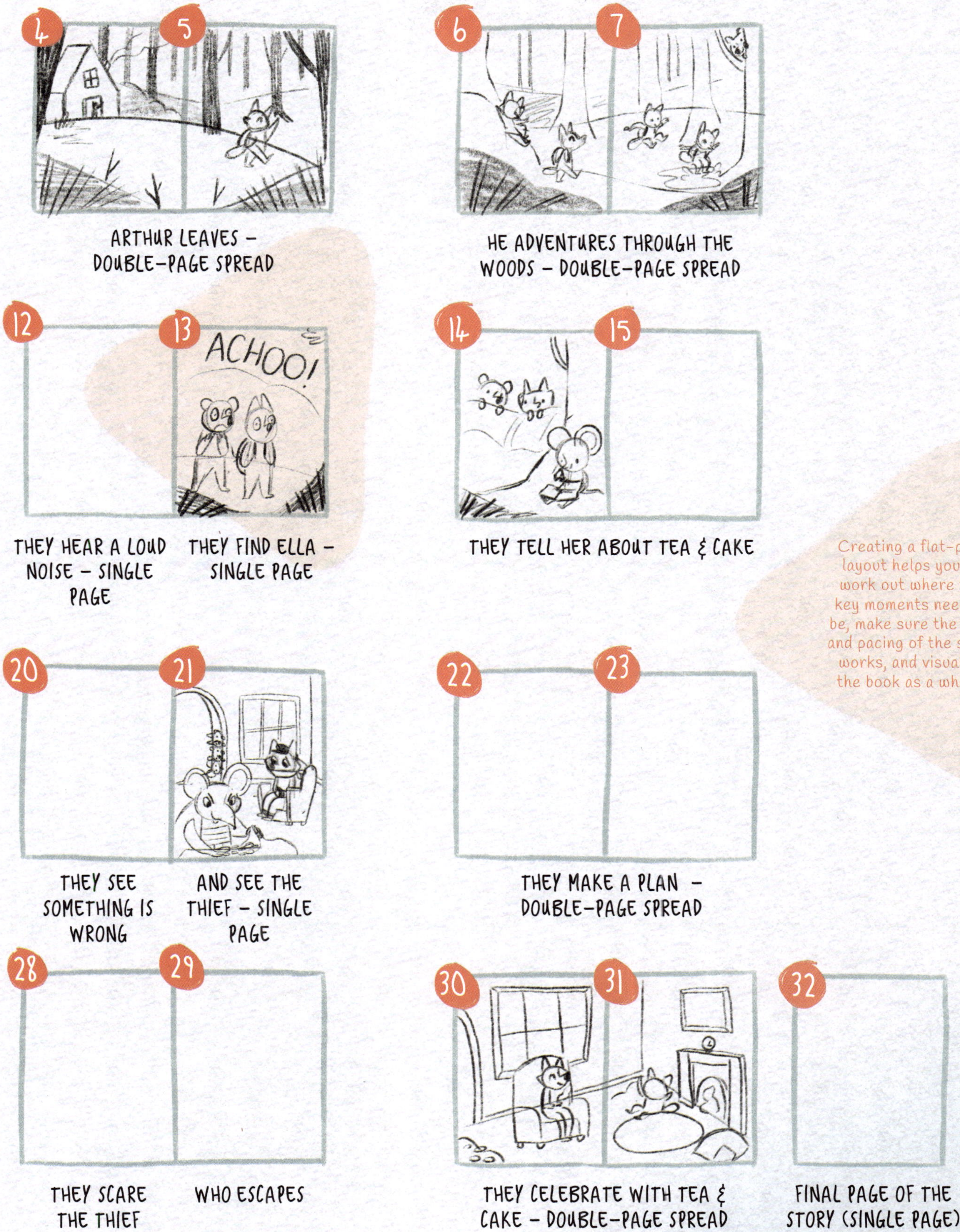


Creating a flat-plan layout helps you to work out where the key moments need to be, make sure the flow and pacing of the story works, and visualize the book as a whole.

# STAGING AND PACING

Next you need to consider the staging and pacing of your illustrations. This refers to the flow and pacing of the narrative and how the illustrations work with it. The spreads will be busier in some parts and quieter in others, depending on what is happening in the story.

Before you can do this, it's important to understand the different types of illustrations and spreads found in a picture book:

- Double-page spread: this is artwork that covers two entire pages, extending to the very edge of the paper (referred to as "full bleed", as the image bleeds right up to the edges of the paper).
- Single page: this artwork is just one page, again extending to the very edge of the paper.
- Vignette/spot illustration: this is a small illustration that "floats" on the page with a small or minimal background.

Including a mix of double-page spreads, single page illustrations, and spot illustrations throughout your picture book will help capture the pacing of the story, as each can be useful for portraying different aspects of the story.

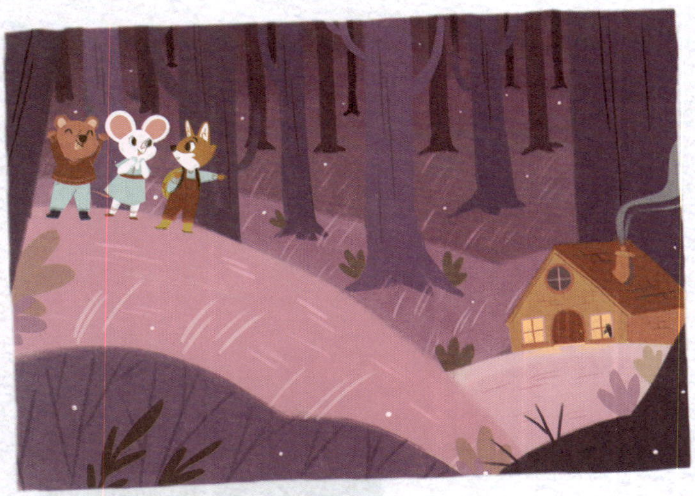

This double-page spread (developed from one of the earlier thumbnails) depicts Arthur and his friends as they find his grandfather's house. Spreads like these are great for setting the scene, but remember not to put important details in or near to the gutter.

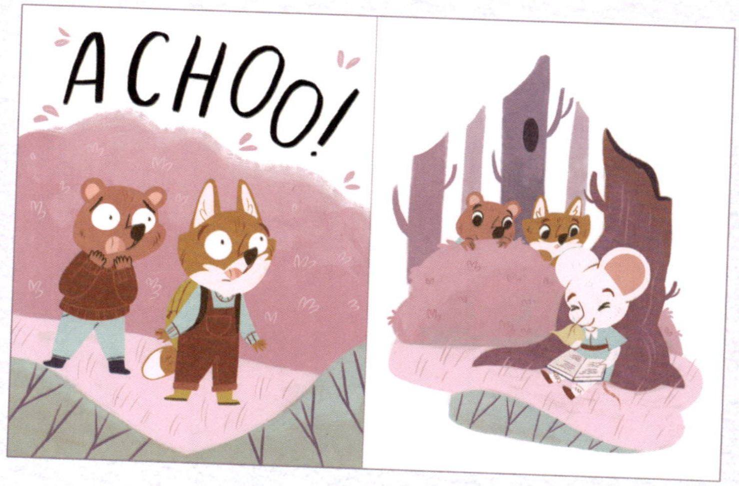


This spread has a single page illustration on the left page, and a vignette on the right page. These pages are much less detail-oriented and are useful for showing character moments and action scenes.

For example, the opening spread is typically a double-page spread to introduce the setting and characters. This is then followed by a mix of single page illustrations, double-page spreads, and vignettes. Double-page spreads are great for setting the scene, but they are also good for capturing key moments or introducing a new setting. While they are generally quite slow-paced in terms of the narrative, they can be filled with lots of detail to keep the reader interested, making them look quite busy.

Vignettes/spot illustrations are useful for honing in on a particular character interaction or emotion, or showing a series of rapid actions. They make the page appear less cluttered and therefore break up the busy feel created by double-page spreads. An entire double-page spread of vignettes can look great, depending on the pace you want to convey, as can a single page of vignettes next to a full-bleed single page illustration.

With single pages and double-page spreads it's important to be aware of the gutter, which is the dip where the spine sits down the middle of the spread. Avoid including important details too close to the spine to ensure they don't get lost in the gutter. Creating a template of the spread, with the spine drawn down the middle, will help avoid this issue, as will creating a dummy book from the page plan you created earlier. A dummy book is a mock-up that is the correct size and number of pages, containing draft spreads to show how the artwork and text looks once laid out. It will make it much easier for you to visualize how your picture book will look in print to help make sure the pacing is right.

# CONTINUITY

While working through these stages, it's crucial to keep continuity in mind. Children will read picture books with their parents, so the books need to be visually captivating for both parent and child. They might read through the same selection of picture books each night before bed, looking at the illustrations and absorbing the details and characters, which will make it easy for them to spot inconsistencies. As an illustrator, it's essential you make sure your character designs and backgrounds are consistent throughout the book to avoid any confusion.

The best way to ensure you avoid inconsistencies is to keep to one simple yet contrasting color palette throughout the book. You should also spend some time practicing drawing your characters from all angles, plus drawing each background numerous times, becoming familiar with the items found there and their positioning in each scene. Try to visualize the characters as actual people, and the backgrounds as places that actually exist, getting to know them and what they look like. As you move through the book, refer back to previous spreads to make sure the illustration you're currently looking at matches the previous illustrations of the same or a similar scene. If a character is wearing a stripy t-shirt, take note of how many stripes their t-shirt has and make sure you draw the correct number of stripes each time you draw the character.

This is Arthur's mouse friend. In the left design she is wearing a short-sleeved dress, little frilled socks, and has a ribbon around her waist.

In the right design, the dress is long-sleeved and there is no ribbon or socks. Ensure your character designs are consistent down to the last detail.

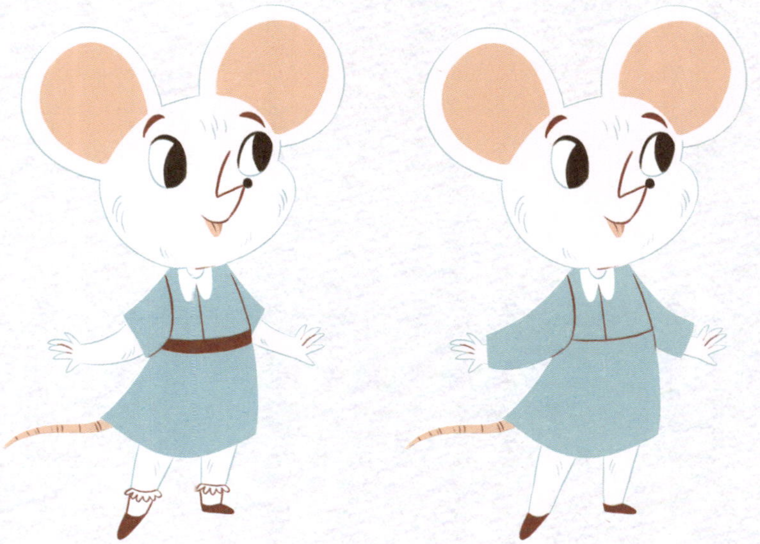

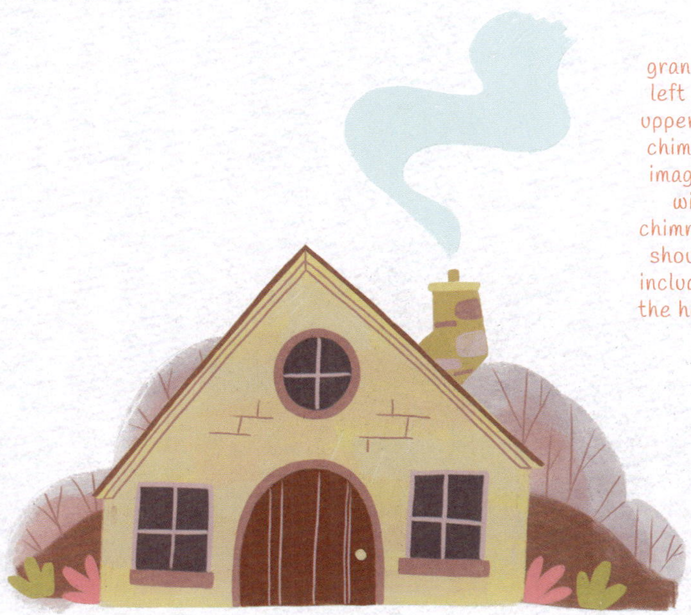

This is Arthur's grandfather's house. In the left image there is a round upper window and a crooked chimney, whereas the right image shows a rectangular window and a straight chimney. These small details should be remembered and included correctly whenever the house or scene is drawn.

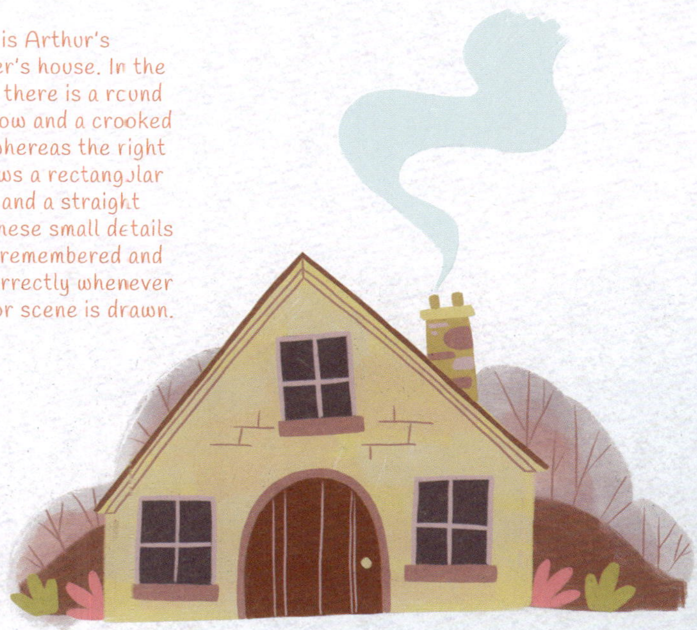

# TELLING THE STORY

Children's books need to have both engaging stories and appealing illustrations to successfully captivate their readers. The story and the world it takes place in should be compelling and well-rounded to ensure they're believable and relatable to the reader. Writers achieve this by using various key narrative devices, such as action, conflict, character, humor, and perspective. It's important for illustrators to take note of the different devices used in a story so that they can reflect them in the artwork to visually carry the reader through the story. By marrying the illustrations with the narrative, you can create a wonderfully fleshed-out body of work that will entice and excite the reader throughout the book.

As well as focusing on key narrative devices, you also need to consider what background characters there might be and what they're doing. What animals might you find in a particular scene? Could they be recurring characters with their own story in the background?

This chapter will explore a range of different narrative and illustrative devices for telling a story, and will demonstrate how you can apply them to your own work.

## KEY NARRATIVE DEVICES

There are many different narrative devices you can use in your illustrations, each one providing a different tone and feel to the story. These include:

- Action
- Conflict
- Page turns
- Humor
- Detail and white space
- Perpsective

### ACTION

When the narrative and illustrations work together to show action, they create a scene filled with adrenaline and conflict, keeping the reader in suspense and therefore engaged. You can show this in your artwork by making use of elements such as different perspectives, dynamic character poses, and emotive facial expressions.

This spread shows a character running away from a large monster. The intensity of the chase is shown through the zoomed-out layout of the shot, the frantic way the character is running, the dust cloud forming behind them, and the size and shape of the monster compared to the tiny character.

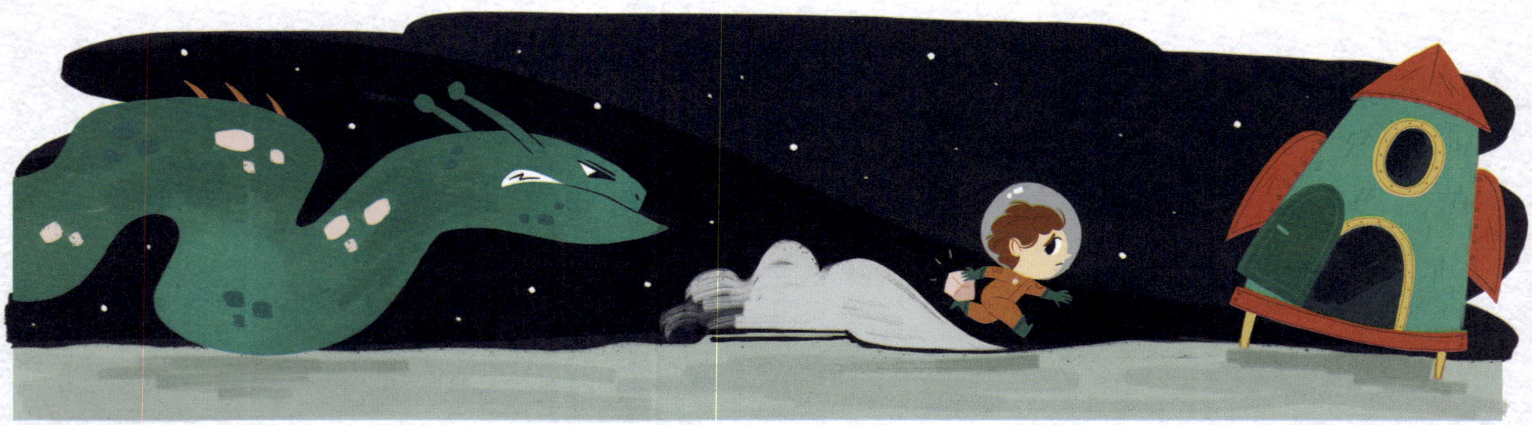

# CONFLICT

Conflict is the challenge characters need to overcome in order to achieve their goals. It allows for character growth, and the reader can be left uncertain at times as to whether or not the character will overcome their challenges. For example, the conflict in a story could be a character conquering a fear. At the start of the story they may appear scared, but by the end they could have grown in confidence and overcome their fear.

This first illustration tells a story of a young girl who is afraid of a monster under her bed.

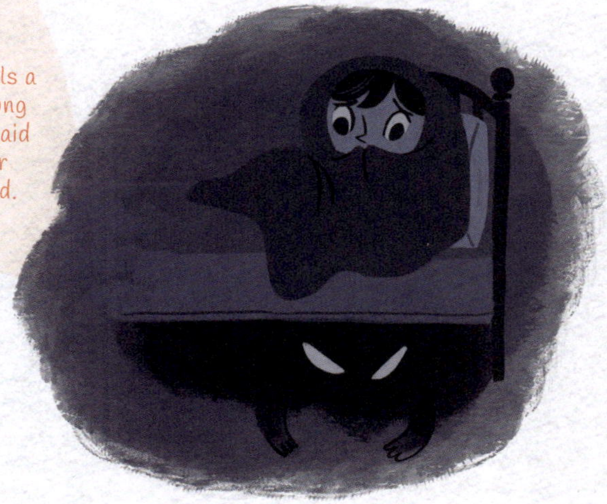

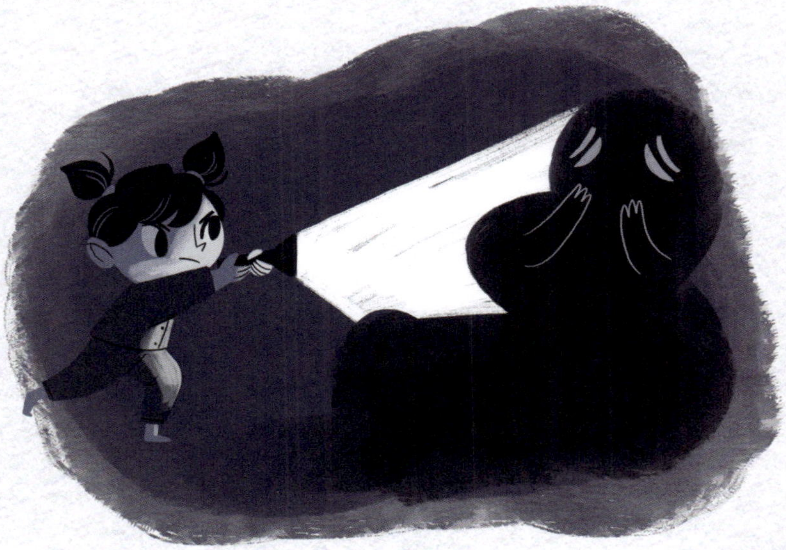

In the second illustration, we see her fighting her fear by shining a light on the monster.

"CONFLICT ALLOWS FOR CHARACTER GROWTH"

In the final illustration the girl is sleeping peacefully, having overcome the conflict.

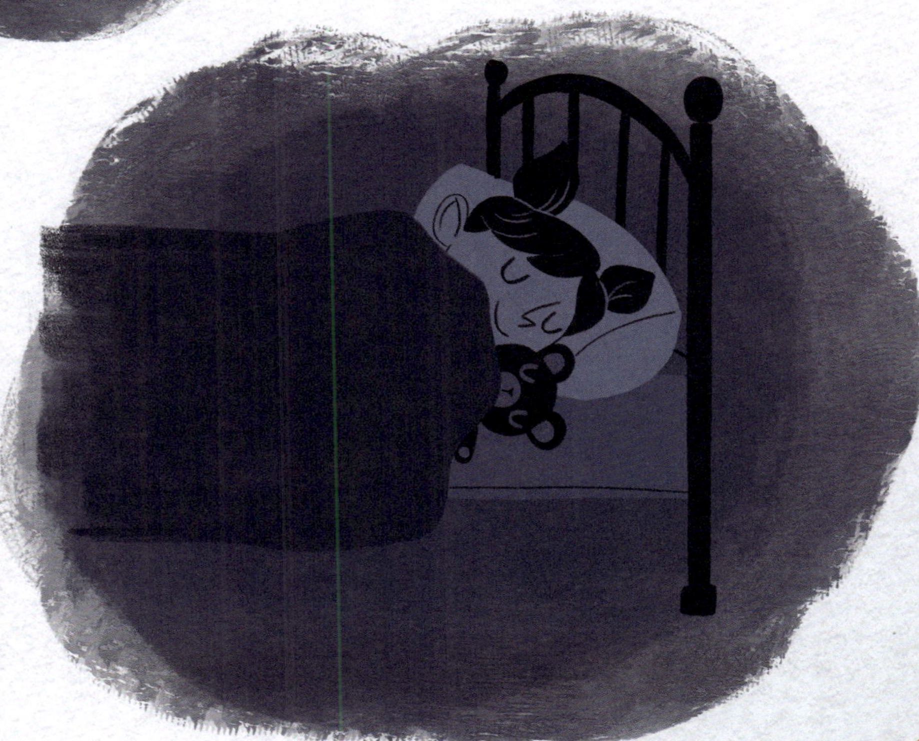

## PAGE TURNS

Setting up dialogue or key dramatic moments where the reader has to turn the page to see what will happen can create suspense in a story. A page containing a powerful image of a key dramatic moment, full of suspense and possibilities, could be followed by a calmer or triumphant page where the drama has been resolved. Suspense is what keeps readers turning the pages!

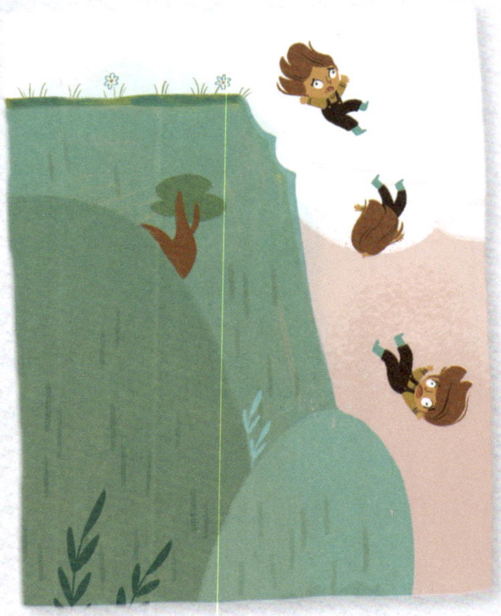

This illustration shows a character as they fall off the edge of a cliff and plummet toward the ground. The scene is full of suspense and worry! Readers will turn the page, anxious to see what happens next...

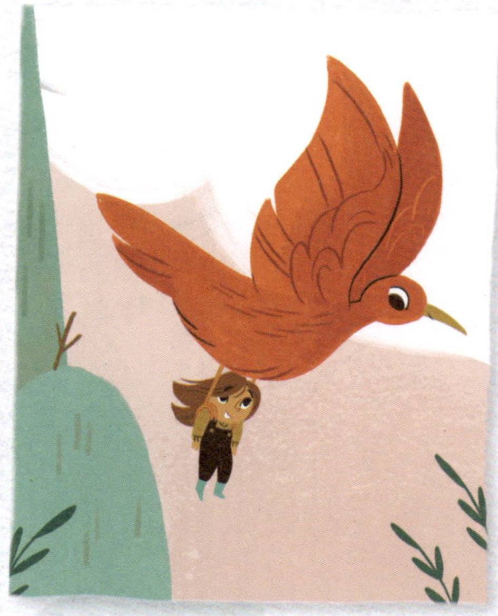

The character is rescued by a big red bird! Readers are left feeling relief for the character after the scary scene on the previous page.

## HUMOR

Humor can help break up tense situations, grounding the story in the children's book genre. It can be shown in character expressions and actions, and you can lighten a more serious scene with something comedic happening in the background.

"SUSPENSE IS WHAT KEEPS READERS TURNING THE PAGES"

This illustration shows puppies who have gotten into a huge bag of dog biscuits and stuffed themselves silly. The comedy and silliness of the image will lighten the tone of any more serious scenes on previous pages of the book.

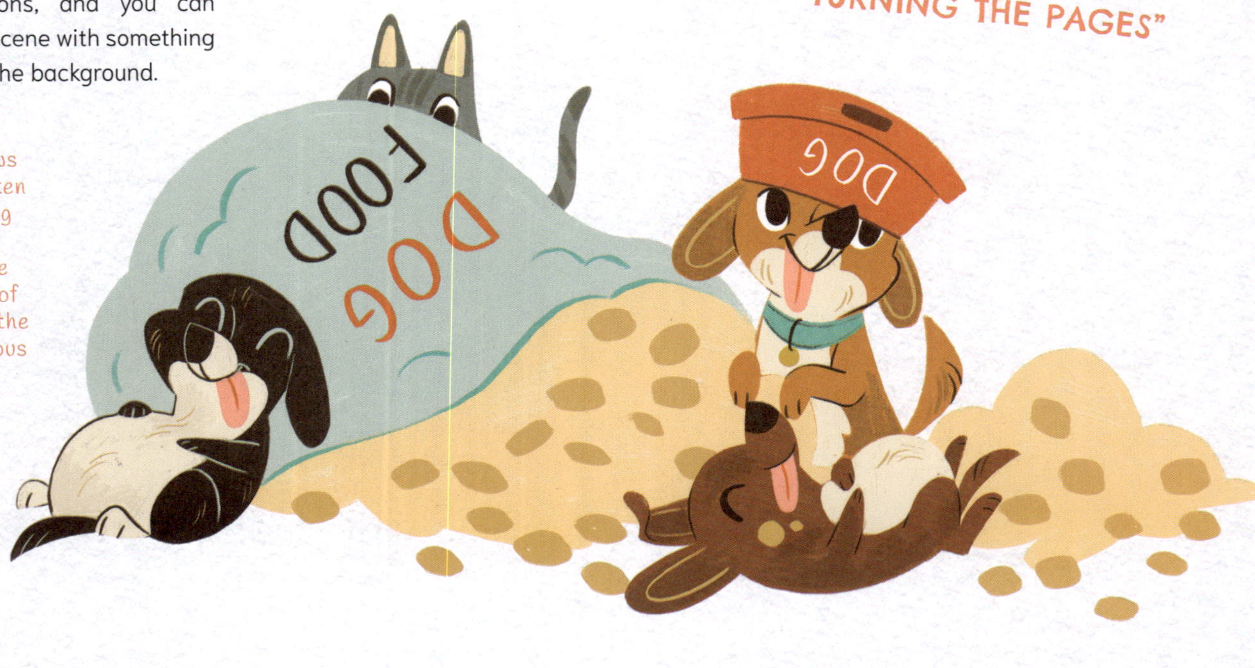

# DETAIL & WHITE SPACE

Attention to detail is important as it creates much more interesting imagery. Children and their parents will look over book illustrations together, picking out the details that excite them in larger spreads. It can also help convey story devices like page turns, showing just how dramatic those moments can be. It's good to balance out spreads containing lots of detail with spreads that contain more white space. This will provide contrast and can help emphasize key character moments in the story.

These two illustrations sit side by side in a book. They show how interesting full bleed (artwork that extends to the edge of the page) double-page spreads can be, and how a vignette with lots of white space around it can be used to break up busier pages.

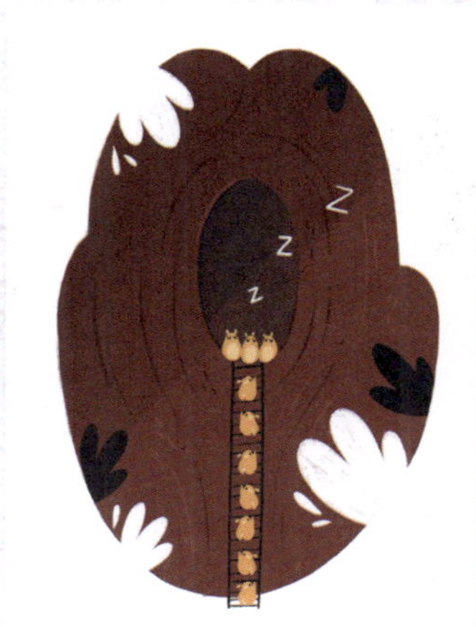

© Ruth Hammond

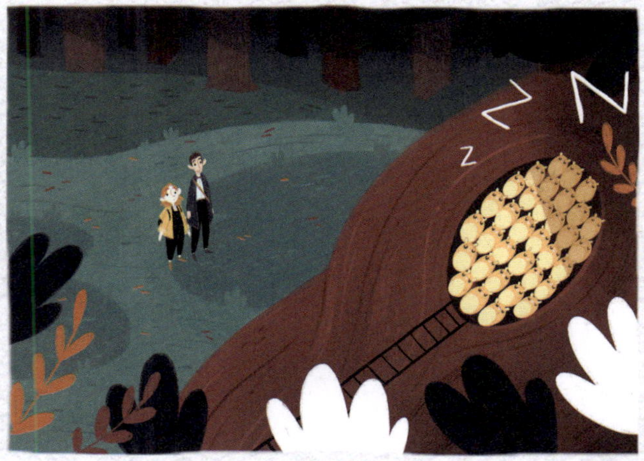

© Ruth Hammond

"BALANCE OUT SPREADS CONTAINING LOTS OF DETAIL WITH SPREADS THAT CONTAIN MORE WHITE SPACE"

# SYMBOLISM

Symbolism is often used as a foreshadowing technique. If there is a particular item that will be important later on in the story, you can subtly add it into the background of earlier spreads. When its function is revealed, you can draw attention to it by making it the focal point of the illustration using color, scale, and perspective.

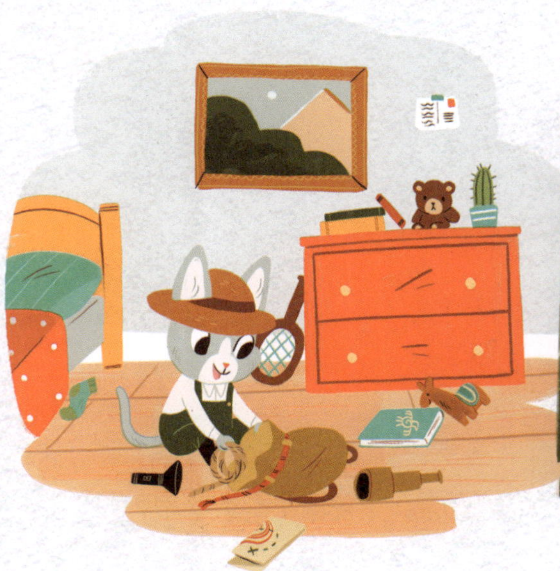

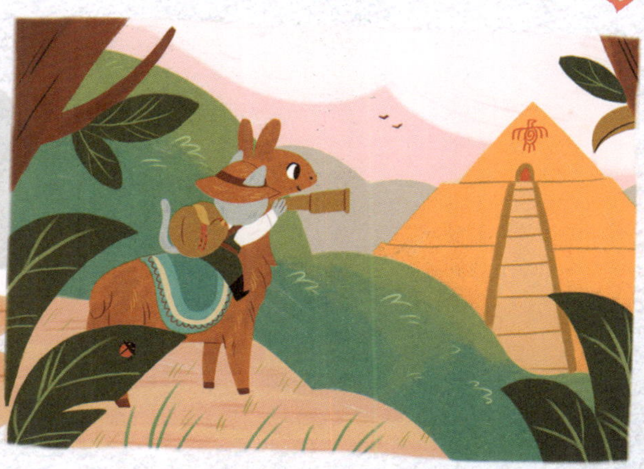

There are subtle clues here in the first illustration that link it to the second, such as the llama toy, the picture on the wall, and the book with the Aztec symbol on it. The first image provides little hints and details for the reader to spot, creating a sense of intrigue about where the character is going on their adventure. The second image resolves the mystery by showing where the character has gone, tying the story together.

## PERSONALITY

Showing personality is important to relatability, allowing the narrative to hook readers as they empathize with the characters. The writing alone cannot portray the nature of a character – you need to show it through your illustrations too. For example, if a character is shy, use timid body language and expressions to show their apprehensive personality. This can help the reader to recognize themselves in the character.

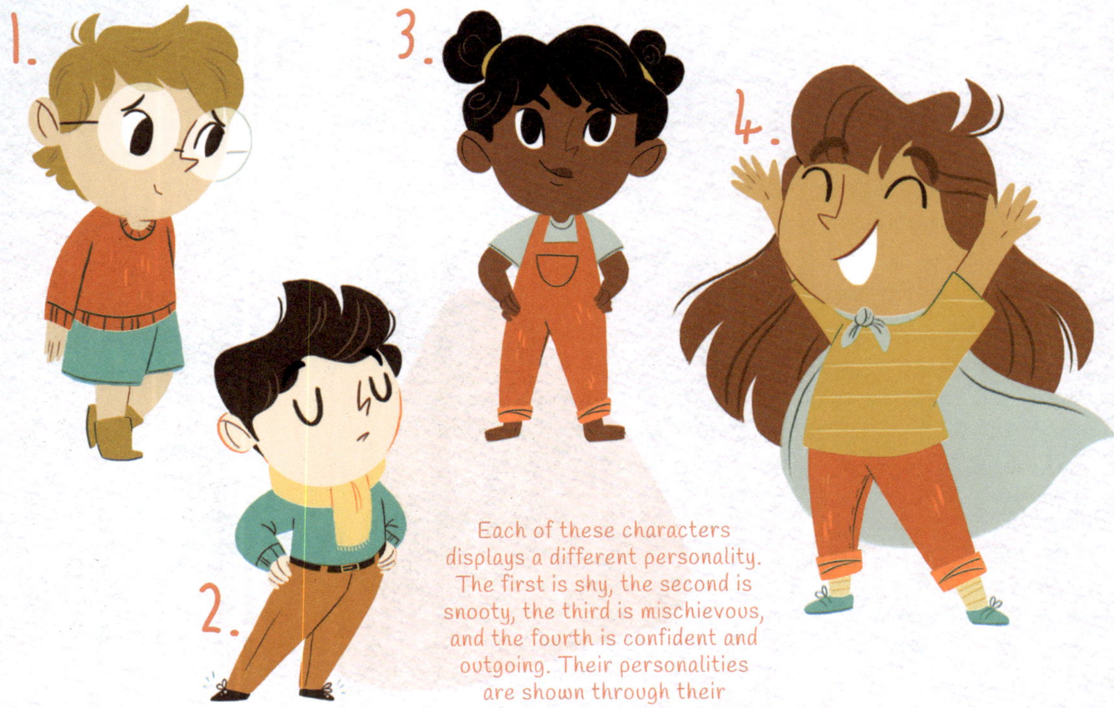


Each of these characters displays a different personality. The first is shy, the second is snooty, the third is mischievous, and the fourth is confident and outgoing. Their personalities are shown through their body language, expressions, and the clothes they wear.

## ENVIRONMENT

The environment is the time and geographic location the narrative is set in. It should create the backdrop and mood of the story, showing the world in which the narrative occurs. To illustrate the environment in a spread, you first need to work out where and when the story is set, and then make sure this is reflected in your illustrations. For example, if the book is set in the Victorian era, take some time to study Victorian buildings, streets, fashion, and interiors to make sure this is accurately portrayed in your environment.

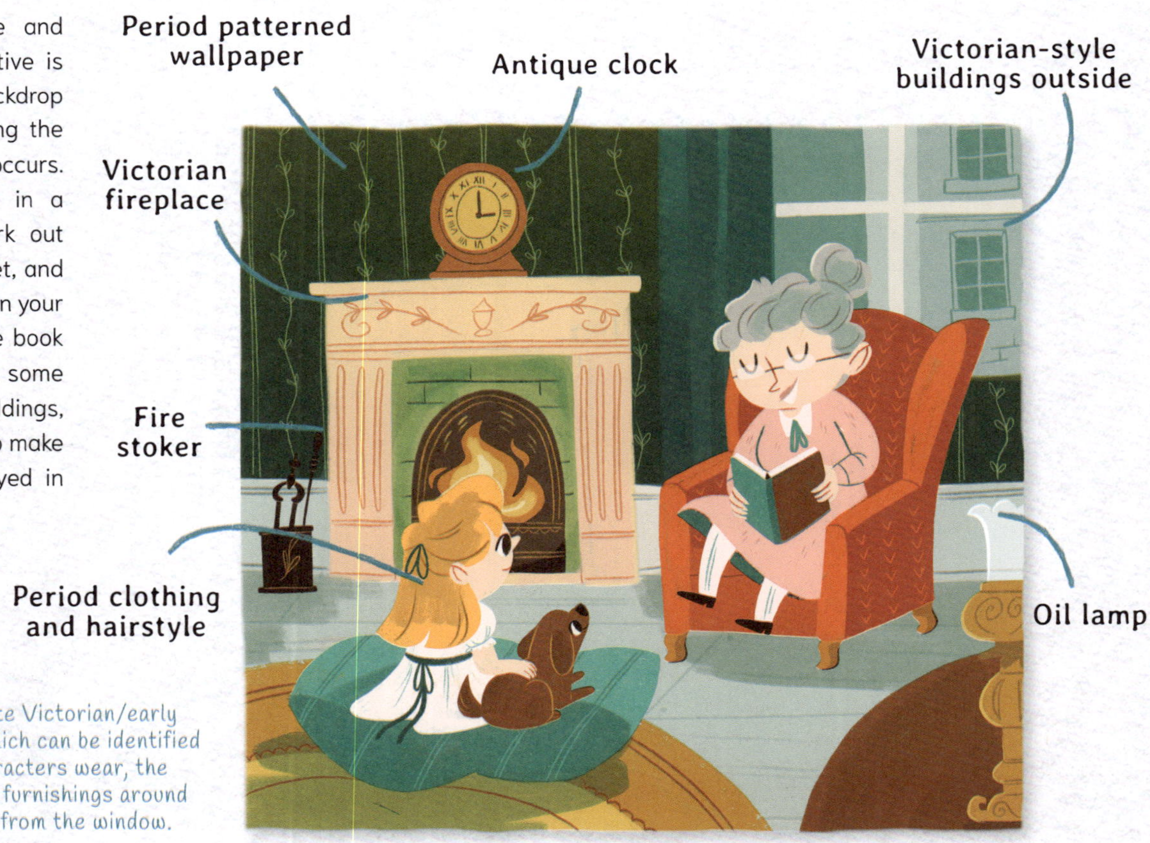


This image is set in a late Victorian/early Edwardian time period, which can be identified by the clothes the characters wear, the little girl's hairstyle, the furnishings around the room, and the view from the window.

## PERSPECTIVE

Perspective provides depth to your illustrations and keeps them interesting rather than monotonous and one-dimensional. It's useful for conveying character emotions and the intensity of action scenes. Instead of showing a character from an eye-level perspective, try drawing the same scene from above or below and notice how it changes the tone of the scene. Sometimes the narrative changes perspective, inviting the reader to see things from a particular character's point of view. This is an ideal time to shift the perspective of the illustration to help the reader understand the character's emotions or what they're experiencing.



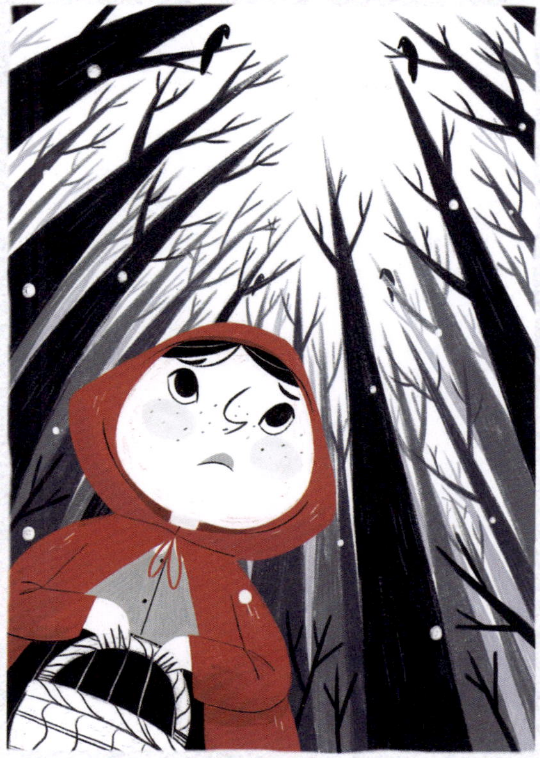

Here Little Red Riding Hood is lost in the woods. Drawing the perspective from below, with the trees reaching up around her, creates a sense of dread and foreboding, emphasizing how lost she feels.

## STORIES WITHIN STORIES

The key narrative plot devices are not the only elements you need to consider when it comes to fleshing out your work. Telling smaller background stories throughout the illustrations can also help to further the engagement of your reader.

Think about the kind of world the story is set in. For example, if you have to draw a crowded scene, consider what the characters in the background are doing. In real life these people would have their own personal stories and would be going about their day-to-day lives, so it's important to show this in your work. Two characters could be having a funny conversation, another character might be walking their dog, or two children could be playing together. This applies to any scene you draw; you should always be thinking about what is going on in the background of each spread and the sort of characters you might find there. You could even choose one of these minor characters and give them their own silly story that plays out in the background throughout the book.

By doing this you create a much more well-rounded world to set the story in, making it feel more detailed, realistic, and therefore more relatable for readers. It also engages young readers and their parents by encouraging them to look out for these small background details on each page, providing them with more than just a story, but an entire world for them to enjoy.

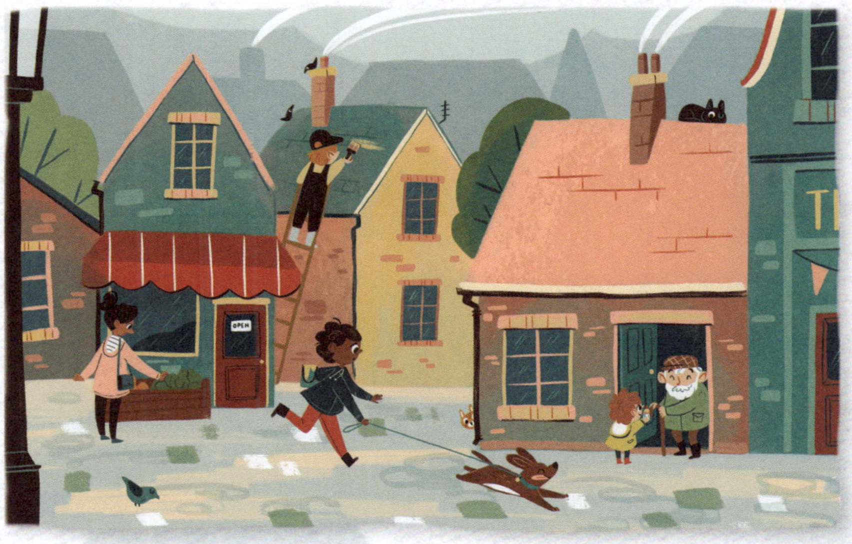

This busy street scene shows lots of different things going on in the village. From left to right, a lady picks a cabbage from the greengrocer, a handyman paints the blue roof yellow, a dog walker is dragged along by her over-excited dog, and a young boy gives an old man a cupcake. In the background there are birds and cats, bunting on the partially hidden shop on the right, a paint tin at the foot of the handyman's ladder, an OPEN sign in the greengrocer's window, and smoke coming from the chimneys. Spreads with lots of detail tell a story of their own, complementing the main narrative and adding to the world that's been created.

# ENGAGEMENT

**Creating engaging and relatable imagery is an incredibly important aspect of illustrating children's books, especially those aimed at younger readers. Picture books in particular will be read night after night, making it crucial that they captivate the interest of young readers and their parents.**

> "CHARACTER APPEAL STEMS FROM THEIR DESIGN, EXPRESSIONS, AND HOW AGE-APPROPRIATE THEY ARE FOR THE READER"

## CHARACTER APPEAL

Characters and their stories are the parts of books readers tend to focus on and remember the most. It's therefore important that they're appealing, which can be accomplished through creating engaging imagery.

Character appeal stems from their design, expressions, and how age-appropriate they are for the reader. For example, when creating a villain for a children's book, you don't want them to be too scary for young readers – they need to be suitable for the book's age group. This can be achieved through their character design and the way you draw their facial expressions. It's important to remember that even a scary or villainous character needs to be redeemable and appealing to the reader!

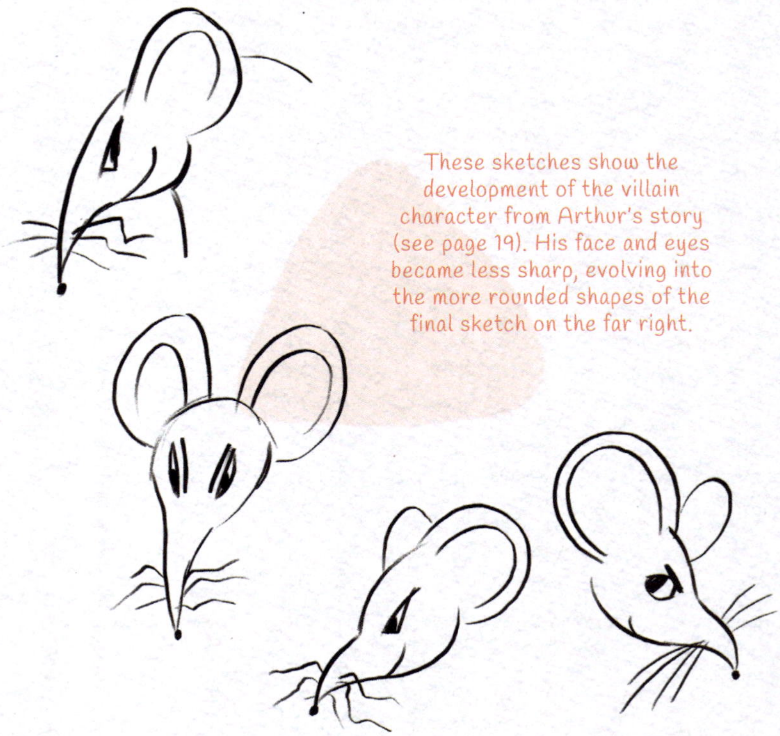

These sketches show the development of the villain character from Arthur's story (see page 19). His face and eyes became less sharp, evolving into the more rounded shapes of the final sketch on the far right.

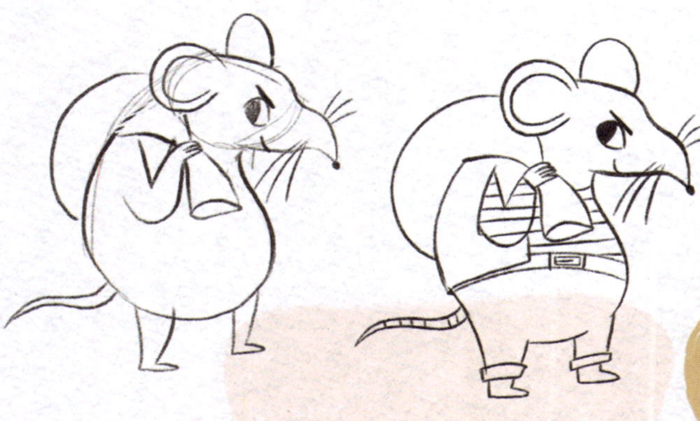

These developmental drawings for the character's final design convey his villainous nature through his slanted eyebrows, pointed nose, sly smile, and hunched back, plus his clothing and sack suggest that he's a thief. Despite looking like a villain, his overall shapes are rounded and the colors used are bright, making him more appealing to a younger audience.

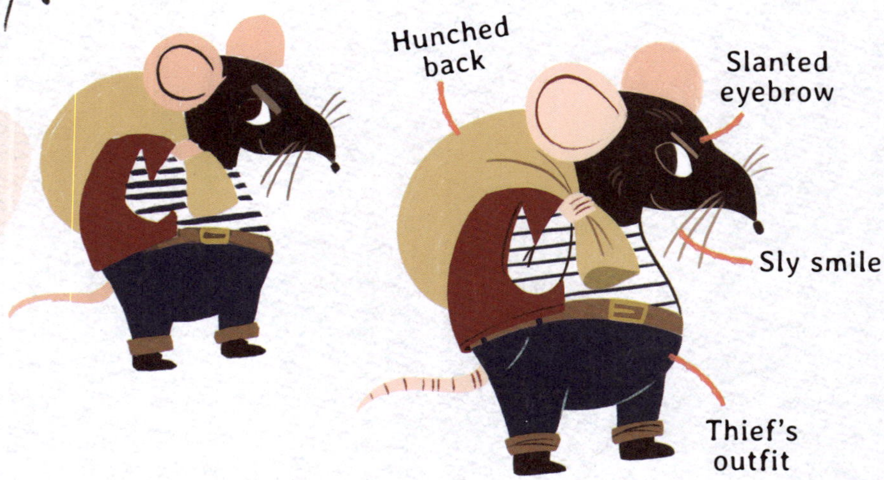

# USE OF COLOR

Use of color plays an incredibly important role in maintaining the engagement of your audience. The style and colors of the illustrations help carry the reader through the narrative, so it's important the color palette you choose remains consistent throughout the book. If you have different color palettes scattered over different pages, the consistency is broken. This makes it hard for the reader to process what's happening in the narrative, as each page will look as though it's part of a different story. In contrast, choosing one color palette to use throughout the book will create a unified and consistent look, making the story much easier to follow and enjoy.

When choosing a color palette, it's a good idea to pick colors that reflect the tone of the book. In general, you want a color palette that's bright but also versatile, so it can portray different scenes and moods in the story. The colors need to be complementary, but also contrasting. The best way to achieve this is by referring to color theory and the color wheel.

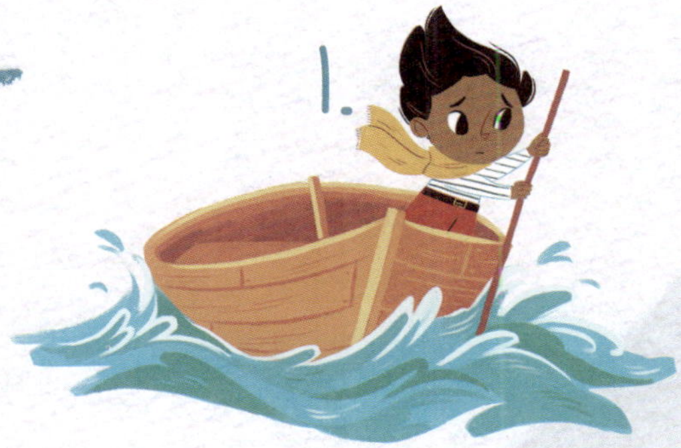


These three illustrations show a little boy who lands on a tropical island. Images one and two use vibrant blues and oranges to emphasize the warmth of the environment, whereas image three uses a cooler blue with purples, which makes the image feel cooler. The use of two different color palettes makes the story feels disjointed and inconsistent, which is hard to follow visually.

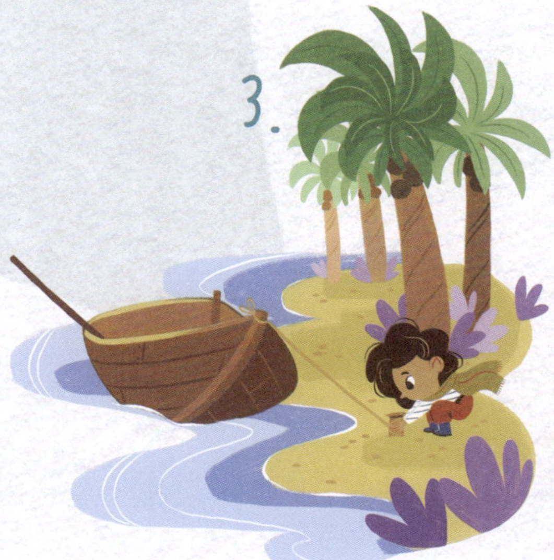


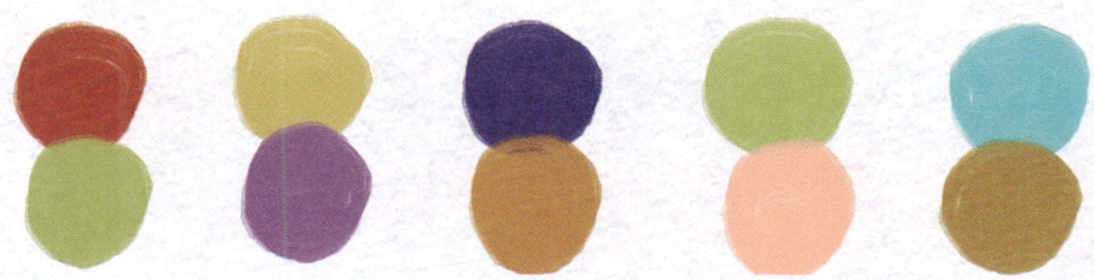

COMPLEMENTARY COLORS

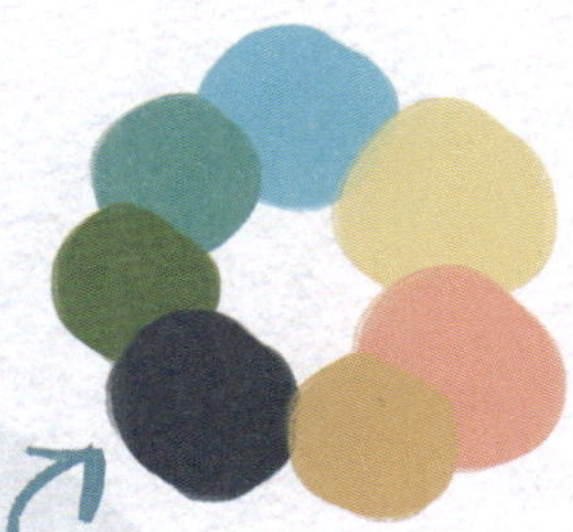

WARM COLORS

COOL COLORS

These two color wheels show the color palettes used for the illustrations above. The top one works beautifully in warm, summer daytime scenes, and the lower wheel would work well in cool, winter, or night-time scenes. For warm scenes, it's best to use colors with warmer tones like peach, red, mustard, and oranges, and to contrast them with teal blues. For cooler scenes, it's best to opt for colors like blues, purples, and lemon yellows.

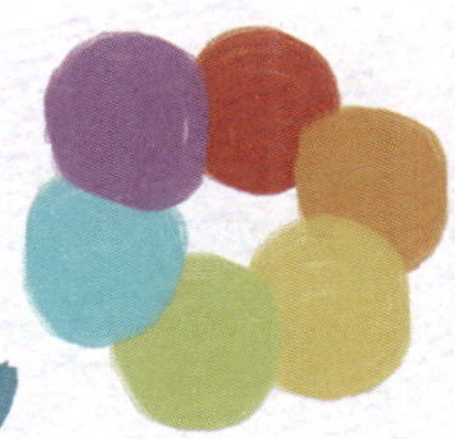

THE COLOR WHEEL

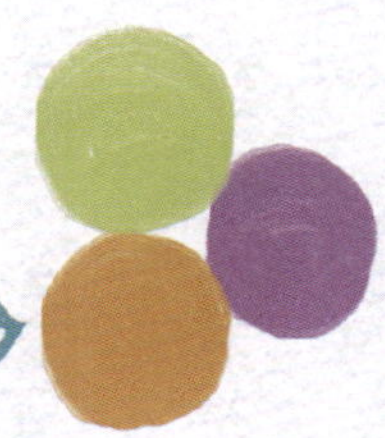

SECONDARY COLORS

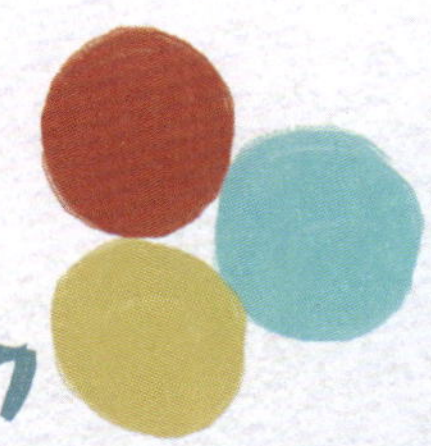

PRIMARY COLORS

When choosing a color palette, it's useful to reference the color wheel (bottom left), which is made up of primary colors (bottom right) and secondary colors (bottom middle). Primary colors alone can be used to make strong color palettes, as can opposing colors on the color wheel. Orange and blue, green and pink or red, and purple and yellow – these are called complementary colors because they complement each other well. They're a good foundation to start building a color palette from.

## LOOK AGAIN

As mentioned, picture books are often read and re-read night after night by parents to their young children. It's therefore important that the illustrations have layers of detail and depth so children can spot new details on their second or third reads that they didn't notice at first. For example, you can hide little items, animals, or minor characters throughout the book, encouraging children to look out for them and giving them a sense of achievement when they find them.

You can also include visual gags by introducing recurring background characters who have their own small stories that play out behind the main story. These little details are not only interesting for children, they also encourage parents to spend time looking through the book with their child so they can have fun spotting details together.

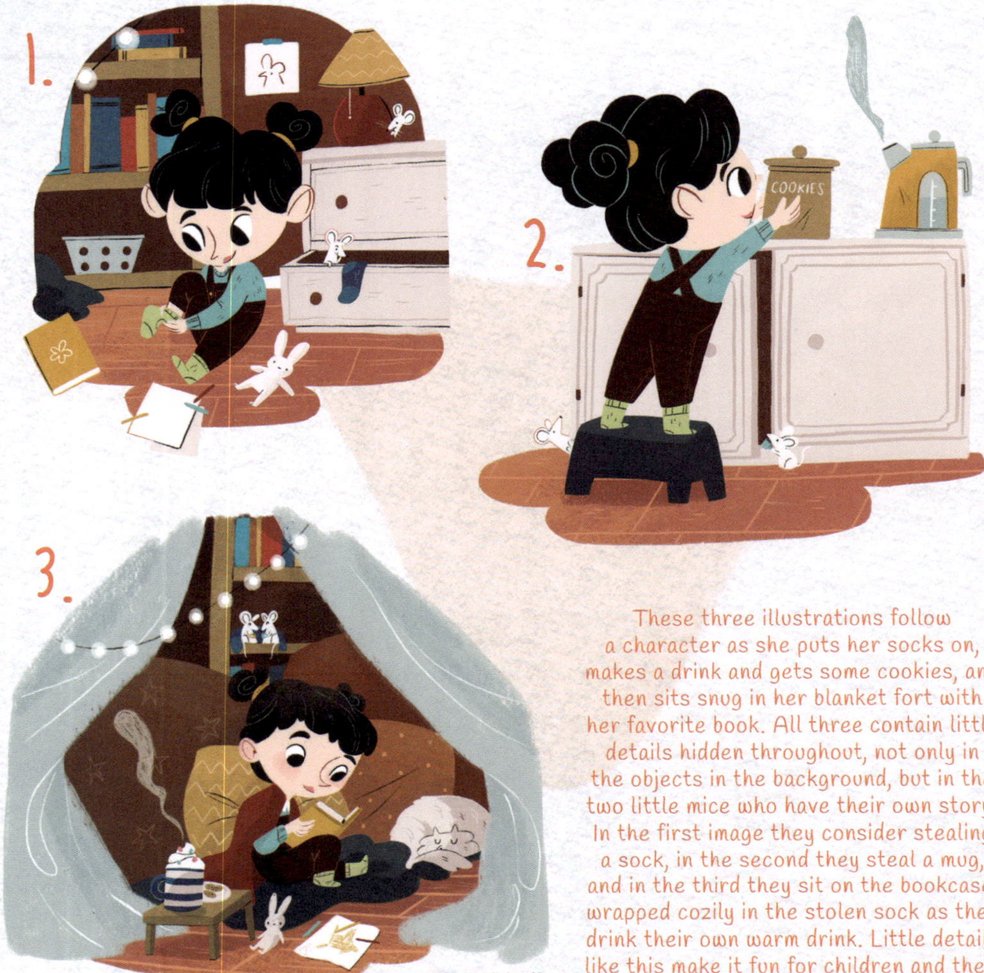

© RUTH HAMMOND

These three illustrations follow a character as she puts her socks on, makes a drink and gets some cookies, and then sits snug in her blanket fort with her favorite book. All three contain little details hidden throughout, not only in the objects in the background, but in the two little mice who have their own story. In the first image they consider stealing a sock, in the second they steal a mug, and in the third they sit on the bookcase, wrapped cozily in the stolen sock as they drink their own warm drink. Little details like this make it fun for children and their parents to read and spot them together.

## EDUCATION AND INTERACTION

Education is important in children's books. Even the most whimsical of stories tend to include some educational themes, teaching children important values and lessons. The values conveyed in a story will generally be those that are important to the author, and will be shared with the illustrator in the brief or through discussions to allow you to fully capture them in the illustrations.

There are a few factors to consider when illustrating educational values in books. You need to ensure accuracy and that the right lessons are being taught to the right age group. If you're creating work for a non-fiction book, such as one based on sea life, then you need to make sure the creatures, environments, and objects are stylized and fun while also accurate to how they look in real life. You can still add fun details in the background and give the creatures different characters – this will encourage parent and child interaction with the book. Young readers are unlikely to find educational books engaging unless the illustrations are fun and bright.

## FARMYARD ANIMALS

Here is a line of farmyard animals. The colors are bright and engaging, and although the animals are stylized, they're easily identifiable as the animals they're meant to be as they have been drawn using references. They are also doing things these animals would normally be doing – the pig is rolling in mud, for example – making them seem more realistic. Children can easily look over this illustration with their parents and name the farmyard animals in a fun and enjoyable way.

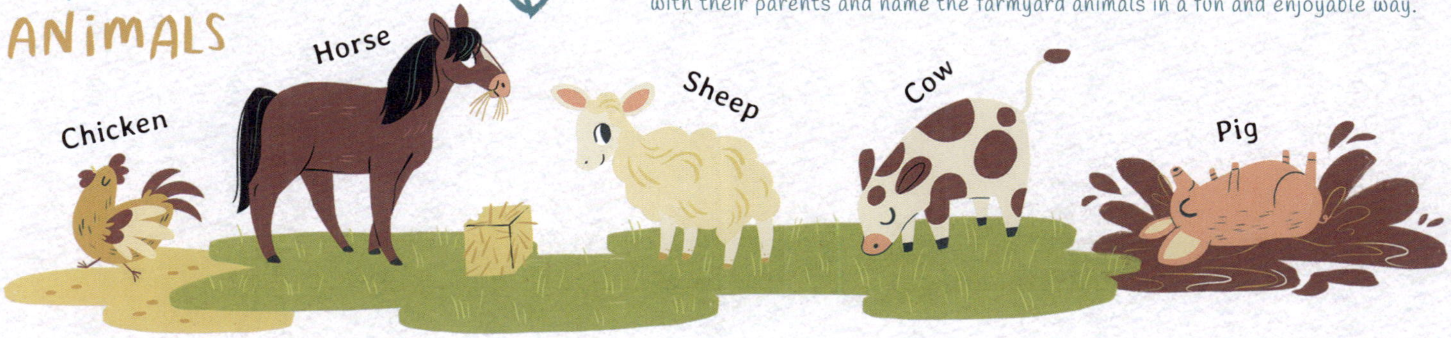


What do pigs like to play in?

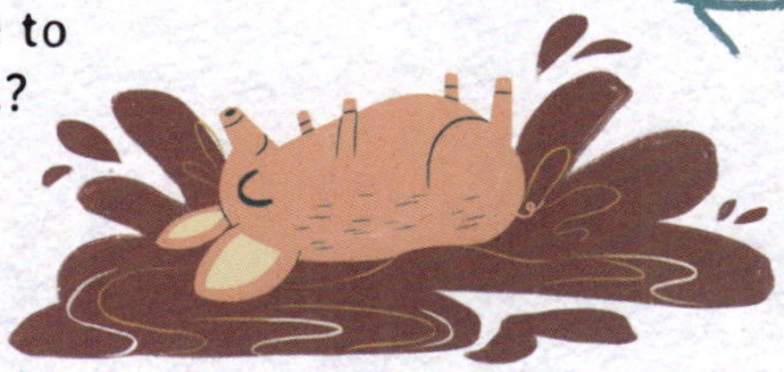

This illustration shows two of the animals from the previous image, but here there are two easy questions for children to answer, encouraging them to interact with the spread and learn at the same time.

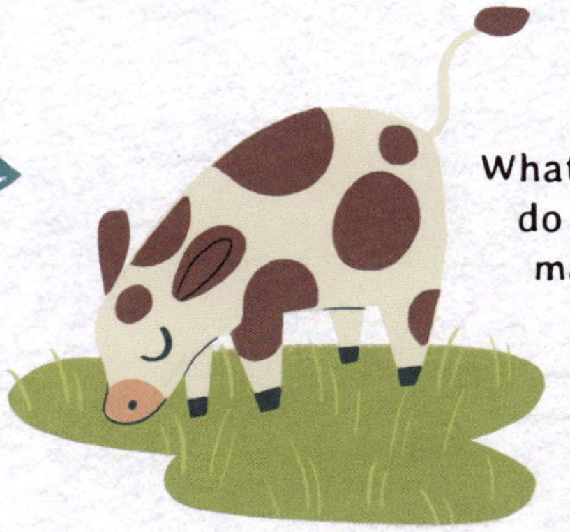

What sound do cows make?

## RELATABILITY

Relatability is the core element that encourages engagement with your audience. The aim is for the reader to be able to see themselves in the story and its characters, and therefore the illustrations need to feature recognizable and familiar elements they can engage with. Even a whimsical fantasy story needs to contain some recognizable features to ground the story and imagery, encouraging the reader to relate to and see themselves in the narrative.

Here are two dragons that have been placed in a real-life setting. Every child can relate to the eagerness and hunger for a long-awaited dinner. Additionally, the kitchen is filled with everyday kitchen items, the characters are wearing normal clothes, and the younger dragon has his toy safely within reach. Even though these fantasy characters don't exist in the real world, this illustration makes their lives look familiar and relatable.

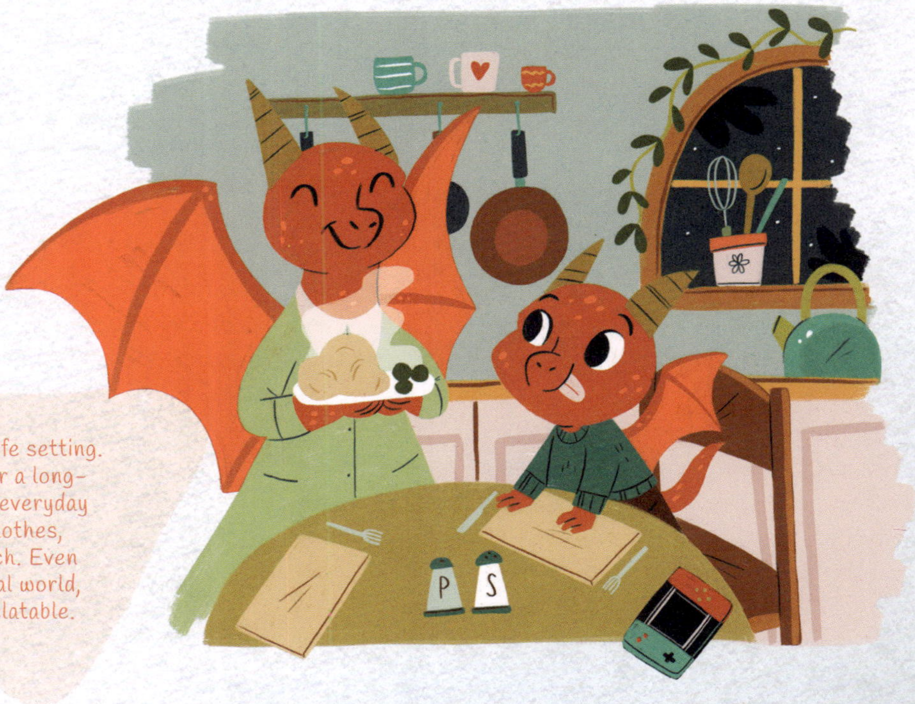

# WORKING WITH WORDS

**When working as a professional illustrator, some jobs may only require you to supply the artwork, working to a template provided by the client, whereas other jobs could ask you to choose the fonts and lay the text out yourself. When tasked with laying out a complete picture book, it's important to think about the position of the text on the page and to consider the type of fonts and typography children will be able to read.**

## MAKING SPACE FOR WORDS

Words play just as important a role as the illustrations in picture books; they tell the story verbally, while the illustrations tell it visually. Illustrations need to work around, and with, the words to ensure both fit comfortably on the spread.

If the client is in control of the typography and text layout, they will usually provide the illustrator with a PDF template of where they want the words to sit on the page so the illustrator can create the illustrations to fit this layout. Alternatively, if the illustrator has been given freedom over the text layout, they will typically be given a PDF template of the page with spread and bleed dimensions (the bleed is the excess bit of page that gets cut off when the book is trimmed to size), plus a separate text document that contains the story.

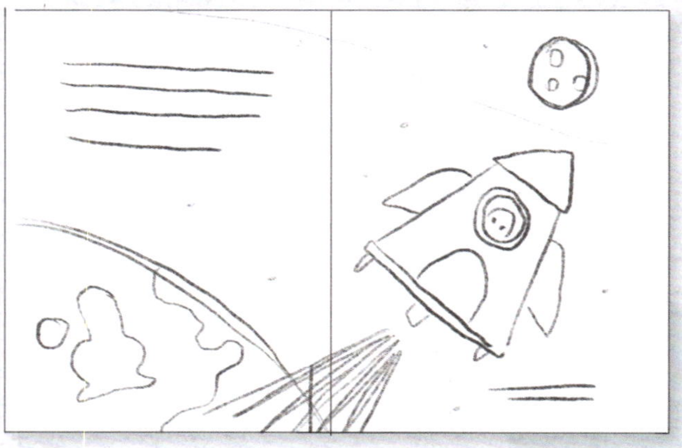

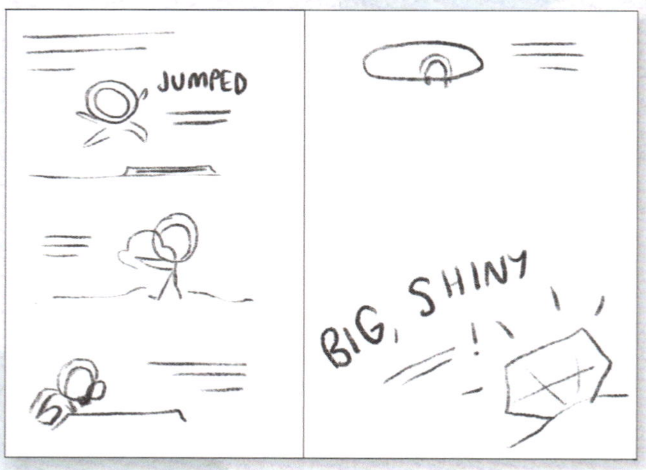


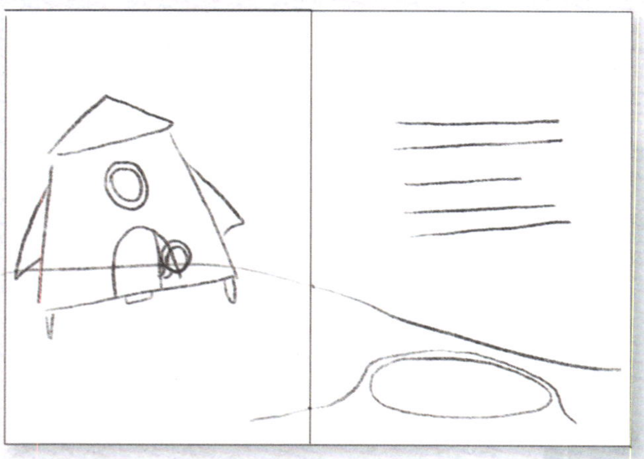

These thumbnails show the rough plan for the layout of the illustrations and text in a book, the horizontal lines representing where the text will sit on the page. It's important to plan the position of the text in the early stages to ensure you remember to leave room for it in the final artwork.

The next step is to work out how to split the text between the pages, separating the key events that need illustrating while still maintaining the overall rhythm of the text. Dividing the text into separate events will allow you to see what actions or conversations need illustrating. How you decide to split the story up will depend on the pace of the narrative. If there are lots of events happening, dividing the text into smaller chunks could work well, allowing you to illustrate each through a series of vignettes and spot illustrations. The points at which the text should be split will depend on how heavy the text is and how many different events it covers.

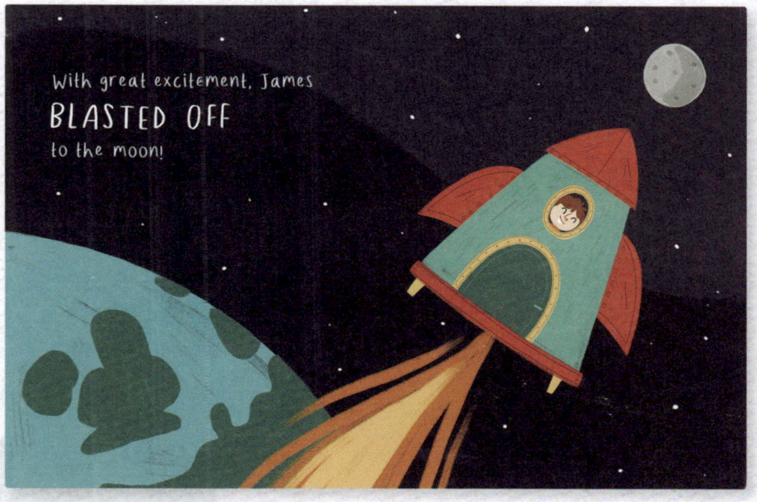


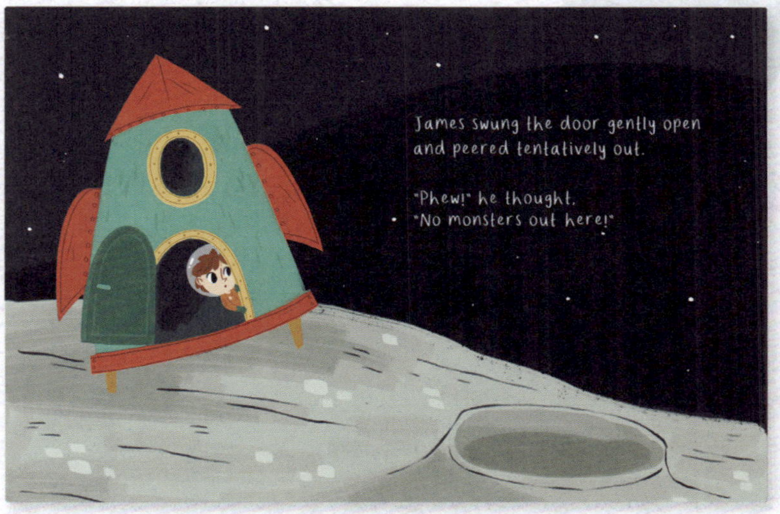


Your illustrations should sit alongside the text, allowing children to read and see what's happening at the same time. Sometimes it's better to split one large block of text into two separate paragraphs to clearly show what's happening in the illustrations. Regardless of whether the illustrator or publisher is handling the text layout, it's important to remember to leave room for the text on the spread, creating the artwork around the space where the text will sit. Whether you're creating a single page illustration or a double-page spread, make sure the space where the text will be added doesn't contain any detail to ensure the text is easily readable. Though in this case there is white text set on a dark background, the text will usually be black due to the printing process. The color of the illustration behind the text needs to contrast, again to ensure the text can be easily read. If this is unfeasible, sometimes allowances can be made to change the text to a lighter color, but it's best to discuss this with the client first before you make any decisions.

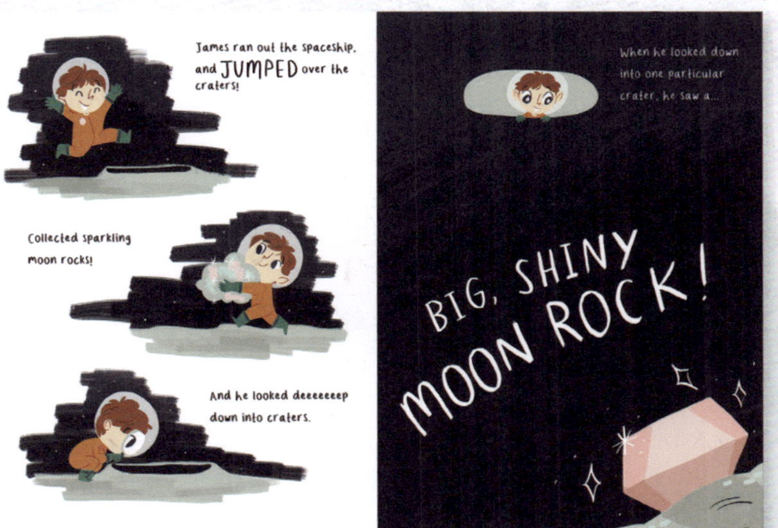


These color illustrations show how the final text is laid out on top of the artwork. The stars have been positioned strategically around the text and certain words have been emphasized in larger lettering to show their importance and so the text looks more interesting.

# TYPOGRAPHY

Typography is an important visual element in children's books. The font needs to be as fun and exciting as the illustrations alongside it, while still being clearly legible for both the parents and children reading it. Remember, the children turning the pages will be learning to read themselves, so they need to be able to recognize the different words and letters.

Handwritten or clean, simple fonts are usually a safe and successful option when choosing the typography style, as they're fun and interesting to look at. While there are plenty of licenses that can be bought for handwritten fonts, it's also easy to make your own using online resources. There are some important aspects to keep in mind when choosing or creating a font, such as the importance of using educational letters, like the correct lowercase "a," and avoiding serif fonts (fonts with small lines or strokes attached to longer strokes) or any with embellishments, particularly for the interior text.

Cover text typography should be bold, fun, and eye-catching. As you can see with these sample fonts, the top two are fairly formal and standard, whereas the bottom two are handwritten and much more fun to look at. The top handwritten font is slightly easier to read and is therefore better suited for use on the book cover.

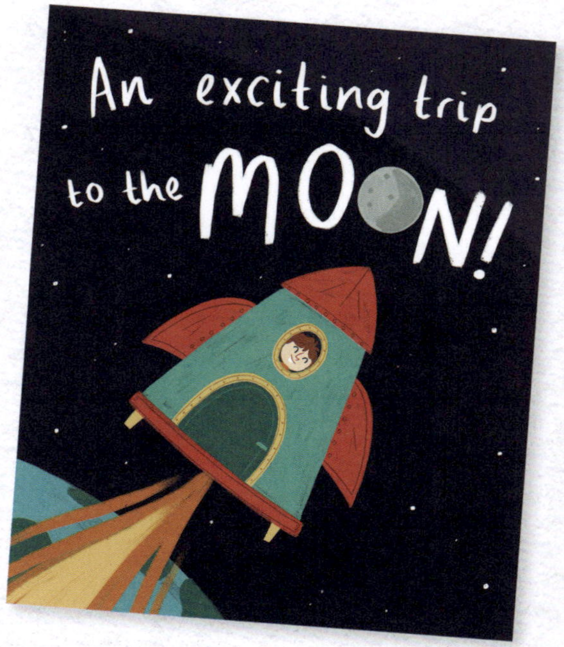


An exciting trip to the MOON!

An exciting trip to the MOON!

An exciting trip to the MOON!

An exciting trip to the MOON!

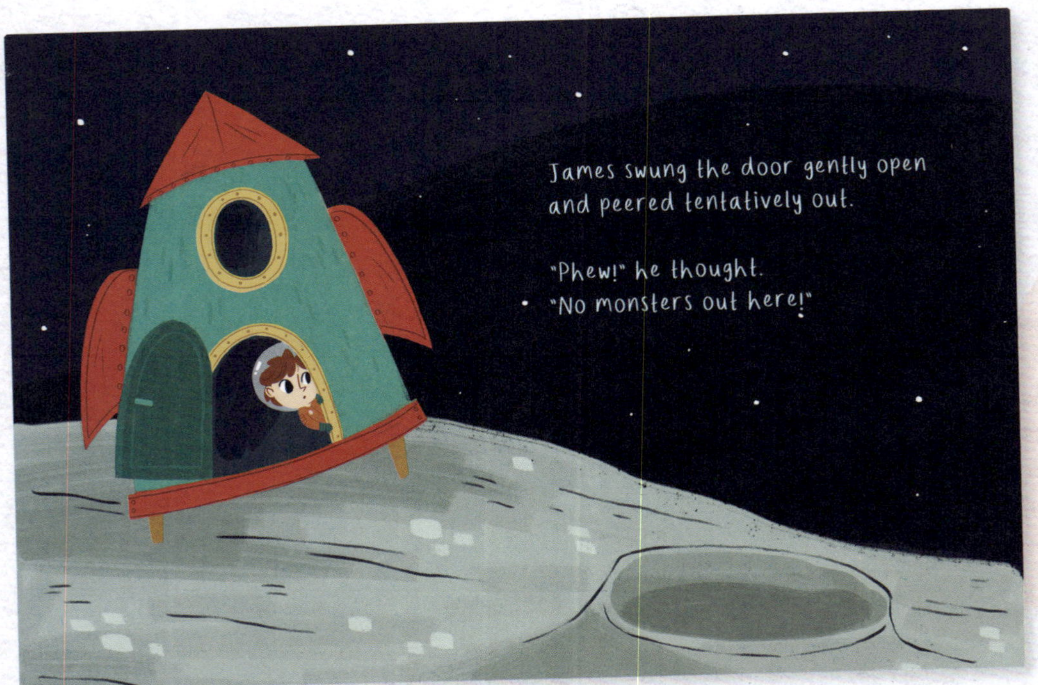


This spread features a handwritten font. It has no embellishments and features the correct form of lowercase lettering, making it very legible and perfect for use in the interior of a picture book.

Font: ruth's hand bold

Additionally, it's important to keep the number of fonts used in the book to a minimum, using one primary font for the interior, with possibly a secondary option for emphasized words, fun quotes, or sounds. The exterior font for the title should be bold, fun, and appealing to the audience to ensure the book stands out on the shelves. For picture books, this is usually a bold handwritten font created by the illustrator, sometimes accompanied by one or two other fonts that are the same as the interior. Continuity doesn't just apply to the color palette and illustrations – it applies to the typography too!

Font: ruth's hand

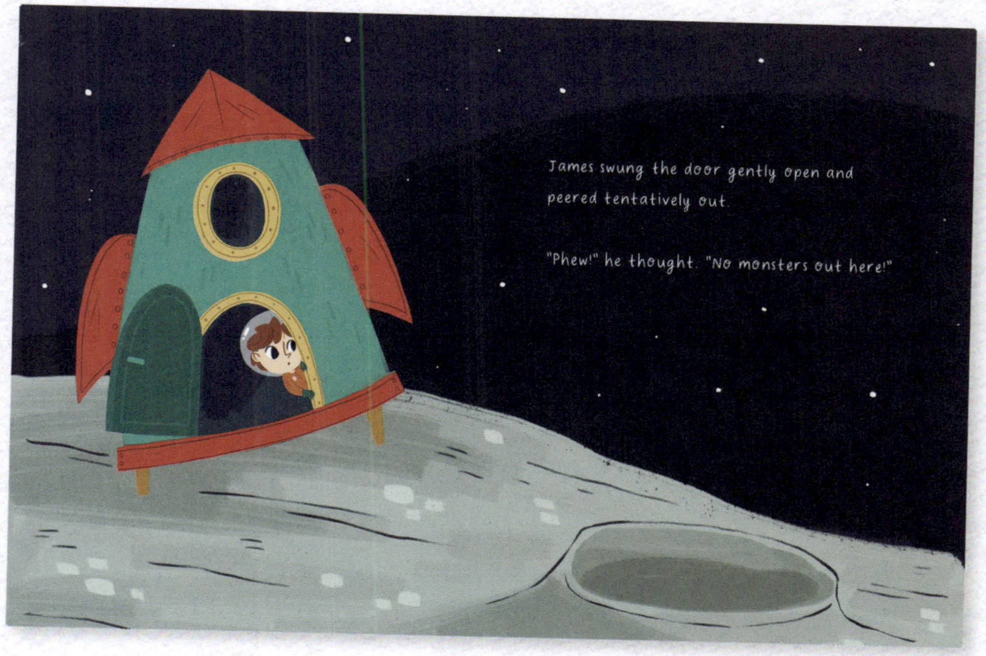


This spread includes a different handwritten font. It's fairly clear and is fun to read, but features embellishments on some of the lowercase letters, such as the "o," "y," and "g." This could confuse young readers, so it may not be the best font to use here.

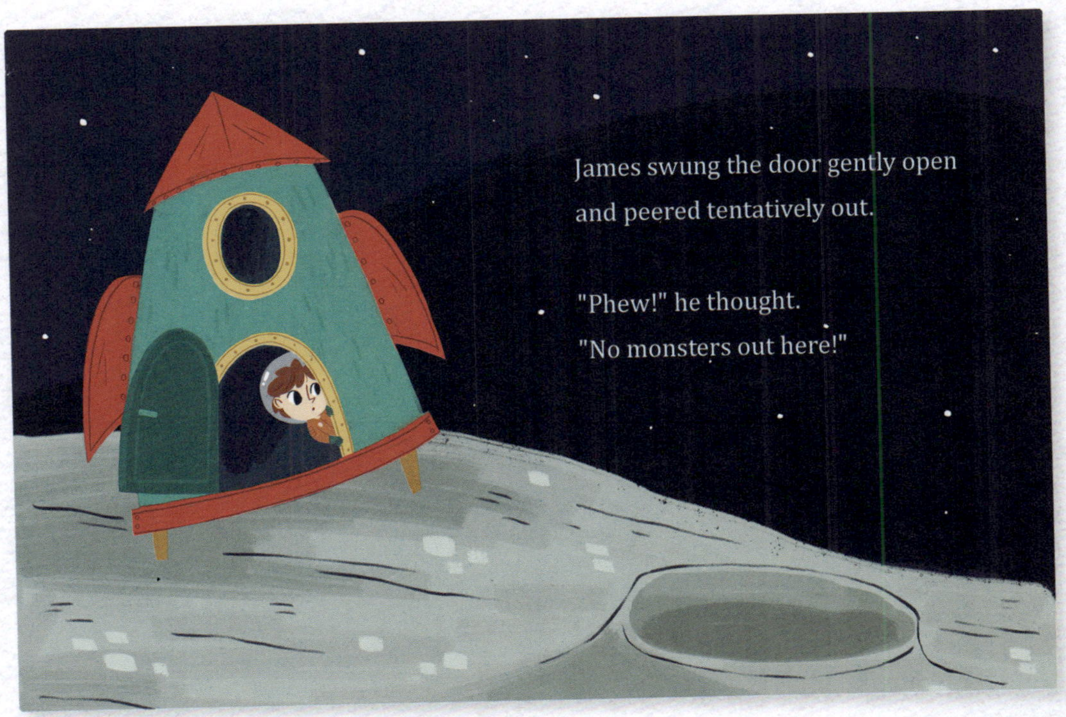


font: cambria

This spread features a standard uniform font. It's clear and easy to read, but does contain a different form of lowercase letter "a." It also doesn't give the impression of a fun and whimsical story, so may not be the best font to use in the interior of a picture book.

# ILLUSTRATION AS A PROFESSION

**If you want to work professionally as a children's book illustrator, there are a number of things you need to consider. Firstly, take some time to think about whether a formal education and university course would be beneficial to your goals, and secondly, consider how you can build a strong and eye-catching portfolio. There is also the difficult task of self-promotion and finding clients, along with working with publishers and all the legalities that come with it. Though it might sound daunting, this chapter will help guide you through each stage of the process.**

Whether you should enroll on a professional illustration course all depends on what you want to learn and take away from it. Studying for a National Diploma in Fine Art followed by a BA in Illustration, or similar, can be incredibly beneficial if you're certain that drawing and illustration are what you wish to pursue as a career. They are often suited to younger artists, fresh out of school or college, who require guidance and structure with deadlines, helping them acquire an understanding of the process of creating illustrations and how to find their style.

A university course will teach you how to juggle numerous different deadlines and projects, and allow you to experiment with different forms of illustration, including children's book, editorial, and advertising. Tutors, who will usually be professional illustrators themselves, will be on-hand to provide feedback on your work, plus there will be the opportunity to attend talks from professional illustrators actively working in the field. A university course can also introduce you to other aspiring illustrators who share similar interests and career goals. Many artists find it encouraging and inspiring to be around so many other creatives who they can share their work with and learn from, as it can introduce you to a variety of different styles and ways of working. Such courses help to lay the foundations many artists need to pursue illustration as a career.

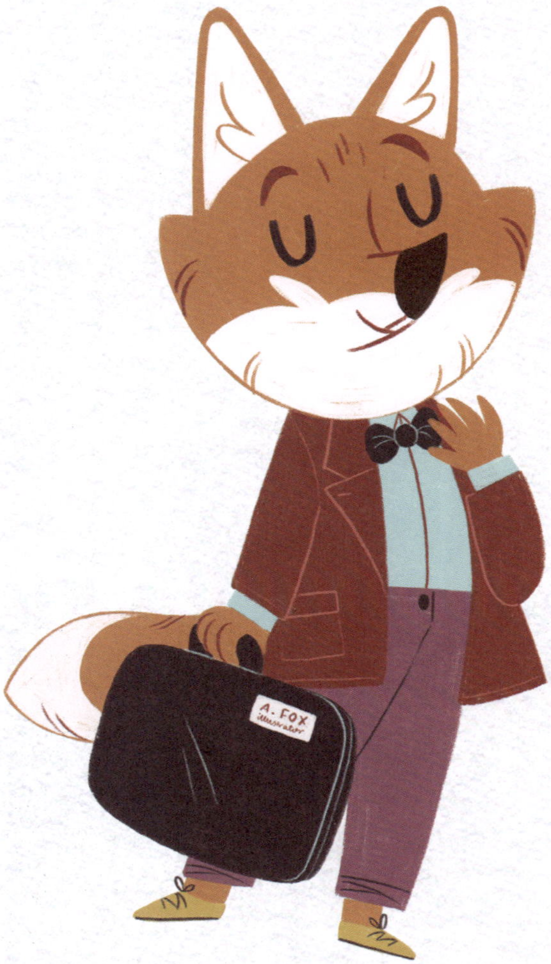

"A UNIVERSITY COURSE CAN INTRODUCE YOU TO OTHER ASPIRING ILLUSTRATORS WHO SHARE SIMILAR INTERESTS AND CAREER GOALS"

Despite all of this, it's important to note that studying illustration at university won't suit everyone. The courses can be very intensive when studied full-time and not everyone will benefit from that sort of environment. If this is the case for you, don't worry – there are plenty of other ways to become an illustrator without studying for a degree in it. The rise of social media and increase in online resources have become incredibly effective in helping artists advance in their professional careers.

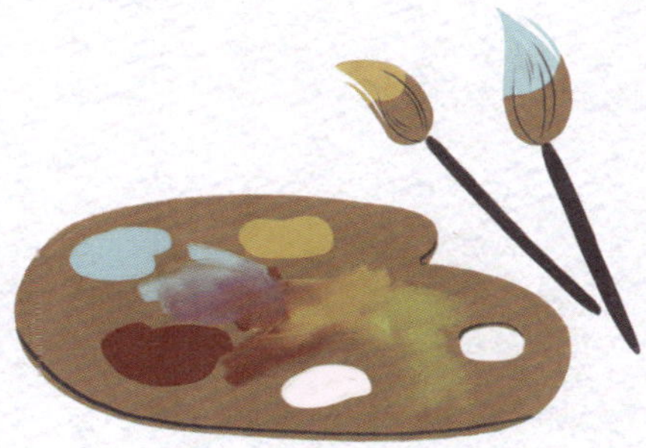

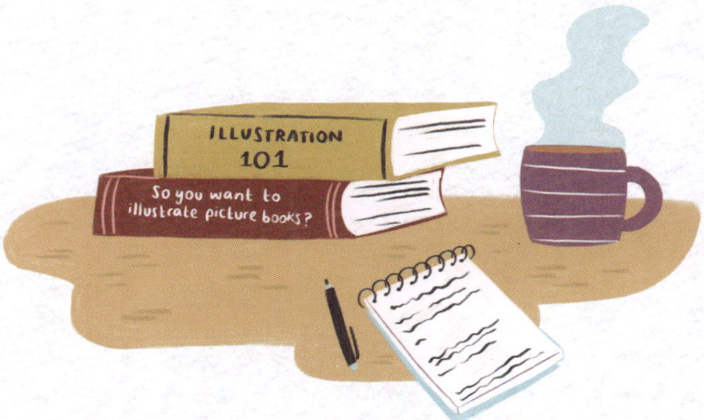


Instagram, for example, is a great social media platform as it has a large art community, allowing you to connect with and learn from other illustrators, both professional and hobbyists, who all specialize in different areas of illustration. Some illustrators provide their own online resources, either directly on their Instagram account or through other platforms such as YouTube and Patreon, where they may share tutorials and create videos full of advice. There are also platforms like Skillshare where leading artists create and share in-depth online courses in their specialist areas, allowing you to learn from them and apply it to your own work – almost like a mini university course from the comfort of your own home!

"THE RISE OF SOCIAL MEDIA AND INCREASE IN ONLINE RESOURCES HAVE BECOME INCREDIBLY EFFECTIVE IN HELPING ARTISTS ADVANCE IN THEIR PROFESSIONAL CAREERS"

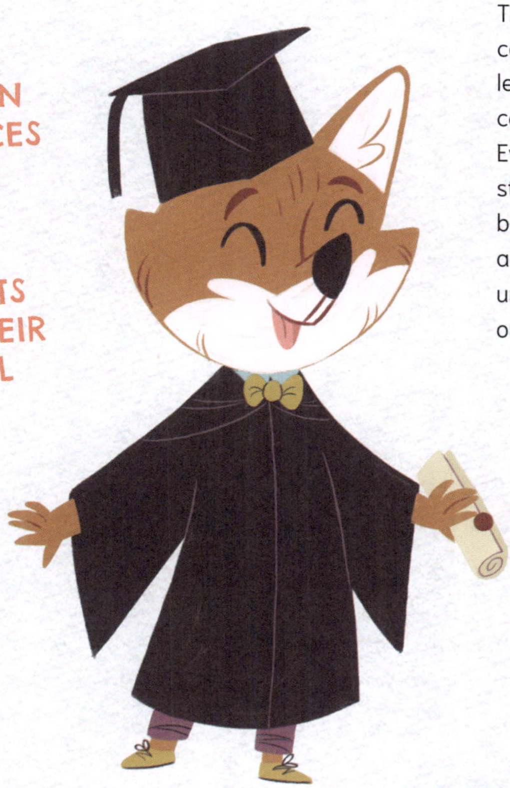

The importance of studying a professional illustration course is subjective – it comes down to what type of learning environment you work best in, as well as what you can fit around any existing commitments you might have. Even if you do enroll to study illustration at university, it's still worth investing time into social media, as it will be beneficial during your degree and when you graduate. An artist's visual signature will continue to develop long after university if they make good use of social media and other online resources.

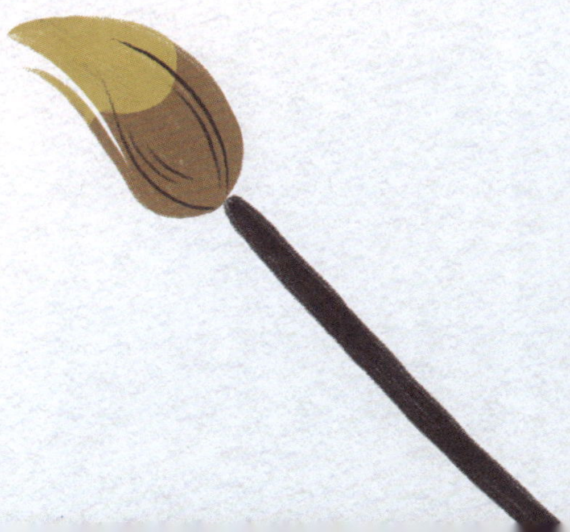

# BUILDING A PORTFOLIO

Building a strong portfolio of work is incredibly important if you want to pursue illustration professionally. Potential clients need to see the type of work you're capable of creating so they know what to expect if they commission you. As the purpose of a portfolio is to showcase your best work, there are a number of things to keep in mind to ensure it's the strongest it can be.

The most important thing to remember when building your portfolio is to tailor it to your client. For example, potential children's book clients won't be interested in a portfolio featuring illustrations for adults, conceptual pieces, or illustrations with serious themes. They will want to see a body of work that is tailored to children's illustration, with child-friendly imagery and bright colors.

"POTENTIAL CHILDREN'S BOOK CLIENTS WILL WANT TO SEE A BODY OF WORK THAT IS TAILORED TO CHILDREN'S ILLUSTRATION, WITH CHILD-FRIENDLY IMAGERY AND BRIGHT COLORS"

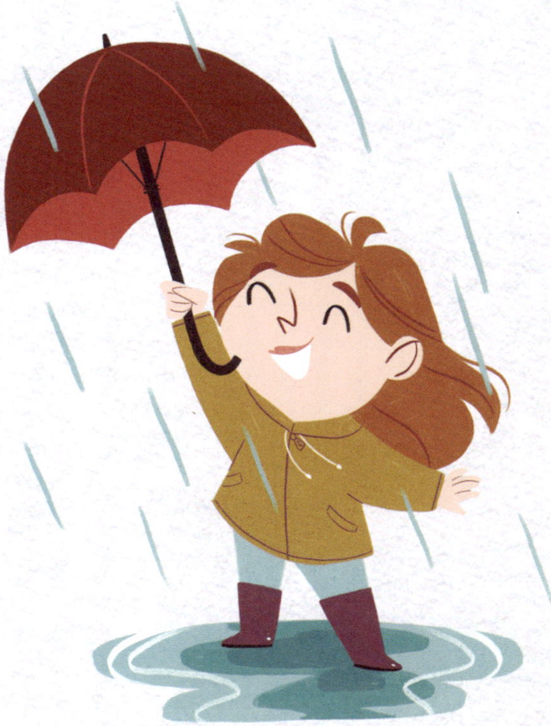

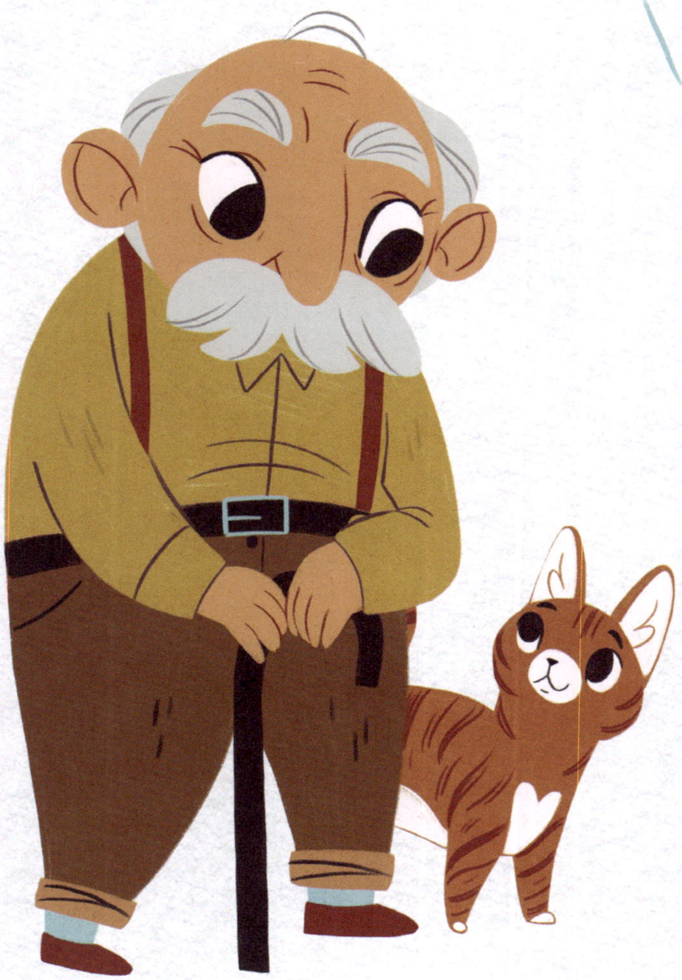

Successful children's book illustration portfolios generally contain thirty to forty strong illustrations that show a variety of different images. The best images to include are:

- character designs, including older characters that children will be familiar with, such as a grandparent
- sample book spreads and covers
- illustrations that feature different indoor and outdoor settings
- various historical periods
- dramatic lighting
- different weather patterns, seasons, and different times of day, including night-time scenes

The sheer quantity of work that has to go into an illustration portfolio can seem intimidating at first. It will take most illustrators a while to build up a strong portfolio, as they will often have other commitments such as a part-time job to sustain them while they freelance. Skill level is also a factor in this, as over time illustrators will hone and improve their craft, meaning that some of their original portfolio pieces will need redrawing to be as strong as their newer pieces.

A useful way to start building a portfolio without becoming overwhelmed is to keep a sketchbook full of thumbnails and loose sketches of potential portfolio illustrations. You may not always have the time to immediately create and finalize every idea you have, so keeping a sketchbook of ideas will allow you to return to older concepts during quieter moments. A strong portfolio is crucial when pursuing a career in illustration, but it's also something that takes time to put together and refine, so don't worry if it isn't immediately up to the highest possible standard.

**"KEEP A SKETCHBOOK FULL OF THUMBNAILS AND LOOSE SKETCHES OF POTENTIAL PORTFOLIO ILLUSTRATIONS"**

It's important to feature a wide range of settings and characters in your portfolio to show variety. For example, weather patterns like rain, older characters that children can relate to (like a grandparent), and night-time scenes.

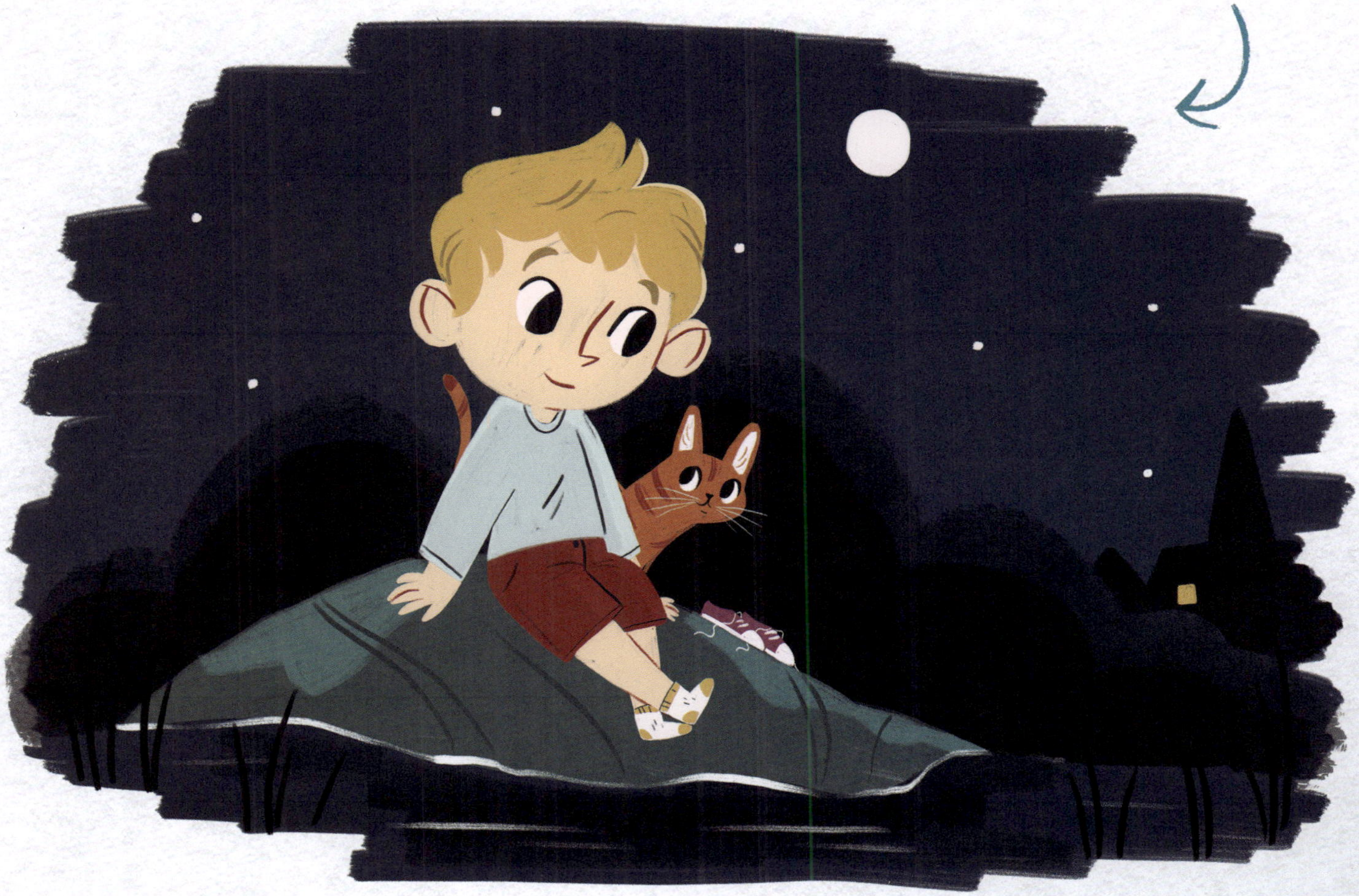

# MARKETING AND PROMOTION

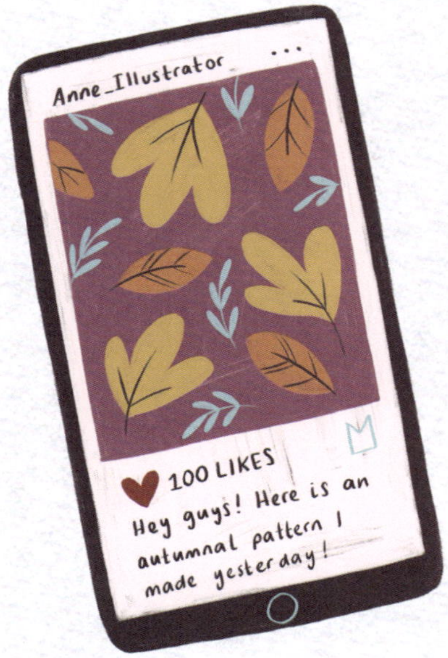


Marketing and promotion was harder to master a few decades ago, but thanks to the invention and increased use of the internet and social media, getting on the radar of publishers and writers has become significantly easier.

Two of the best ways to get noticed online are to post your work on social media and to ensure all of those posts link back to your website. Building a website to showcase your portfolio is crucial, as it allows potential clients to browse your best work, find out more about you as an artist, see who you have previously worked for, and find your direct contact information. There are plenty of user-friendly website-building platforms that allow you to build a website, upload your work, and link a custom domain for a small monthly fee.

In regards to social media, having a large social media following is not necessarily important to a client, but it does help in gaining their interest. A large following gives you more exposure to being found by more people, including potential clients. Building a following online takes time and is helped by posting regularly, interacting with your followers, and using hashtags, including taking part in and using trending hashtags. If you want to be noticed by specific kinds of clients, tailor your hashtags and posts to the sort of client you wish to attract.

"BUILDING A WEBSITE TO SHOWCASE YOUR PORTFOLIO ALLOWS POTENTIAL CLIENTS TO BROWSE YOUR BEST WORK AND FIND OUT MORE ABOUT YOU AS AN ARTIST"

Print business cards to hand out at industry events. Make sure they include your website, contact details, and social media handles.

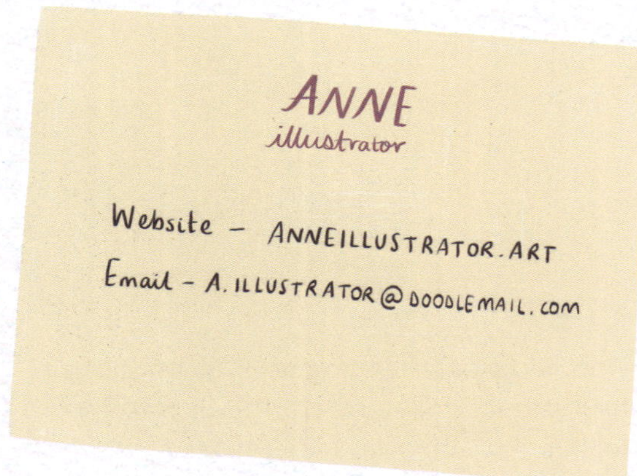


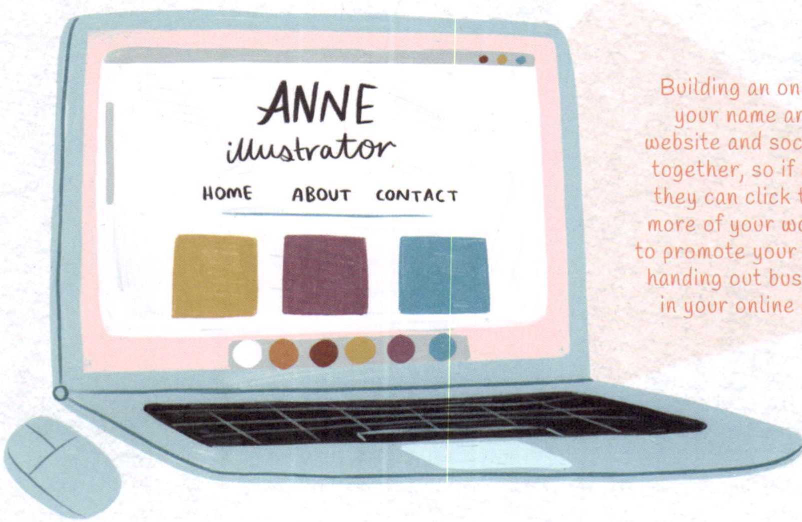


Building an online presence is a useful way to get your name and work noticed. Create your own website and social media accounts, then link the two together, so if a potential client finds your website they can click the links to your social media to see more of your work, and vice versa. It's also possible to promote your website and social media in person by handing out business cards at fairs, or packing them in your online orders if you sell your work online.

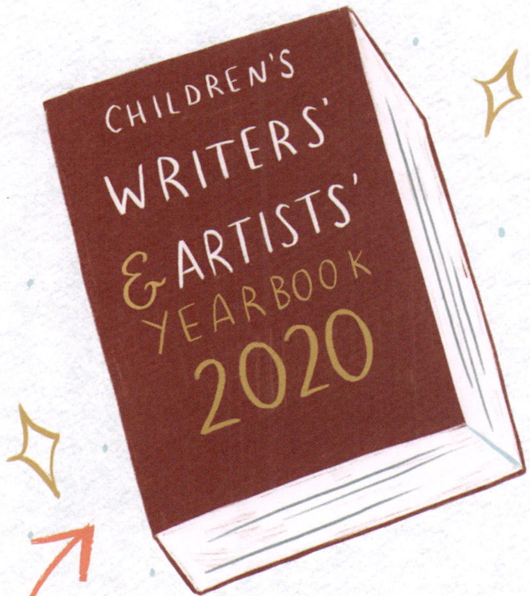


Browsing the *Children's Writers' & Artists' Yearbook'* will give you lots of useful advice about the sort of work publishers are currently looking for, plus contact details and the best ways to approach them. See if your local library has a copy!

Gaining representation with an illustration or literary agency is also beneficial when pursuing illustration as a career, as agencies have direct contact with publishing clients and will be able to share your work with the clients you want to work with. They will also be able to promote your work on their agency social media accounts, as well as on their websites. Before approaching an agency, it's best to check first whether they are accepting submissions, and if they are, to follow the submission guidelines on their website. If you already have contact with someone working at the agency, it's possible that you could send them your portfolio so they can make sure it gets seen by the right people. Agents are not for everyone though, and finding the right one for you may take time. Some artists can feel lost in a huge agency and prefer to be represented by a smaller one. In contrast, a smaller agency may not work for some artists who want a larger agency with a bigger name and wider reach. Some artists even find they get more work without having an agent and so don't feel the need to seek one out.

The *Children's Writers' & Artists' Yearbook'* is a helpful resource to refer to when contacting clients. A new edition of this book is published every year in July and contains helpful advice and contact details for publishers, plus how they prefer to be contacted. There is also the Association of Illustrators (AOI) who champion illustrators and the illustration industry with education, promotion, and campaigning to achieve a thriving industry for everyone. Memberships are available for illustrators, agents, and colleges, with discounts for students and represented artists.

When it comes to contacting publishers yourself, it's common for illustrators to send out postcards of their illustrations that feature new work every few months, making sure to include their name and contact details on the reverse side. This is a useful practice to keep up, as it shows initiative and can make your work more memorable to publishers. Most art submissions publishers receive will occur online or by email, so having something physical will stand out against other submissions. It also shows publishers what your work looks like in print, which is incredibly important in book publishing.

Overall, there are many different ways you can reach out to and be noticed by clients, it's just a matter of working hard and testing the water to see what works best for you.

Try printing your work onto postcards and sending them to children's book publishers you would like to work with. This will show them what your work looks like in print, plus the reverse side will list your contact details so they can get in touch for more information or visit your website to view your portfolio.

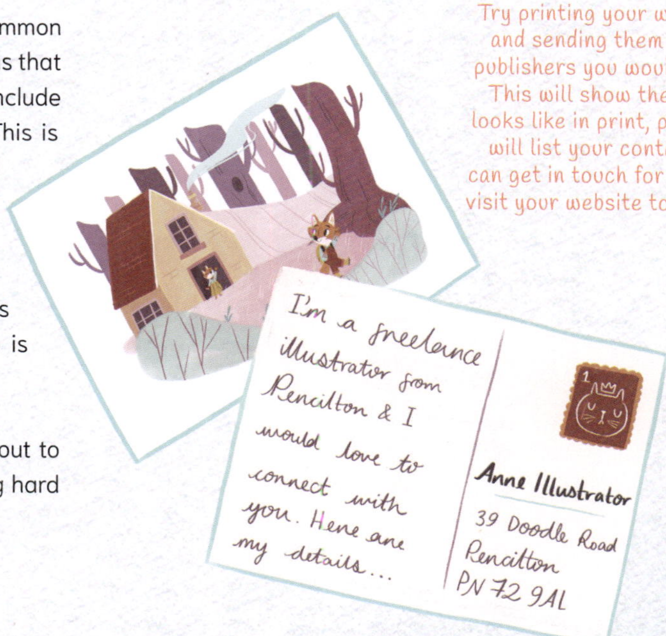

# WORKING WITH PUBLISHERS

There are a couple of different scenarios in which you could find yourself working with a publisher; either you have approached them with your own story and illustrations, or they have approached you with a story they would like you to illustrate. Hearing back from a publisher you have pitched your own story to can take time, sometimes up to a month, as the story is often shared with a number of different editors in the office to get various opinions before they make a decision. When a final decision is made, they will let you know whether they want to publish it or pass. If they pass on your work they will usually explain the reason for their decision, and sometimes even provide detailed feedback on how you can improve it. If your pitch is successful, however, then it's okay to do a happy dance! The publisher will start outlining their proposed financial deal for your book, any changes they might want you to make, and the legal process and deadline arrangement will begin.

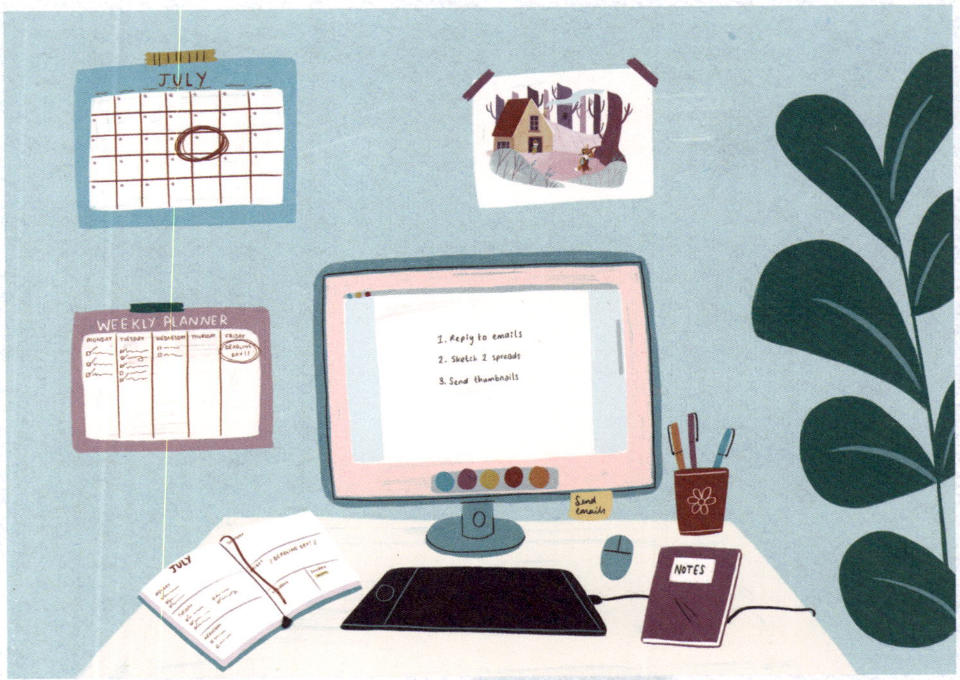


If you have been approached by a publisher to illustrate a book for them, they will usually provide the specifications of the brief detailing the fee, deadlines, and quantity of work. Sometimes they may send you a copy of the story manuscript for you to read through before you make your decision, allowing you to see exactly what the story is about and whether it's something you would like to work on. Once you accept, the publisher will usually ask you to start work on the project while they sort out the legal details and draft up a contract for you to sign. One important thing to note is that when a publisher contacts you, you should be prepared to create sample artwork for the story before committing to the project, as publishers sometimes want to see how your art style will work with the project. While it may be common for them to ask you to do this for free, you need to consider how much work they are asking for and whether you are comfortable with not being paid for it. If you are not, you should discuss any concerns you have with them, politely explaining that you're not happy creating so much work with no payment. It may seem like an awkward thing to bring up, but so long as you are polite and professional when discussing it, the publisher will be understanding.

*Keeping an organized and (somewhat) tidy workspace is an effective way of staying on top of your deadlines. Clearly marking your monthly, weekly, and daily tasks and goals, either digitally on your device or physically pinned to your walls, will help keep you focused and on target, creating a constant reminder of what you have to get done.*

Whether you have approached a publisher yourself, or they have approached you, deadlines will typically be the first thing discussed, as publishers have a schedule that needs to be adhered to in order to get the book printed on time. These deadlines can be quite tight, or sometimes quite long, but all require a level of organization, especially if you are working around other deadlines and commitments. When it comes to time management, start by being realistic about the amount of work you can get done in the set amount of time, and whether the set deadlines will be possible to meet. If they aren't, speak to the publisher to discuss potential extensions.

Once resolved, start by making a long list of everything you need to get done in the upcoming months, marking all deadlines on your calendar or in your diary. If you're a pen and paper sort of person, you may prefer your lists, calendar, and diary to be physical. There are also online resources you can use to manage your time digitally, such as Google Calendar and apps on your phone. Next, break up the month, planning your time week by week and making note of your weekly goals. After that, work day by cay, making a list of small tasks you need to complete each day. It's quite a meticulous system, but it will keep you organized.

Once you have met your deadlines, your artwork will be shown to the design team and editors, and they will contact you with ary feedback. The publisher's main concern is to create a book that will sell, which means their feedback is usually sales-driven and isn't something you should take personally. Typical feedback might include being asked to tweak characters' expressions or actions to make them more readable, altering the composition to better suit the text, or tweaking the colors so the scene and characters are easy to read. The deadline for changes can be quite short, so it's best to prepare for this in advance and plan your time wisely to allow enough time to make any requested edits.

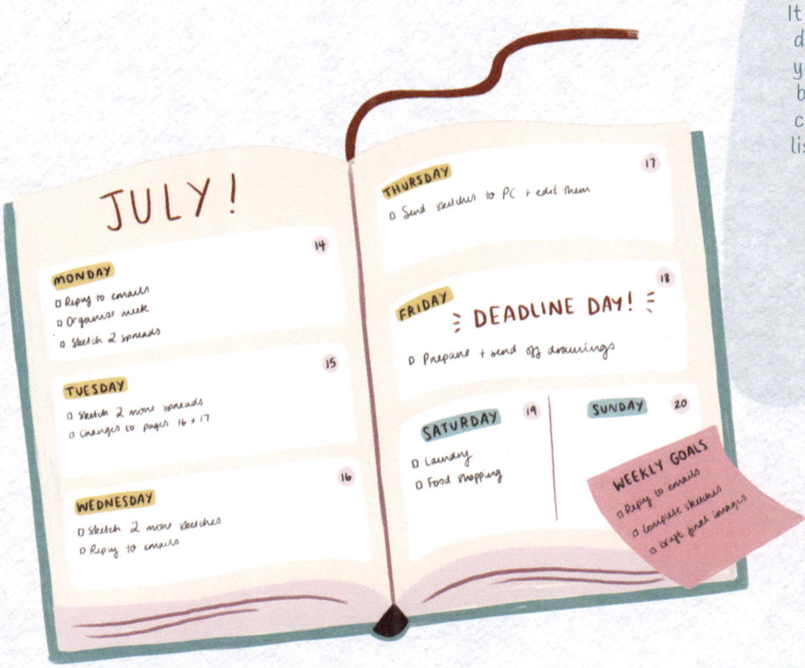


It can be helpful to keep a monthly calendar listing all the deadlines for the month, showing exactly how much time you have to get everything finished. The month can then be divided into weekly and daily "to-do" lists, which you can keep in your diary or on sticky notes. These smaller lists can keep you focused week by week, and day by day, making sure you stay on target for the big deadline.

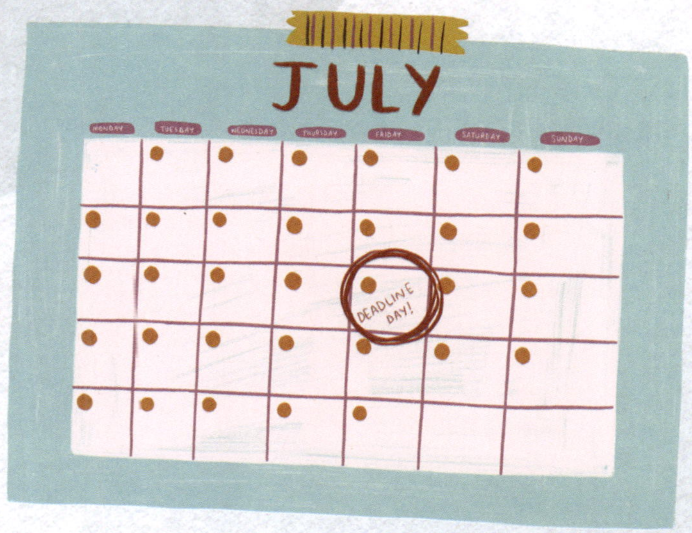

## SELF-PUBLISHING

Self-publishing is becoming an increasingly popular method of publishing due to its ease and affordability. Some of the avenues available for this are ebooks and hard copies, both of which can be sold online or through physical retailers. For a small fee, some online booksellers will allow you to self-publish and sell your book via their platforms, making it more likely for your book to be discovered. Some provide a branded ebook publishing platform, which allows you to simply upload your book and sell it. There are also print-on-demand distributors who will print a copy of your book when someone orders it, which will save you money in the long run, and offer distribution services, saving you time in finding retailers to stock your books.

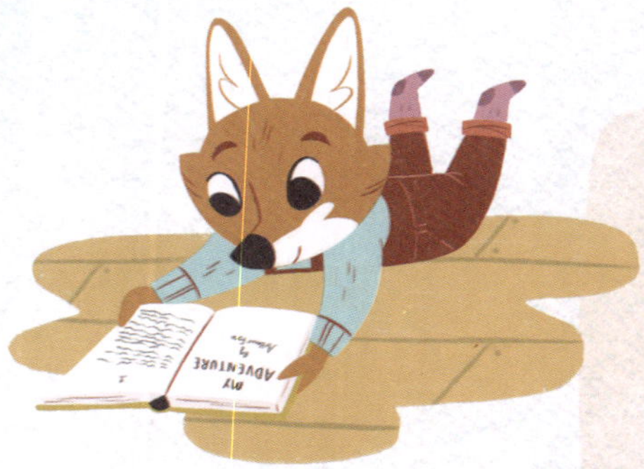

"CONTRACTS ARE THERE TO PROTECT BOTH YOU AND THE CLIENT"

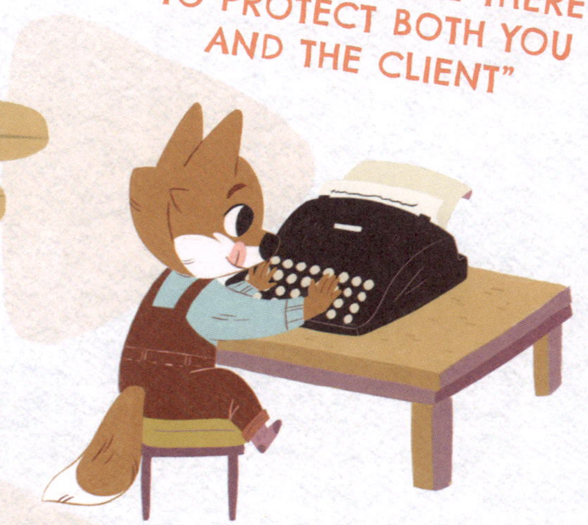

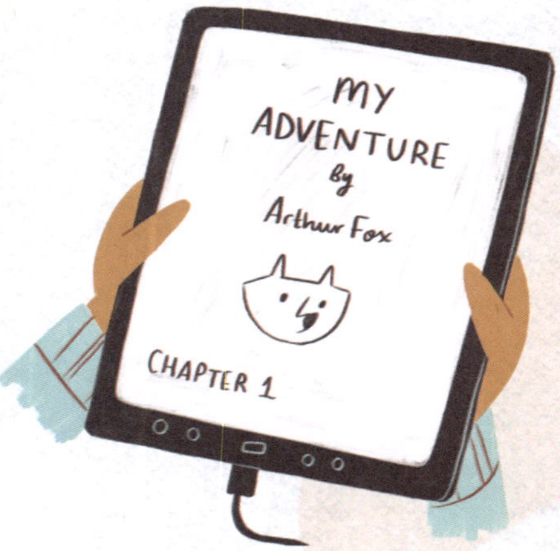


Self-publishing is a great way to print the book you have lovingly written in small quantities. These can then be sold in small bookshops, through your own online shop, and in the form of ebooks, all without having to go through an external publishing house.

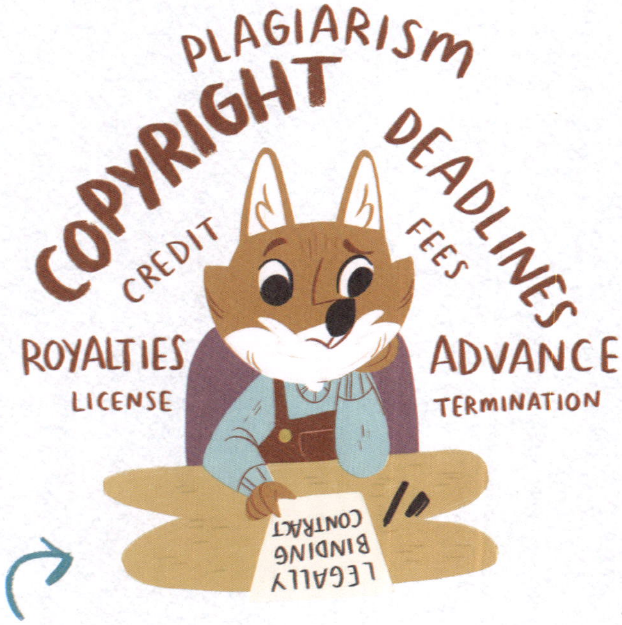


It's okay to feel a little confused or overwhelmed when reading a contract for the first time. If there is anything you feel unsure about, addressing it directly with the publisher should help clear up any concerns you have. And if there is anything you don't agree with, it's reasonable to politely negotiate certain aspects of it.

## THE LEGAL BIT

When it comes to working with a publisher and other clients, there are some legal aspects that need to be considered and worked through. It might sound daunting, but contracts are there to protect both you and the client. They determine the copyright details of the artwork, protect the client against plagiarism, outline the deadlines of the project, and ensure you will get paid the agreed fee at the end of the job.

One of the biggest factors outlined in the contract is the copyright details. This explains who can use the artwork, for what purpose, and where. If the client is commissioning you to illustrate a story, it's normal to be required to sign over the rights for your artwork to them. This will mean they can use the artwork to publish the book, sell copies, create later editions, and create promotional material to publicize it. The publisher will usually agree to let you use the artwork in your portfolio and to promote the book on your social media, but it's always best to discuss this with them before signing the contract, as contracts sometimes mention exclusivity, which restricts where you can share the artwork.

If you have developed a picture book yourself, or with an author, and then taken it to a publisher, you are more likely to retain the copyright to the artwork and be given an advance and royalty deal. The advance is the sum of money the publisher will give you to create the artwork, and royalties refer to the percentage of profits you will get from sales of the book.

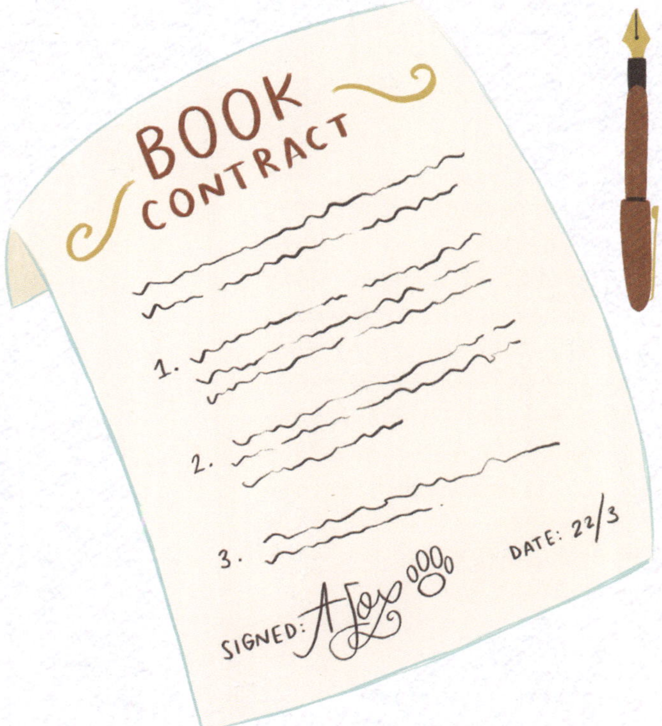


Plagiarism is another important point that can be found in a client-to-illustrator contract. This declares that all the artwork you will provide for the project is entirely original, created by yourself, and does not belong to anyone else. This is very important to the client as they will want to avoid any legal issues regarding the copyright of the artwork when they publish it. When you create the illustrations for a book, make sure you create everything yourself from scratch; don't use pre-existing artwork, don't use artwork that is owned by someone else, and don't submit artwork that you have copied or traced. It's okay to be influenced and inspired by other artists' work for the project, but you have to ensure the artwork is entirely your own.

Another section to look out for in the contract is the deadline, so you can make sure it's feasible for you to create the artwork in the outlined schedule. It will also mention the fee the client will pay you and when to expect the payment. Clients will usually pay you at the end of the project, on completion of the work, though some may offer to pay you a percentage of the total fee at the start and the rest at the end. This section will also mention what will happen in the event of the termination of the contract, and how much you will be entitled to if the client cancels the project. It's important that the terms of the fee are outlined in the contract, as this ensures you will be paid for the work you do for them. Credits are also sometimes outlined in the contract, telling you where your name will be printed in the book, such as on the cover and the imprint page (the page at the start of the book listing the details of publication), to let readers know who illustrated the book.

If you're happy with the original or negotiated contract, fill out the appropriate spaces and sign your name, then send it to the publisher to process.

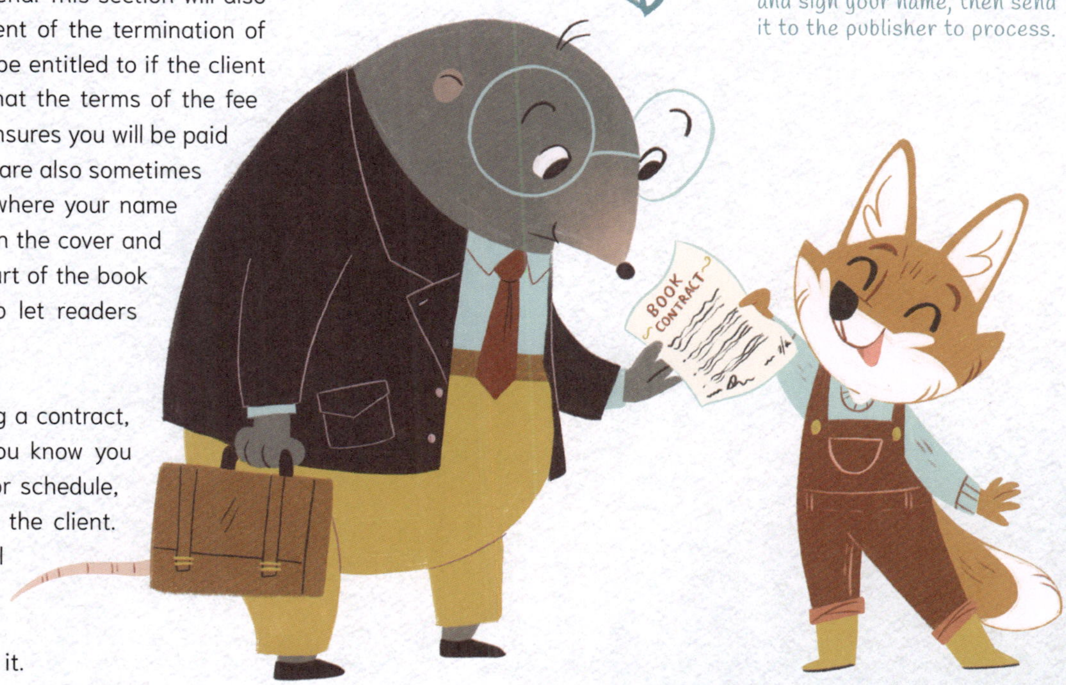


If you have any queries after reading a contract, or if there are aspects of it that you know you can't keep to, such as the deadline or schedule, you can discuss your concerns with the client. They are usually open to making small changes to the contract. Make sure any discussed changes are added into the new contract before you sign it.

# TROUBLESHOOTING

**There are a number of issues and obstacles you may encounter as a children's book illustrator, from handling challenging themes to rejection from a top publisher, or simply a case of artist's block. These issues can be difficult and sometimes frustrating, but every illustrator will face such challenges over the course of their career – experiencing them is completely normal. Despite their difficulty, there are a number of ways to manage and overcome these obstacles, which will be discussed in this chapter. So don't worry and keep going – everything will be okay!**

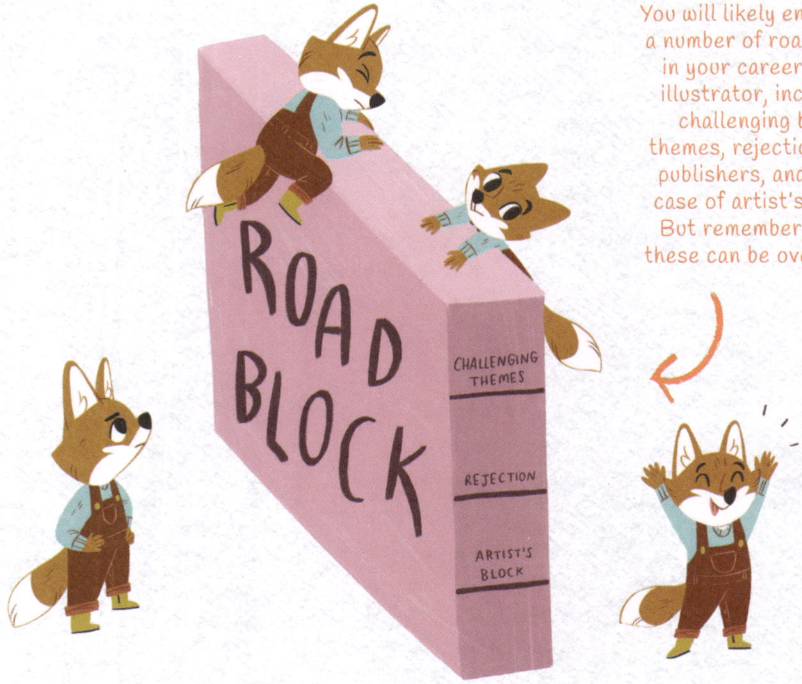


You will likely encounter a number of roadblocks in your career as an illustrator, including challenging book themes, rejection from publishers, and a bad case of artist's block. But remember, all of these can be overcome!

## DEALING WITH CHALLENGING THEMES

Children's books cover a wide variety of themes that promote life lessons and moral values, some of which can be quite serious. The main goal for an illustrator is to convey these messages through their artwork, while maintaining a light-hearted tone that's suitable for young readers.

Common themes found in children's books include friendship and bullying, belonging and identity, family, loss and grief, racism, and gender identity, all of which are issues many children will experience in their lives. The message that children's books with these themes try to get across is that children are not alone in experiencing these issues, and to have hope that things will work out okay in the end.

As many of these themes are situational, it's difficult to give a precise explanation of how to approach them. However, one of the best ways to begin tackling them is to have a conversation with the author or publisher to find out exactly what they want their book to achieve. By doing this you can establish their vision for the illustrations and the kind of tone and mood they would like you to convey.

Once you have established this you can start to think about how you can convey their ideas in your illustrations. A good way to do this is to keep their theme as the main focus of the artwork. This will draw the reader's attention to the serious situations that occur and how the character overcomes them, showing the significance of everything that happens.

"COMMON THEMES FOUND IN CHILDREN'S BOOKS INCLUDE FRIENDSHIP AND BULLYING, BELONGING AND IDENTITY, FAMILY, LOSS AND GRIEF, RACISM, AND GENDER IDENTITY"

However, it's important to remember that the book is still for children, and so the overall tone of the illustrations can't always be serious, otherwise you may upset the reader in a way neither you nor the author intended. While the serious themes need to be kept at the forefront of the artwork, you also have to make sure the illustrations are child-friendly. You can do this by utilizing the illustrative techniques explored throughout the previous chapters.

These three illustrations deal with the concept of a loved one getting sick – in this case, the family dog. This is an upsetting situation for anyone to deal with, especially a child, but it's one they will likely experience at some point in their life.

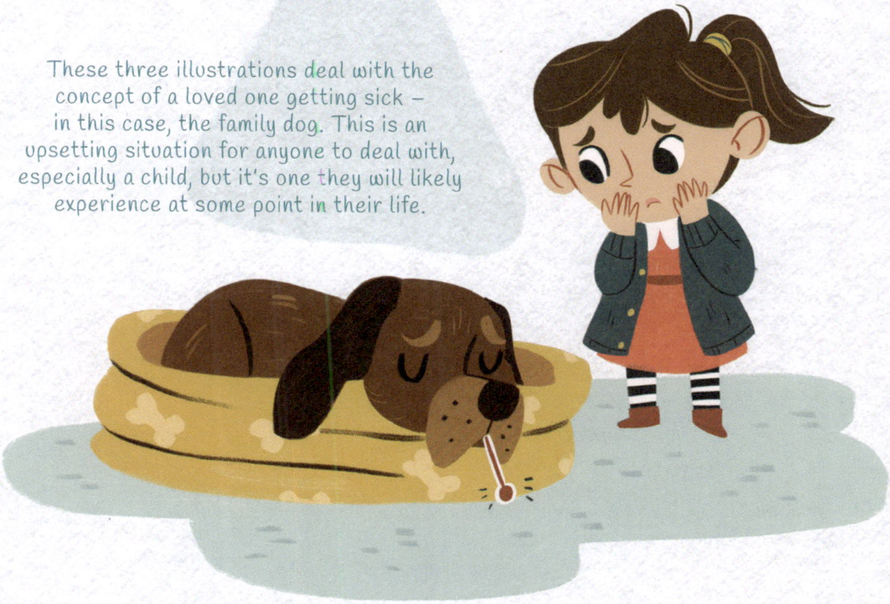

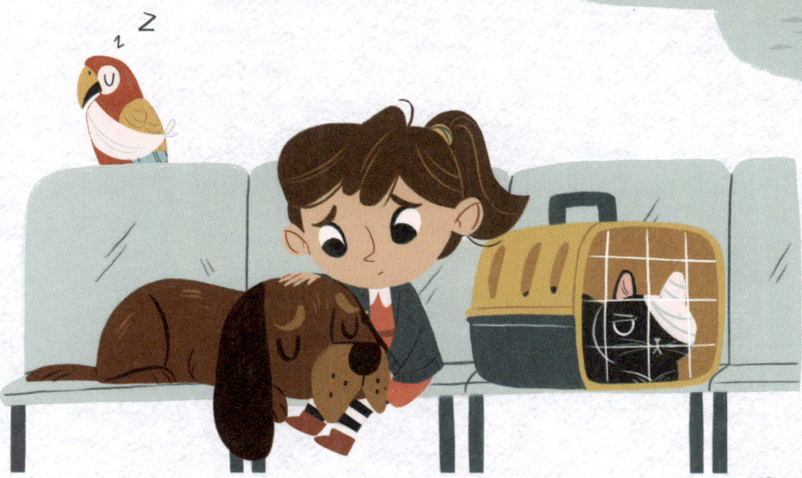


For example, you should keep the color palette simple and bold; create age-appropriate and relatable character designs; occasionally provide some comic relief through the introduction of background characters; and carefully plan out the pages to ensure there is a balance of more serious pages followed by lighter pages to provide readers with some respite from the heavier tones. By combining serious or challenging themes with strong, child-friendly imagery, you can create a beautiful and thought-provoking book that children will enjoy reading with their parents.

The illustrations show the severity of the situation, with the dog looking poorly in the first two images. The young girl's worried expression tells the reader there is cause for concern. Though the reader doesn't know whether the dog will be okay, the situation is made somewhat lighter by the grumpy cat and sleeping parrot.

There is a happy ending as the dog gets his treatment and is well again. By making the serious situation the main focus of the illustrations, but using background characters to make the illustrations a bit lighter, you can address challenging themes while still keeping them child-friendly.

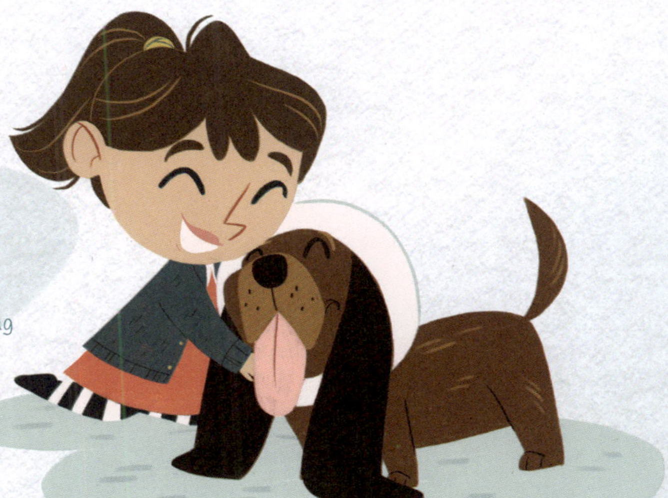

# REJECTION FROM PUBLISHERS

Rejection from publishers is not an uncommon thing to experience when pitching your book. It's something that happens to many writers, and although it can be disheartening, it shouldn't be taken personally. A rejection simply means the book is either not the right fit for the publisher it has been sent to, or that the story needs improving to make it more marketable. As we have already established, selling books is incredibly important to publishers.

There are various reasons publishers may pass on your work. The story may not match their target market; they may only be looking for specific themes at that time, which perhaps don't feature in your work; or they may want something more from your story and have specific thoughts on how you could achieve those.

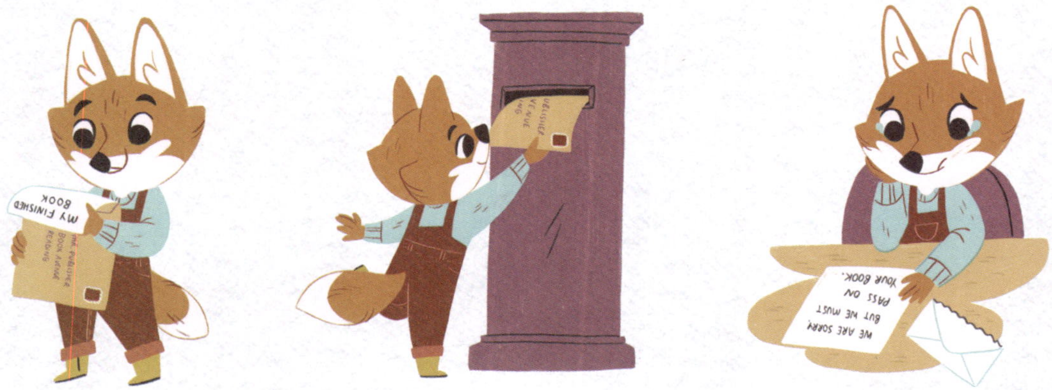


Receiving a rejection from publishers is a common occurrence, whether it's for a book you've written and illustrated yourself or one created in collaboration with an author. It's okay to feel upset when receiving disappointing news.

If a publisher turns down your story, they will usually provide some kind of feedback. This could be a single sentence or a more detailed reply, stating what they feel the story is lacking or simply explaining why the story is not a good fit for them. If you feel like their response doesn't contain sufficient feedback, it's acceptable to kindly ask for more details on their decision so you can implement their notes in your work. If you agree with their comments, there is no harm in applying the changes to your work and resubmitting, as doing this may lead to publication. However, it's important to consider whether the changes they are asking for are worth it, as they may want to change your work into something completely different from your original vision, in which case working with them may not be a good fit for you. This is why it's worth sending your manuscript to as many different (yet relevant) publishers as you can. This will increase your chance of success in finding a publisher who's a good fit for your story, and to get as much professional feedback on your work as possible.

The best way to deal with a rejection is to take the criticism on board and apply it to your work (if you agree with it). Making a publisher's suggested edits will make it more likely that you will receive more positive news if you resubmit the book at a later date.

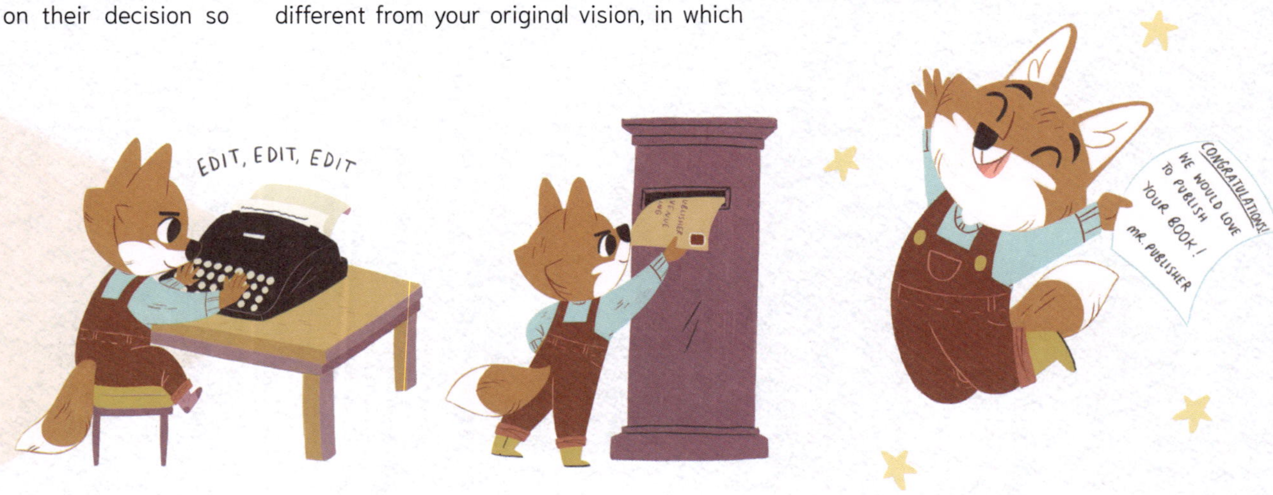

# ARTIST'S BLOCK

Artist's block is something all artists suffer with from time to time. It often stems from burnout, when you've taken on too much work, when you're drawing similar things repeatedly over a long period of time, or just general stress. It's a frustrating thing to experience, but there are a few tricks you can use to overcome it.

Firstly, if you're working to a deadline, the only thing you can do is to keep going – you won't meet your deadline if you stop. Continuing to draw can also help. You don't have to be drawing anything "good" or finished; simply finding time to doodle mindlessly in a sketchbook without a goal in mind can relieve the pressure and allow you to create whatever you like in that moment. Additionally, experimenting with a medium you don't usually use, like working traditionally instead of digitally, or using oil paints instead of watercolor, can help free up your creativity and give your mind a break from the monotony of how you were working before. Artist's block often comes from burnout and repetition, so breaking away from that can provide artistic relief.

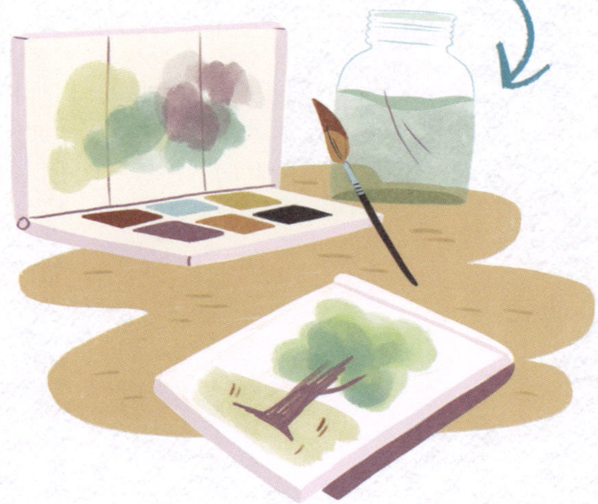


If you are in a position to do so, try stepping back and taking a break. This could be going on holiday to somewhere new, or simply taking a few days out from drawing to do something you enjoy. Resting in this way can help to reset and rejuvenate your mind and body, and you may even experience a burst of inspiration as a result. When you feel ready to start again, pick up a pencil and start doodling something fun that's just for yourself. Hopefully all the frustration you were feeling will have melted away.

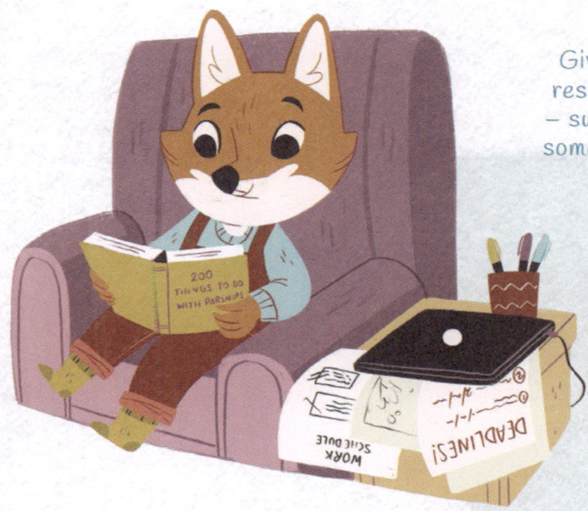


If you aren't able to take a few days break from drawing, try doing something else for an hour or two when you find yourself becoming frustrated with the piece you're working on. Your mind will appreciate the break and will feel better equipped for the task of finishing the piece.

Try not to feel too dejected or disheartened if you experience artist's block. It's a perfectly normal thing to happen and usually just means you need to take a break or work in a different way to reset your creativity.

> "ARTIST'S BLOCK OFTEN COMES FROM BURNOUT AND REPETITION, SO BREAKING AWAY FROM THAT CAN PROVIDE ARTISTIC RELIEF"

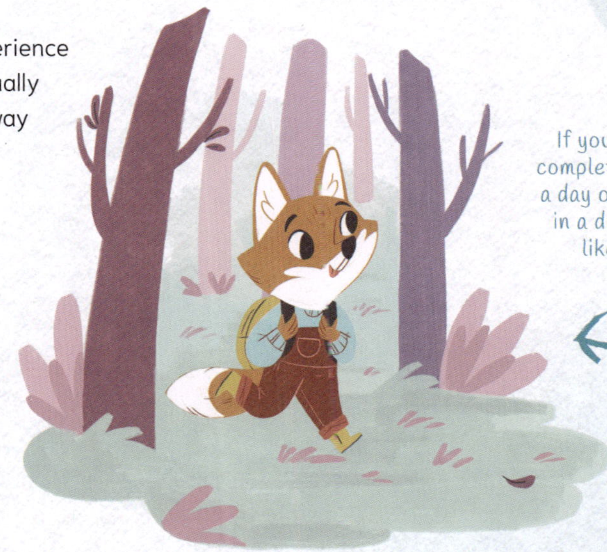

# SAMPLE STORIES

The following chapters contain eight specially commissioned and fully illustrated stories, each told in full as you would find in a real-life picture book. After each story, the artist has provided an insightful behind-the-scenes look at how they created the illustrations, sharing how they went about developing key features, ranging from characters to environments. Everything they discuss (including use of color, tailoring illustrations to a target age group, audience engagement, and working with the story text) has been explored in full in the previous chapters, allowing you to refer back to those fundamental considerations. Plus, each artist shares additional tips and advice. They then provide an analysis of the process of illustrating the book, sharing challenges they overcame along with even more nuggets of wisdom for how to begin illustrating your own book.

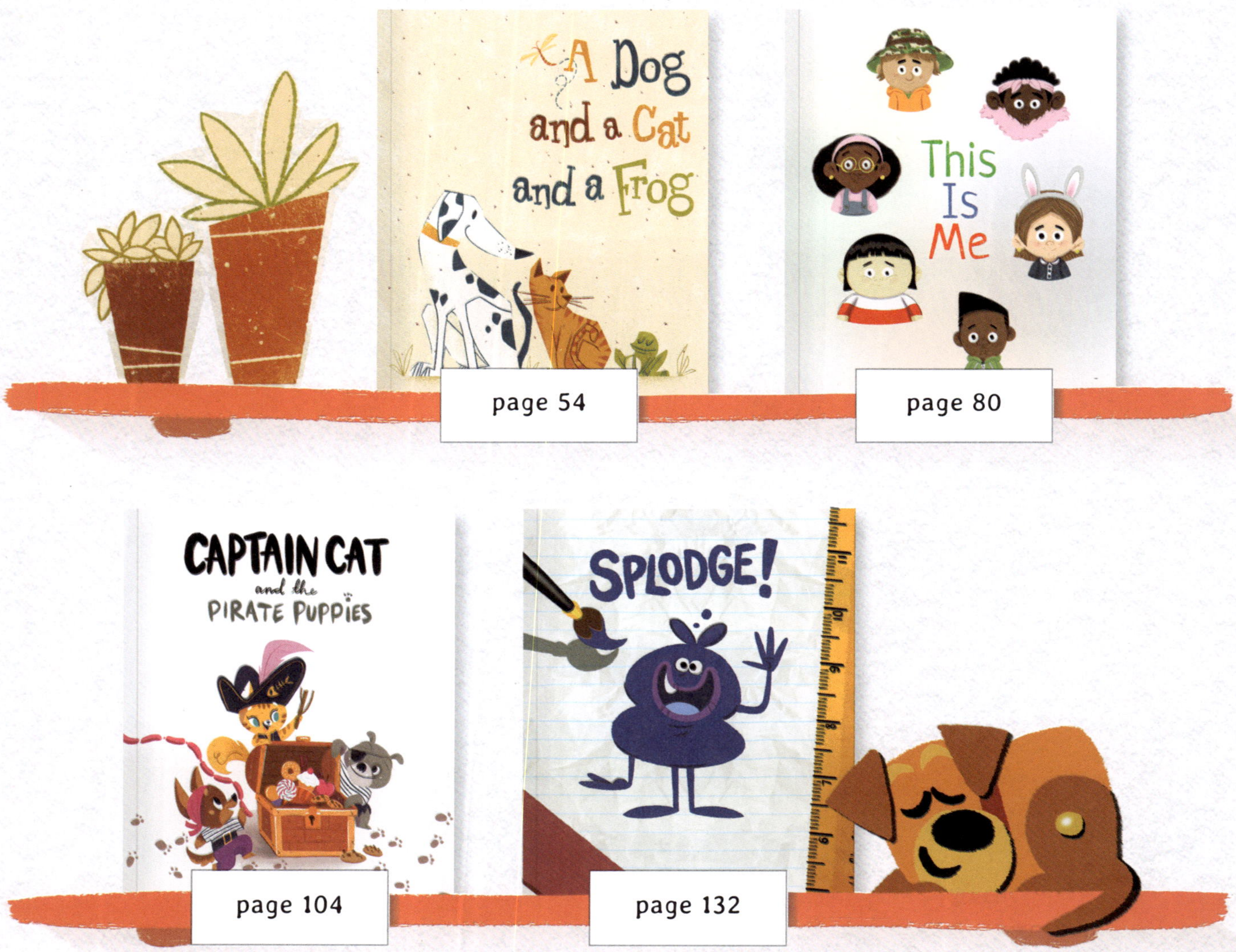

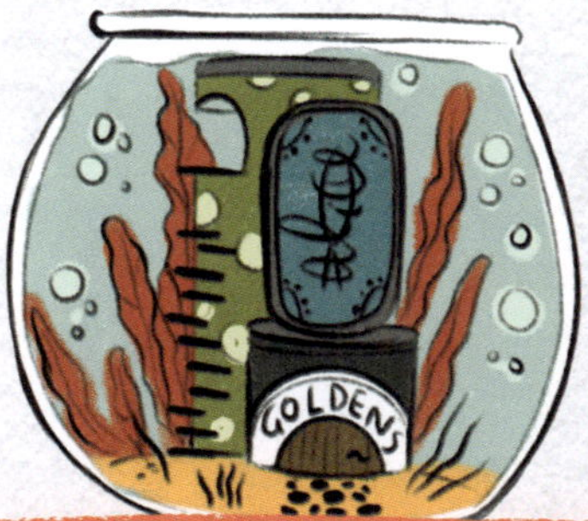


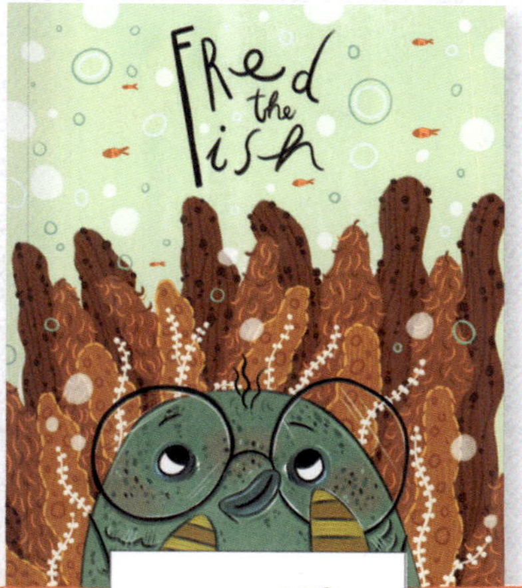


page 158

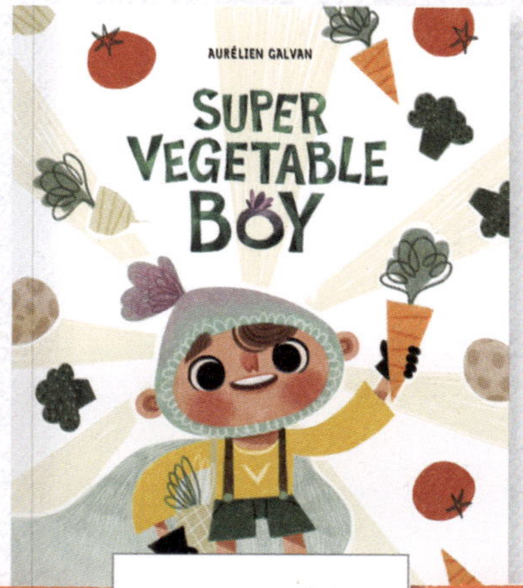


page 186

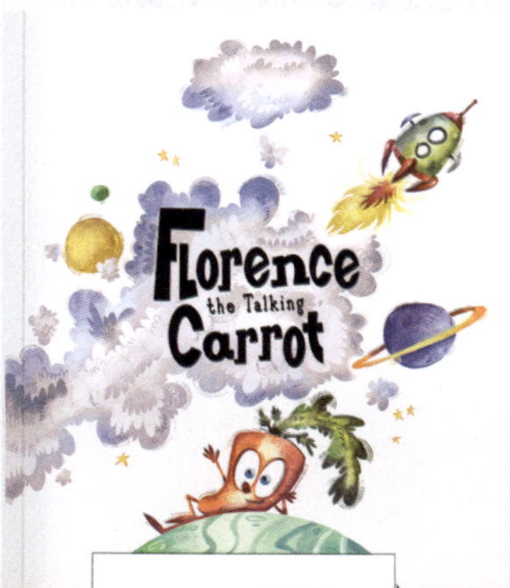


page 214

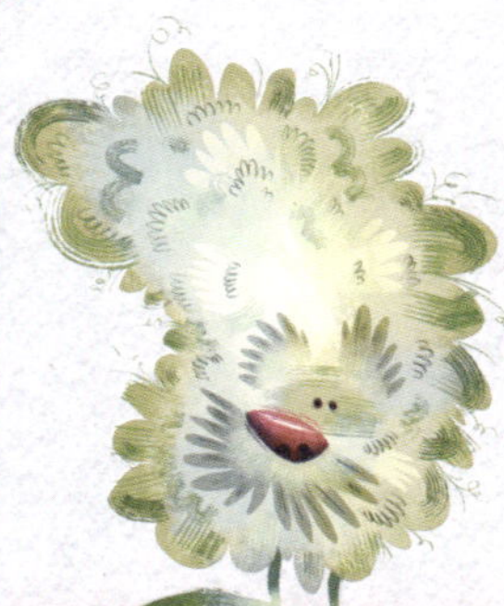

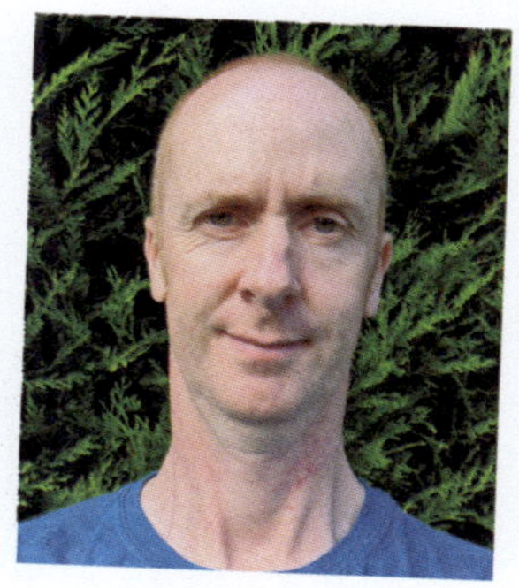

Stories written by

# GREG DOBBINS

Children's book author

**facebook.com/GregDobbinsWriter**

Greg is a published children's writer. His books include *The Positively Pleasant Pirates* and *The Grumpy Teddy*.

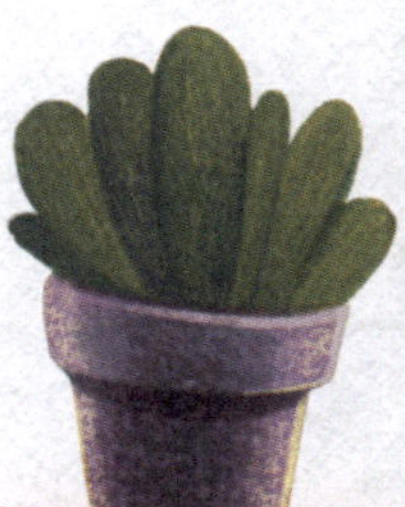

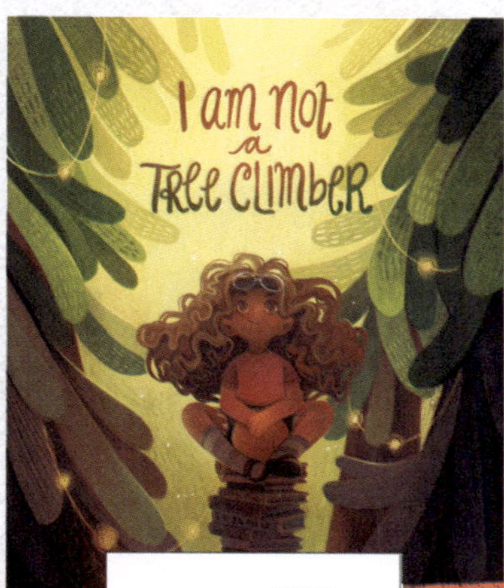


page 238

A Dog and a Cat and a Frog

Written by

GREG DOBBINS

Illustrated by

CRIS RAMOS

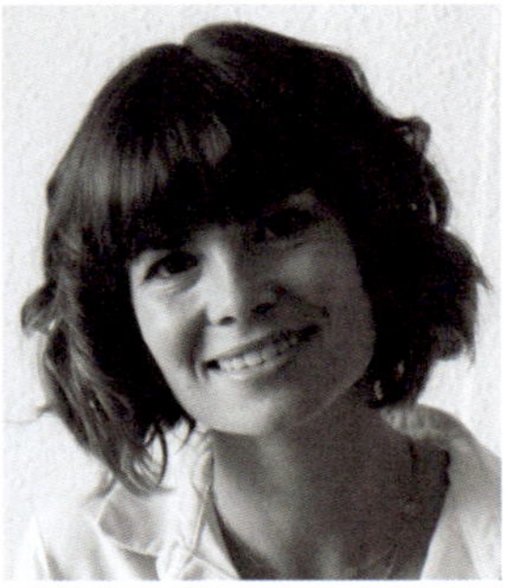

Illustrator

**crisramosillustration.com**

Cris is an illustrator and social educator from León, Spain, now living in the northern sierra of Madrid. She is dedicated to the creation of educational content and illustrated books.

A STORY FOR AGES 0–24 MONTHS

# A Dog and a Cat and a Frog

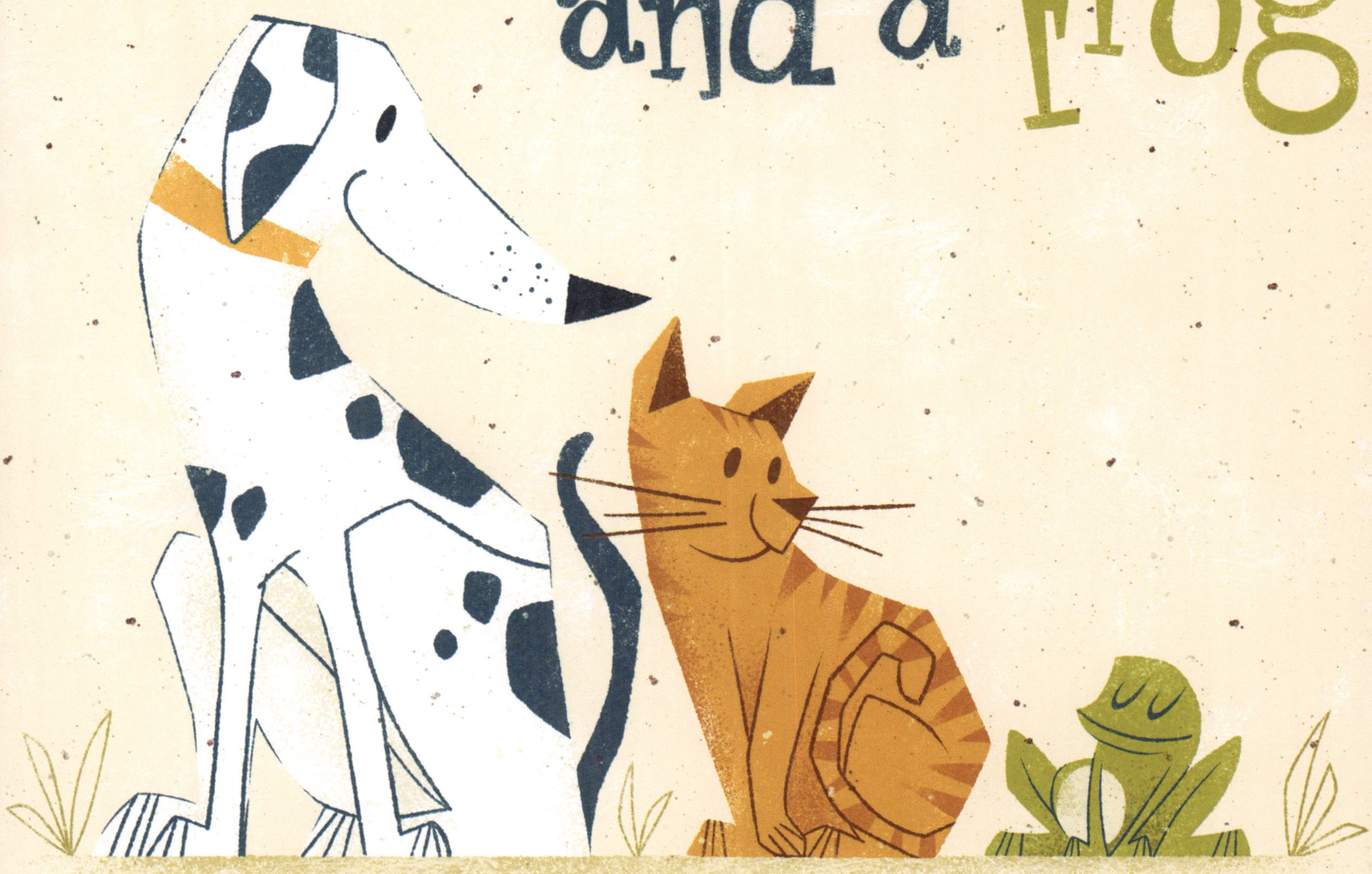

A dog and a frog.
And a cat, on a mat.

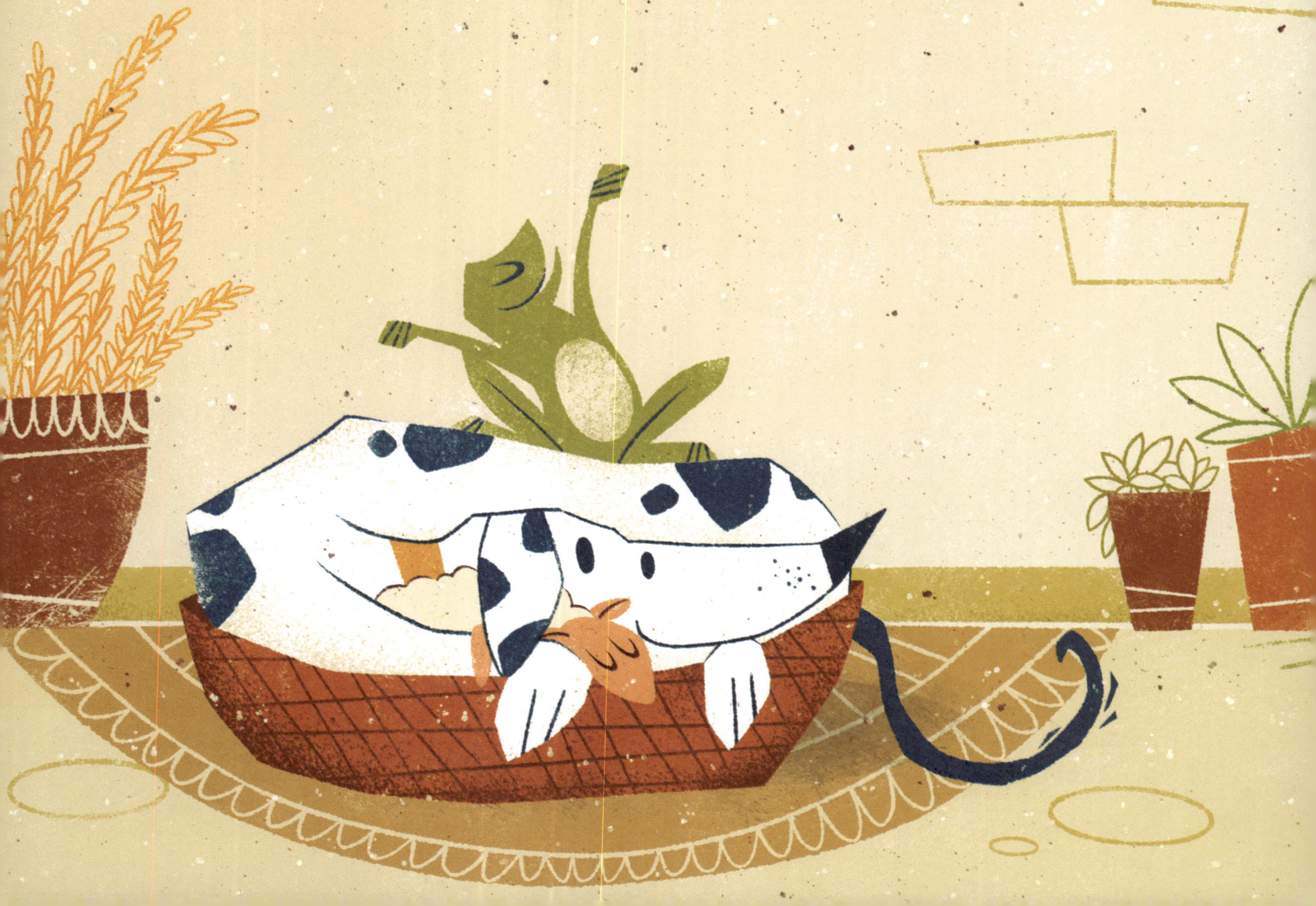

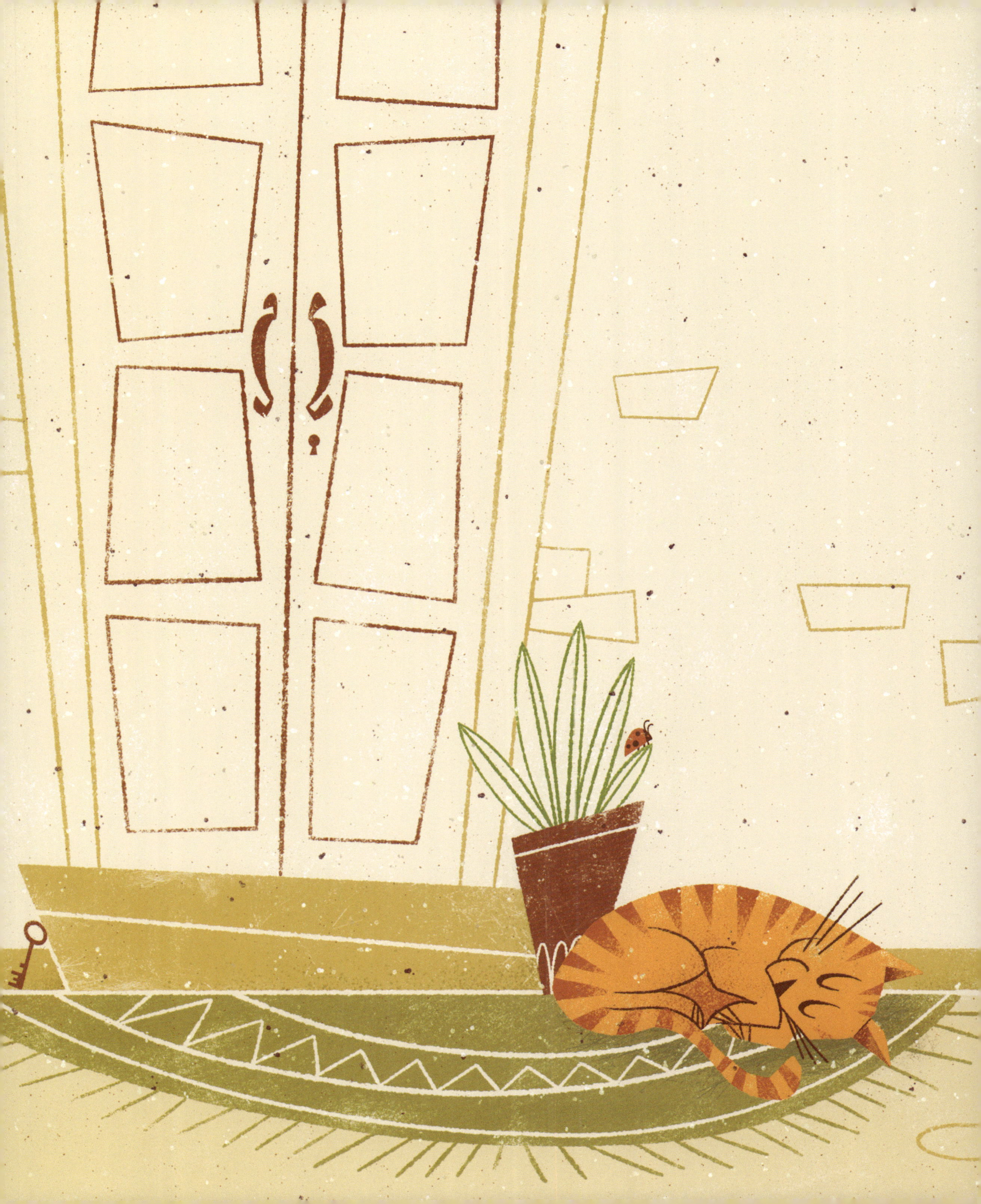

A dog on a mat
and a frog on a cat.

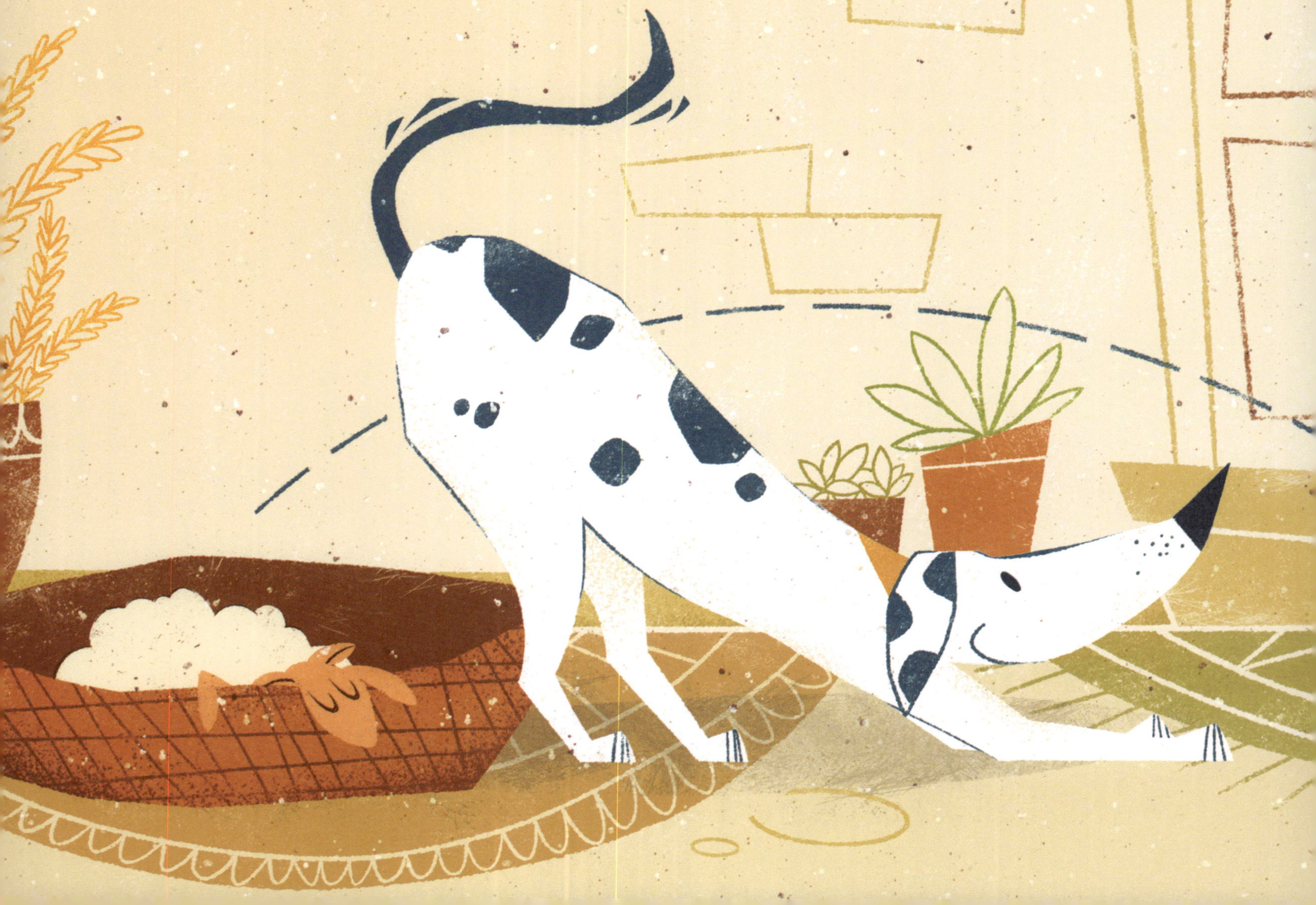

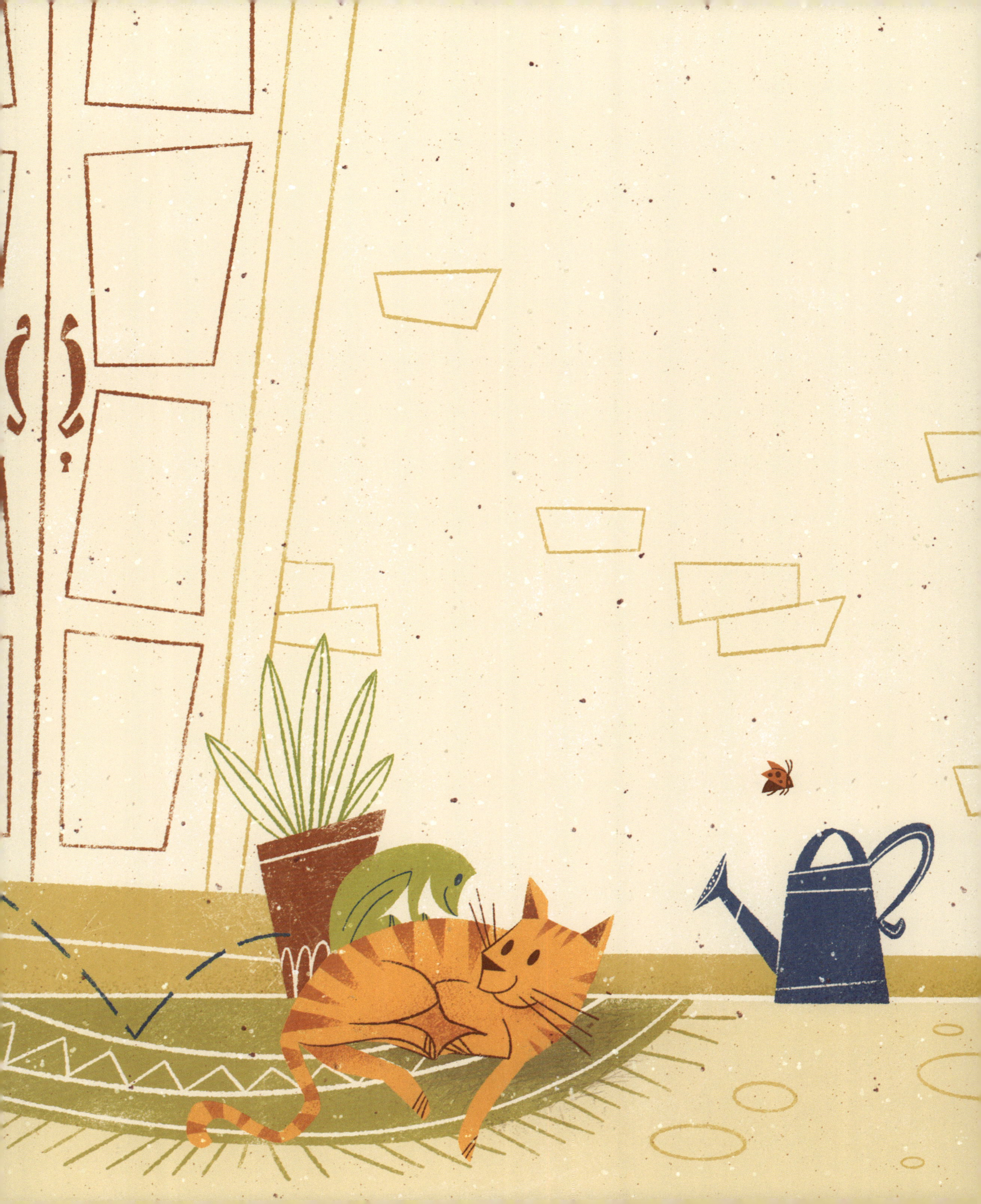

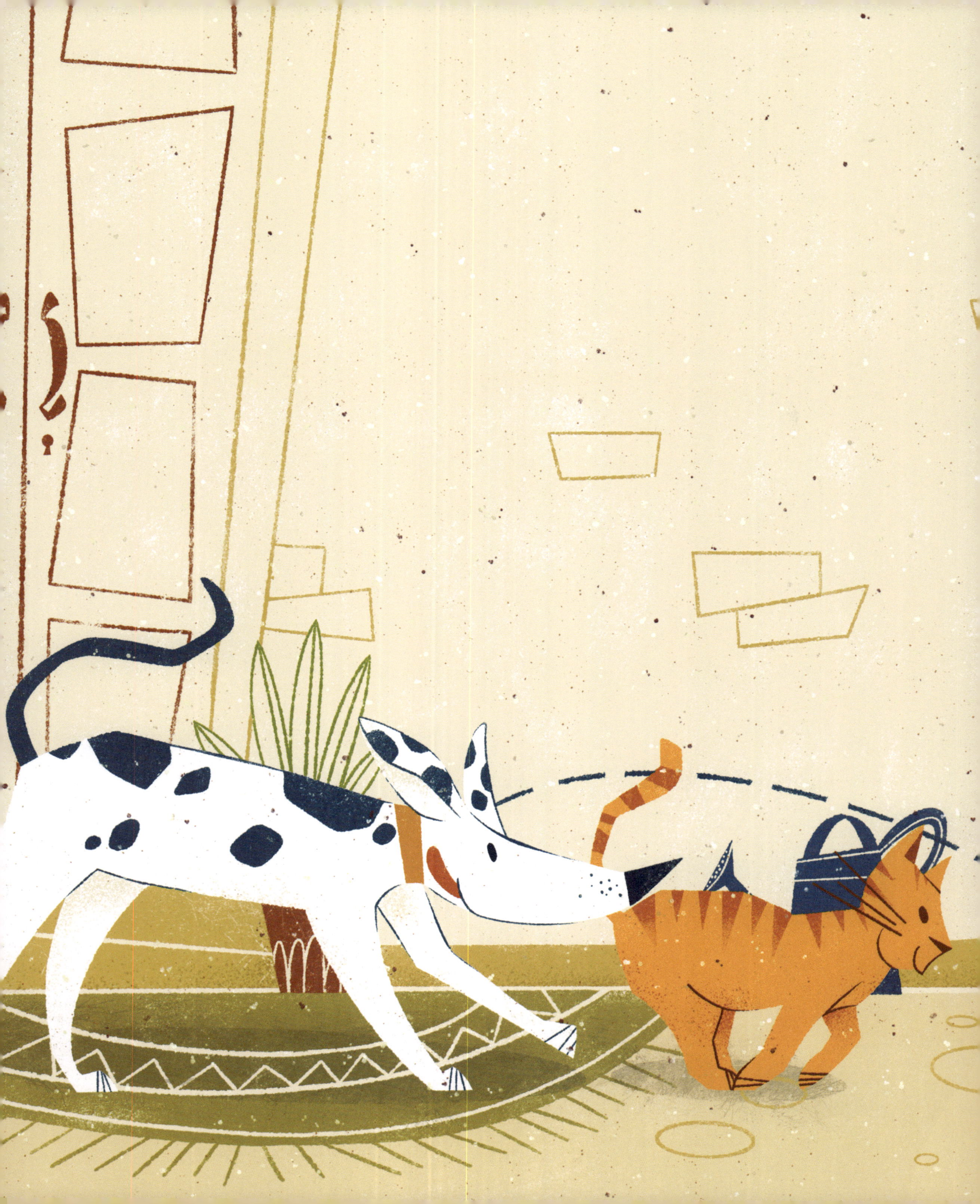

The cat and the dog chase after the frog.

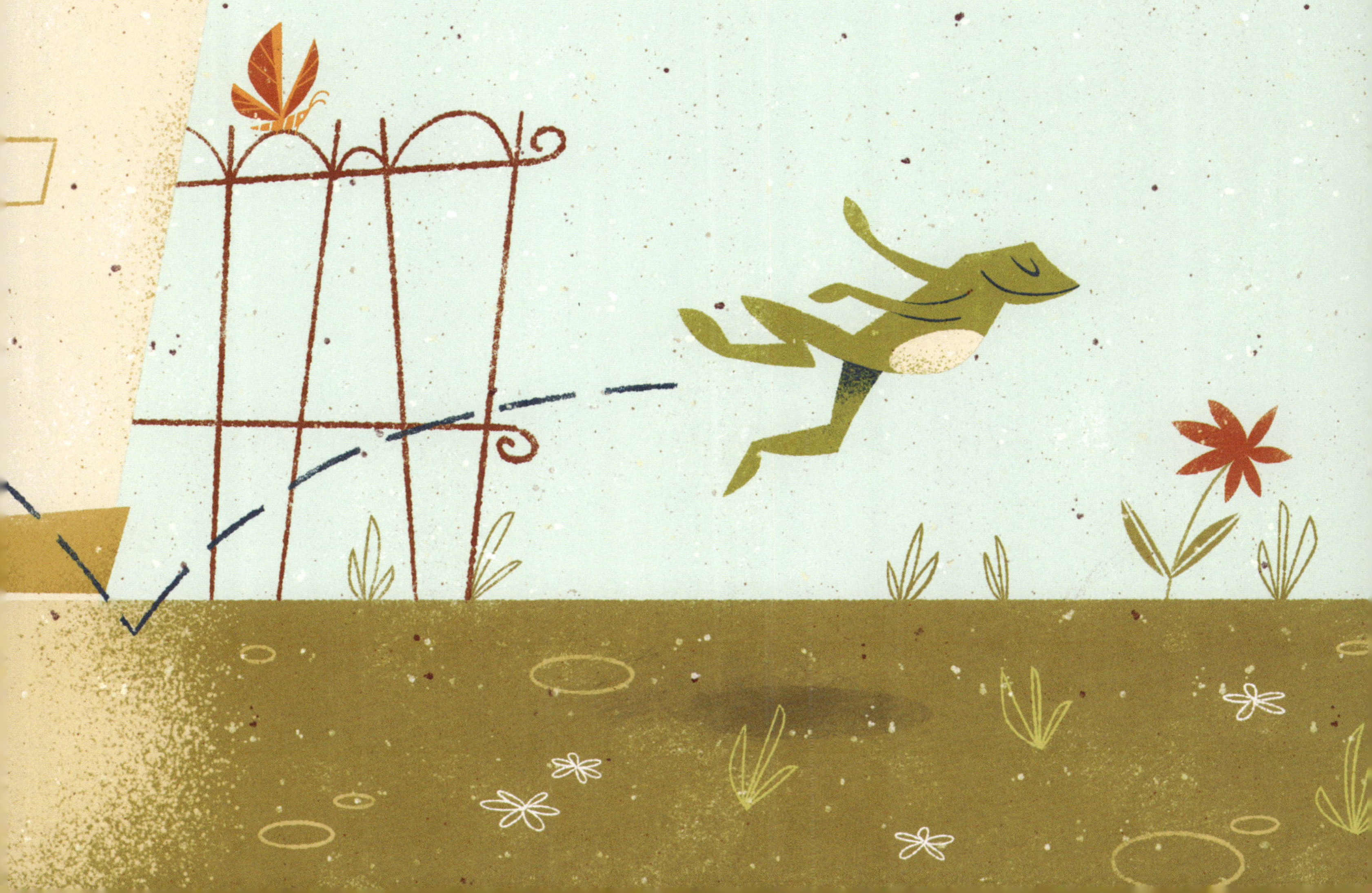

The frog and the cat...

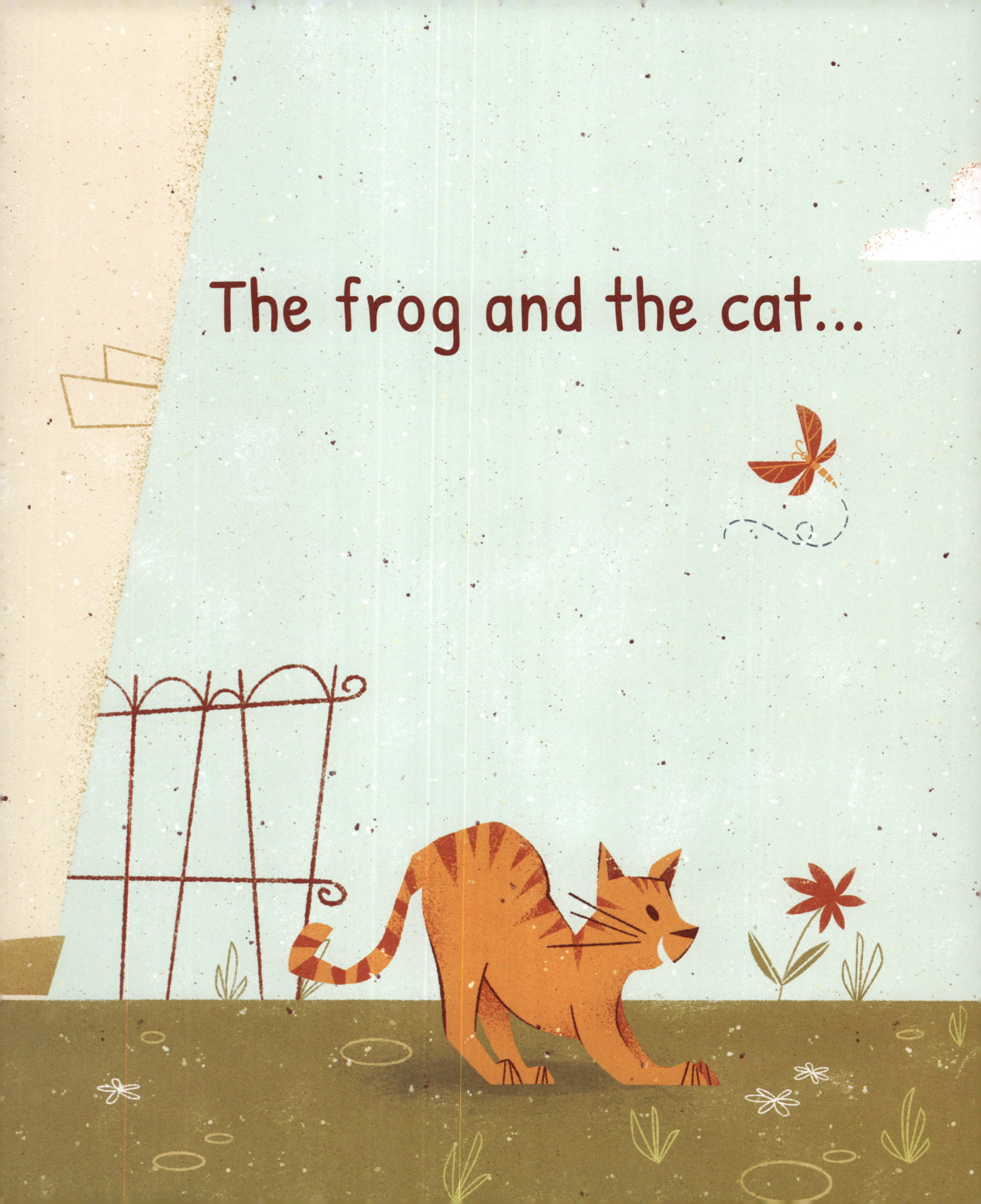

...stop for a chat.

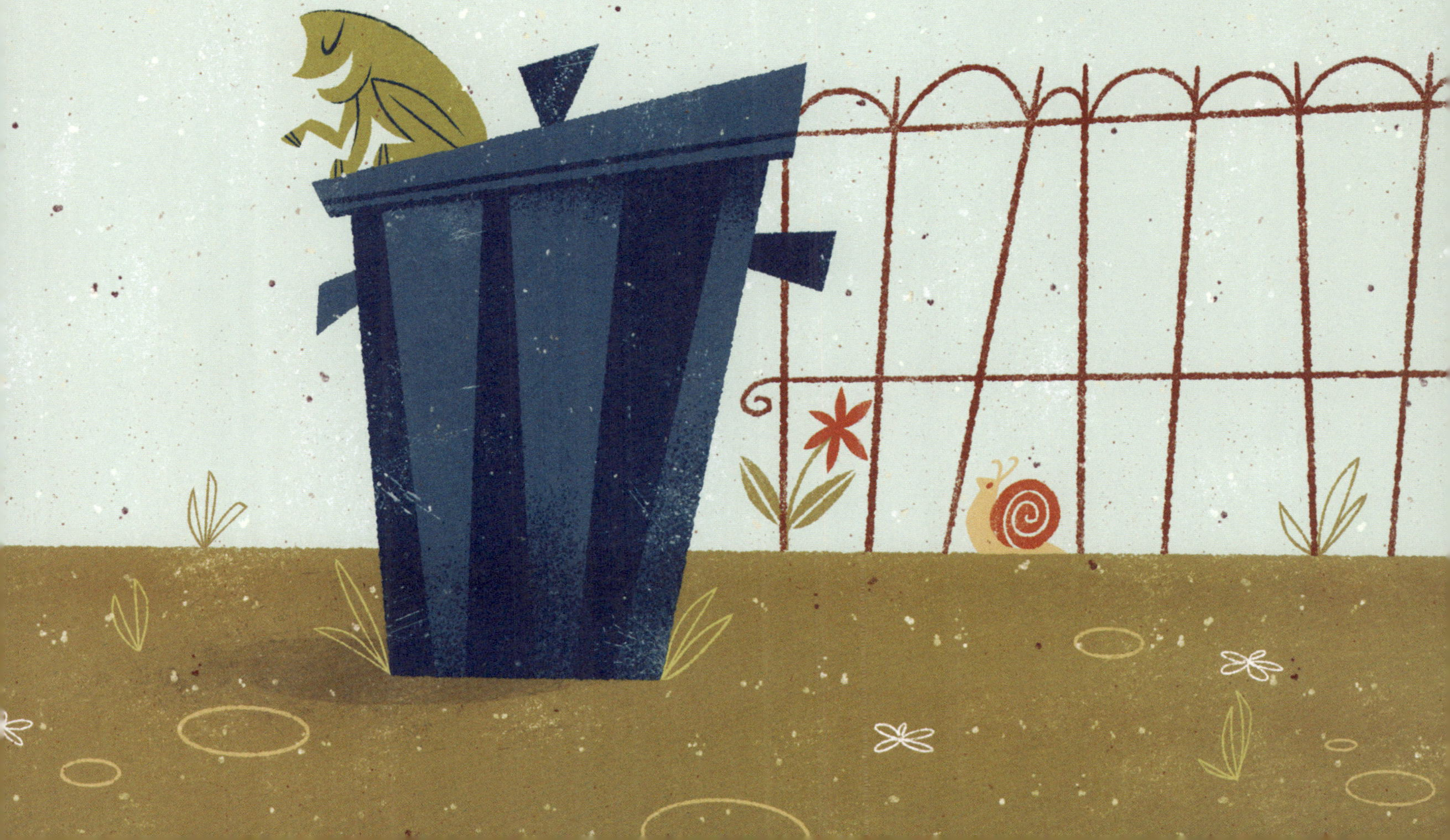

The dog runs around...

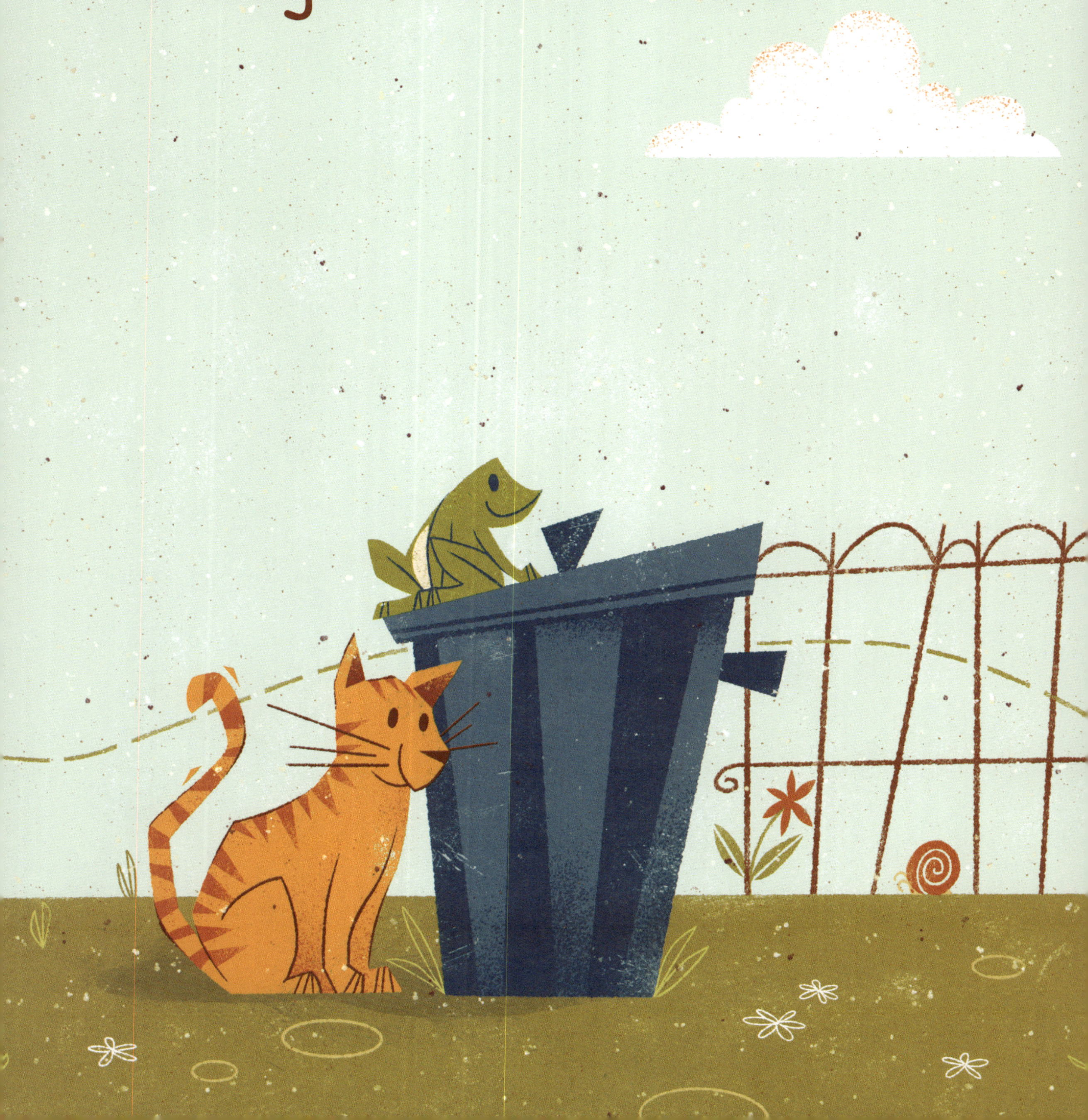

...and then rolls on the ground.

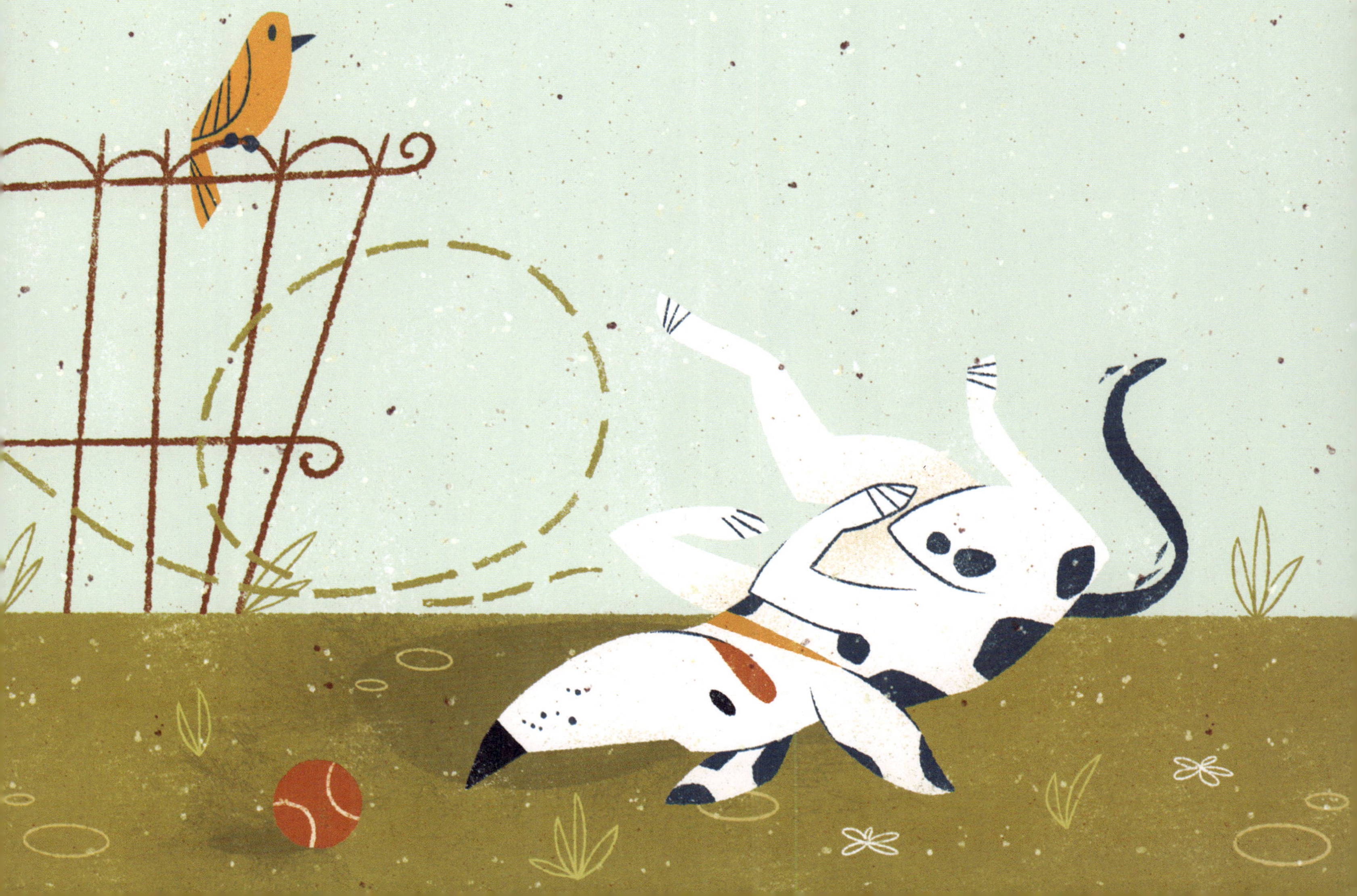

The cat and the frog...

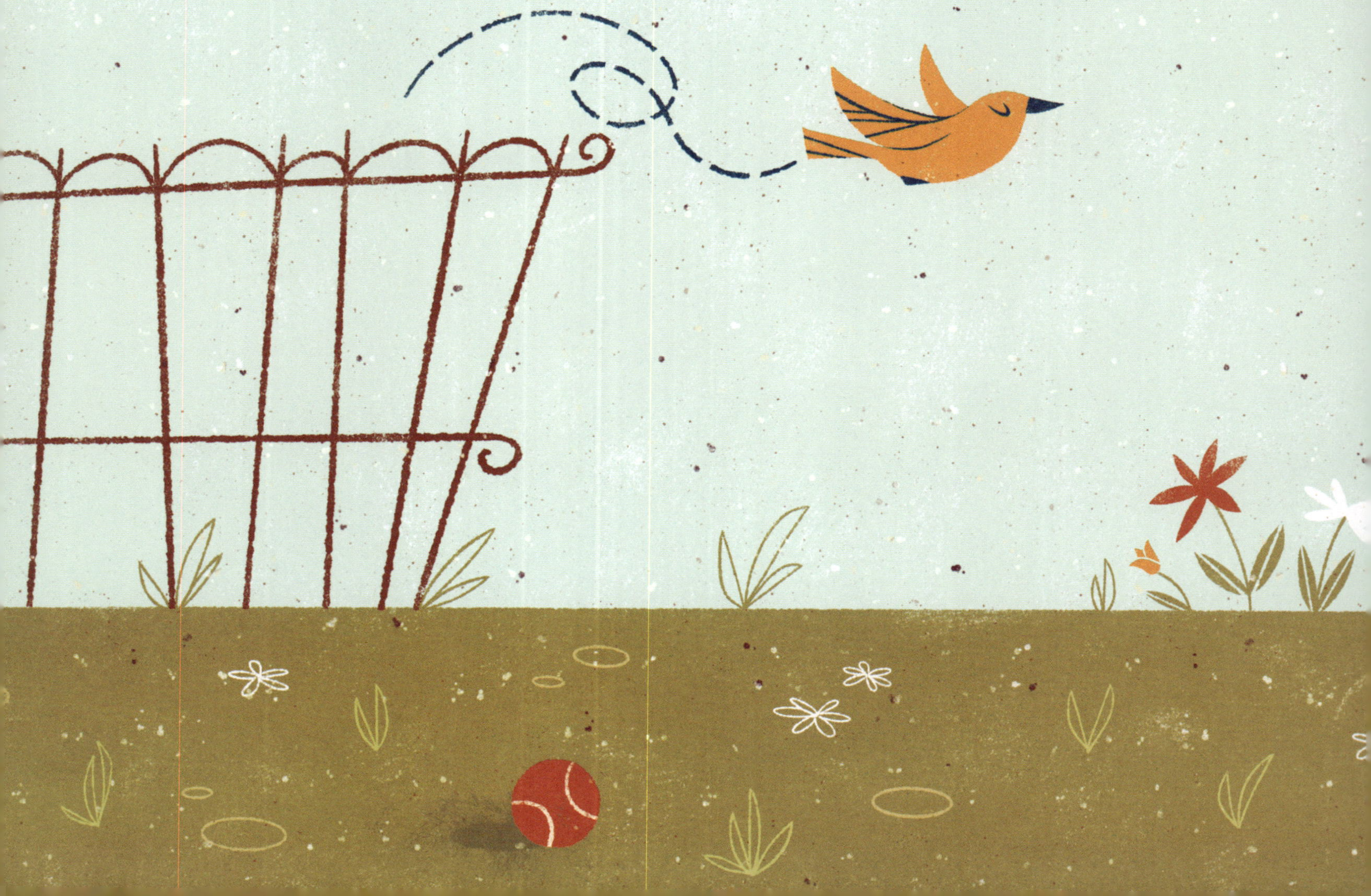

...roll around with the dog.

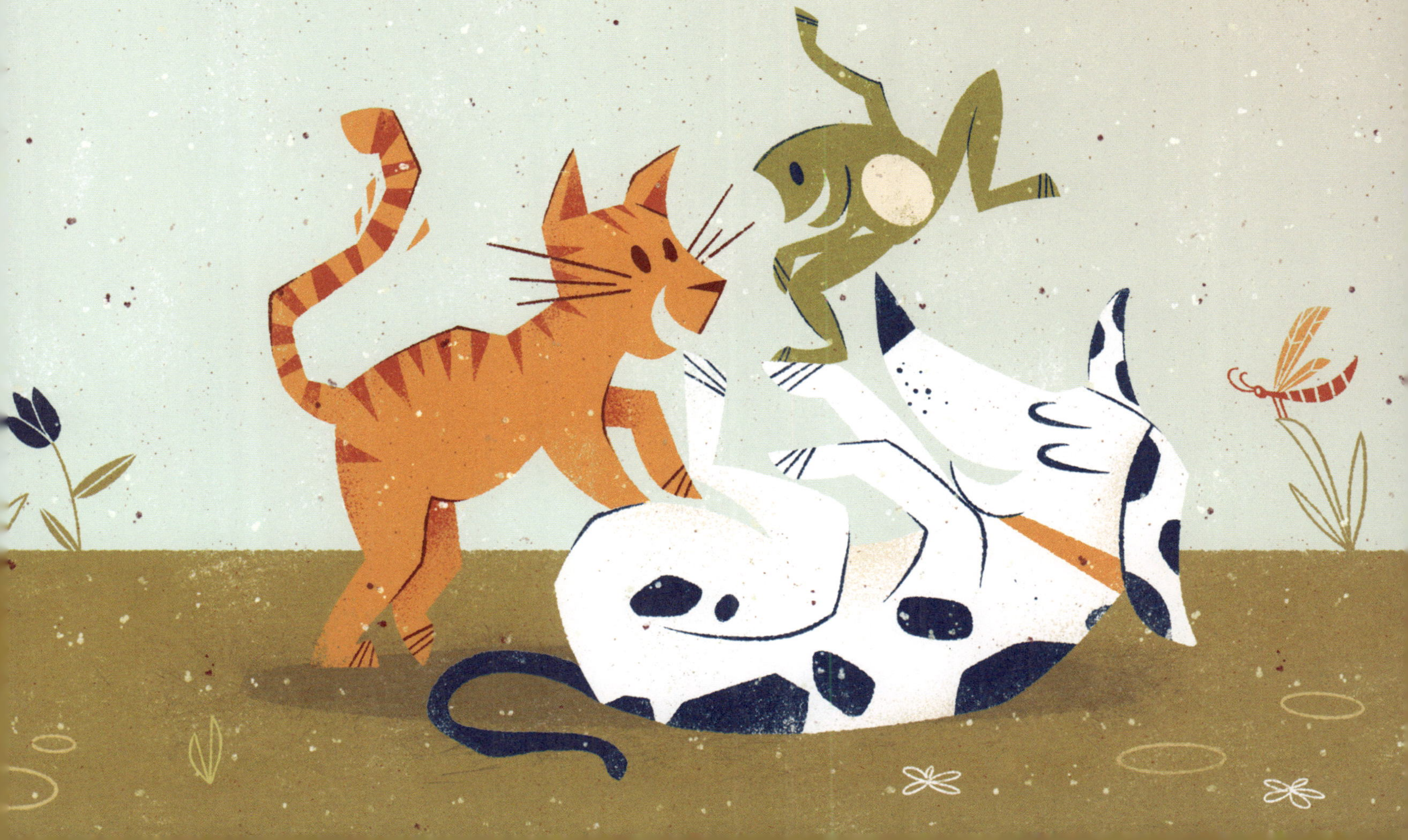

The dog and the
frog and the cat
walk back to the mat.

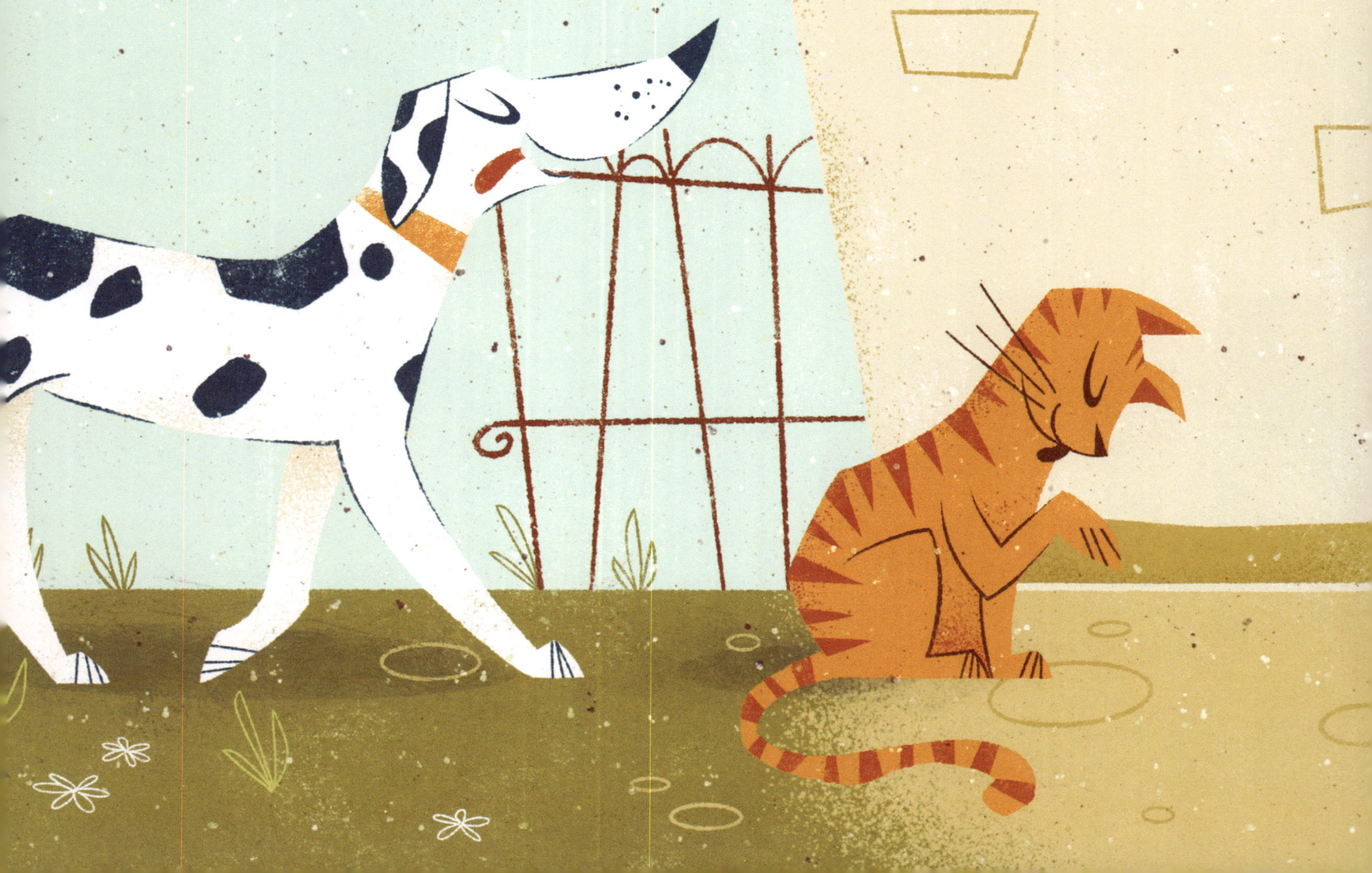

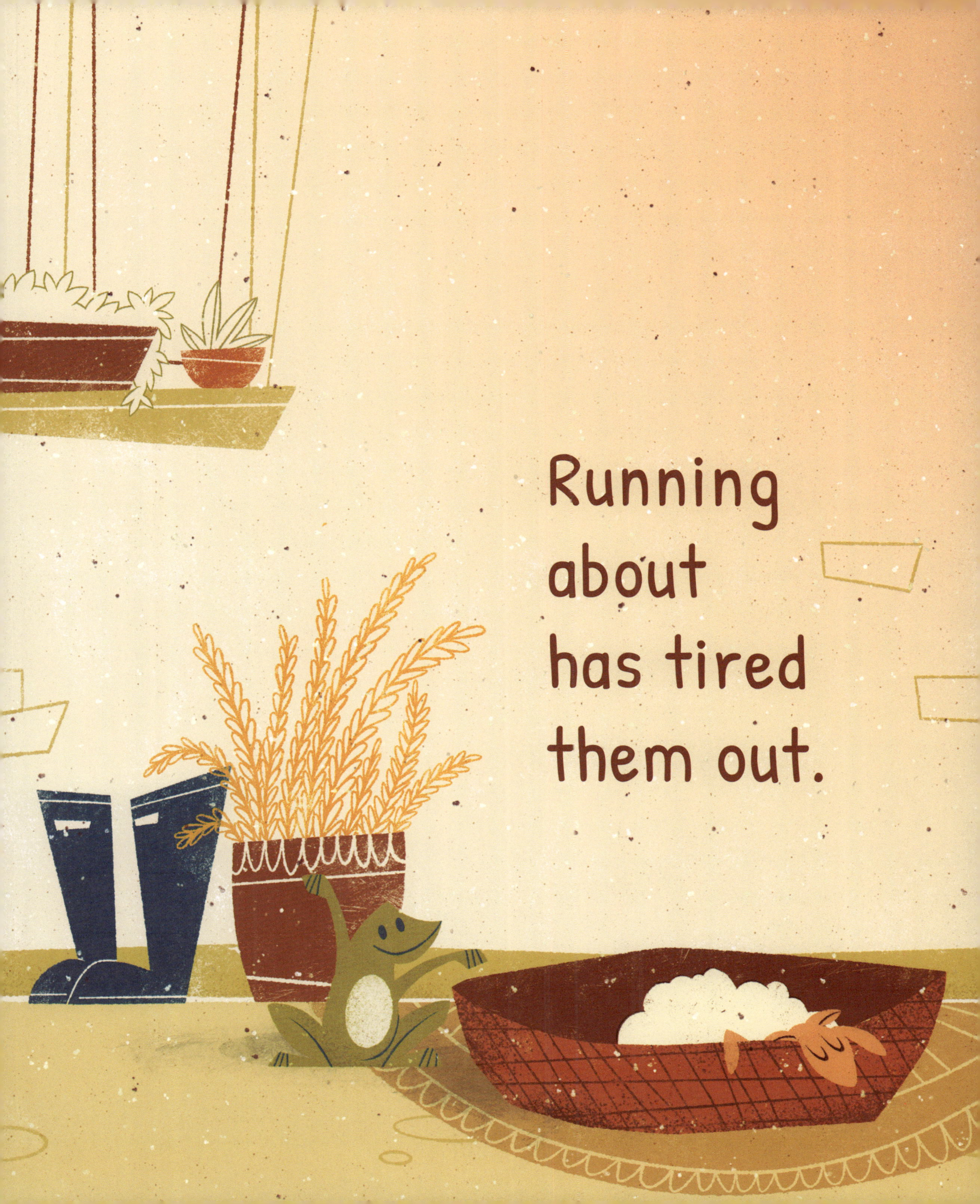

Running about has tired them out.

The frog and the cat
curl up for a nap.

And the dog goes to sleep,
with his cuddly sheep.

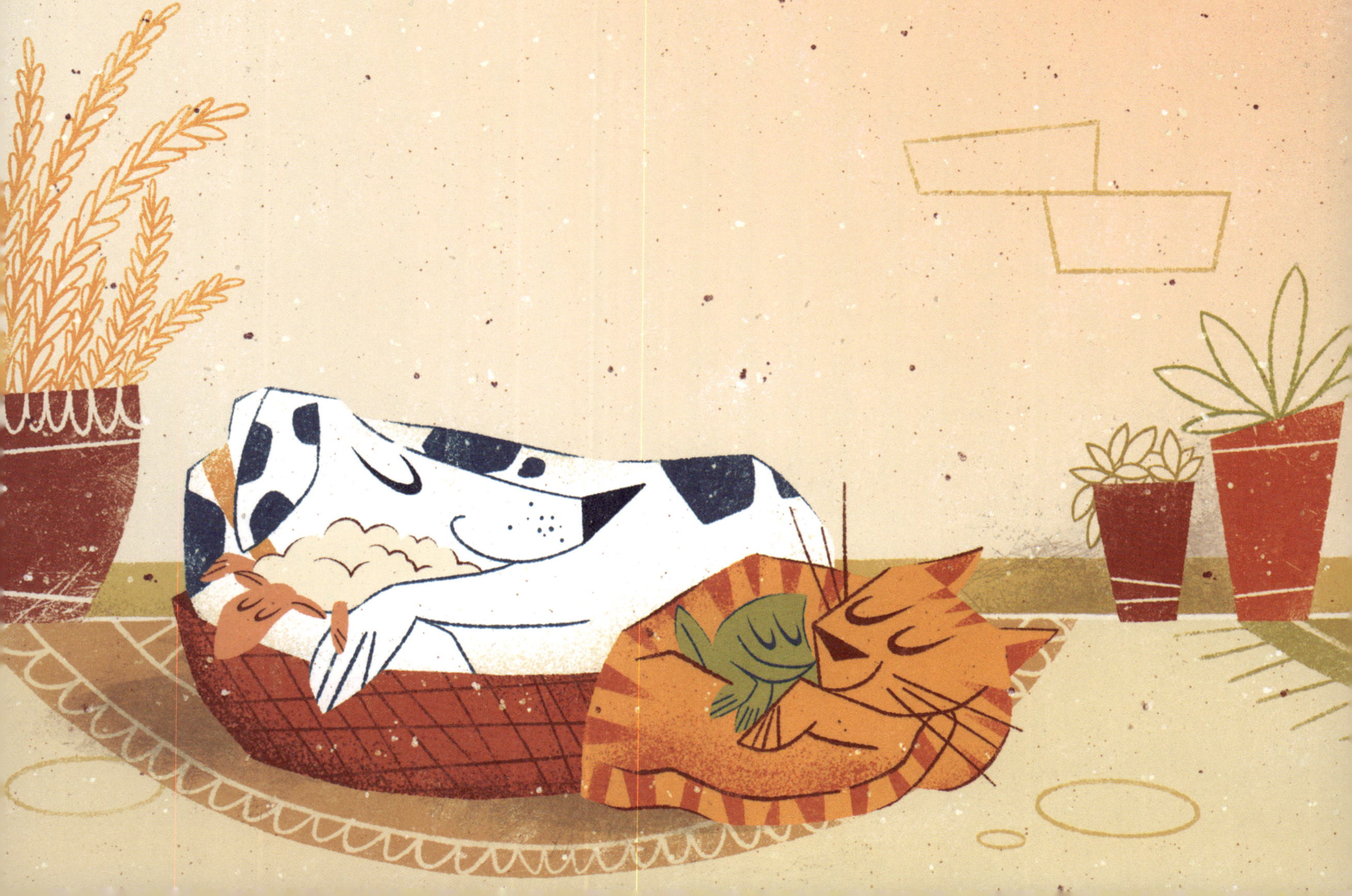

TURN THE PAGE FOR
INSIGHTS FROM THE ARTIST

# A Dog and a Cat and a Frog

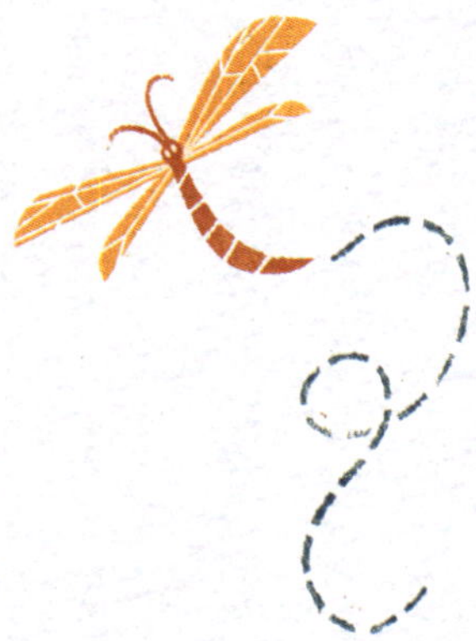

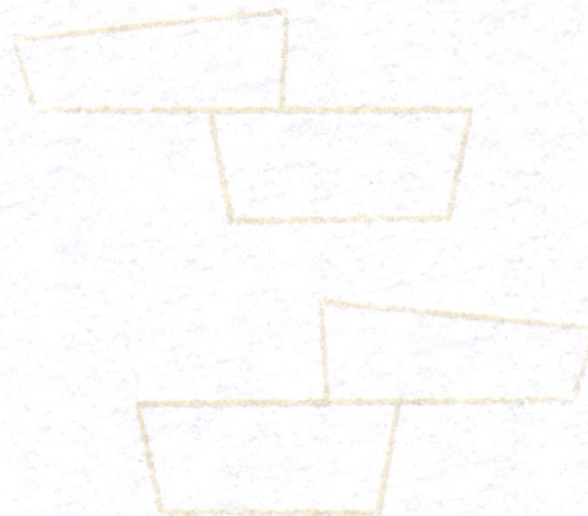

## DEVELOPING KEY FEATURES

### ENVIRONMENT

Before you begin working on the illustrations for a children's book, it's important to carefully read the story through several times. Make sure you understand it well and consider what environment would make the most appropriate setting. In *A Dog and a Cat and a Frog*, the options were endless, as the text does not specify where the action takes place. However, given the target age range is 0–24 months, it was clear that a fairly simple background would be best. I decided that the whole story would take place outside a country house, allowing me to draw a cozy background for the scene where the characters are sleeping, and a bright, flowery garden for when they are playing. I also included objects to help set the scene, such as plants, a watering can, and a garbage can.

Incorporating details from a Provençal-style house offers a unique and inviting color palette.

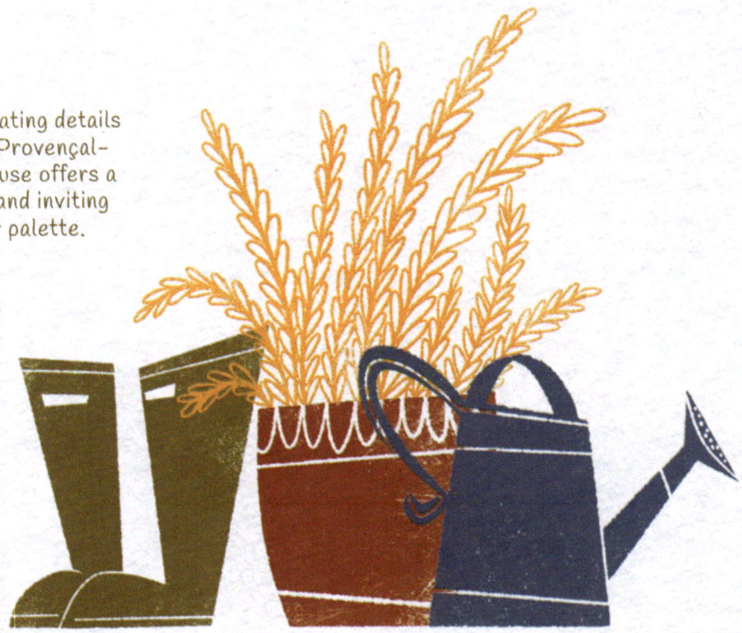

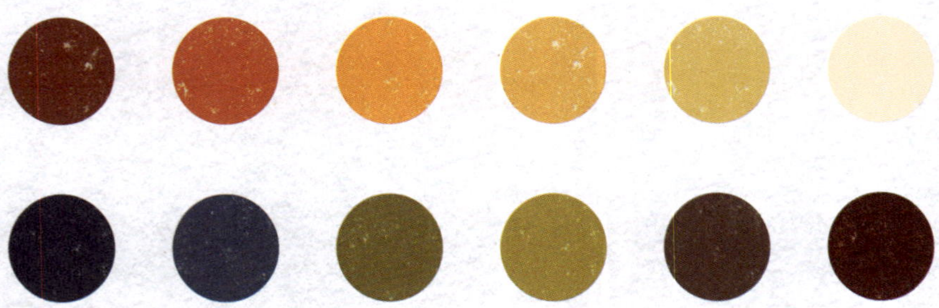

Using natural tones – such as beiges, browns, oranges, and greens – adds warmth to illustrations. But the choice of color palette is something very personal!

To make clear that it's an outdoor setting, we can add flowerpots, bricks, and windows. They don't need to be very detailed as they're just part of the background.

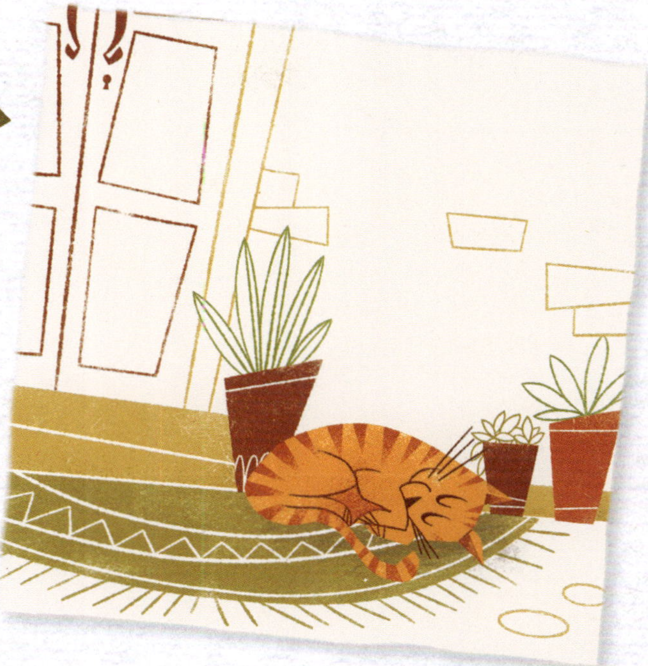

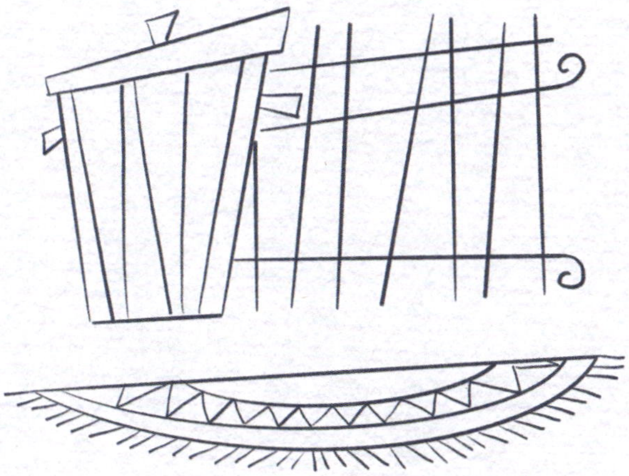

It's important to include all the elements that are named in the text, since a certain logic in the story is necessary for young children.

Consider how the characters will interact with the environment chosen for the story.

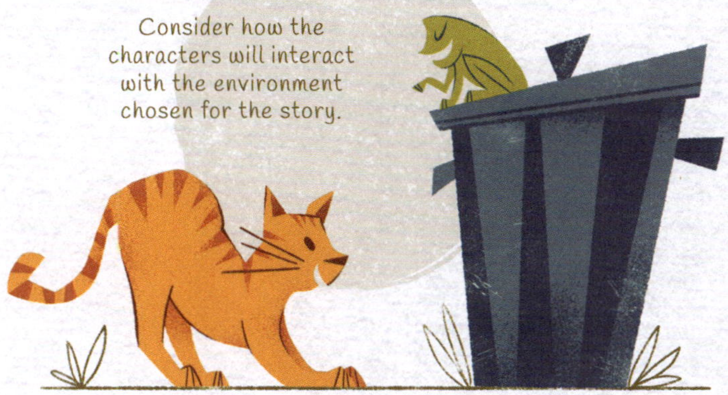

During the sketching stage it's essential to consider how the characters are going to stand out from the environment, establishing the color palette and the organization of the background elements.

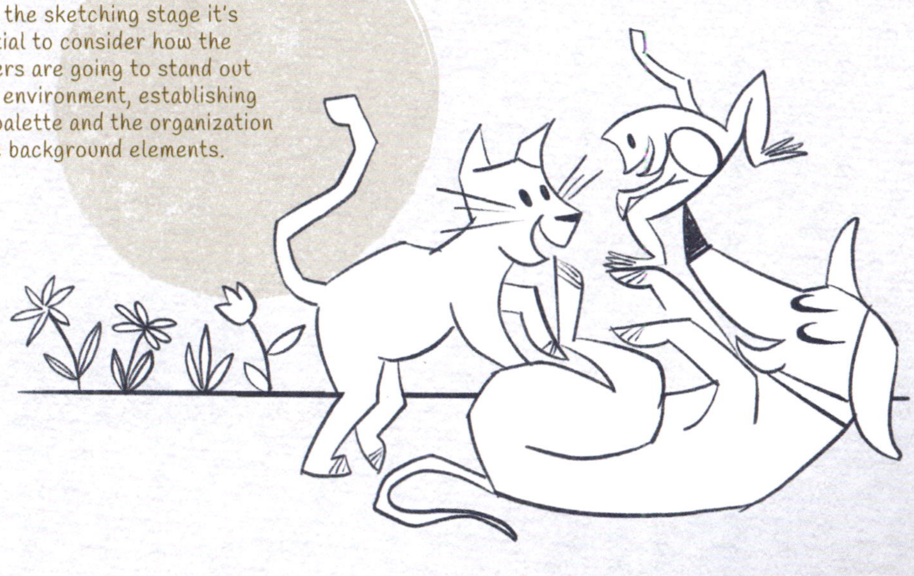

## CHARACTERS

In this story, the three main characters must attract the attention of the child. Books for babies usually have simple stories, meaning the characters are often the focus. Sketching different movements, imagining their reactions and how they relate to each other, will help define your characters' personalities. It will also help you to hone their design and color palette. Some of your initial ideas may vary greatly as you experiment.

I used a greyhound as a reference when sketching the dog: a cute puppy, lanky, funny, and curious. Play with the proportions to make the design more memorable and unique.

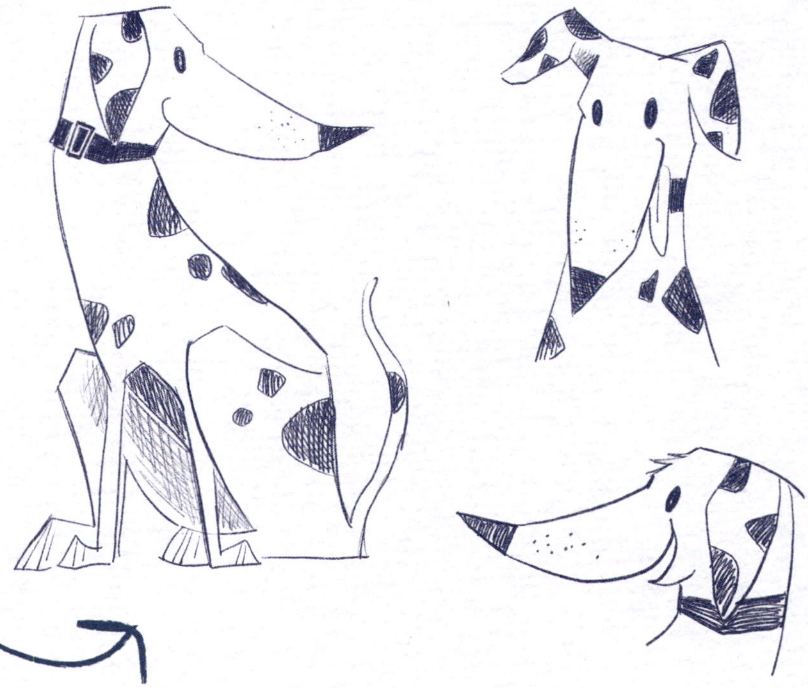

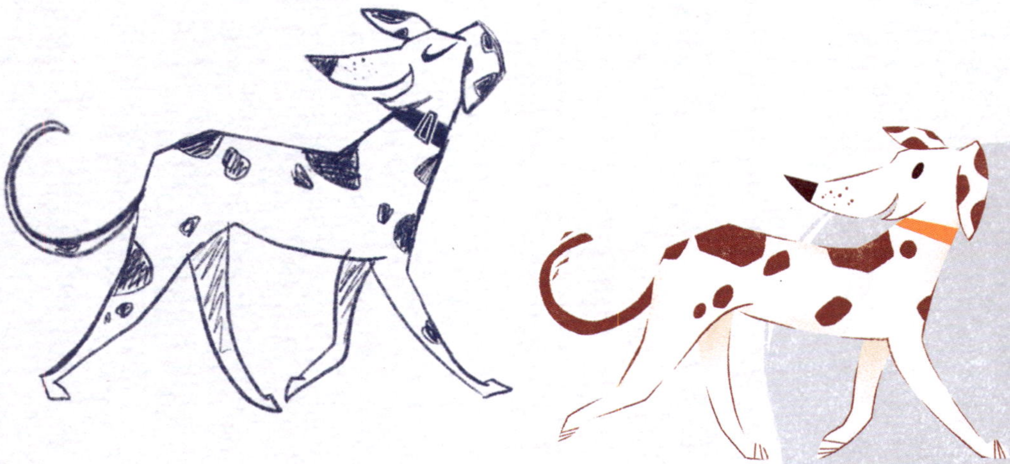

Try out different color palettes for each character. A dog could be yellow, blue, or purple! Forget about real-life color palettes and push out of your comfort zone. Using color in a different way will bring life and personality to your characters.

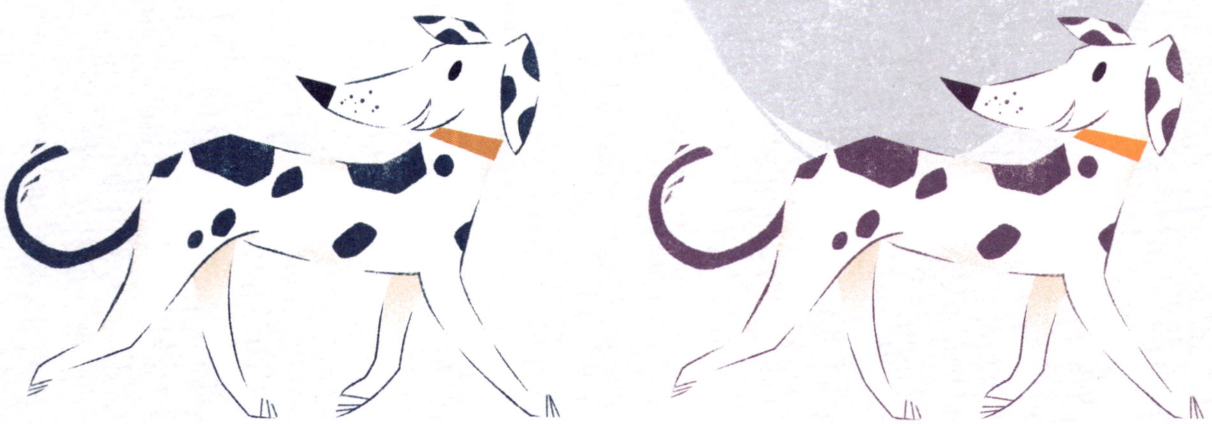

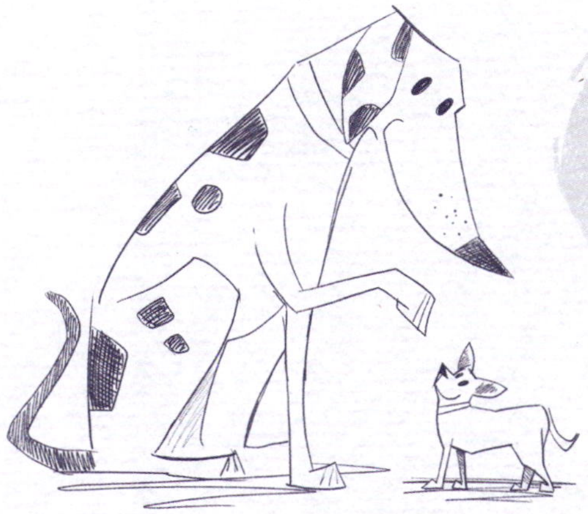

Investigate the characteristics of each animal and what differences exist between different breeds. A greyhound moves very differently to a Chihuahua!

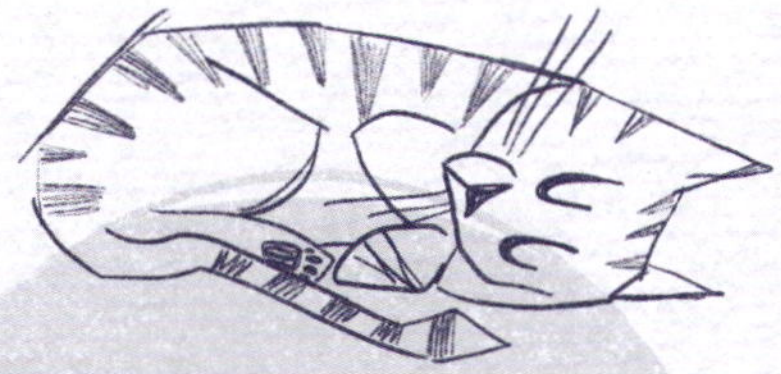

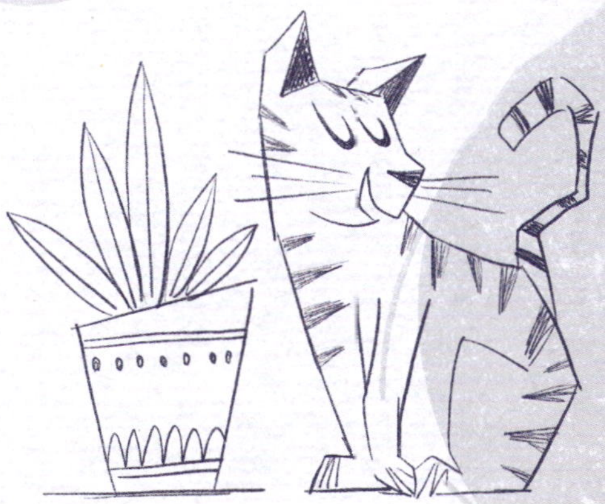

Analyze their way of moving, sleeping, or playing. The design does not necessarily have to be realistic, but it does need to be logical and consistent with the physiognomy of the animal.

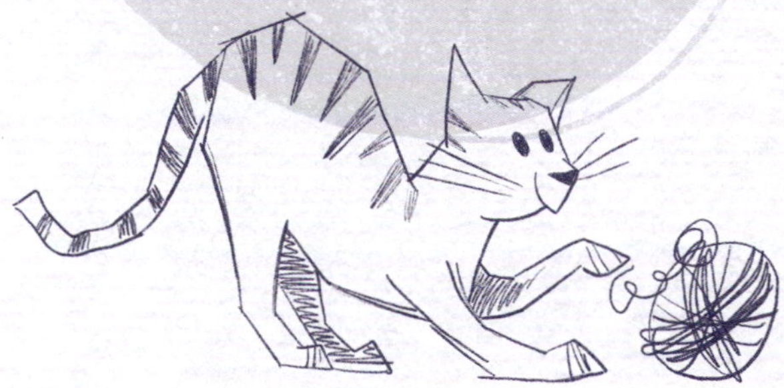

Sketching digitally can make it easier to try out different color palettes, or different positions for the eyes or mouth. Even so, sketching with pencil and paper can often get you drawing more freely, motivating your imagination and the development of ideas. A combination of both techniques is often the best approach. This part of the process takes time, but when it comes to creating the final art it will make all the difference. Working out the gestures and positions of the characters in advance will be a big help.

The color of the characters needs to stand out from the background, so young children can easily identify the key elements of the story.

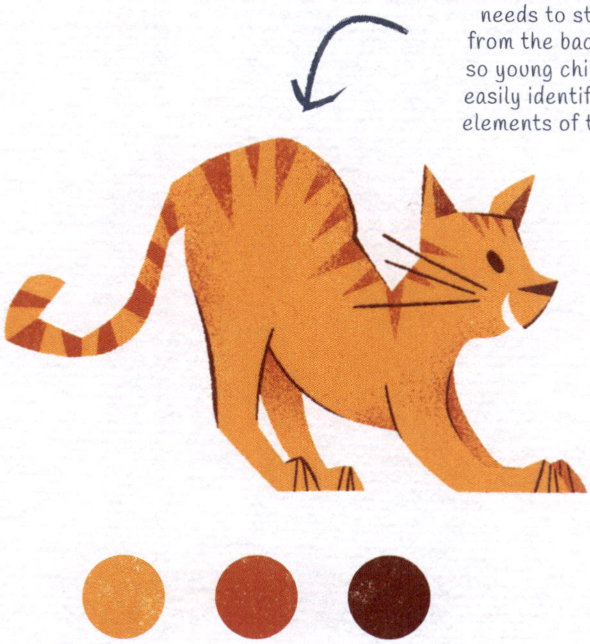

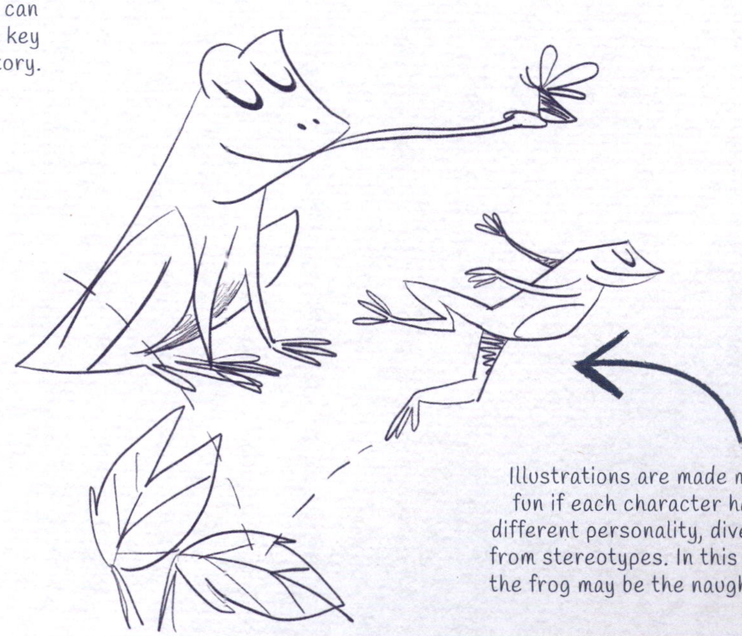

Illustrations are made more fun if each character has a different personality, diverging from stereotypes. In this story, the frog may be the naughtiest!

## MOVEMENT IN THE STORY

The illustrations in a children's book should create a sense of movement. In real life, everything is continually moving. People and animals don't have a static posture, not even when sleeping. Movement is essential in the illustration to ensure the reader wants to turn the page to see what will happen next. In *A Dog and a Cat and a Frog*, movement is one more element to consider. Though the background is very simple, each page shows a different perspective, so it seems as though the reader is slowly turning, seeing the whole scene. In addition, the characters spend the day playing, moving around the house and garden until they fall asleep at the end.

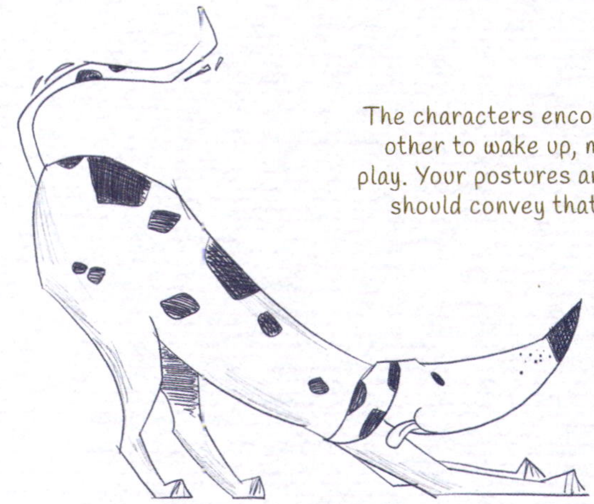

The characters encourage each other to wake up, move, and play. Your postures and gestures should convey that feeling.

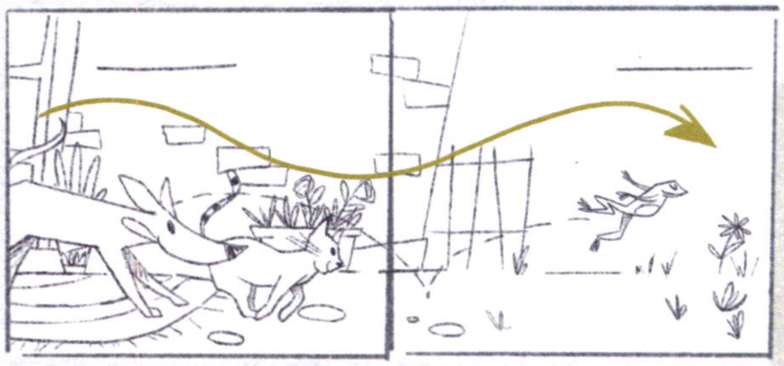

In the design of each double-page spread, the idea is that the characters are always moving to the right. This invites readers to keep turning the page and follow the natural reading line.

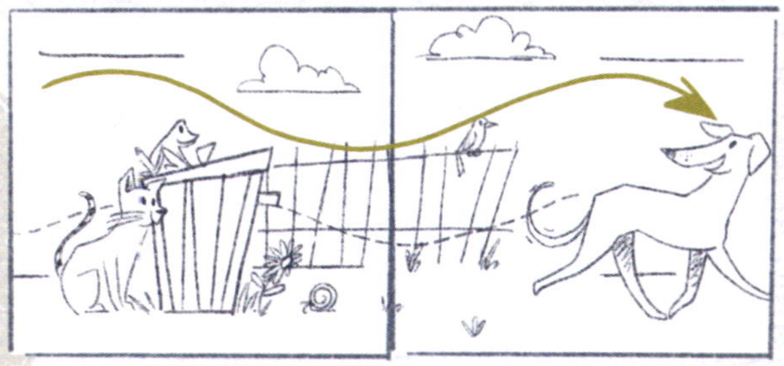

Each character has a different way of moving, giving them personality and diversity. The frog, for example, moves by jumping with great energy.

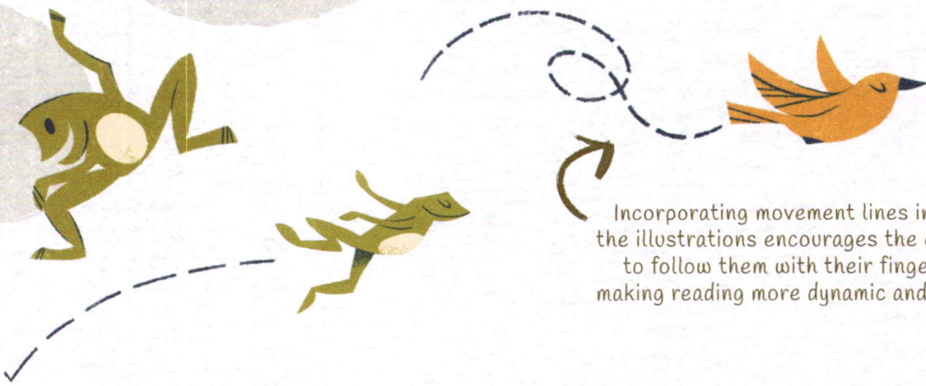

Incorporating movement lines into the illustrations encourages the child to follow them with their finger, making reading more dynamic and fun.

A simple background is not incompatible with creating a sense of dynamism. In this story, the characters move through different areas of the garden.

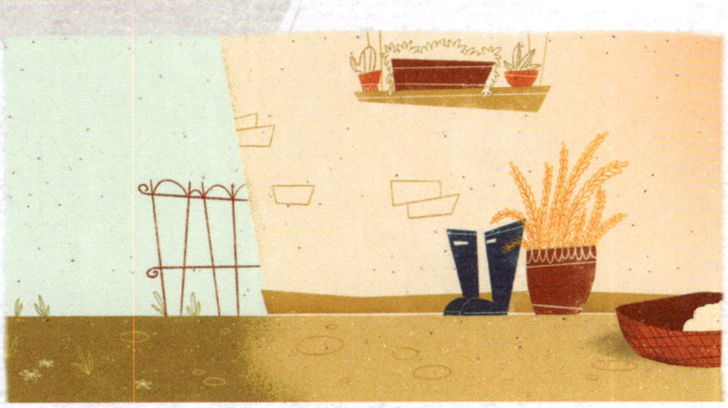

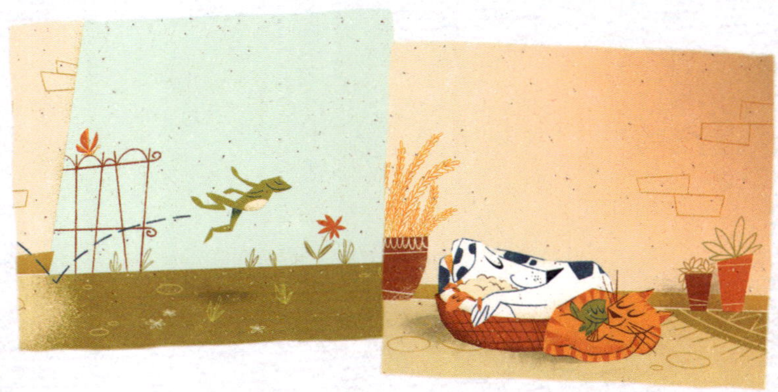

The color palette also seeks to create a sensation of movement. The characters play throughout the day, the light and shadows changing as day turns to dusk.

## DETAILS FOR CHILDREN

Picture book illustrations need not be limited to what the text says. More elements can be incorporated; details that tell their own story without stealing all the attention. I always like to add other small animals, insects, or objects that allow readers to discover something new every time they look at a page. Children take a lot of interest in these fun details and enjoy looking out for small objects in the background. In this story, which takes place in a garden, there were lots of opportunities to add garden-related elements, such as butterflies, dragonflies, or birds. It can be fun spotting a little key or discovering a scary snail.

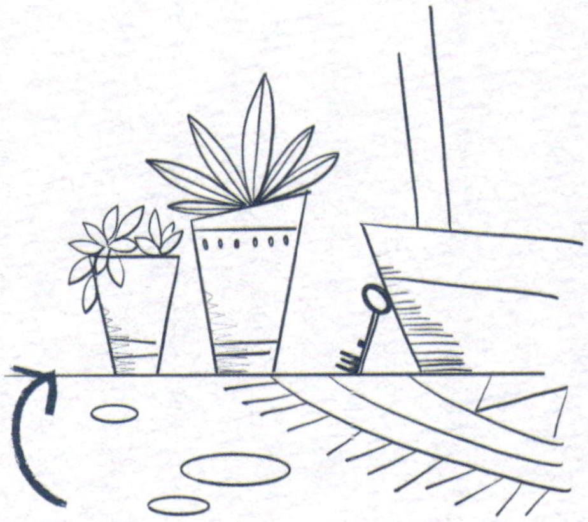

A hidden key can be a fun discovery for a child. Depending on age, more items can be added into the illustration.

Many of these elements didn't appear in the initial sketch, but were added as the final art developed and I evaluated the space on each page or the action that takes place.

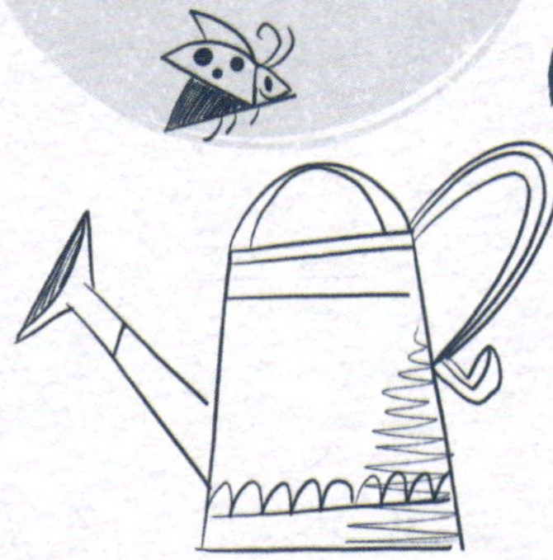

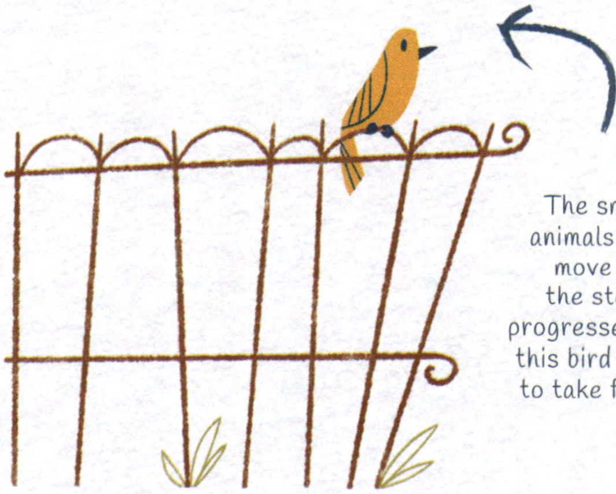

The small animals also move as the story progresses, like this bird about to take flight.

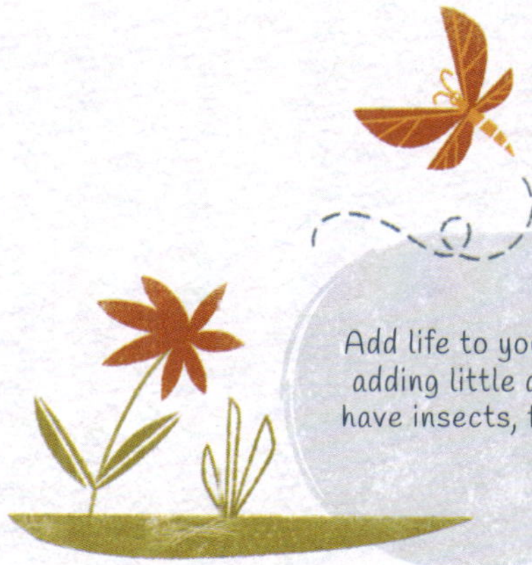

Add life to your story settings by adding little details. All gardens have insects, flowers, and stones.

Younger children can identify simple objects, such as wellies, and relate them to the context of the story.

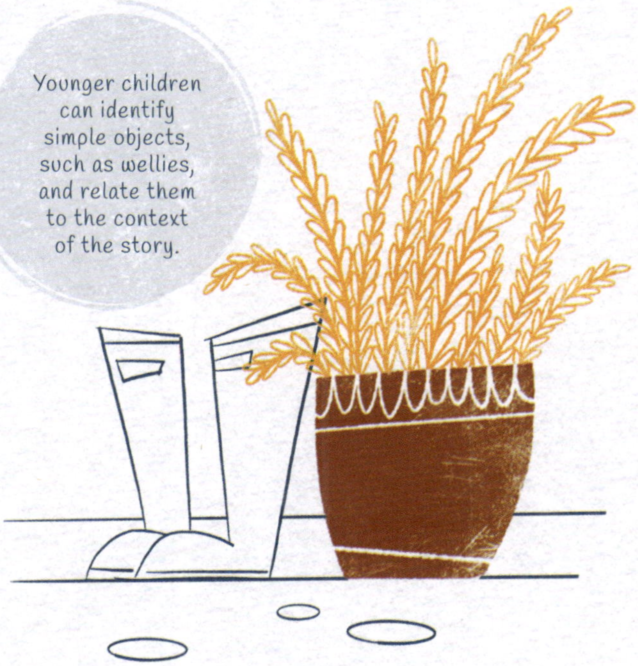

Some elements do appear in the text and it's the illustrator who decides the prominence given to them in the illustrations.

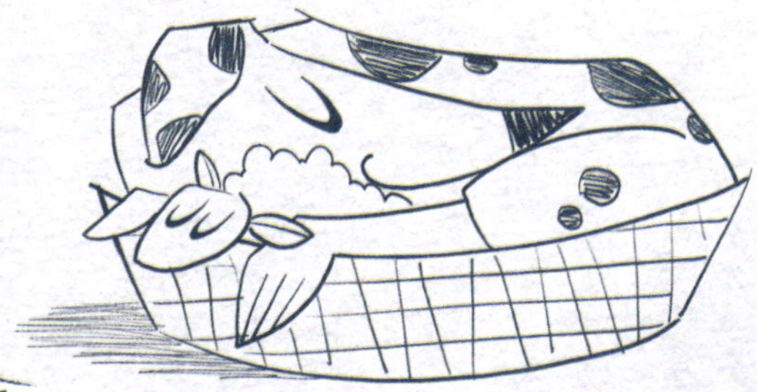

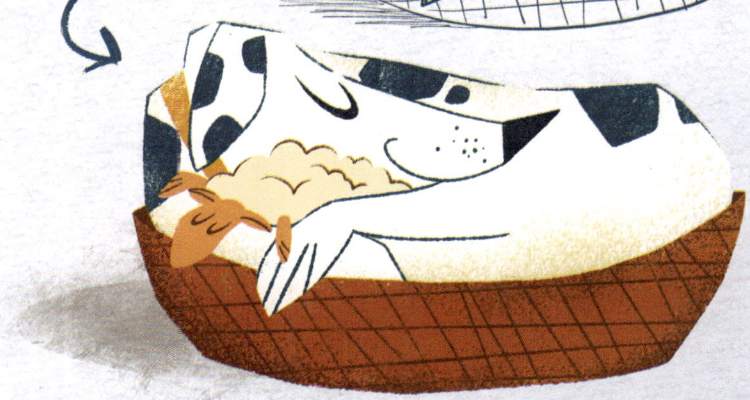

# ANALYSIS

Each illustrated story is a unique experience – I find my initial ideas always change throughout the development. I try not to stay with the first idea that comes to mind. Instead I prefer to force myself to try different color palettes and different perspectives for each scene. This way the creative process gives more of itself, offering more original ideas.

*A Dog and a Cat and a Frog* is a story that can offer many possible ideas for illustrations; I just had to find the one that best fit my way of seeing the story. I use the technique of creating five to eight quick sketches for each concept, then developing the one I like most in detail. It's a slower creative process, but it pays off when you start developing the final color art with the assurance that you're drawing the best idea you can offer the reader. It also means you make fewer changes in this part of the development and can fully dedicate yourself to drawing, painting, and developing the texture you imagined for the illustration. Carrying out a preliminary sketching and character study process allows you to work more calmly and confidently, knowing that you have already made the right decisions.

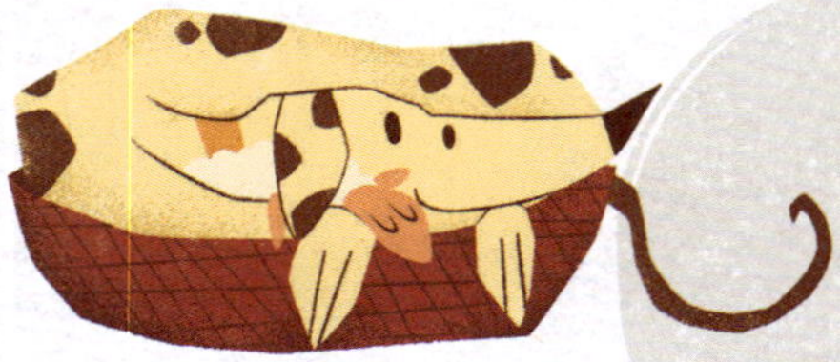

While my ideas for the cat and frog were clear from the beginning, I tried out different color palettes for the dog until I was convinced I wanted a white dog with blue spots that would jump off the page.

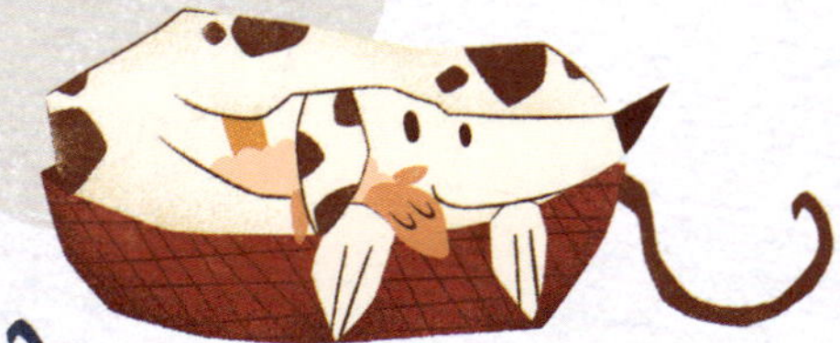

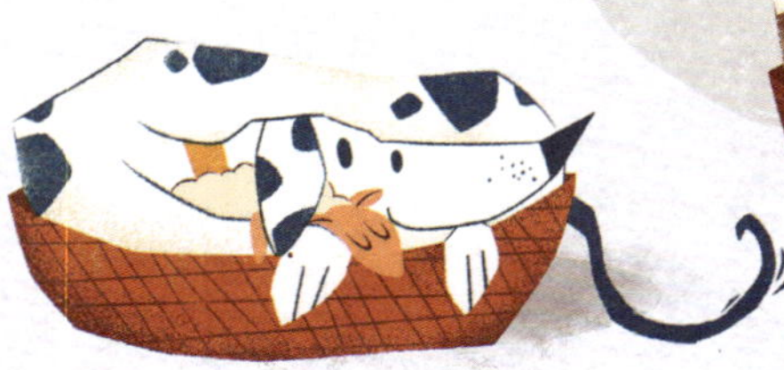

Working with a white-haired character forced me to modify the background color and include some linework to achieve enough contrast.

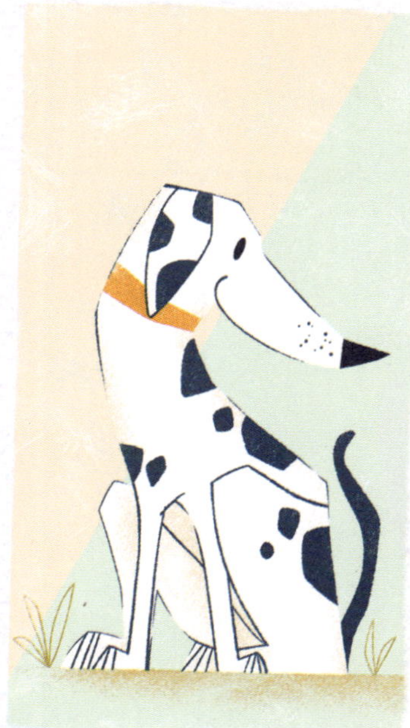

I wondered whether the elements in the background, like pots and plants, should be full color, or just a simple line. In the end I opted for an intermediate option.

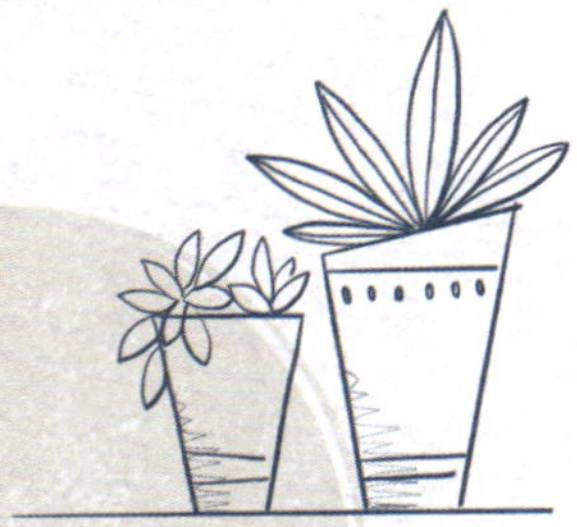

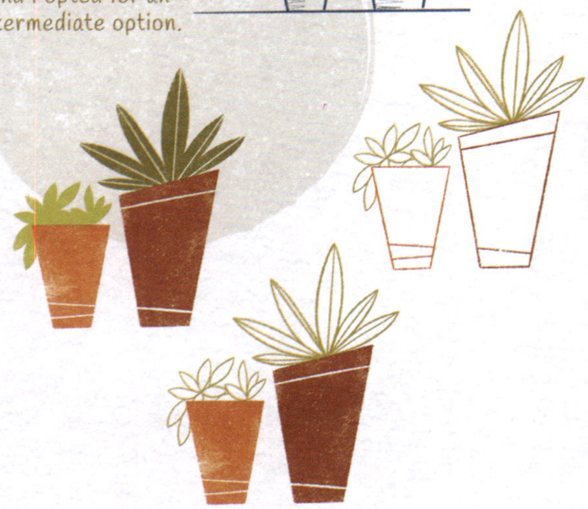

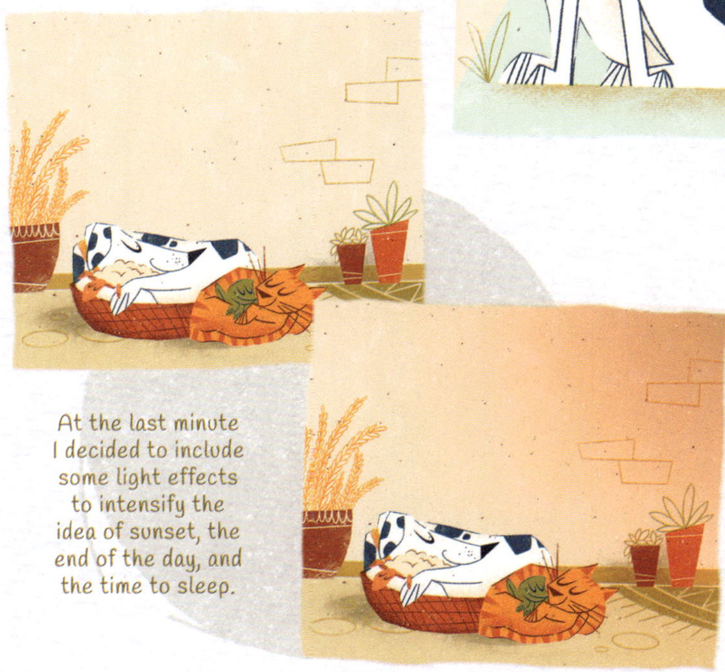

At the last minute I decided to include some light effects to intensify the idea of sunset, the end of the day, and the time to sleep.

Board books may seem simpler to illustrate than other children's books, but in reality their simplicity requires complex illustration work. You need to take into account how to attract the attention of younger children, or even babies, while also attracting the eyes of their parents, as they will usually be the ones who choose the book and read it.

Fairly simple backgrounds, well-defined characters, and clear actions all help children to understand the message of the story. Personally, I prefer to use minimalist color palettes and natural hues, but this depends on the style of each illustrator. Many board books are full of vibrant colors, while others prefer pastel shades. There are no rules or limits, as long as the illustration is consistent and has enough contrast to engage the reader.

As always, the cover should be the star of the book. It needs to jump off the shelves and attract the attention of young readers. For board books, a simple but charming cover with cute and fun characters is usually preferable.

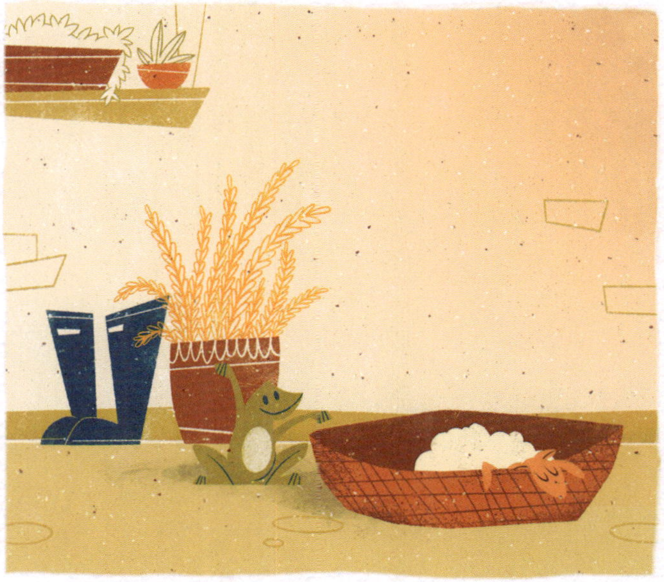

Simple and warm color palettes create a cozy feeling.

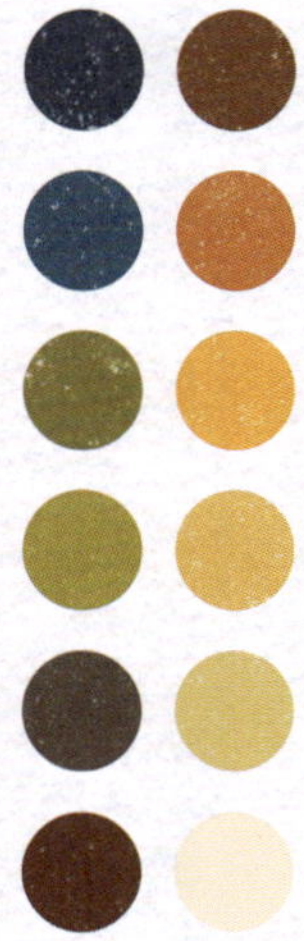

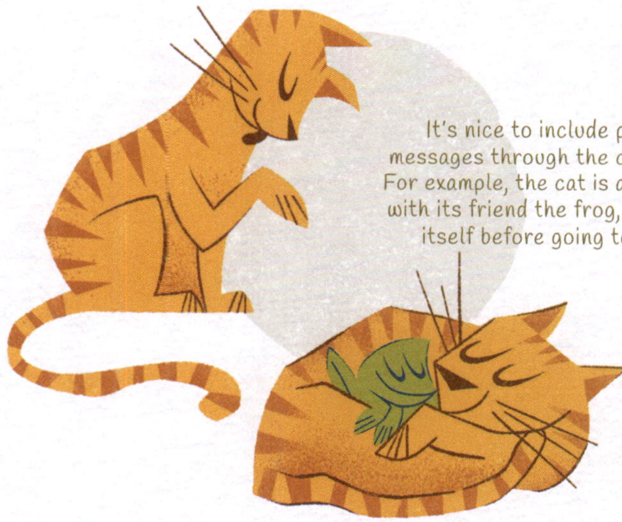

It's nice to include positive messages through the characters. For example, the cat is affectionate with its friend the frog, and cleans itself before going to sleep.

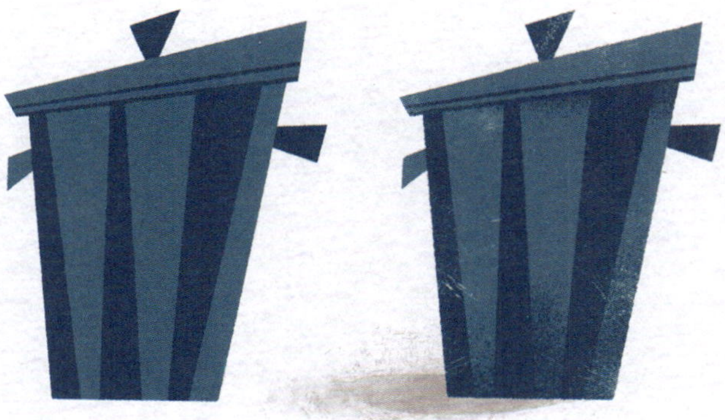

Using textures is always interesting, but in books for babies they should be used sparingly to ensure the characters and actions are well defined.

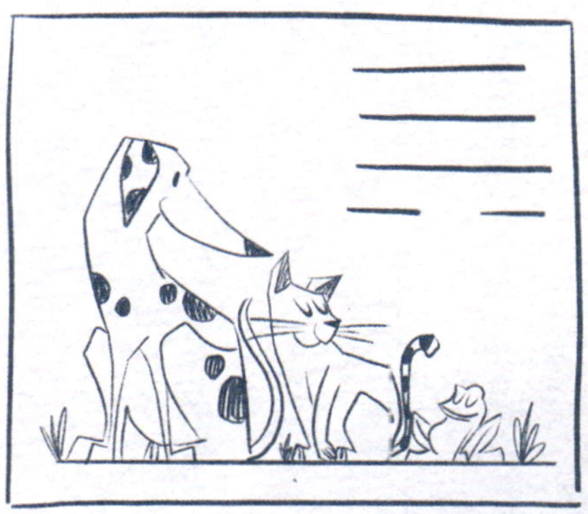

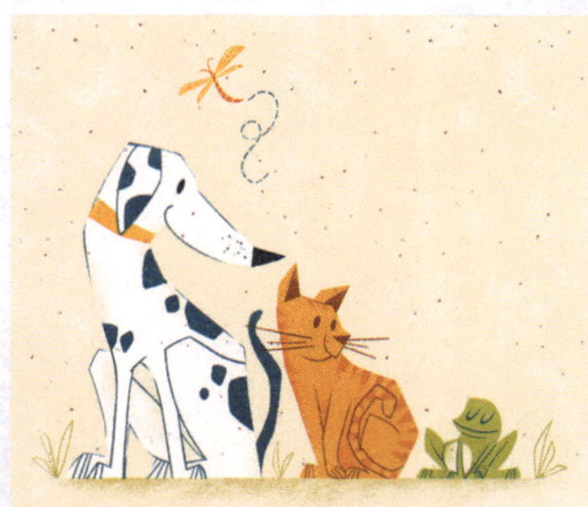

I decided to make the three characters the focus of the book cover, looking from one to the other as they hint at the playful game to follow.

# This Is Me

Written by

**GREG DOBBINS**

Illustrated by

**DAPO ADEOLA**

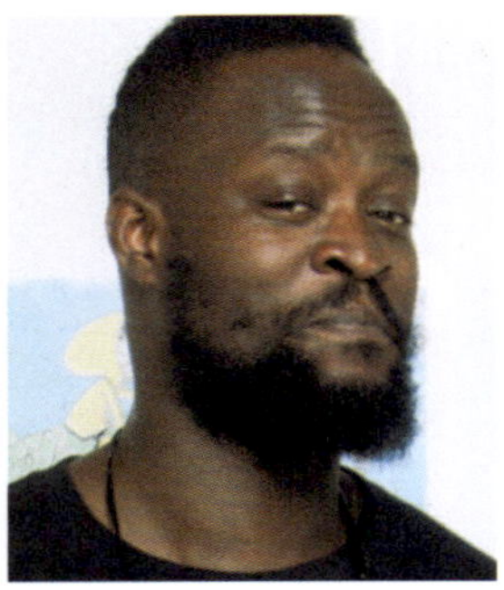

Character designer &
children's book illustrator
**instagram.com/dapsdraws**

Dapo is a self-taught illustrator and character designer whose bestselling debut picture book *Look Up!* won the Waterstones Children's Book Prize 2020.

A STORY FOR AGES 2–4 YEARS

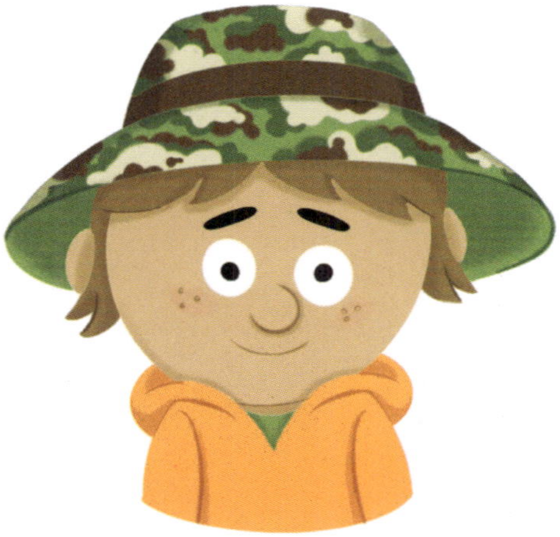

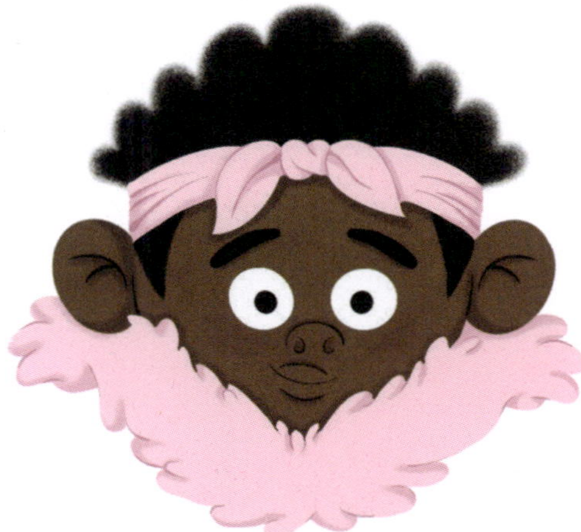

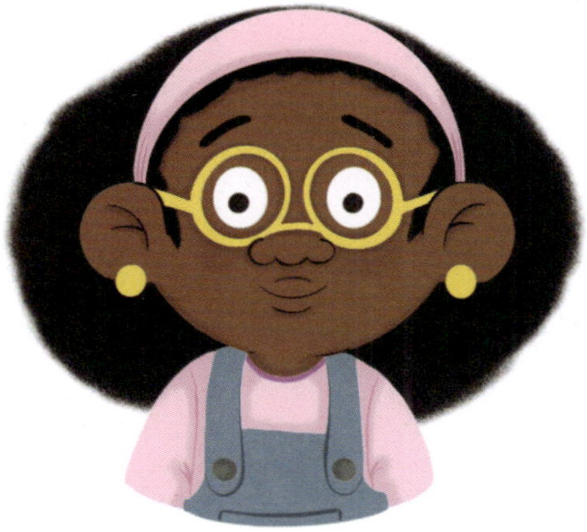

# This Is Me

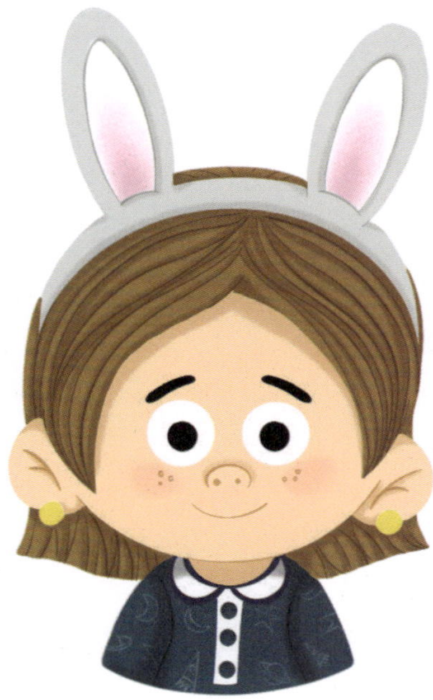

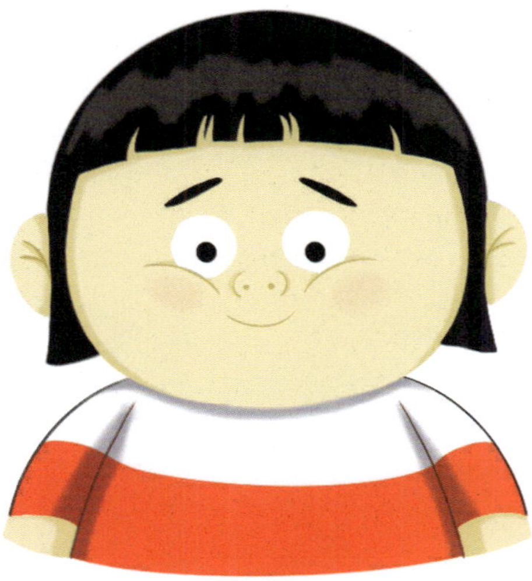

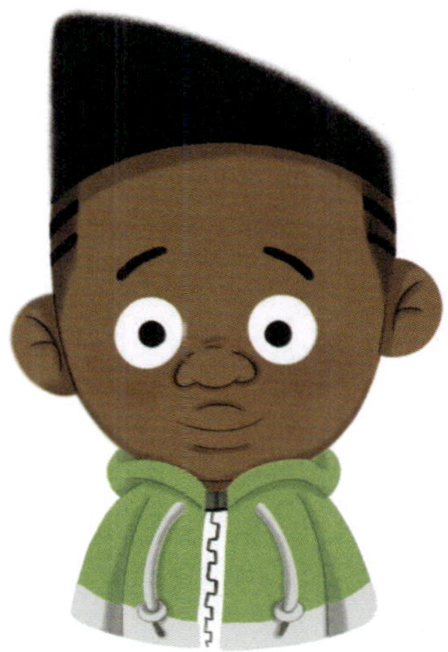

I can...

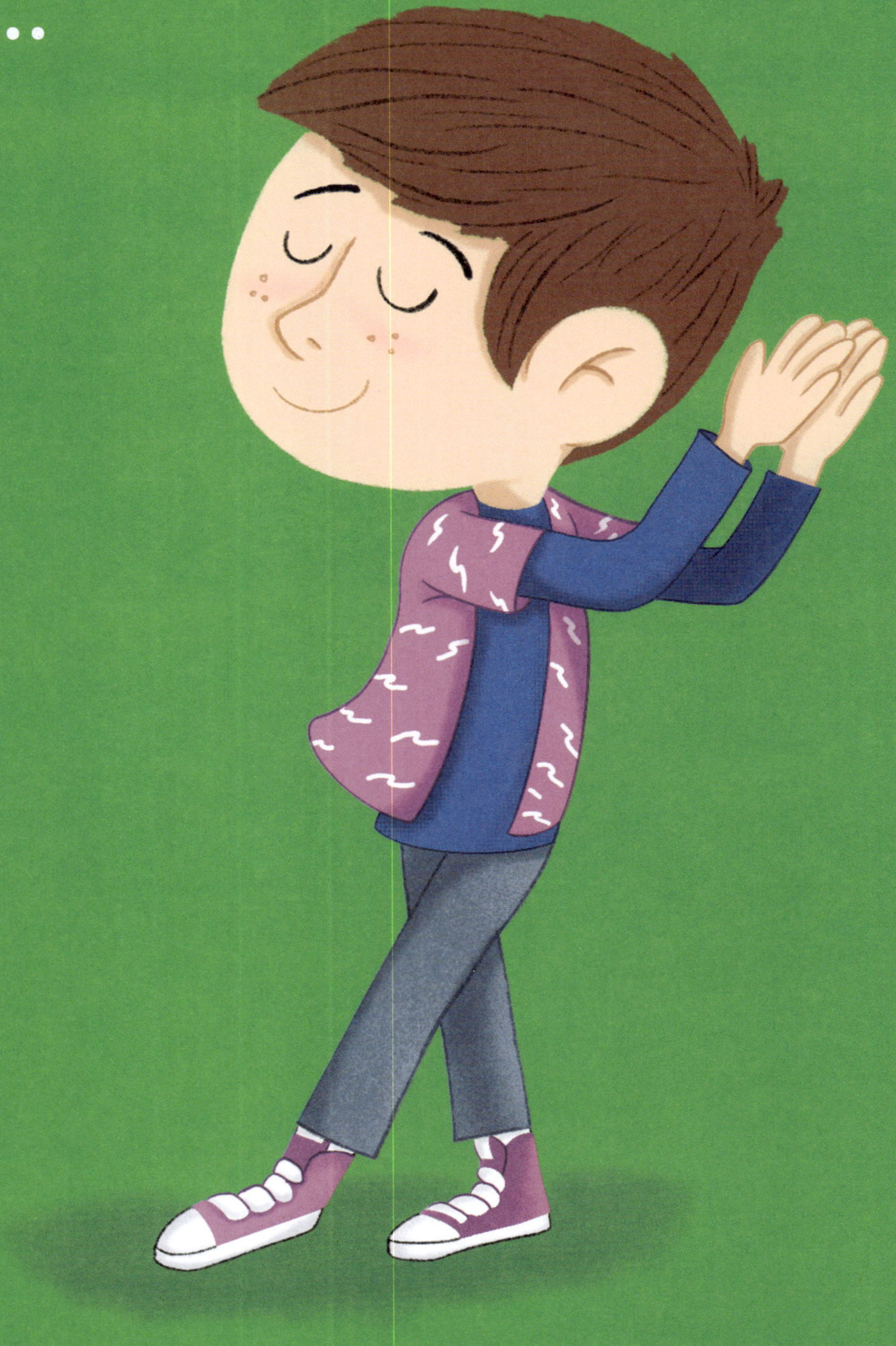

CLAP my hands

I can...

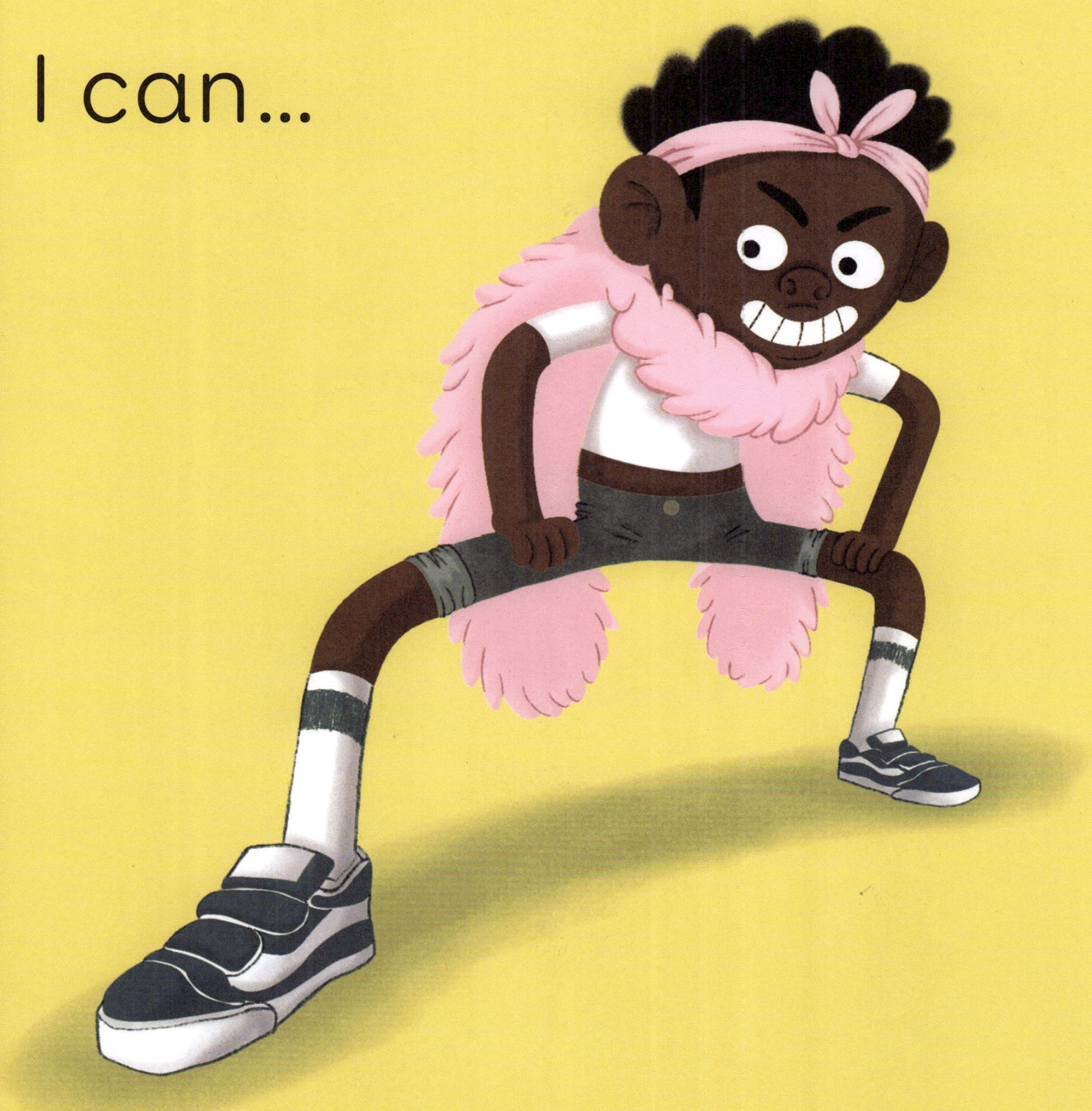

STAMP my feet

I can...

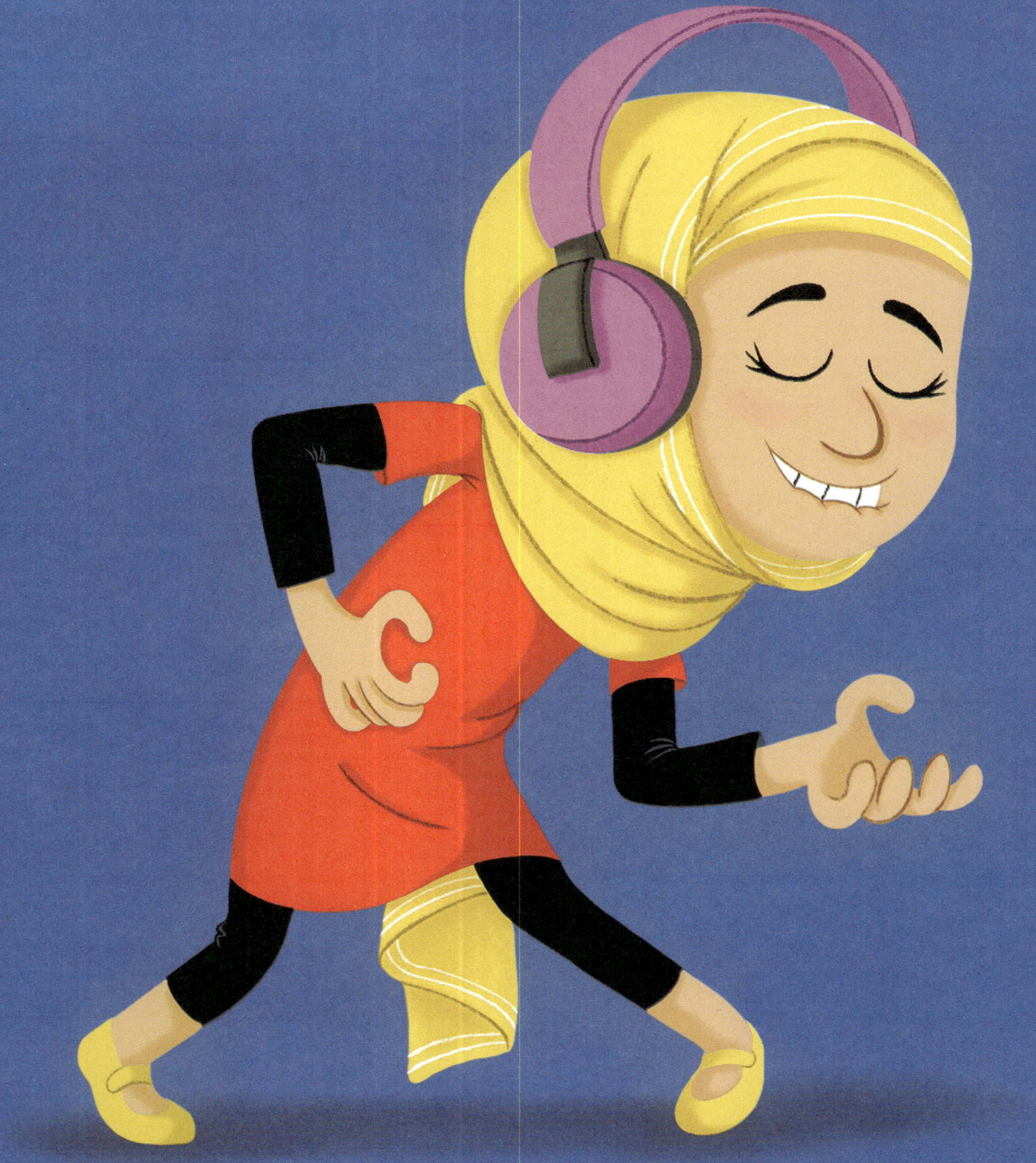

NOD my head

I can...

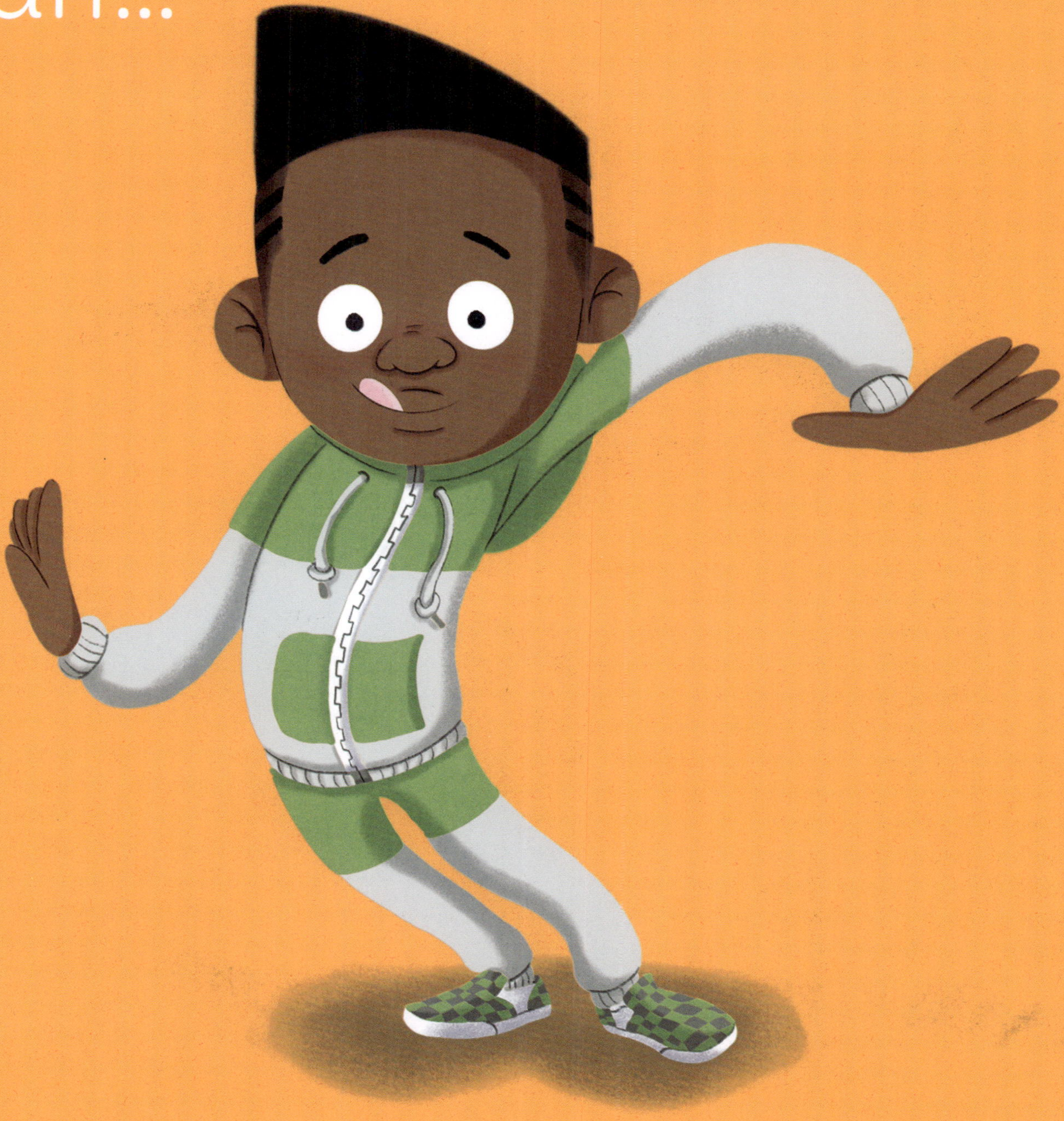

WIGGLE my body

I can...

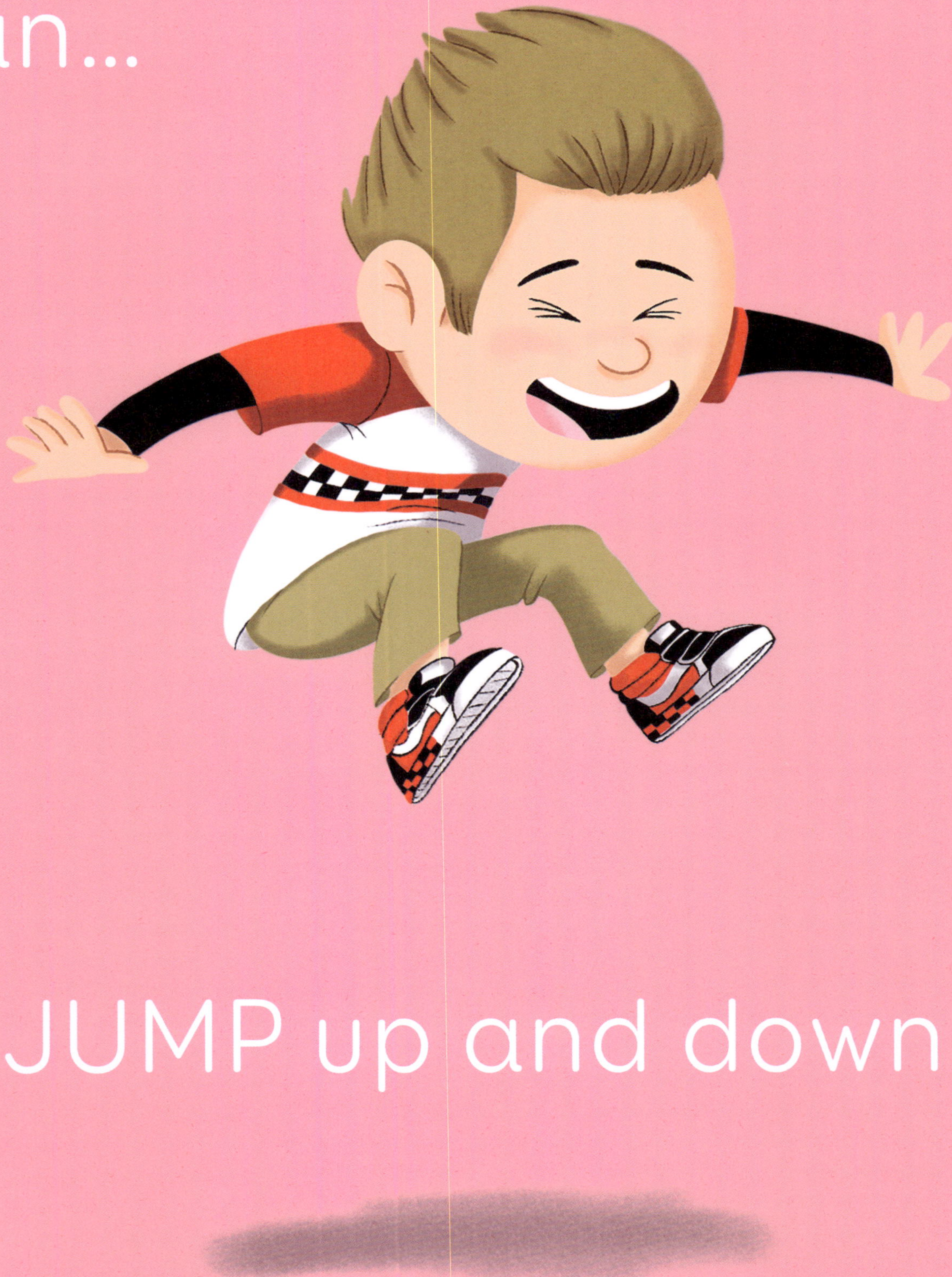

JUMP up and down

I can...

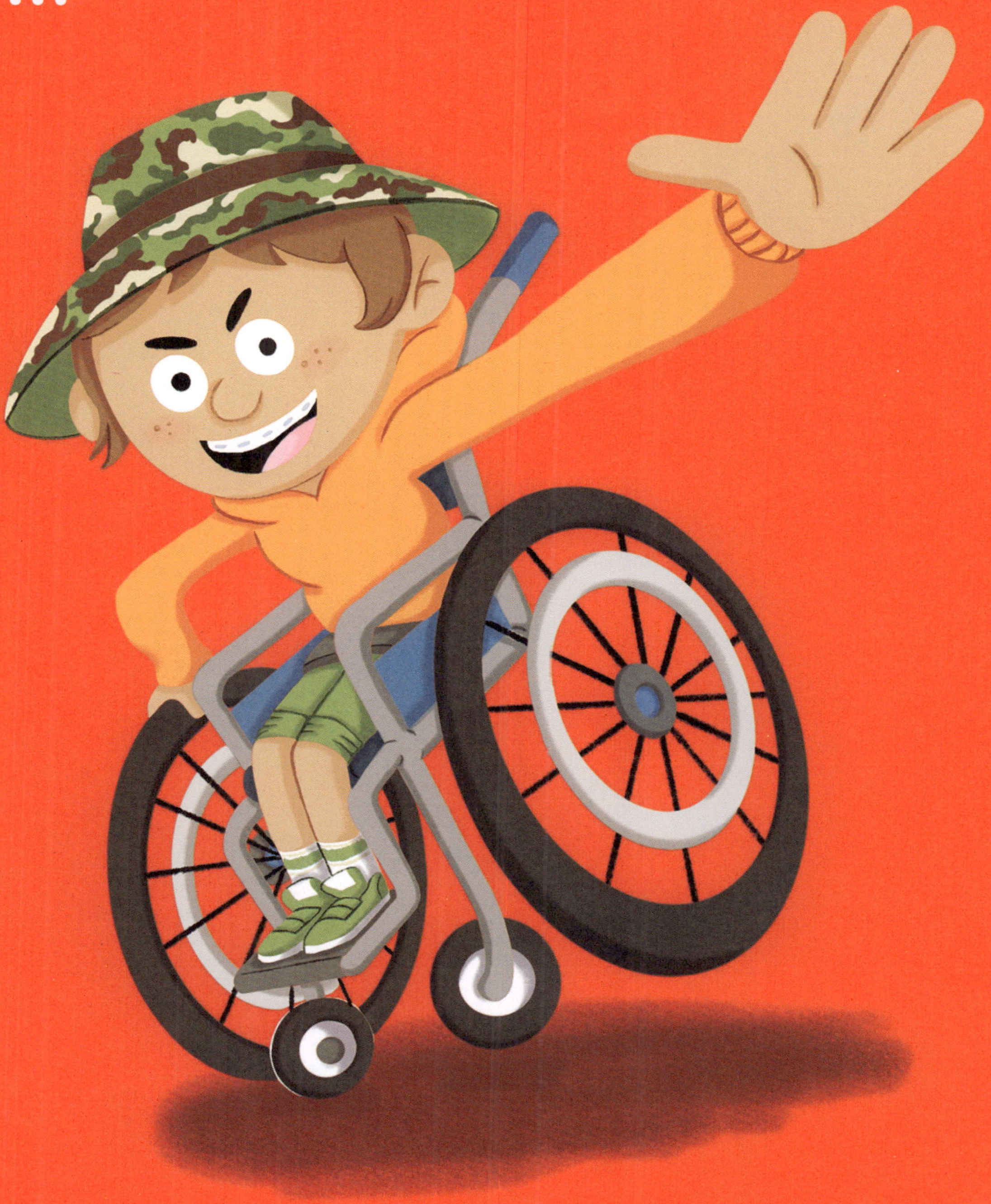

SPIN around and around

I can...

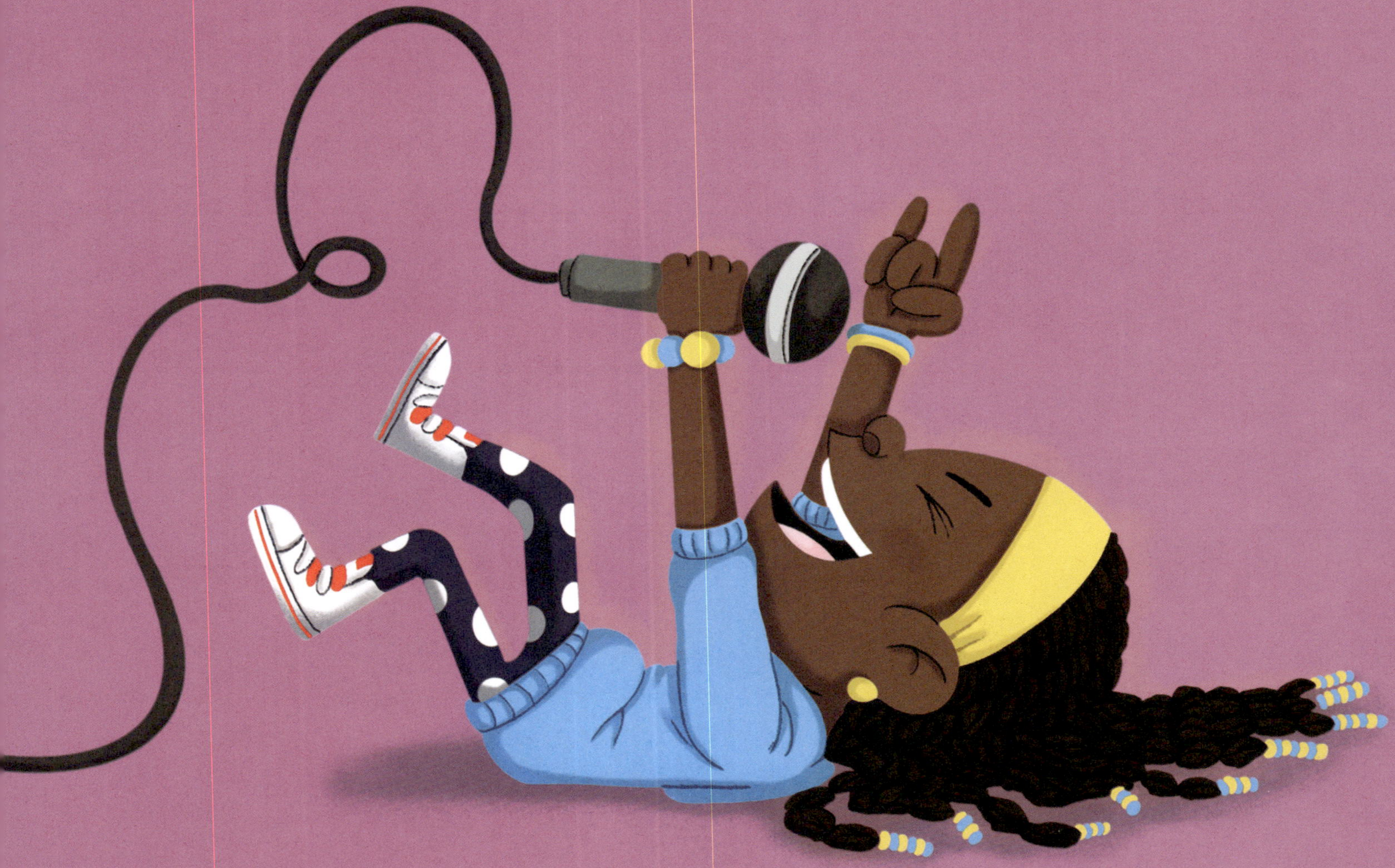

SING a song

I can...

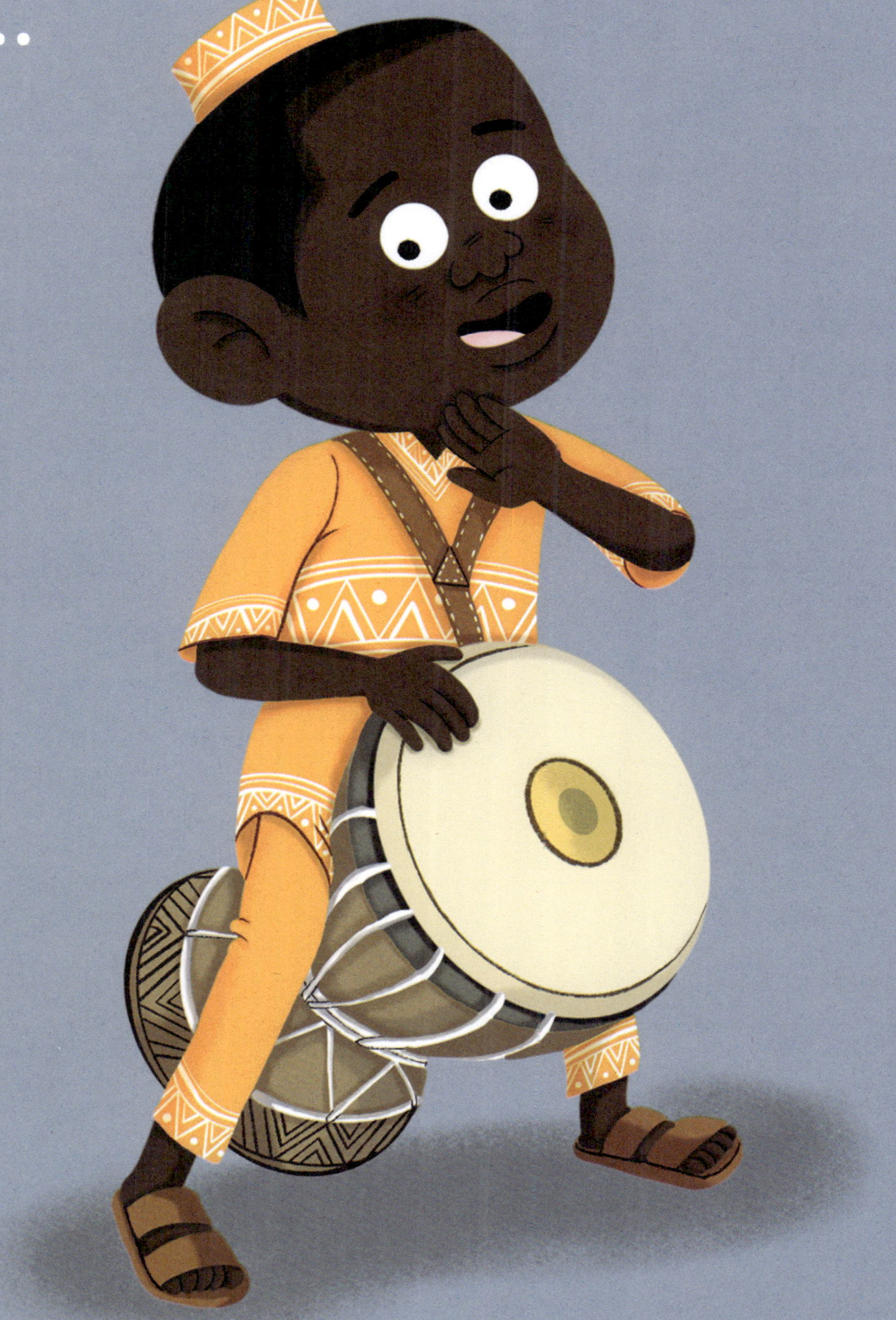

BANG a drum

I can...

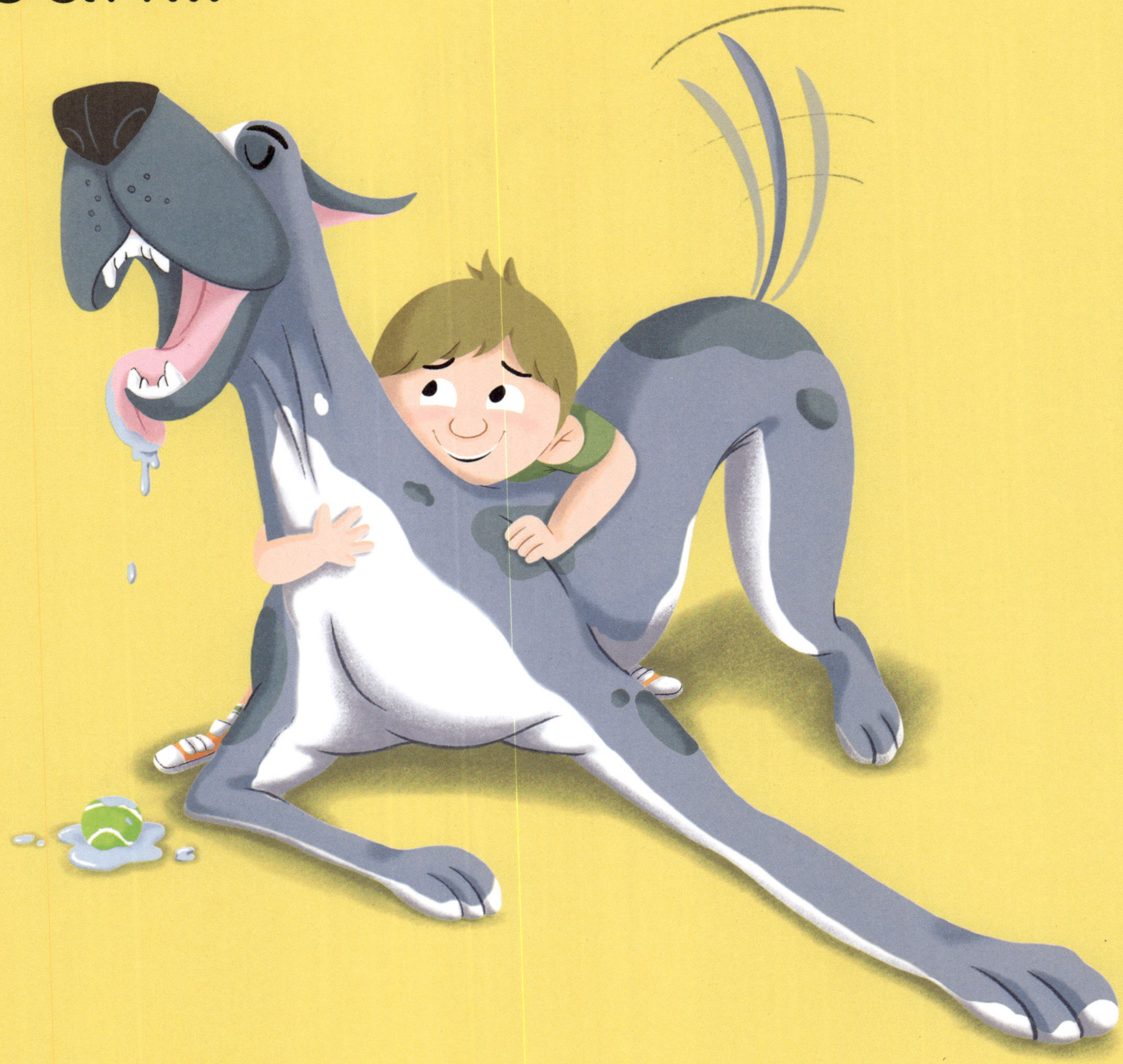

STROKE my dog

I can...

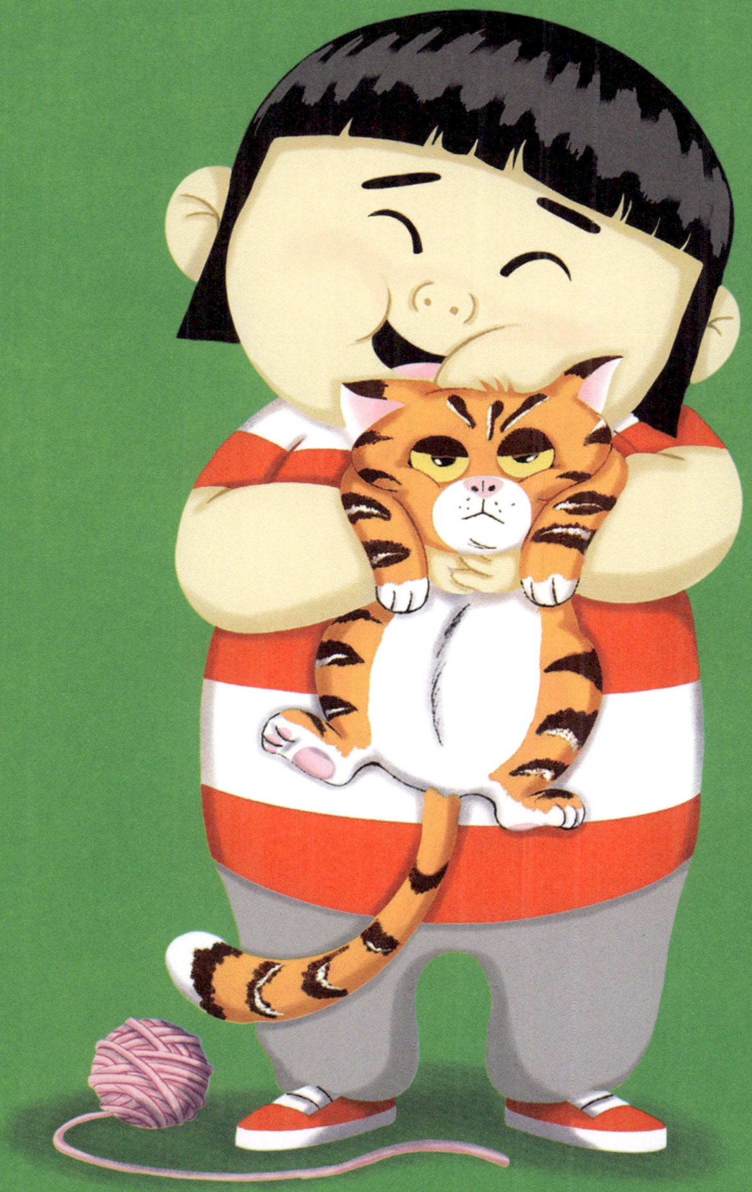

CUDDLE my cat

I can...

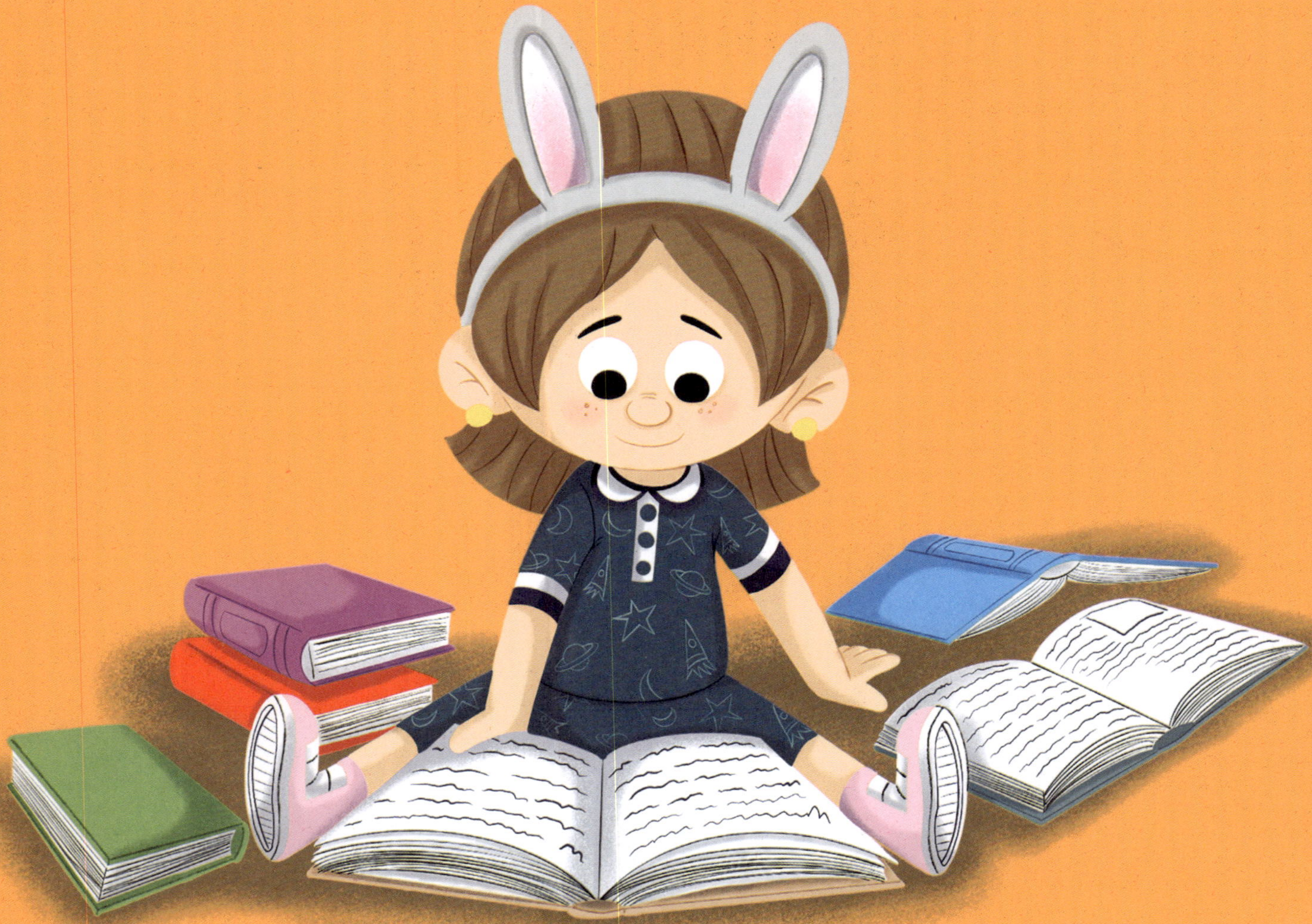

READ a book

I can...

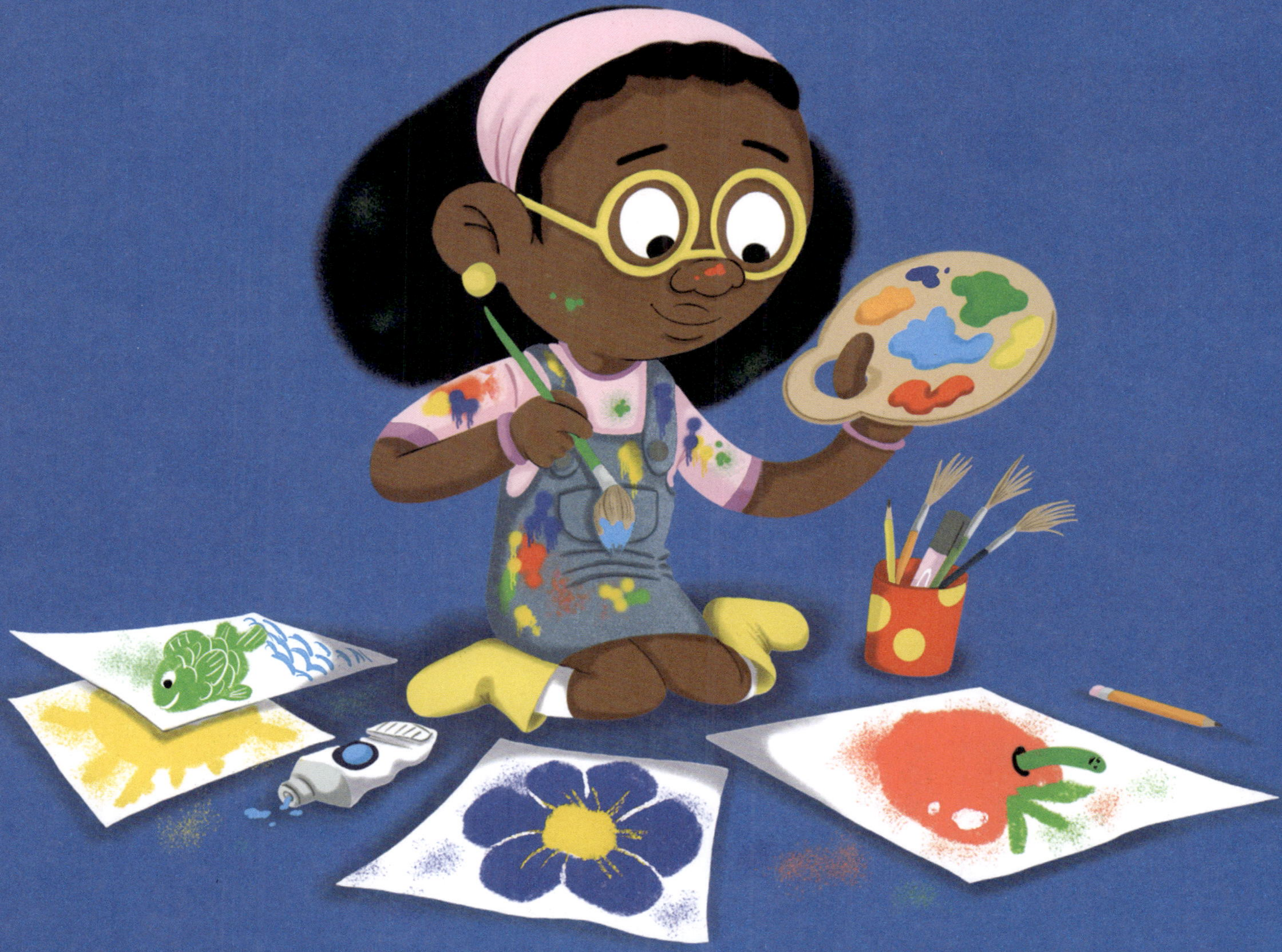

PAINT a picture

I can...

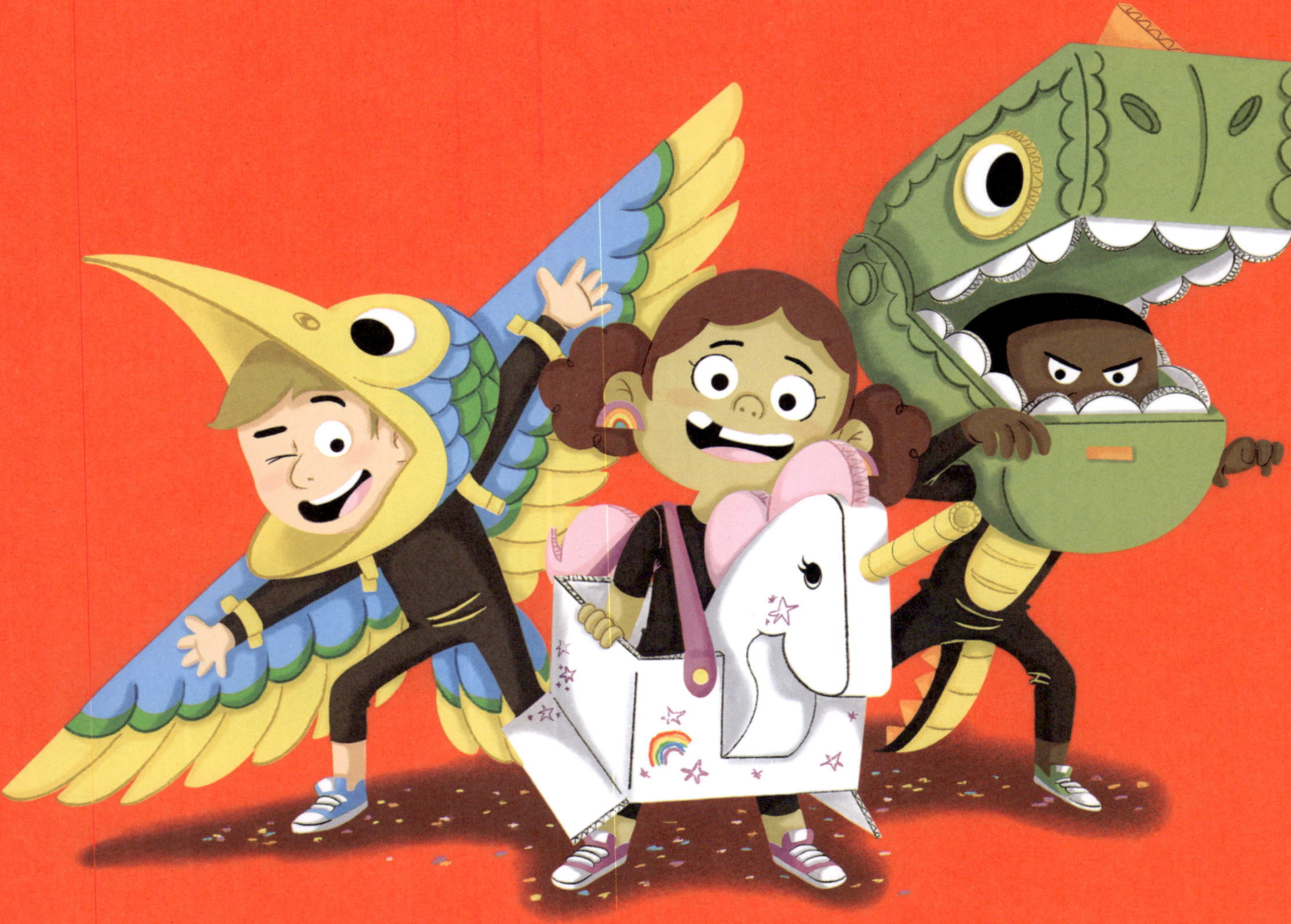

PLAY with my friends

I can...

HUG my family

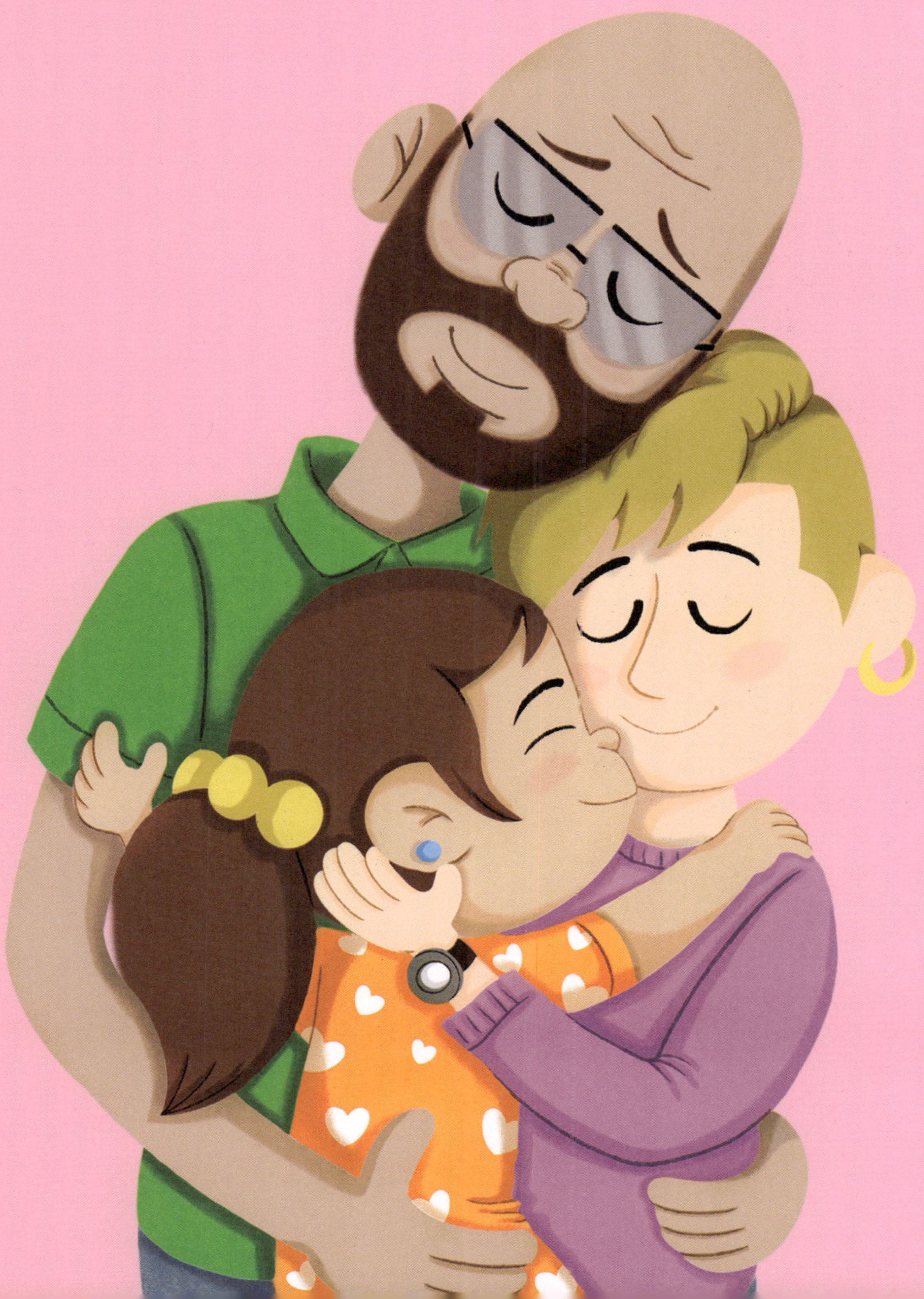

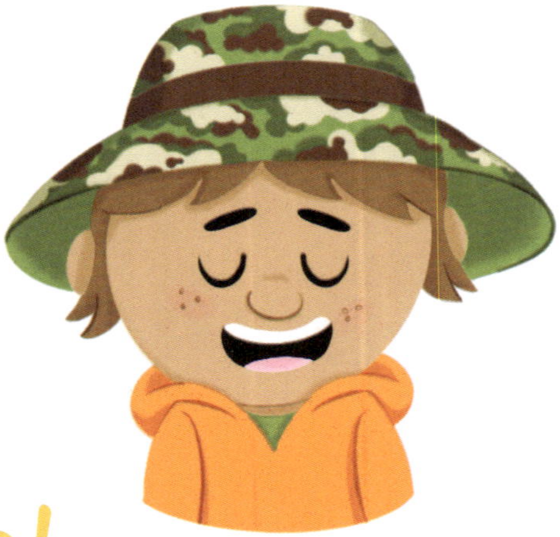

And me!

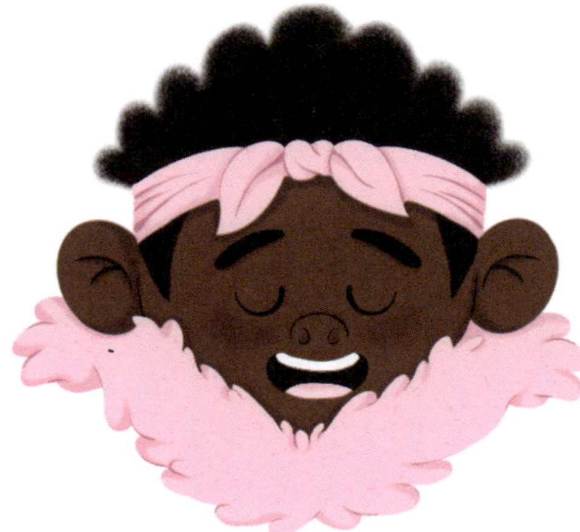

And me!

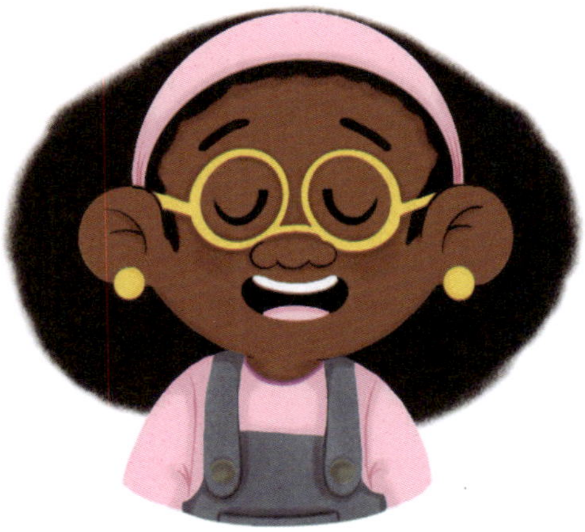

# This Is Me

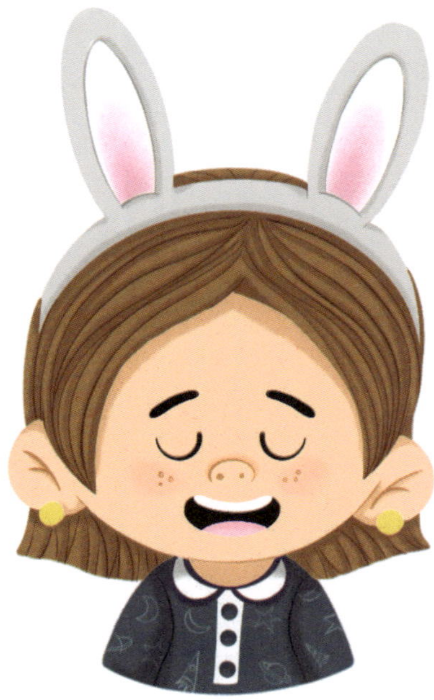

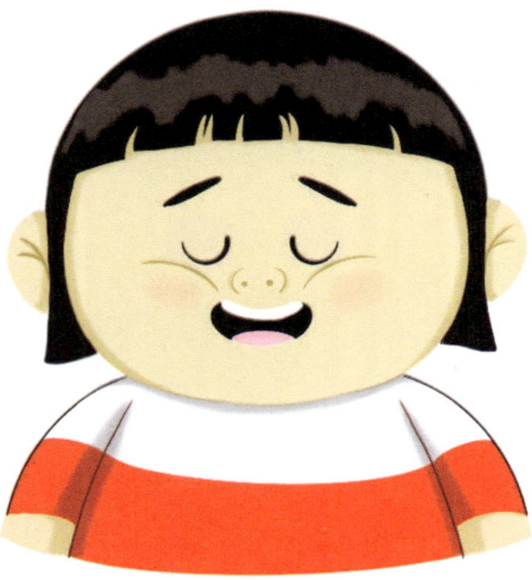

And me!

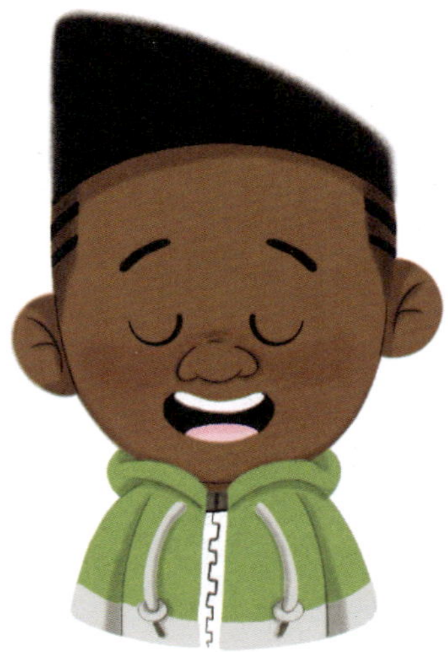

And me!

TURN THE PAGE FOR
INSIGHTS FROM THE ARTIST

# This Is Me

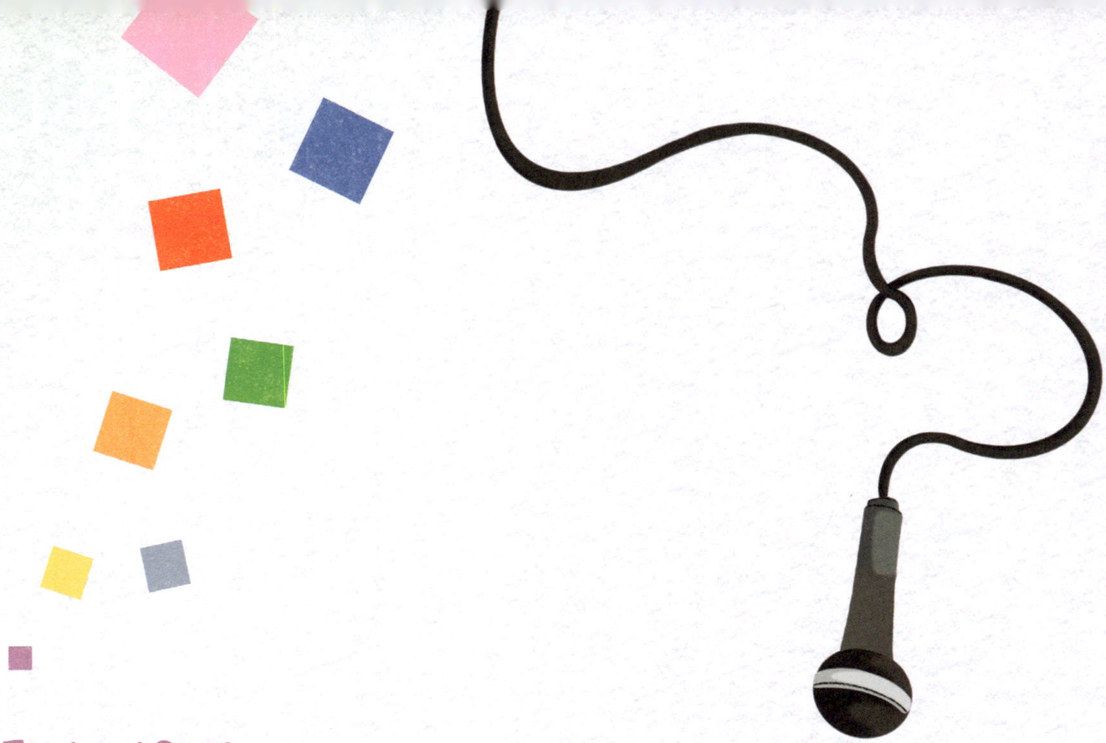

## DEVELOPING KEY FEATURES

### TARGET AGE RANGE

The target age range for *This Is Me* is 2–4 years. The story is perfect for this age group; not only is it short but it's action-packed too, providing numerous directions in which I could illustrate it. This was a little challenging to begin with, as I normally work on stories for children aged 4–8 years. I adapted to the younger age range by making simpler choices with background elements and color.

When working on stories for this age range, it's important to make sure your artwork reads clearly so young readers are able to make sense of what is happening. I decided to keep my illustrations character-focused, using simple shapes within the characters and ensuring each had a clear, readable expression.

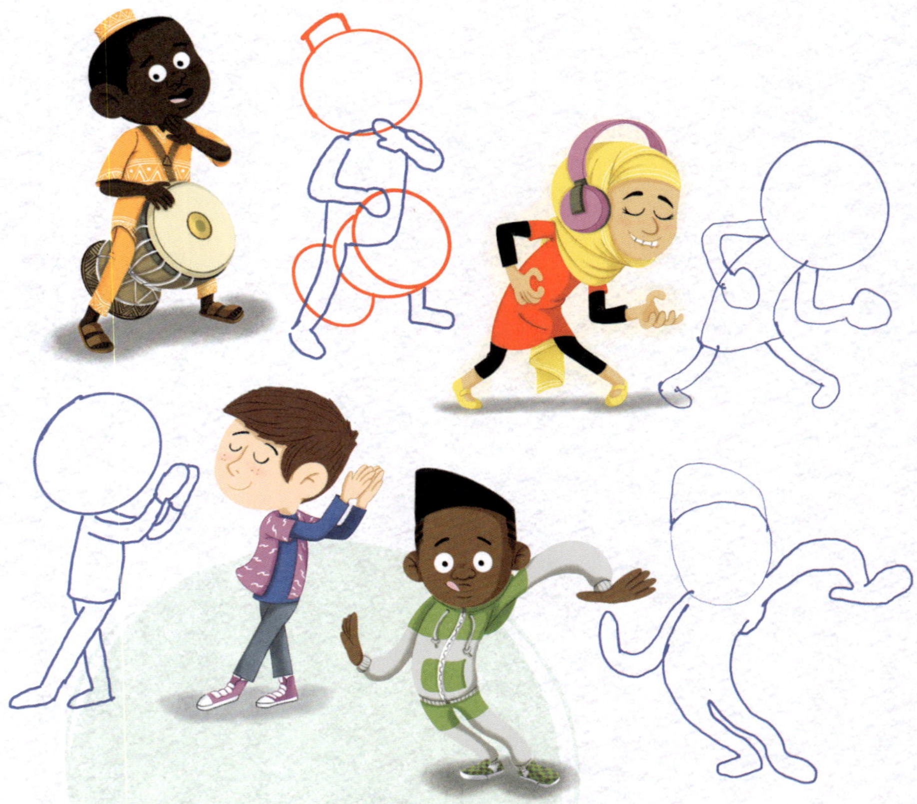

Here are some examples of the shapes found within the character designs. The use of curves and very few angles makes the shapes friendly, warm, and inviting. This is key with illustrations aimed at younger children, especially if the story is intended to be fun.

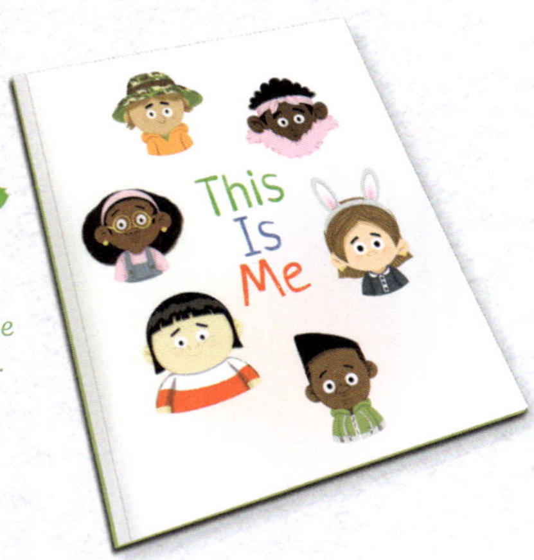


The final title page design.

## CHARACTERS

The project called for a diverse cast of characters, so I started by dividing the fourteen illustrations up, making sure there was a good ratio of diverse characters in the mix. I compiled a mood board of various images I found online to help me decide how the different characters would look. The story text was simple, which gave me a lot of room to play when it came to deciding which characters I could draw doing which action. This lack of constraint really helped drive the initial stages along.

Thumbnail sketches are the perfect stage to work out your characters. There's a good chance sketches drawn at this stage might not end up in the final image, but they're always a great jumping-off point. This is the time to try things and make mistakes in order to figure out what works.

The text for this page reads "*I am me... I nod my head.*" The first-pass sketch is what instantly came to mind, but I couldn't get it to work in a way that did justice to the text while also fitting well with the other illustrations. I then had an idea to try an air guitar pose instead, which worked much better. This illustration captures the joy and love of music, enhancing the playful mood of the book as a whole.

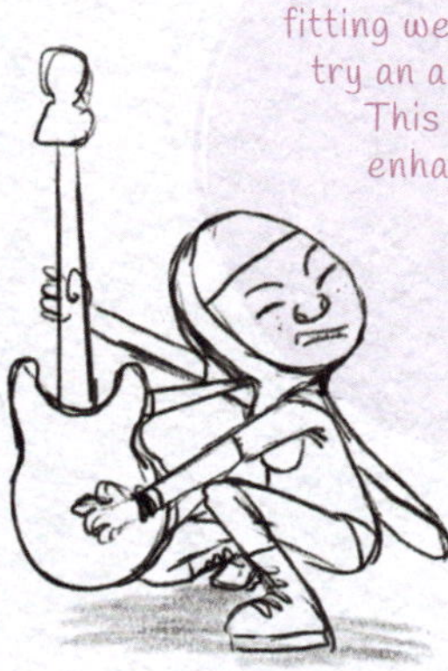

**1ST PASS**

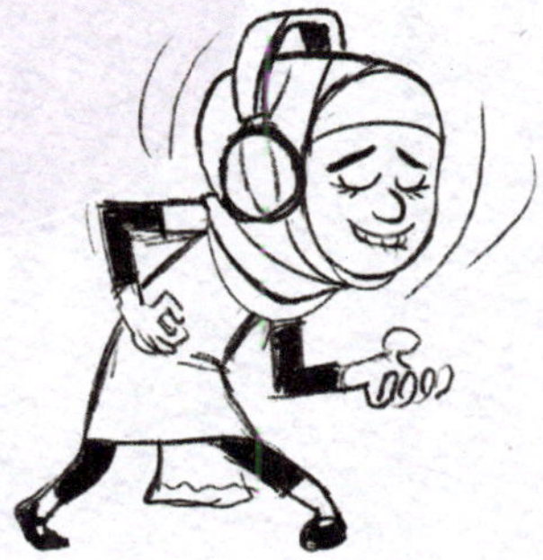

**2ND PASS**

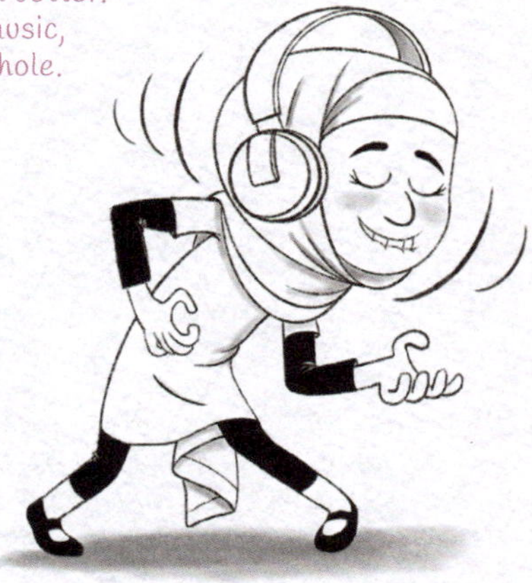

**FINAL DRAFT**

The young target age range meant bright, eye-catching colors that popped were a must. I also used the colors as another opportunity to push the diversity of the characters. I used as many gender-neutral colors as I could in the characters' clothing to avoid perpetuating gender stereotypes, while showing a range of children from diverse demographics. When it came to choosing the colors for the complexions of the black and brown characters, it was important to deliberately show the different shades and skin tones that can be found within people from these cultural backgrounds to ensure the representation being depicted was accurate.

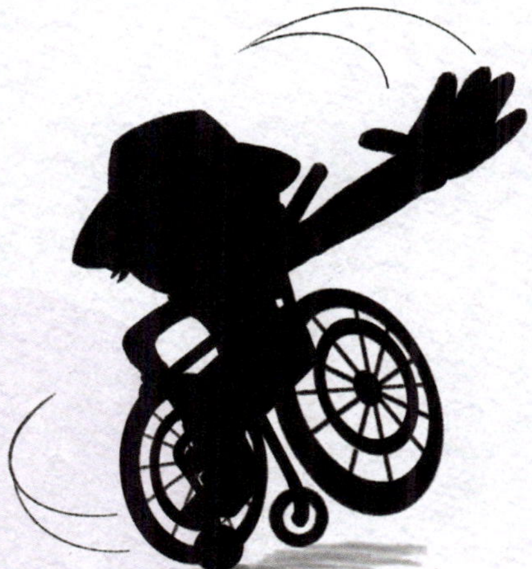

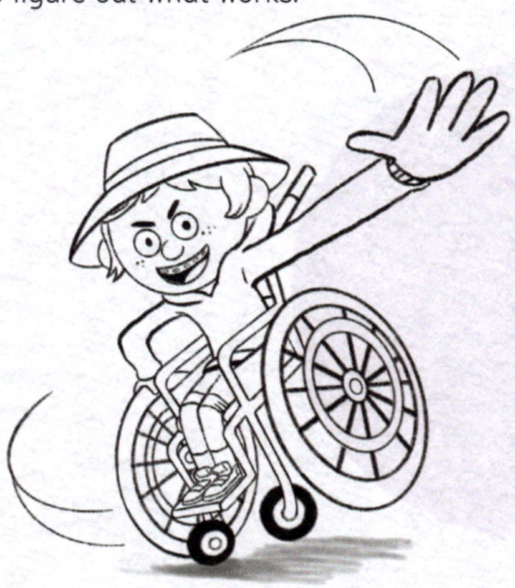

The tone of this story is energetic and very kinetic, which meant the characters needed to have tons of personality. Their shapes needed to be bold and their poses strong and easy to read. A useful trick to check this is to turn the pose into a silhouette after each one has been drawn. If the silhouette is strong and easily readable, you know the pose is good.

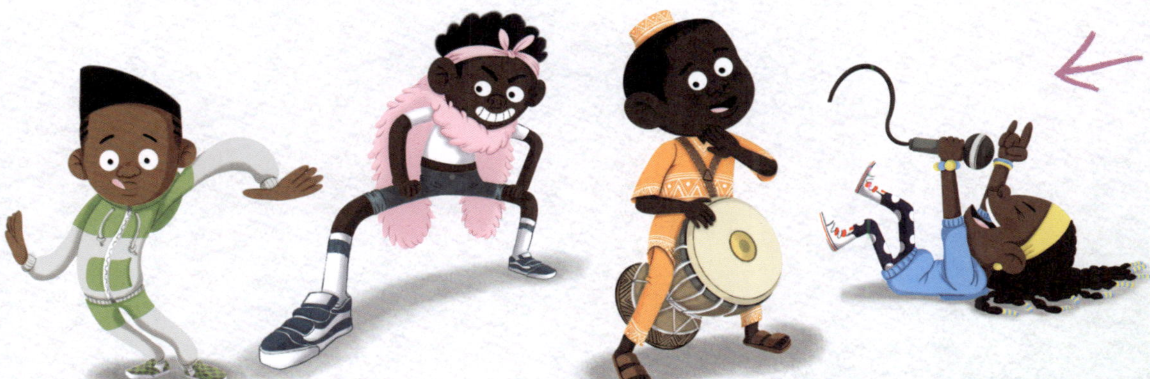

As a black man myself, my knowledge of the variety of complexions that exist within the black diaspora serves me well when accurately depicting black people in my work. My advice when depicting other ethnicities is to do your research to ensure you're doing so accurately, and to avoid straying into negative stereotypes or portrayals.

## BACKGROUNDS

I decided to use solid blocks of color as the backdrop for the characters instead of detailed environments. This would work well for the young age of the target audience, as well as the simple format of the text. I kept it relatively simple by choosing eight bold colors and creating a repeating sequence. When the illustrations are viewed side by side, each color works to enhance the one on the opposite page, as well as the individual characters.

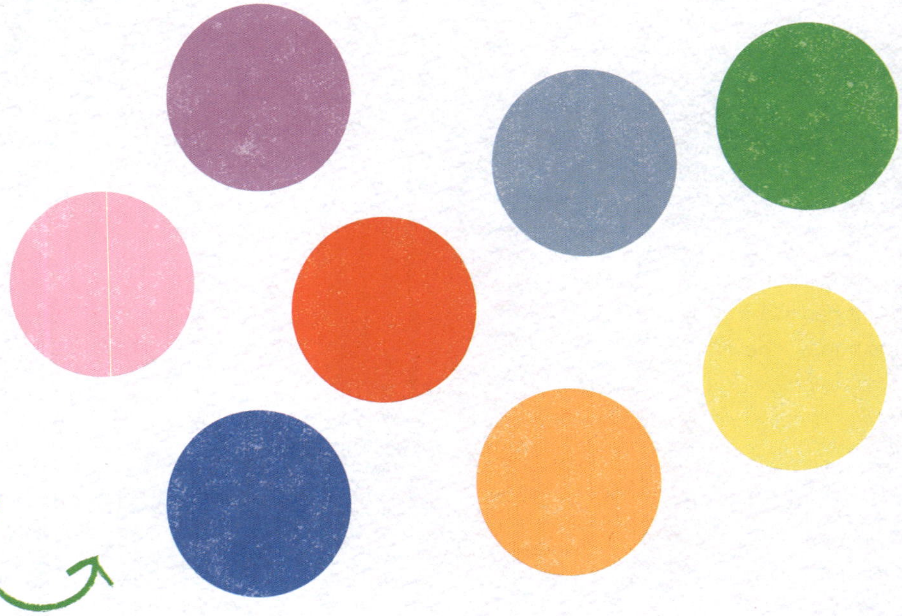

My idea to use solid block color backgrounds was inspired by a YouTube music series called *Colors* that features musicians performing against a backdrop of solid color. Draw inspiration from other disciplines when looking for ideas for your illustrations!

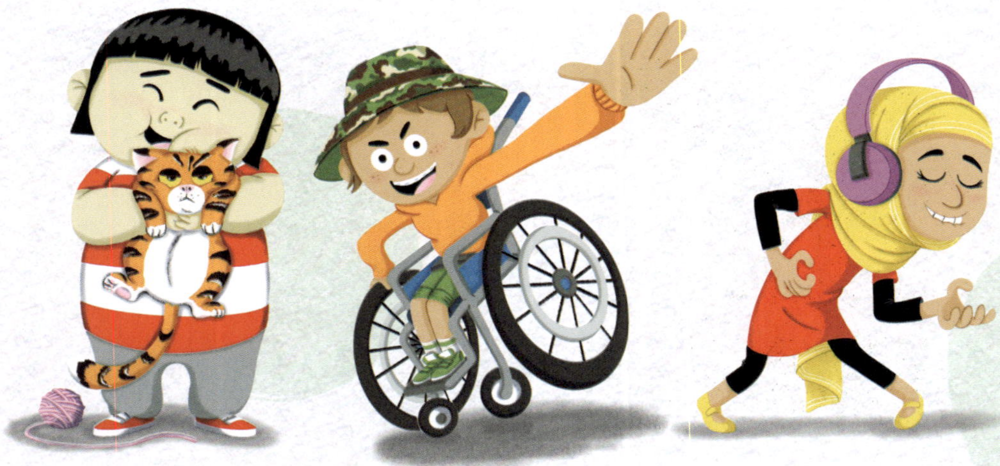

Gender-neutral color palette

I chose gender-neutral background colors, as well as choosing colors that would complement the skin tone of the character on the page. Take another look... you won't find many pages with boy characters on blue backgrounds or girl characters on pink backgrounds.

The color choices helped create the energetic tone I was aiming for. The joy of the text being so simple is that it leaves room to create a kind of narrative through the illustrations. I chose to depict play and joy throughout, which the vivid color choices helped to portray.

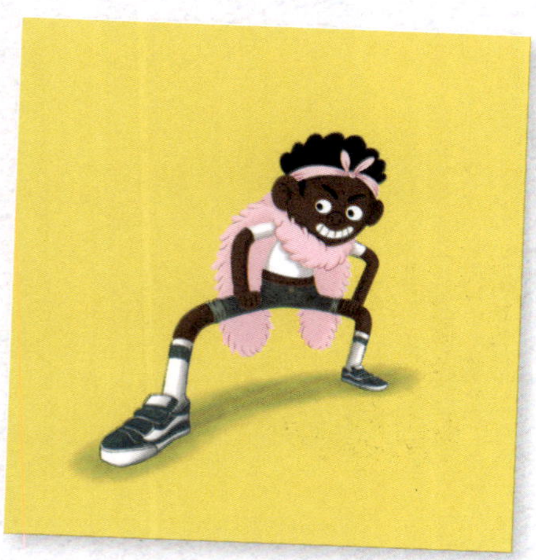

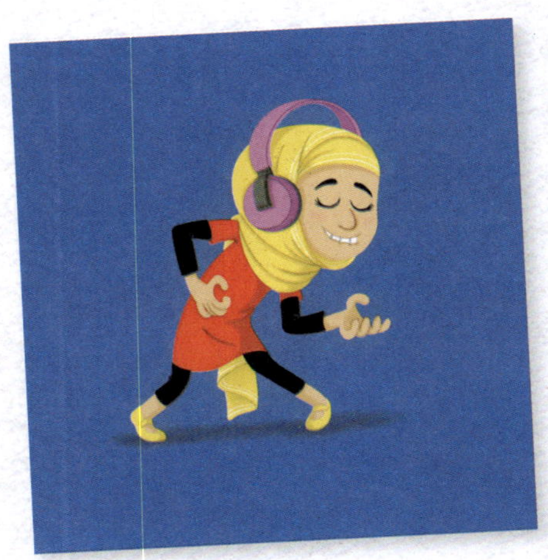

As well as using browns, oranges, reds, and other gender-neutral colors, I also played with using colors commonly associated with one gender for another.

## POSES AND GESTURE

Due to the simpler style of background, it was important the characters really jumped off the page. I made sure of this by giving each character a clear line of action. First I sketched the pose until I was happy with how well it communicated the action, and once I was happy, I developed the draft further.

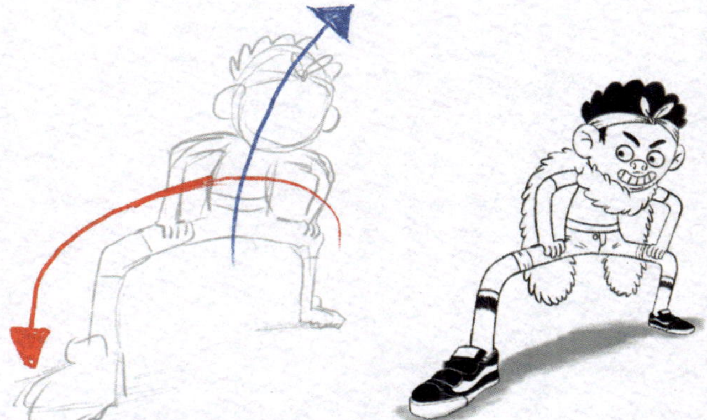

LINE OF ACTION

I've drawn in the line of action here to show the direction of the flow of movement in this pose. This is a great way to make sure the audience's focus goes where you want it to.

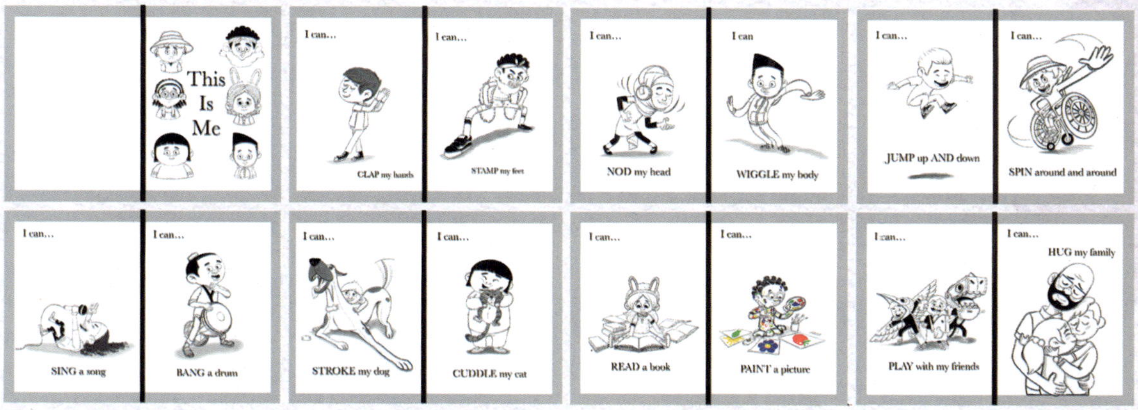


I applied the line of action process to each character in turn. Before starting the coloring stage, I put together a quick flat-plan of the book with the story text to make sure everything sat as I needed it to. Every picture book should have a rhythm and a clear flow from one page to the next. Putting all your draft pages together like this is a great way to check this.

As I use flat color in all my work, it's important that the linework is strong and solid. It's also crucial the poses have enough space in them for the colors to breathe so the image doesn't feel too stiff or lifeless.

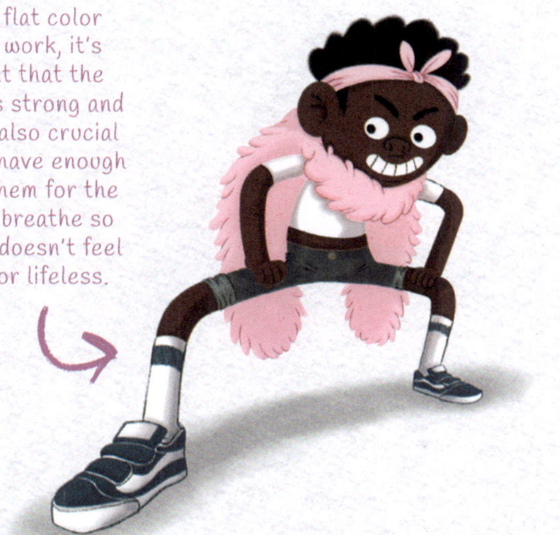

Your character poses should aim to capture the right tone for the story. The tone of *This Is Me* is playfulness and joy, and as such each character is shown enjoying their activity. An easy way to show this is through their facial expressions. Strong gestures combined with believable facial expressions will go a long way toward helping the audience to connect with your characters.

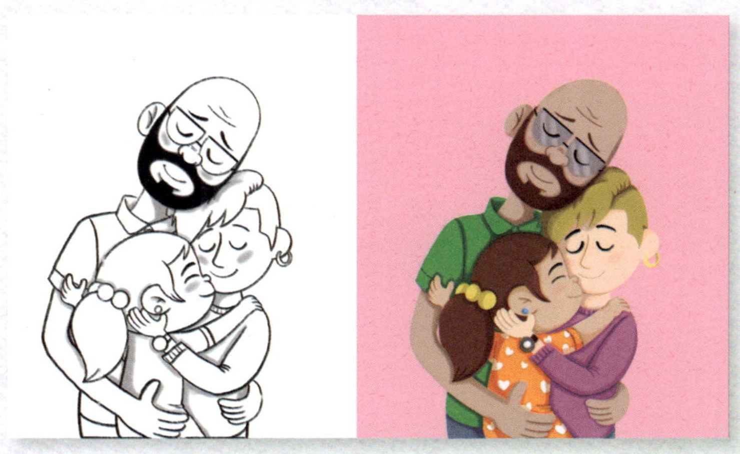

Here you see the transition from rough to color. The energy of an image can get lost from draft to color stage if the decisions made during the draft stage aren't solid and well thought through. The full-color pose in the final illustration conveys the warmth and love of a family hug.

# ANALYSIS

All my design choices were successful and had the intended impact. From color to character to page layout, everything clicked into place and had the desired effect. My first interpretation of the story remained intact throughout, which was helped by the simple and fun nature of the story text.

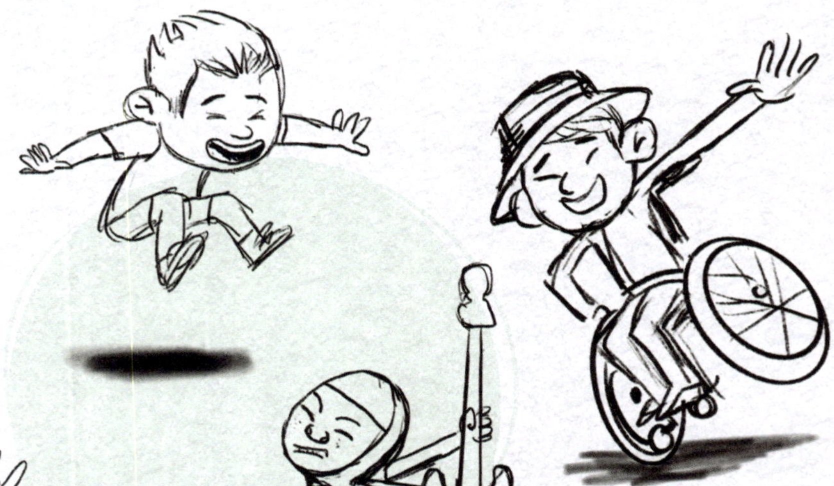

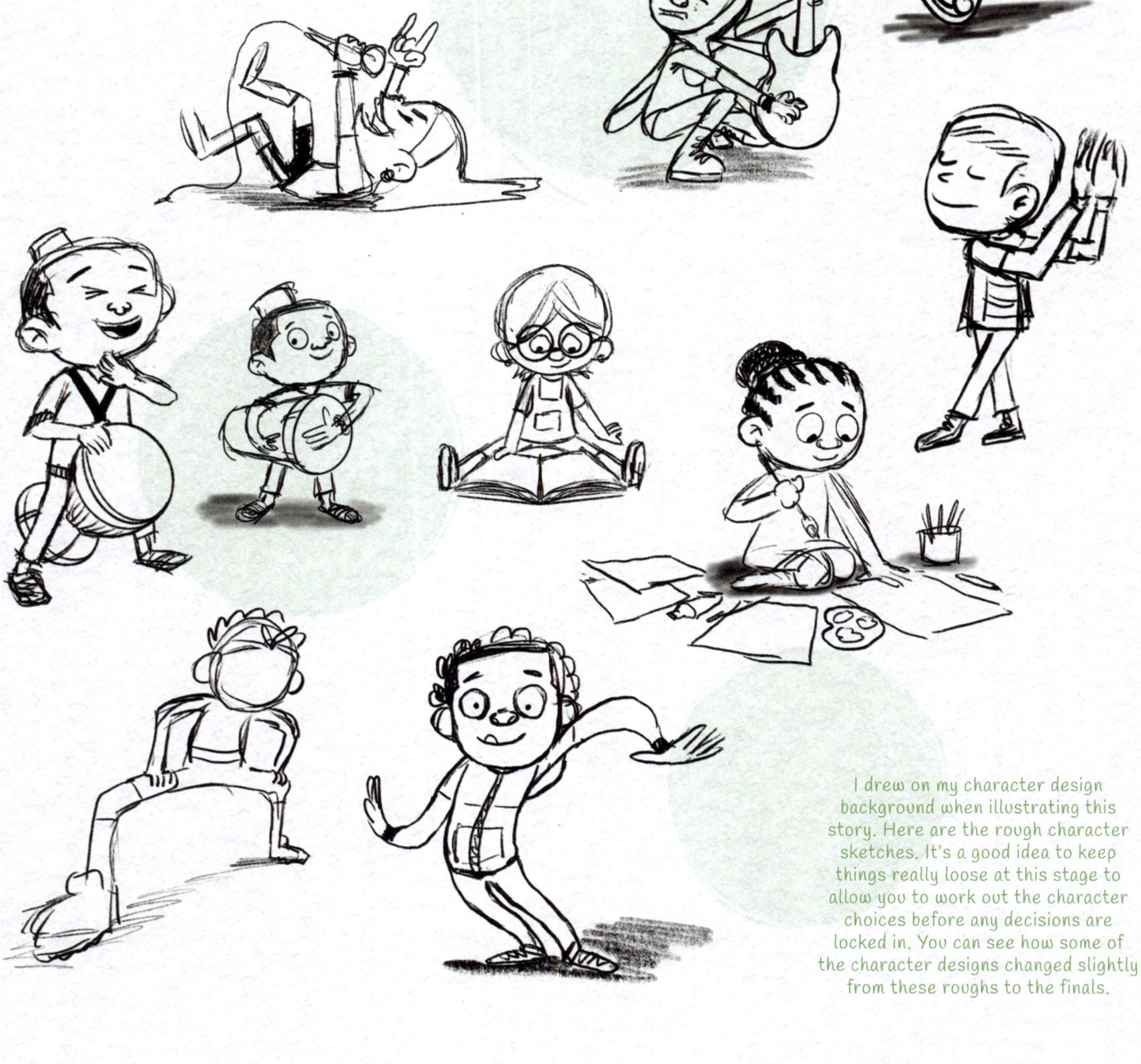

I drew on my character design background when illustrating this story. Here are the rough character sketches. It's a good idea to keep things really loose at this stage to allow you to work out the character choices before any decisions are locked in. You can see how some of the character designs changed slightly from these roughs to the finals.

The biggest challenge was taking into account the various design considerations necessary for illustrating for a preschool audience and thinking about what would engage such young readers. The easiest part was the character design, as this is my background.

My advice to any artist looking to get into children's book illustration would be to play to your strengths. While it's fun to try new things, if you're up against a tight deadline, see if you can tailor the brief to allow you to work to your illustration strengths. However, it's also good to be versatile and to learn new skills – it's always beneficial to push yourself to grow as an artist.

This is the stage where my design decisions were locked in as I cleaned up the roughs. I think through designs carefully to ensure I don't have to spend time making corrections when coloring and finalizing the illustrations.

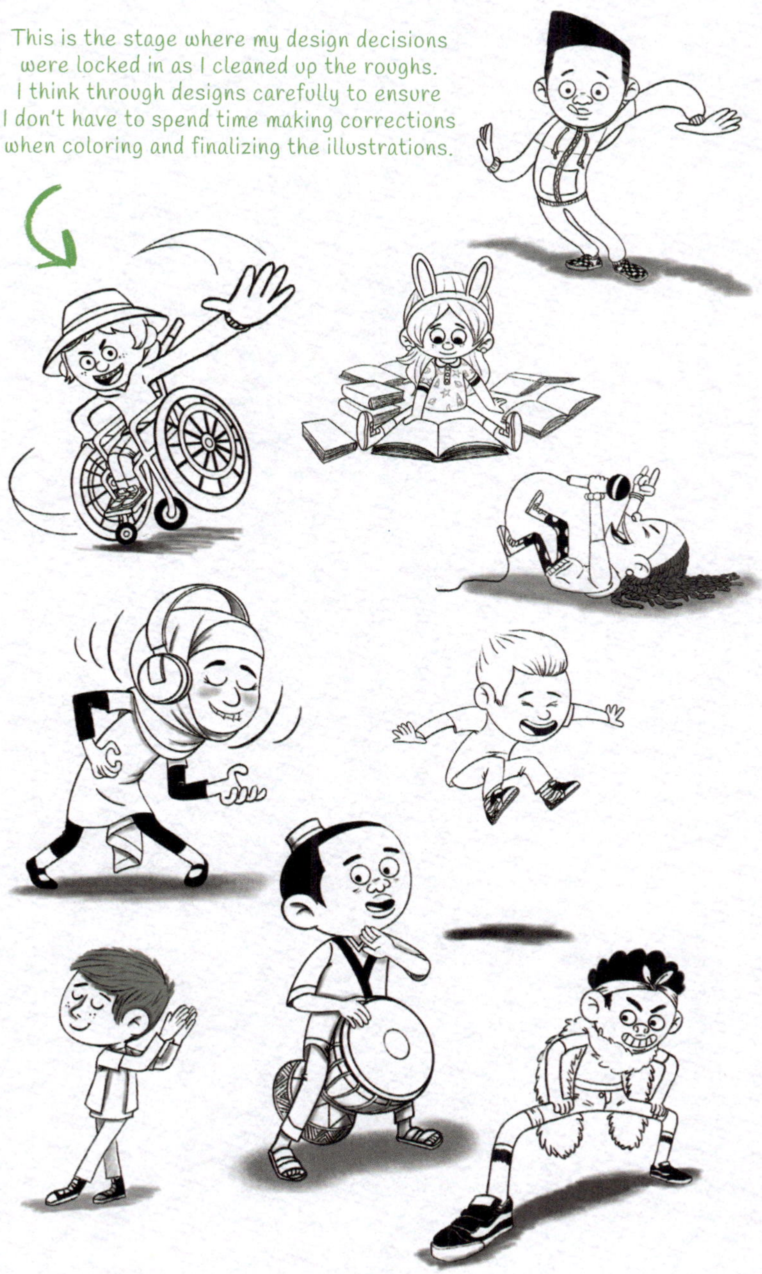

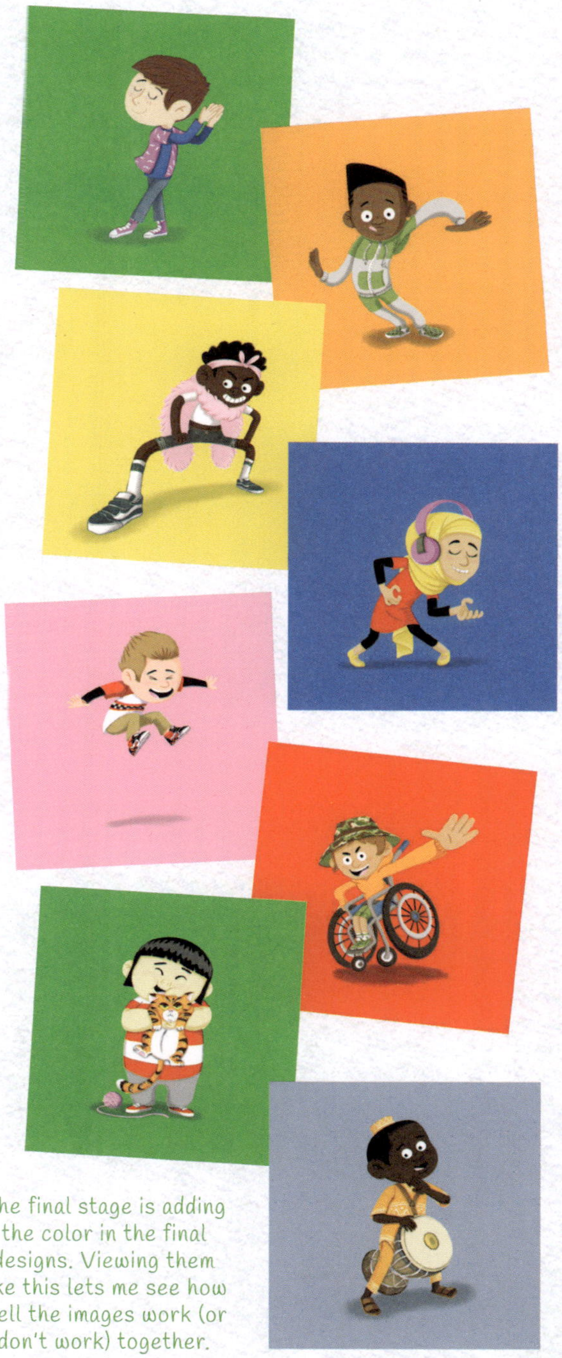

The final stage is adding the color in the final designs. Viewing them like this lets me see how well the images work (or don't work) together.

Another key piece of advice would be to read, read, and read again! There's so much to be learned from reading and being aware of the wide variety of children's books that have been and are currently being published. Plus, it's hard to create children's book illustrations when you don't understand the mechanics of how children's books work. You need to know the rules before you can bend or break them!

# CAPTAIN CAT and the PIRATE PUPPIES

Written by

GREG DOBBINS

Illustrated by

SAOIRSE LOU



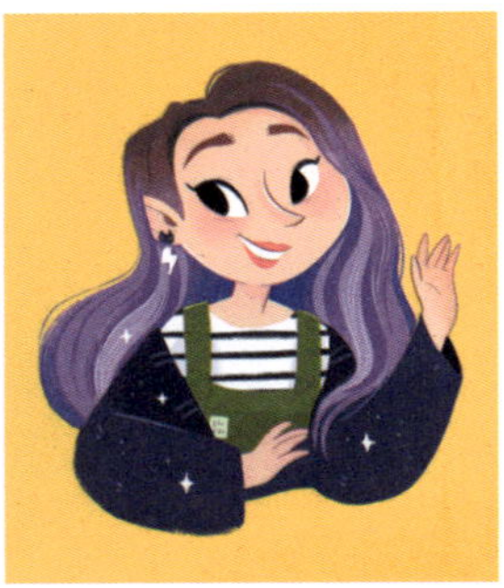

Illustrator

**saoirselou.com**

Saoirse is a children's illustrator based in Poole, UK. She loves making quirky, colorful artwork for children's books and has a keen interest in nature and mythology, which appear frequently in her illustrations.

A STORY FOR AGES 2–4 YEARS

# CAPTAIN CAT and the PIRATE PUPPIES

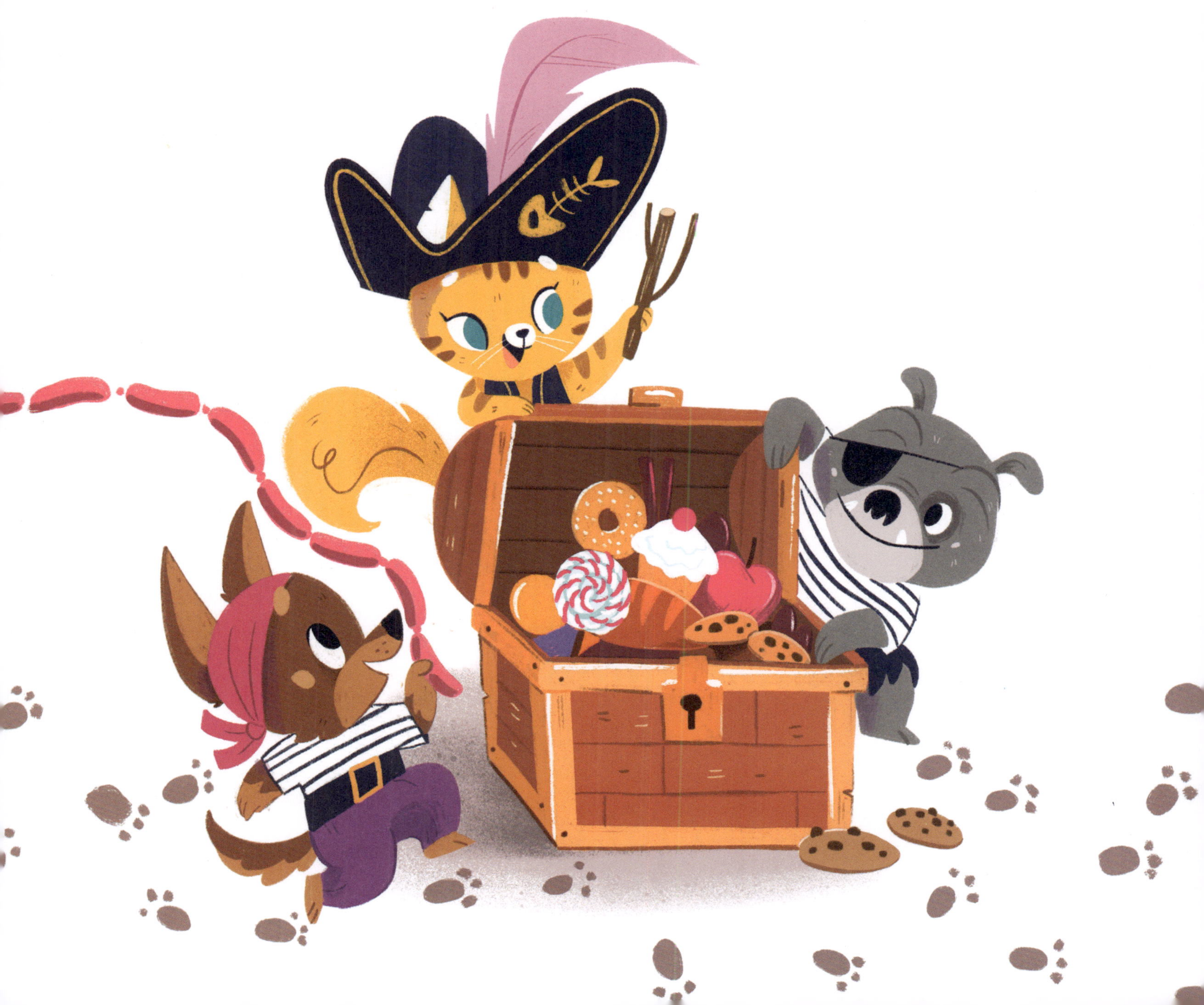

Pirate puppies, One, Two, Three!
On the good ship Golden Hound,
heading out to sea!

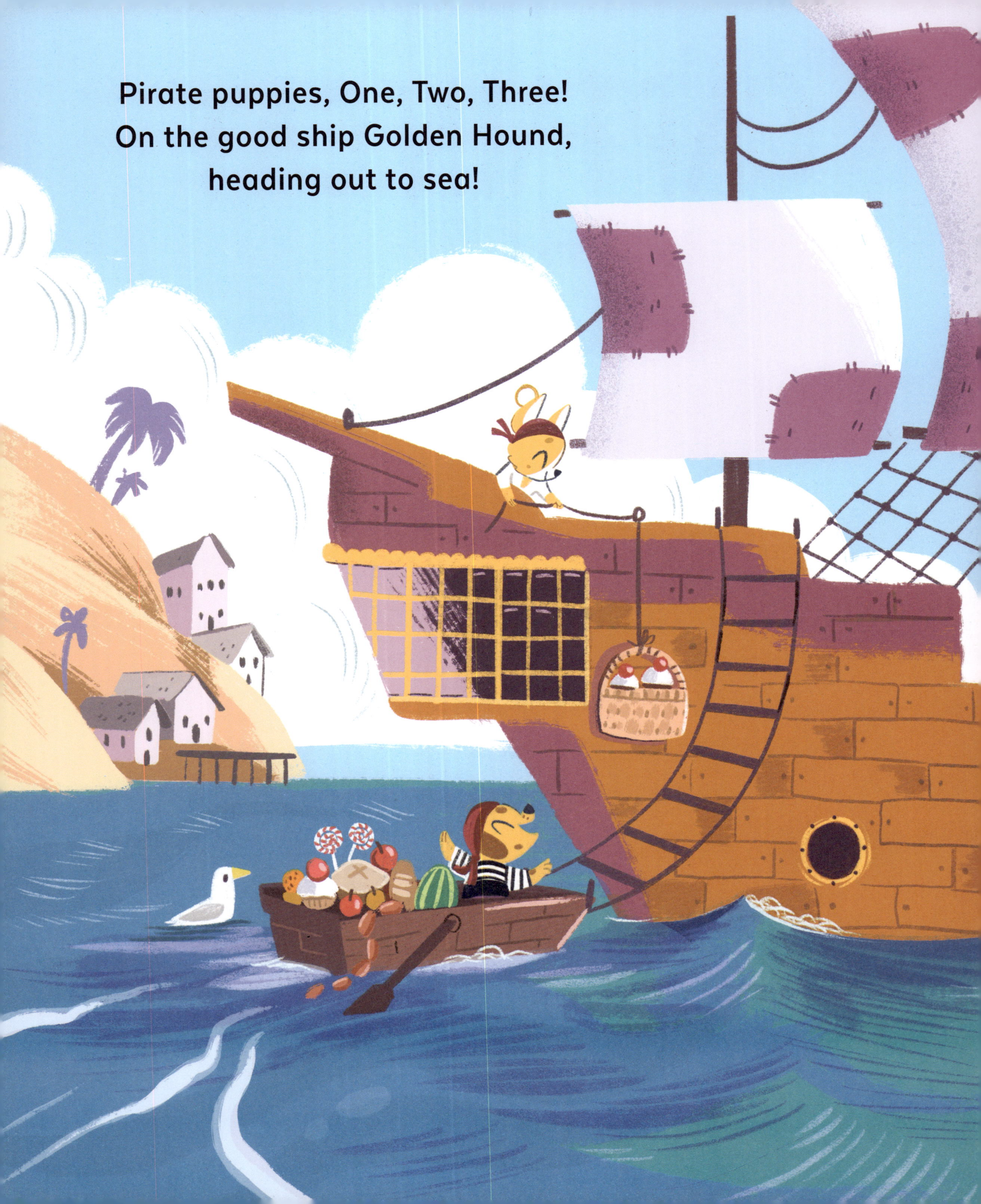

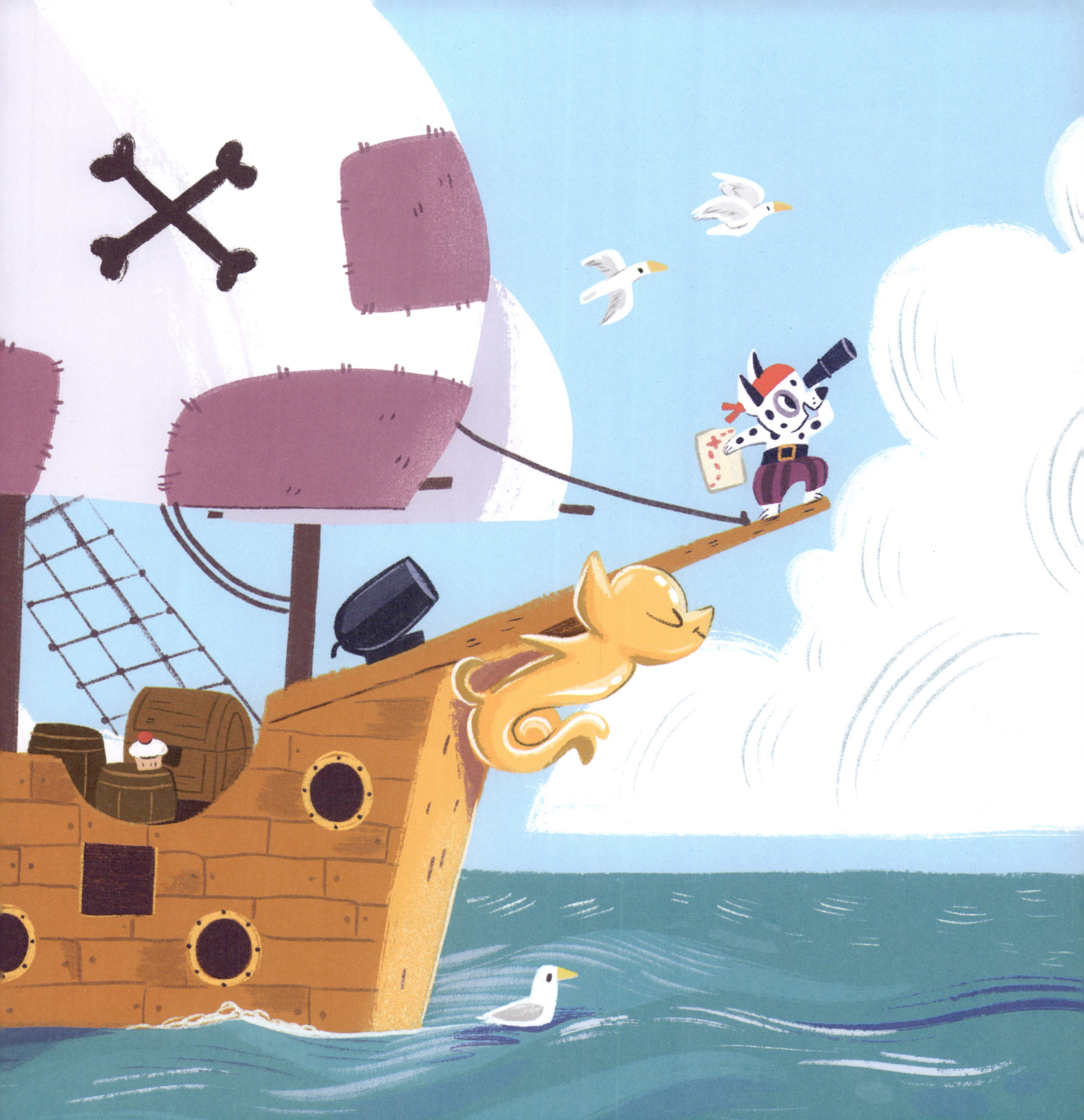

Looking for **adventure**, playing in the sun.
A hold full of tasty treats,
they're having lots of fun.

Pirate puppies, **Four, Five, Six!**

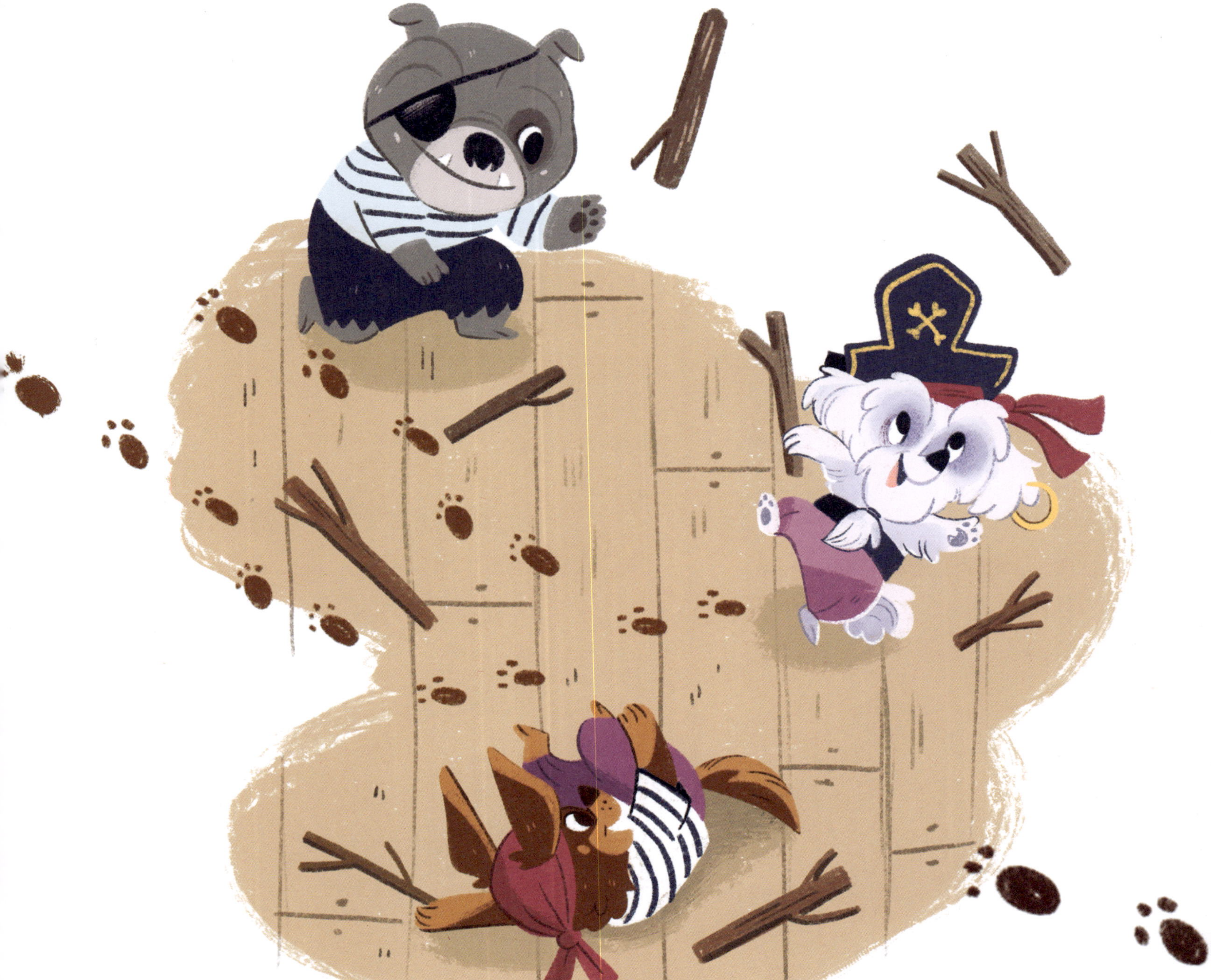

Should be on the lookout, but they're
chasing after sticks.

Running around the deck,
hiding behind the sails.
Woofing and yapping happily
as they wag their little tails.

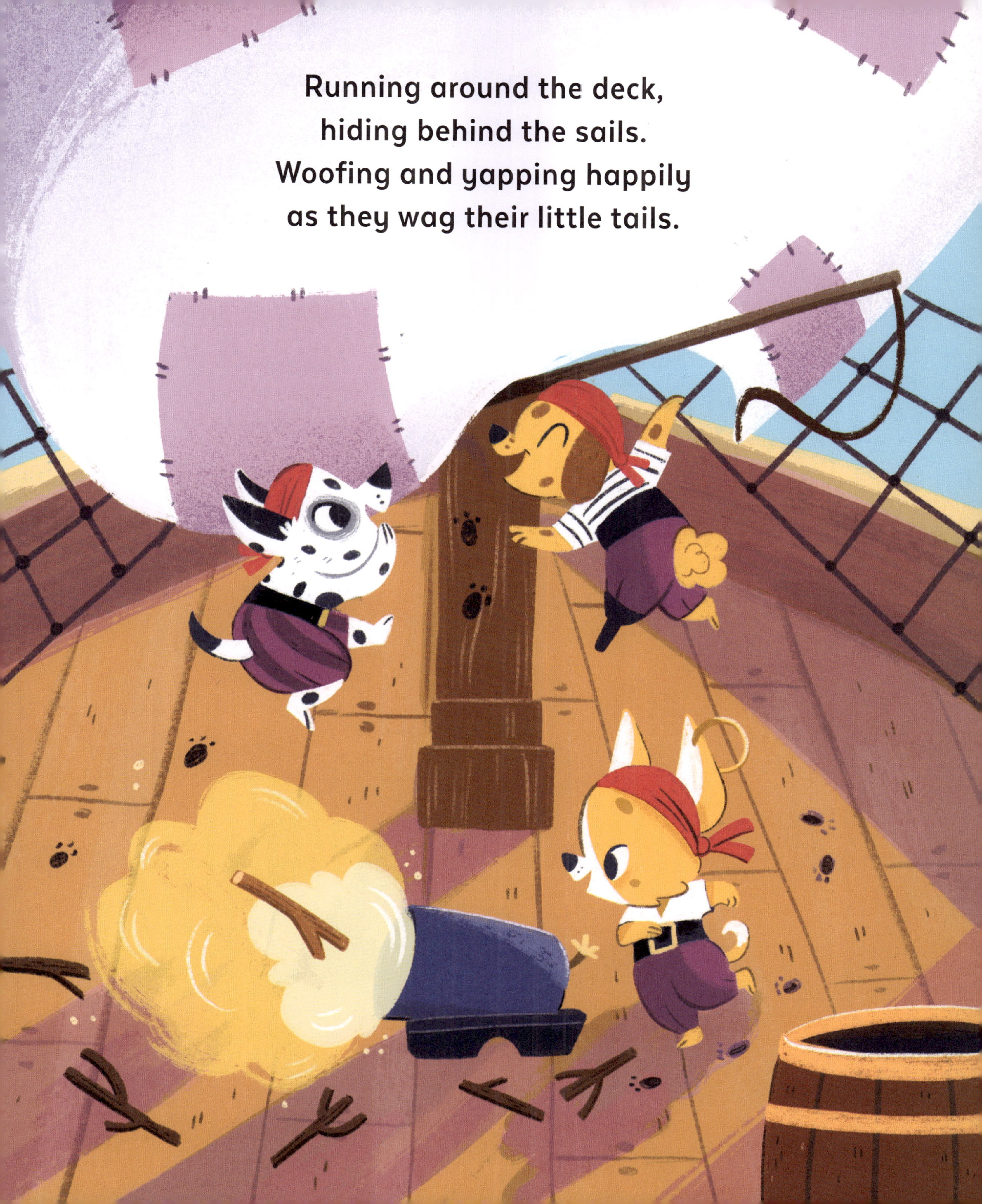

Pirate puppies,

**Seven, Eight, Nine!**

All tired out, it must be
sleepy time.

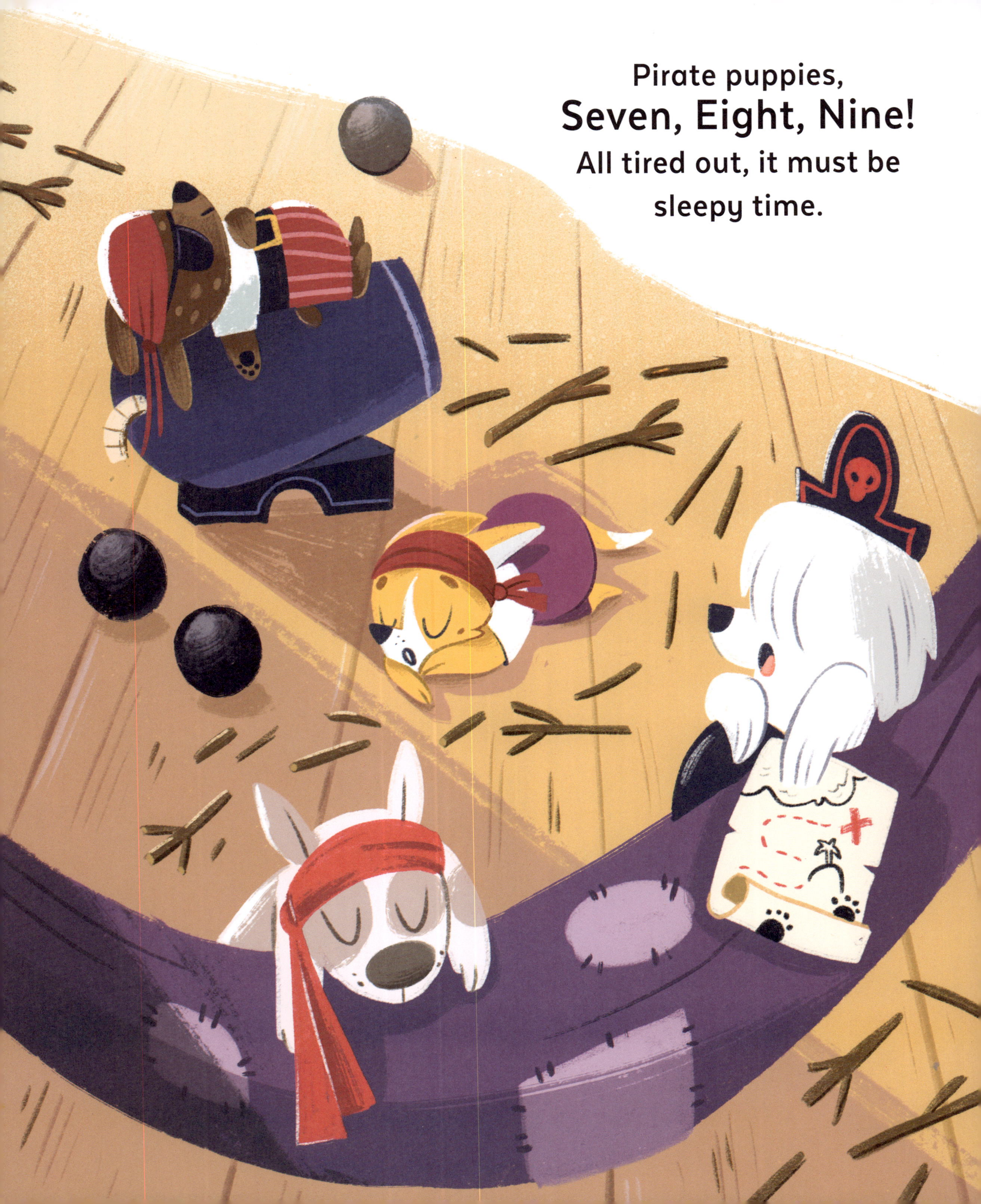

**Snoozing** in their hammocks,
**lazing** in the rigging.
Dreaming of a beach where they can
all do some digging.

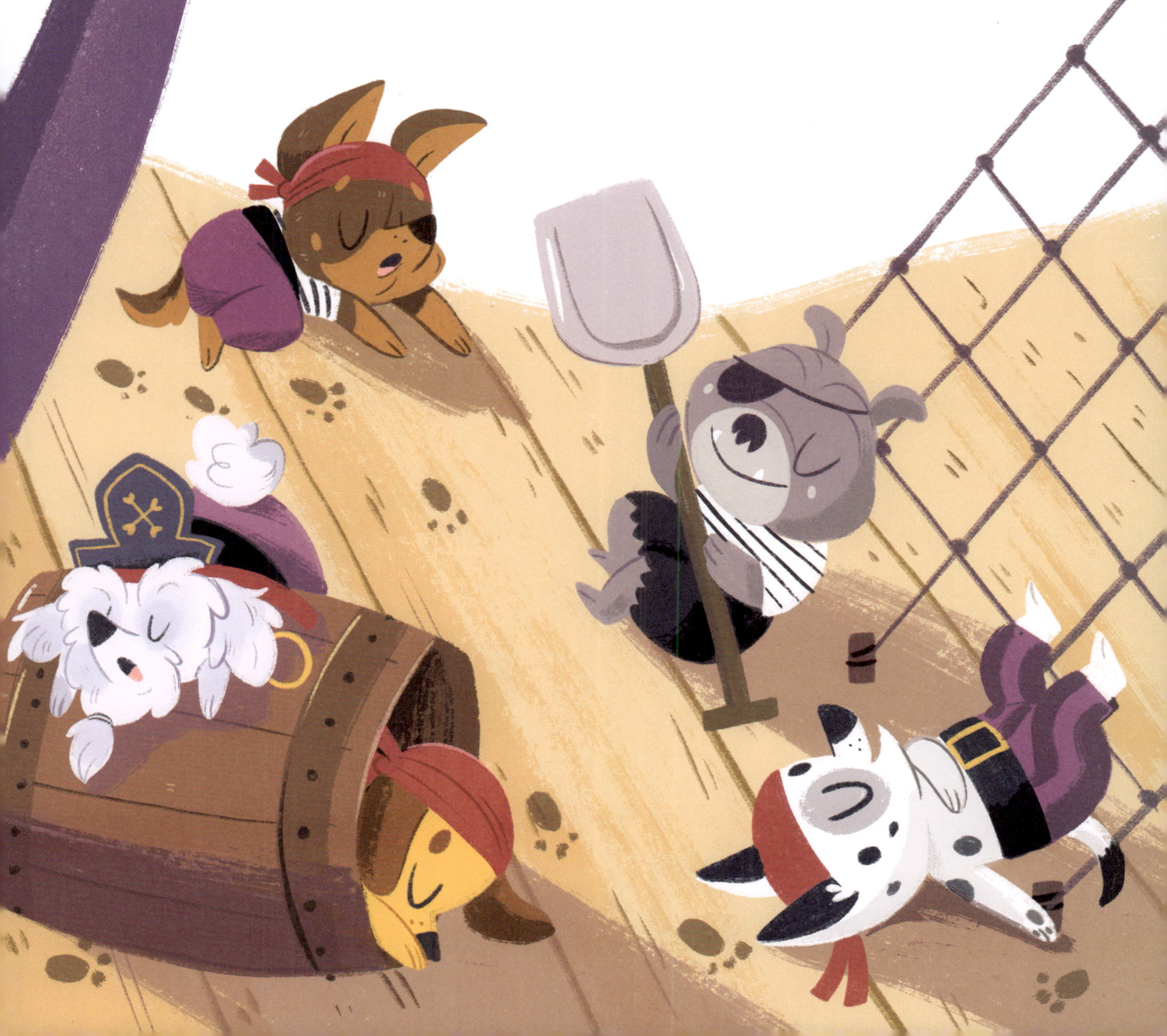

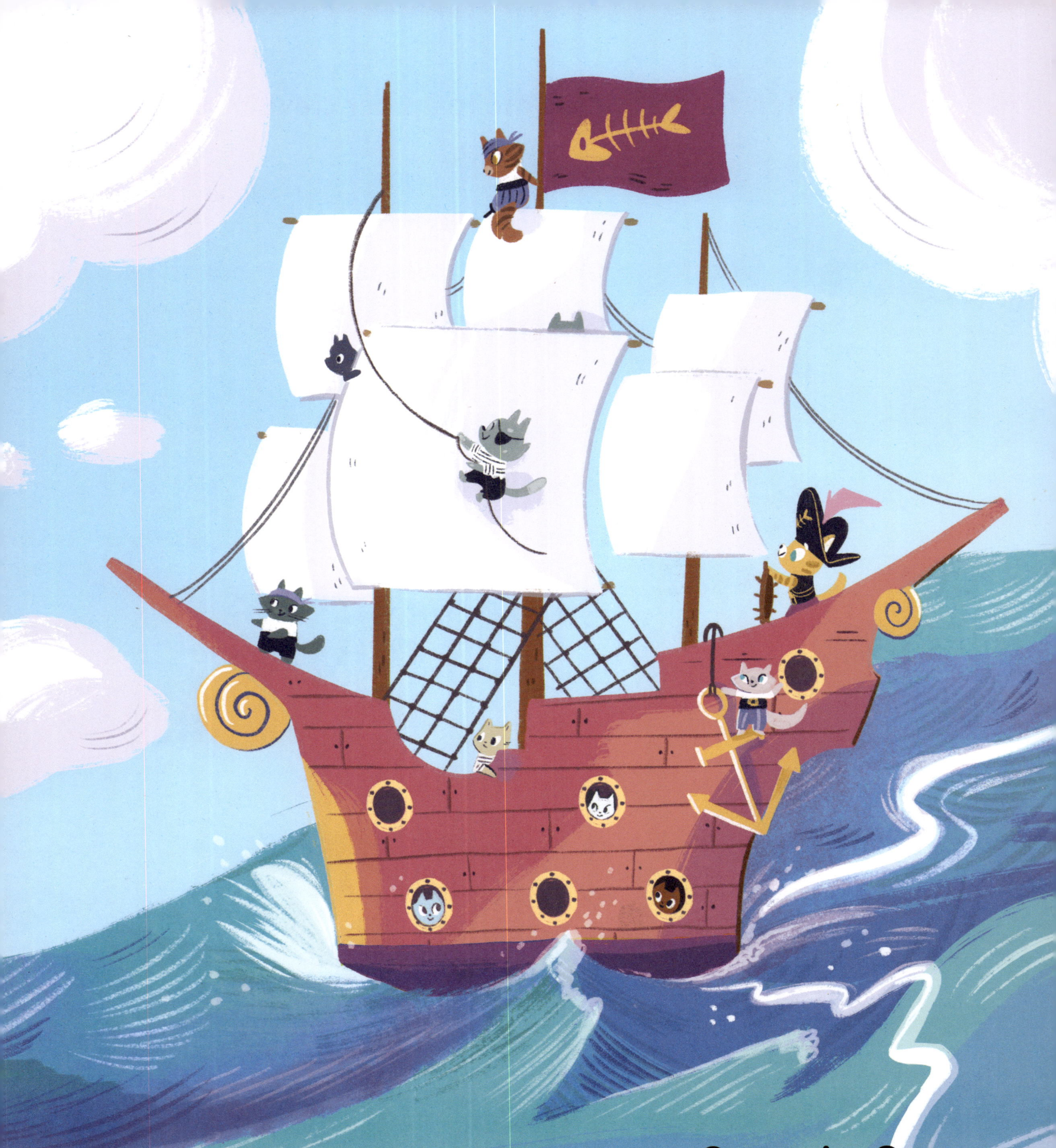

Sailing on the Kitty Sark, here comes **Captain Cat**,
standing at the wheel in her special captain's hat.

Ten fluffy kittens make up her crew,

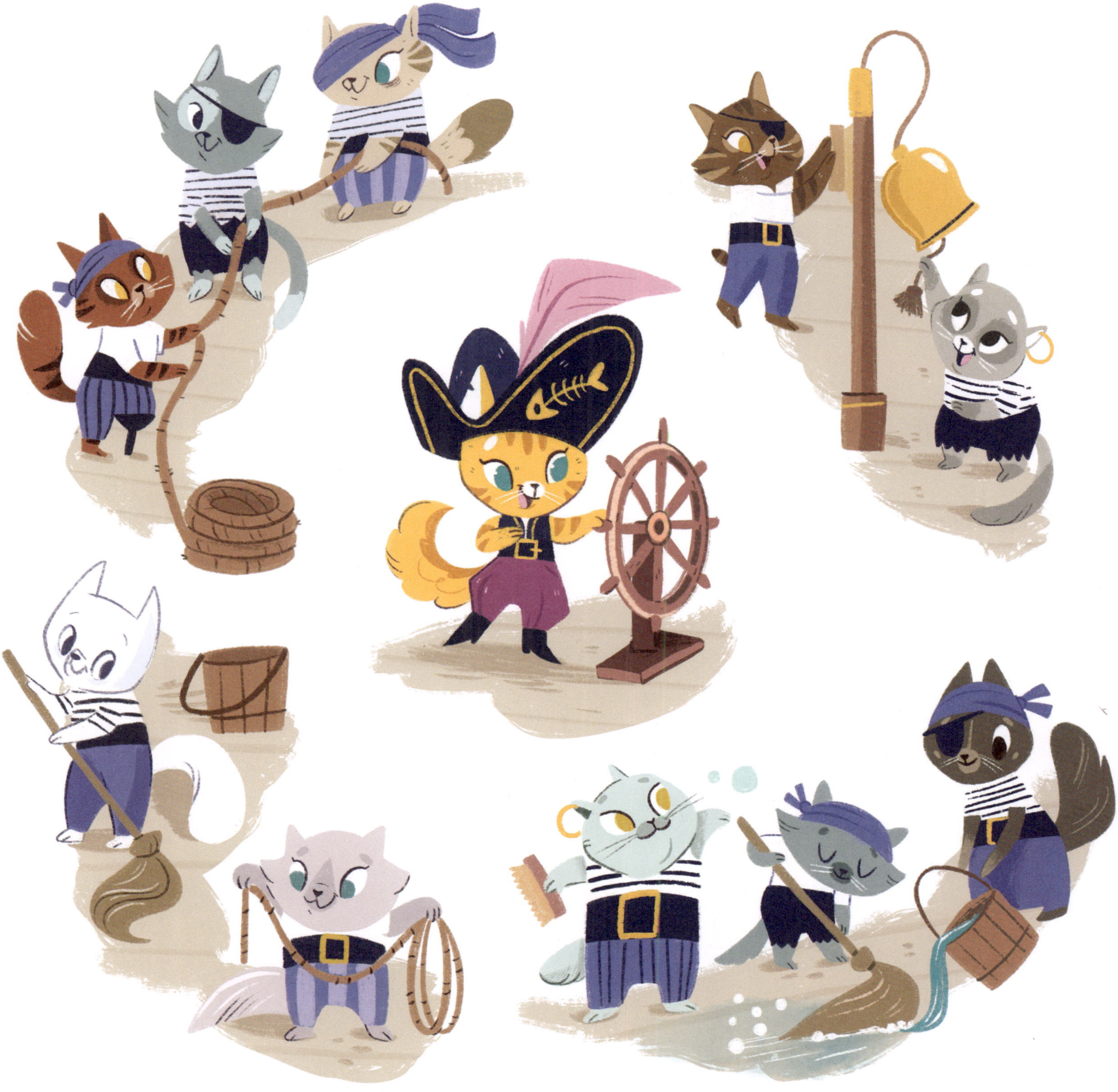

all **working hard** as they sail the ocean blue.

Pirate puppies, still dreaming away.
They're heading for some **rocks**,
can the kittens save the day?

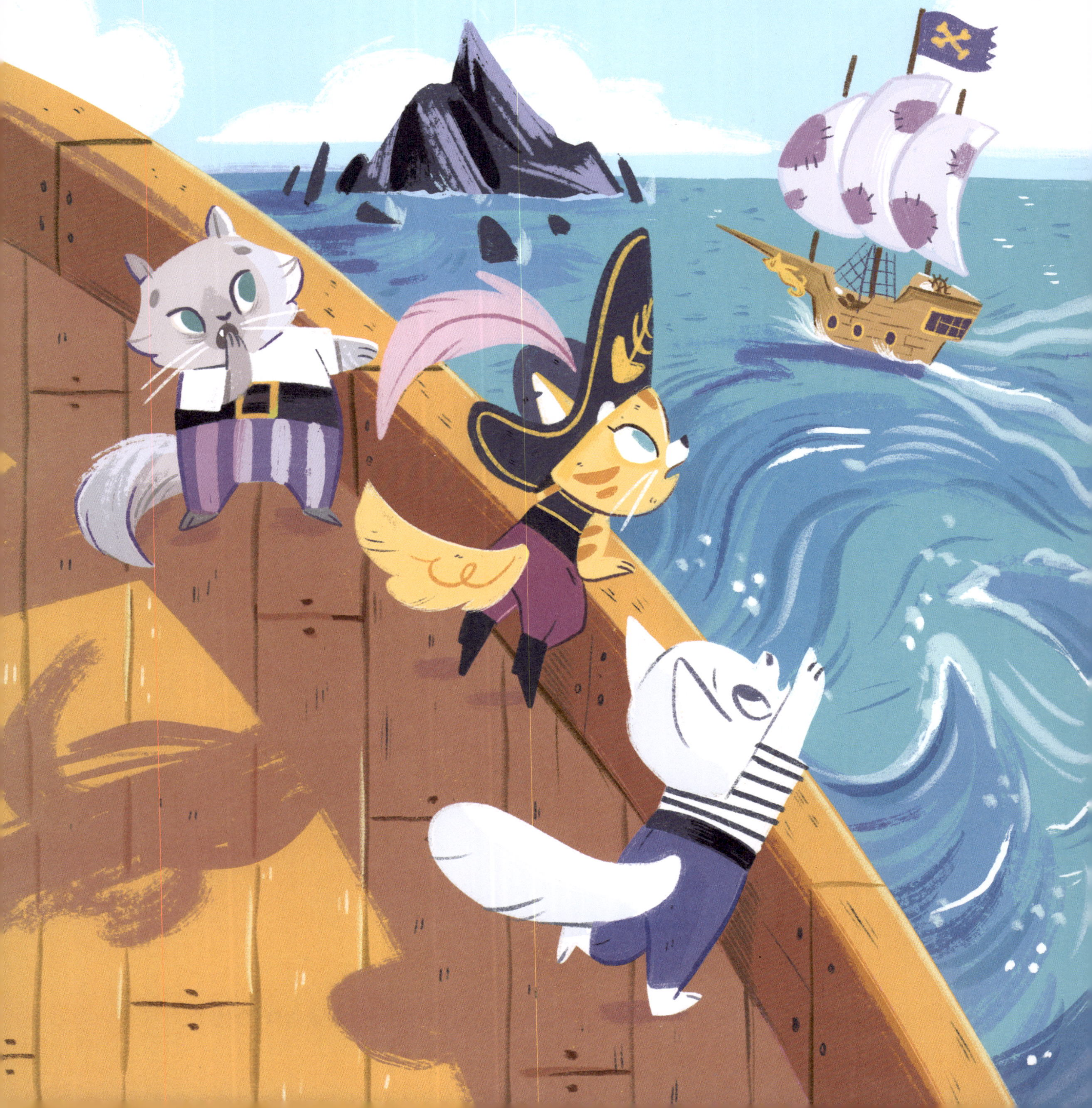

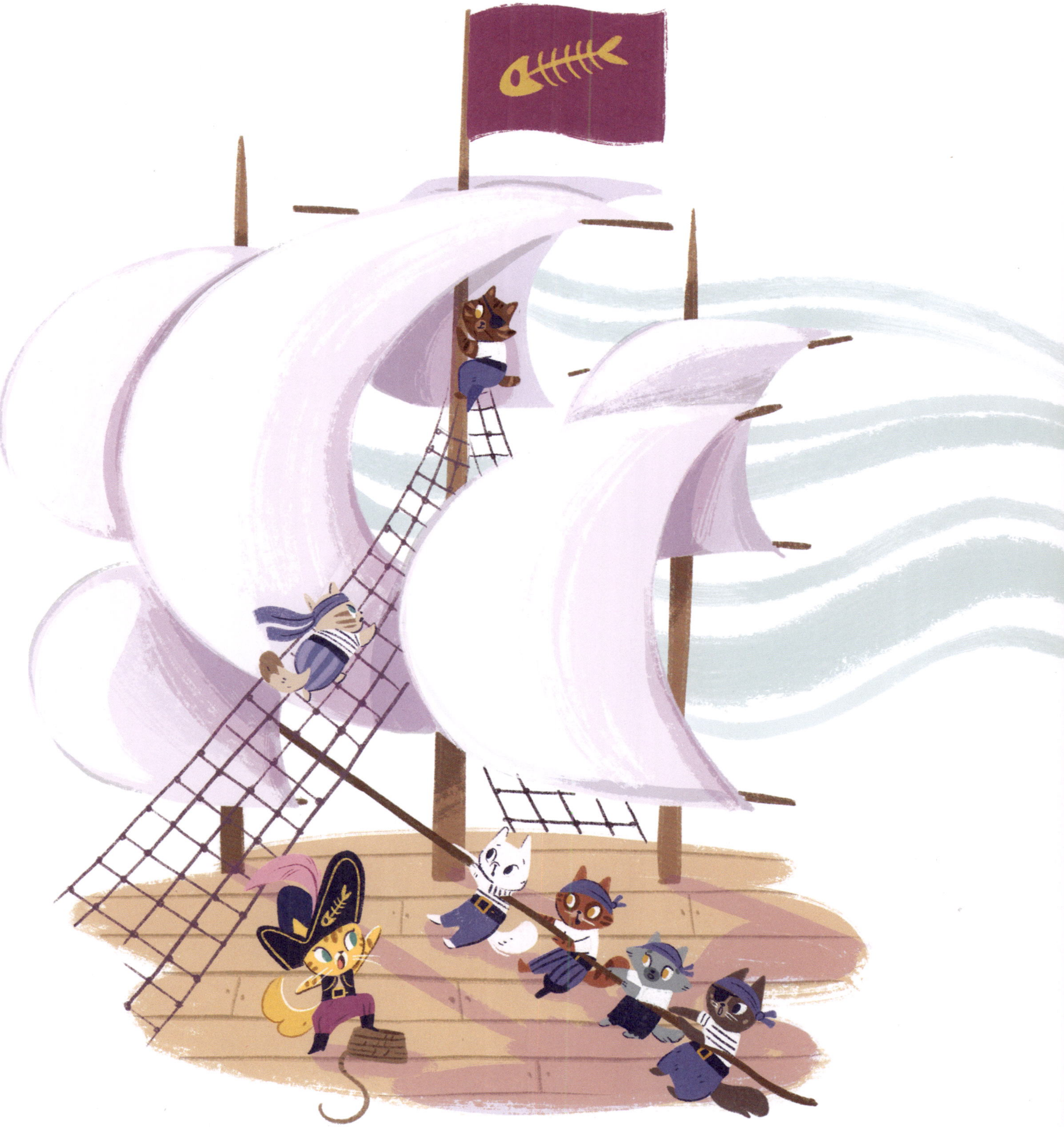

Hauling on the ropes and climbing up the mast.
The sails catch the wind, and they're going really fast.

Captain Cat turns the wheel, and then gives a **shout**.
At last the puppies wake up, and they all run about.

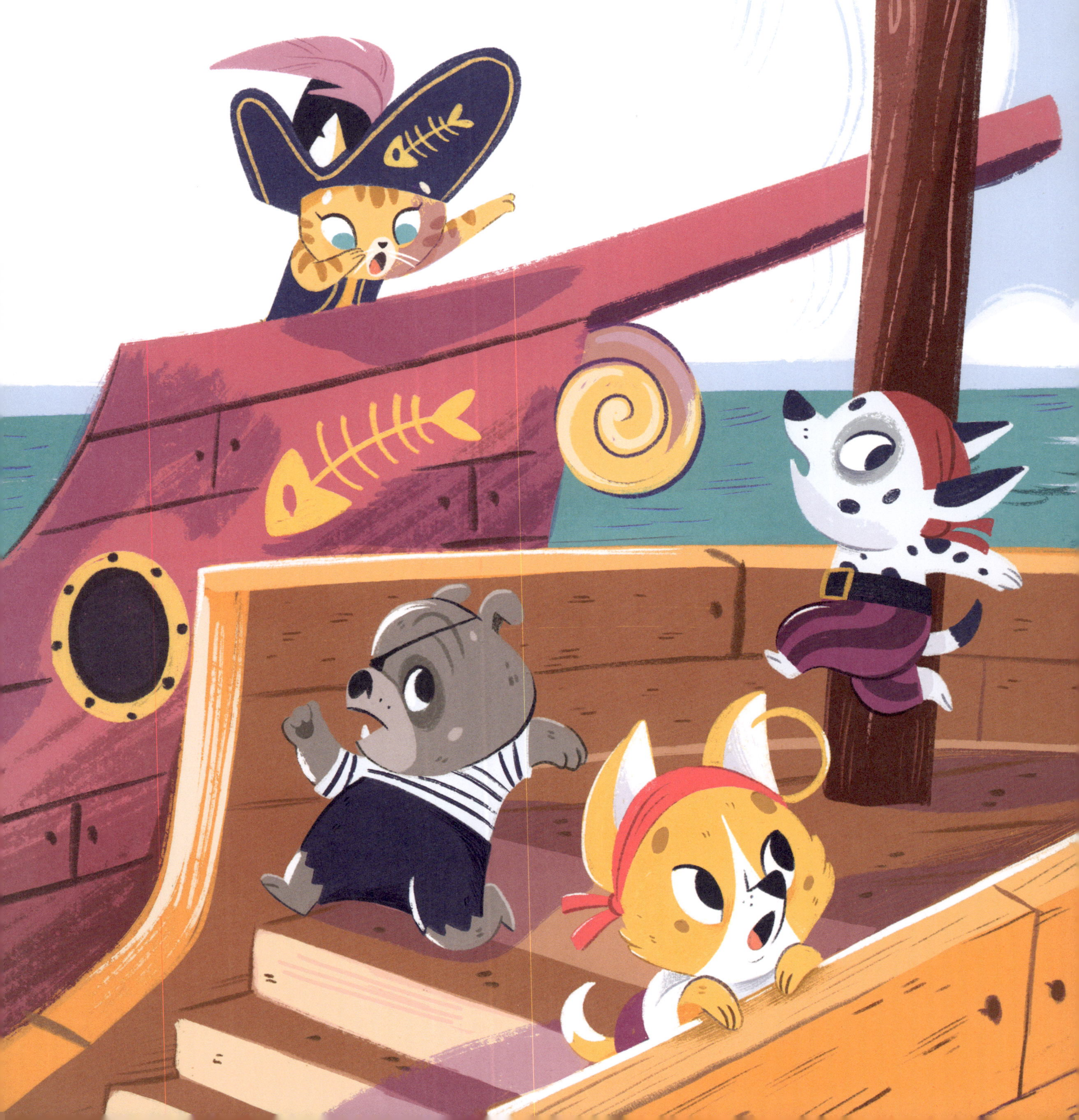

"Turn the wheel, hard to port!
Look sharp, on the double!
If we crash into those rocks,
we really are in trouble!"

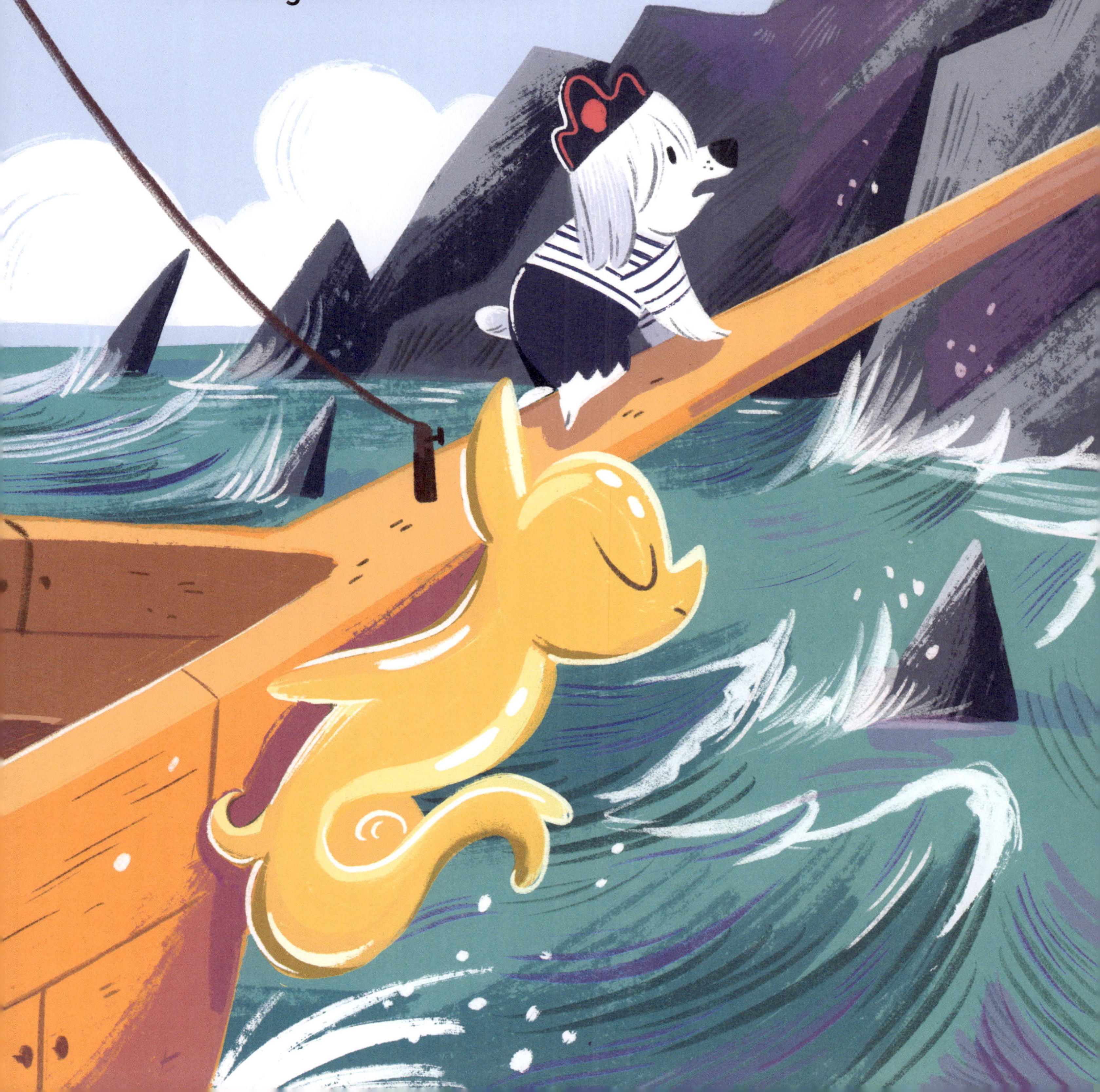

Pirate puppies close their eyes
and all hold on tight.
Here come the rocks...

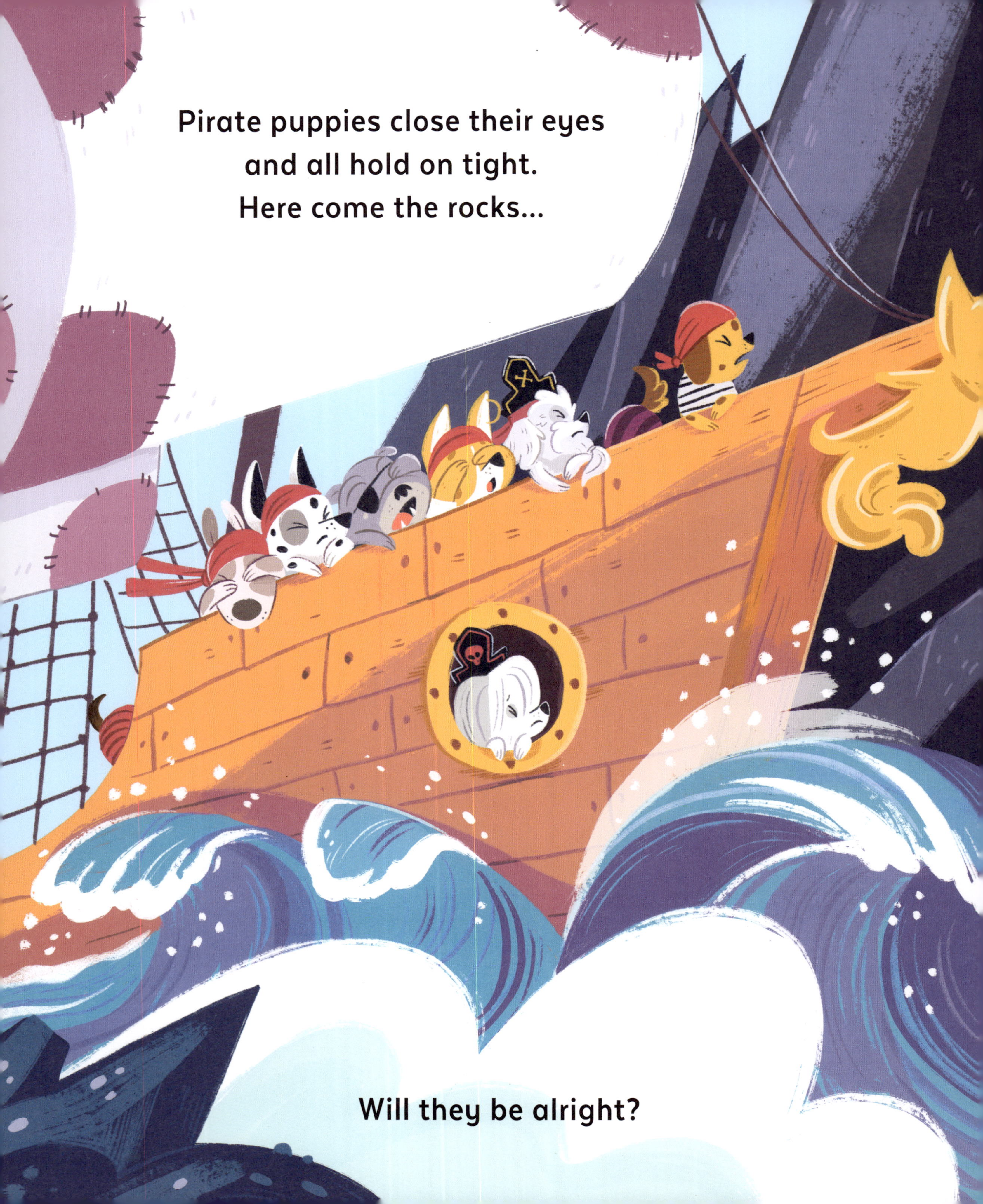

Will they be alright?

They miss them by a whisker, sailing safely by.

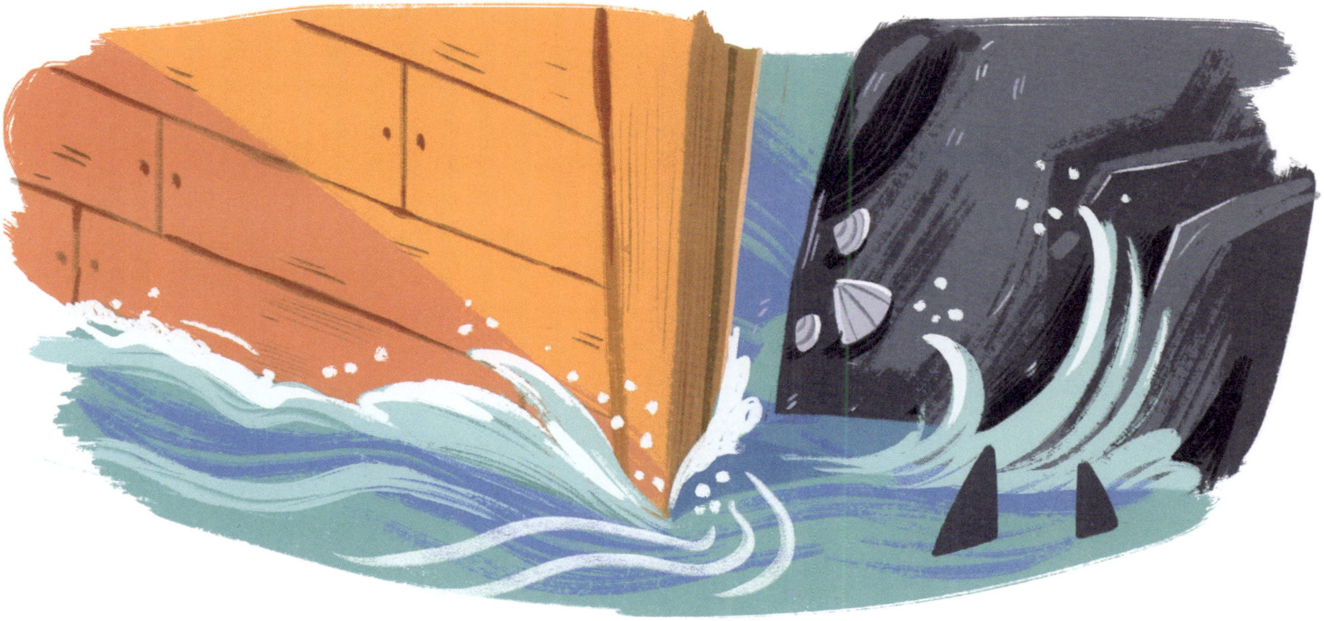

"Thank you, Captain Cat!" the pirate puppies cry.

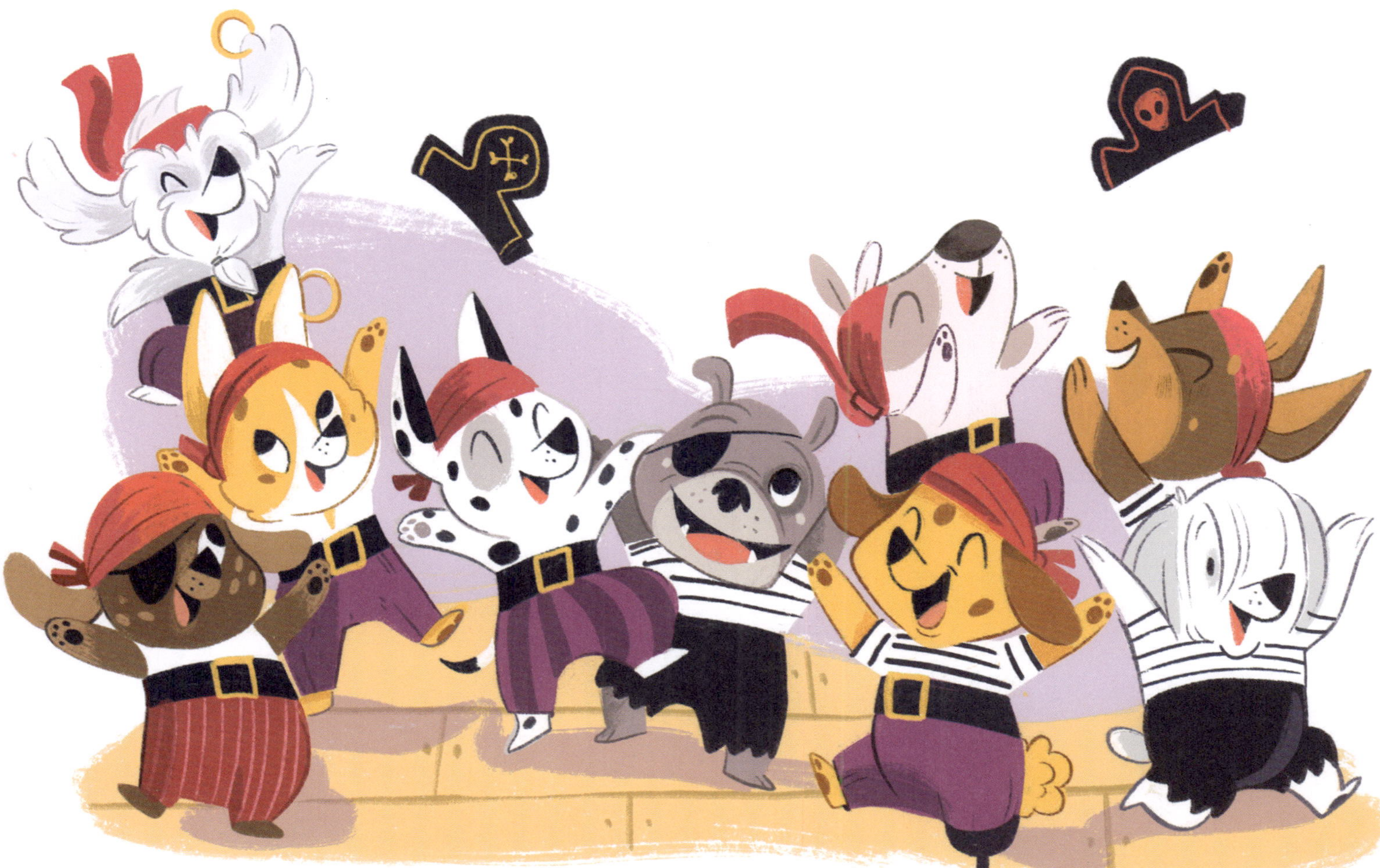

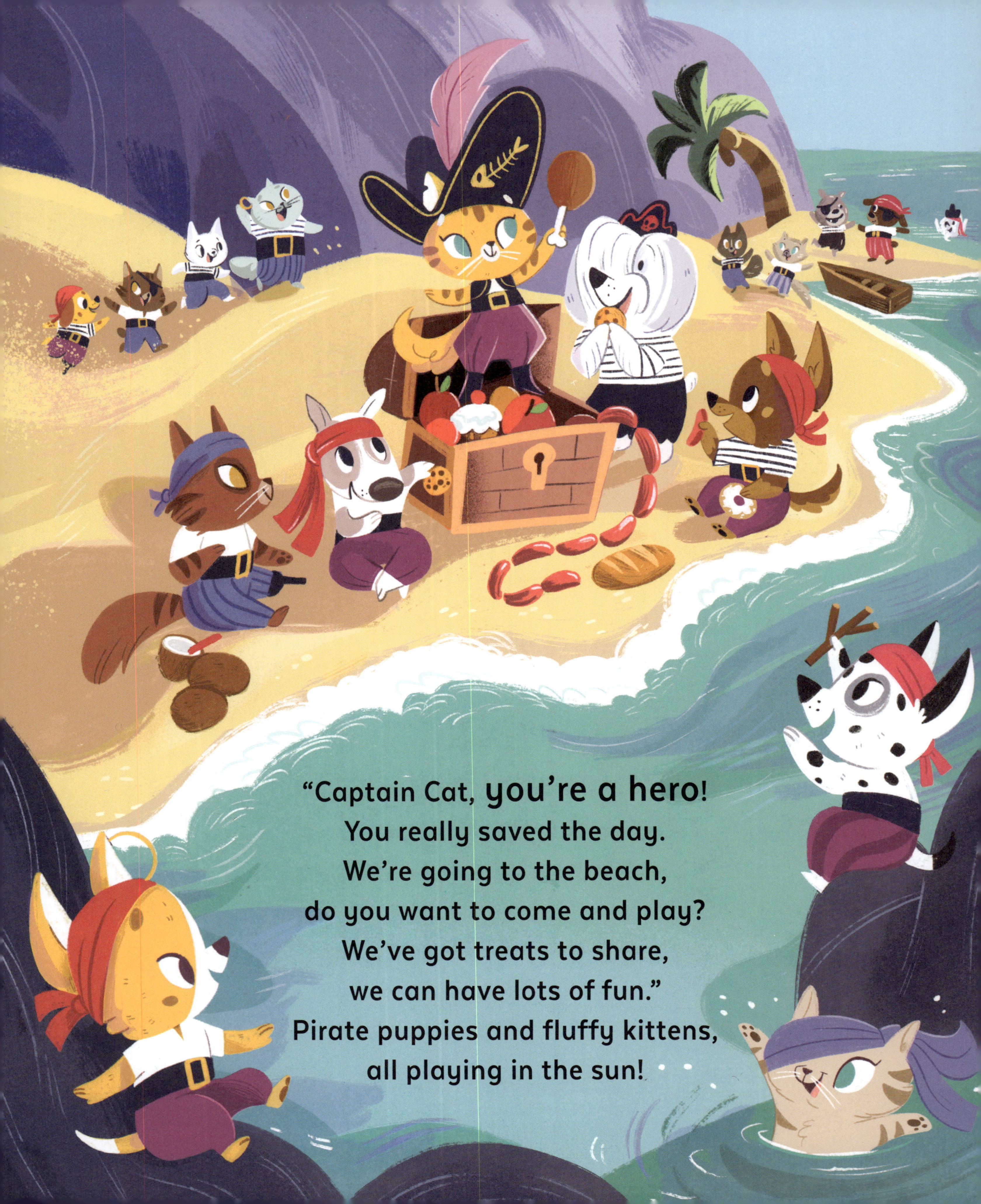

"Captain Cat, **you're a hero**!
You really saved the day.
We're going to the beach,
do you want to come and play?
We've got treats to share,
we can have lots of fun."
Pirate puppies and fluffy kittens,
all playing in the sun!

TURN THE PAGE FOR
INSIGHTS FROM THE ARTIST

# CAPTAIN CAT

## and the PIRATE PUPPIES

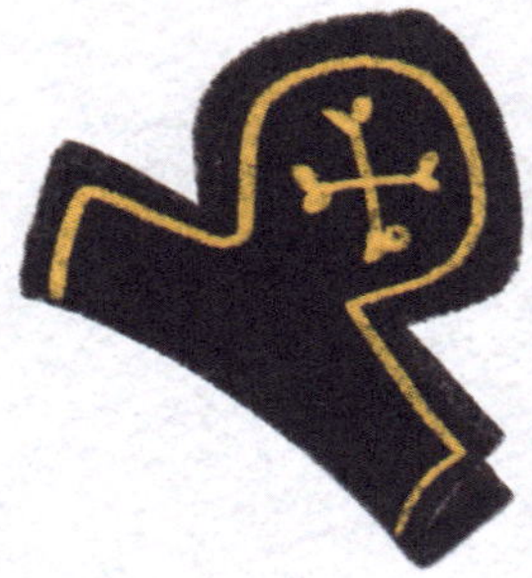

# DEVELOPING KEY FEATURES

## CHARACTER

When designing a character for a children's book, it's important to consider the target audience. For a book aimed at children aged 2–4 years, the character's proportions should reflect that of the children reading the book to help them relate to the story. Preschool children are likely to have the story read to them by an adult, so the characters should be bright, engaging to look at, and distinguishable from their environment. I kept this in mind when designing Captain Cat, giving her a larger head in proportion to her body, soft rounded features, and a mouth designed to easily convey emotion. I also used bright, cheerful colors and recognizable pirate clothing that is simple but bold. This story has a cheerful, adventurous tone, with a hint of mild peril, so the characters and setting can be kept bright and bold to capture the reader's attention.

The proportions of your characters should reflect that of the intended reader – in this case, children aged 2–4 years. As these characters are kittens and puppies, there is some flexibility in experimenting with different leg, arm, and torso sizes.

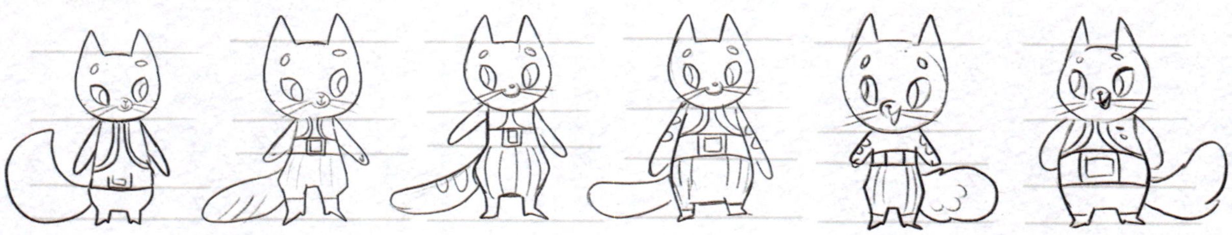

Reading the text carefully and making good inferences about the characters will help to inform your design. For example, Captain Cat is described as wearing a "special captain's hat." This is a distinguishing feature that needs some careful consideration to help the character stand out from the other characters who may also be wearing pirate hats.

Color choice plays an equally important role. It's essential to consider the environment the characters will inhabit throughout the story. Captain Cat is mainly found on her ship, but there is sea and sky in the background as well. Her colors need to complement the environment and allow her to stand out against it.

Once you've decided on the general shape of your character, it's time to explore in more detail. Use thumbnails to experiment with different details such as fur markings, outfits, and expressions to fine-tune the character.

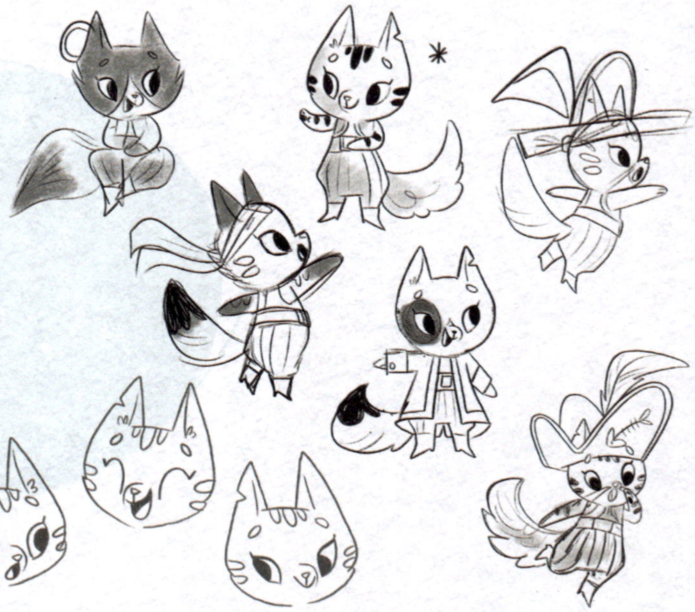

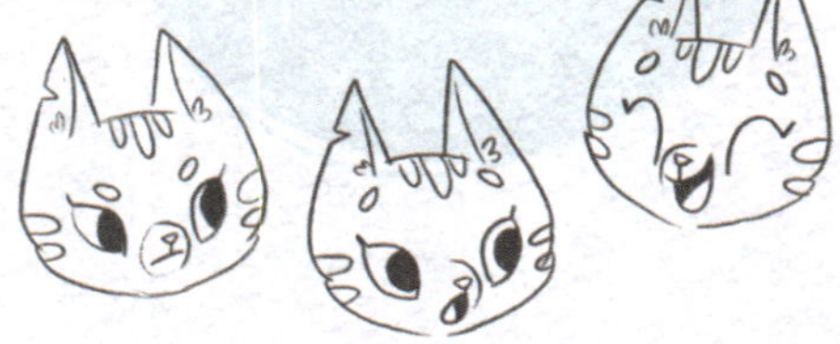

Captain Cat's hat is a key element of her design. It must allow the reader to recognize the character is a cat, but be large and bold enough for a captain. Consider the personality of the character; Captain Cat has a hardworking crew, so you can infer her character is likely to be quite sensible and organized. A crooked hat may not best represent her levelheaded character.

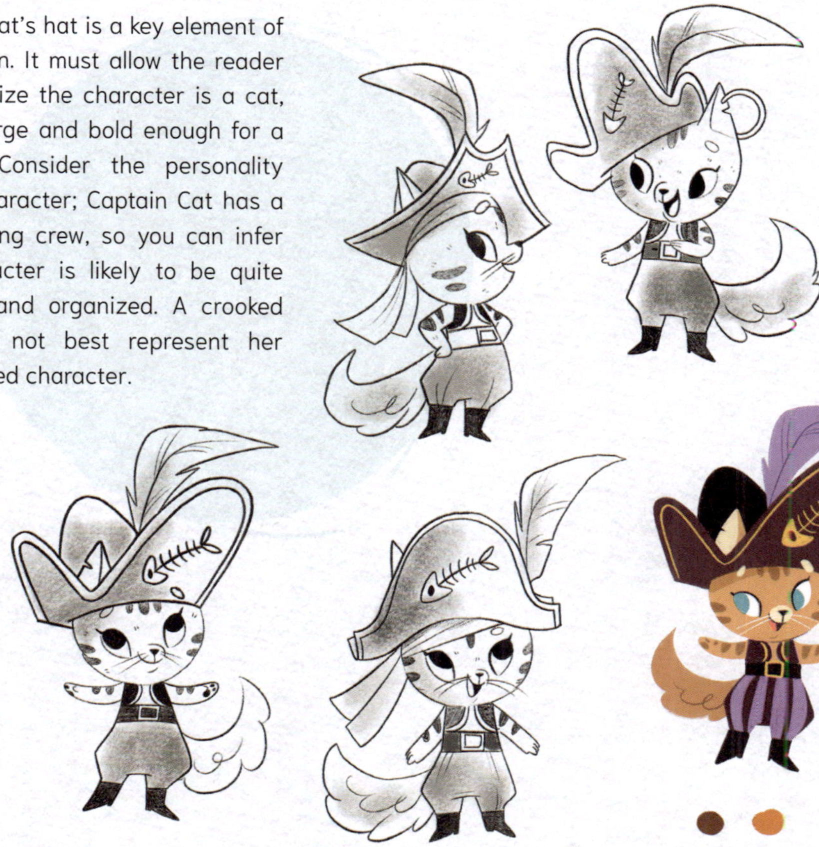

Try out different color palettes next to each other so you can compare and contrast. This character needs to stand out against wooden decking, sea, and sky, so the brighter yellow fur is the best option.

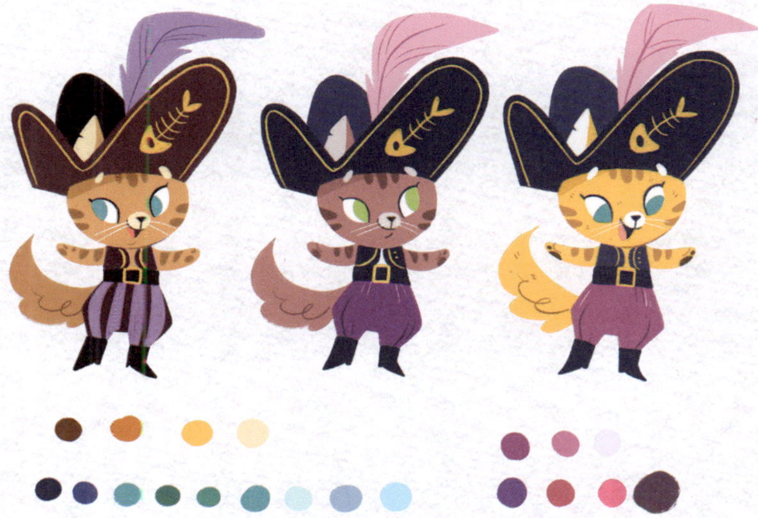

You can also try out different color options by roughly laying out a thumbnail of a page where the character features. This will allow you to see which colors work best within the environment.

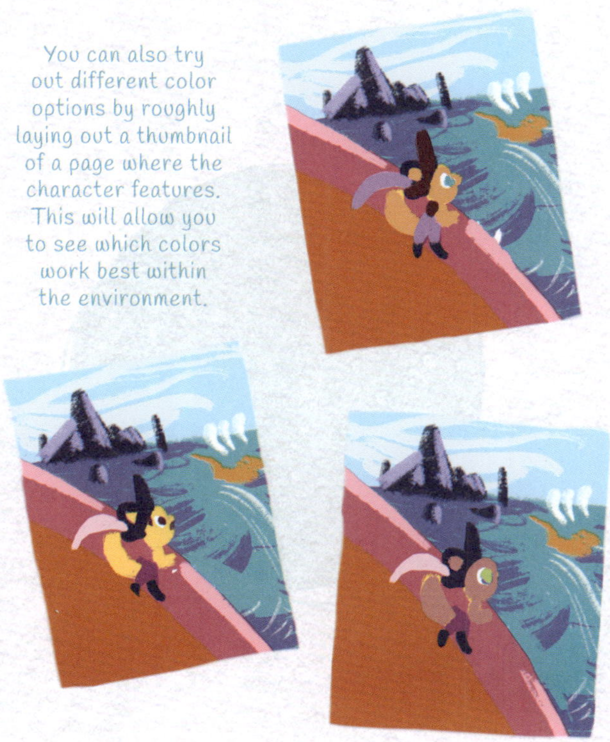

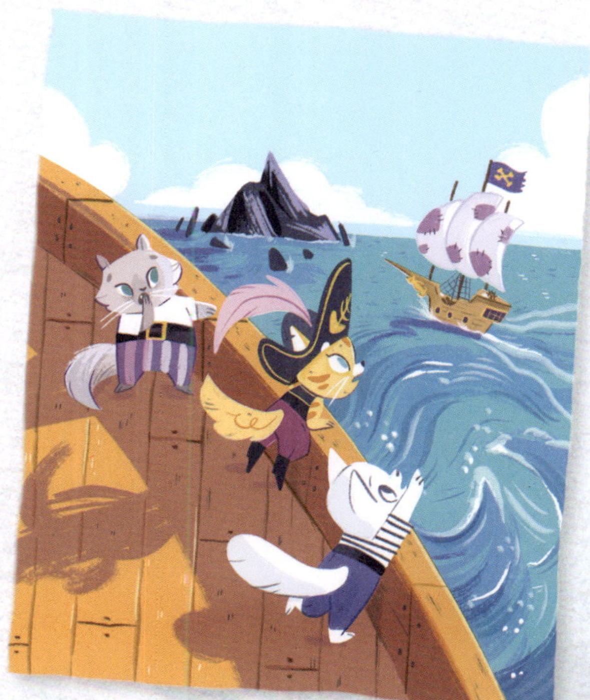

After working through the previous steps, you can then start to draft your spreads with a good understanding of the shape and color of your character. This will help you when making composition or lighting choices.

## THE PIRATE PUPPIES' SHIP

The pirate puppies' ship, the *Golden Hound*, is a key element in the story. It's one of the first things you read about and reappears throughout the narrative. The ship must therefore be interesting and engaging for the target age group, have a shape that works well with the events of the story, and reflect the personalities of the puppies.

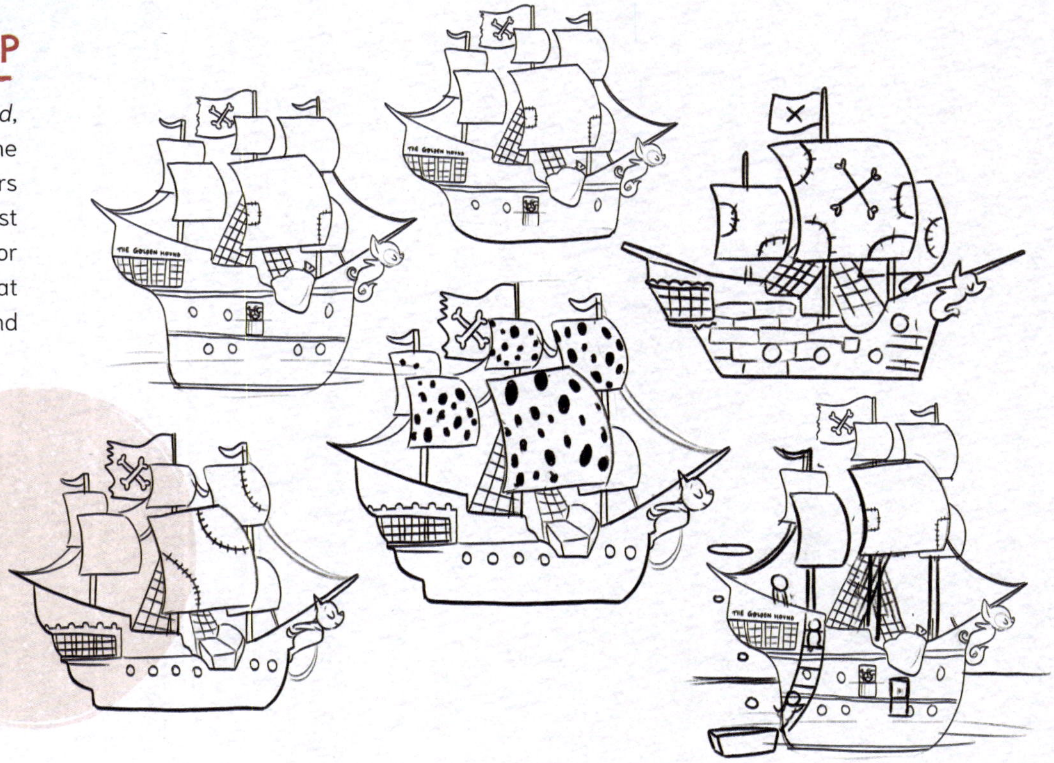

The first double-page spread sets the scene by including the pirate puppies' ship. Taking the dimensions of the pages into consideration, a long, pointier ship is a good choice. The sharper shape will add drama later on in the story.

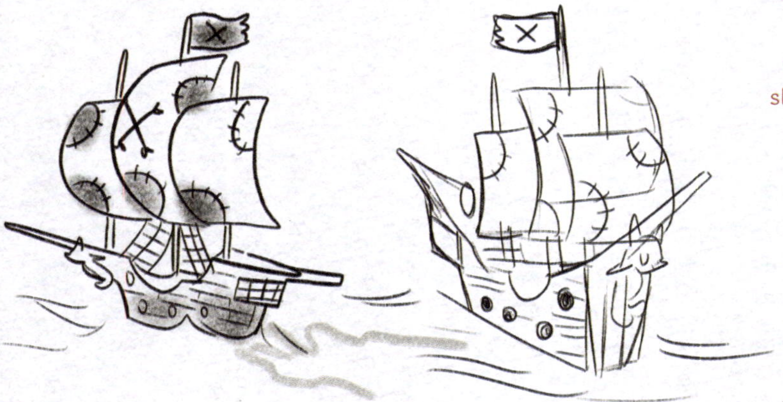

Consider the puppies' personalities; the story tells us they're fun-loving but accident-prone. The ship should therefore include details that hint at their previous mishaps. The sails have been repaired with big patches, which will also make the ship distinguishable from the kittens' ship later on. Large, visible planks help to add detail, even when seen from a distance, and provide interest and texture for a younger audience.

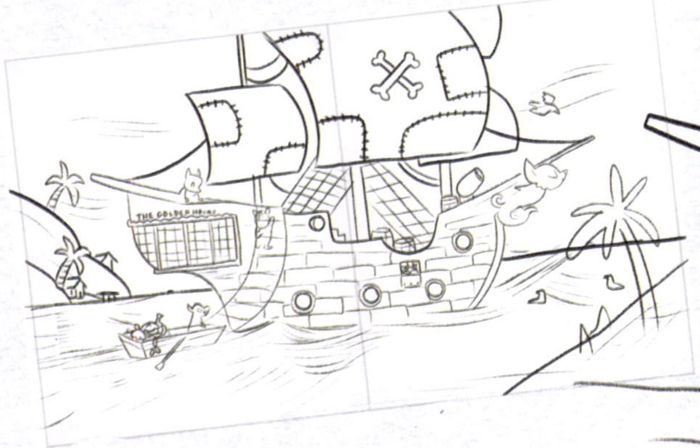

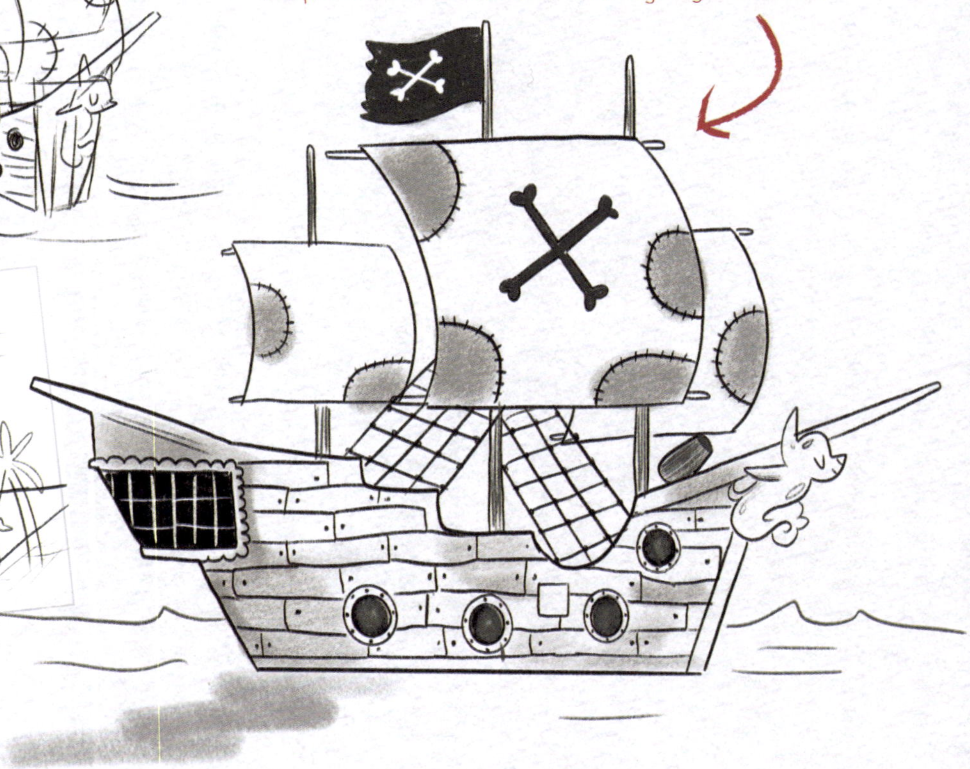

Using the chosen color palette as a base, you can play with different options to fit the tone of the story. The brighter, fresh colors will stand out well against the blue hues of the sea and the dark rocks, creating a positive, adventurous feel.

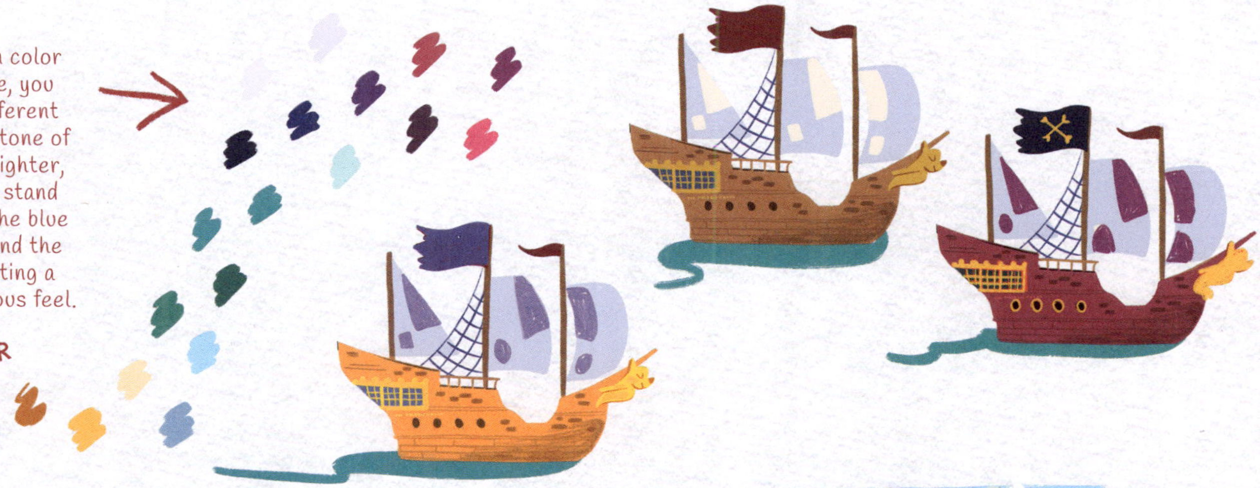

BASIC COLOR PALETTE

It's always a good idea to start with research. Studying various kinds of ships, sails, and rigging, then beginning by drawing from reference, will give you an advantage when experimenting with the shapes and details. Even if you intend a highly stylized design, researching first will help you discover key details that will keep your overall design believable.

The colors shown in the middle image are the most successful. Warm and inviting, they provide contrast with both the sea and the surrounding sand. As they're mid-tone, they allow for both light and shadows to be cast across the boat to create depth.

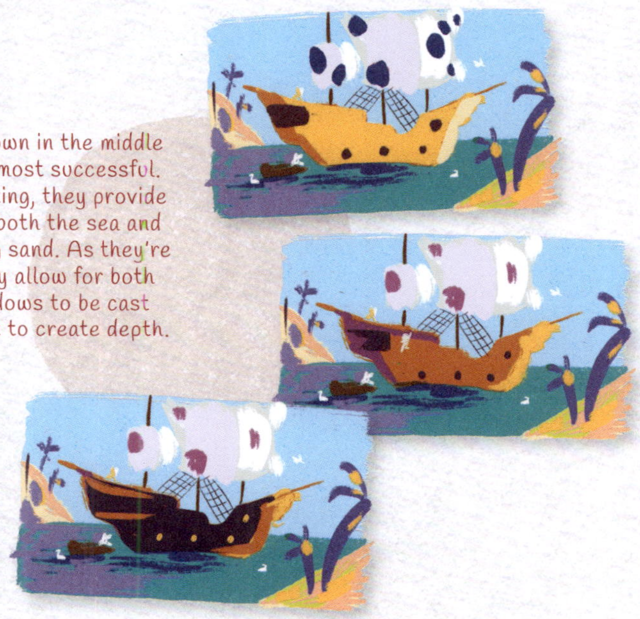

For shadows cast across the ship, you can keep the artwork vibrant and avoid muddiness by using a color that complements the wooden cladding. Purple is used to create a shadow effect, keeping the tone light.

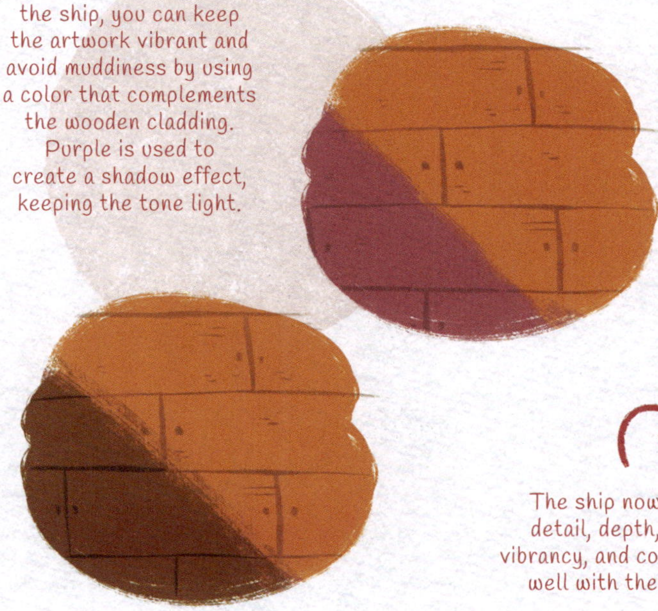

The ship now has detail, depth, and vibrancy, and contrasts well with the sea.

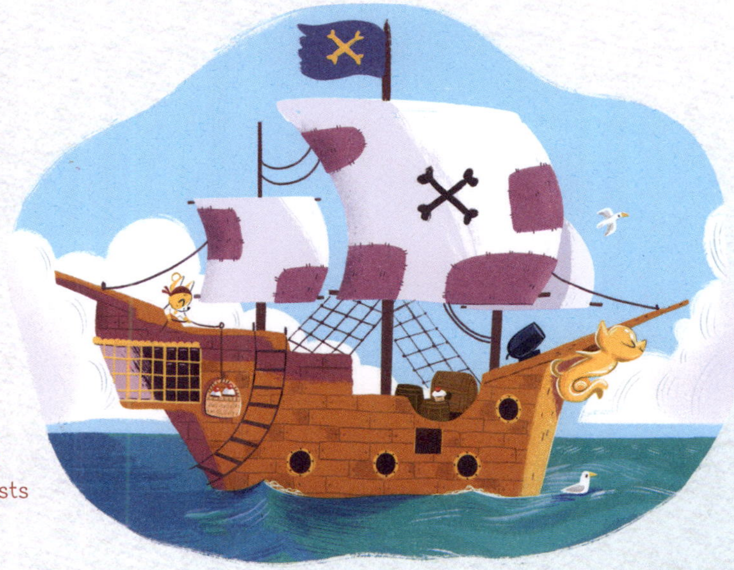

## THE ROCKS

The rocks represent the "antagonist" element of the story, so they need to be somewhat threatening in tone. Considering the age group of the reader and the style of the story, there is a little balancing that must be done. You want to show danger, while avoiding being too scary.

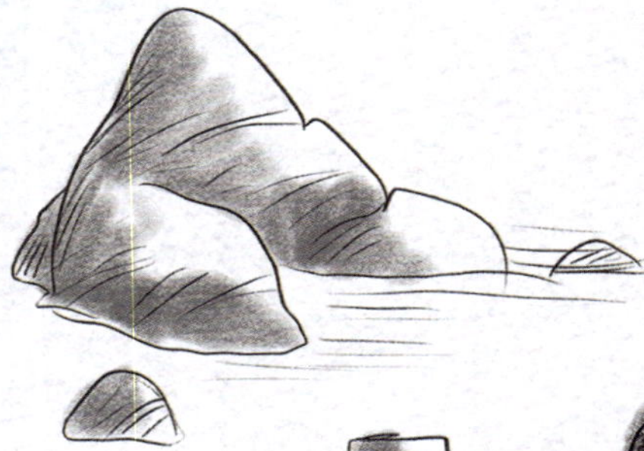

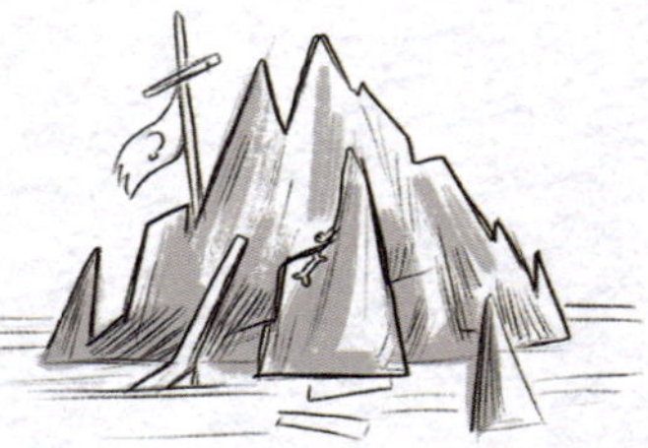

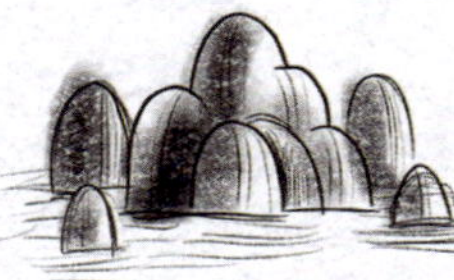

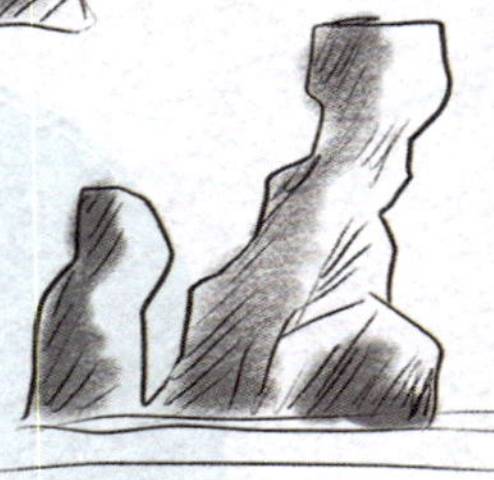

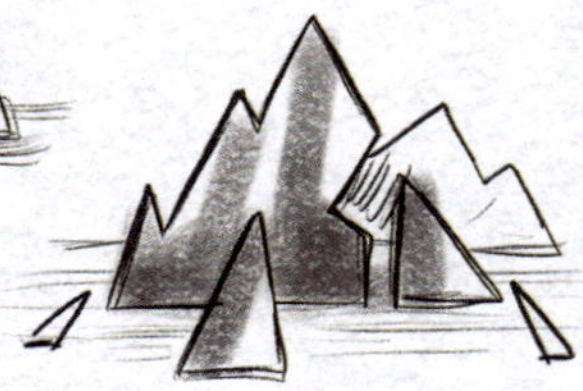

As with previous elements, drawing from references is key. Research cliffs and rocks, then draw as many different kinds as you can to find something that fits well with the story.

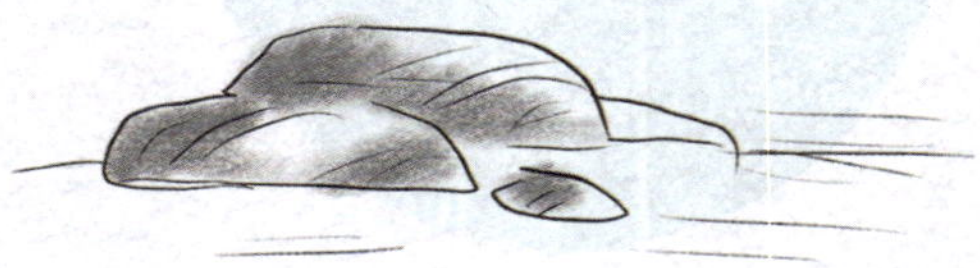

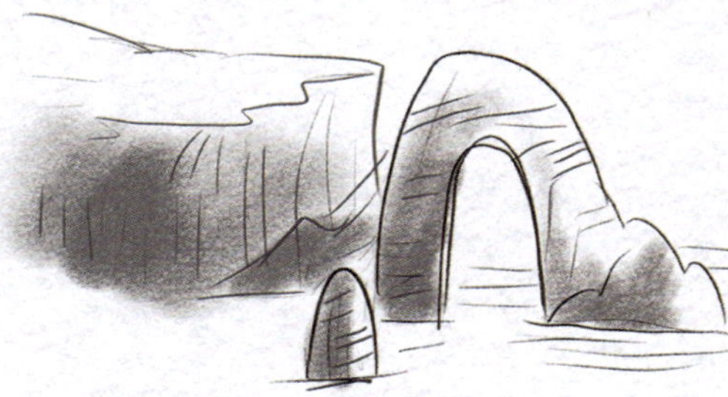

The curved shape and warm colors make these rocks appear too friendly in tone. They wouldn't work well within the context of this story where the rocks represent drama and action.

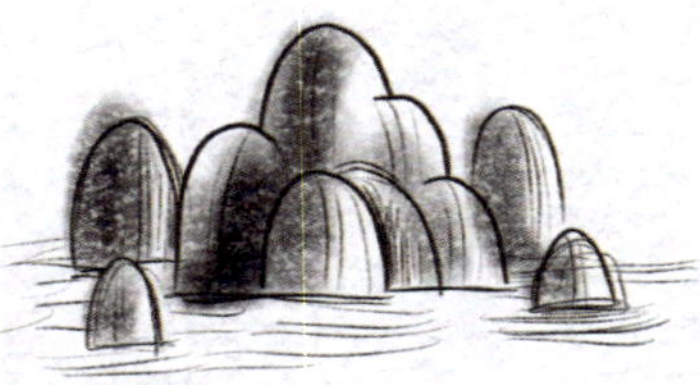

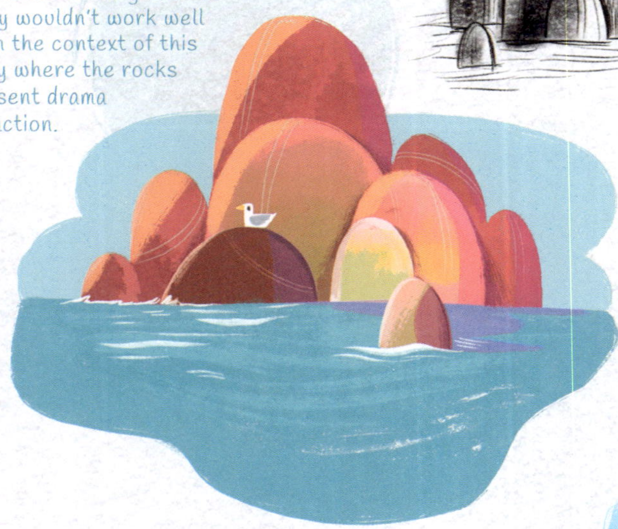

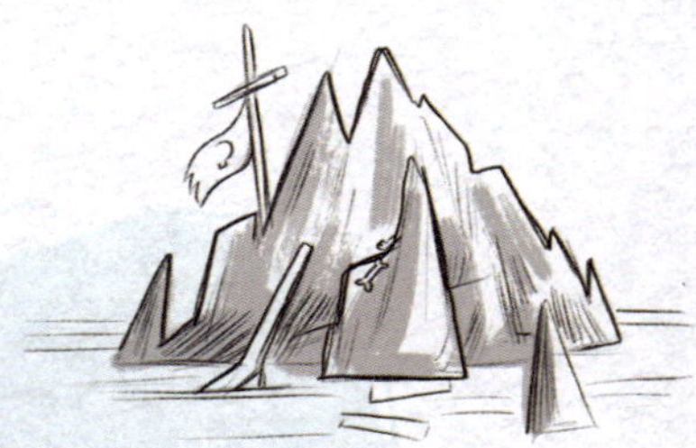

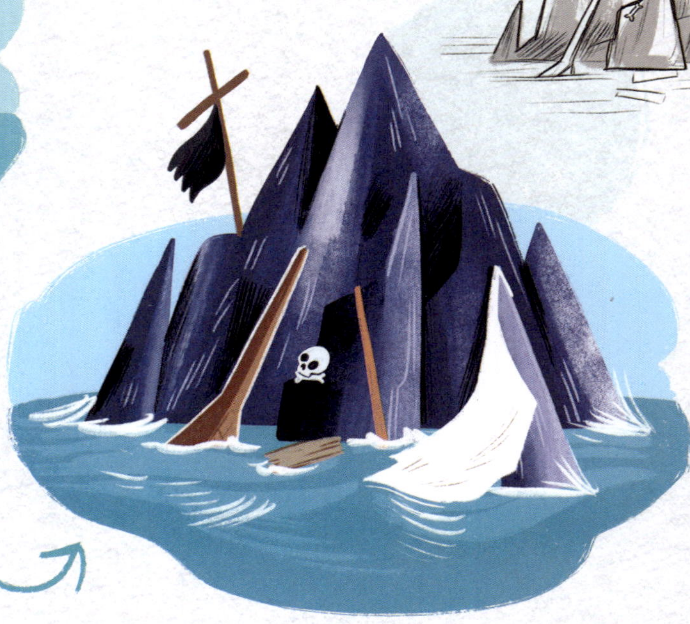

These rocks are more successful in conveying danger due to their sharp lines and angular shapes. While the general shape is preferable to the previous example, the evidence of previous wreckage plus the skull and bones make the tone a little too dark for this adventure story and age group.

You can create drama and movement in the rocks with your choice of brushstrokes and textures. Quicker, more painterly strokes work well here and create the impression of sharper edges and slopes.

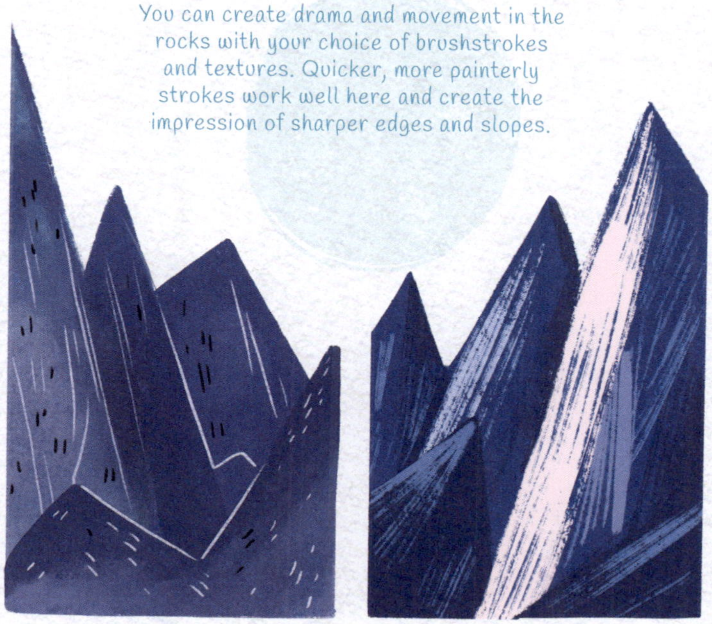

Although in keeping with the choice of palette, the warm highlights on the first rocks, shown here, diminish the threat and don't create enough contrast with the boats and water. Pulling back on the warmth plus contrasting and desaturating the colors creates a more dramatic effect and makes them a little scarier.

COLORS TOO WARM

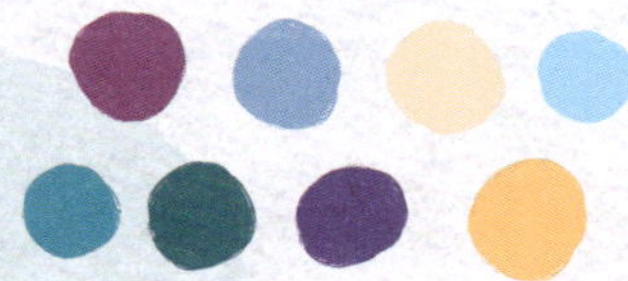

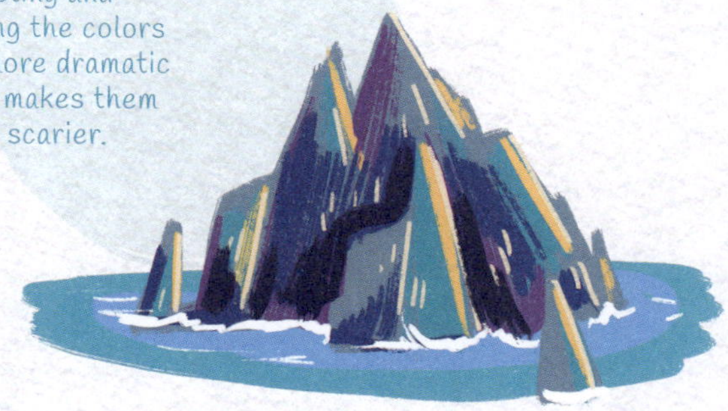

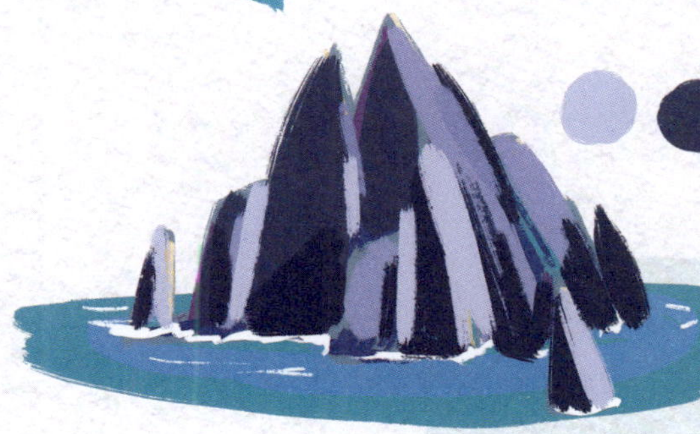

IDEAL COOL COLORS

Consider factors such as shape and color. A curved, rounded rock is friendlier-looking than a jagged rock made up of straight lines and angles. A rock with greenery, plants, and animals on it gives an impression of safety, whereas a barren rock where nothing grows conveys a harsh and inhospitable feel.

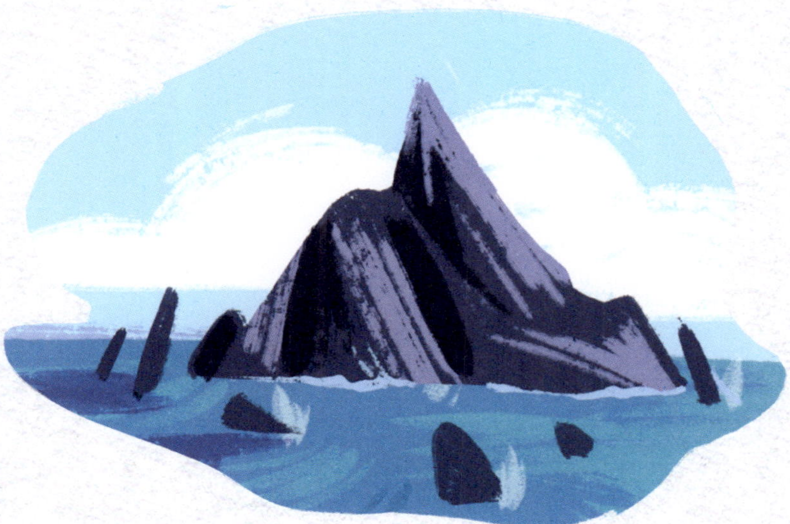

The rocks that appear in the story.

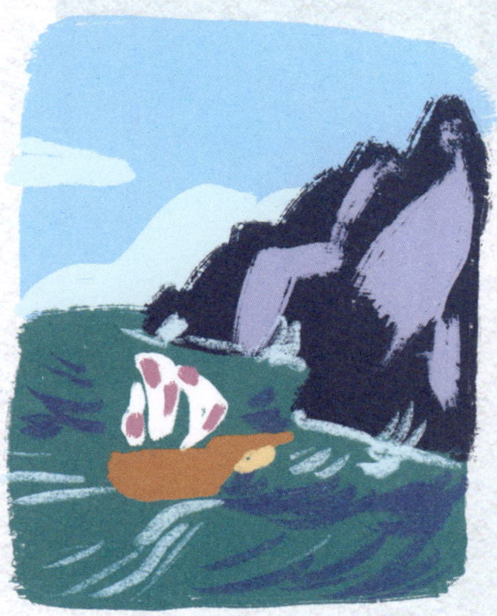

## THE SEA

The sea is a constant element throughout the story and can be used to portray the events and help set the tone. Starting by looking at the different plot points, there is calm before the puppies set out, adventure and excitement when the kittens arrive, and then peril when the puppies' ship nearly hits the rocks. Using linework, color, and the sea's various states can aid the narrative in these different sections. The sea can be smooth and calm, rough and choppy, or have undulating, crashing waves. As young children are highly visual, you can use the sea to help them follow the story's events.

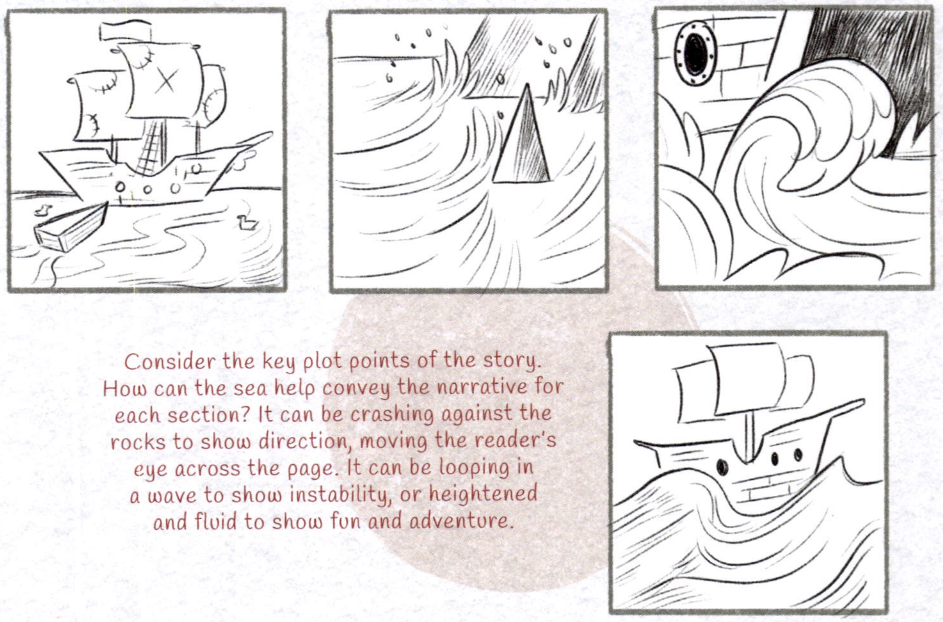

Consider the key plot points of the story. How can the sea help convey the narrative for each section? It can be crashing against the rocks to show direction, moving the reader's eye across the page. It can be looping in a wave to show instability, or heightened and fluid to show fun and adventure.

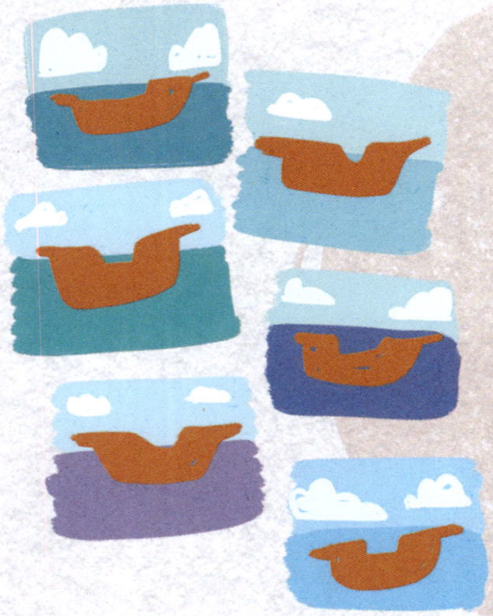

Creating more contrast between the colors will provide some drama, while keeping the colors fresh and vibrant for young children. Using a varied palette of light and dark purple and teal hues will allow for contrast where it's needed, and the deeper teal works well and looks richer against the ship and sky.

NOT ENOUGH CONTRAST

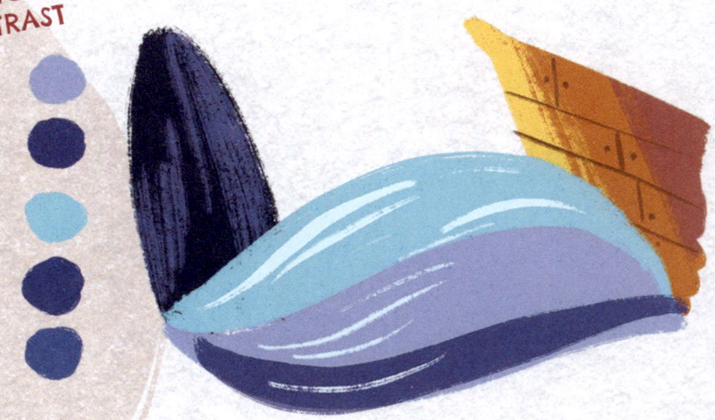

EFFECTIVE CONTRAST

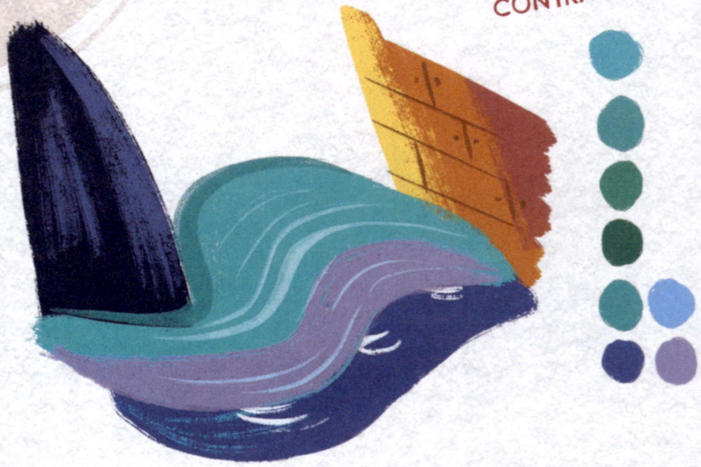

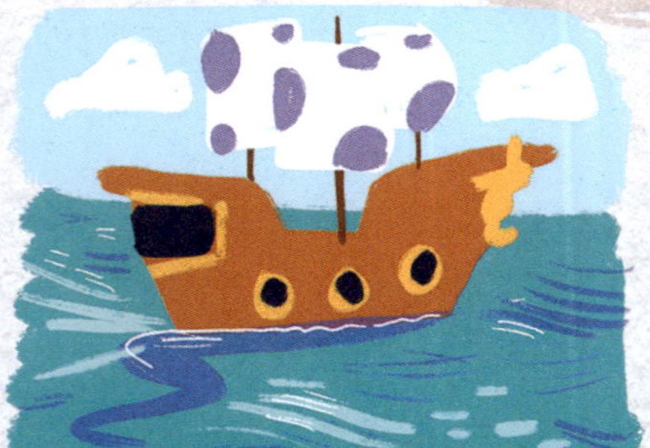

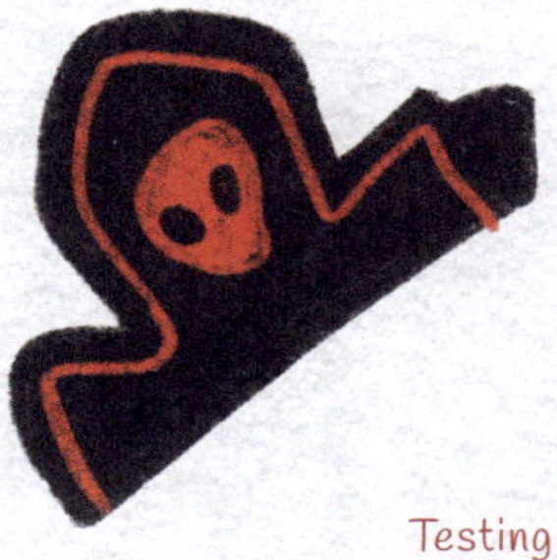

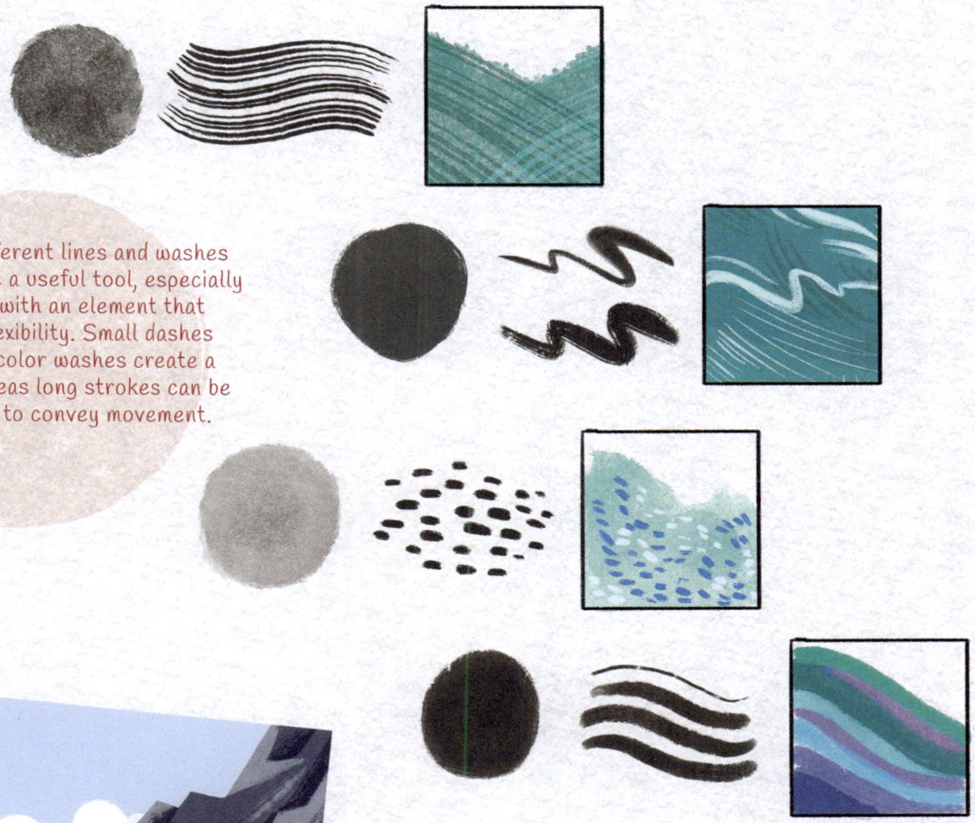

Testing the way different lines and washes work together can be a useful tool, especially if you're working with an element that requires a little flexibility. Small dashes and dots on watercolor washes create a sense of calm, whereas long strokes can be used more flexibly to convey movement.

Using rough color sketches of the environment will help you decide if the style of the element fits. This style is not well suited to showing the waves crashing against the rocks as there is minimal room for extra details.

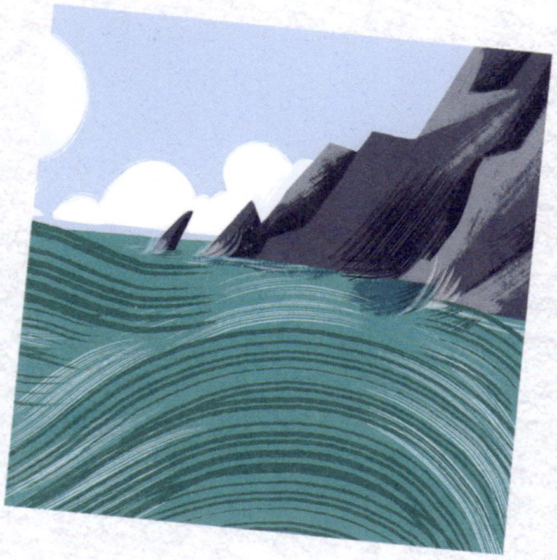

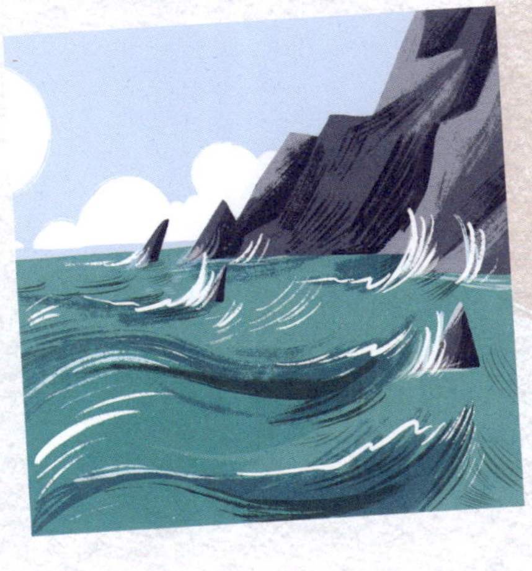

This style works well for showing a variety of different sea states, so is ideal for this story. Colors and brushstrokes can be varied to show all kinds of movement within the sea.

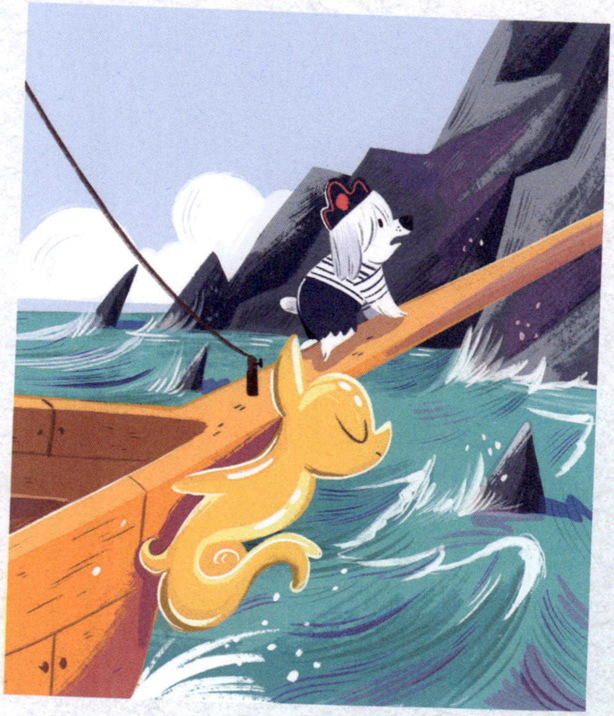

The final images of the sea use color and linework in a variety of ways to aid the narrative.

# ANALYSIS

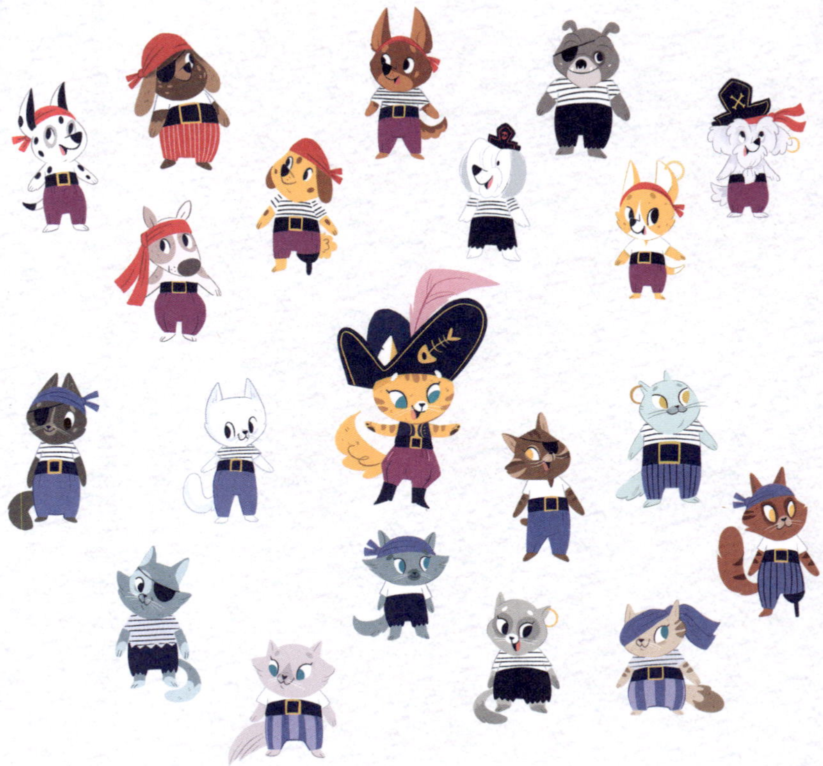

This was a fun and engaging story to work on, with exciting characters to interpret and space for lively, colorful scenes. With children aged 2–4 years, counting is an important part of their learning, so I wanted to create artwork that made it easy for them to count the characters on each page. The characters needed to be engaging and noticeably different from one another. Creating the characters was great fun, but having twenty different kittens and puppies meant I had to take care to make sure they looked consistent throughout the story. I found it helpful to create a character reference sheet containing every puppy and kitten character, which I was then able to refer to when drafting the spreads and during the final render.

The first draft showed the puppies sleeping on the ship, but I felt some of the puppies were too distant. This pulled focus from the puppies and put too much focus on the ship, which was not the right feel for this spread.

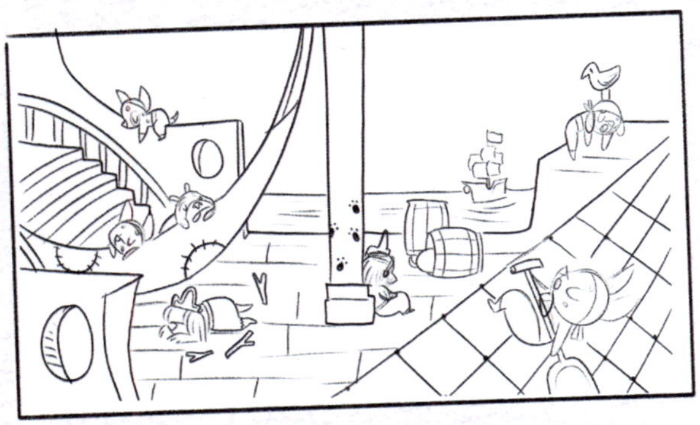

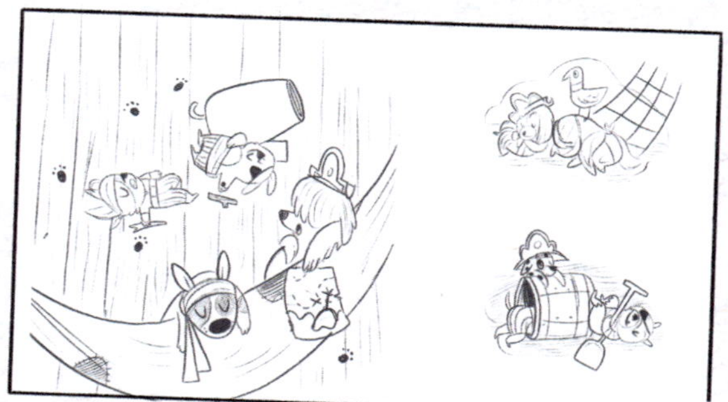

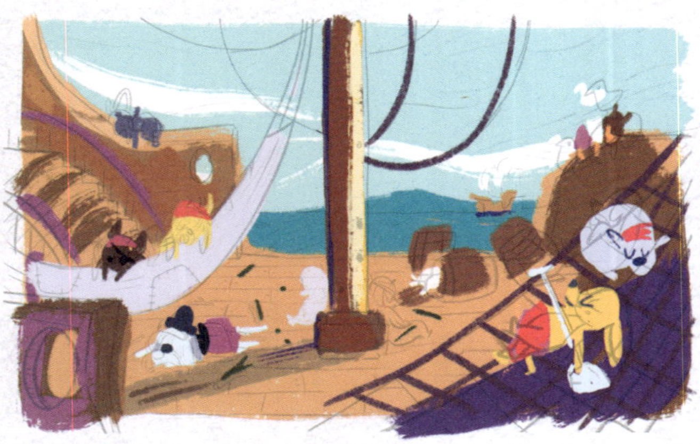

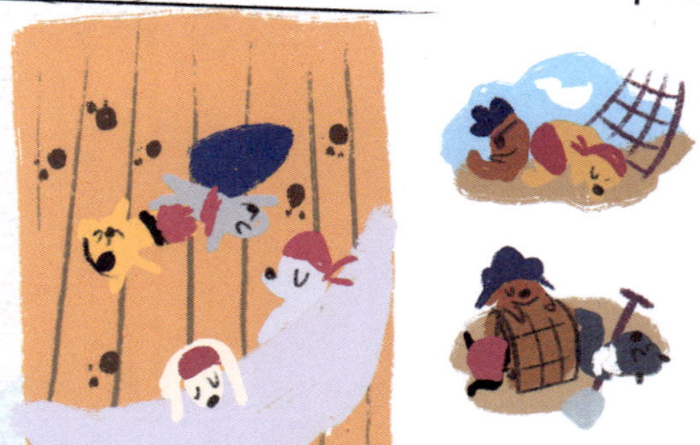

This draft put the focus on the puppies, but when I printed it to read with the rest of the story, I realized it didn't have the right flow. The puppies are all doing the same thing and the tone is sleepy and calm, so the reader's eye should flow gently over the scene, but here the eye jumps from one image to the next.

One of the easiest elements to work out was the color palette. This story needed a bright palette, and having the sea and sky as the environment allowed me to choose a rich teal and then work on finding colors that complemented and contrasted against this.

I faced a few different challenges during the drafting process and while painting the final illustrations, particularly regarding the flow and focus of some parts of the story. A useful way to check whether your drafted roughs work well together is to print and examine them all together. You can line them up in a row, or even make them into a small book and test-read it. Using this method, I noticed that the page with the nine sleeping puppies was broken up into too many vignettes. I realized that turning this into a double-page spread would make it easier for young children to count the puppies, allowing the eye to gently move across the page and take in the sleepy scene.

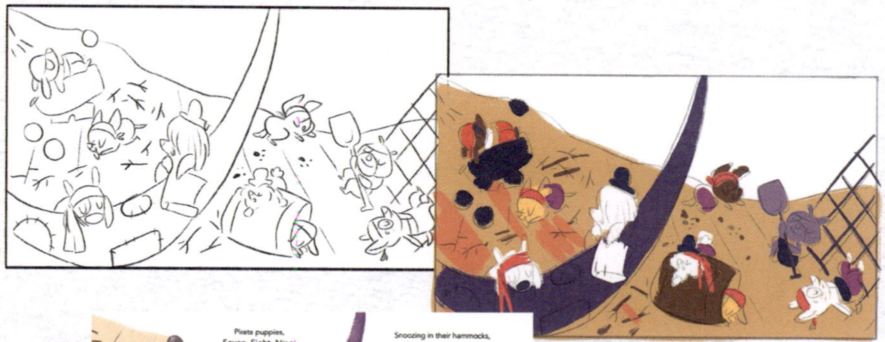

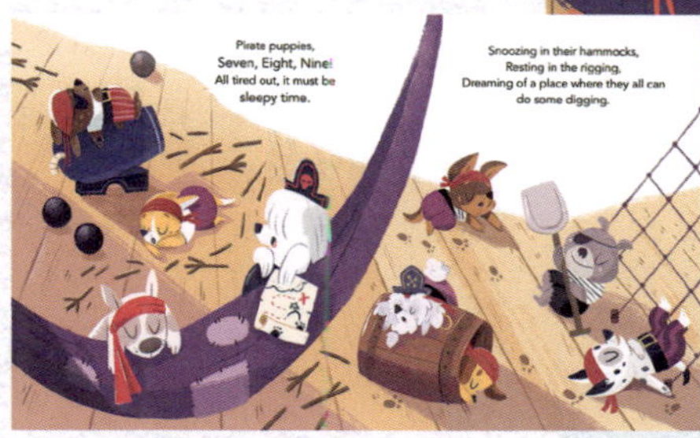


In the final draft I removed the vignettes to improve the flow of the page and extended the single-page illustration to create a double-page spread. To put the focus on the puppies, I zoomed right in on the decking so less of the exterior ship is visible.

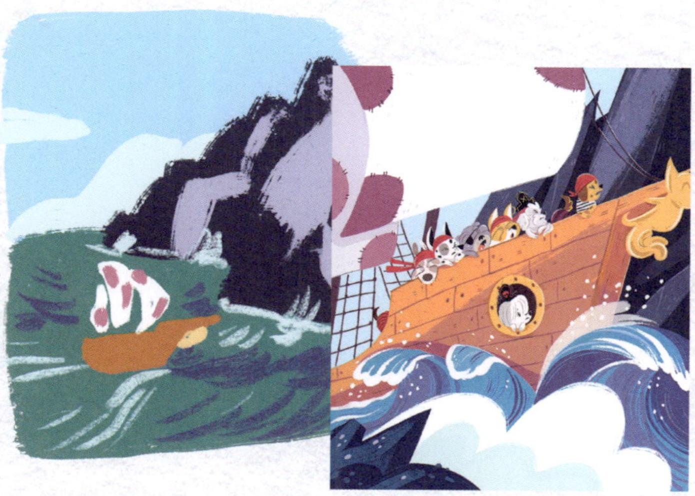

As the puppies approach the rocks, I had to decide whether to focus the attention on the rocks or the puppies' faces. At first I decided to build suspense with a scene of the small ship approaching the giant rocks, but I realized the younger age group would relate more to seeing the puppies faces as they close their eyes in fear and hold on to the side of the ship.

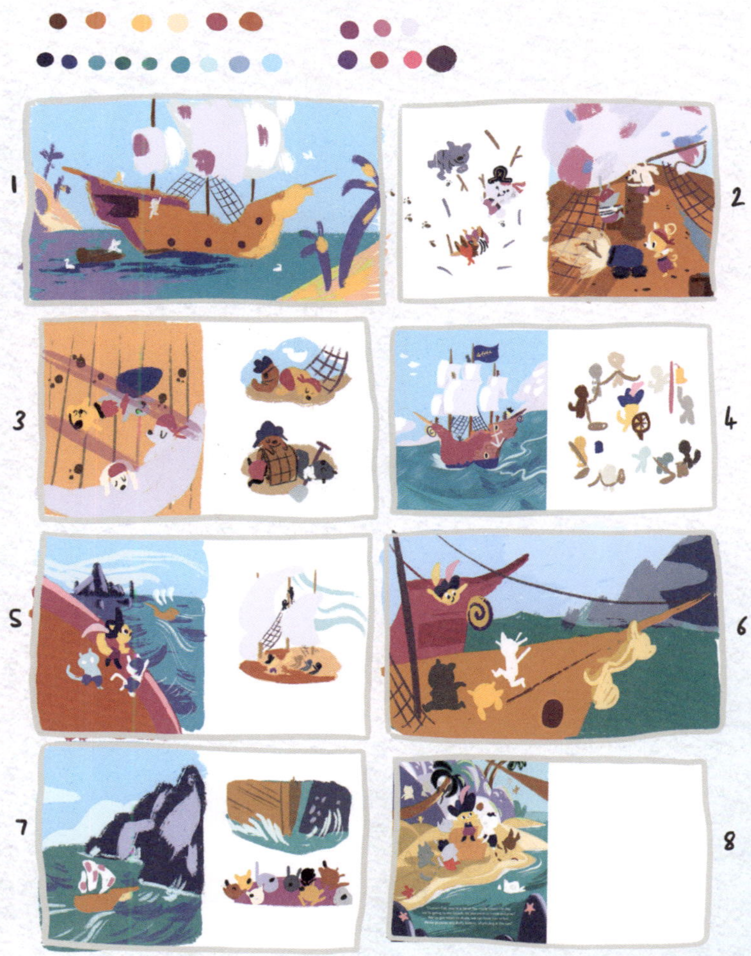


Viewing your draft spreads together throughout the process will help you see the flow of the whole story and address any focus or flow issues.

# SPLODGE!

Written by

GREG DOBBINS

Illustrated by

DOM "SCRUFFY" MURPHY



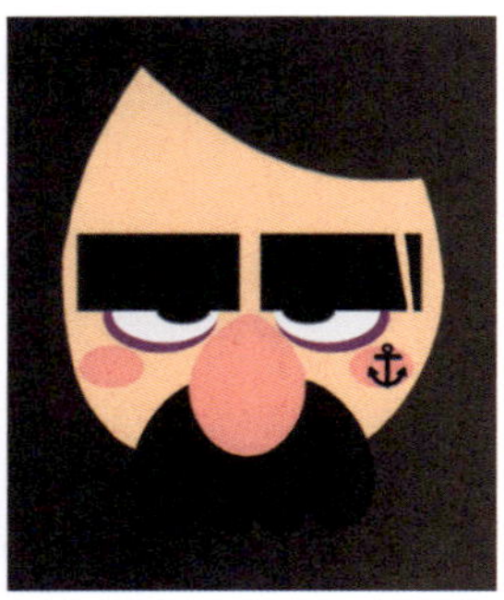

Character designer
**instagram.com/scruffyshenanigans**

Dom is a character designer for animation, an illustrator, and a lifelong sufferer of chronic "doodle-itis." He uses humor to soften the hard edges of life.

A STORY FOR AGES 4–6 YEARS

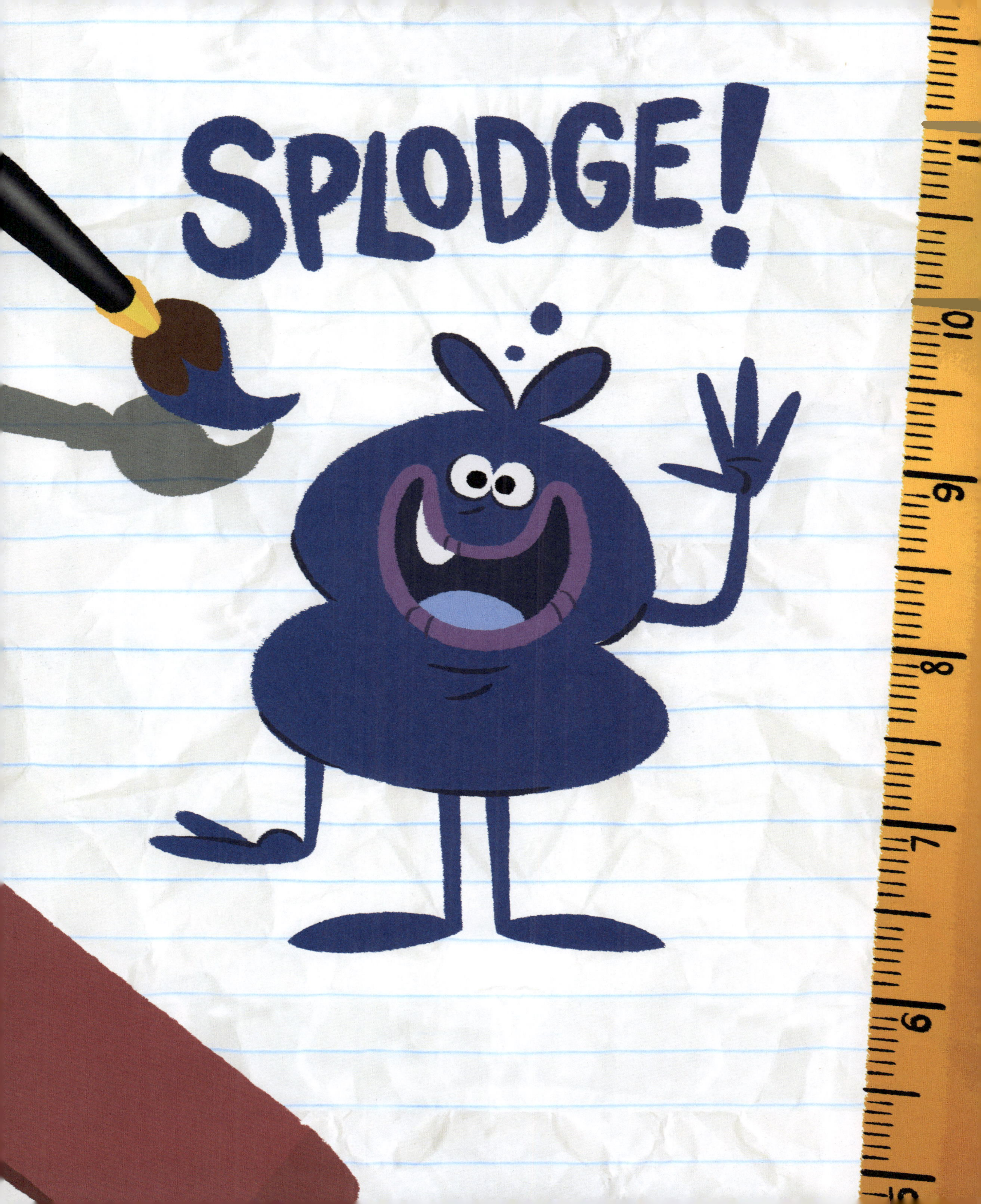
SPLODGE!

Splodge is an inky
splodgy blob of ink.

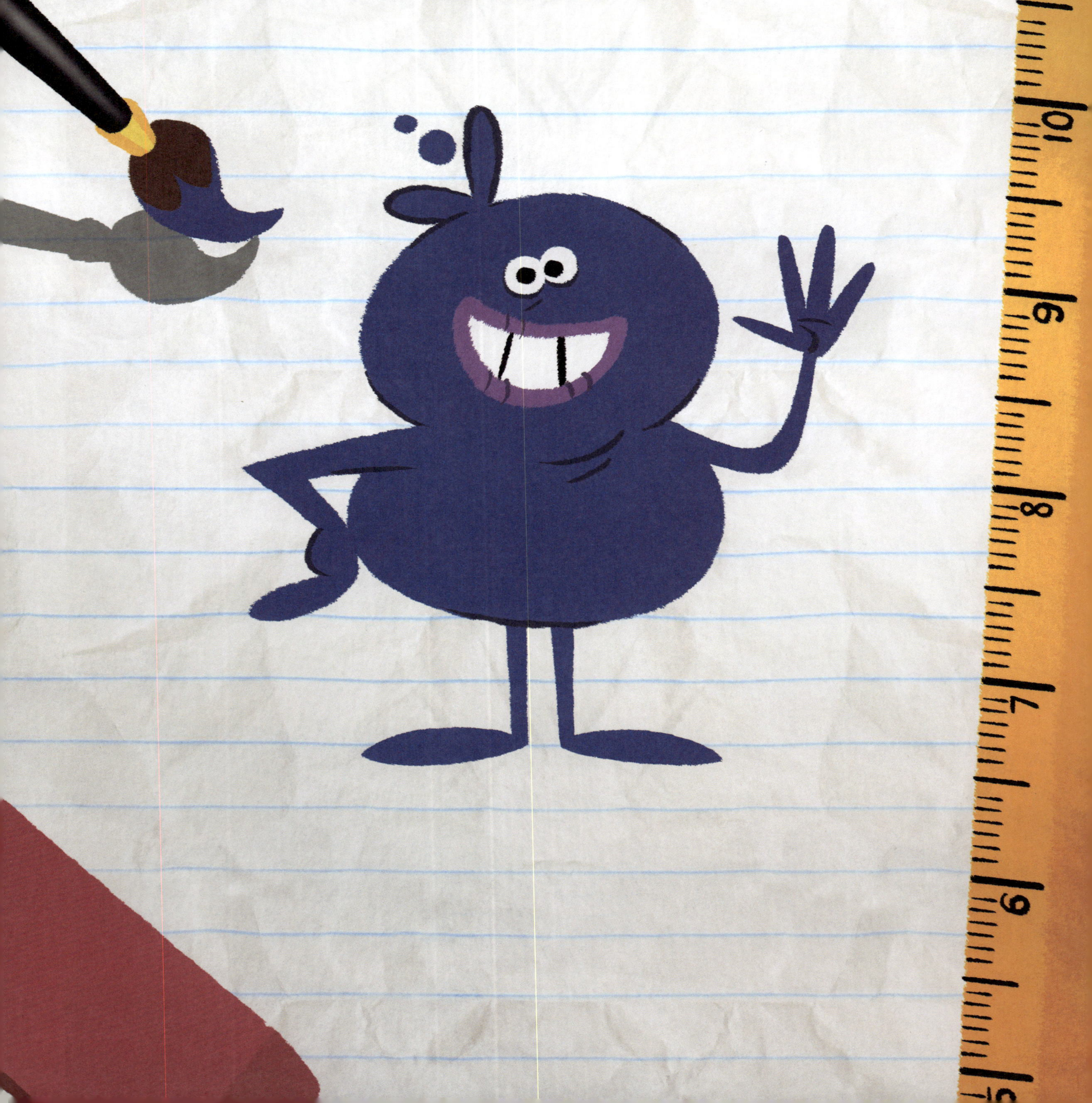

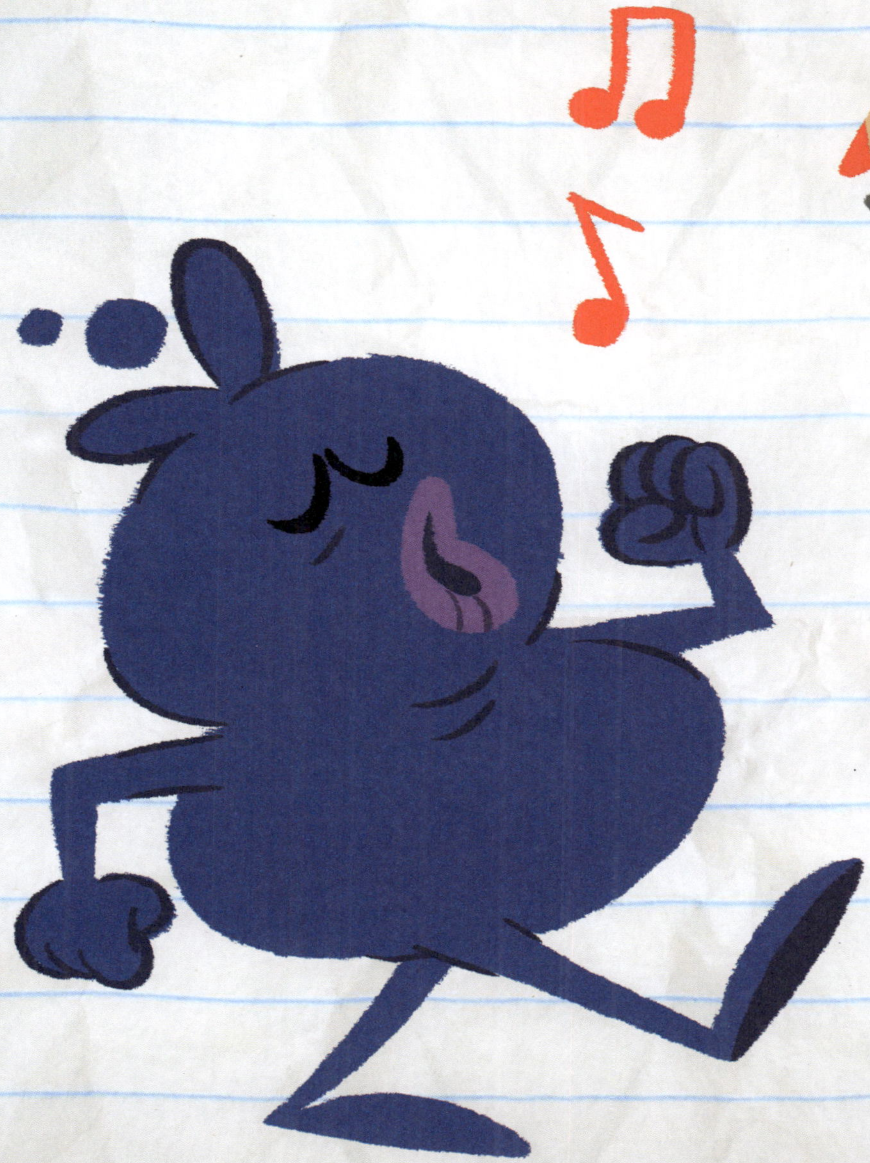

Splodge is going for a walk –
why don't we go too?

Look, Splodge – there are some Scribbles.

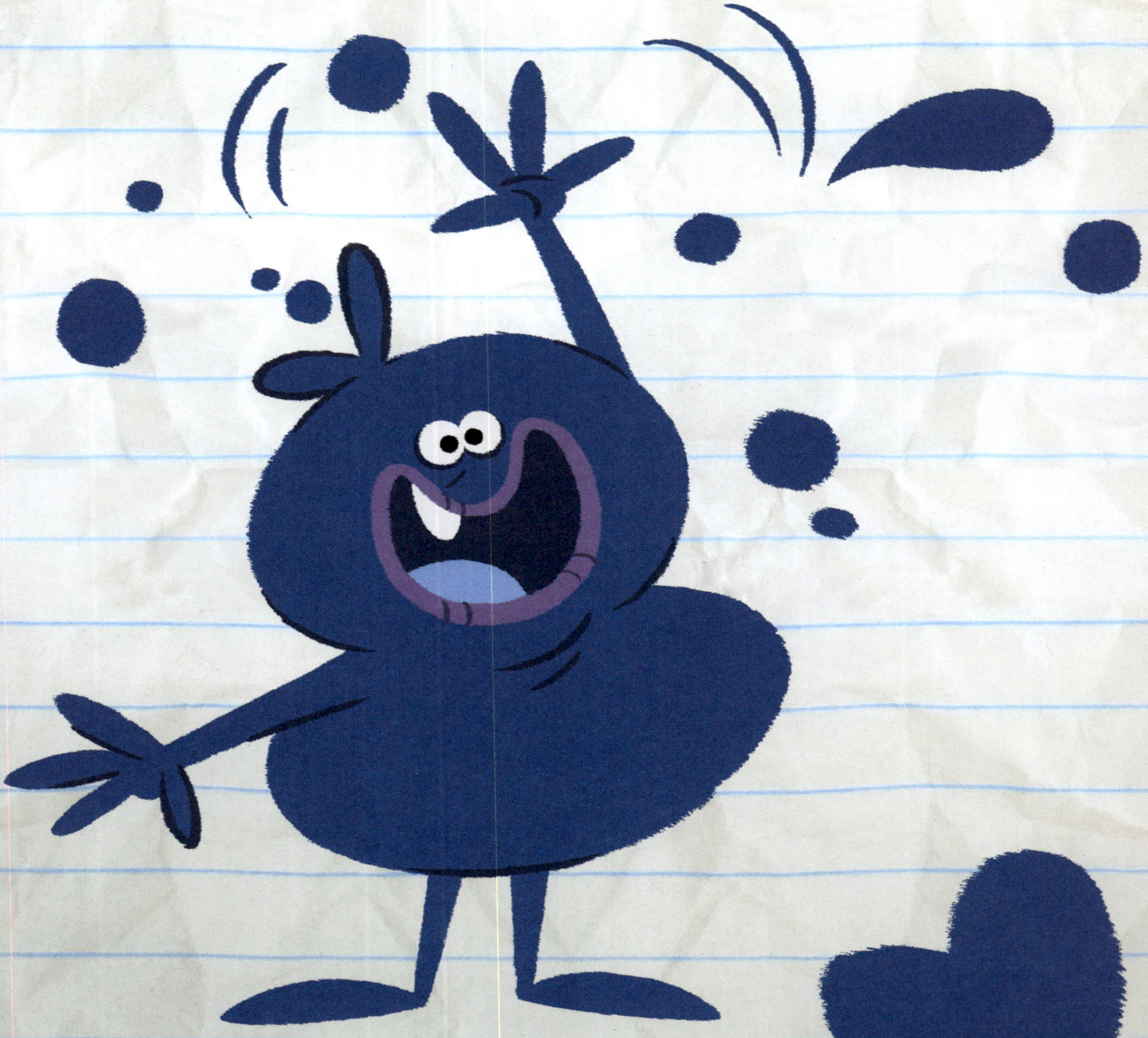

"Hello, Scribbles!"

"Who are you?"

"I'm Splodge!"

"Yes, we thought so. You're not a Scribble like us, are you? You're just a splodge. Go away! We don't want your ink spoiling our lovely squiggles."

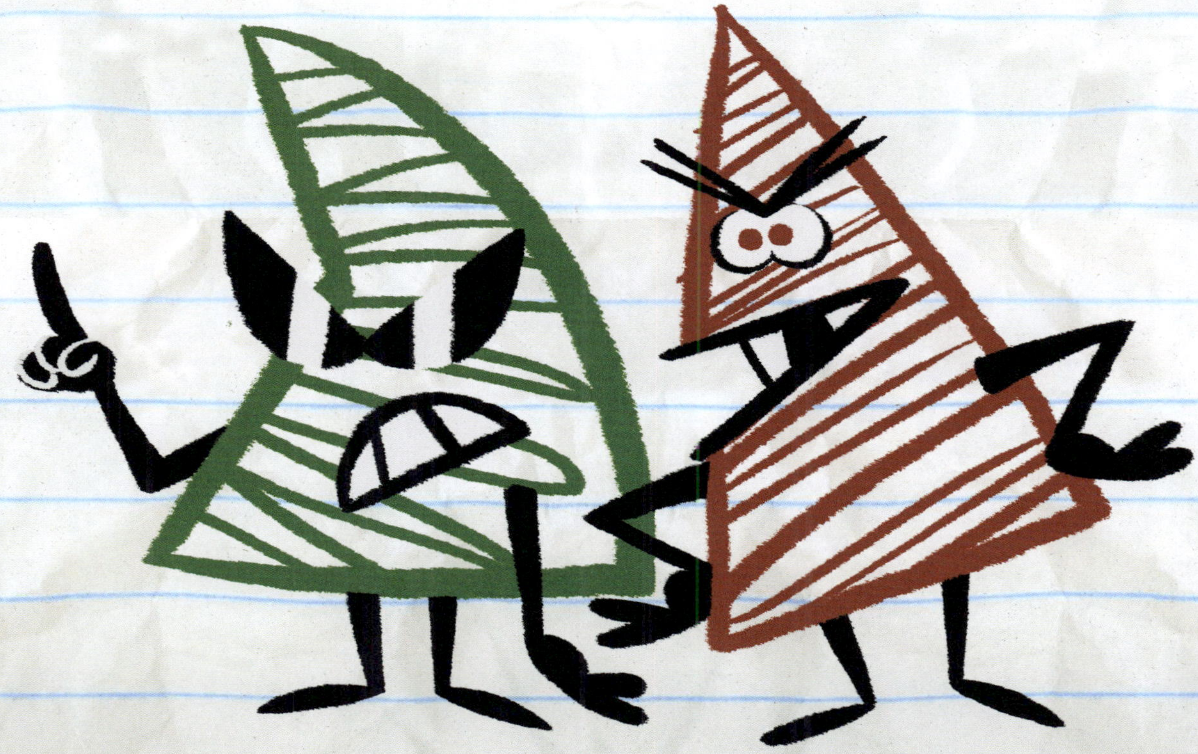

Oh dear, Splodge. They're not very nice, are they? Shall we carry on walking?

Look, Splodge – it's a dog.
What a lovely drawing!

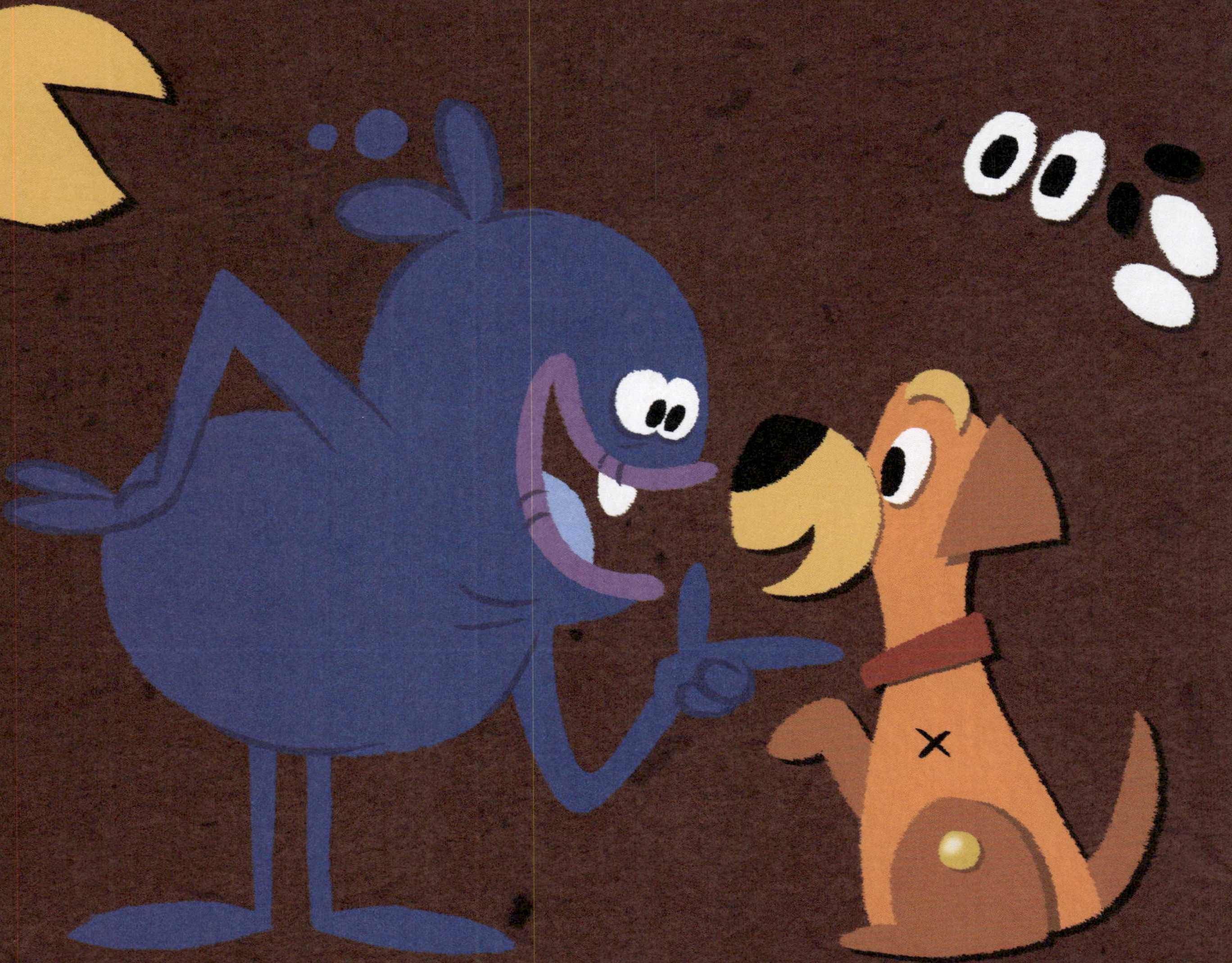

"Hello, little dog, what's your name?"

"I'm Doggy. Will you be my friend?"

"Of course I will!"

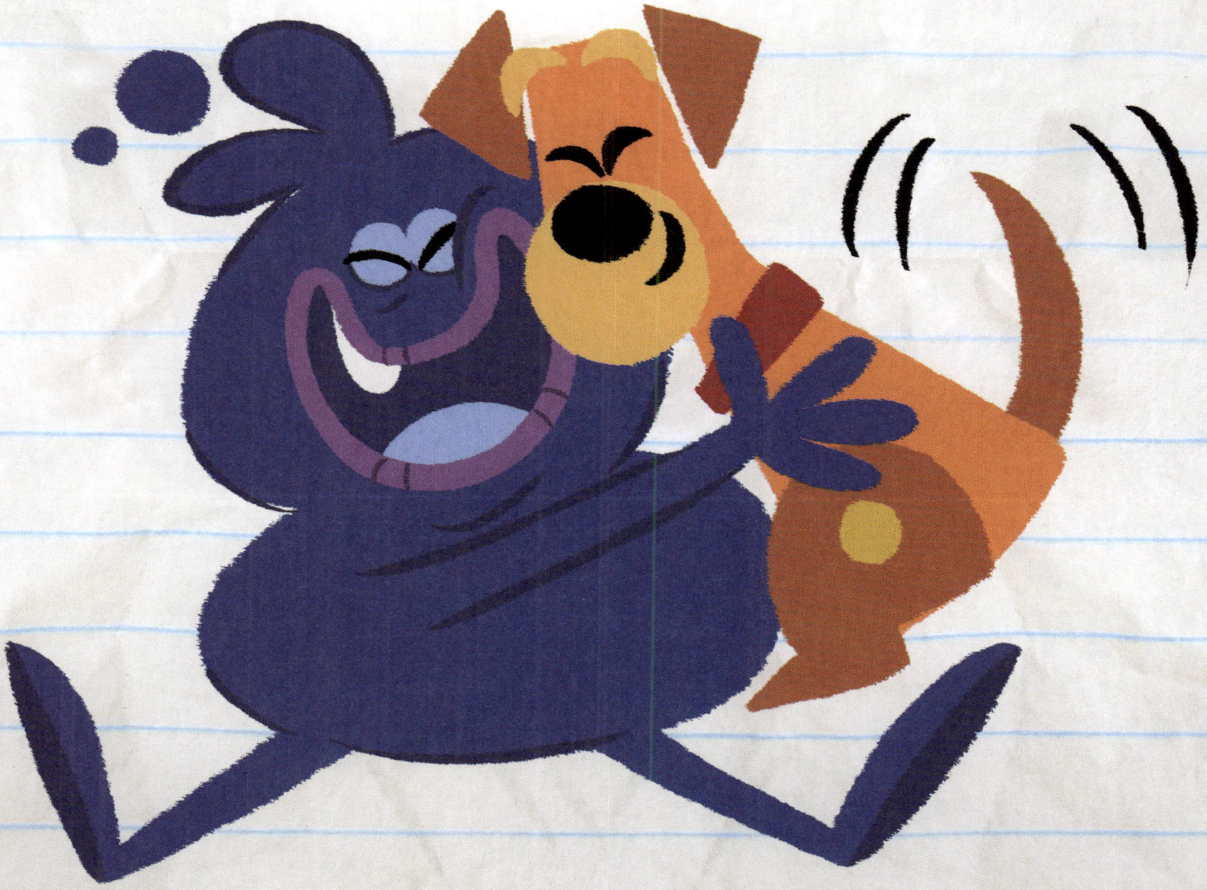

Splodge and Doggy are friends.
Doggy is very nice, isn't he?
Doggy is coming on our walk too.

Look, Splodge –
it's another Scribble.
"Stay away from that Scribble,
Doggy. The Scribbles are mean."

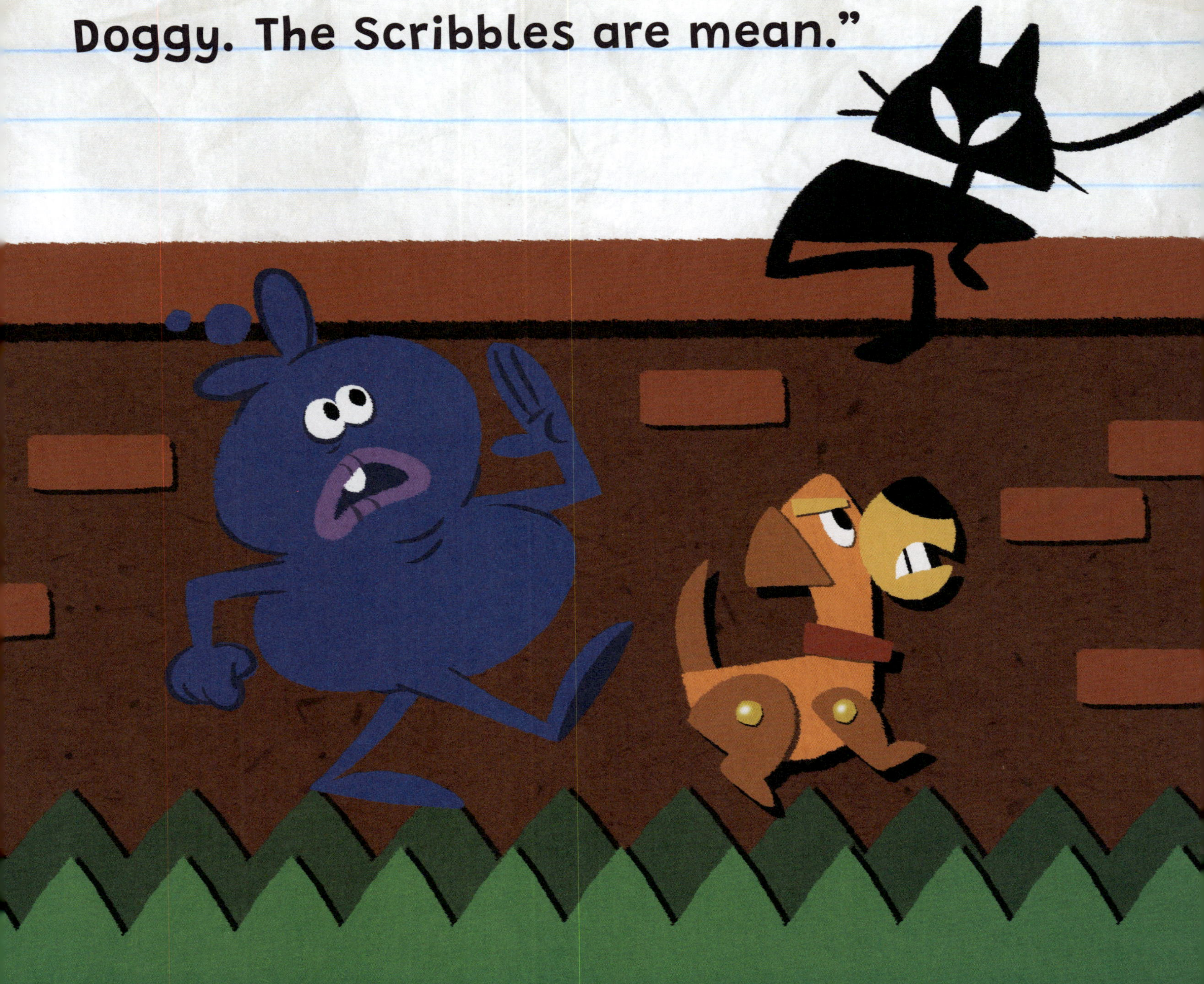

Oh no, it's a Scribble Cat!
"Come back, Doggy! Come back!"

Doggy chases the cat.
Oh no! It's the rest of the Scribbles.

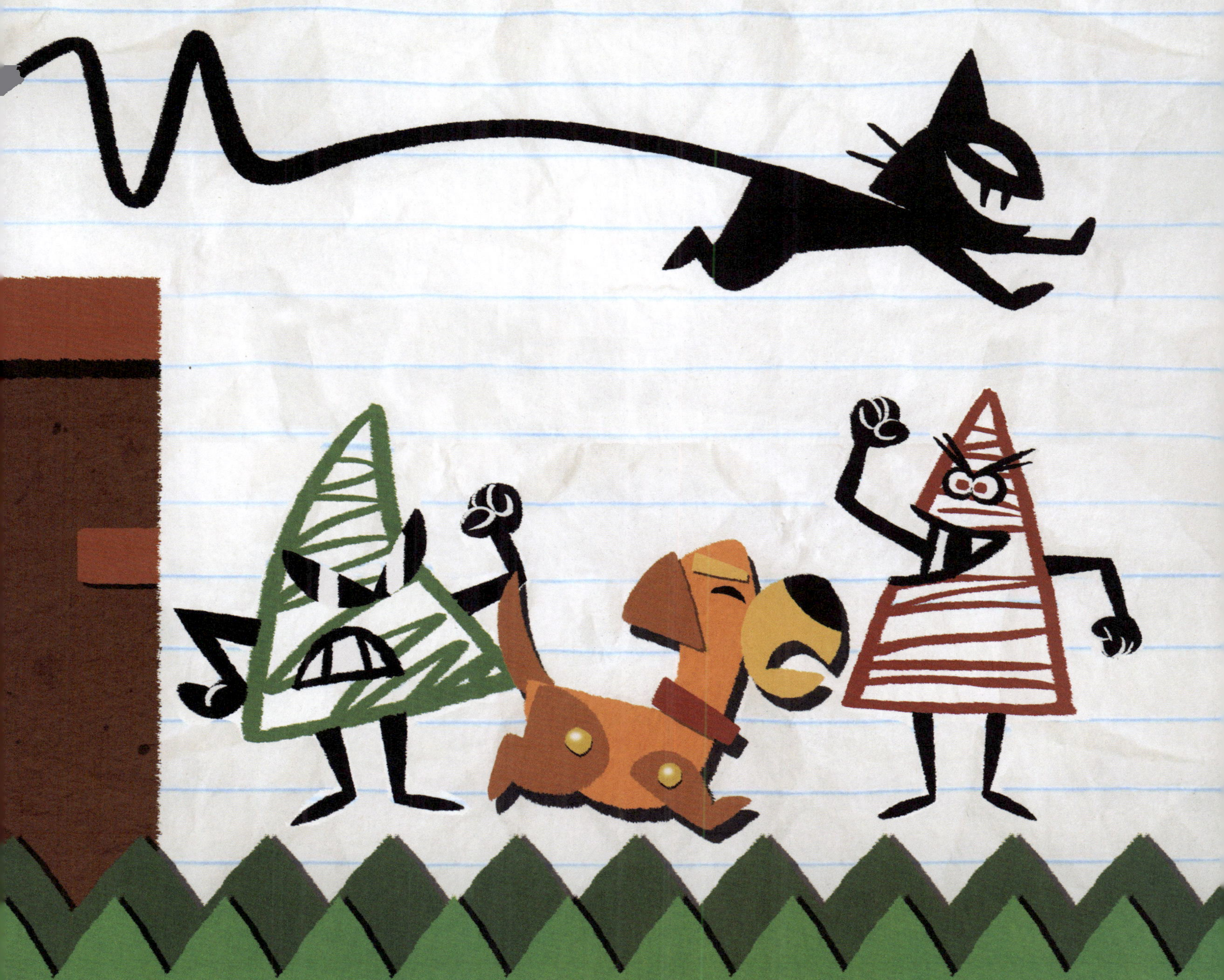

"You again? We told you to clear off.
And take your dog with you. He isn't even a
real dog – look, he's only got three legs!"

Doggy is sad.
Why are the Scribbles so mean?
"Come on, Doggy, we don't need them.
We can have fun together."

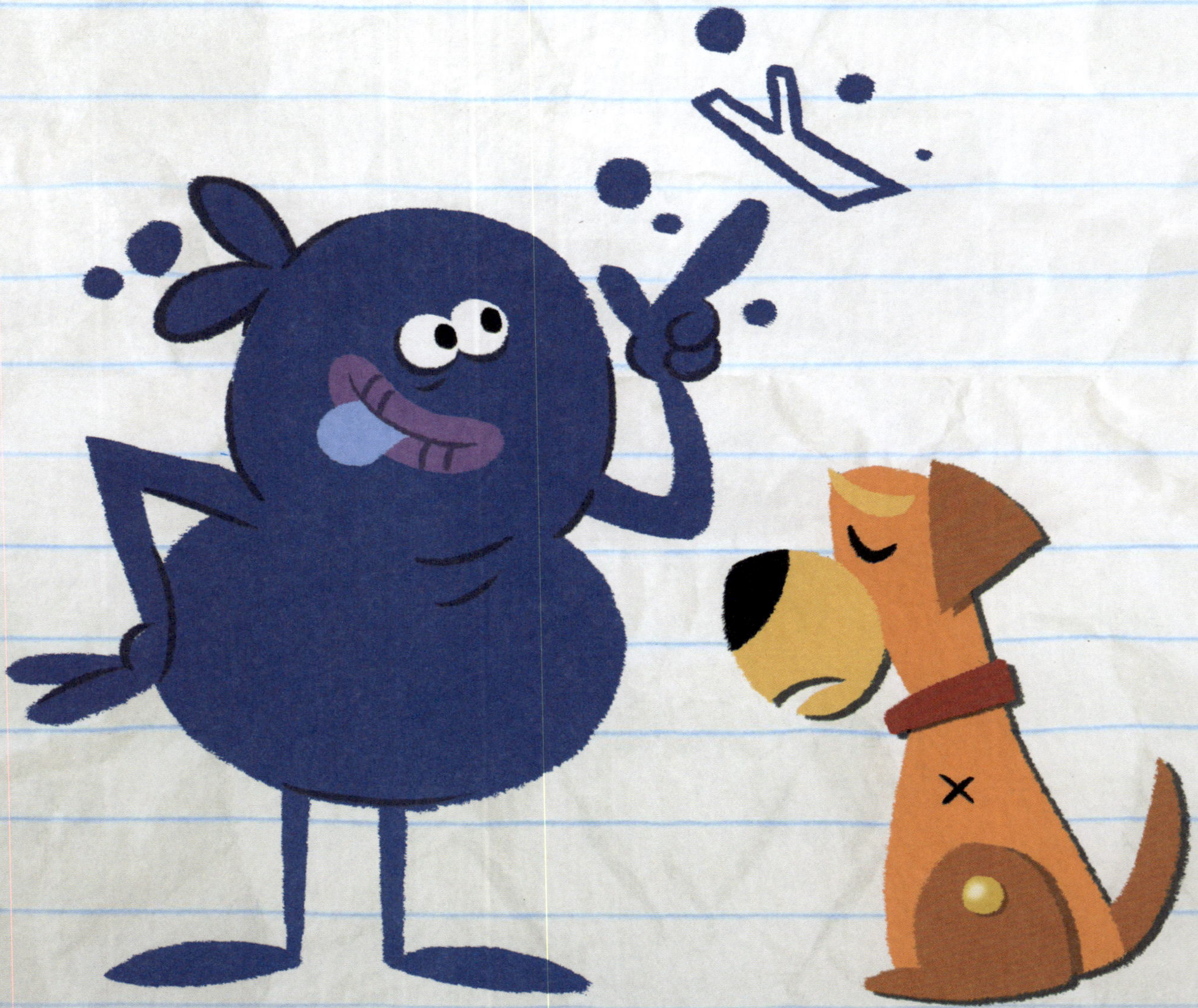

Using an inky finger,
Splodge draws a stick.

"Fetch, Doggy!"
Doggy fetches the stick.
Throw it again, Splodge!

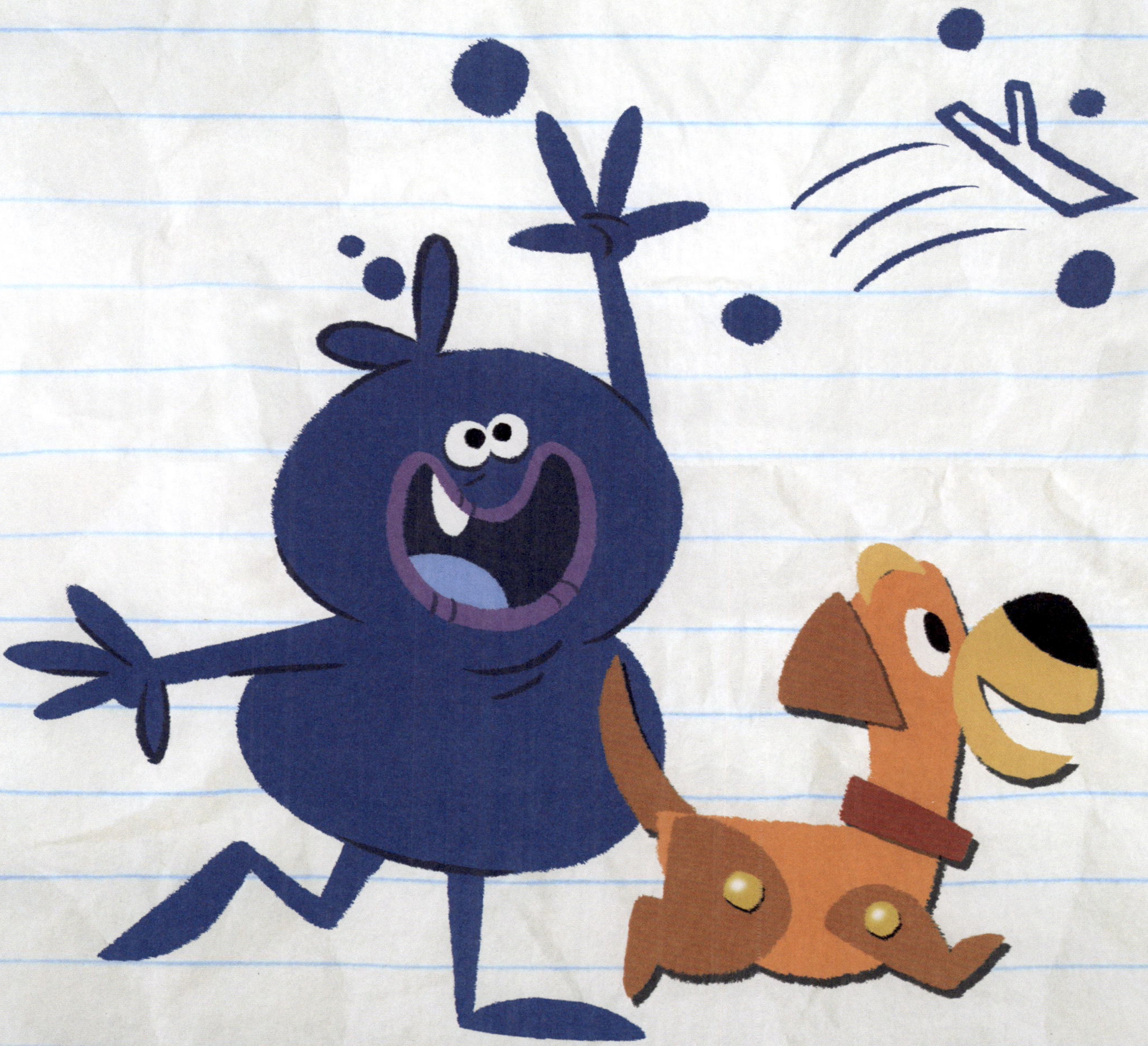

**Oops!**
**You've thrown it onto the next page!**

Doggy has found a crayon.
“Ah, that gives me an idea!”

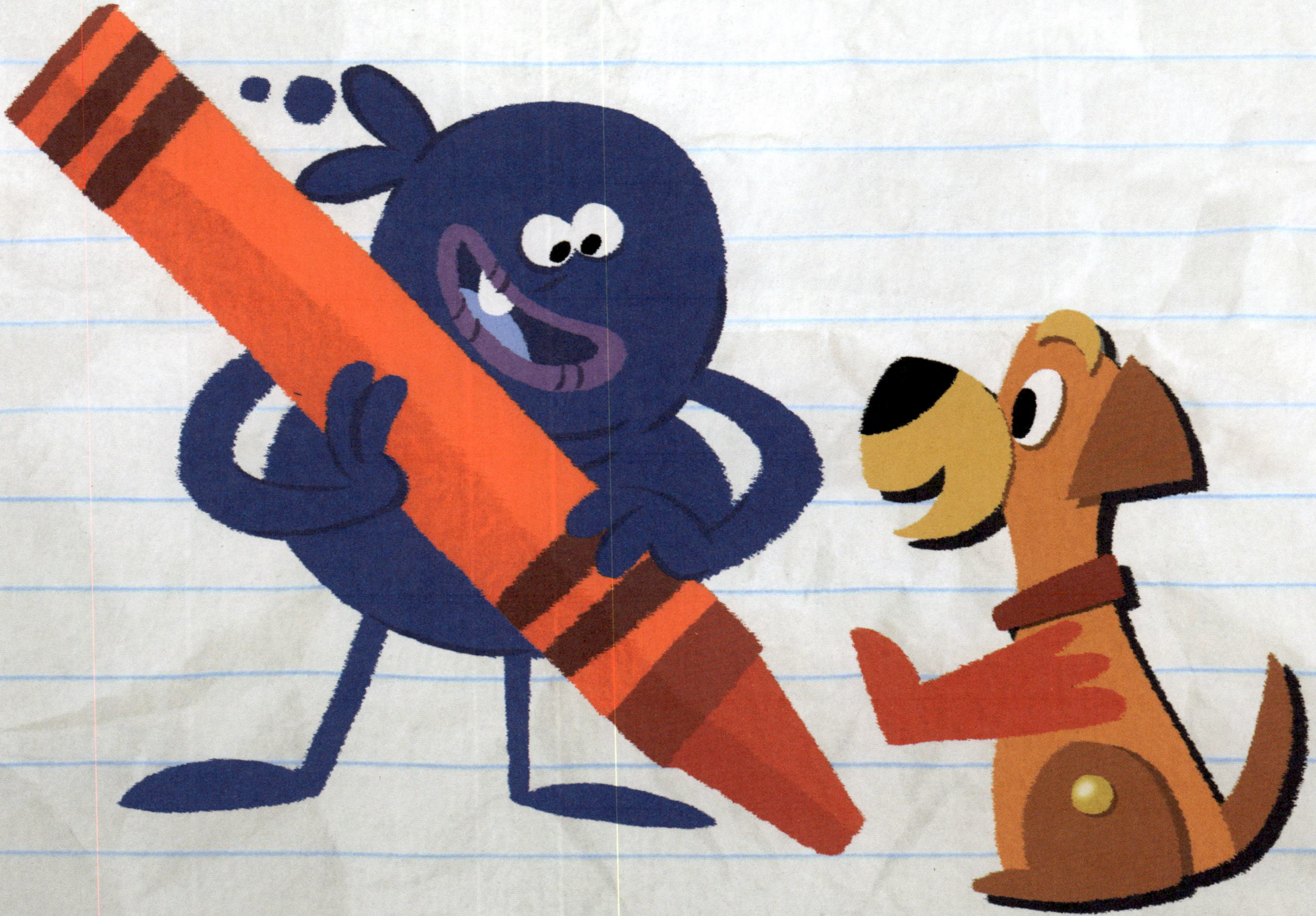

Splodge is drawing
another leg on Doggy.

"Come on, Doggy, keep up!"
Doggy is sad again.
"I don't like having four legs.
I don't feel like me anymore."

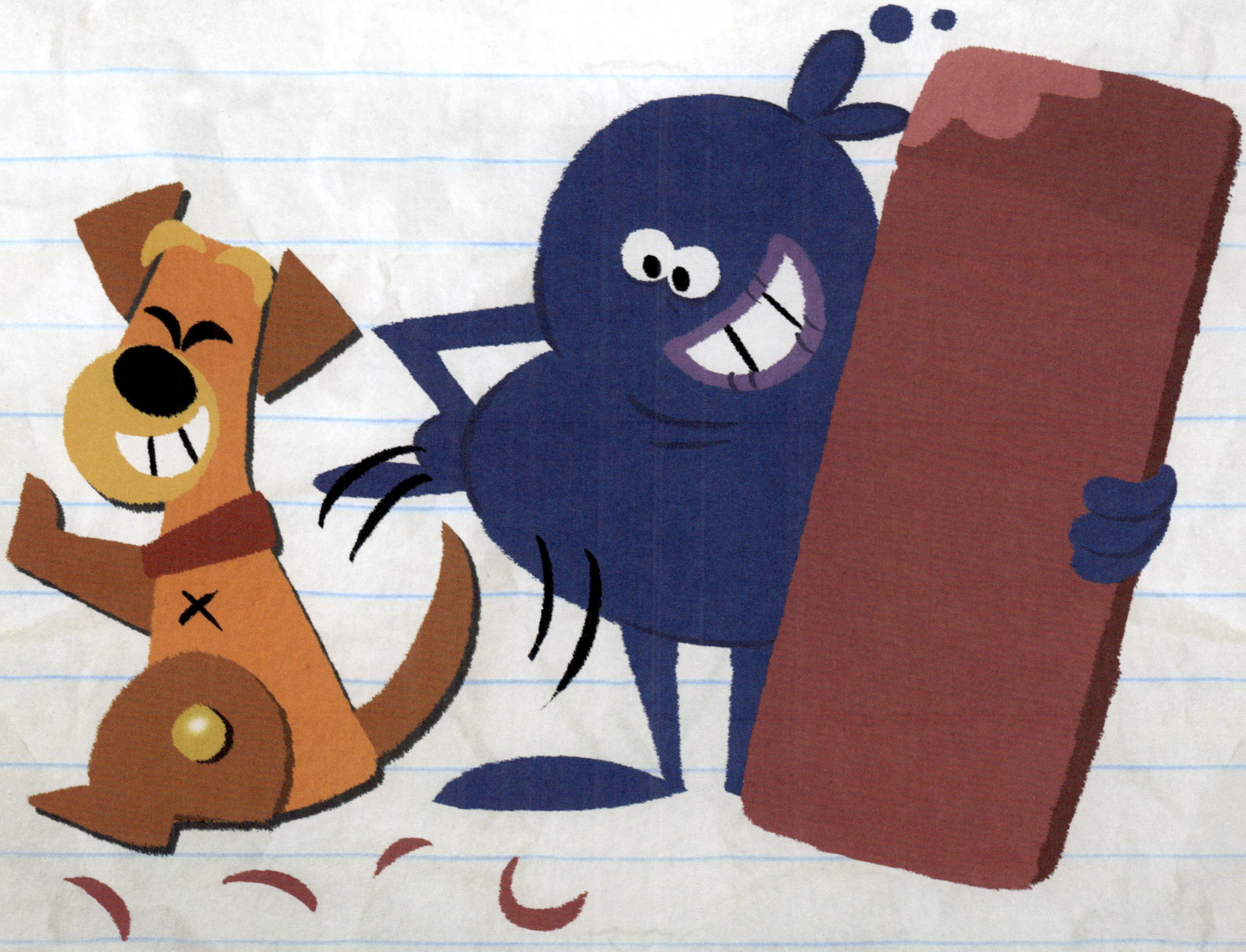

Splodge rubs out the new leg.
Doggy is happy again!

Look, Splodge –
it's nearly the end of
the book.

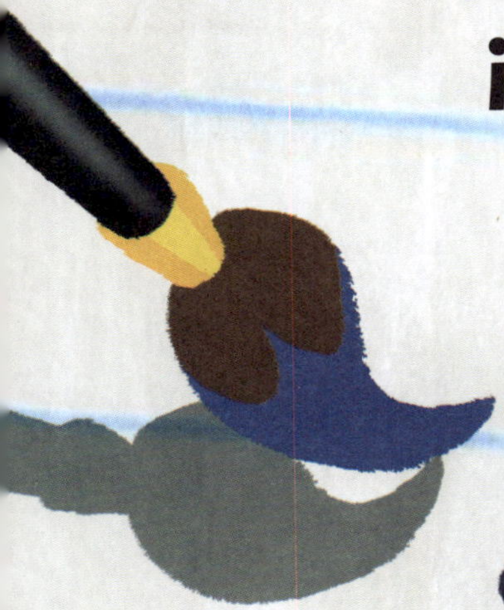

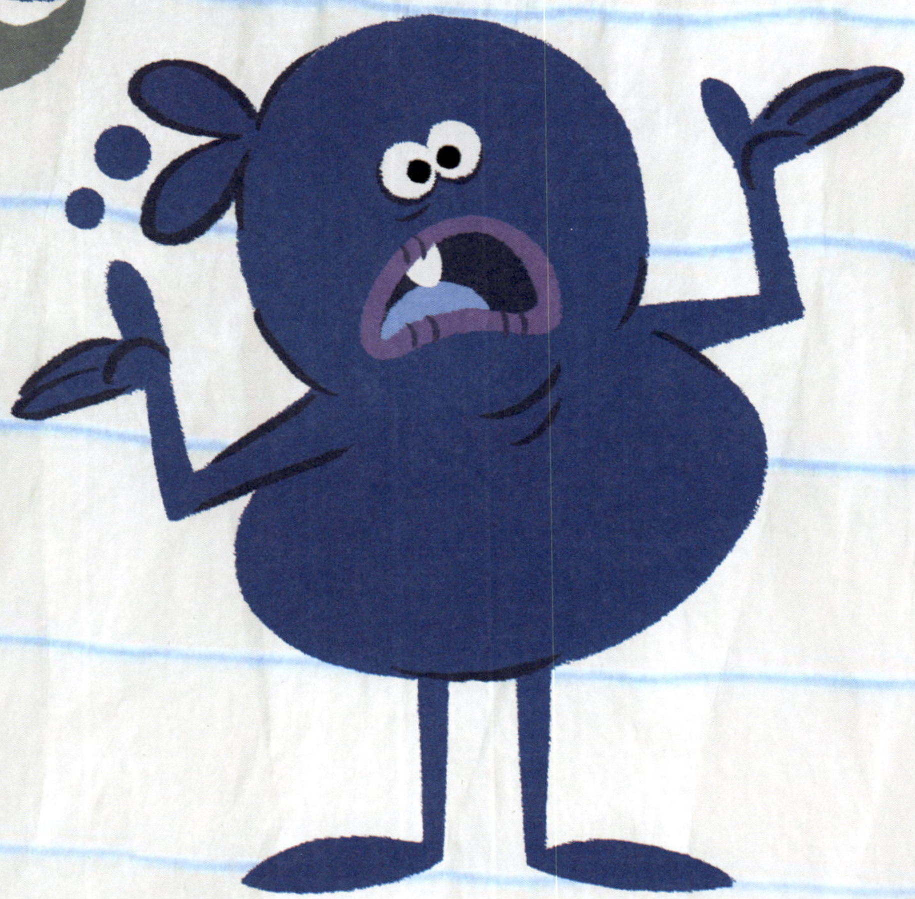

"But where can we go?
It's nearly time for bed."

It looks like Doggy has found something.

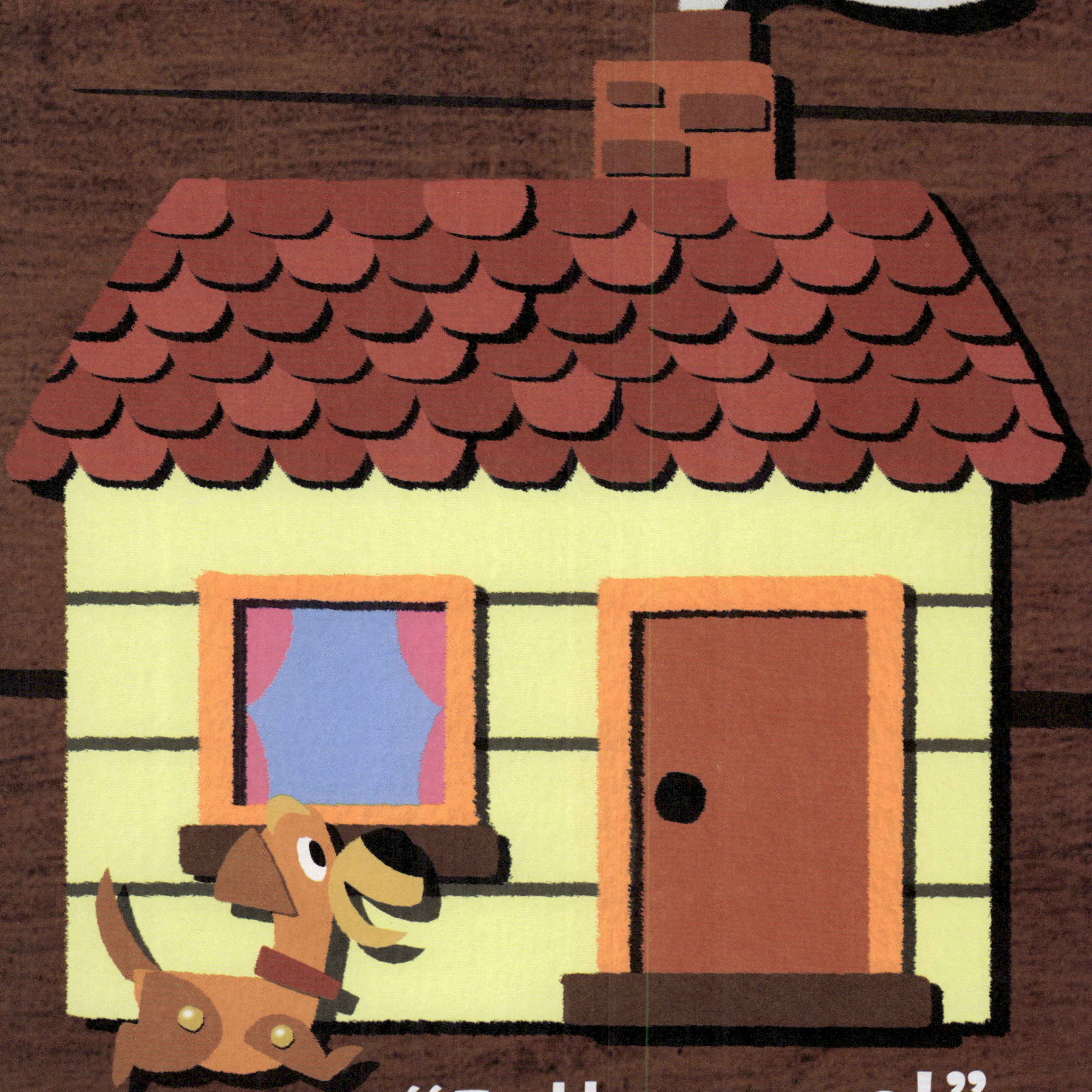

"Follow me!"

A house for
Splodge and Doggy!

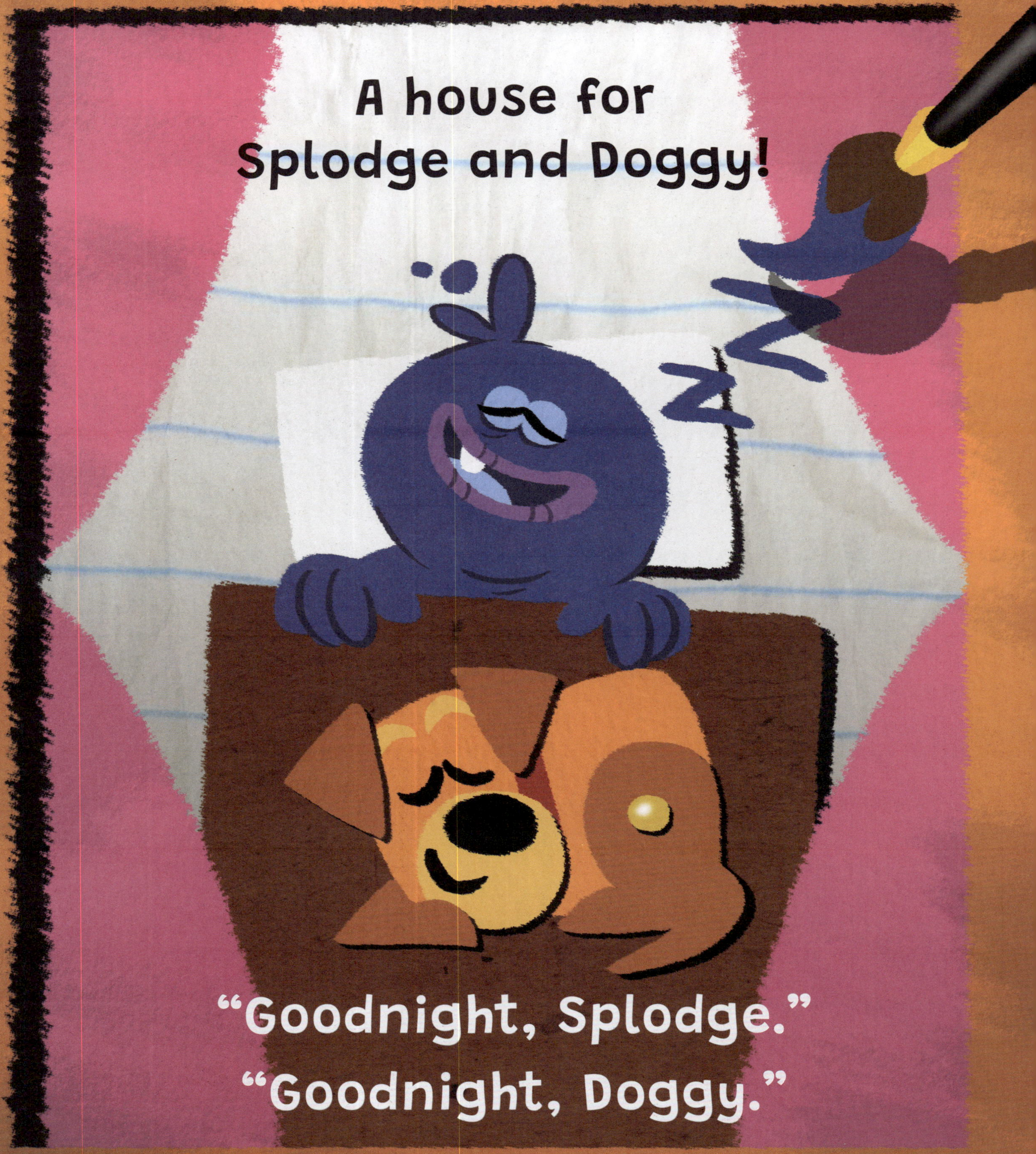

"Goodnight, Splodge."
"Goodnight, Doggy."

TURN THE PAGE FOR
INSIGHTS FROM THE ARTIST

# SPLODGE!

## DEVELOPING KEY FEATURES

### CHARACTERS

*Splodge!* may seem like a fairly simple story, centering on an ink blot and scribbles in a bookish world, and yet the characters have a lot of personality and heart. It was important that I established as much of their character as possible in their designs to showcase their personalities and bring them to life. With the main character, Splodge, the challenge was to bring an ink blot to life. I carefully thought through his design in order to make him memorable and unique to help capture the attention of young readers. I drew a simple splodge of ink to start with; however, this design conveyed little to no emotion. For my second attempt I made him rounder and friendlier, using bright colors and animated emotions and gestures.

For the character of Doggy, the description was a drawing of a dog with only three legs. This provided a good starting point, which developed into ideas of paper-craft cutouts, allowing Doggy's character to take on a personality of his own and contrast nicely against Splodge's ink-blot look. I decided to draw the Scribbles as more of a uniform gang to emphasize the feeling that Splodge and Doggy were being left out.

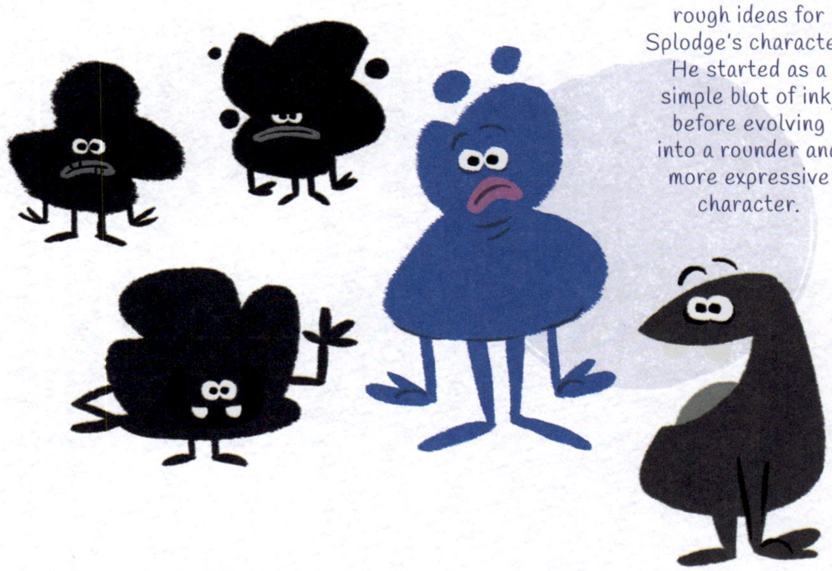

Here are various rough ideas for Splodge's character. He started as a simple blot of ink, before evolving into a rounder and more expressive character.

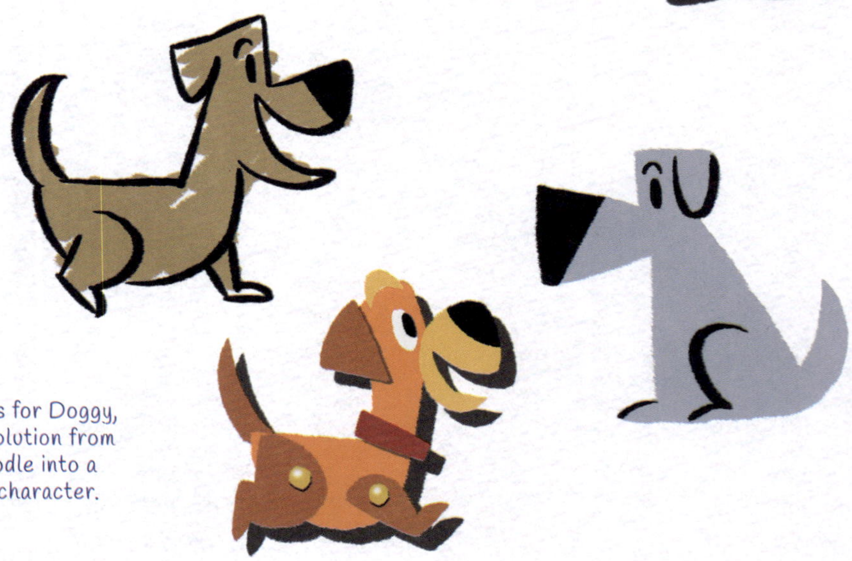

Rough sketches for Doggy, showing his evolution from the initial doodle into a cutout-style character.

Initial sketches for the Scribbles and their different shapes, exploring how they would contrast against each other and Splodge.

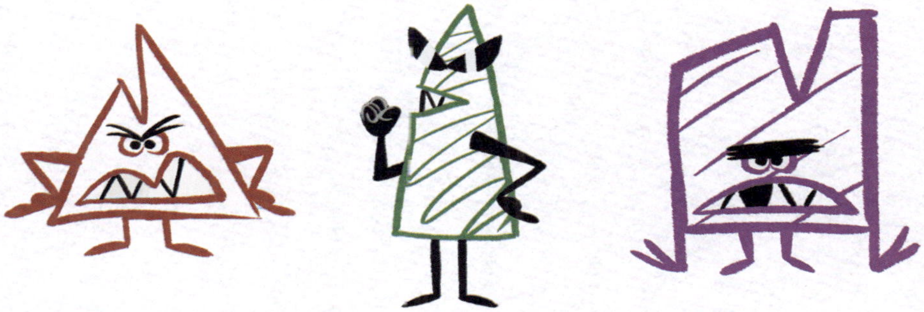

My idea for Scribble Cat included one continuous scribble or line, running from one page to the next.

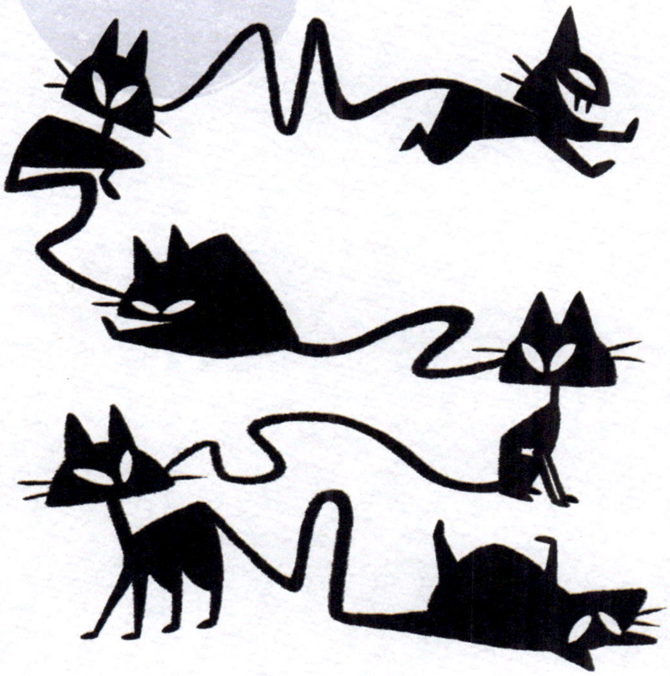

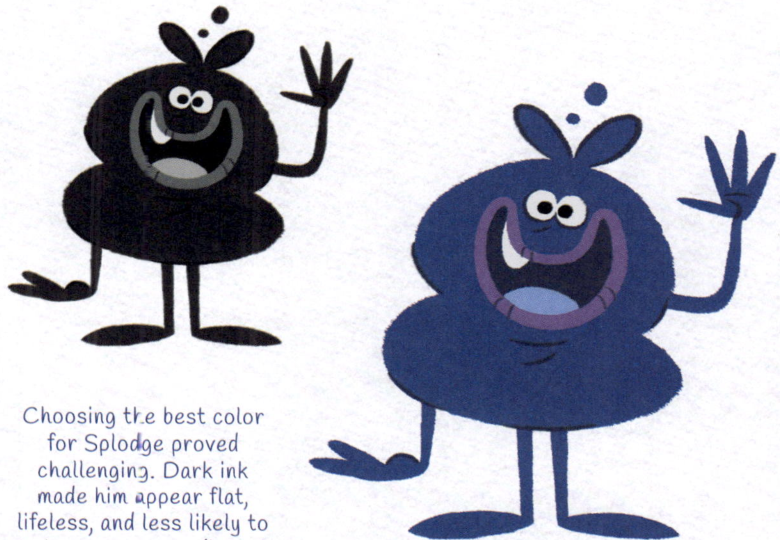

Choosing the best color for Splodge proved challenging. Dark ink made him appear flat, lifeless, and less likely to capture a young audience's attention, so I opted for a vivid blue instead.

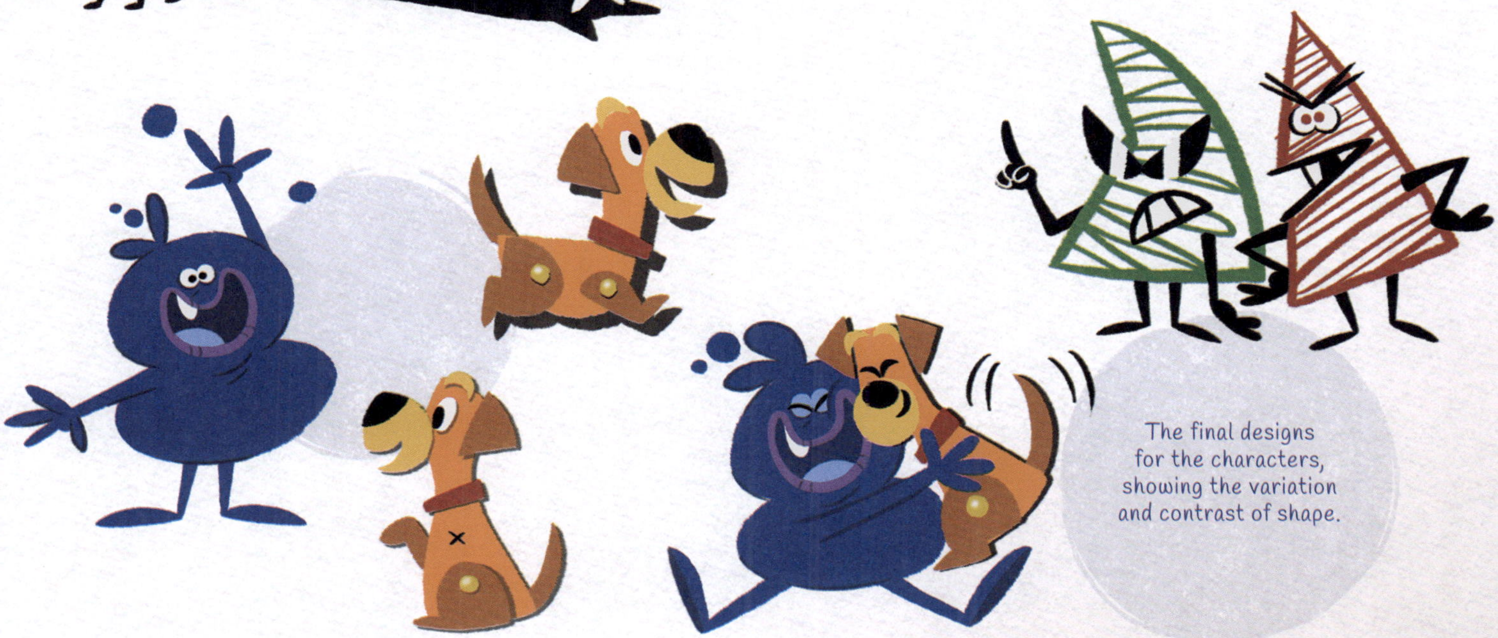

The final designs for the characters, showing the variation and contrast of shape.

## SETTING

Once I had established initial character designs, I moved on to exploring the overall look and feel of the story, including the tone and where it would be set. The idea for setting it in a bookish world conjured images of old, traditional-style illustrated books. Maybe the book was a work in progress, which would explain the ink blots and other half-drawn and scribbled characters. I also thought of setting it in a child's notebook. From that concept came the idea of someone creating the book as the story progresses. It seemed only natural to construct the page as seen from the point of view of the person creating the book, with pencils and other art materials creating fun boundaries and objects for the characters, and the reader, to interact with.

Here is a rough pass at the old, traditional-style ink storybook direction. This concept would have led to fairly repetitive pages and would struggle to keep the attention of a young reader.

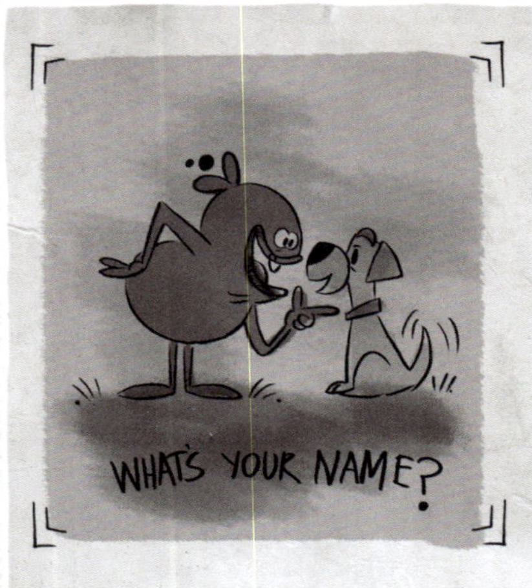


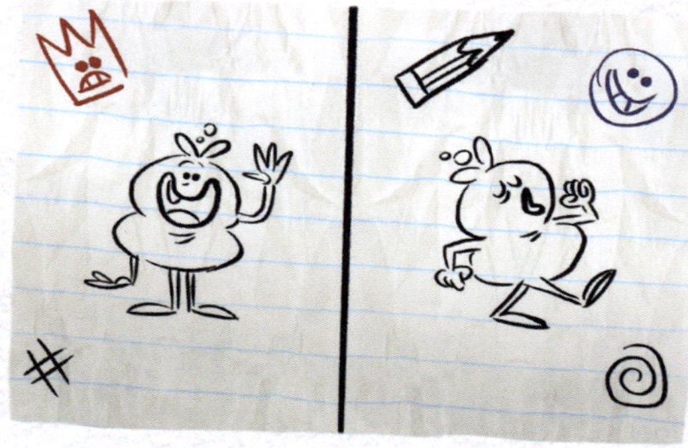

This draft shows the idea of setting the tale on the pages of a child's notebook, with doodles telling the story.

I started to explore and map out the pages from this point of view, adding the artist's materials to the pages. "X" marks where the characters will go.

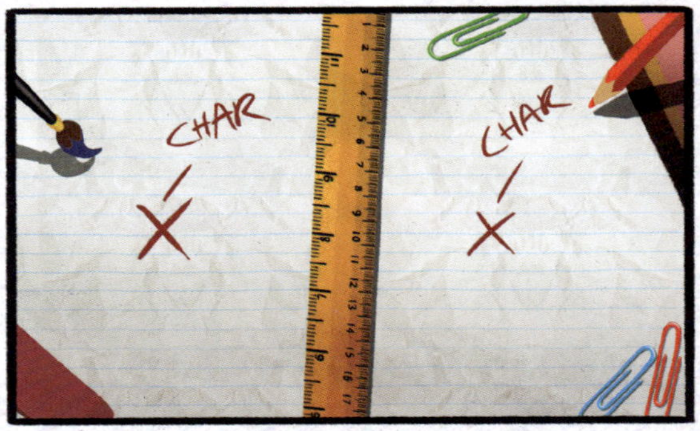


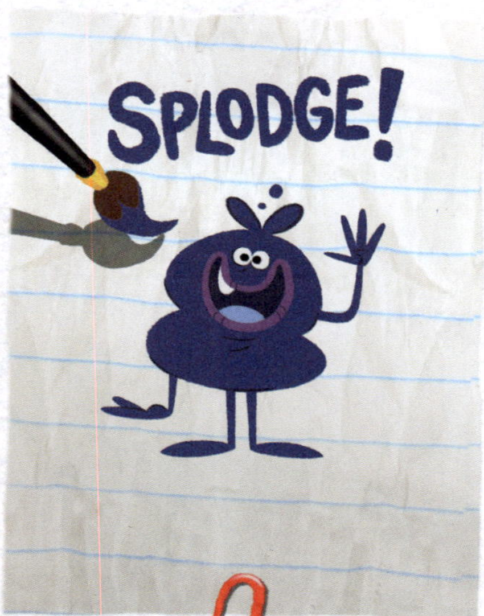


My ideas for the setting progressed to this concept, where the reader sees the pages from the point of view of the artist creating the story.

I added the art materials to create the impression that the reader is watching the book being made.

PAINTBRUSH INKING SPLODGE

MUSIC NOTES BEING DRAWN

The first spread from the book.

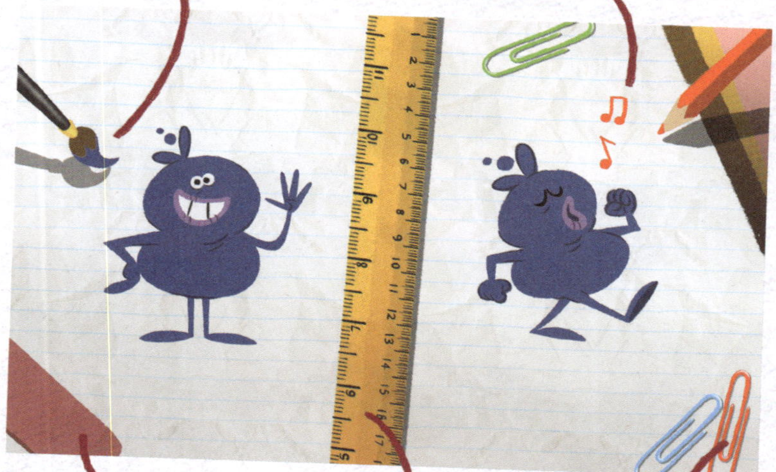

ERASER

RULER

PAPER CLIPS

## PAGE LAYOUT

Another important factor to consider was how I would construct the pages to start to bring the story to life. Keeping the intended audience in mind, I made creating a lively, eye-catching look my main priority when laying out the page. Sketching out a number of different thumbnails is really helpful for giving you an idea of how the page will look and read. After drawing various versions of the initial thumbnail, I moved on to color blocking. Next I began to rough out a more detailed layout of how the final page would look, adding in the final details before completing a final pass.

I roughed out some initial thumbnails to give me an idea of how the page layout would work.

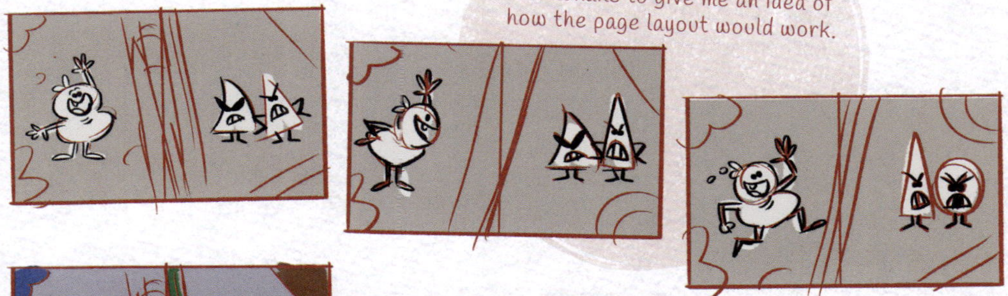

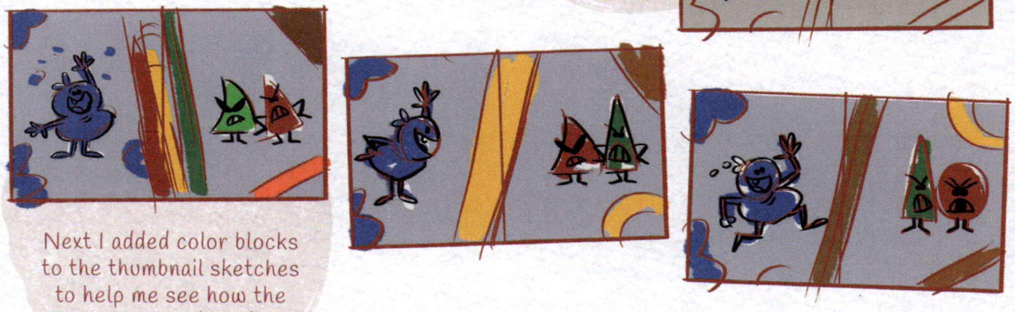

Next I added color blocks to the thumbnail sketches to help me see how the pages would read.

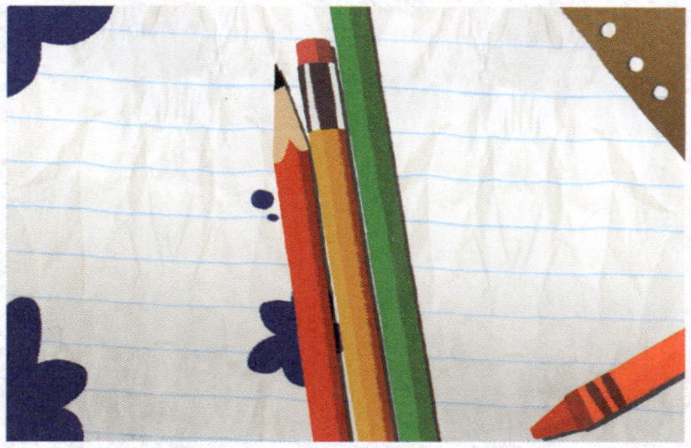

This thumbnail provided an overall idea of how the page would look.

Next I added in the characters, keeping in mind the spread dimensions and bleed.

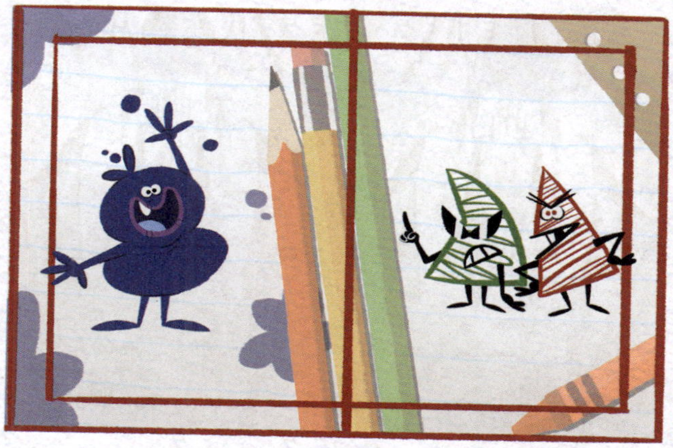

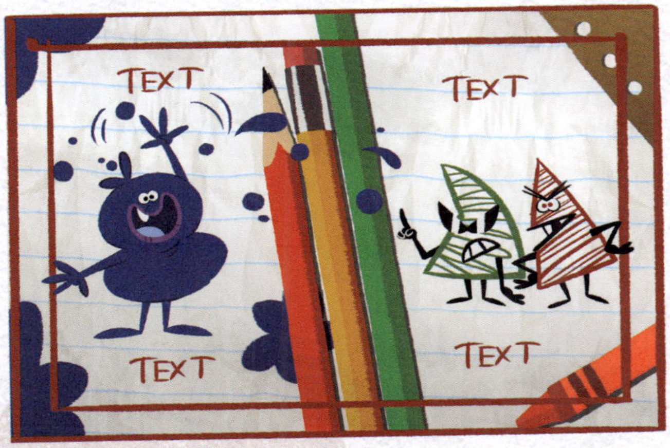


I then decided where the story text would sit on the page and how the rest of the artwork would work around it.

A final spread design, ready for the addition of text.

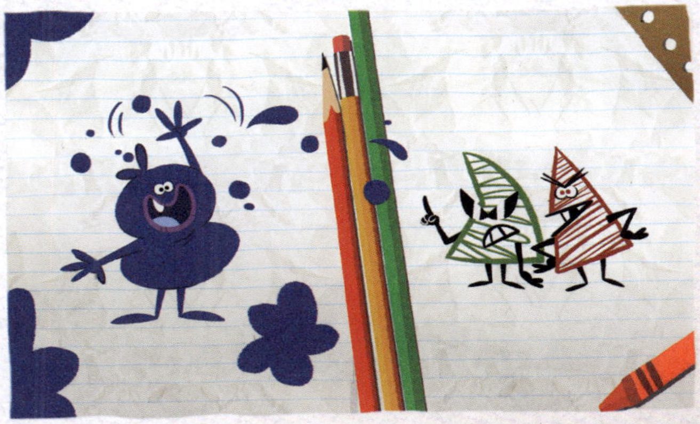

## CUTOUT STYLE

Once the initial character designs and overall look of the book was formed, I moved on to developing the characters in more detail and exploring their contrasting origins: Splodge as an ink blot, the Scribbles as scribbles, and Doggy as a cutout paper-craft. Their different styles fitted the playful tone of the book and provided visually interesting ways to tell the story. It also made it more engaging for young readers, inviting them to spot the different types of character and their details. While Doggy's character had to fit within his paper-craft cutout design, he also needed to have enough personality and energy to interact with Splodge. I explored a number of different colors for his design, settling on one that would fit well with the light-hearted tone of the story. Another element of the paper cutout theme was Splodge and Doggy's house at the end of the story. The inclusion of details like the scissors and ruler on the spreads all hint that the artist is making something: the house.

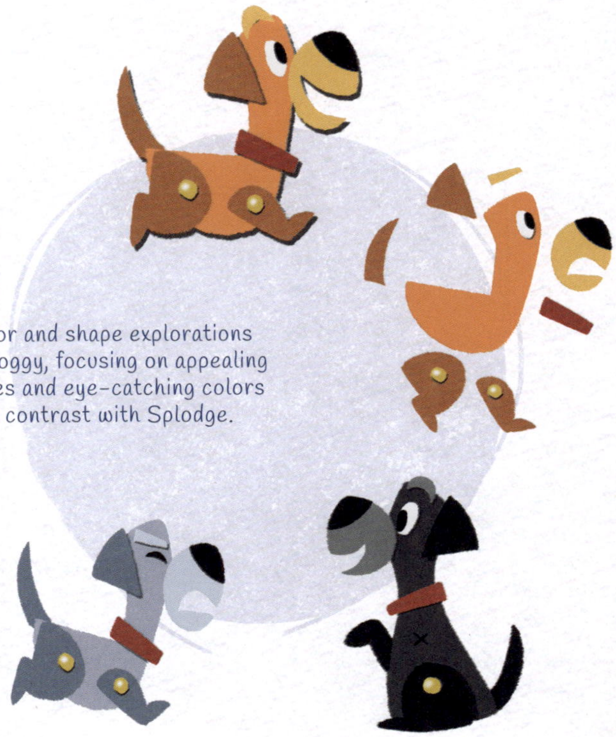

Color and shape explorations for Doggy, focusing on appealing shapes and eye-catching colors to contrast with Splodge.

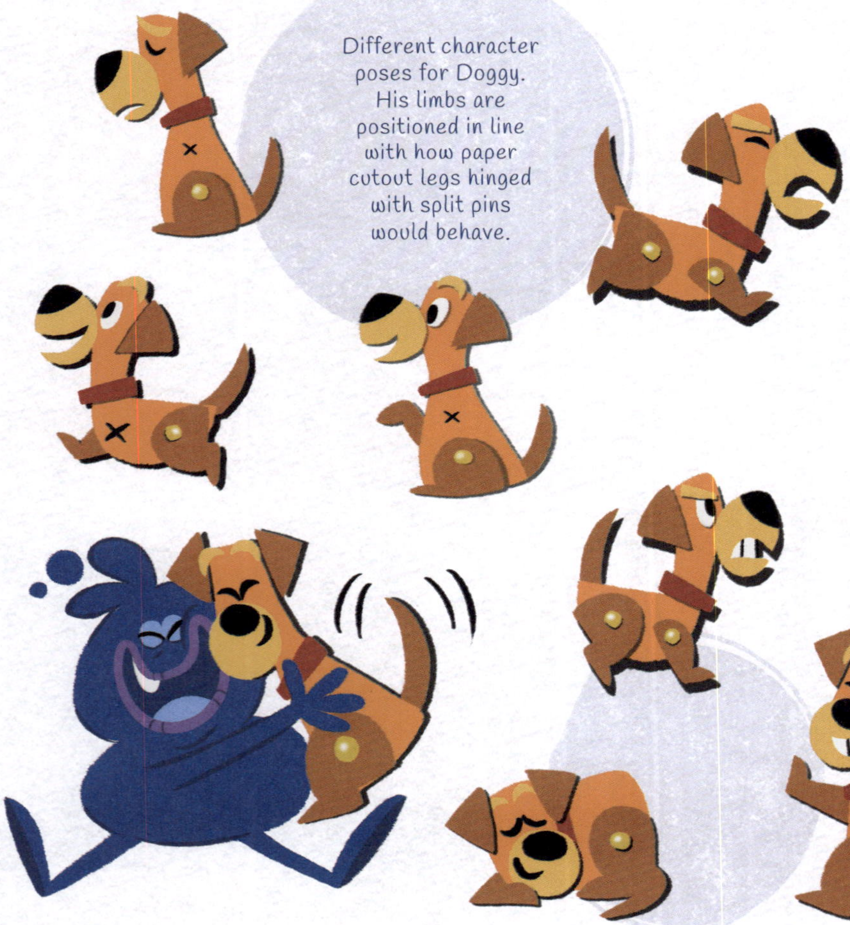

Different character poses for Doggy. His limbs are positioned in line with how paper cutout legs hinged with split pins would behave.

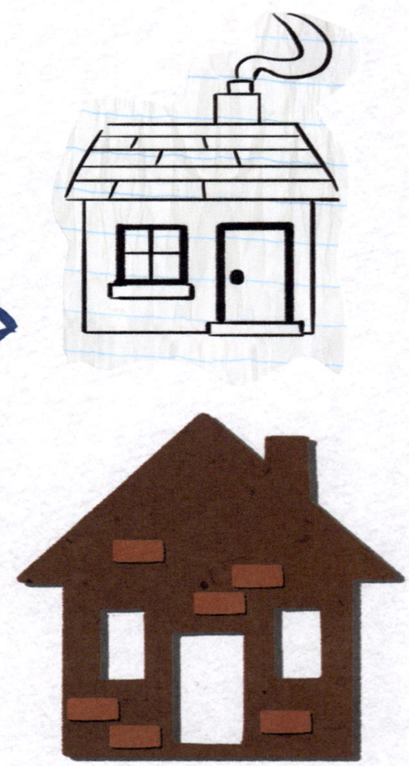

Initial ideas for the house, evolving from the initial ink drawing to cutout-style look.

Eye-catching color variations for the cutout house.

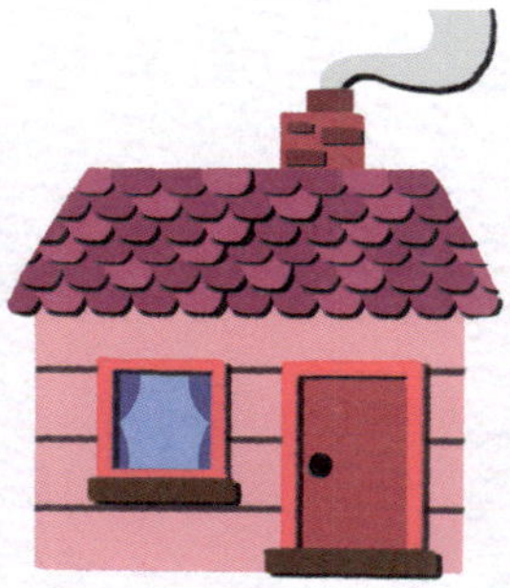

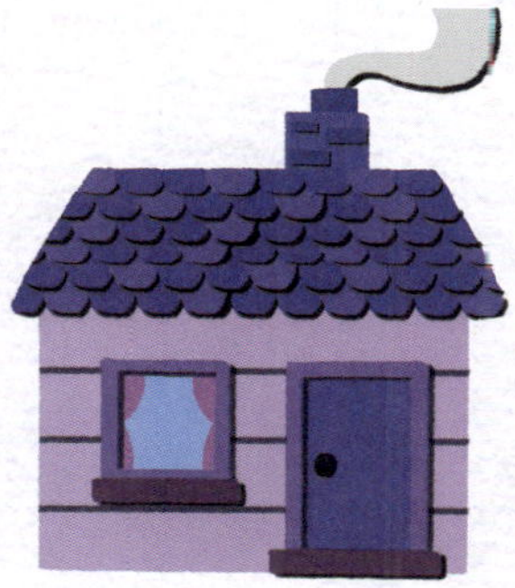

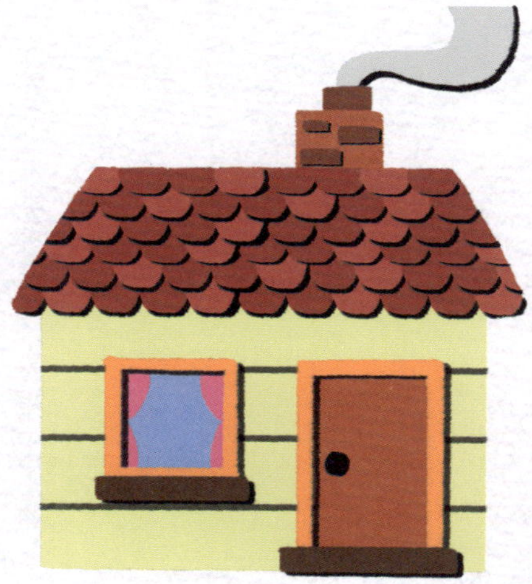

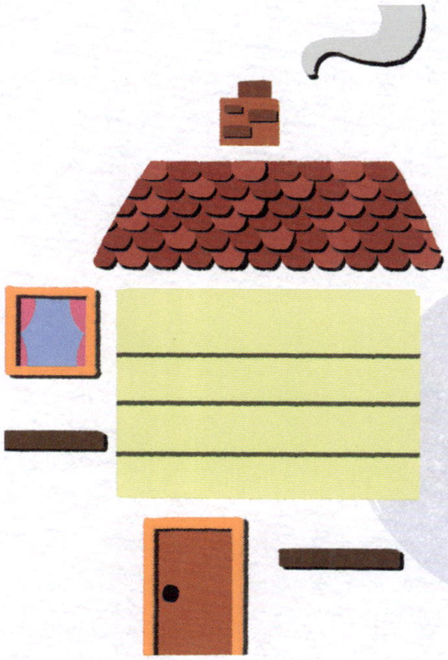

Breakdown of the paper cutout house, exploring how it fits in the world.

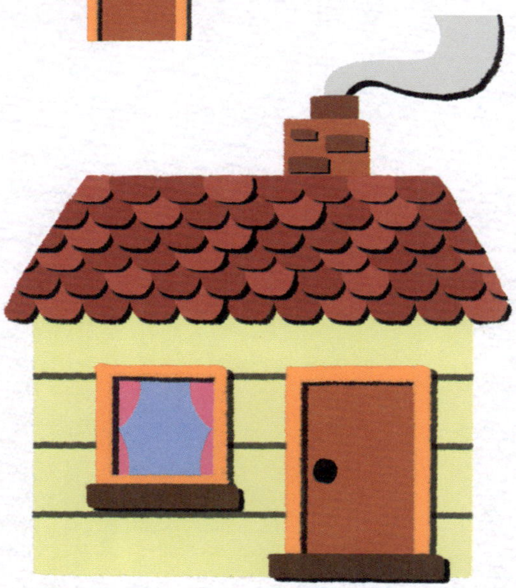

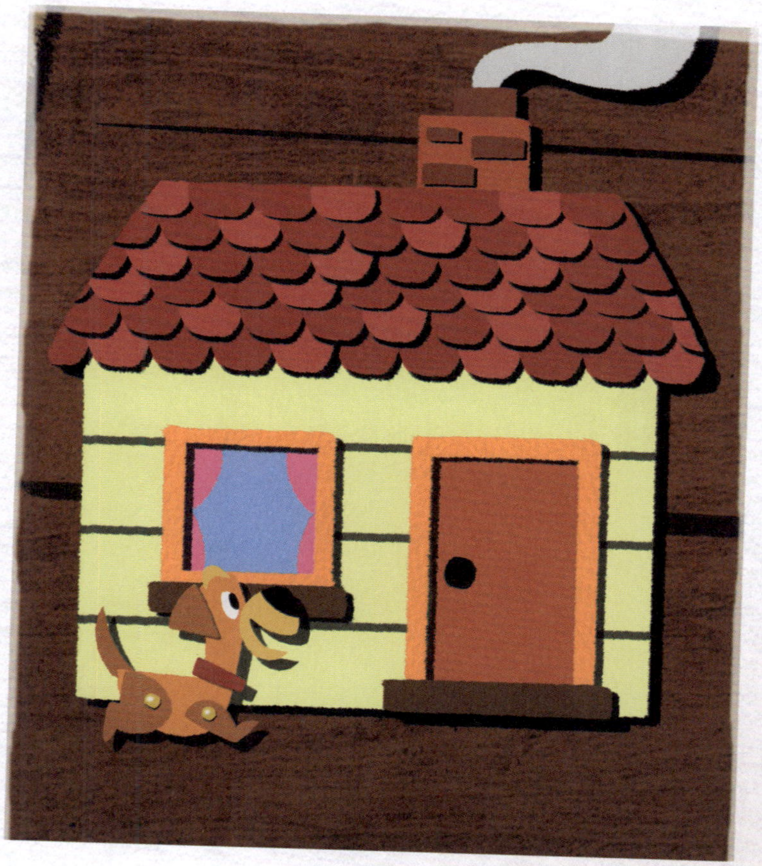

The house as it appears on the final spread.

# ANALYSIS

Bringing the story of *Splodge!* to life was a fun journey. How I envisioned the characters and story changed over the course of the design process; the characters almost helped create their own world as the project progressed and as the paper-cutout style of Doggy's character was introduced. Splodge's character was a delight to create and added much personality and comic relief to the story. While the story itself was pretty straightforward, condensing the illustrations into sixteen pages proved challenging, as it meant some aspects of the story were not as fleshed out as I would have liked them to be.

My advice for illustrators working on a similar story for children would be to know your audience and play to its strengths. For stories aimed at young children, opt for friendlier and more welcoming visuals to capture and hold their interest. Additionally, find what you love in the story and emphasize it. It will show in the finished product and make it all the more special.

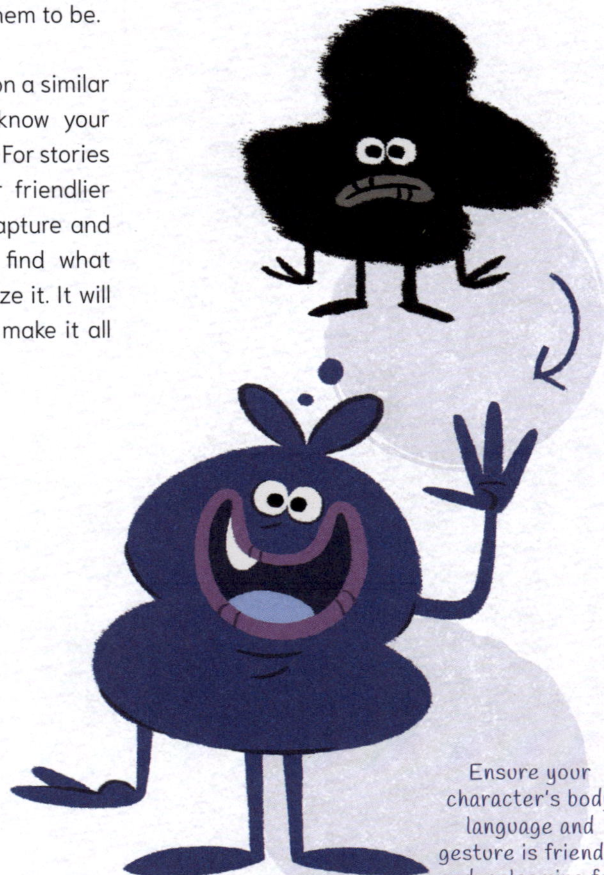

Ensure your character's body language and gesture is friendly and welcoming for young readers.

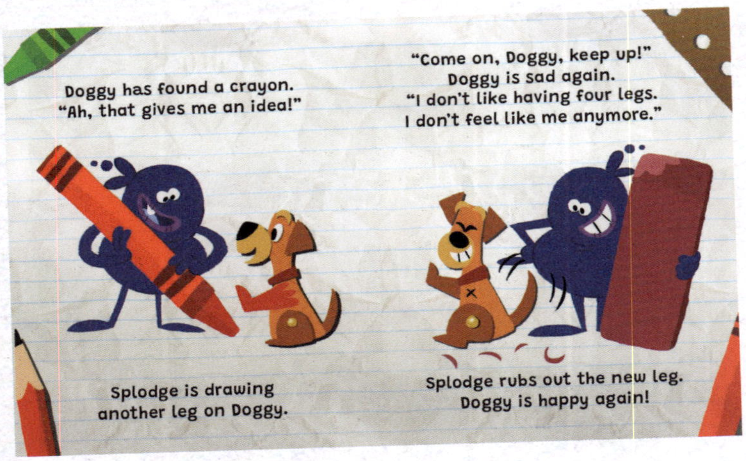


When laying out your pages, think carefully about how you can best represent the key story moments.

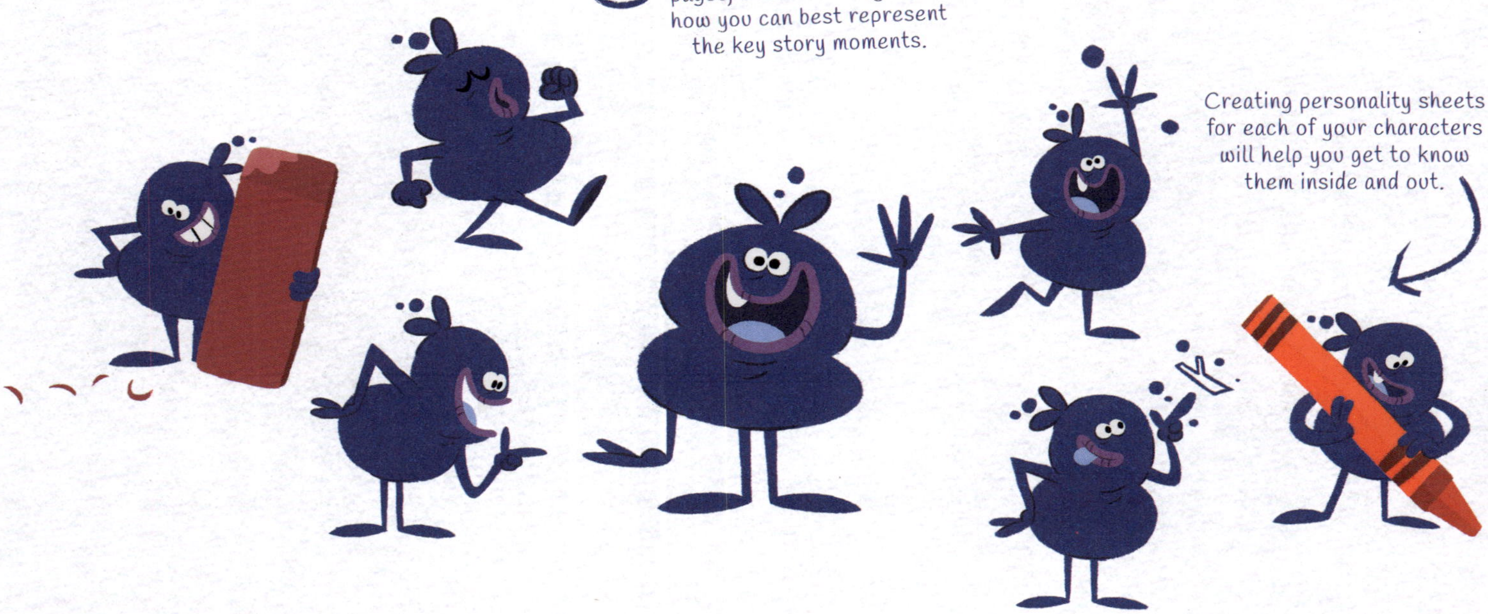

Creating personality sheets for each of your characters will help you get to know them inside and out.

Make sure you know your character from every angle.

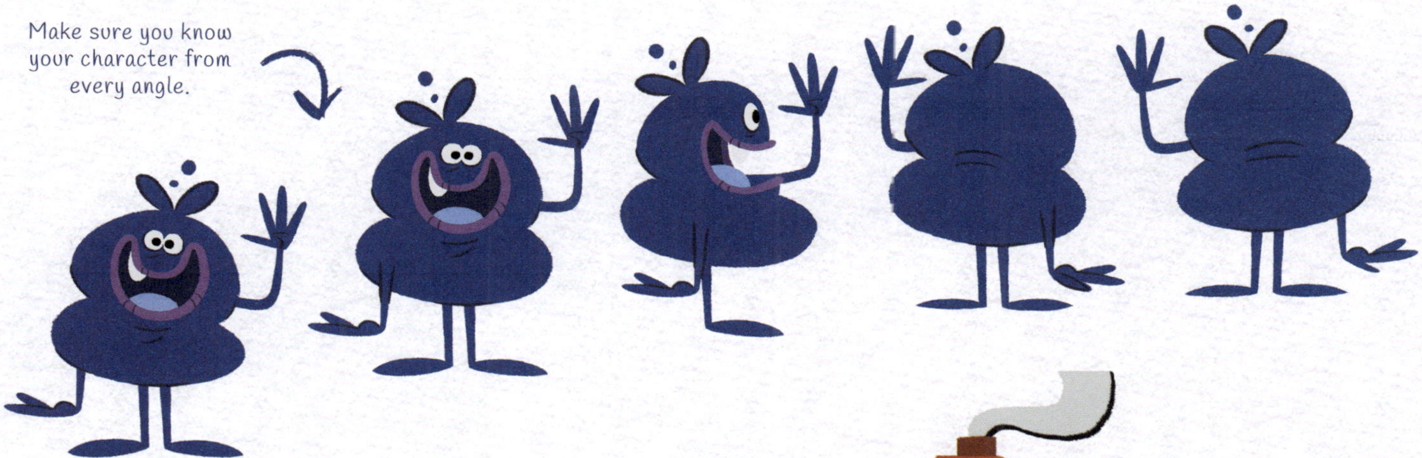

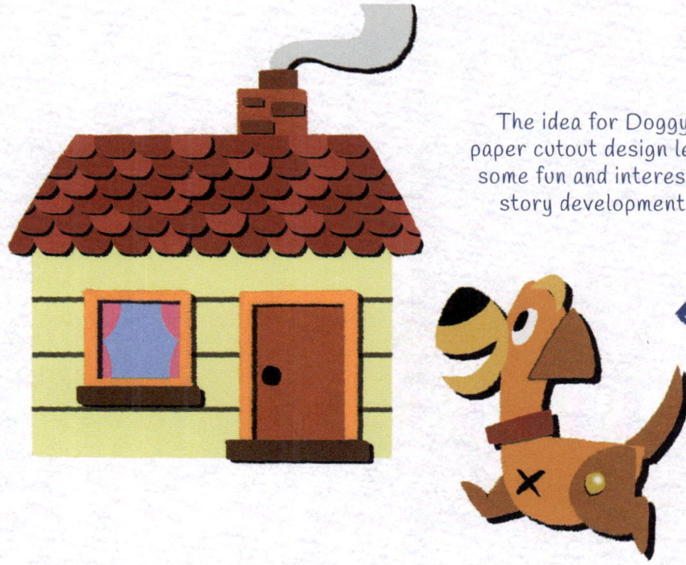

The idea for Doggy's paper cutout design led to some fun and interesting story developments.

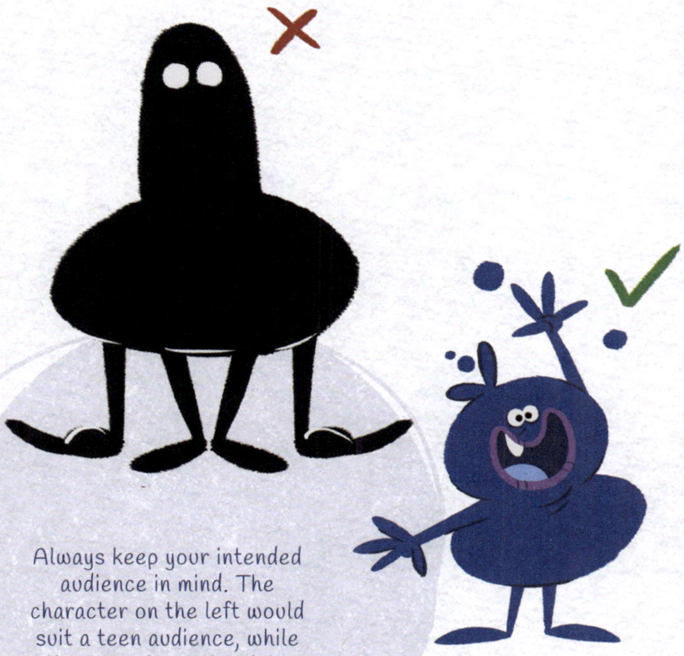

Always keep your intended audience in mind. The character on the left would suit a teen audience, while the example on the right is more child-friendly.

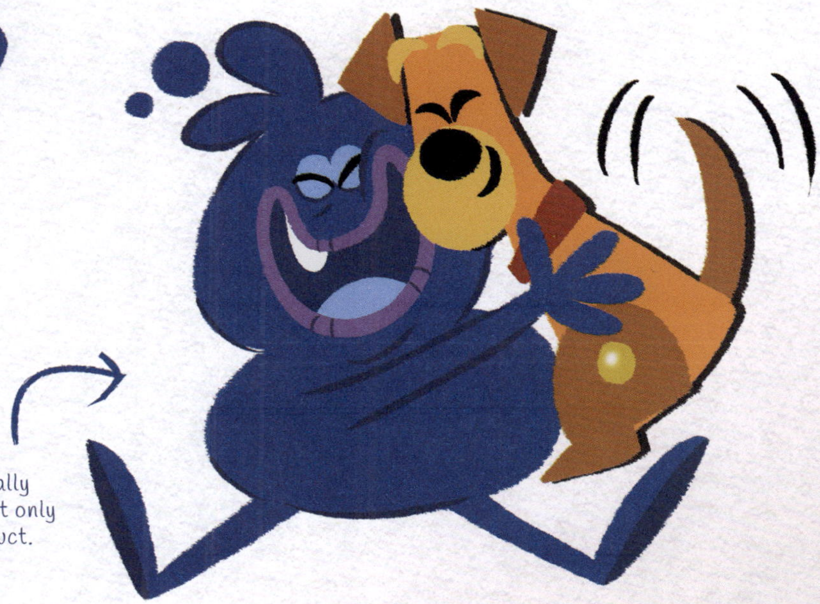

The friendship between Splodge and Doggy was really heartwarming – emphasizing it only enhanced the finished product.

# Fred the Fish

Written by

GREG DOBBINS

Illustrated by

LAURA PROIETTI

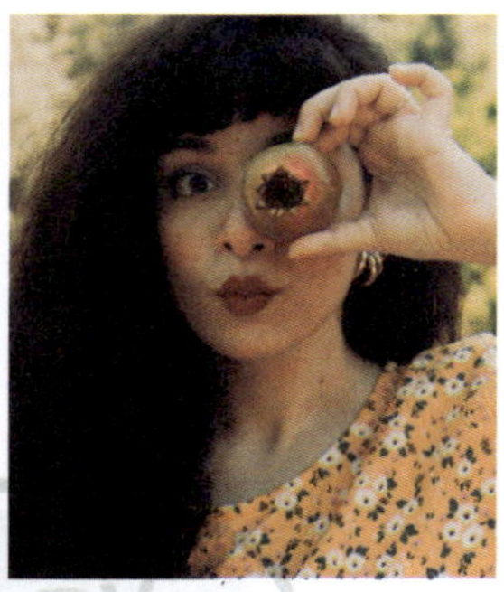

Illustrator

**instagram.com/laura_illustrator**

Born in Sicily, Laura graduated from art school before studying illustration and animation at the School of Comics. She now works as an illustrator for various Italian and international publishing editorials.

A STORY FOR AGES 4–6 YEARS

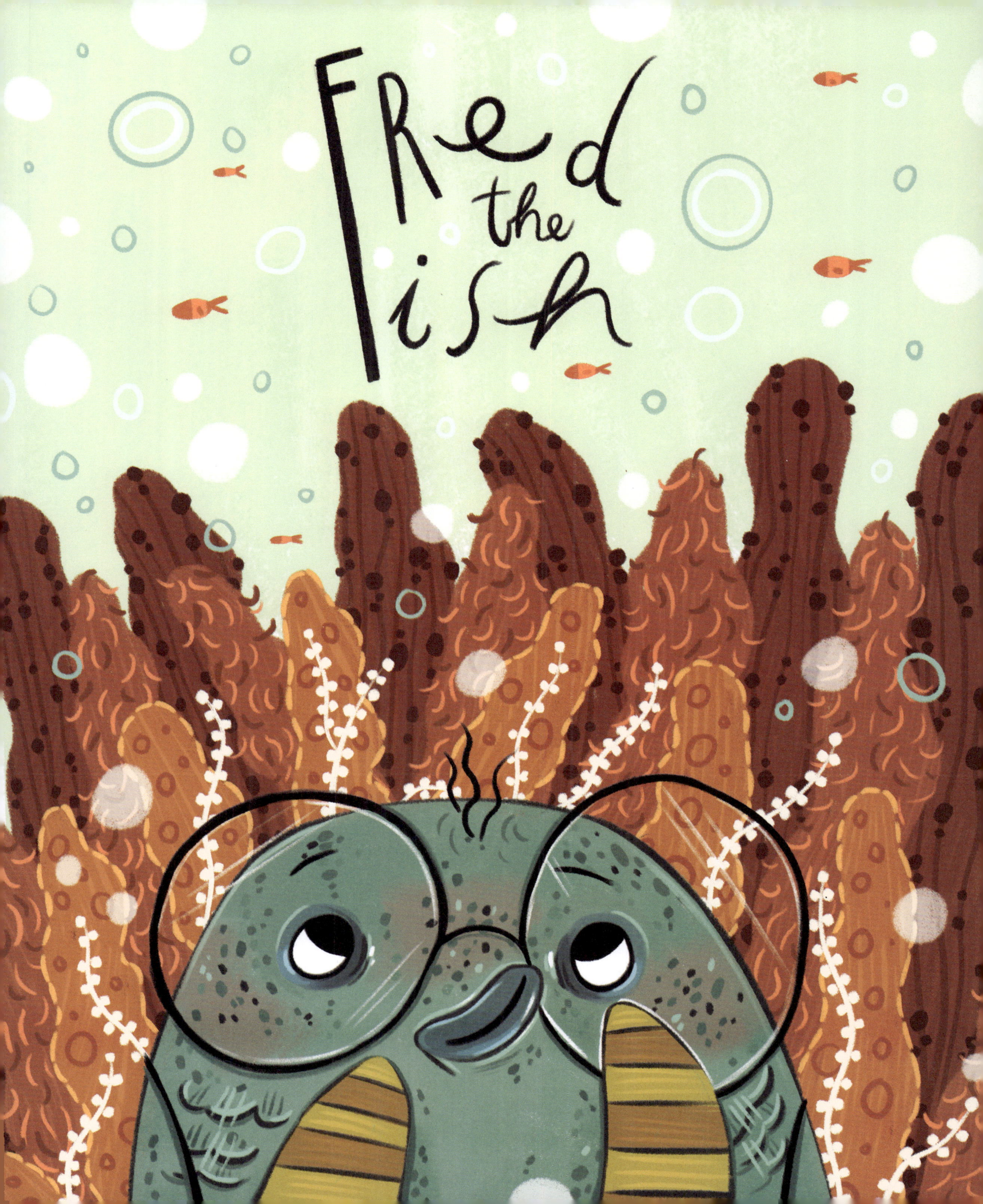
Fred
the
Fish

Fred the Fish had just one wish:
his fish tank needed a satellite dish.
He really wanted his own TV,
to watch some films about the sea.

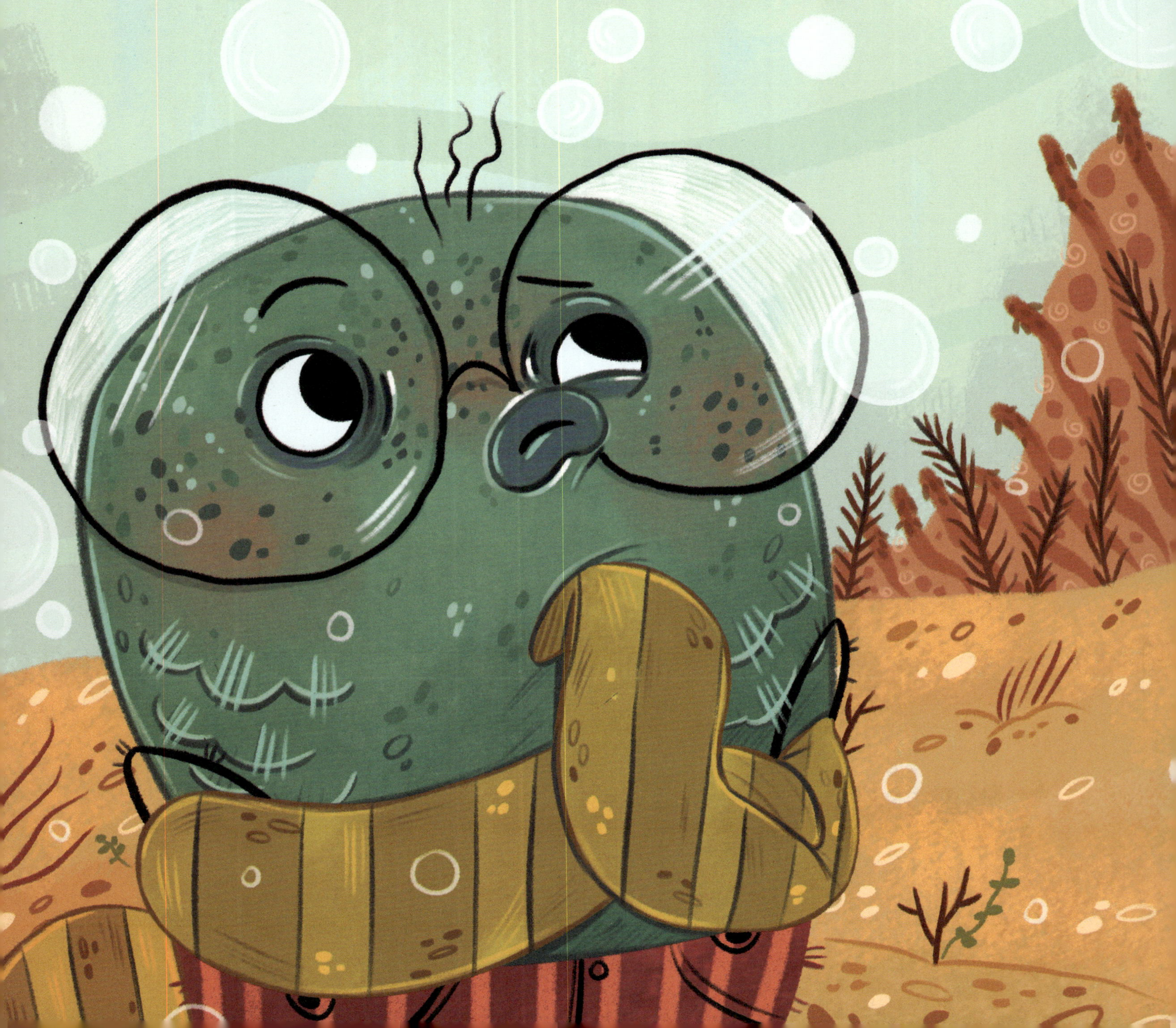

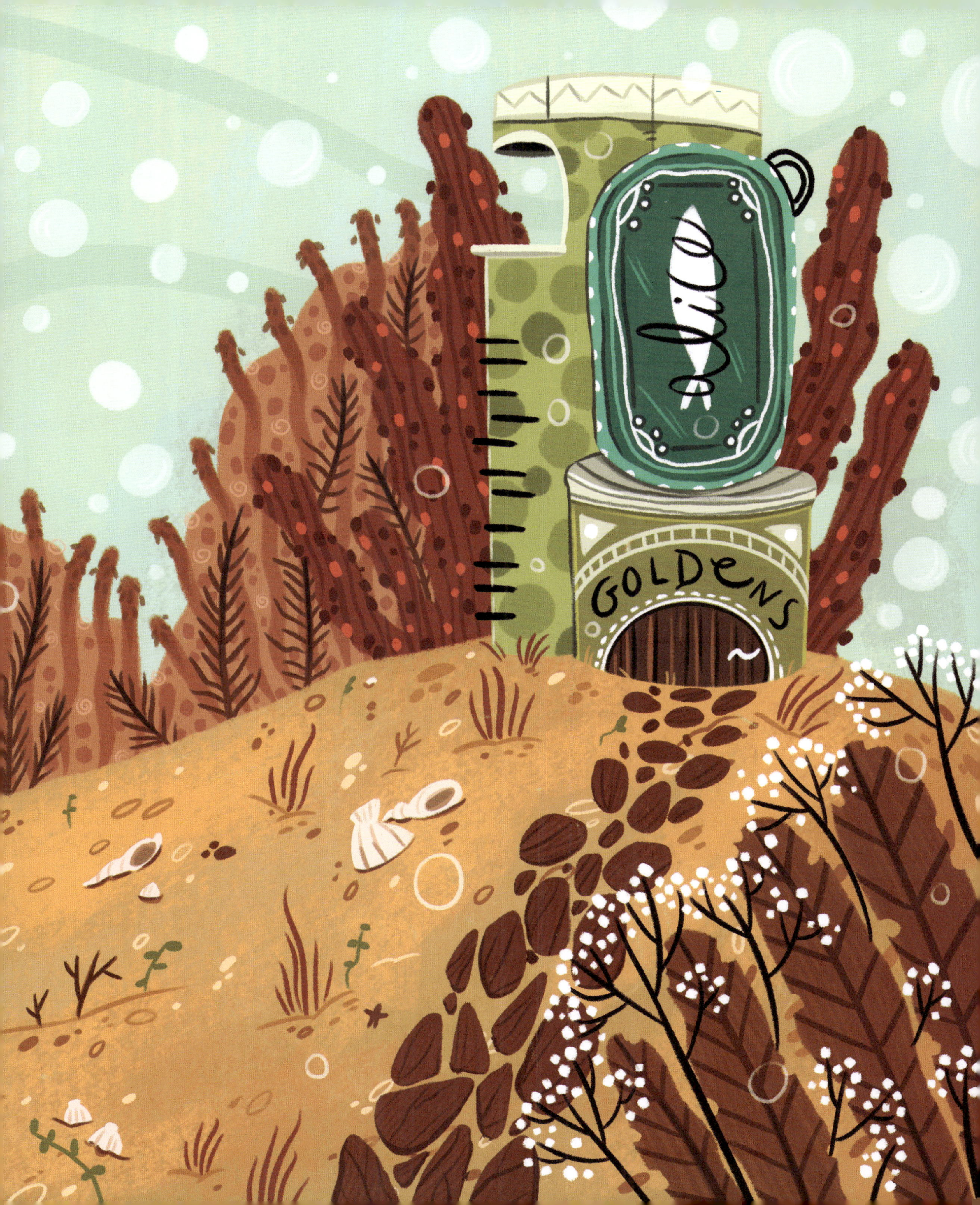
GOLDENS

So off he went on a special mission,
for something to help with this ambition.
Searching the kitchen, looking in drawers,
for something special to help his cause.

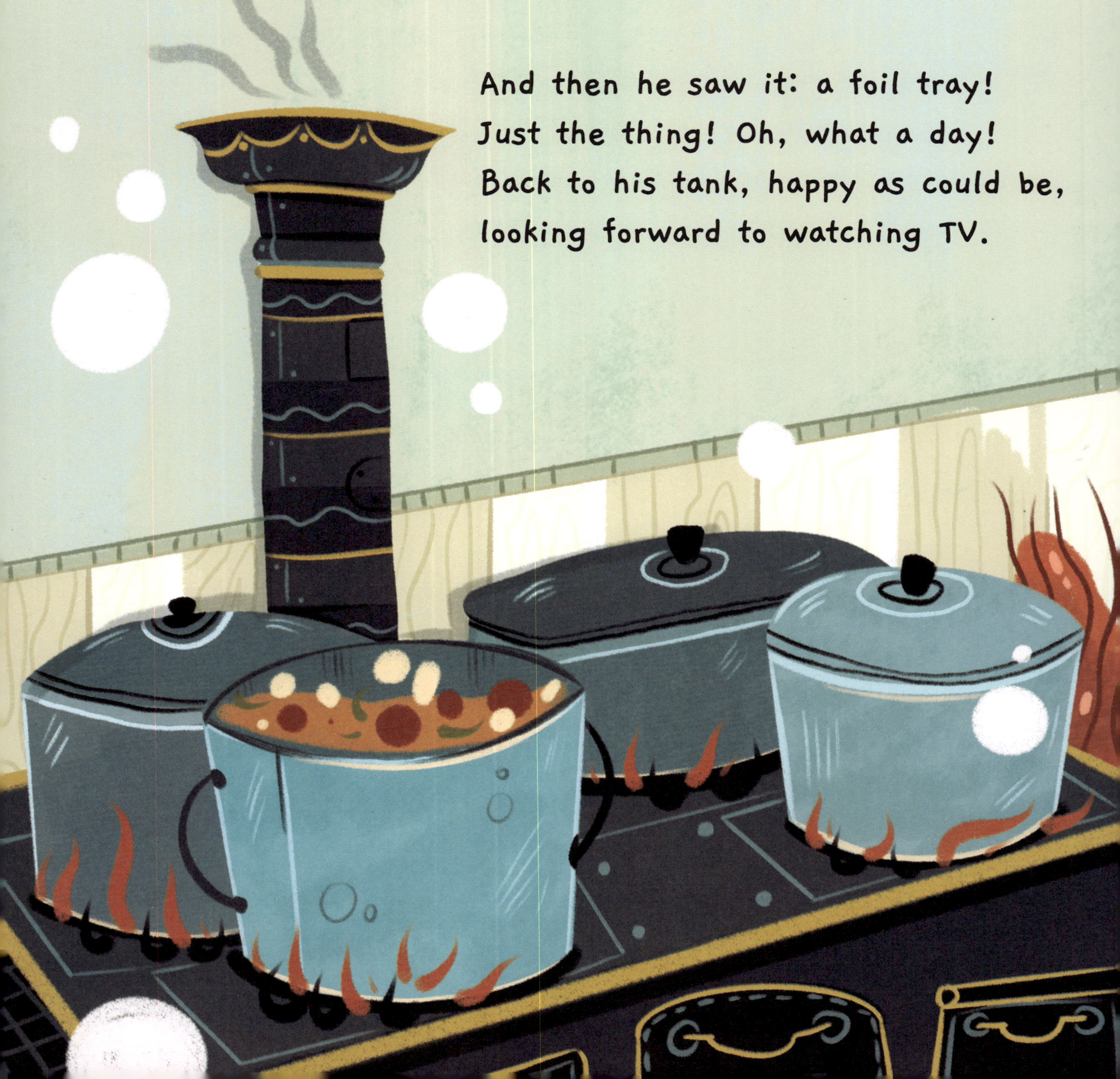

And then he saw it: a foil tray!
Just the thing! Oh, what a day!
Back to his tank, happy as could be,
looking forward to watching TV.

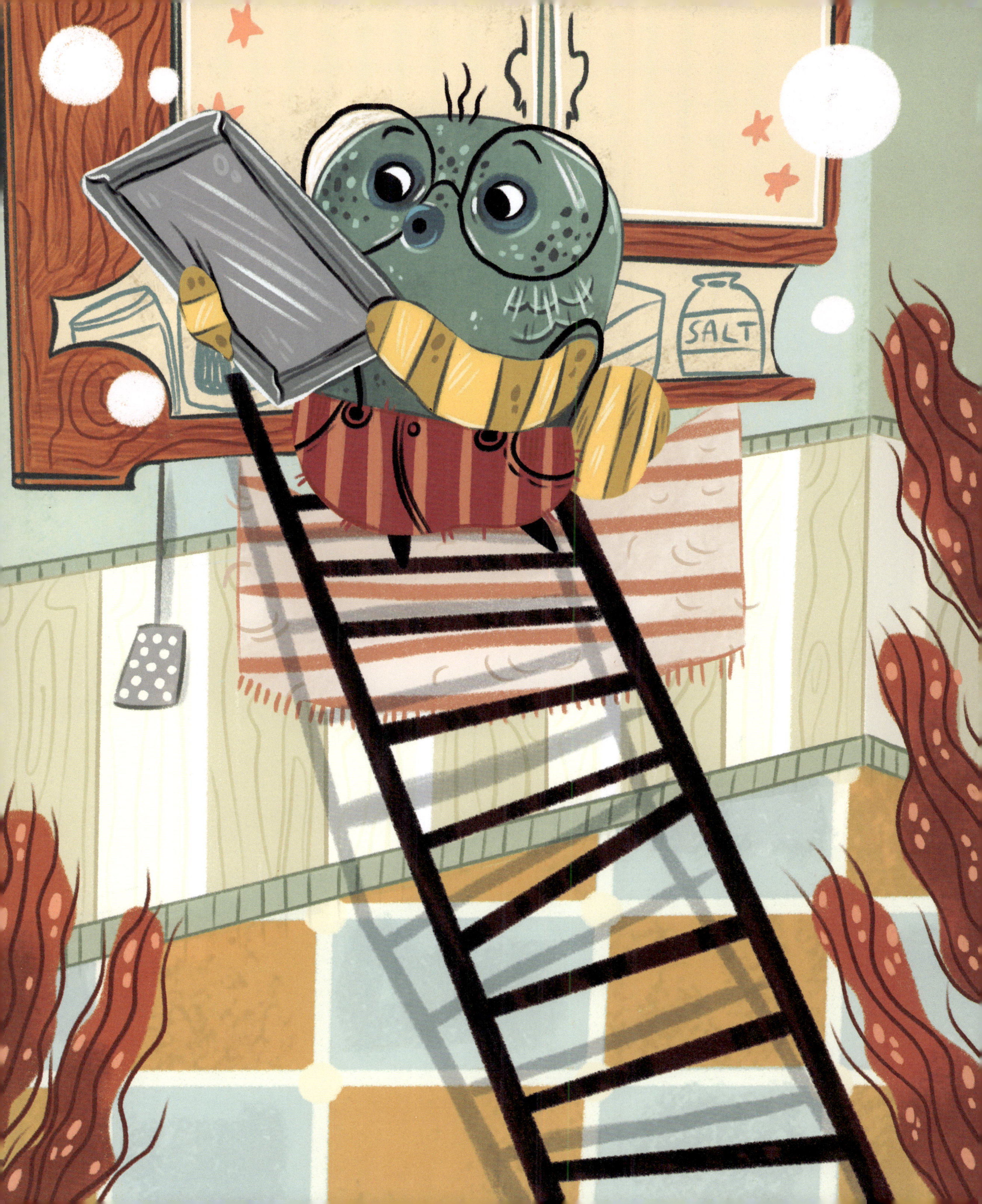
SALT

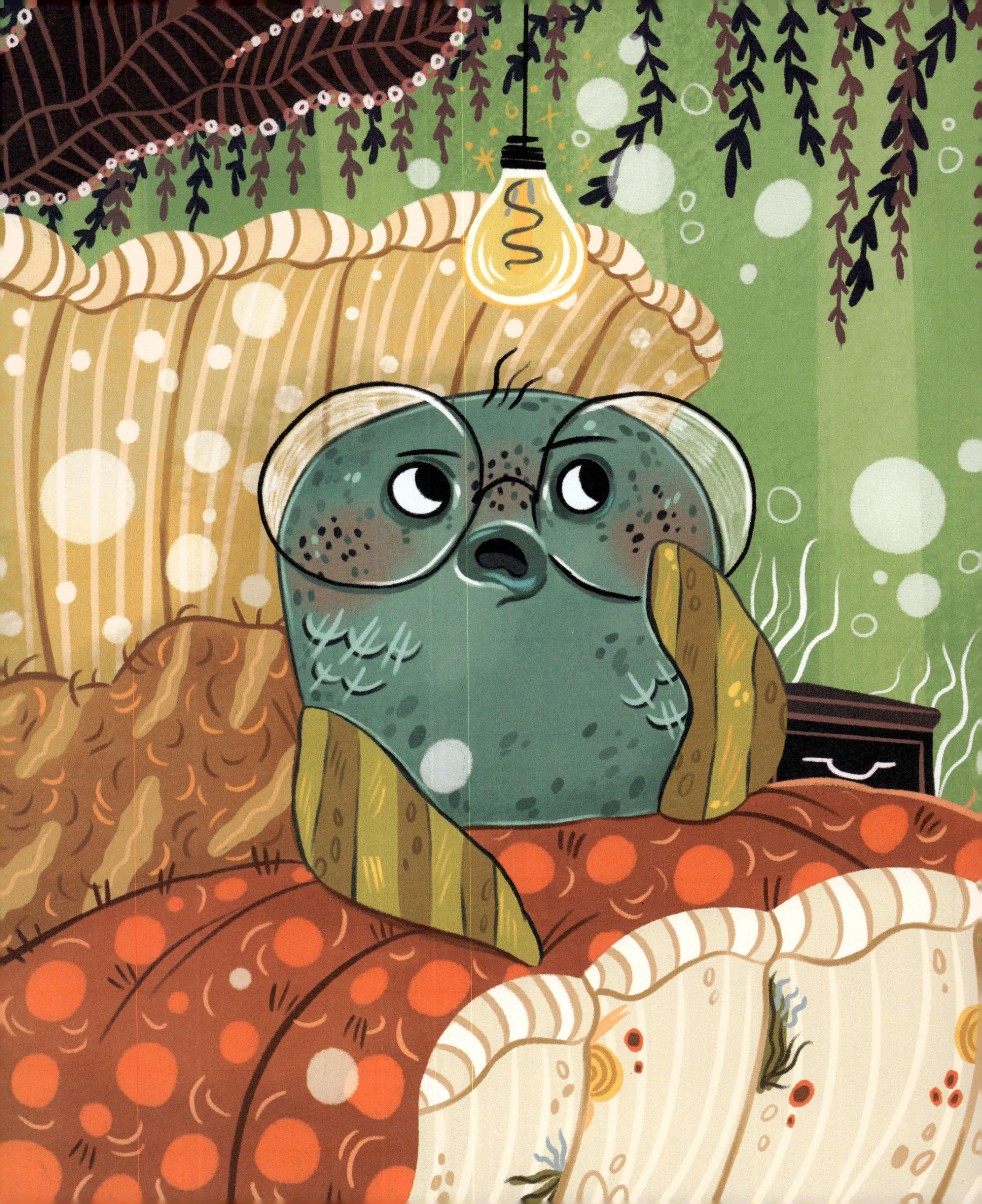

But in the morning, when he got out of bed,
he saw the satellite dish and said,
"Who put that thing on my tank?
I really don't like it, to be quite frank!"

CAN YOU BELIEVE THAT FRED'S FORGOTTEN?
HIS MEMORY IS RATHER ROTTEN!

"But I hate TV, I'm a sporty fish –
a skipping rope is my one true wish!"

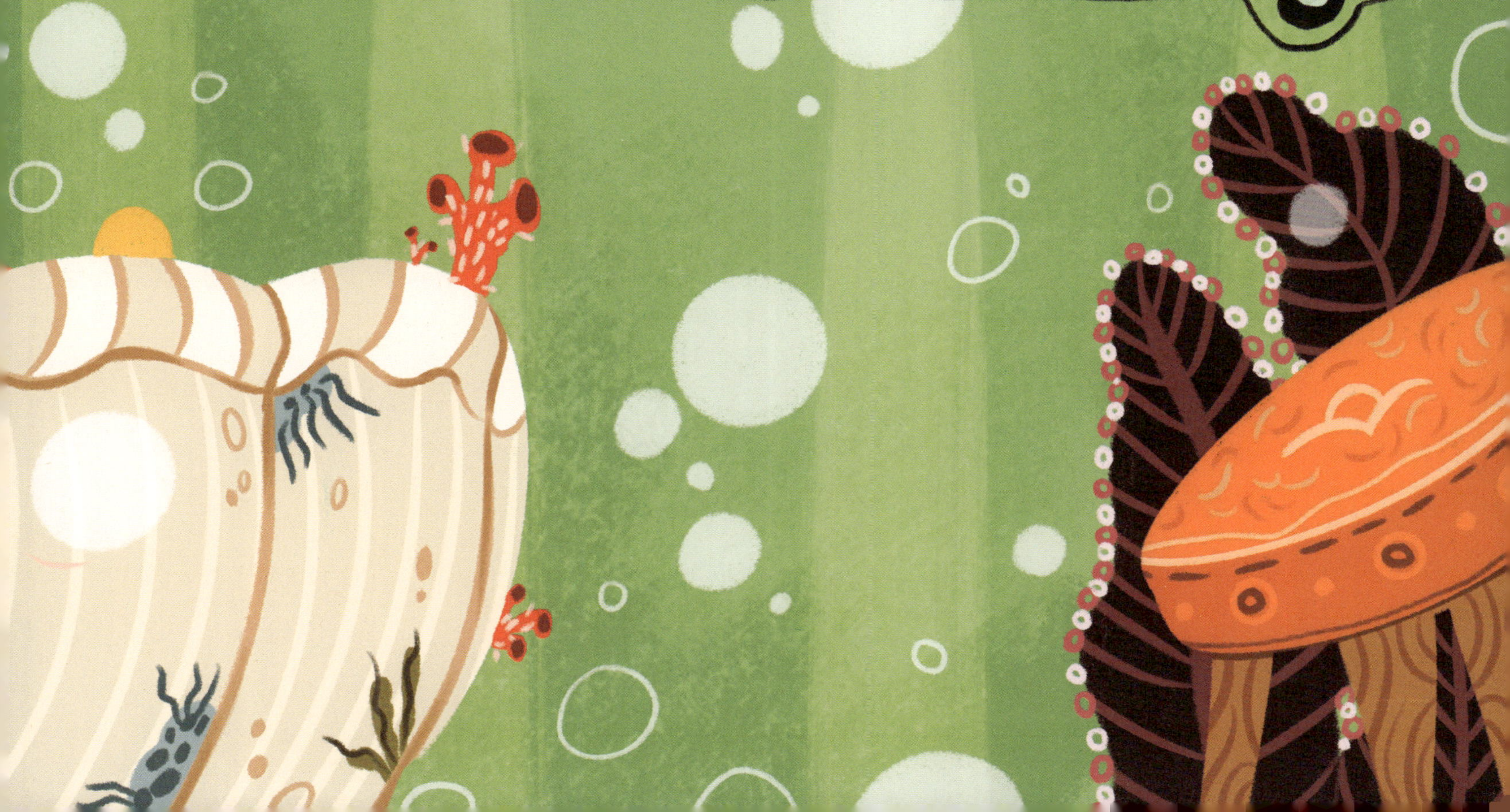

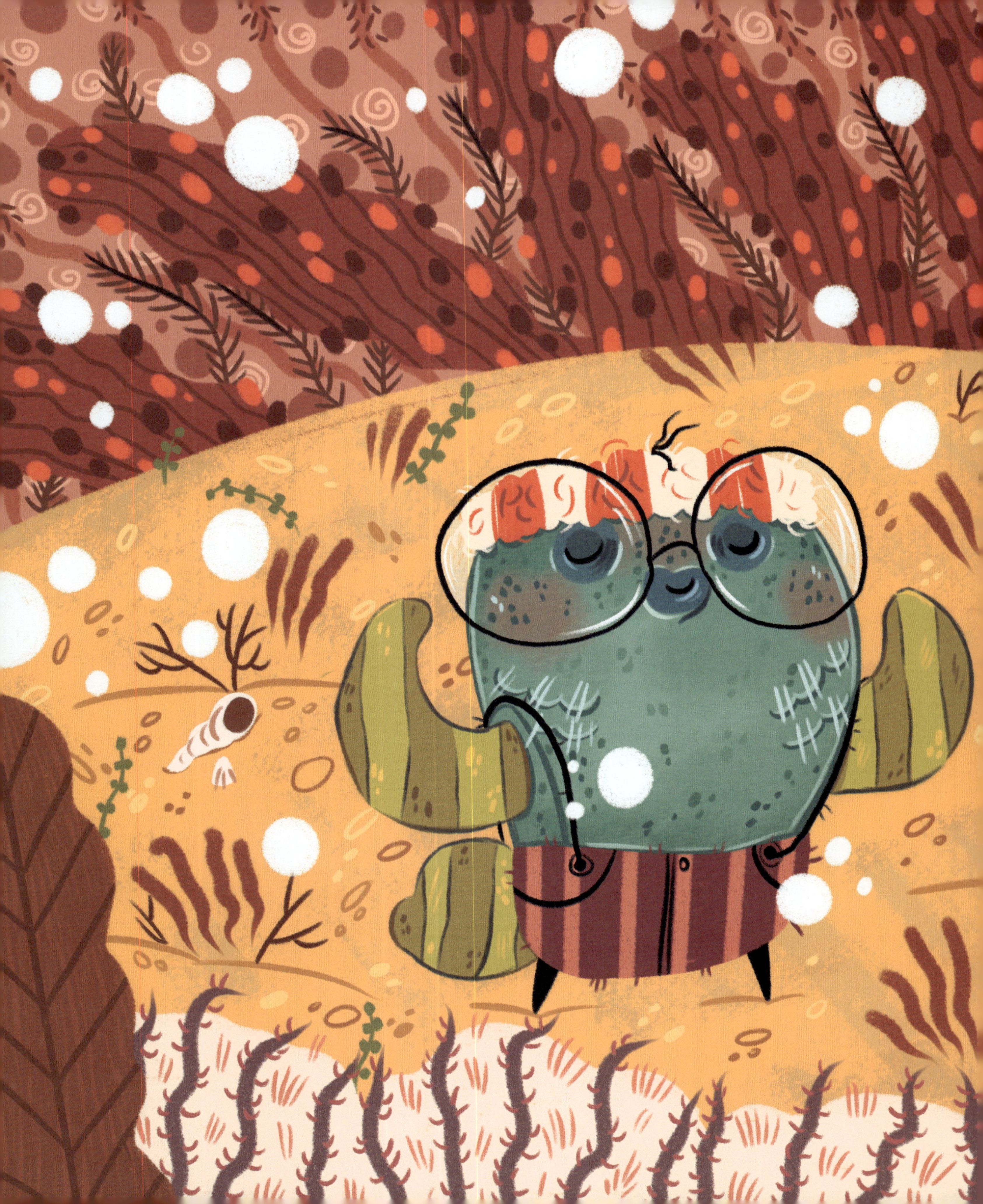

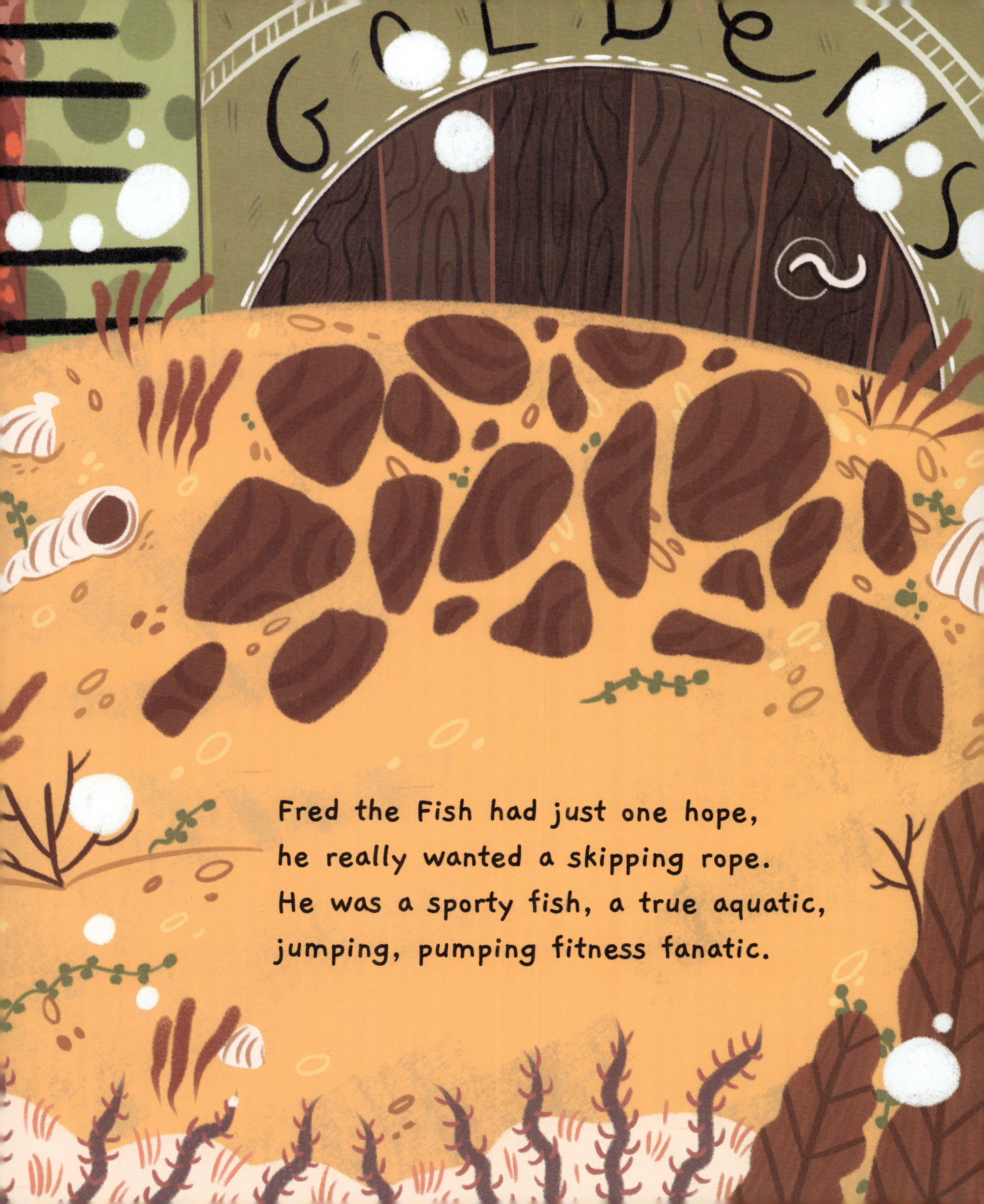

Fred the Fish had just one hope,
he really wanted a skipping rope.
He was a sporty fish, a true aquatic,
jumping, pumping fitness fanatic.

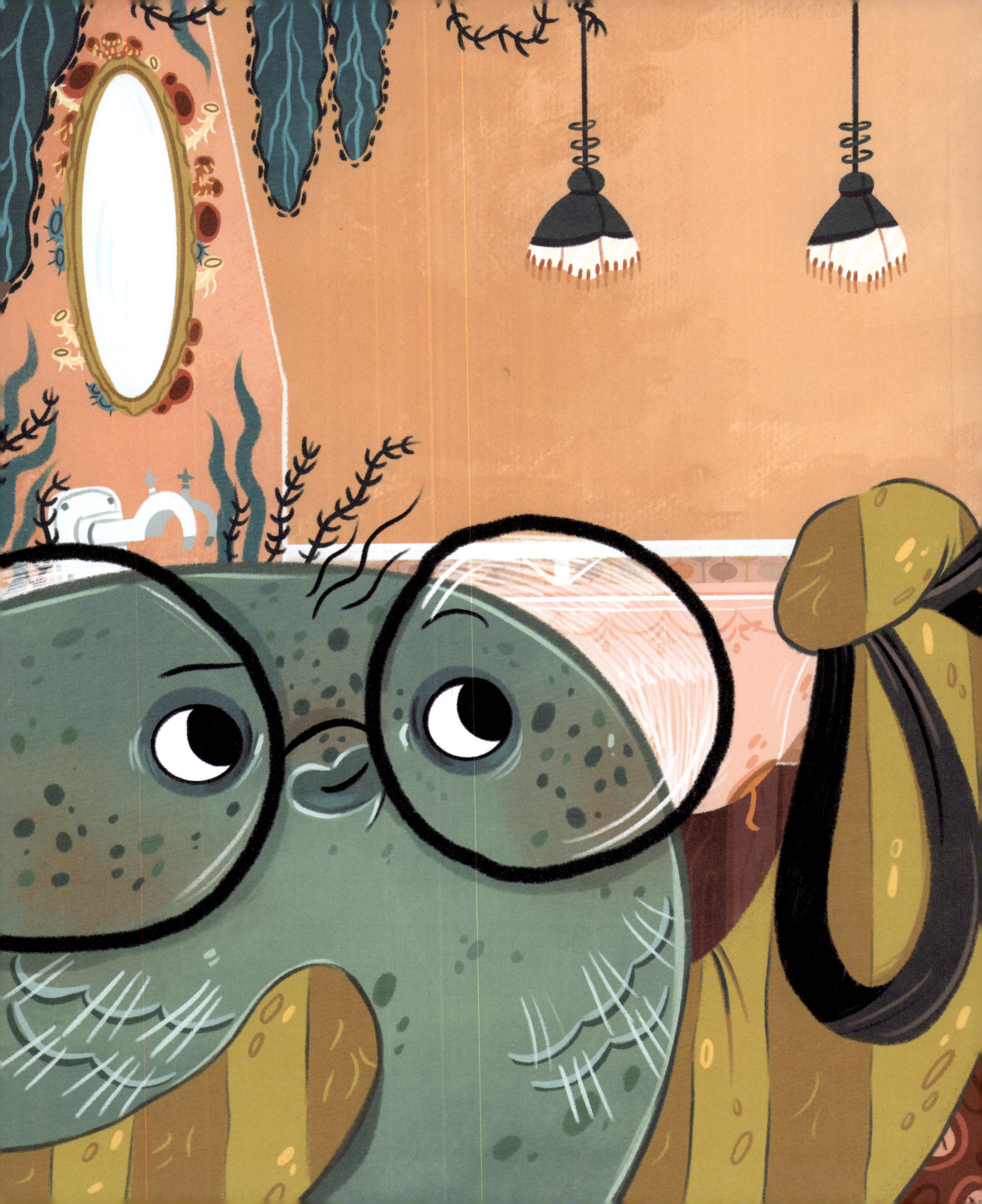

So off he went on a special mission,
for something to help with this ambition.
Searching the bathroom, looking in drawers,
for something special to help his cause.
And then he saw it: an elastic band!
Just the thing! Oh, how grand!
Back to his tank, with his prize,
ready for his exercise.

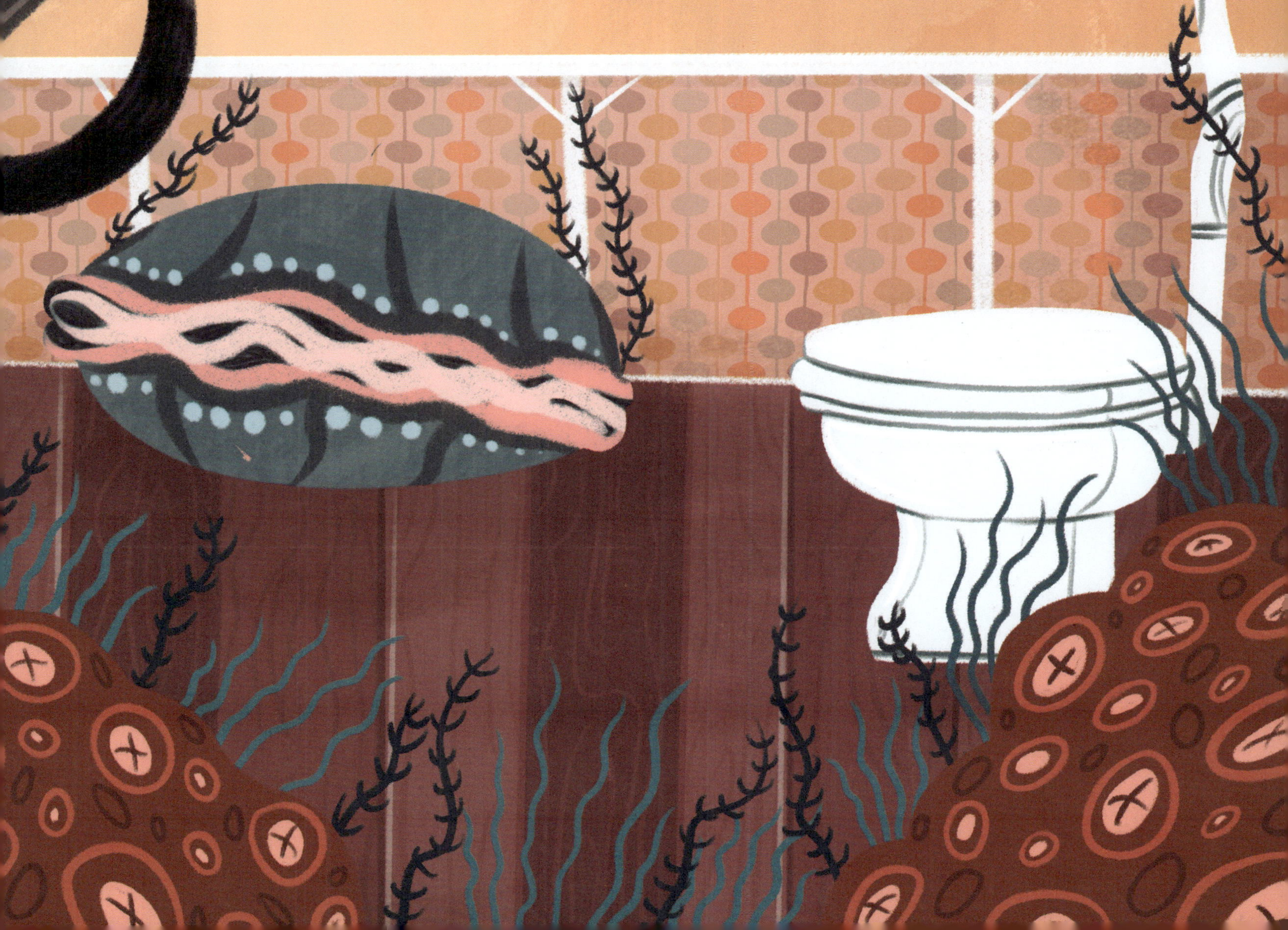

But in the morning when he got out of bed,
he saw the elastic band and said,
"Who put that thing over there?
What a mess, I just despair!"

CAN YOU BELIEVE THAT FRED'S FORGOTTEN?
HIS MEMORY IS REALLY ROTTEN!

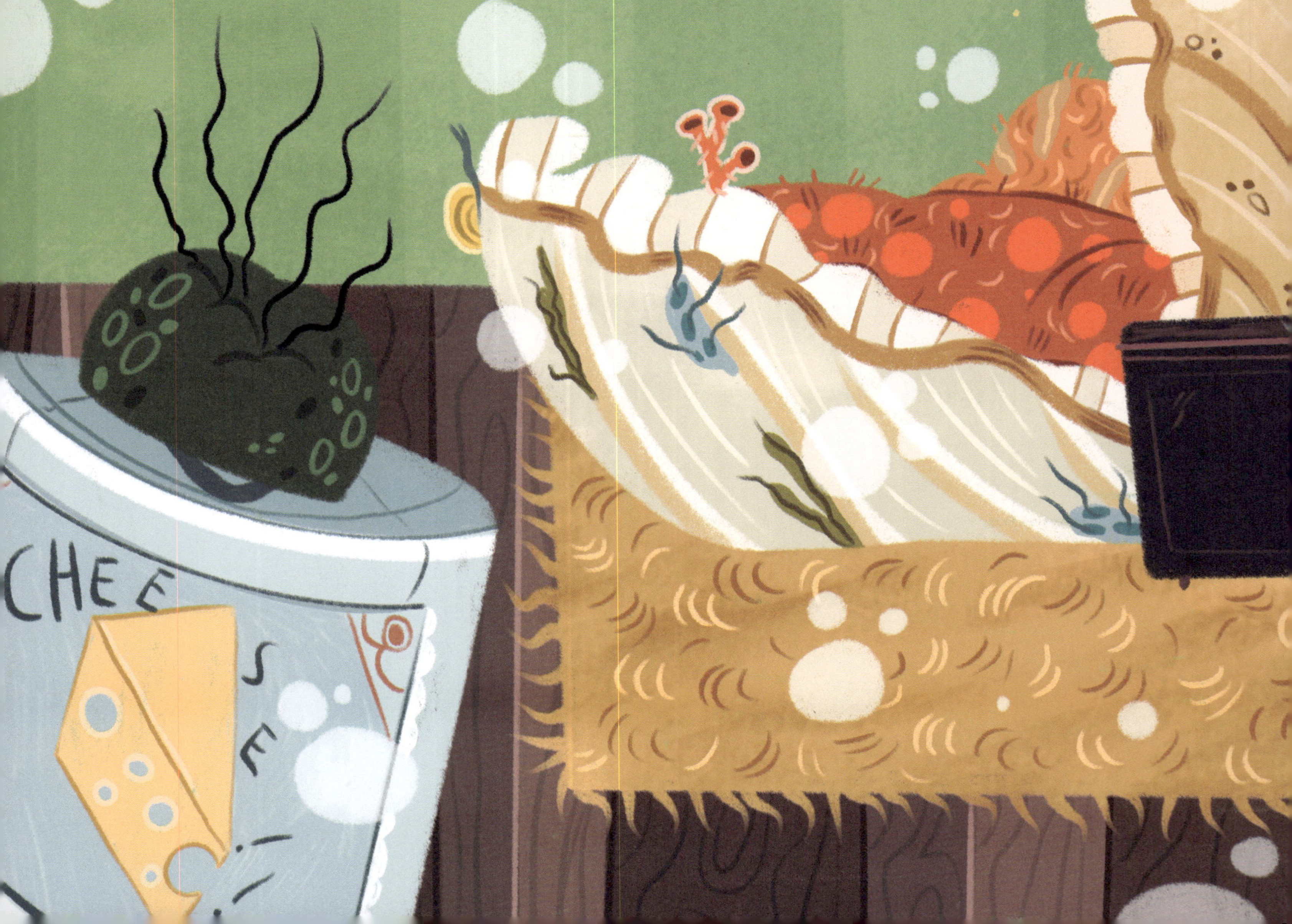

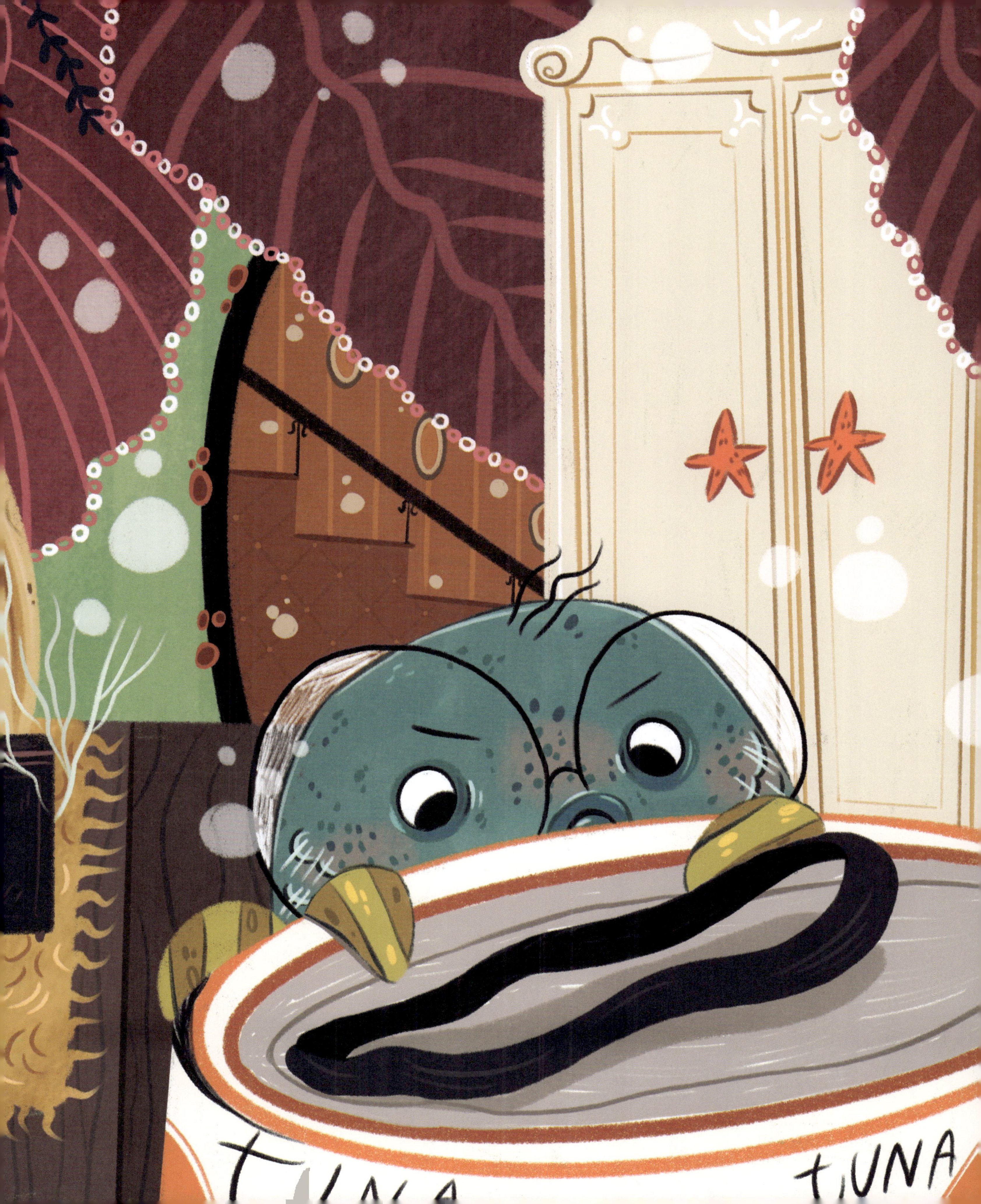
TUNA

Fred the Fish, he loves a moan!
In his tank, all on his own.
He's a grumpy fish, but I think he oughta
look behind him in the water.
For his owner has bought him something new...
Another fish – now there are two!

"Another fish! Well hello my friend!
My loneliness is at an end!
It's just like I've always said,
I'm a friendly fish. I'm Friendly Fred!"

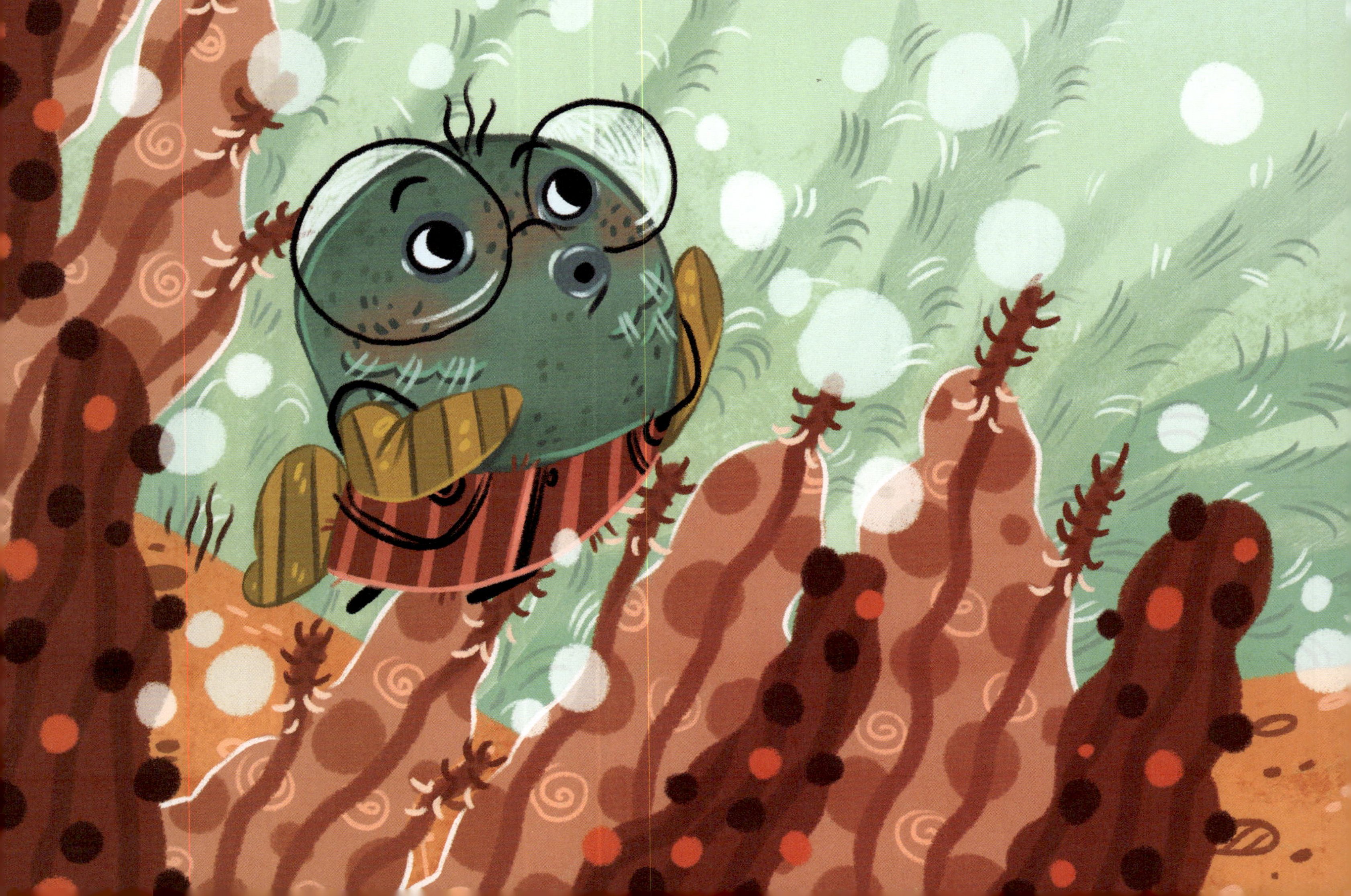

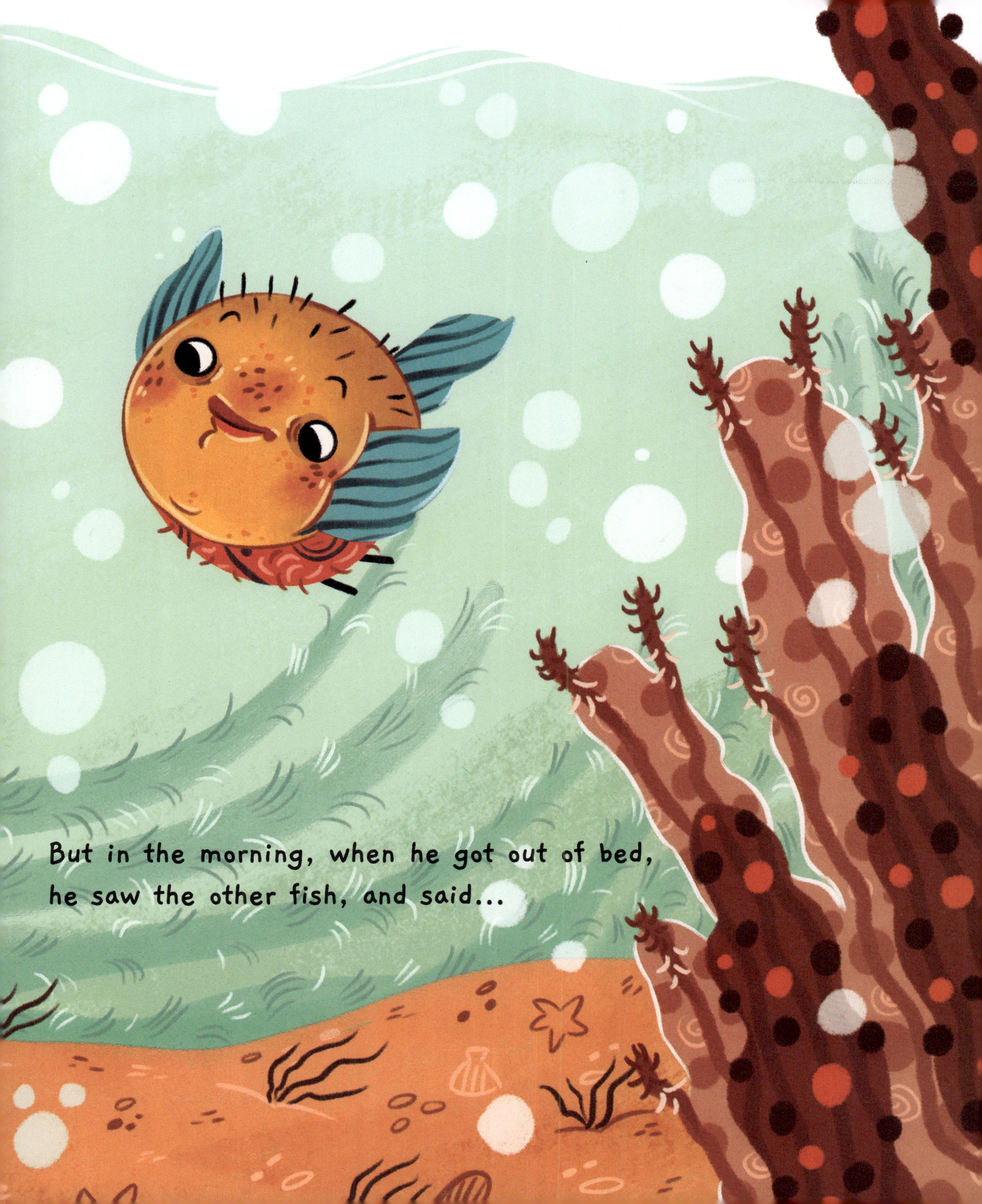

But in the morning, when he got out of bed,
he saw the other fish, and said...

"Hello again. Still here? Hurray!
What are we going to do today?
Do I still remember you?
Absolutely, of course I do!
We're fishy friends, a joyful duet,
and that's something I'll never forget!"

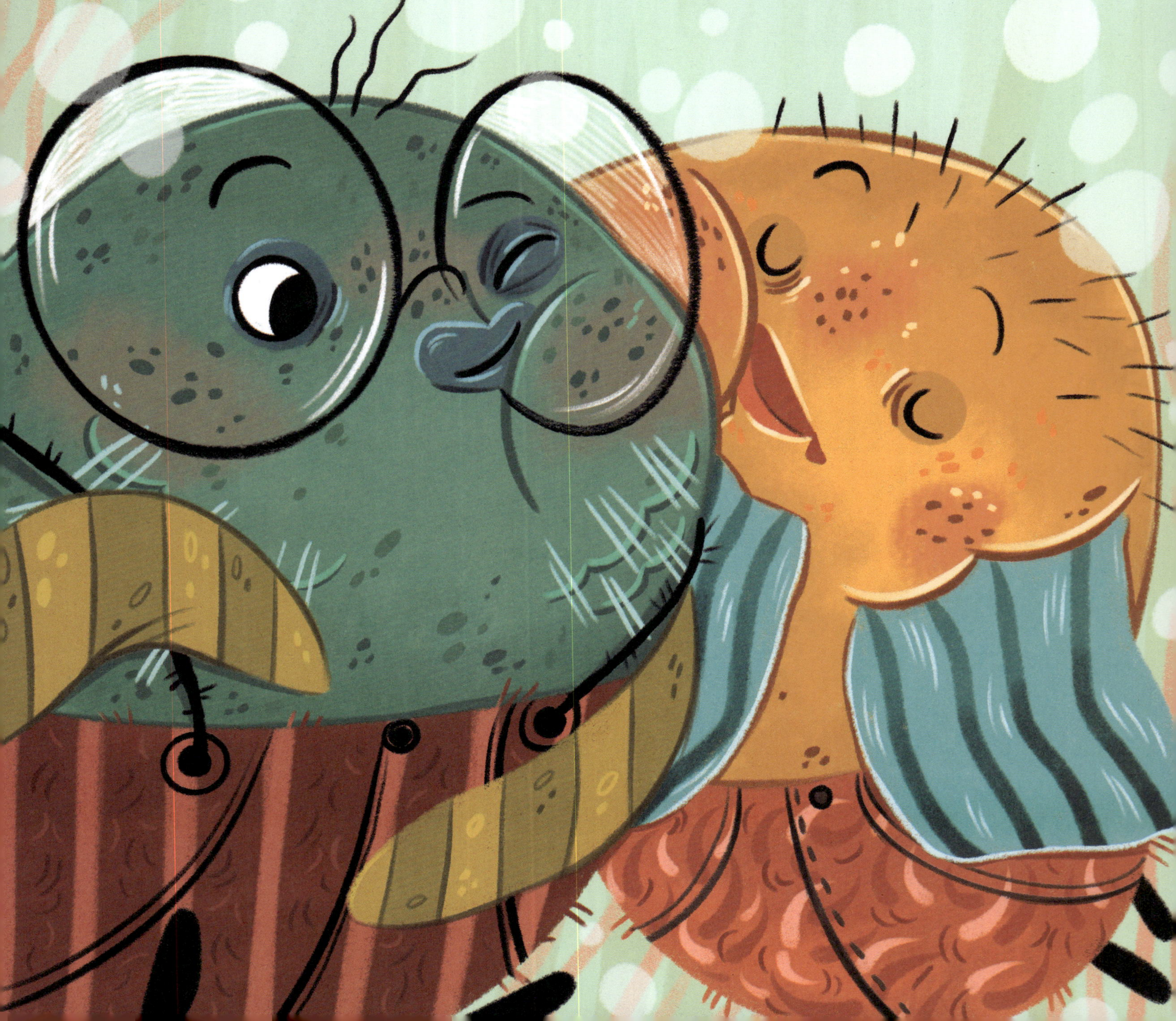

TURN THE PAGE FOR
INSIGHTS FROM THE ARTIST

# Fred the Fish

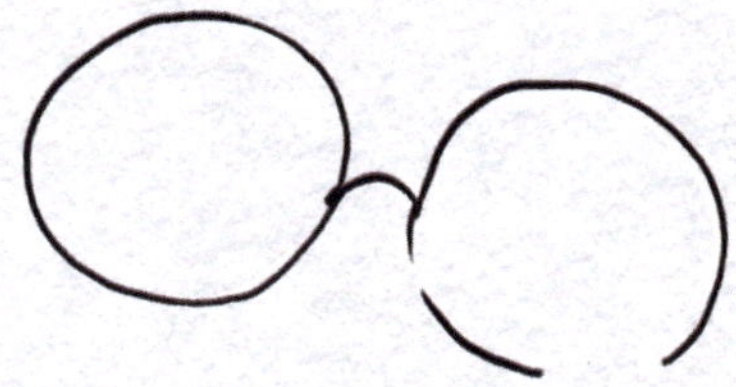

## DEVELOPING KEY FEATURES

### INITIAL CHARACTER DESIGNS

It's important to take the target audience into account before you begin work on your illustrations. *Fred the Fish* is aimed at 4–6 year olds, so I took some time to consider various factors including color, characterization, proportions, and methods of narration. With children's books, the design decisions need to be simple but effective. The story is funny and tells of a forgetful little fish who forgets the tasks of the previous day and reinvents things to do each morning. I wanted to convey the lighthearted mood by using bright colors and creating vivid combinations.

While Fred is a bit of a grumpy character, he also needed to be original, eye-catching, and fun to grab the reader's attention. I gave him glasses and braces to help make this little fish truly unique. I paid close attention to the story while sketching out initial designs for Fred, as it helped me understand how much I could push the character.

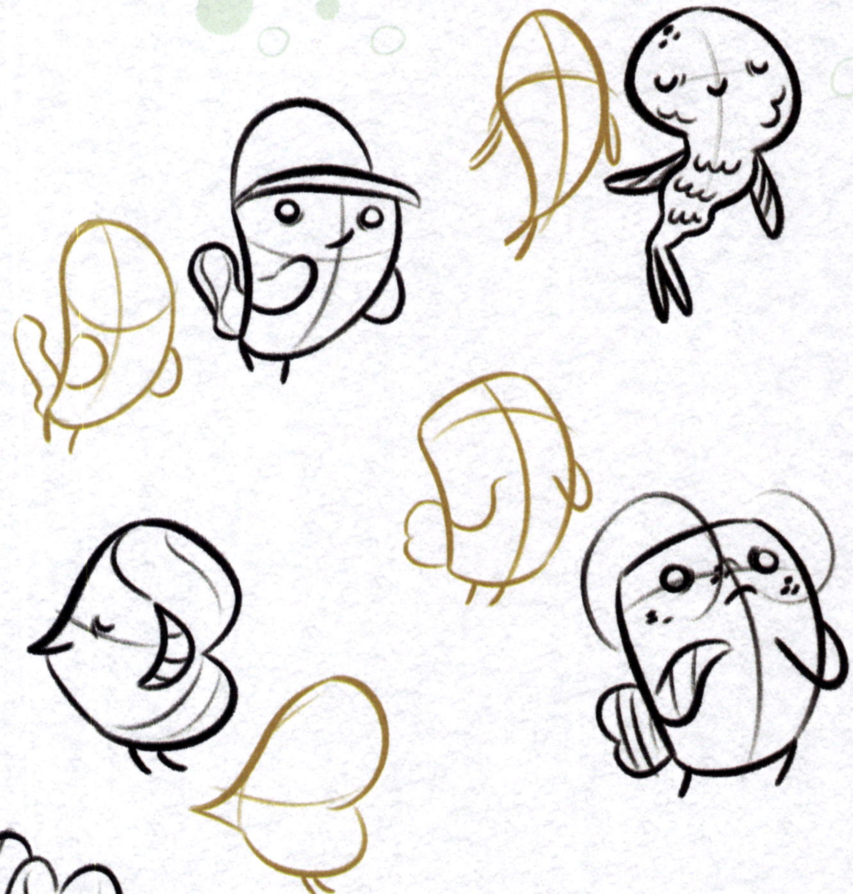

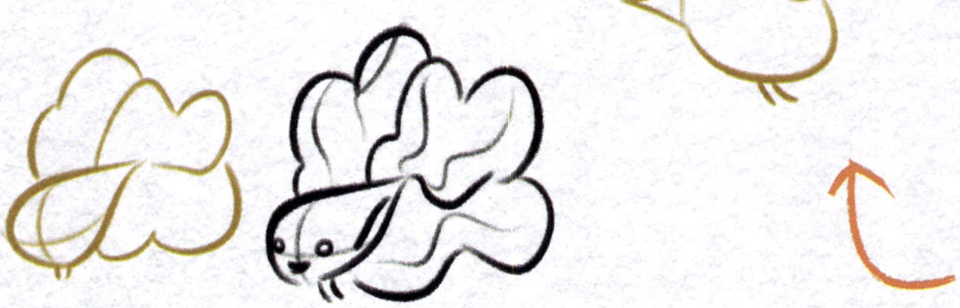

When drawing the main character, I usually start with a search for shapes. I looked up different types of fish for reference to help make the character design believable and realistic, before refining the shape in my style.

Once I'd found the basic shapes, I slowly defined the shape of the fish. I then added character, clothes, and expressions, creating an identity that helped me to understand who Fred was and what I wanted to achieve with his design.

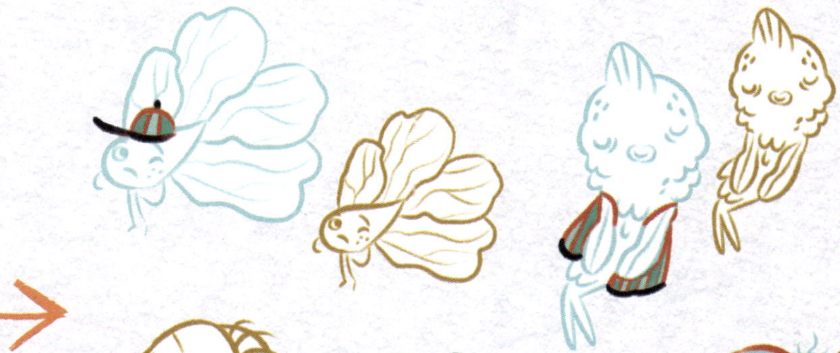

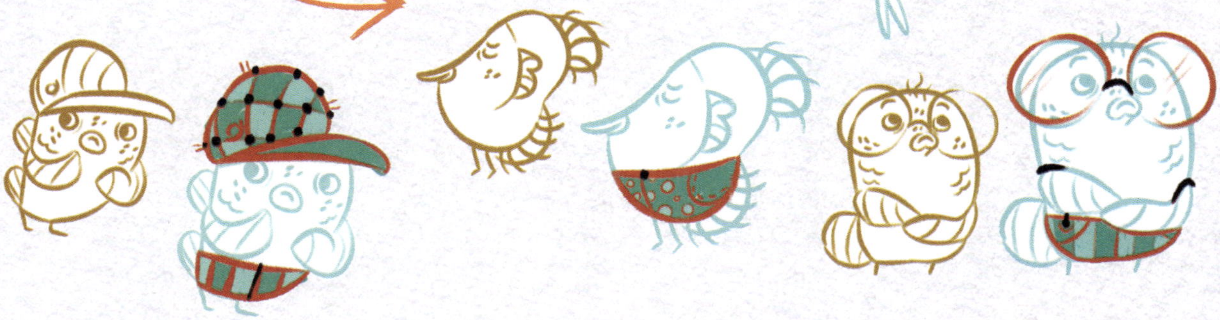

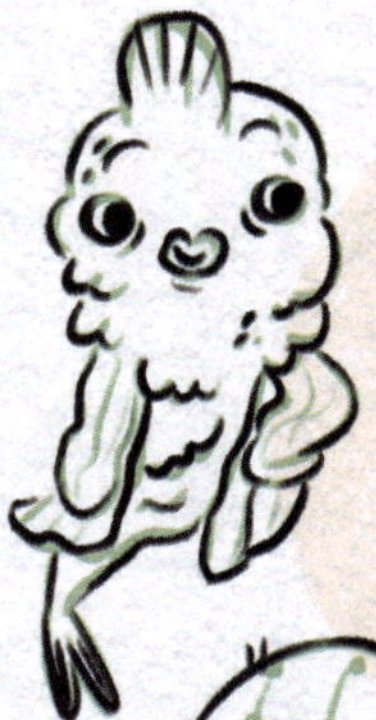

At this point I found myself with many possible characters, each with different characteristics, shapes, and appeal. I paused to compare the different designs and reflect on which would be the best fit for the story. Sometimes I will keep creating and merging shapes for a while longer, whereas at other times the first sketch wins.

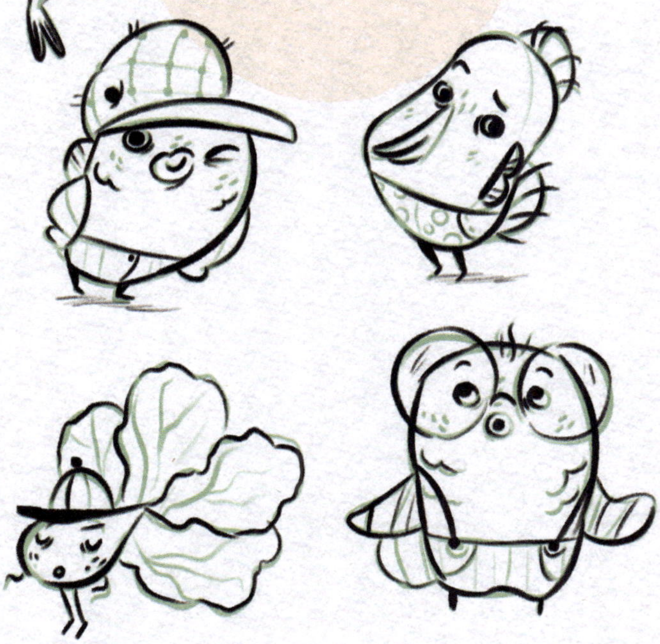

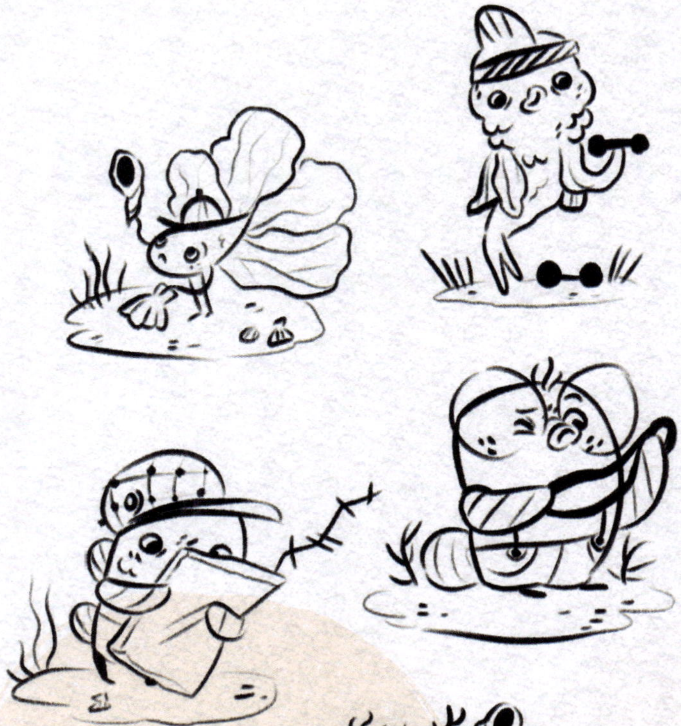

I sketched many different Fred designs to help me to work out which was most suitable.

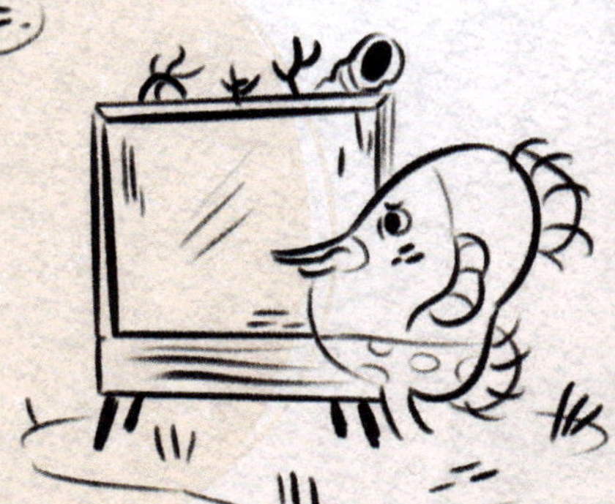

## CHARACTER DEFINITION

Once I had chosen the shape and attitude for Fred's character, I continued my research for his design. Fantasy is often based on real life and what we see every day. It was important to start from something that existed before adding my own imaginings. I wanted to anthropomorphize Fred's design and create a somewhat vintage mood, so after some research I gave him human accessories like glasses and braces.

I decided to make Fred a bit squat to create a funny appearance in keeping with the story. I also gave him glasses for added personality and quirkiness, choosing accessories that would help to communicate his happy, sweet, and gruff character.

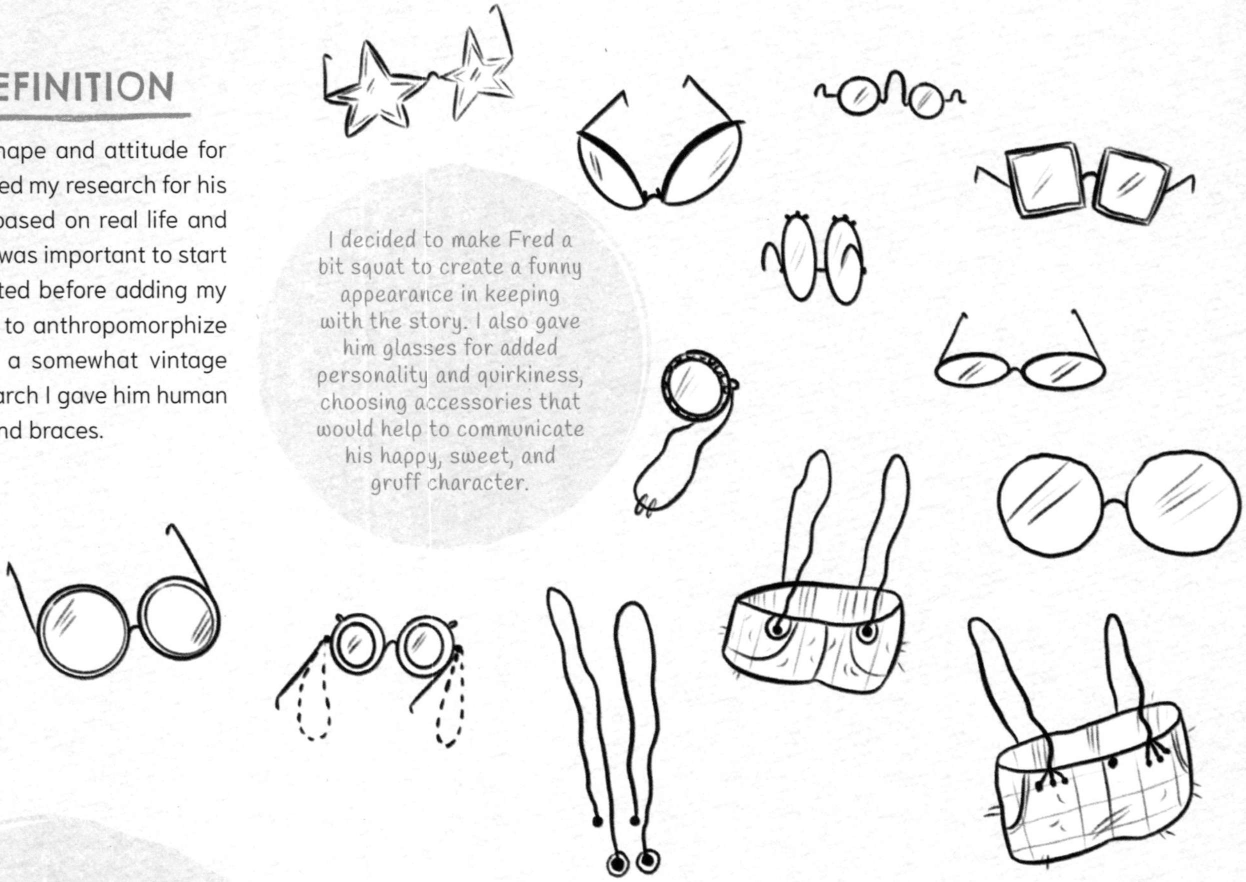

When sketching a character, I always draw them with various expressions to help me work out how they will look and react throughout the story. In this case, I needed to understand how to make Fred's glasses functional with a smile or pout.

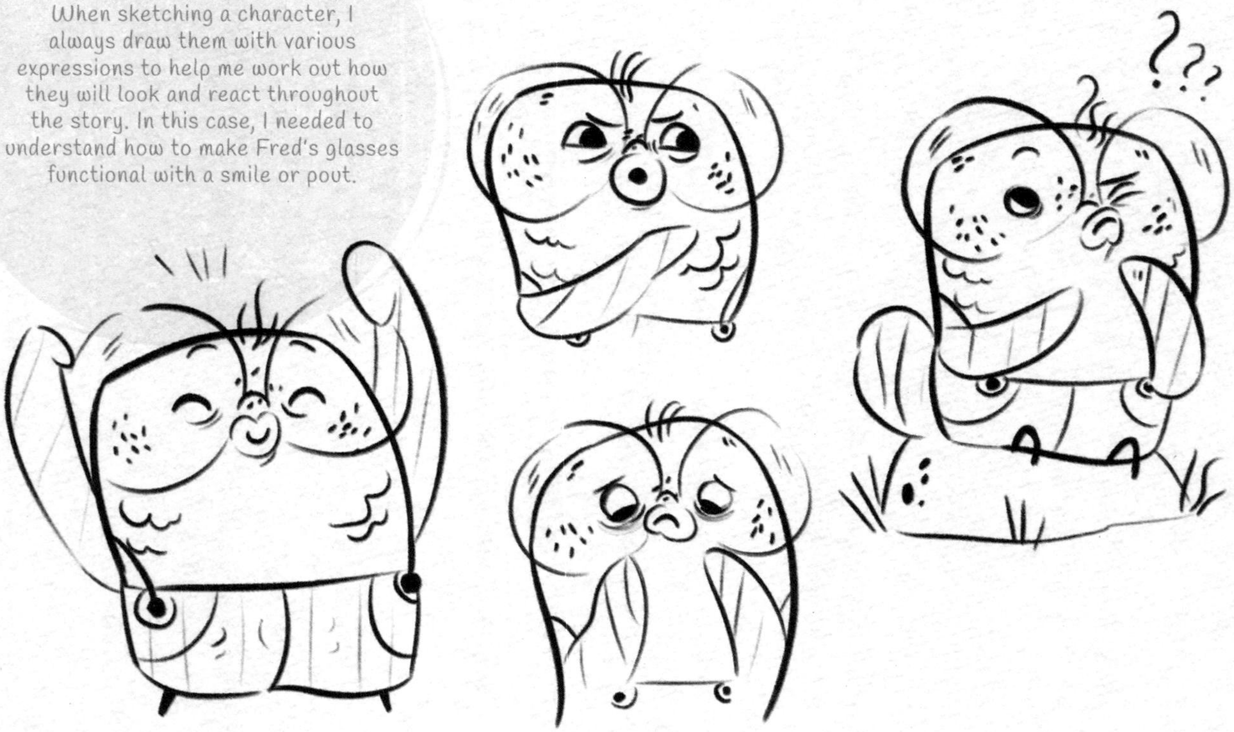

The choice of colors is crucial in serving the story. I never imagined the fish tank with typical colors, such as blue water and green algae. I wanted to see if I could use a warmer color palette and create stronger contrasts. Similarly with Fred's design, I used a petrol green for his scales, contrasting red shorts, and mustard yellow fins.

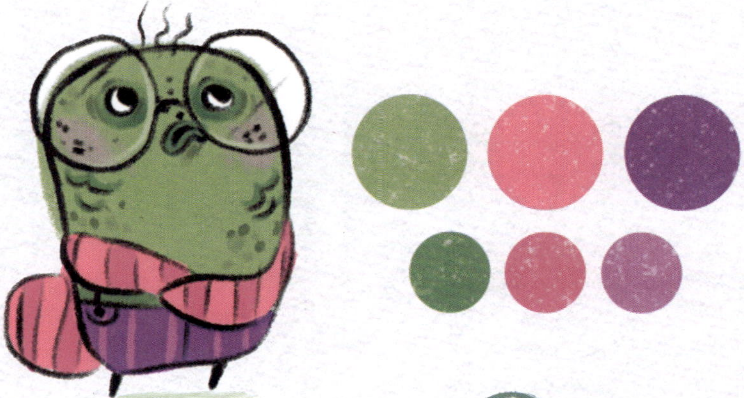

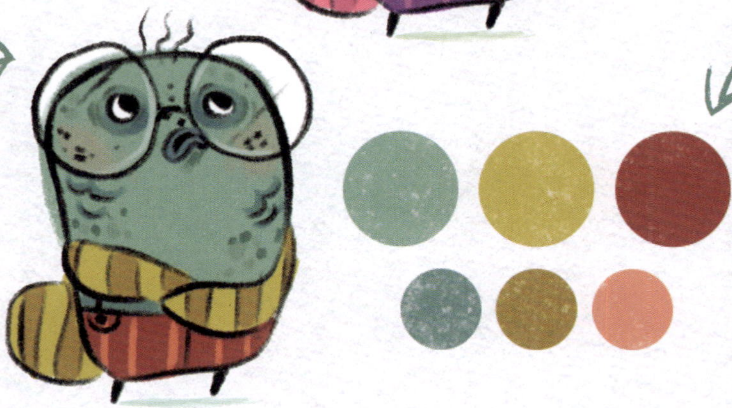

I placed Fred's colors next to each other to get an idea of the different shades and combinations. I generally like to compare my chosen palette to other possible ones, but without dwelling on other options for too long. Once decided, I then applied a filter to turn the palette even hotter or colder, to see if I liked the result.

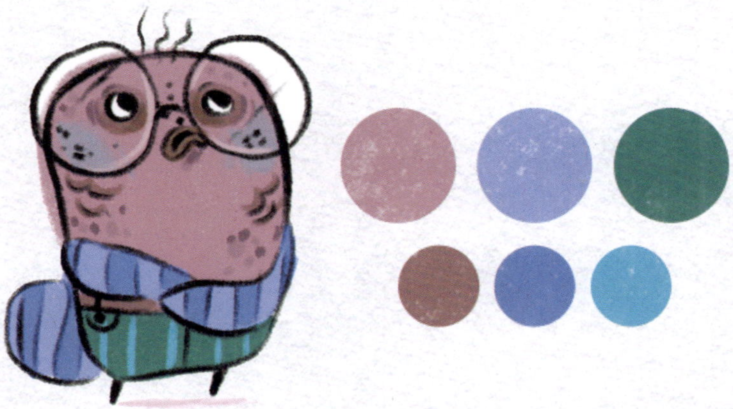

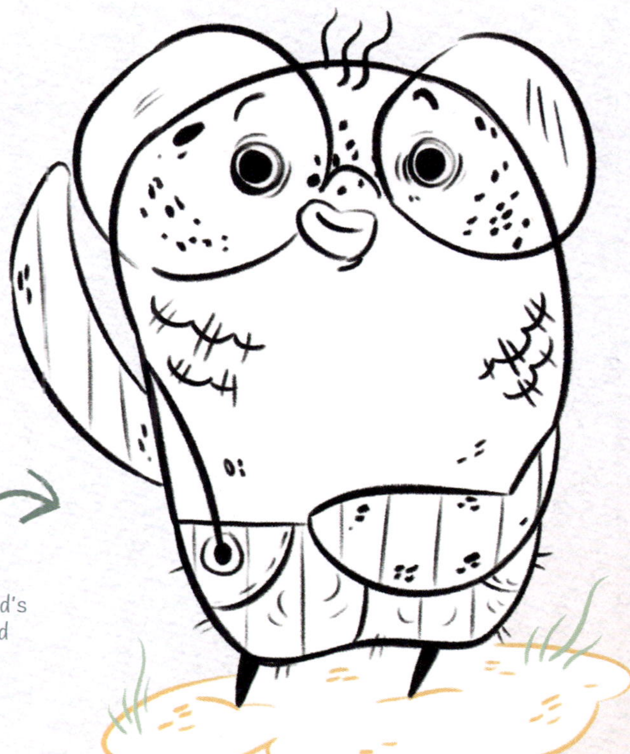

Once I finished Fred's design, I continued with the other design elements.

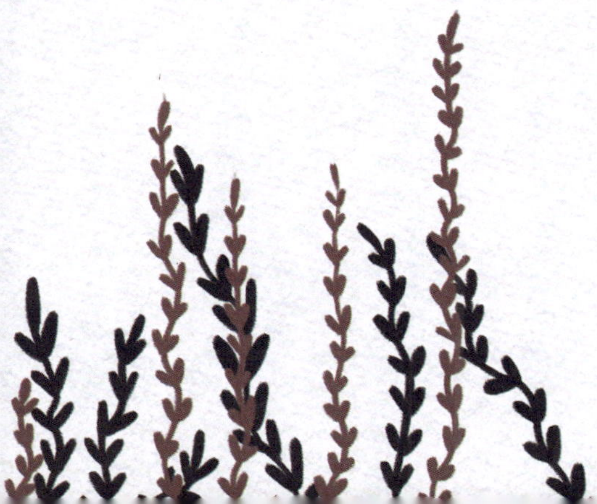

## ENVIRONMENT & INTERIOR DESIGNS

When coming up with ideas for Fred's house, I reread the story carefully. The story text mentions various rooms, such as the kitchen and bathroom, which made me consider just how big his home could be. As Fred is an aquarium fish, I found it fun to combine the classic fish bowl with more house-like features. I decided his house would be made up of a series of small tins within a fish bowl, which would make separate rooms.

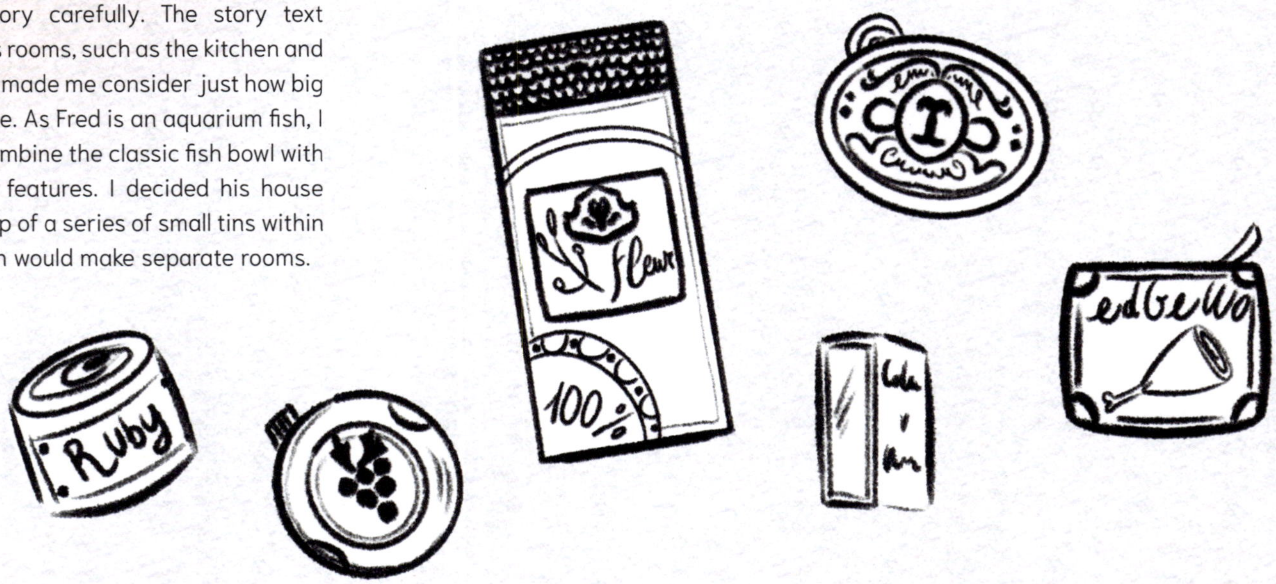


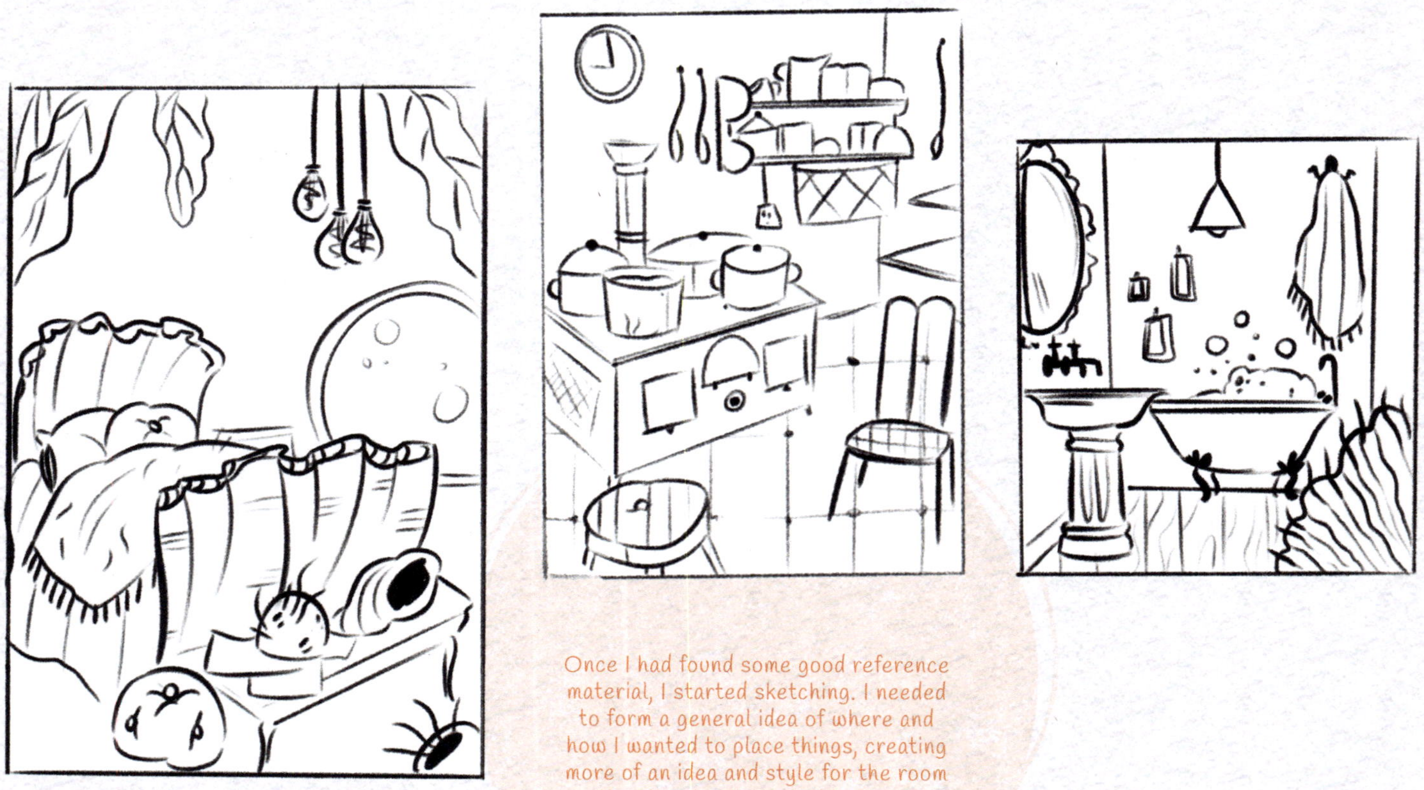

Once I had found some good reference material, I started sketching. I needed to form a general idea of where and how I wanted to place things, creating more of an idea and style for the room than its structure at this stage.

Research is crucial when illustrating home interiors and any environment that contains many objects. When designing Fred's home, I researched typical fish bowls and aquariums, as well as vintage, dollhouse-style kitchens. I used references when sketching the designs to add recognisable details and give everything the same vintage touch. Children love detailed environments that are full of little things to discover.

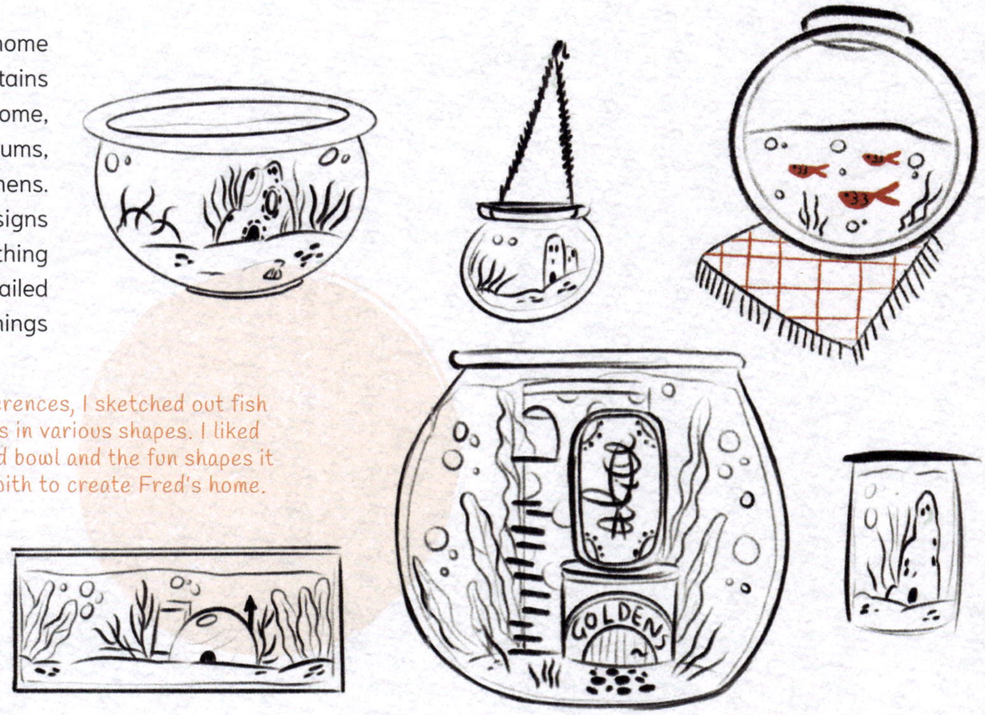


Referring to my references, I sketched out fish bowls and aquariums in various shapes. I liked the style of the round bowl and the fun shapes it allowed me to play with to create Fred's home.

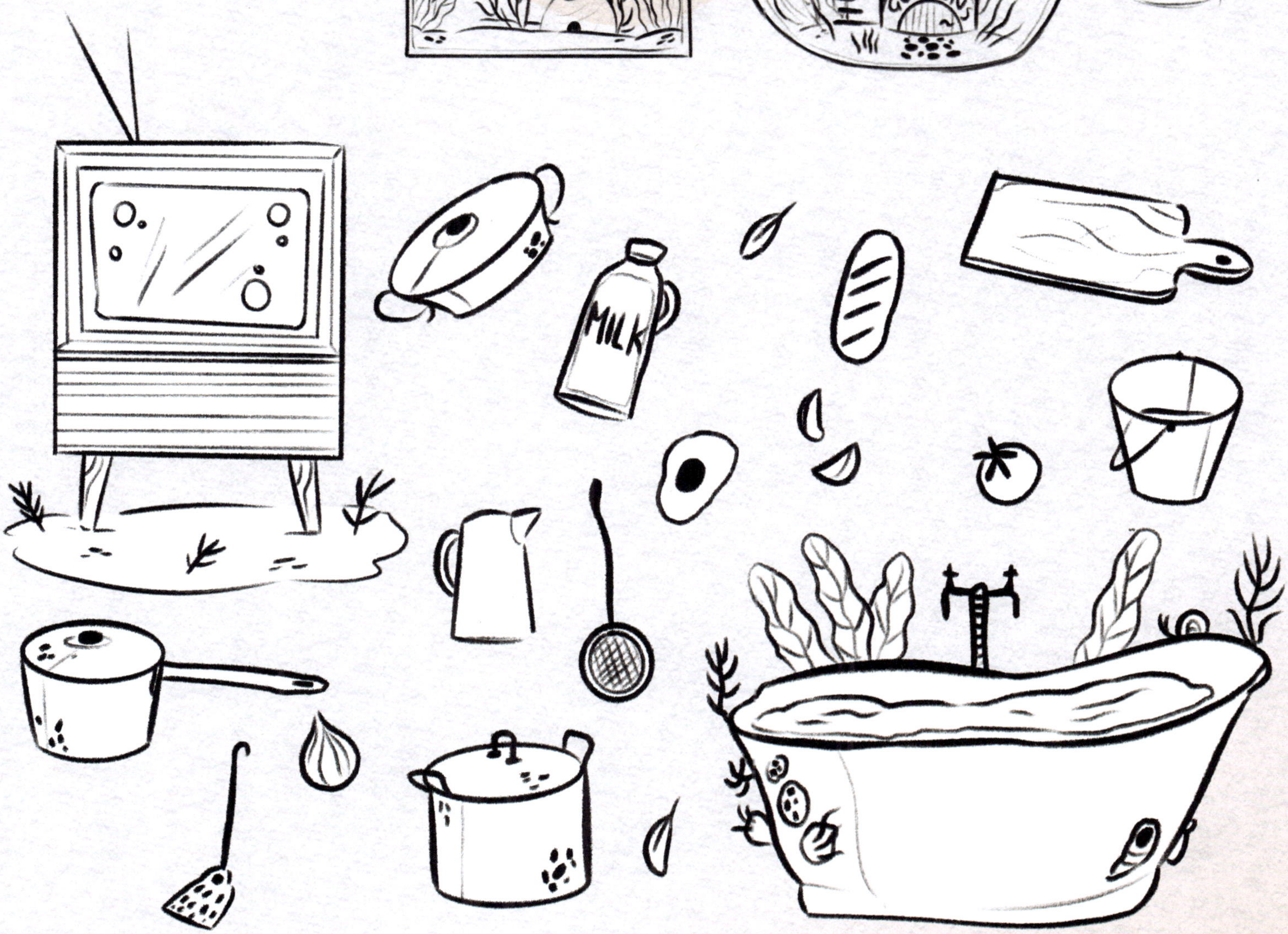

As this is a children's picture book, the interiors needed to be well characterized, rich in detail, and interesting to look at, without containing too many objects. As with the color palette, I decided the items in Fred's home didn't fully need to be those of a typical fish tank. I decided to use both expected elements (such as coral and seaweed) and unexpected elements (such as a bed, toilet, and stove) to make the environment interesting yet easy for children to understand. Illustrating an environment children are familiar with helps them to connect to the story and fosters even more curiosity.

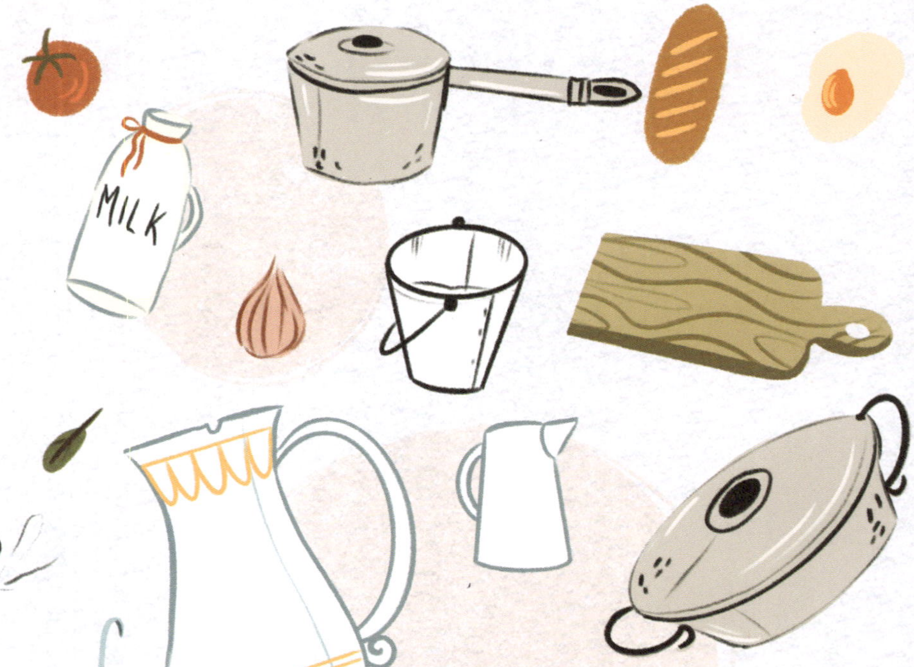


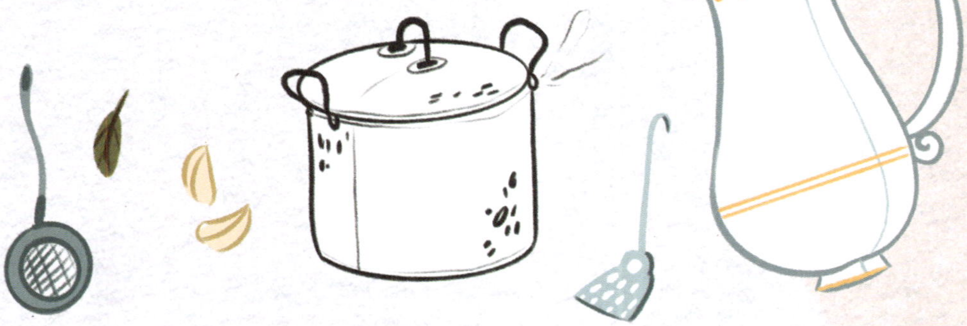

When coloring the household items, I started to bring in some of the warmer shades I wanted to use. Refining the designs helped me to form a clearer idea about Fred's environment.

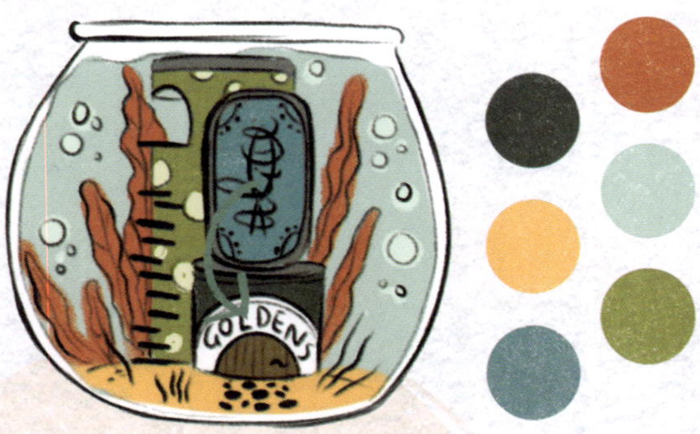


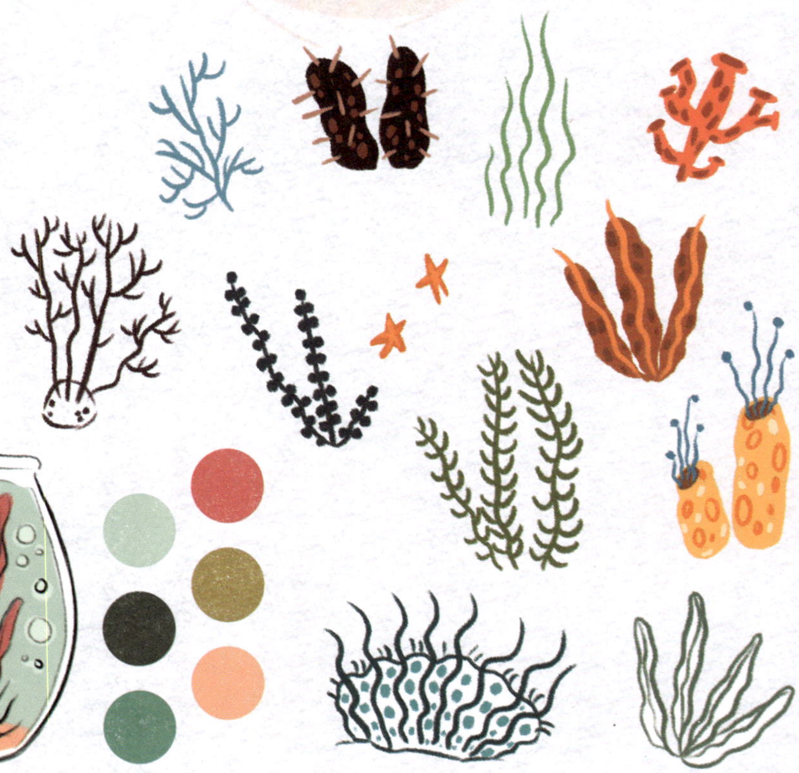

I researched various types of algae to create a garden for Fred's home. Adding the aquatic plants helped make it appear more believable and like a fish bowl.

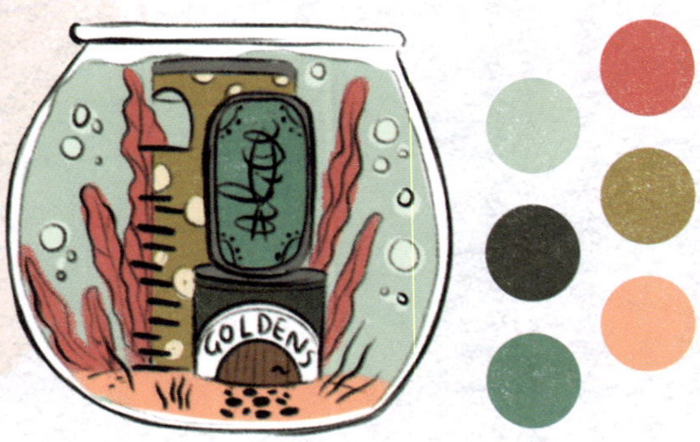

The colors were clear in my mind by this stage and I wanted to avoid straying into other color palettes that could weaken the overall look of the spreads.

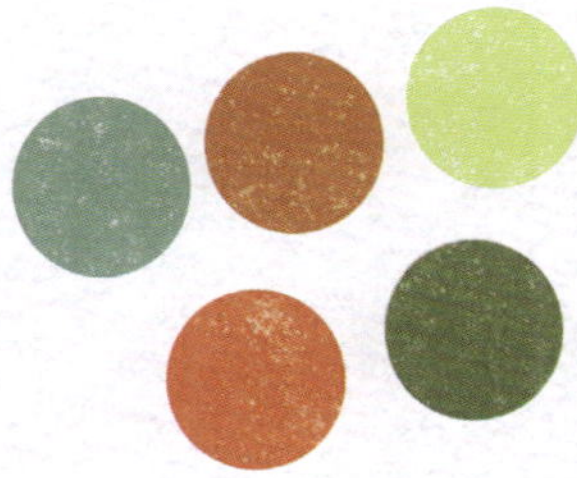

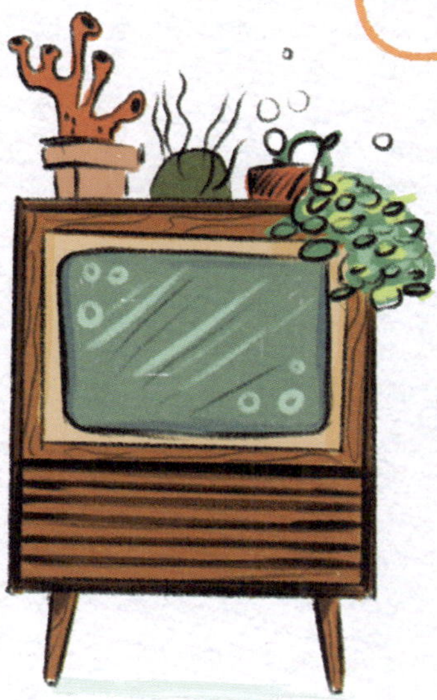

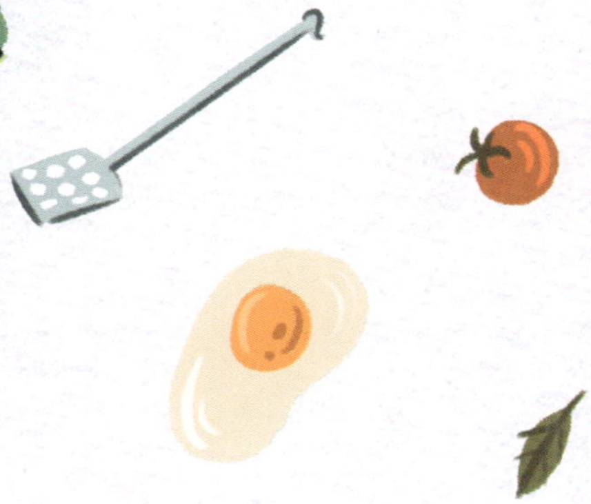

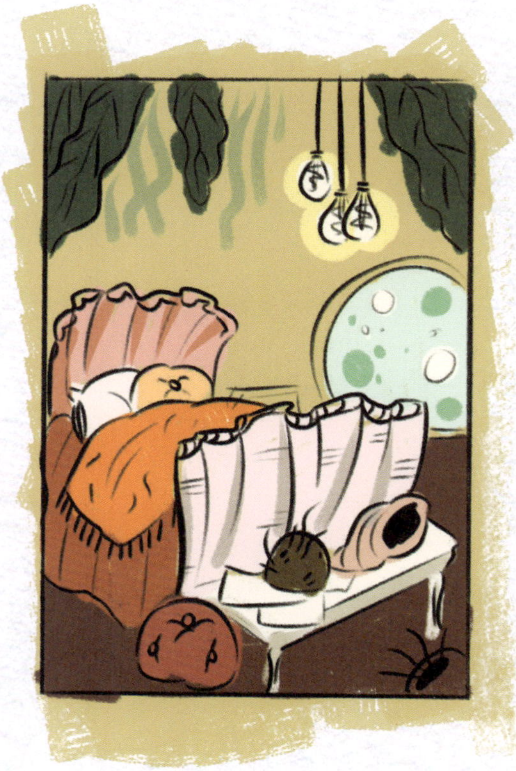

Before finalizing a design, I gather together various elements and designs to look at them as a whole to see if anything appears out of place, is not relevant, or requires more work. This kind of comparison is important at each stage in the design process. Once happy, I was able to finalize the design.

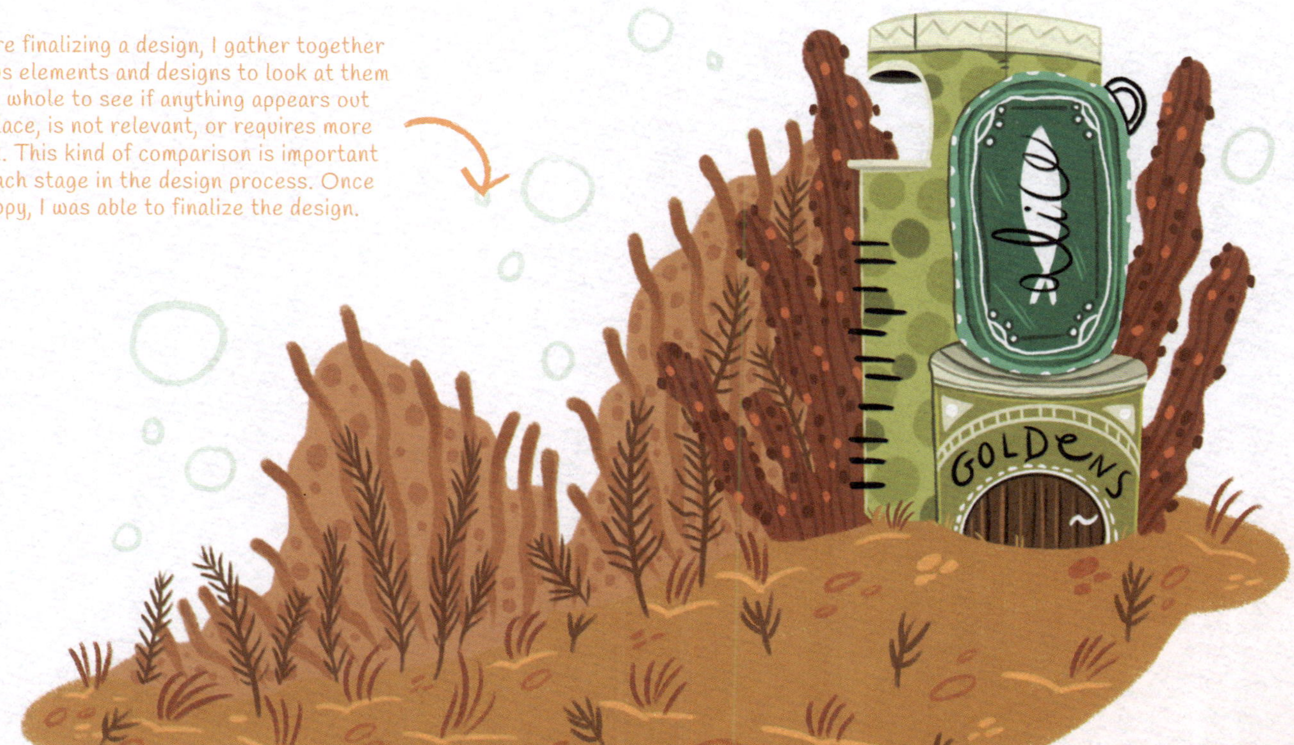

# ANALYSIS

The part I love most about illustrating children's books is designing the characters. Whether they're animal or human, I enjoying watching them come to life on the page – from the hairs on their head down to their clothing and shoes. When I first read the story I imagined Fred as an anglerfish – a gruff character who lived in the depths of the sea. As I read on, I realized Fred was an aquarium fish with a few memory problems. While I immediately abandoned the idea of the anglerfish's pendant light, I still wanted to give the character a robust appearance. The first idea that comes to mind is often the one I end up pursuing, though I never stop at the first idea. I always experiment with different designs, in this case, different types of fish, shapes, styles, and character attitudes. My idea for Fred was fairly formed from the start: a squat, forgetful little fish with glasses and freckles.

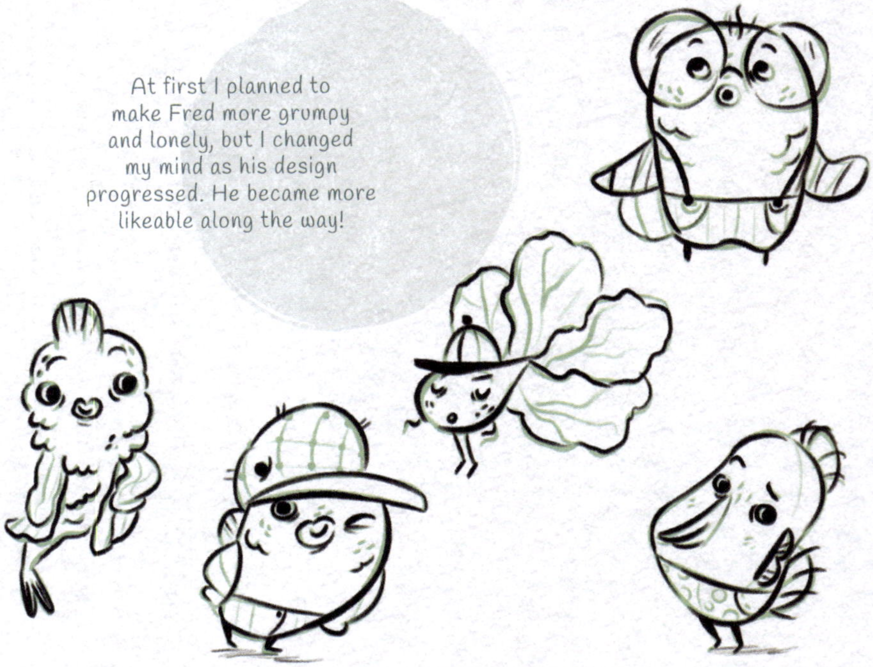

At first I planned to make Fred more grumpy and lonely, but I changed my mind as his design progressed. He became more likeable along the way!

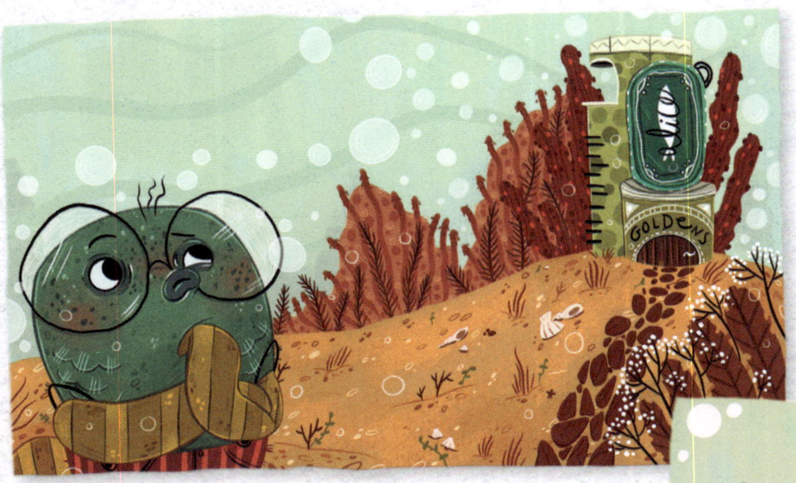

Empathizing with the story and its characters is key. It's like reading a good book and seeing the movie play out in my head. Connecting with the story allows me to see it on the page. From a technical point of view, references make a big difference. You can't create anything of your own if you don't start from something that already exists, to help make the object look credible and real – though of course your work should always be your own.

I wanted to show Fred in the foreground of the opening spread to introduce his character and show the reader the world in which the story takes place.

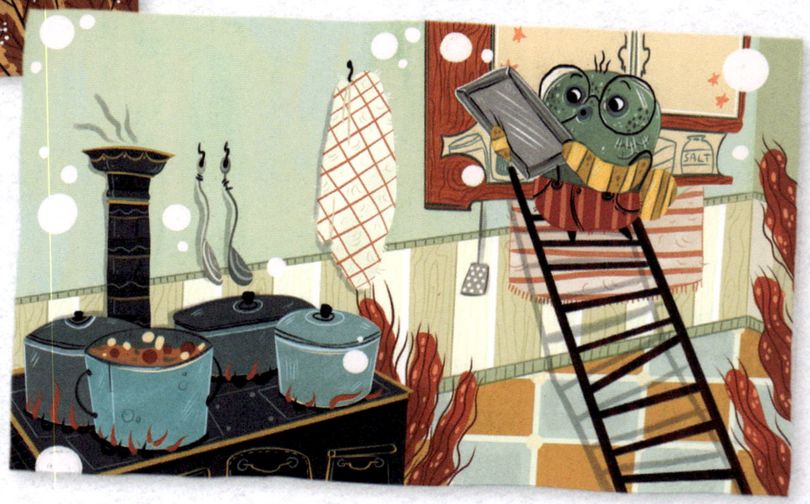

The second spread shows Fred at home in his kitchen. I think any child would be amused to see a kitchen with a lit stove underwater!

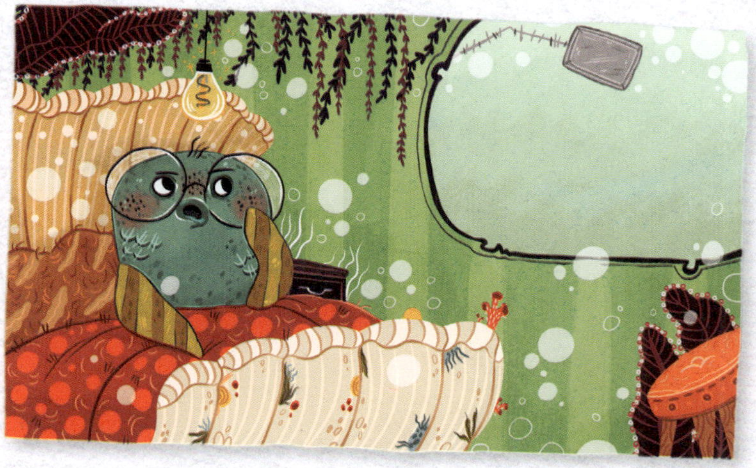

I wanted the bedroom to show that Fred's home is underwater. I did this by introducing sea elements, such as a seashell bed adorned with colorful coral, alongside other typical bedroom objects.

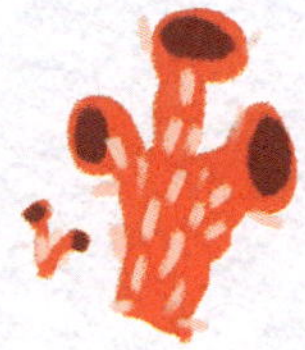

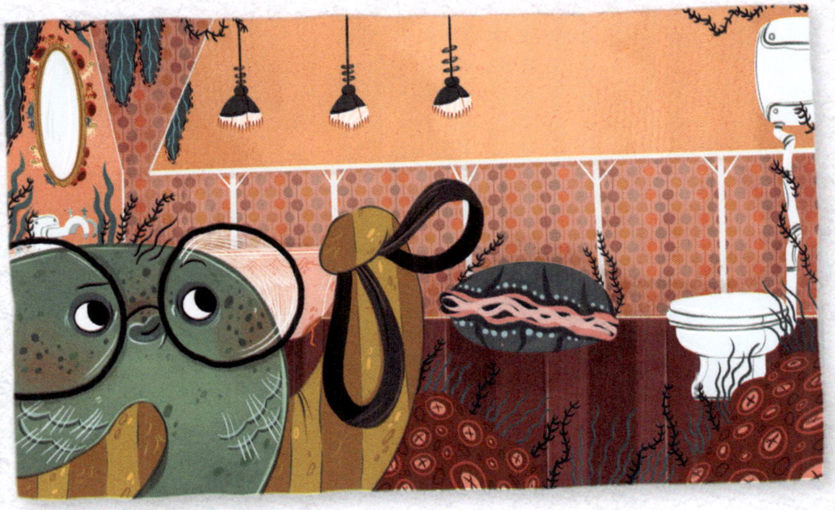

Fred's bathroom is full of typical bathroom objects, along with more marine-like items such as the shell and seaweed. Give your backgrounds importance and space on the page so they can serve the story and character.

This spread shows the meeting between Fred and his new friend – a key moment in the story. I put them on opposite pages, either side of the central binding, their gazes transfixed on each other. The direction of the algae frames the spread and almost pushes them together.

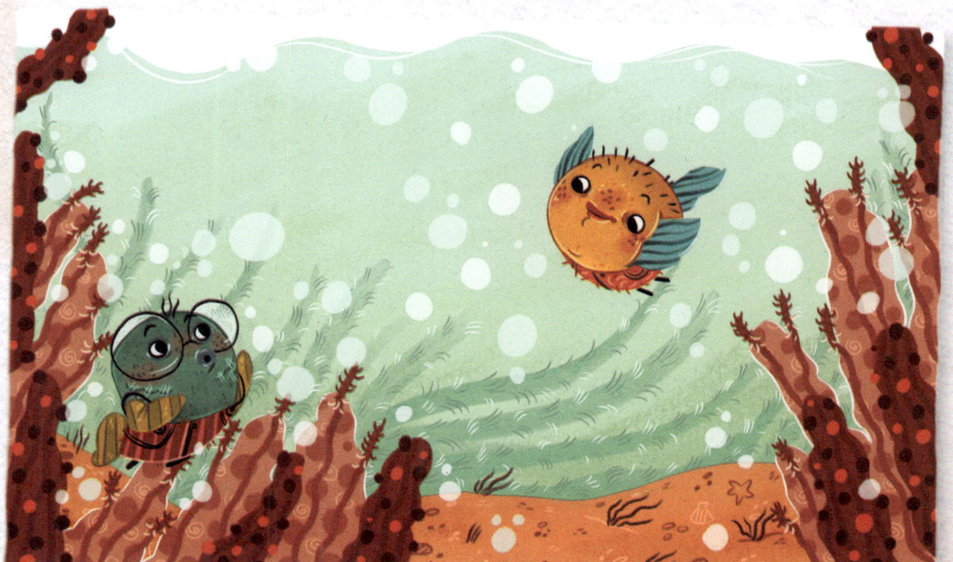

Take inspiration from illustrators you admire. I like going to bookstores to look at picture books and seeing the range of different styles of illustrations made for children. Children love these books and it is our job as illustrators to excite and impress them with our artwork. In those moments I feel like a superhero with a pencil in my hand!

# SUPER VEGETABLE BOY

Written by

GREG DOBBINS

Illustrated by

AURÉLIEN GALVAN

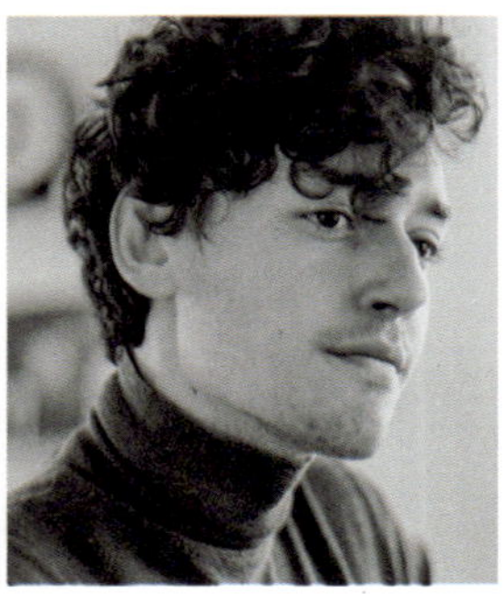

Author & illustrator

**aureliengalvan.com**

Originally from the south of France, Aurélien has been living in Canada for over ten years. His work is mostly digital, incorporating textures and techniques reminiscent of traditional mediums such as colored pencils, pastel, or watercolor. His passion for children's illustration grew with the arrival of his two daughters.

A STORY FOR AGES 6–8 YEARS

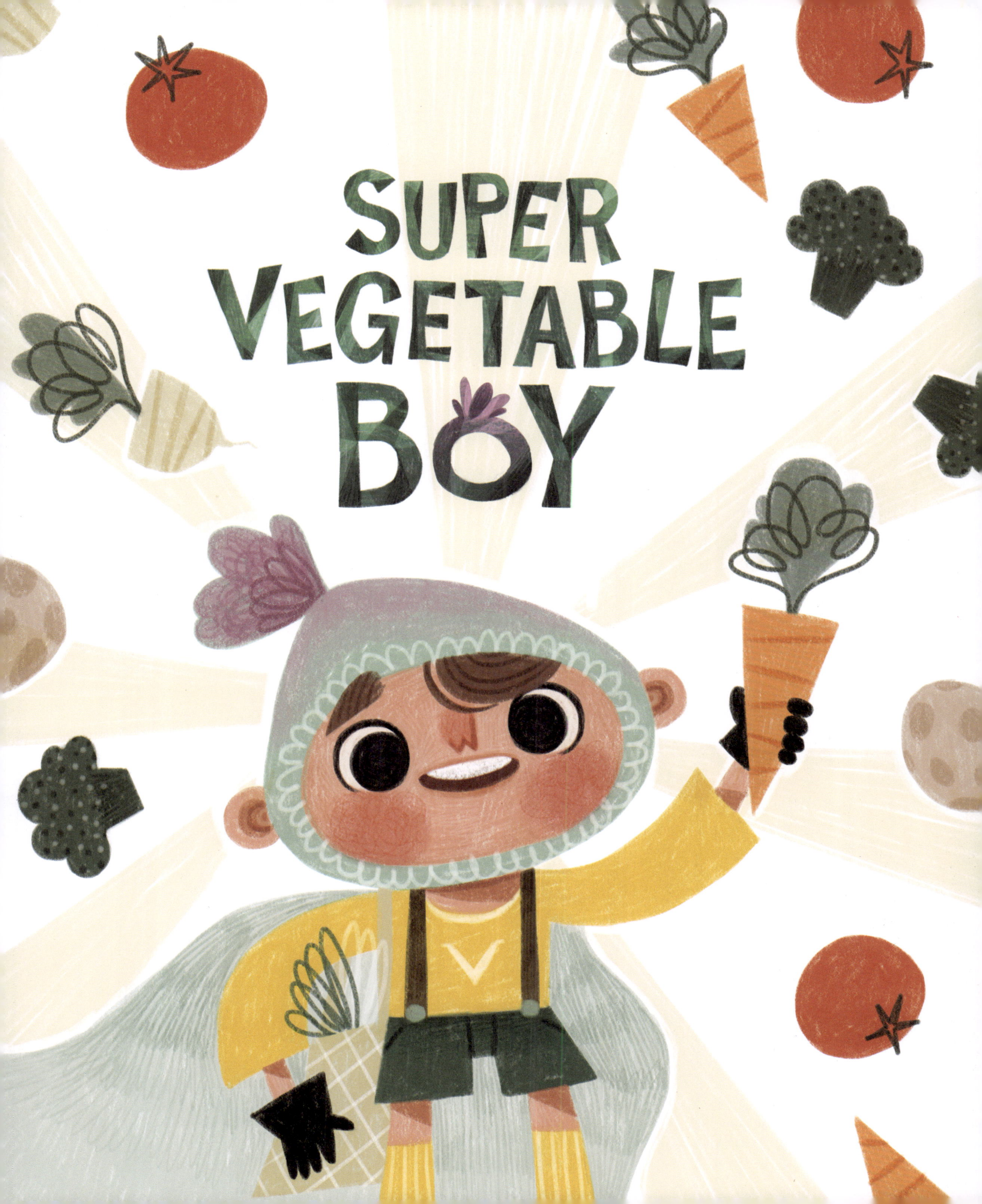
SUPER
VEGETABLE
BOY

It's an ordinary day in Oopsville... or IS IT?
Danger could lurk around every corner.
Disaster could hide behind every door.

But do not fear, residents of Oopsville,
for a hero watches over you.
He's alert and ready, he's strong and brave,
he's... carrying a big bag of vegetables.
It's SUPER VEGETABLE BOY!!

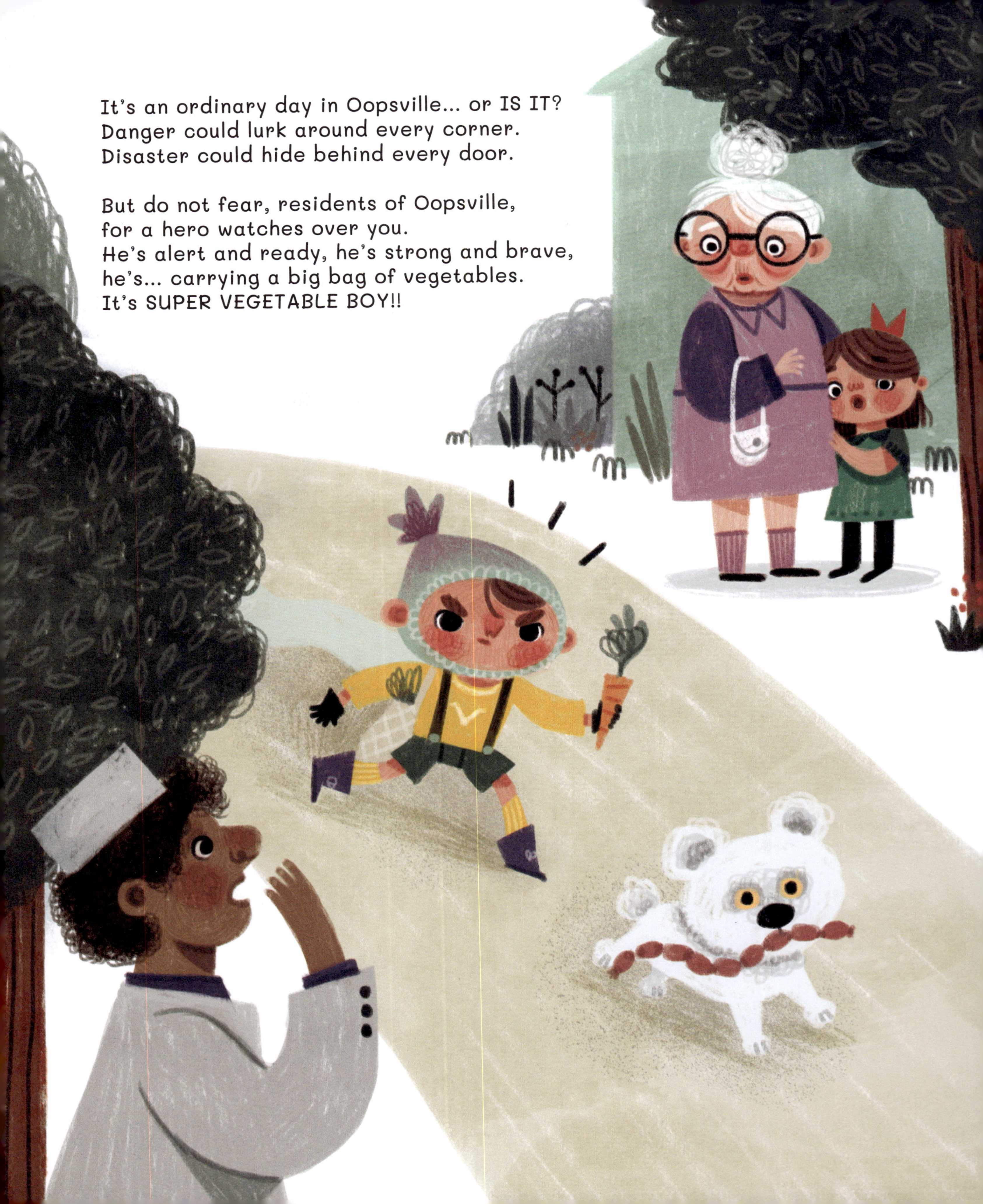

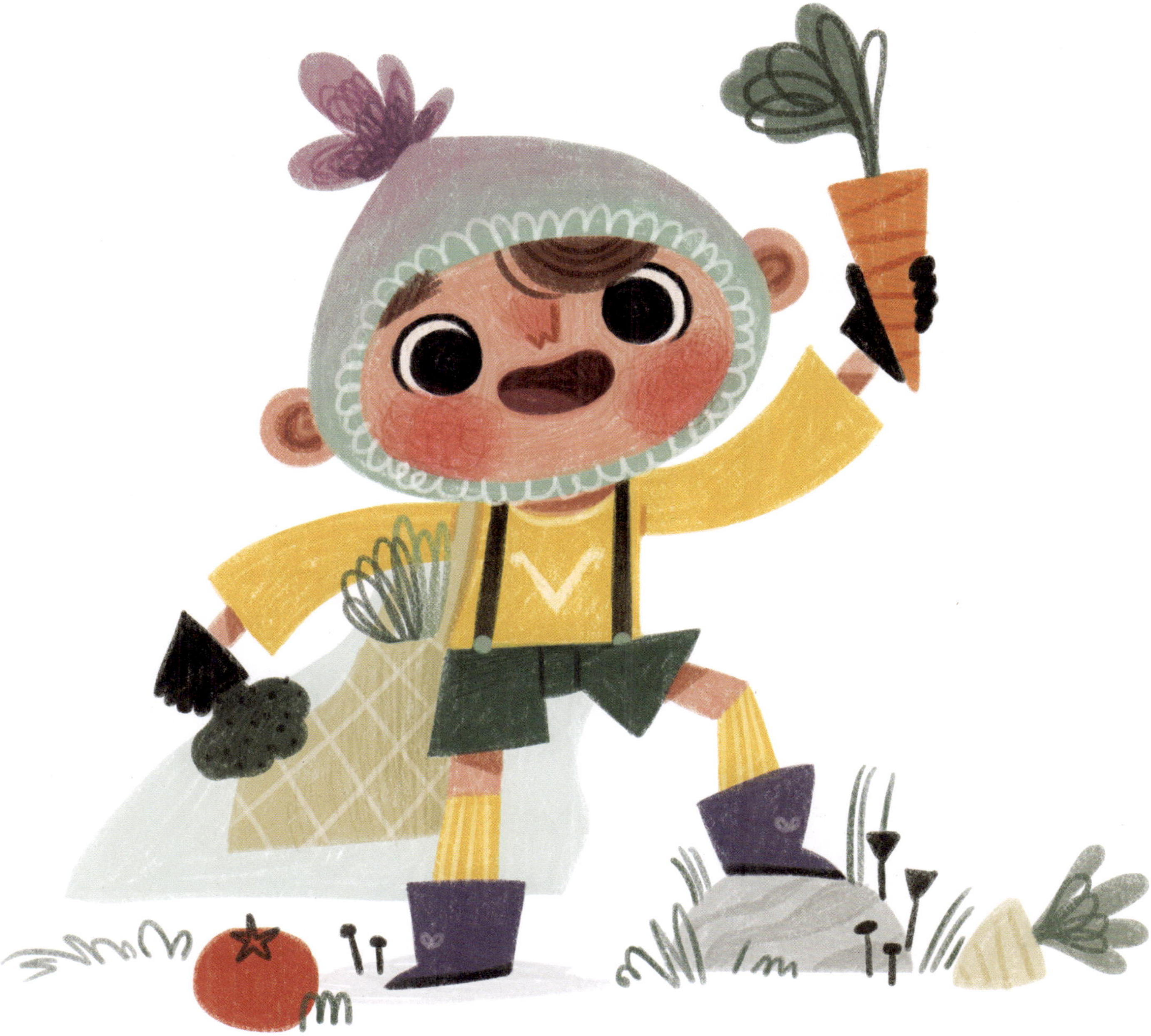

"Yes, I am Super Vegetable Boy,
and I am brave at least five times a day.
I patrol the streets of Oopsville,
on the lookout for peril,
properly prepared with my parsnips and potatoes,
bravely battling bother with my broccoli and beetroots,
controlling commotions with my carrots and cauliflowers."

"OH HELP!
The wind has blown my hat off
and it's stuck in that tree.
What am I to do?
Whoever can help me?"

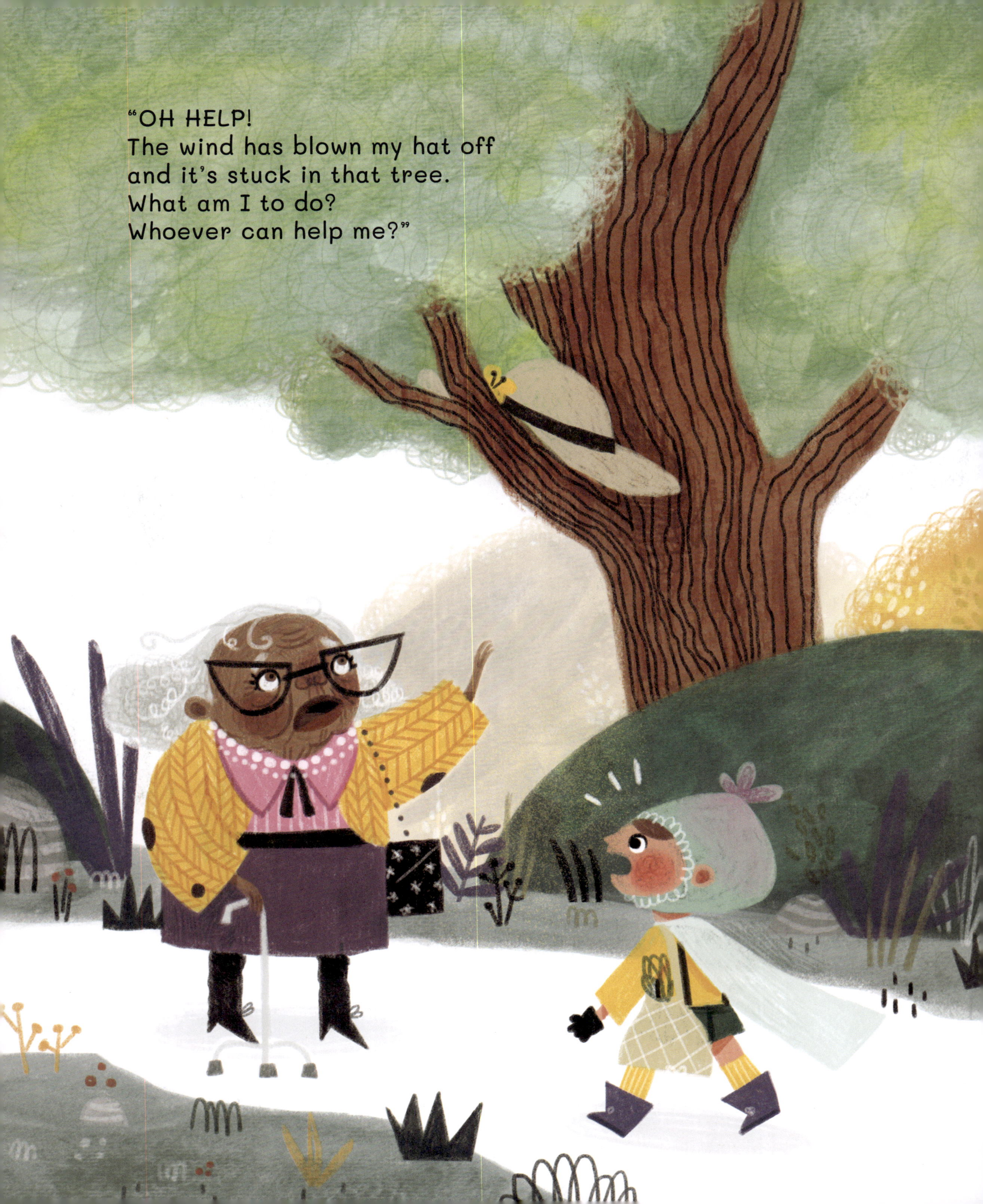

Could it be... is it...? Yes, this looks like a job for... SUPER VEGETABLE BOY!

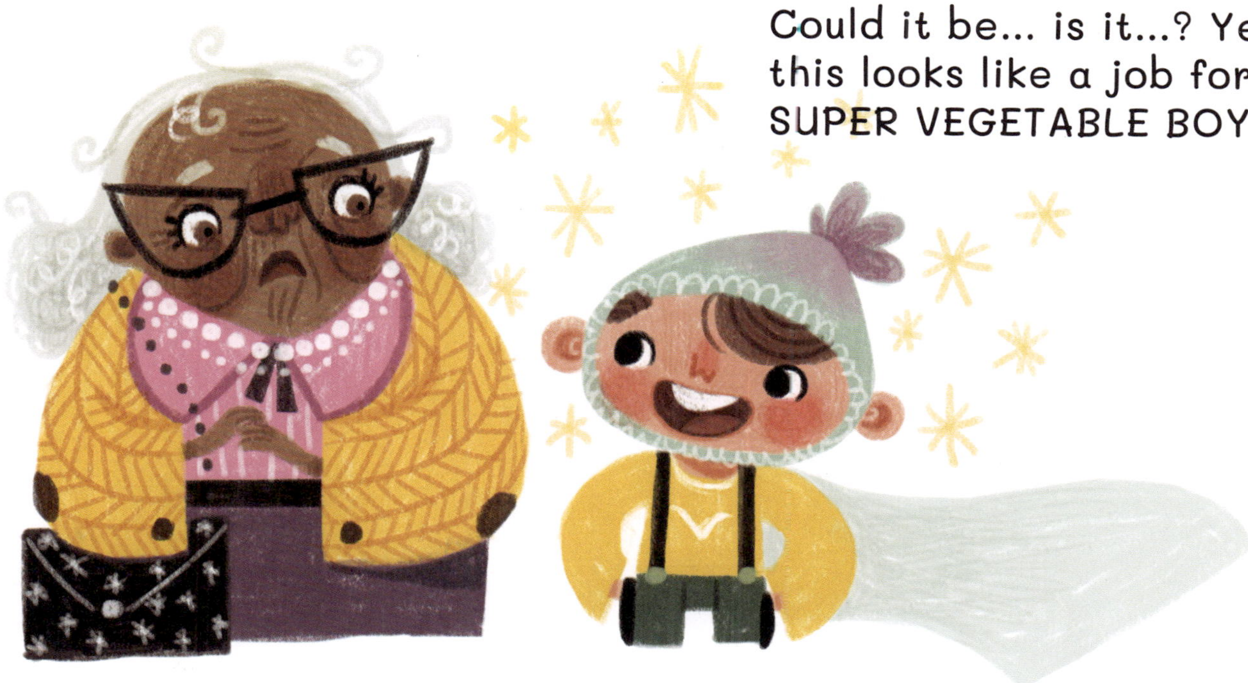

"Stand back Ma'am,
and I, Super Vegetable Boy,
will retrieve your hat in the blink of an eye.
Tomato! Tomato Tomato Tomato!"

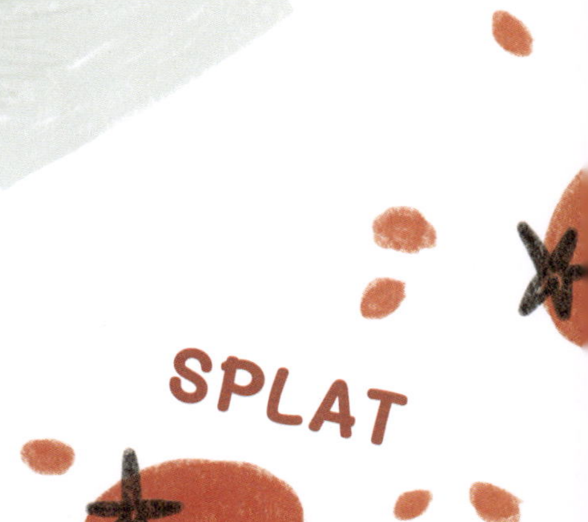


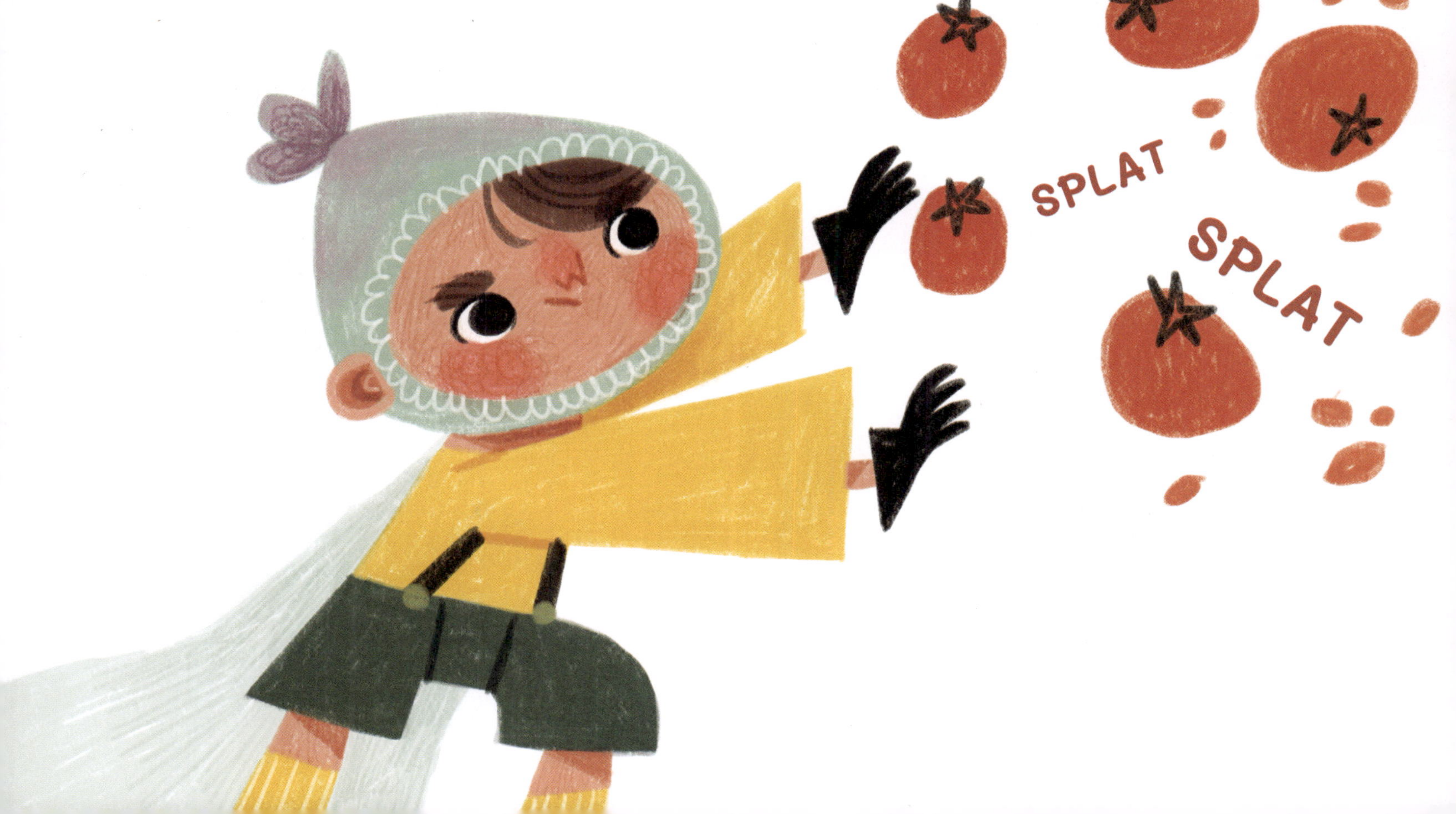

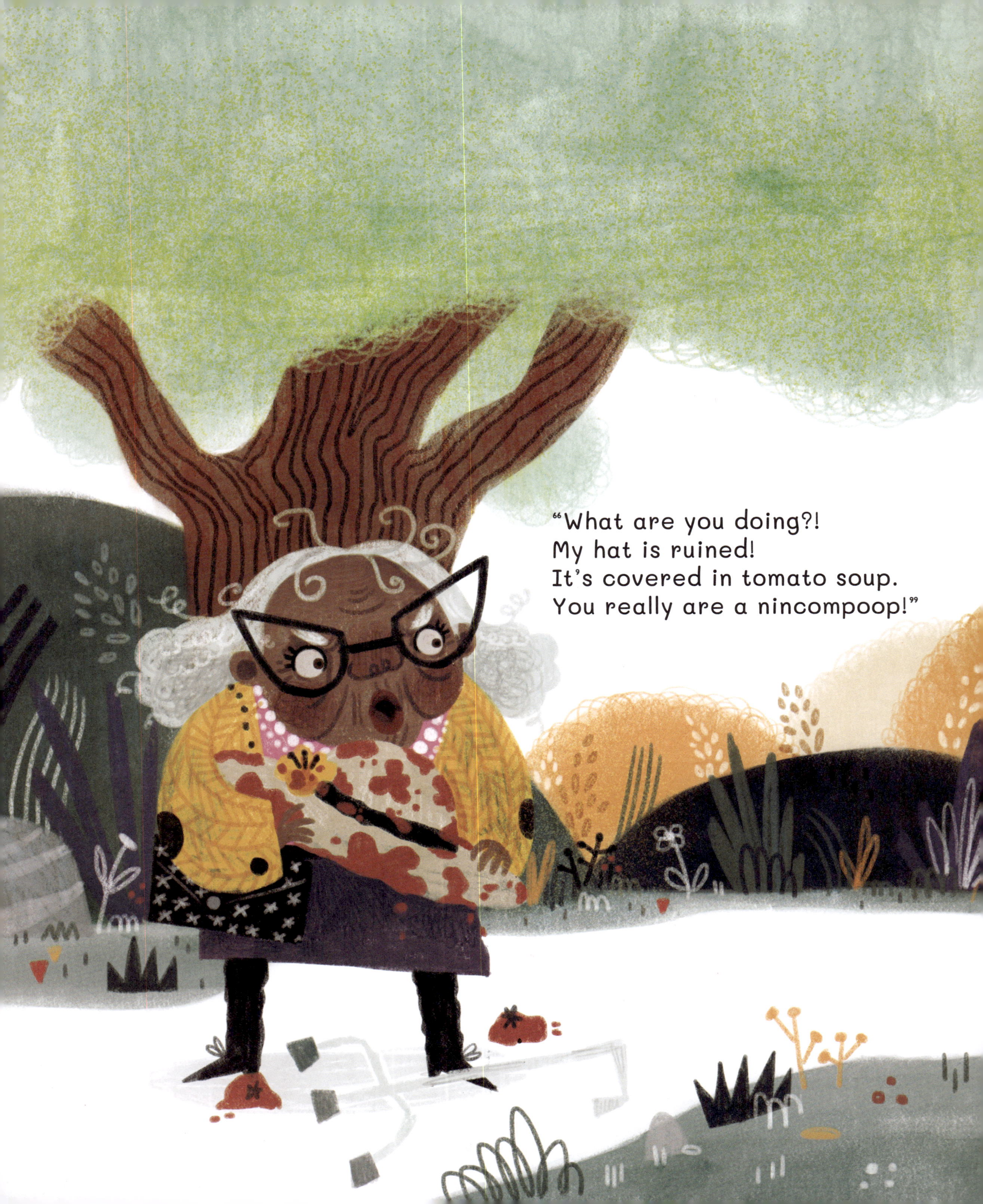

"What are you doing?!
My hat is ruined!
It's covered in tomato soup.
You really are a nincompoop!"

"Well really!
Some people are so ungrateful.
But do not fear!
For I, Super Vegetable Boy, will continue on my way,
protecting the residents of Oopsville from danger and disaster!"

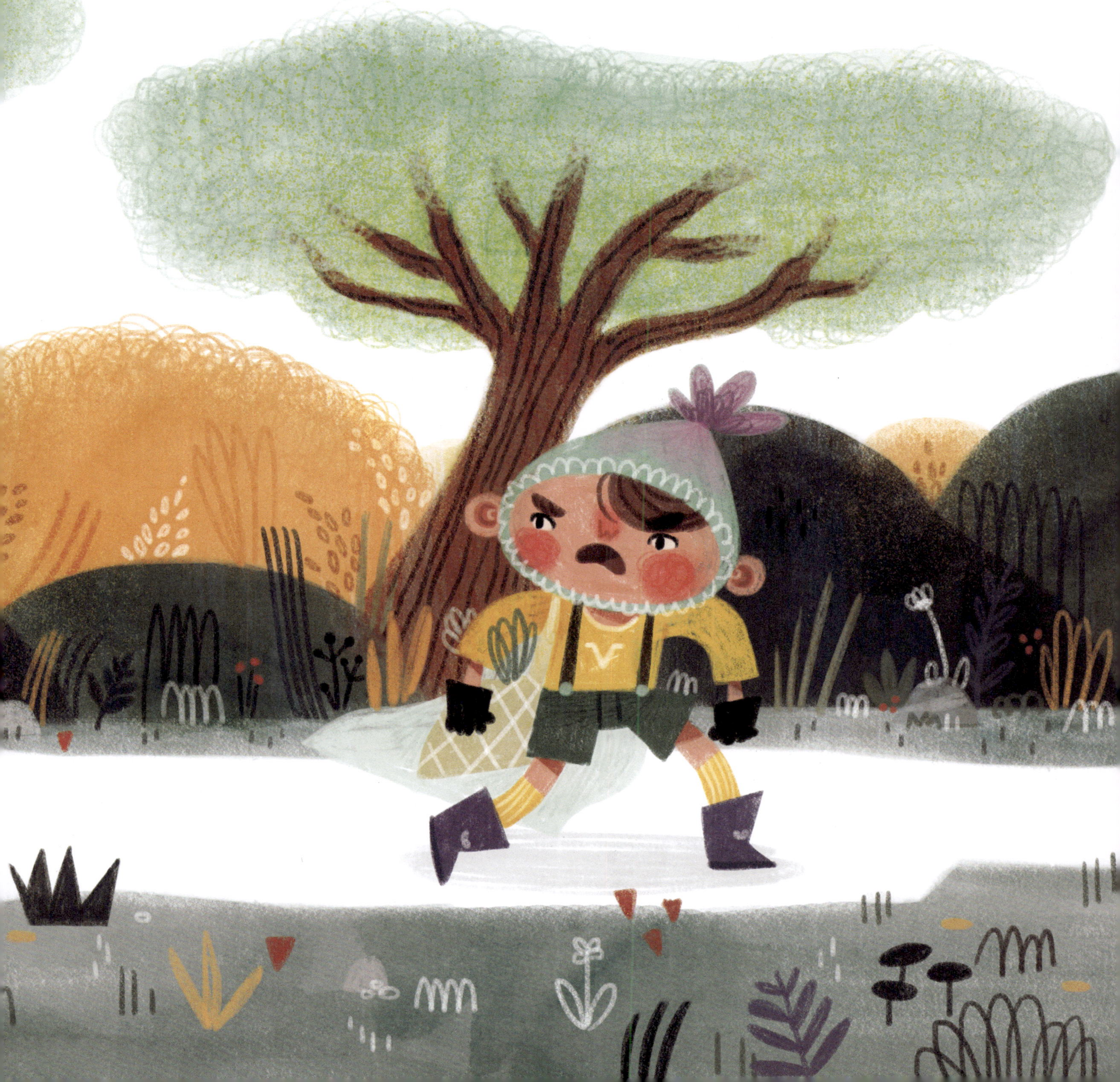

"OH HELP! My car
is stuck in the mud.
What am I to do?
Who will rescue me?"

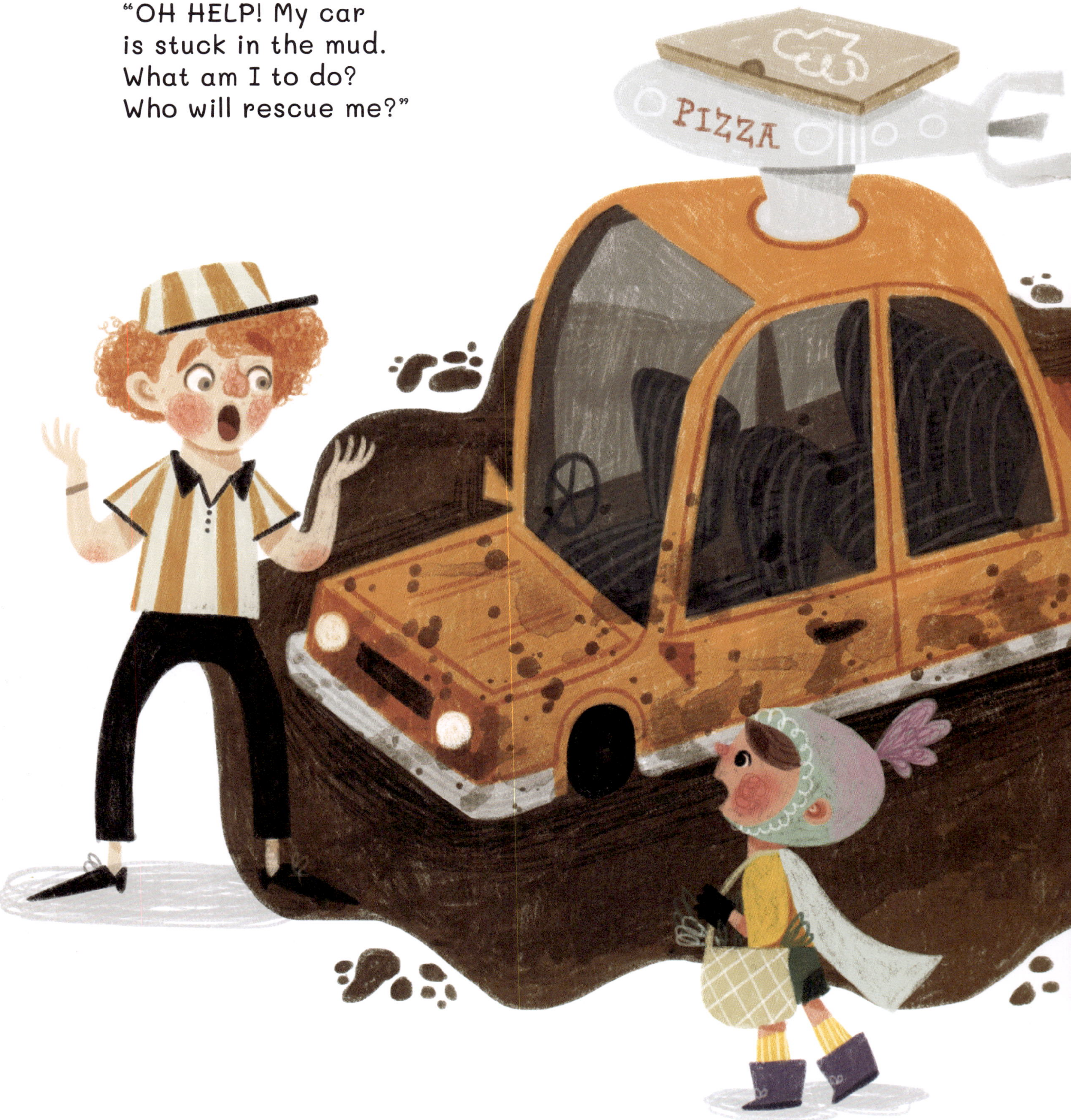

Could it be... is this the one... ?
Yes, this looks like a job for...
SUPER VEGETABLE BOY!

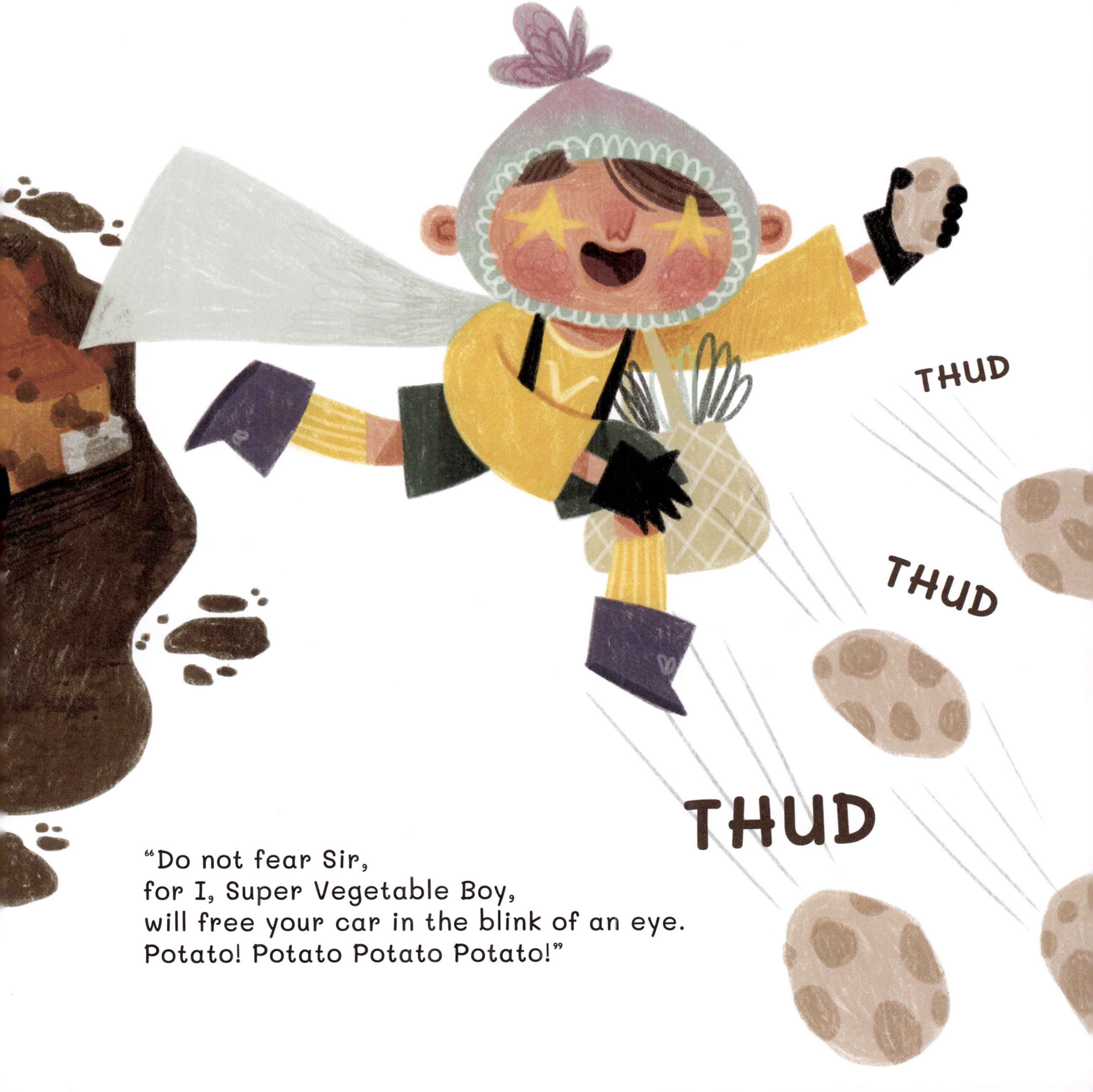


“Do not fear Sir,
for I, Super Vegetable Boy,
will free your car in the blink of an eye.
Potato! Potato Potato Potato!”

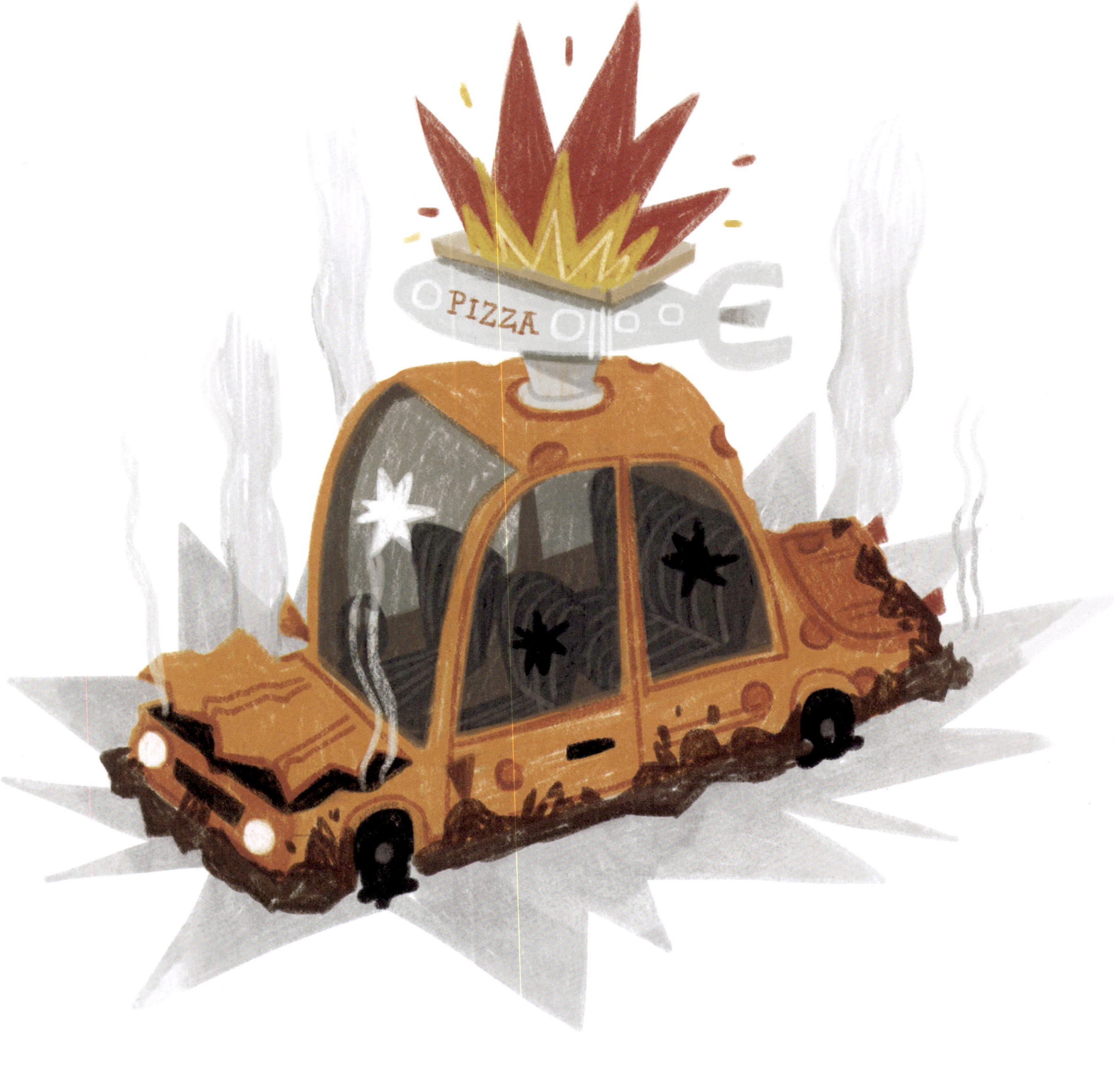
PIZZA

"We're most discontented –
our car is all dented!
Your potatoes were no help at all.
You're driving us all up the wall!"

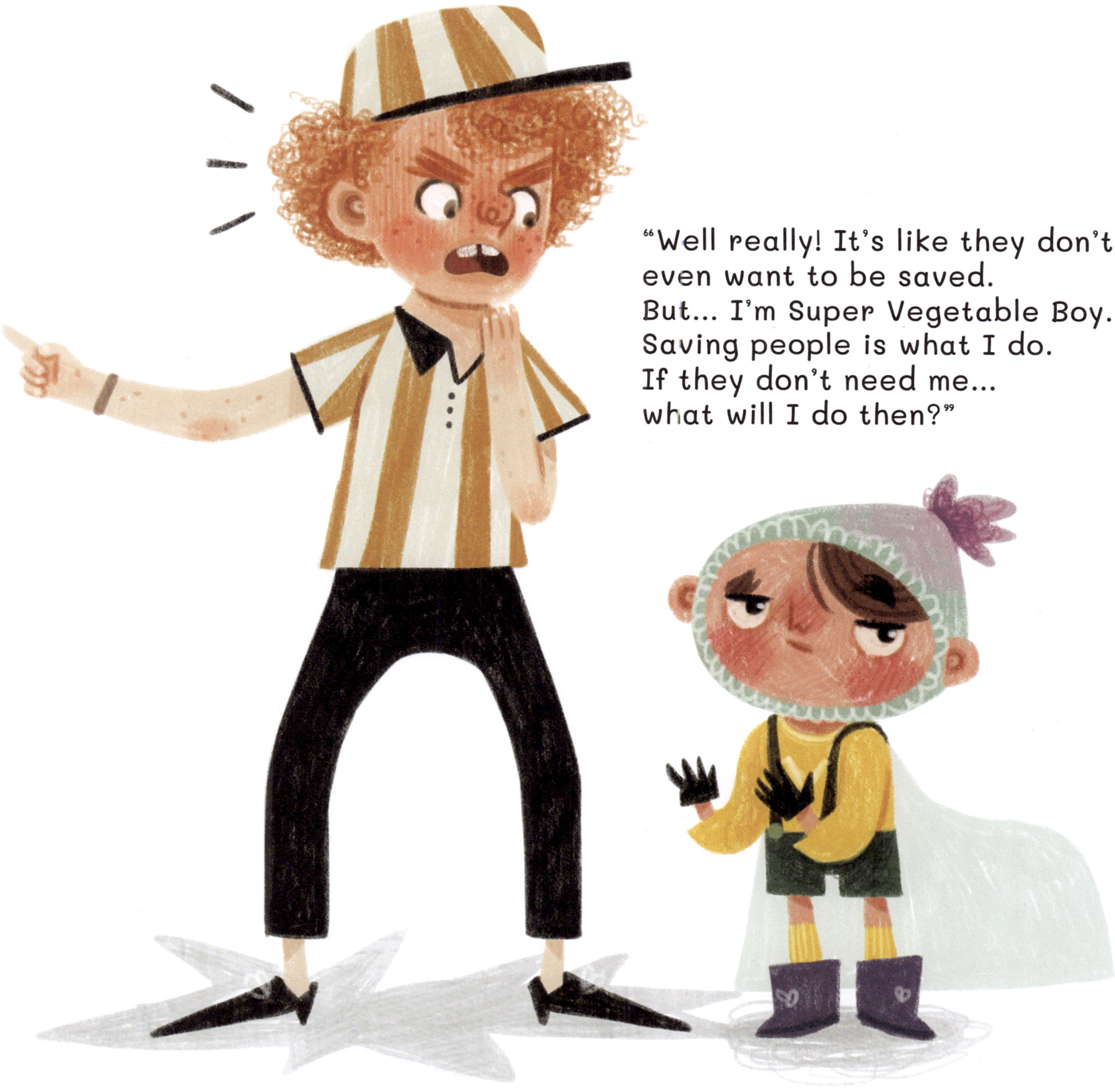

"Well really! It's like they don't
even want to be saved.
But... I'm Super Vegetable Boy.
Saving people is what I do.
If they don't need me...
what will I do then?"

Is this the end for our salad savior?
Time to call it a day, our green guardian?
Please don't give up, we're all rooting for you!

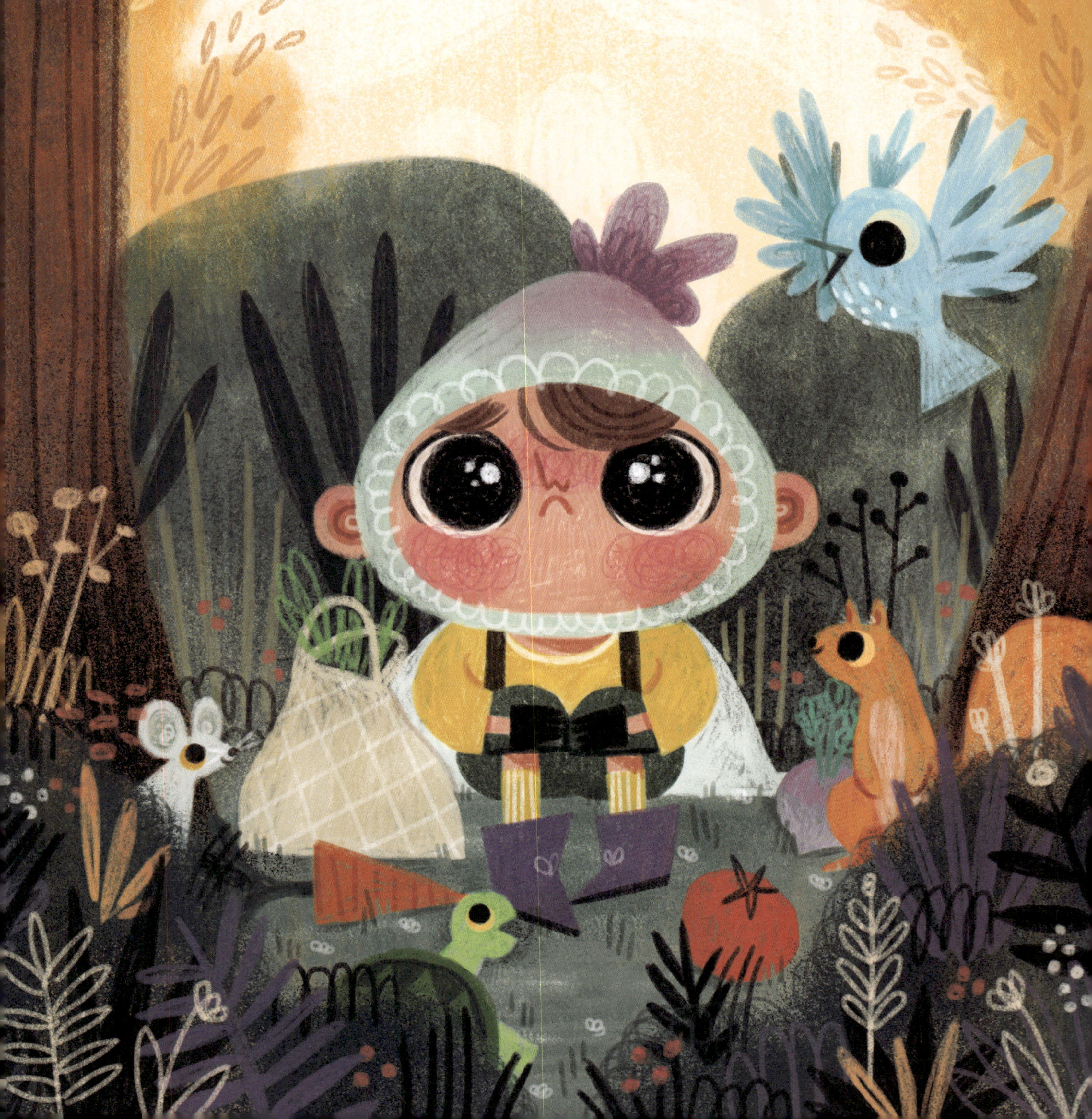

"Nope. It's just no good, I keep making things worse. I might as well go home and cook up a nice vegetable stew."

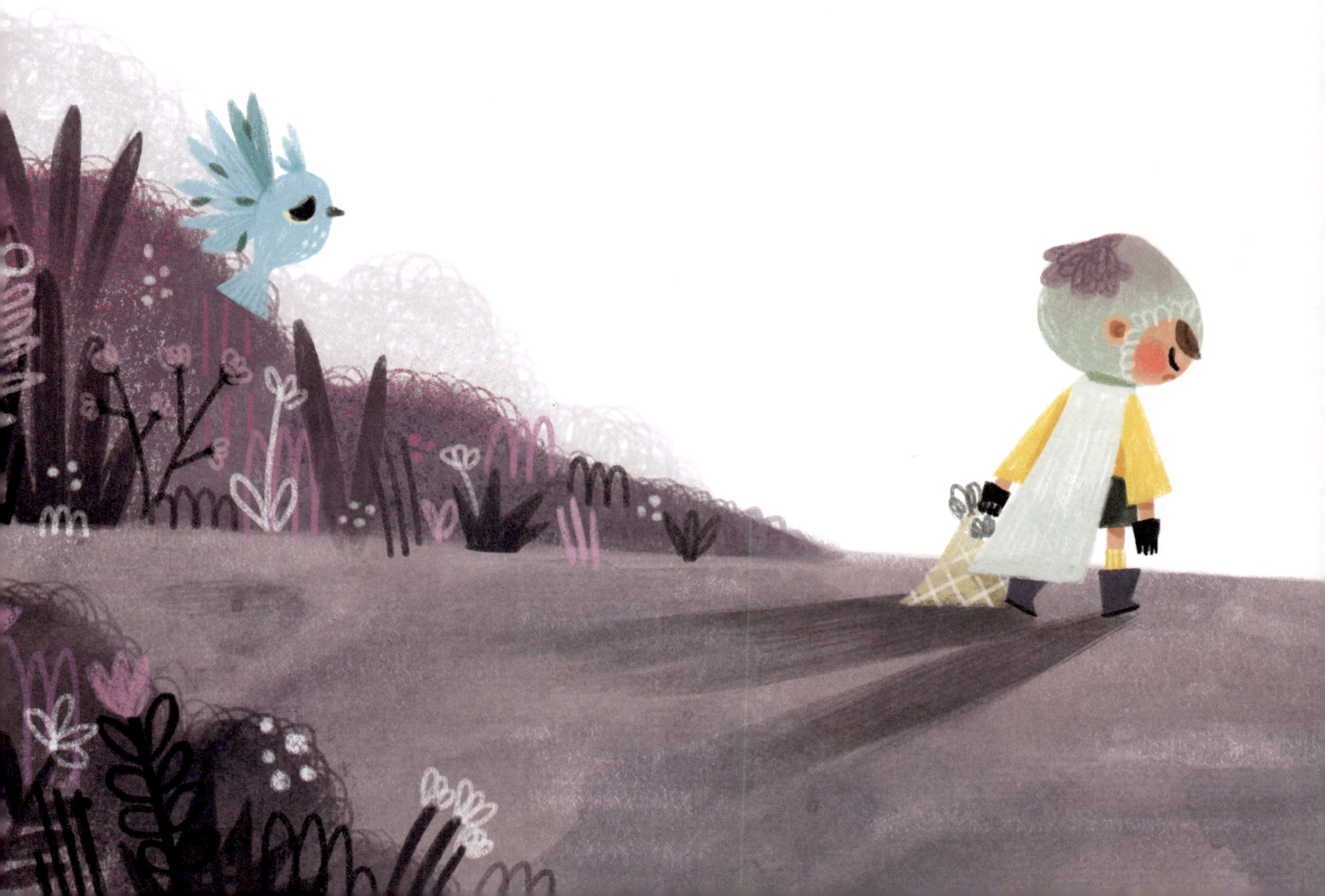

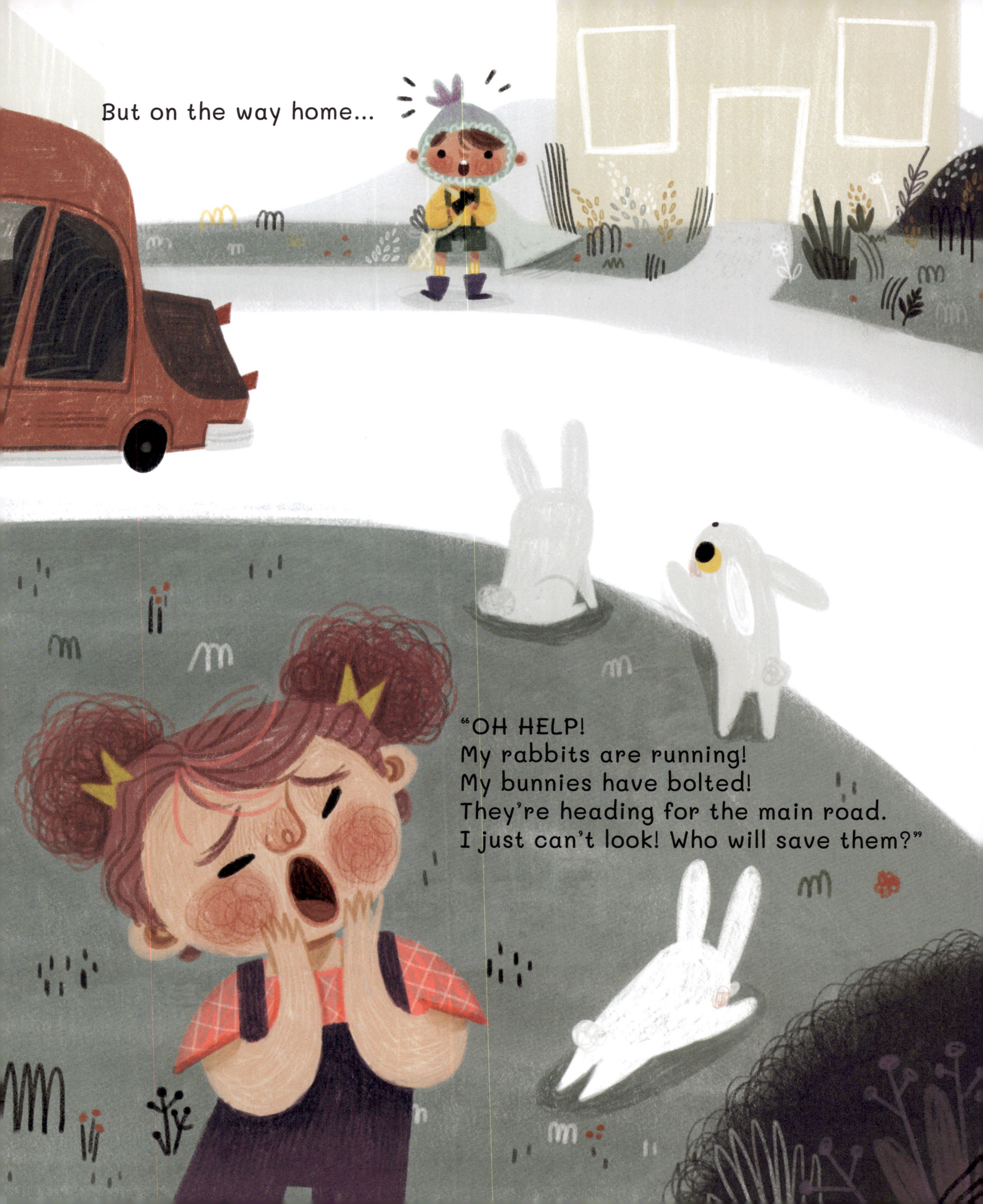

But on the way home...

“OH HELP!
My rabbits are running!
My bunnies have bolted!
They’re heading for the main road.
I just can’t look! Who will save them?”

"But what can I do?
Unless... of course!
My vegetables! Carrot!
Broccoli! Curly kaaaale!"
MUNCH! MUNCH! MUNCH!

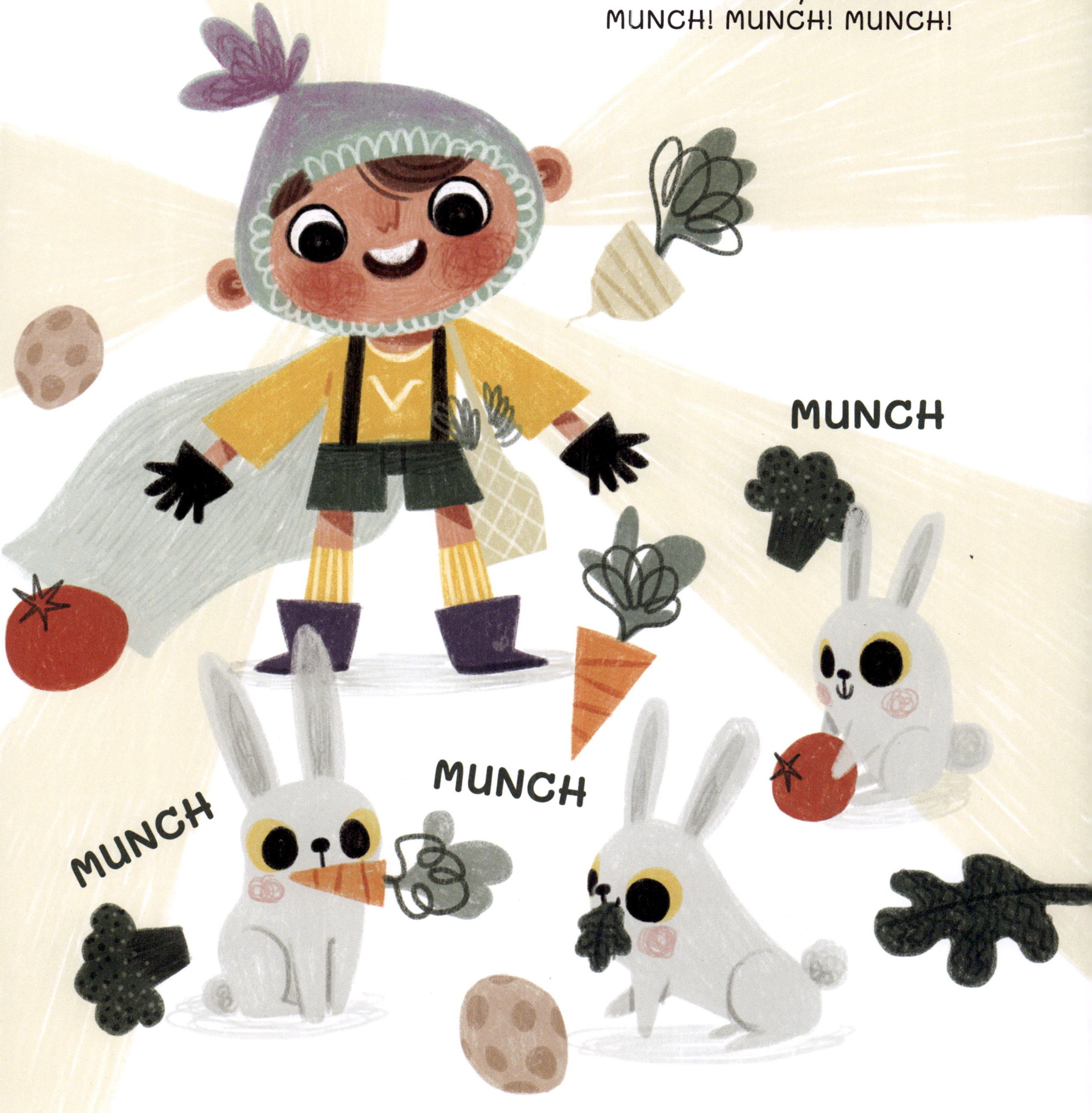

"My hero! You saved them,
with the vegetables you gave them!
I just want you to know,
you really are a SUPERHERO!"

"Yes, I am, aren't I?
I'm... SUPER VEGETABLE BOY!
Carrot! Potato! Broccoli! Parsnip!
TOMATOOOOOOOOO!!!!!"

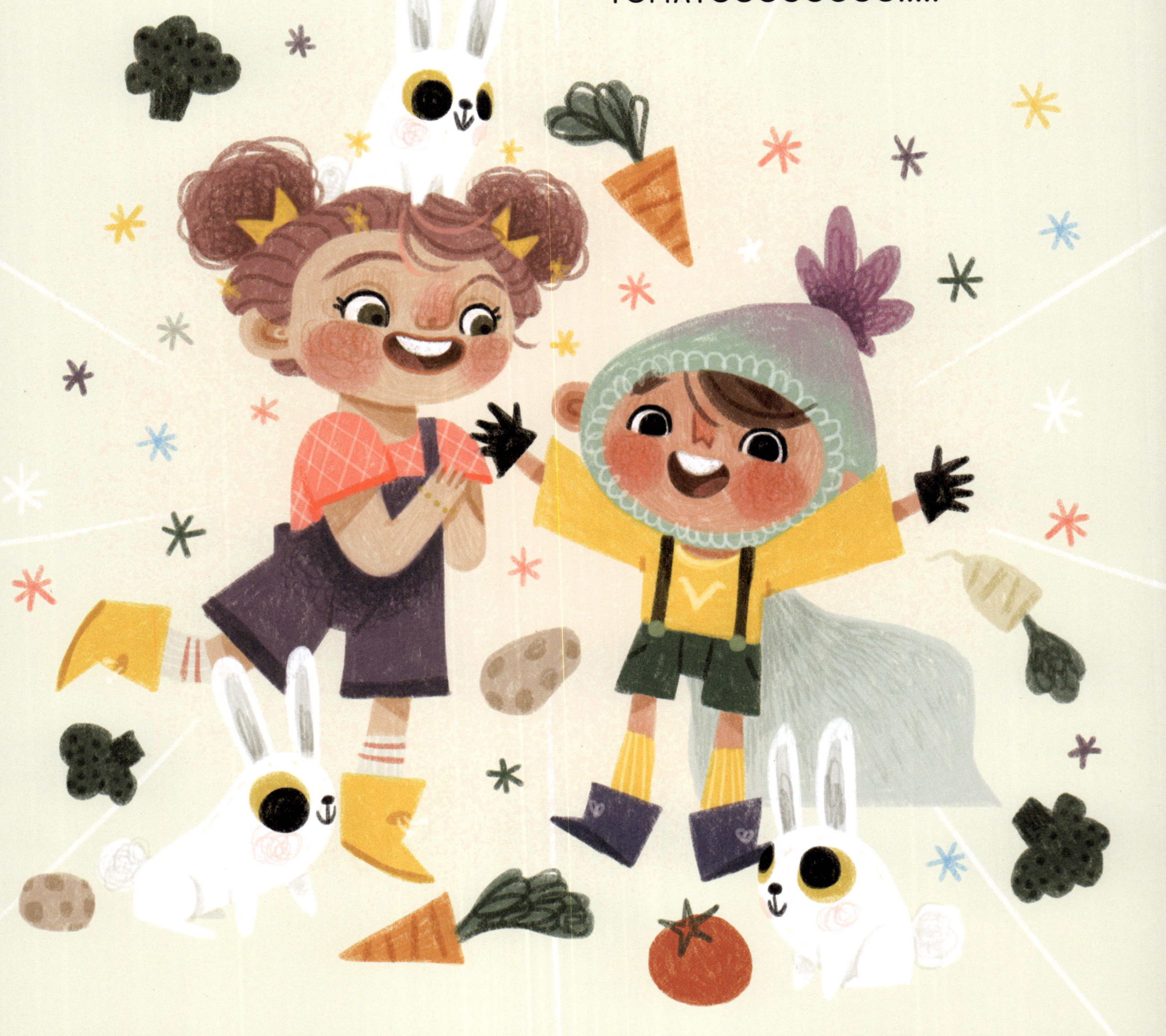

TURN THE PAGE FOR
INSIGHTS FROM THE ARTIST

# SUPER VEGETABLE BOY

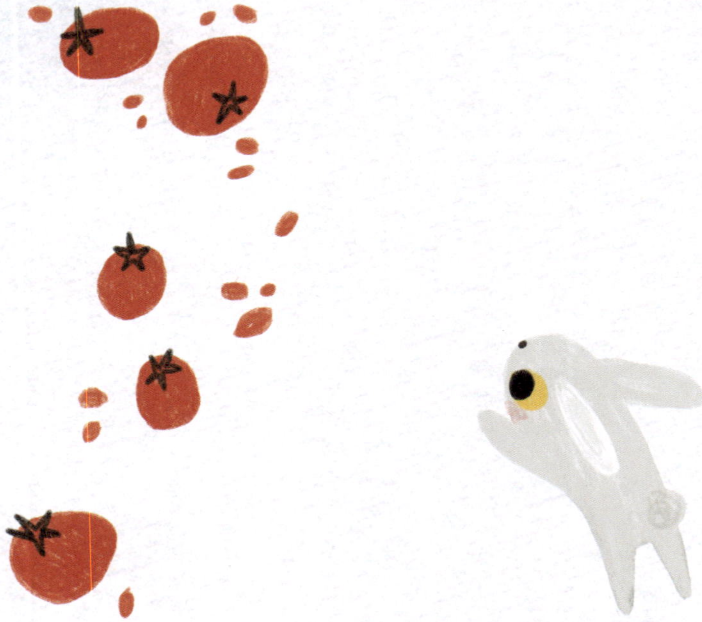

## DEVELOPING KEY FEATURES

### CHARACTER

The design of the main character is one of the most important factors when illustrating a children's book. You want readers to identify with the character immediately, making them more likely to enjoy and relate to the story being told. Have fun designing your main character – children are drawn to creativity and imagination, and will be keen to follow the character's adventures. Remember to keep the story in mind when working out your character's design, and don't hesitate to introduce additional details and visual elements. This will give your character credibility and depth, and will help bring them to life.

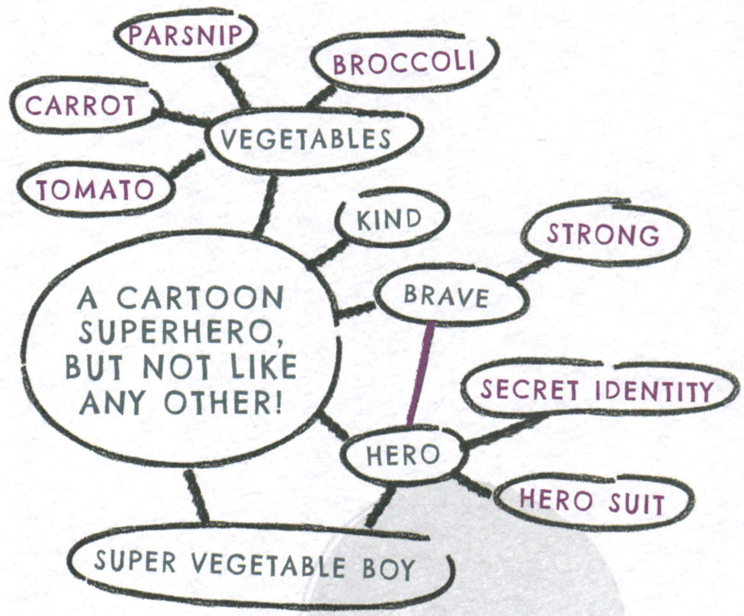


Create a mind map to jot down keywords that describe your character. Draw branches from the central word or character brief, exploring any ideas the character evokes and using each word to generate further ideas. Keep the ideas that will help develop your design.

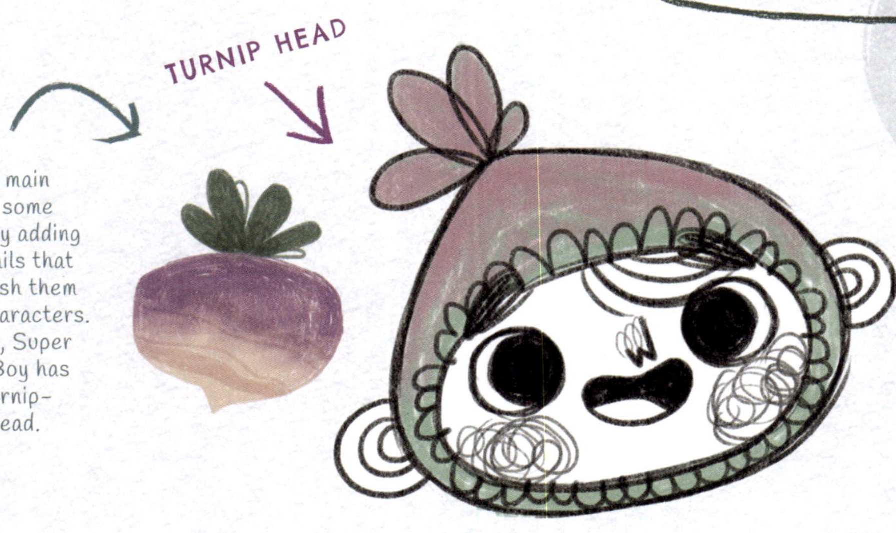


Give your main character some personality by adding original details that will distinguish them from other characters. For example, Super Vegetable Boy has a large, turnip-shaped head.

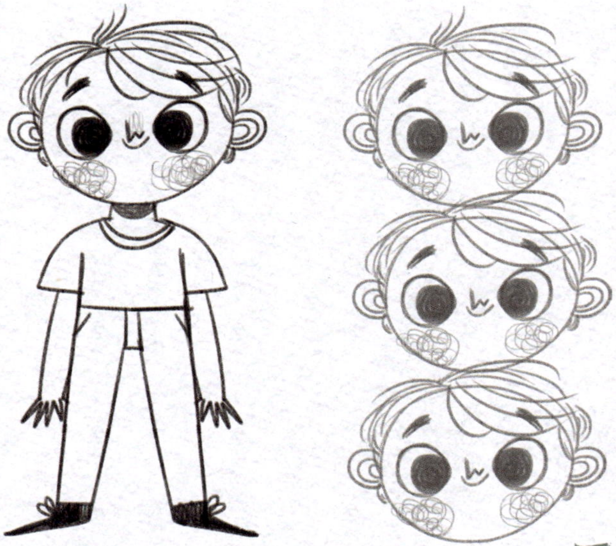

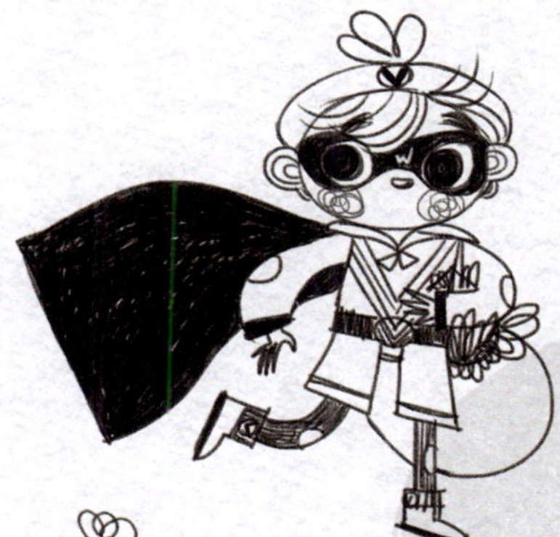

Have fun experimenting with different styles. For a superhero-type character, consider using typical superhero accessories such as a mask, cape, gloves, or boots. Include elements that will add motion, like a cape or pompoms on a hat.

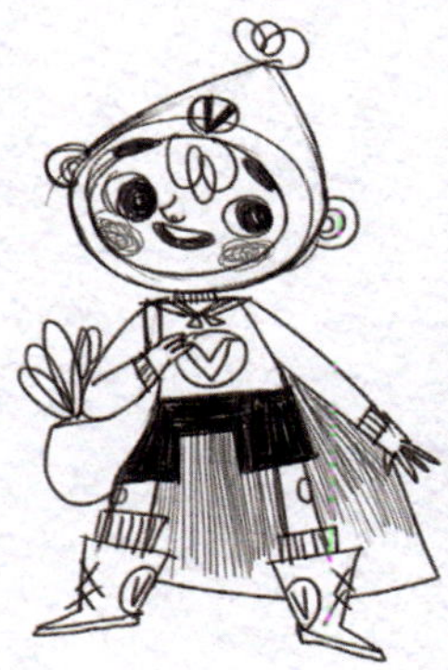

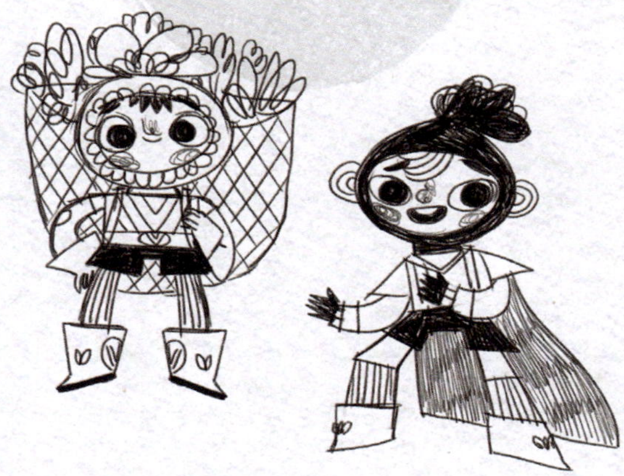

Child characters often have small proportions and exaggerated features. One way to create this cute look is to draw a three-heads-tall figure with a large round head, big expressive eyes, and ears that stick out.

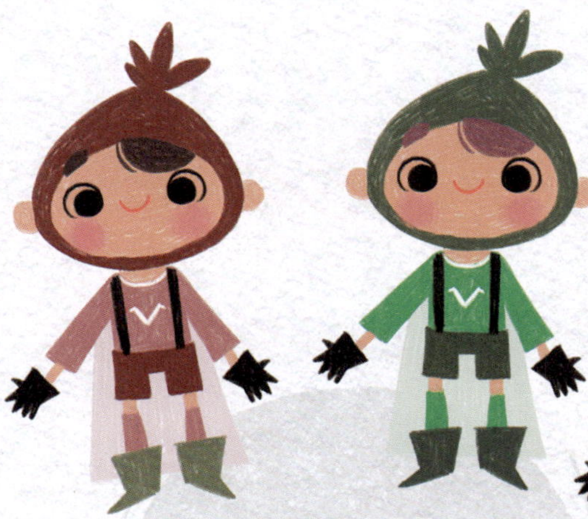

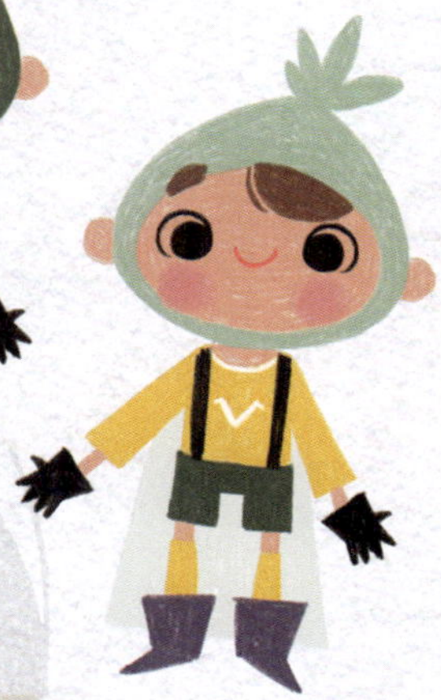

Identify the mood of the story and personality of the character when experimenting with and choosing their color palette. A benevolent, willful, and dynamic character like Super Vegetable Boy calls for a colorful and bright color palette, with shades of green to convey his vegetable obsession.

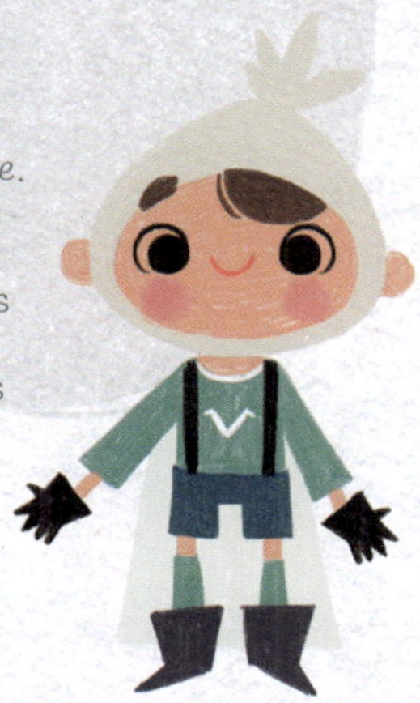

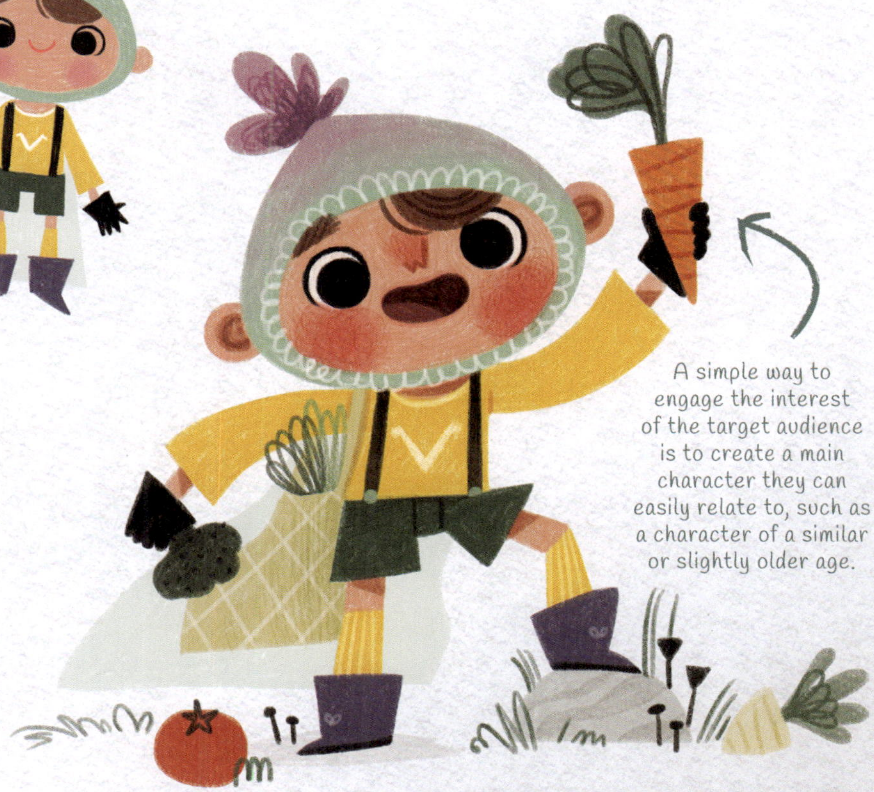

A simple way to engage the interest of the target audience is to create a main character they can easily relate to, such as a character of a similar or slightly older age.

## ENVIRONMENT

The environment in which the characters evolve must provide information to enhance and further the story. Environments should communicate an atmosphere or create a feeling, for example of calm or chaos, emptiness or grandeur. While the environment is complementary to the characters, it should never steal the spotlight. For that reason, it can help to situate the characters and story action against a simple or white background for scenes where you want to emphasize or focus on their emotions and intentions. It's also necessary to experiment with different perspectives and layouts to best serve the story. Keep an open mind and be creative to fully immerse your characters and readers in an environment that helps tell the story.

HOME

OOPSVILLE

MUD

TREE

THE MAIN ROAD

Note down keywords to determine the kind of environment needed for each scene. Create a mood board by collecting relevant images such as photos, textures, illustrations, and scenes from movies.

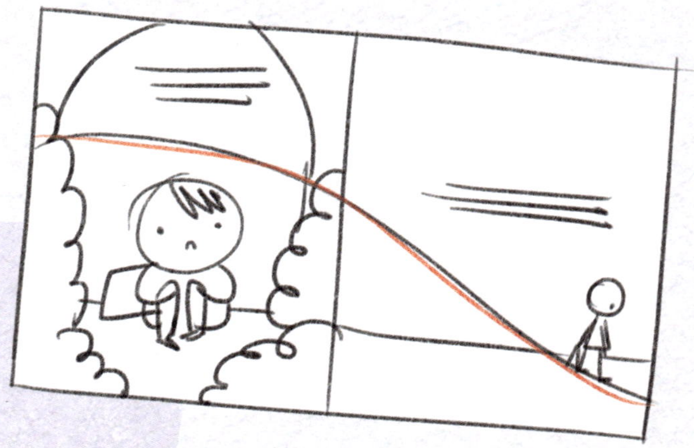

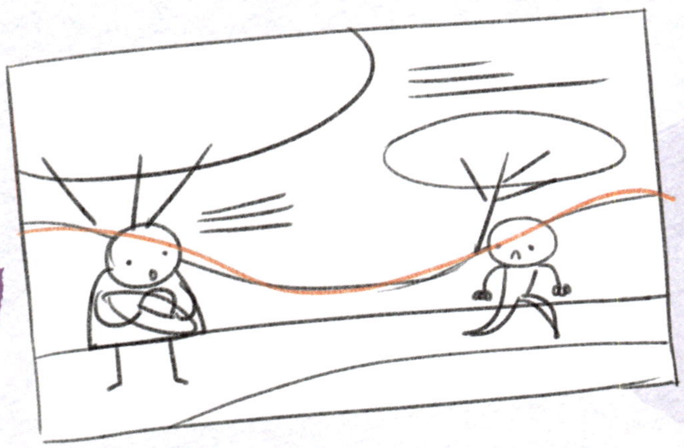

COMPOSITION GUIDELINE

Create a storyboard by drawing small frames to the scale of the book and making rough sketches to get a general idea of what will go on each page. Use the environment to create guidelines in your compositions. Try out different compositions, angles of view, and framing, such as close-ups, vignettes, and full-page scenes.

Refine your sketches, roughly placing different elements of scenery. Leave white spaces to lighten the images and remember to leave a clear space for the text.

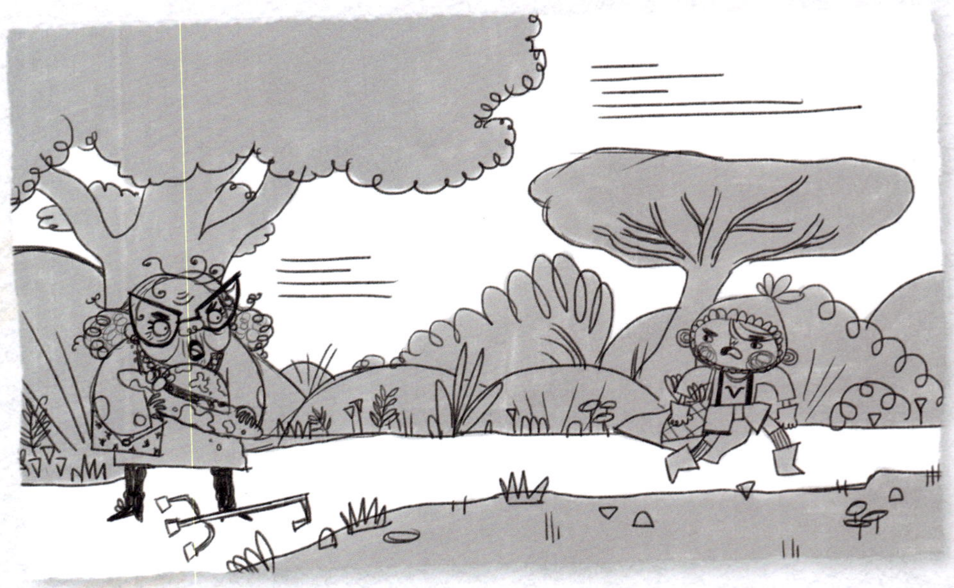

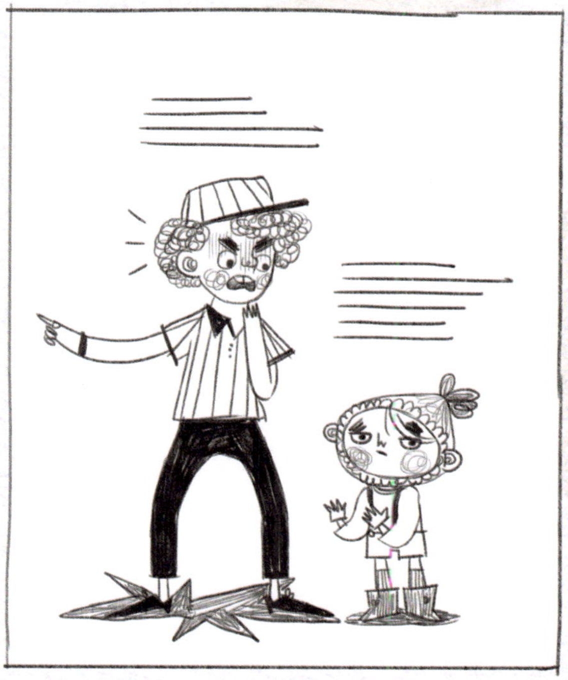

Close-up framing or a white background can help focus on action, a particular object, or a character's facial expression. Alternatively, a large frame can emphasize a striking landscape or show the distress of a character lost in a huge space.

Create a color palette to ensure consistency throughout the book. A change of color palette can communicate a change of mood, emotion, season, or time of day. Purple, for example, can convey solitude.

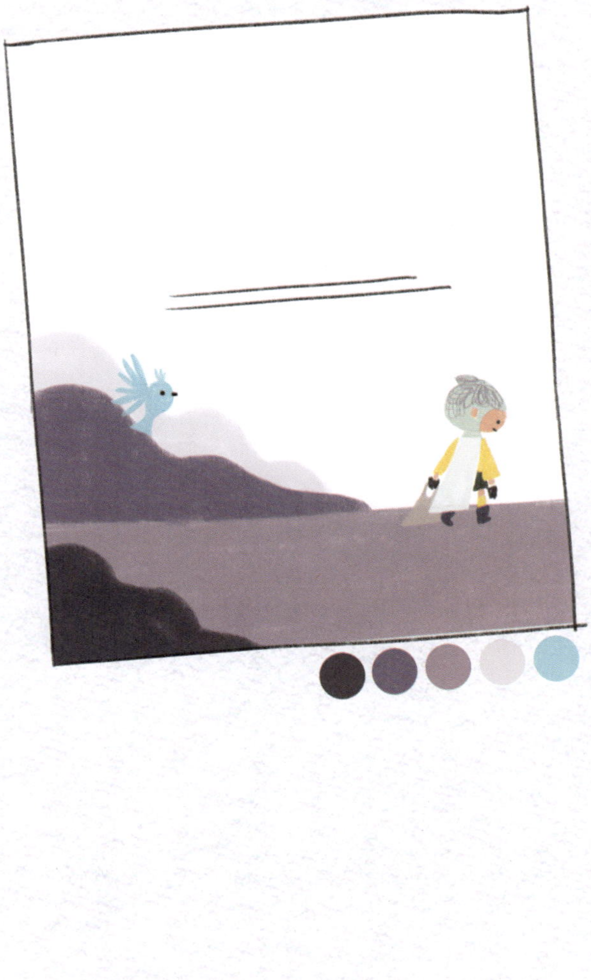

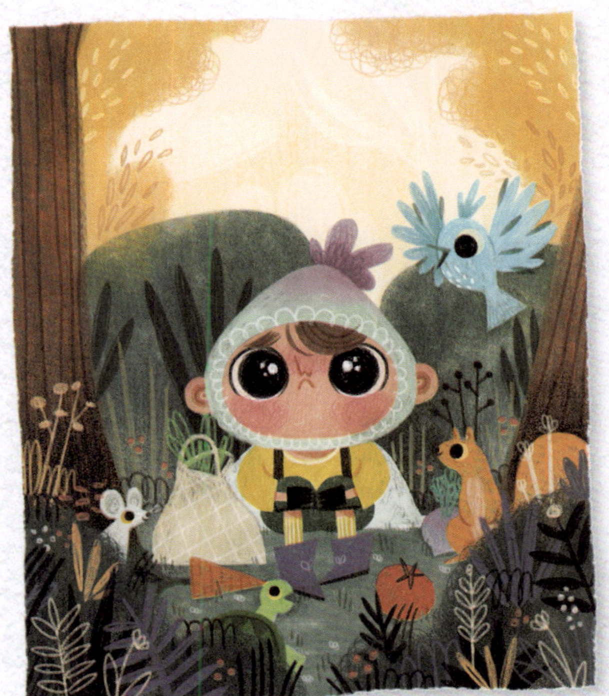

When designing the environment, don't simply draw what the story text says. Your illustration should enhance the text. Through your own interpretation of the story, choose key moments and visually add that "something extra" that will keep young readers captivated.

## VEHICLE

Vehicles are one of the elements in an environment that will immerse the reader in a particular style.

If the story doesn't specify the type or model of vehicle, have fun choosing one from a past or futuristic era. Keep in mind the story's target age range and try to create a vehicle unique to the story, playing with exaggerated shapes, funny details, and bright colors. This will be more entertaining for young readers than a realistic car. The large exaggerated windows of the main car shown here are a good way to show the driver and his expressions, if he is inside it. Alternatively, small or tinted windows could help hide a character and create suspense. Use the thumbnail stage to experiment and figure out what brings the most to the story.

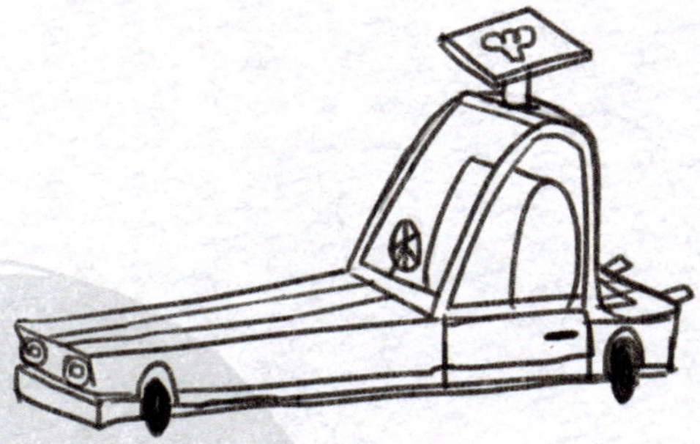

A car's design can help define the style of your illustrations. Choosing between a retro or futuristic model can completely change the mood of the story.

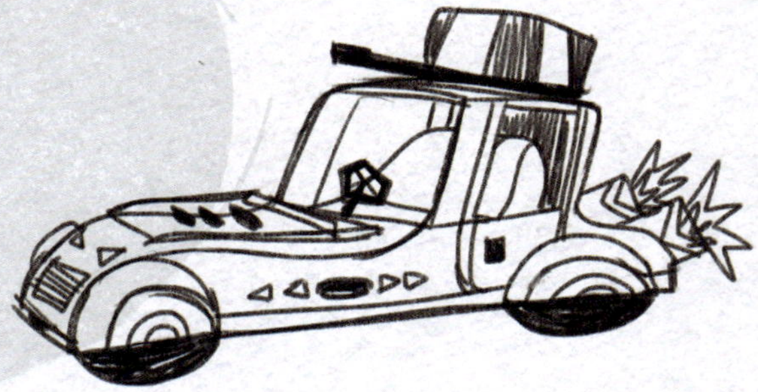

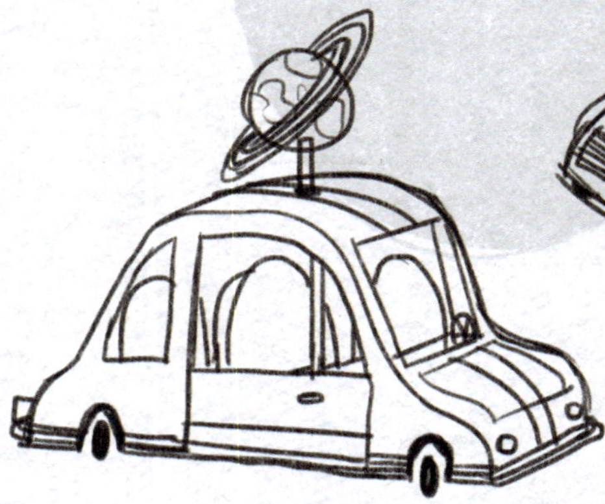

Experiment with shape. Soft and round or sharp and angular lines convey different personalities. Consider adding funny details such as large windows, tiny wheels, or a rocket on top.

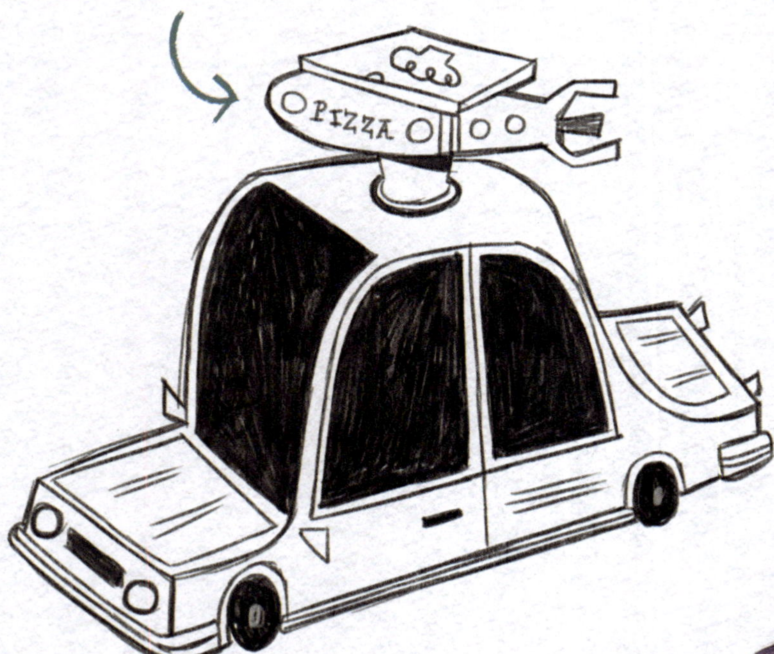


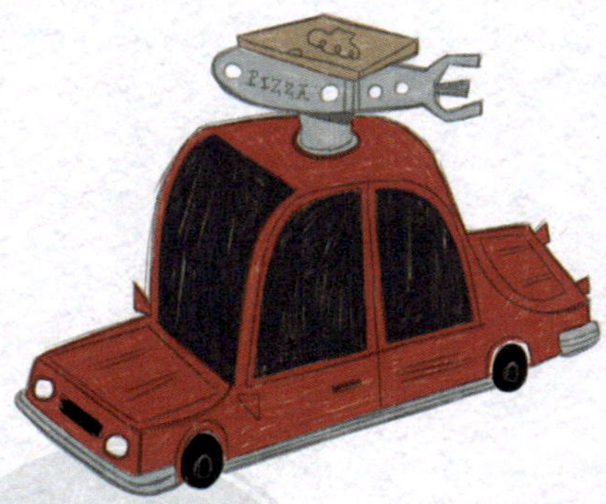

Use color to add meaning to a scene. For example, a red car can express danger, whereas a blue car could express safety or comfort.

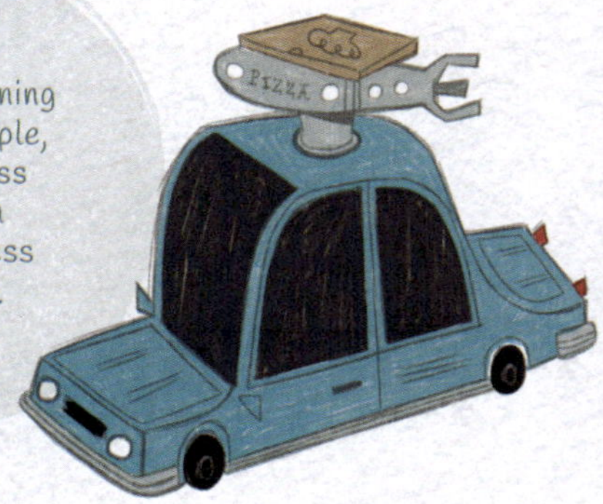

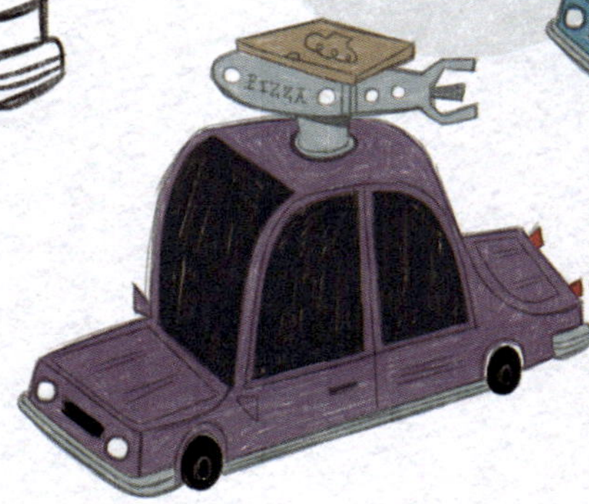

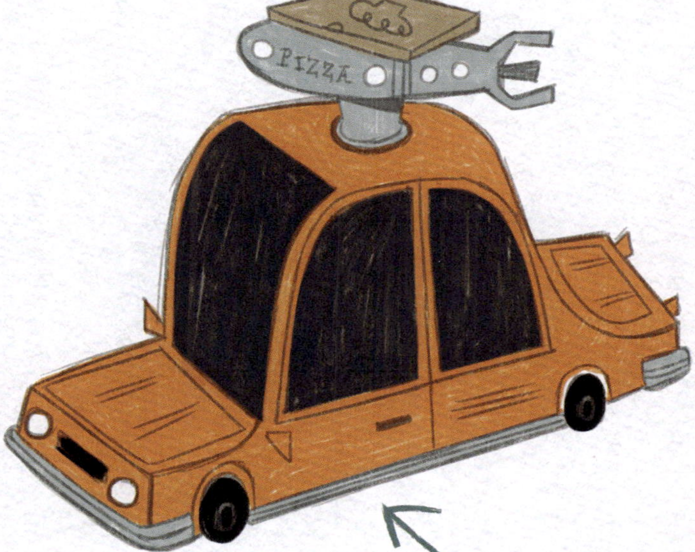


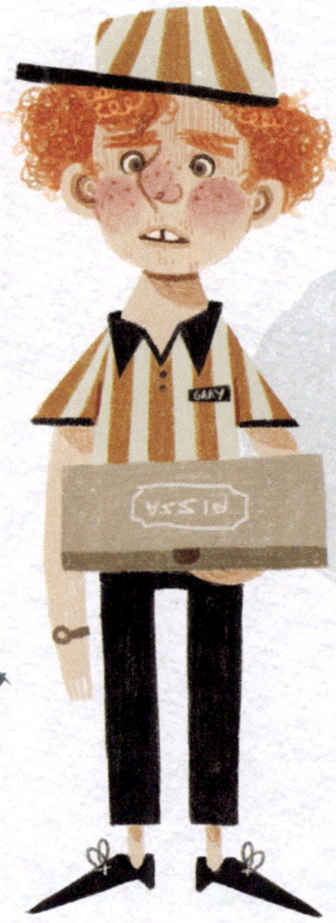

It's always fun to make a car match its owner.

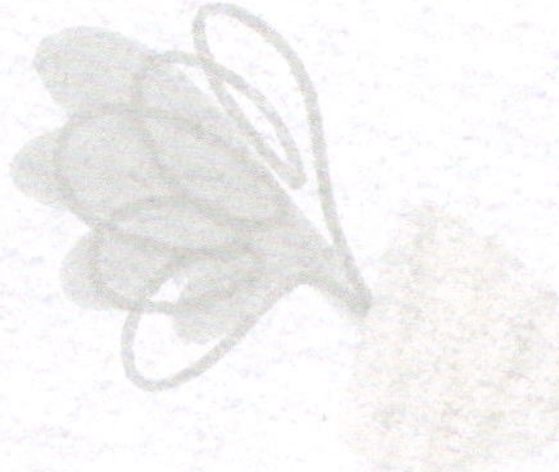

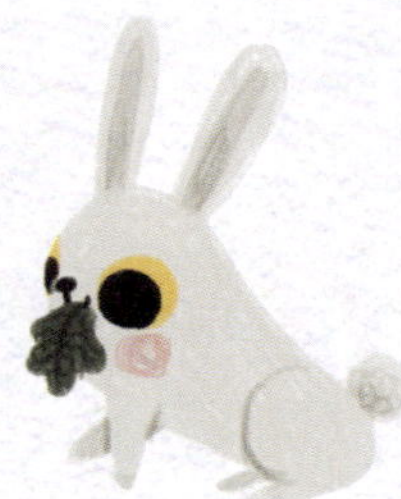

Create scenes that further the story. Add to the drama with disproportionate consequences. Here the dented car is also on fire!

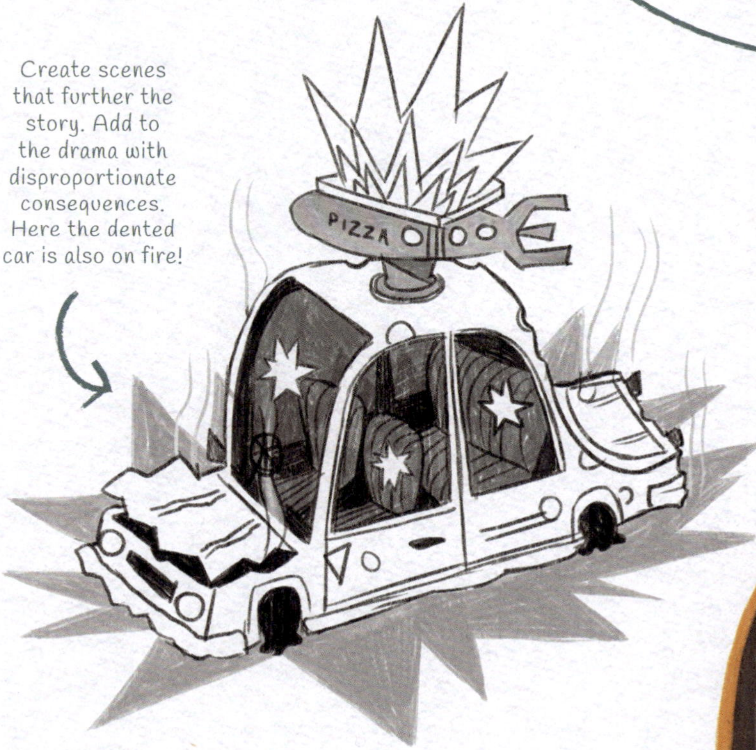


Retro design inspiration was key in the creation of the rocket pizza-delivery car.

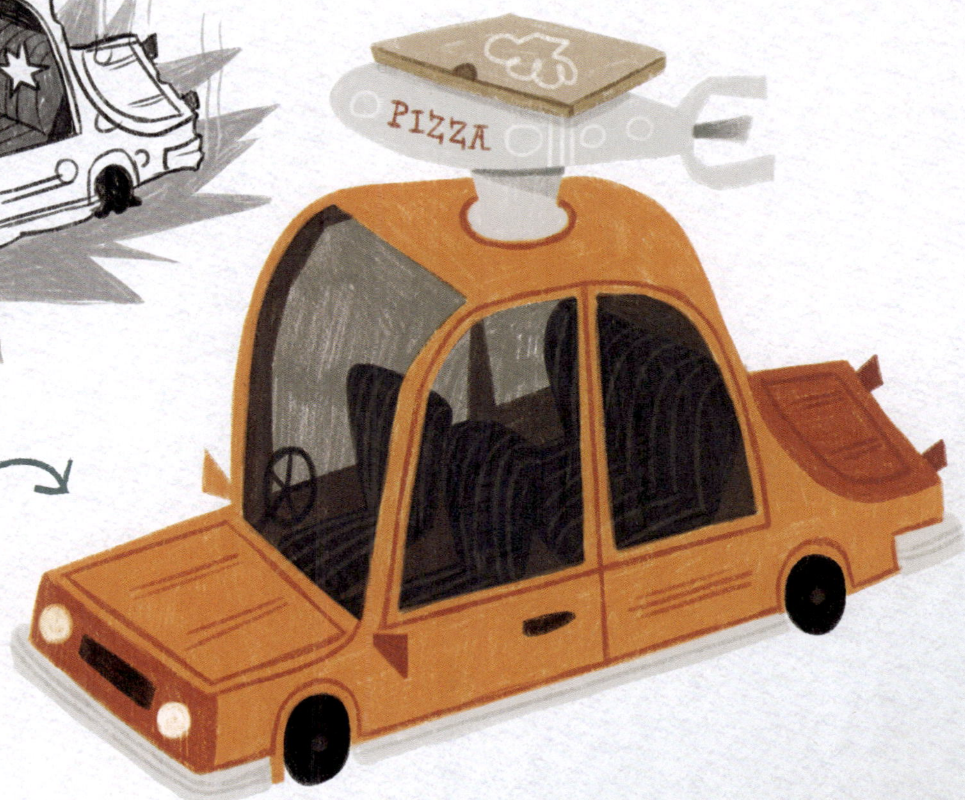

## BOOK COVER

The book cover is the first thing readers will see, so it must be captivating and eye-catching. The colors should be appealing to children, but keep in mind that it's parents who have the final word when it comes to choosing a book. It needs to be attractive to them too! Pay attention to the fact that the book can also be a decorative object in itself. Including the main character and focusing on their face is often a winning recipe. Remember to include elements that communicate the main theme of the book, but without revealing too much.

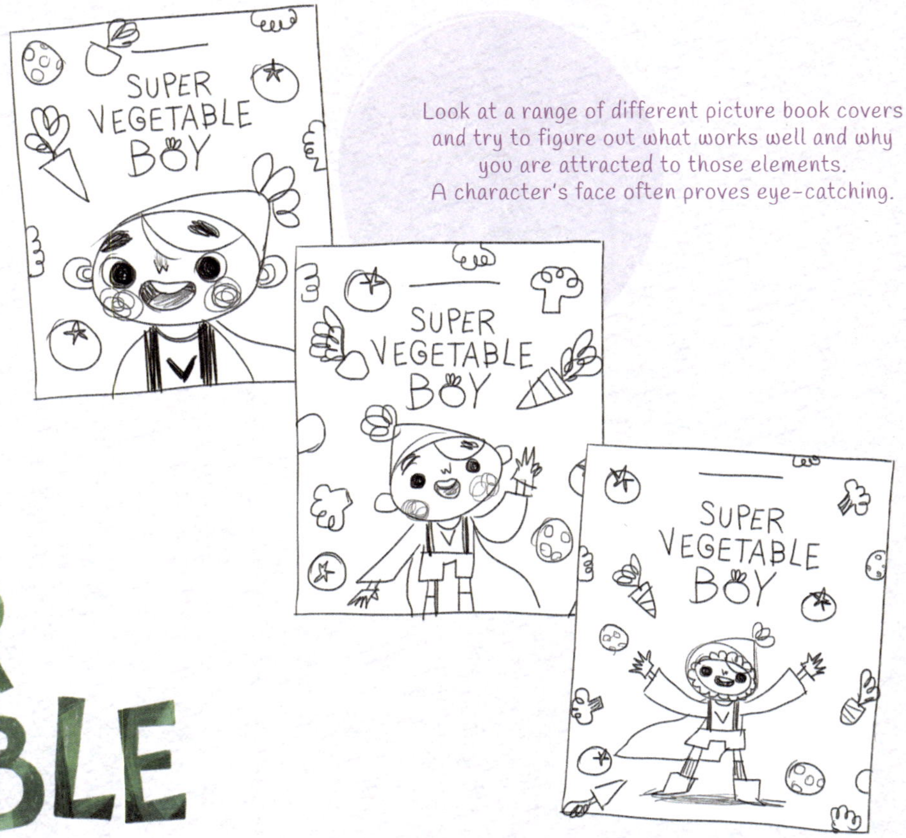


Look at a range of different picture book covers and try to figure out what works well and why you are attracted to those elements. A character's face often proves eye-catching.

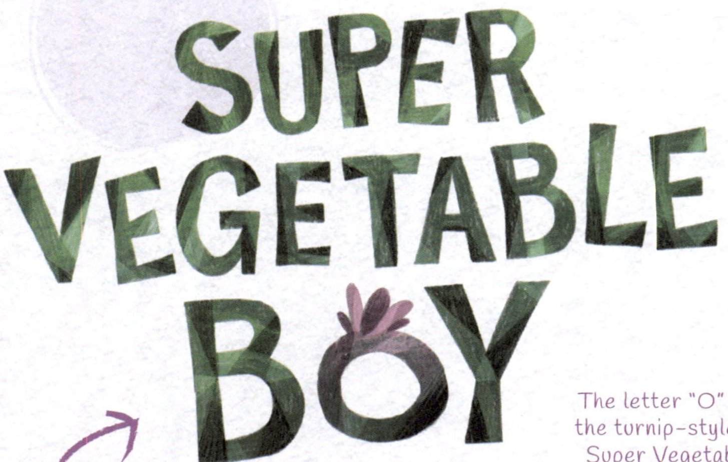


The letter "O" matches the turnip-style head of Super Vegetable Boy.

The title is as important as the illustration. Choose simple and clear typography. You can add small details or add texture to connect it to elements of the story, but ensure the title remains clear and readable.

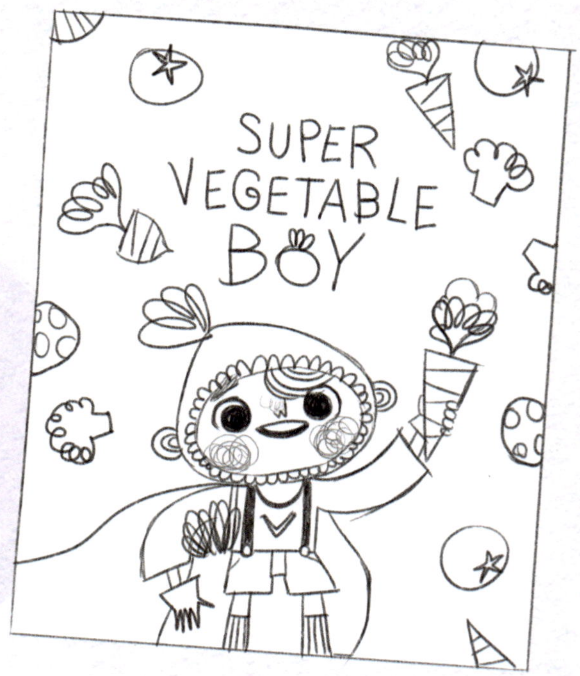


A simple cover design will introduce the main character and give some clues about the theme of the book.

## GENERAL COLOR PALETTE

Corresponding to the color scheme of the main character.

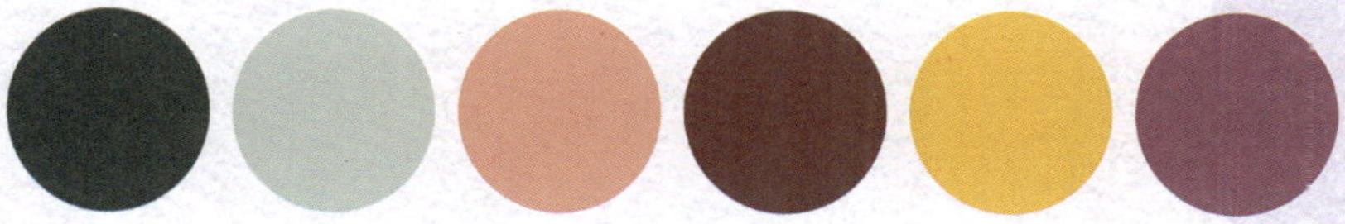

The color palette should match the theme of the book. Remember, paler shades will communicate different emotions and moods to brighter, more vivid shades. Bright, colorful palettes are usually best for a younger audience.

## COLORS OF VEGETABLES

The book cover is the most important illustration, as it's the first thing readers will see. People should be able to figure out the theme at first glance, but be careful not to spoil the story.

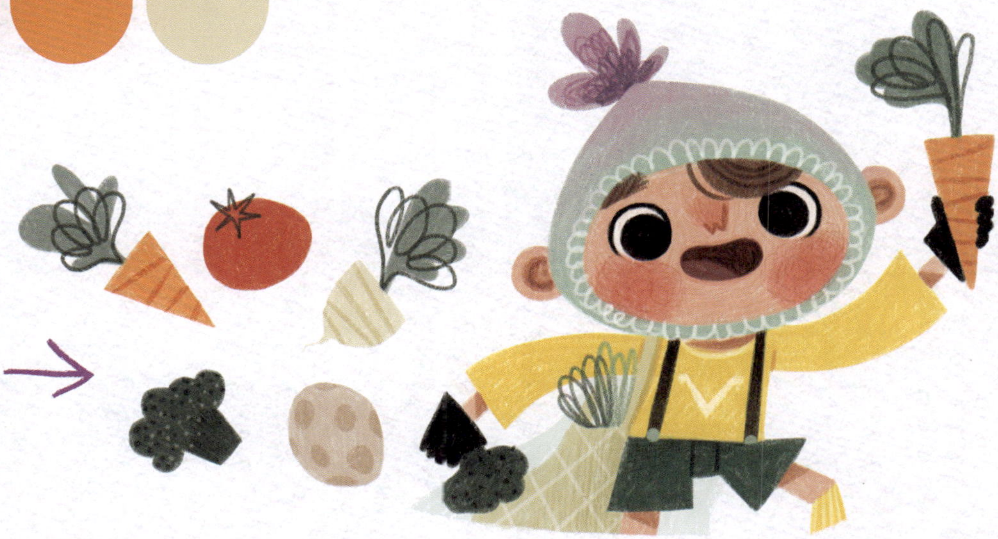

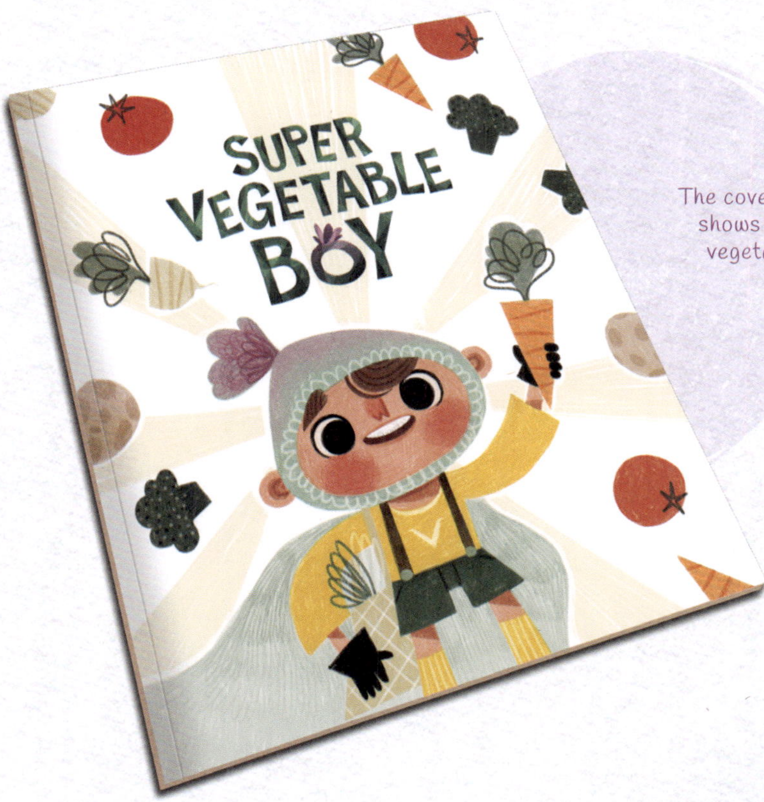


The cover of *Super Vegetable Boy* shows the main character with vegetables flying around him.

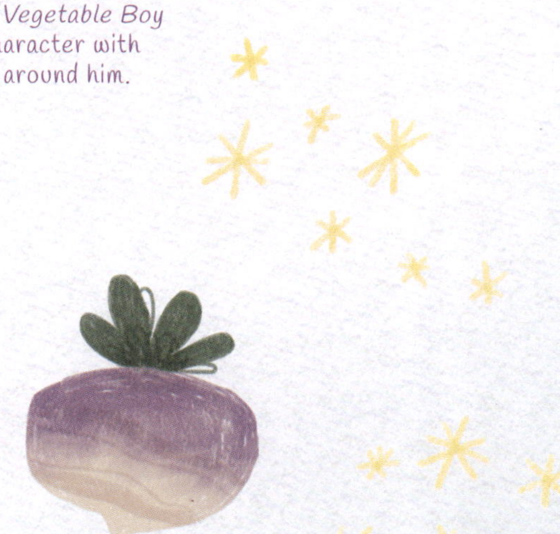

# ANALYSIS

At first I imagined the character of Super Vegetable Boy like a real kind of superhero, but then I decided to make him a child in a homemade costume who sees himself as a superhero. Kids can relate to this type of character. I also made him more sensitive to begin with, almost crying at every failure, before making the decision to give him some attitude instead. Nothing is set in stone – you can change your interpretation of the character throughout the process if it improves the storytelling or the visual of your artwork.

The design for a self-proclaimed superhero with a handmade costume.

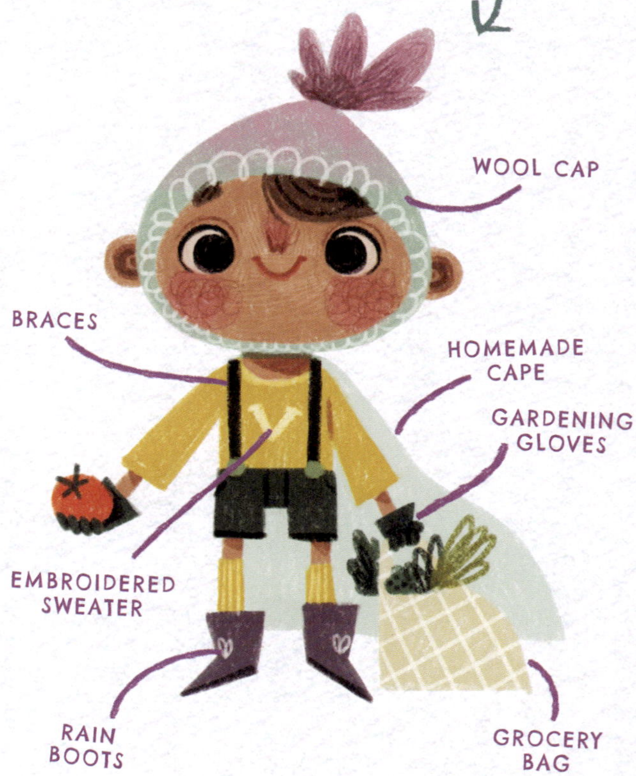


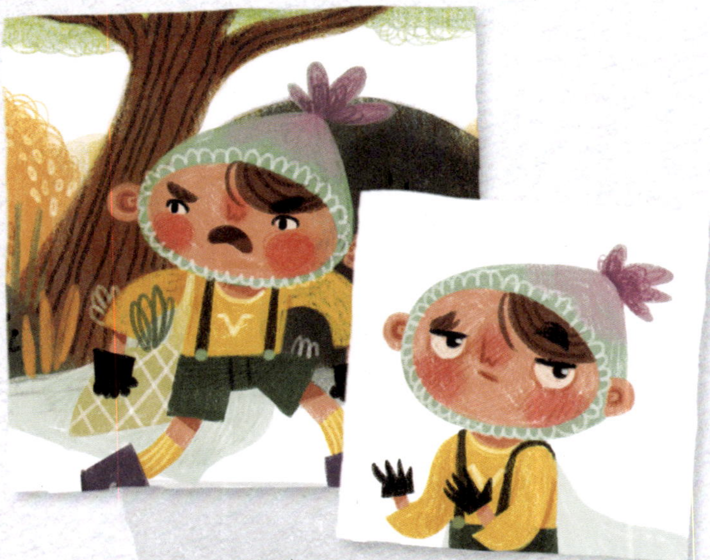

Showing some attitude: a sideways glance and bemused expression.

While I had a good idea of where I was going with the main character design, I experimented with a variety of different options for his bag. I first drew a really big backpack as I wanted all his vegetables to fit in it, before I realized it didn't need to be completely realistic. You don't have to be entirely constrained by reality – children have a lot of freedom in their imagination.

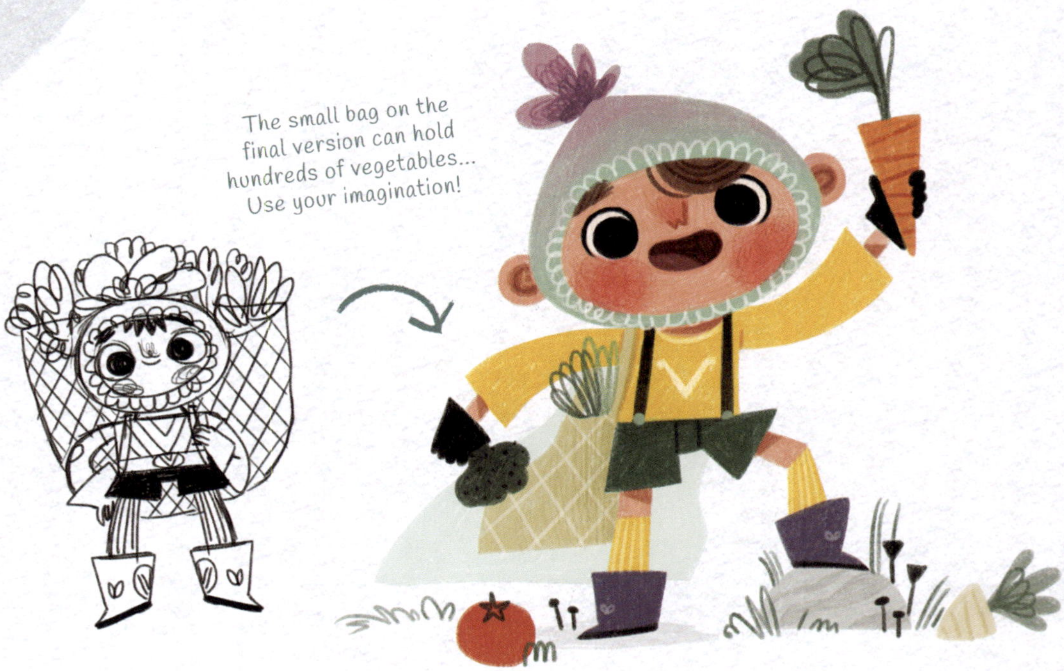

I found designing the different characters in the story to be the easiest and most enjoyable part of the process. I love bringing characters to life with my own vision of their personalities. The part I can find most challenging is showing a sequence of action on a single double-page spread. While I love drawing spreads as one big illustration, it doesn't always fit the story. Including a variety of different layouts can be more entertaining for the reader. When working with story text, don't hesitate to split the action across two or three drawings – this can help accelerate the pace.

Final character designs for the girl with the rabbits, the elderly lady, and the delivery man.

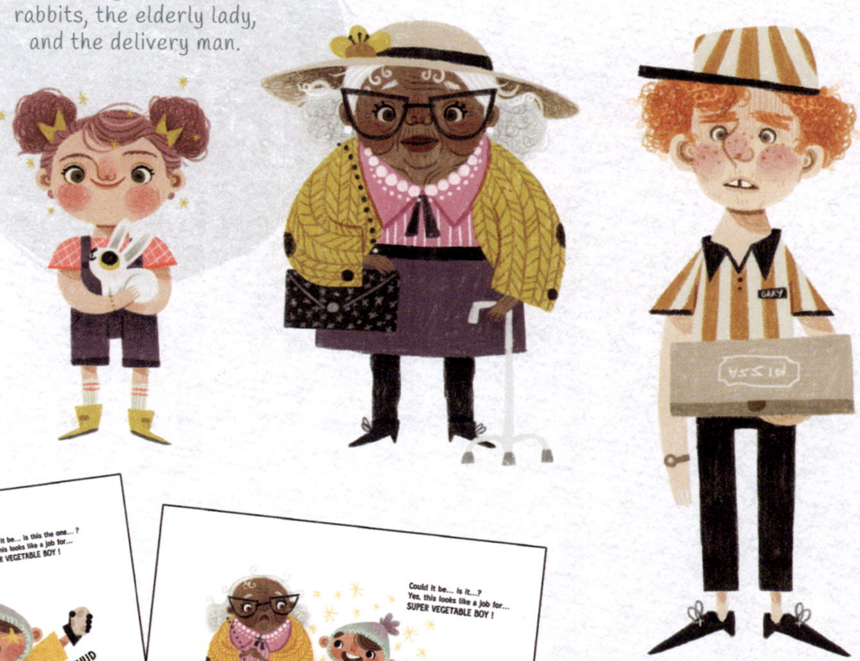

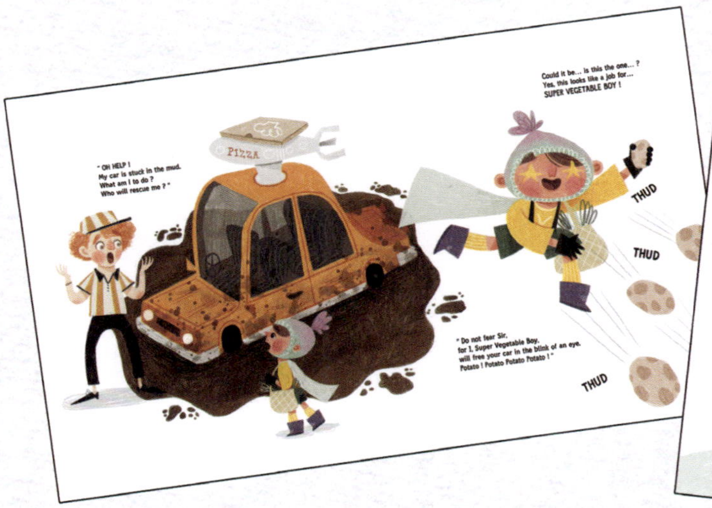


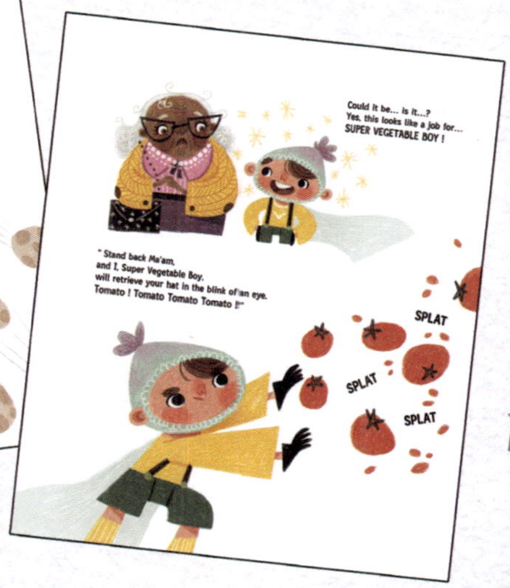


Some spreads are broken up into several areas of action.

Final tip – add some animals! Children love animals. Even if there aren't any mentioned in the text, adding a few animals into some of your scenes will entertain and catch the attention of young readers.

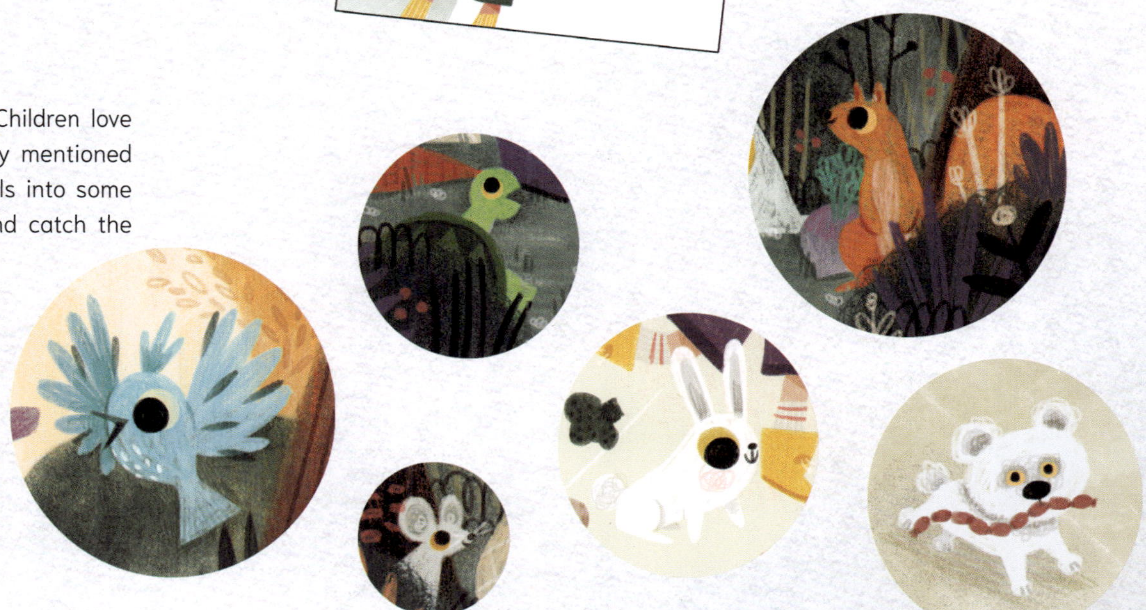

The wild animals encourage Super Vegetable Boy when he doubts himself.

Florence the Talking Carrot

Written by

GREG DOBBINS

Illustrated by

KYLE BECKETT

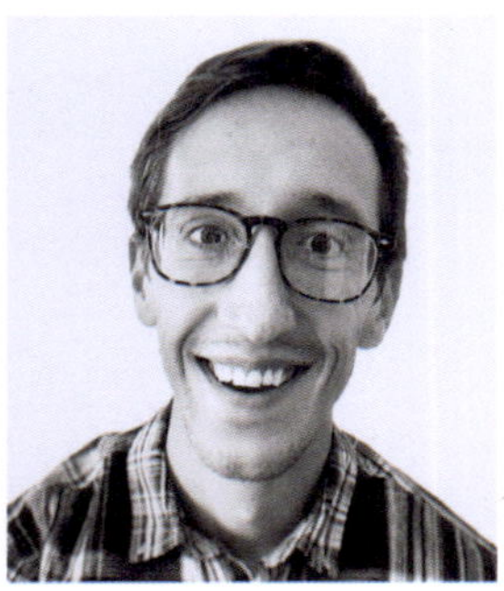

Children's book author & illustrator

**kbeckett393.wixsite.com/illustration**

Kyle grew up in Rockford, Illinois, and attended Ringling College of Art and Design. He now lives and works from Atlanta, Georgia, with his wife Lauren and their dog Goose.

A STORY FOR AGES 6–8 YEARS

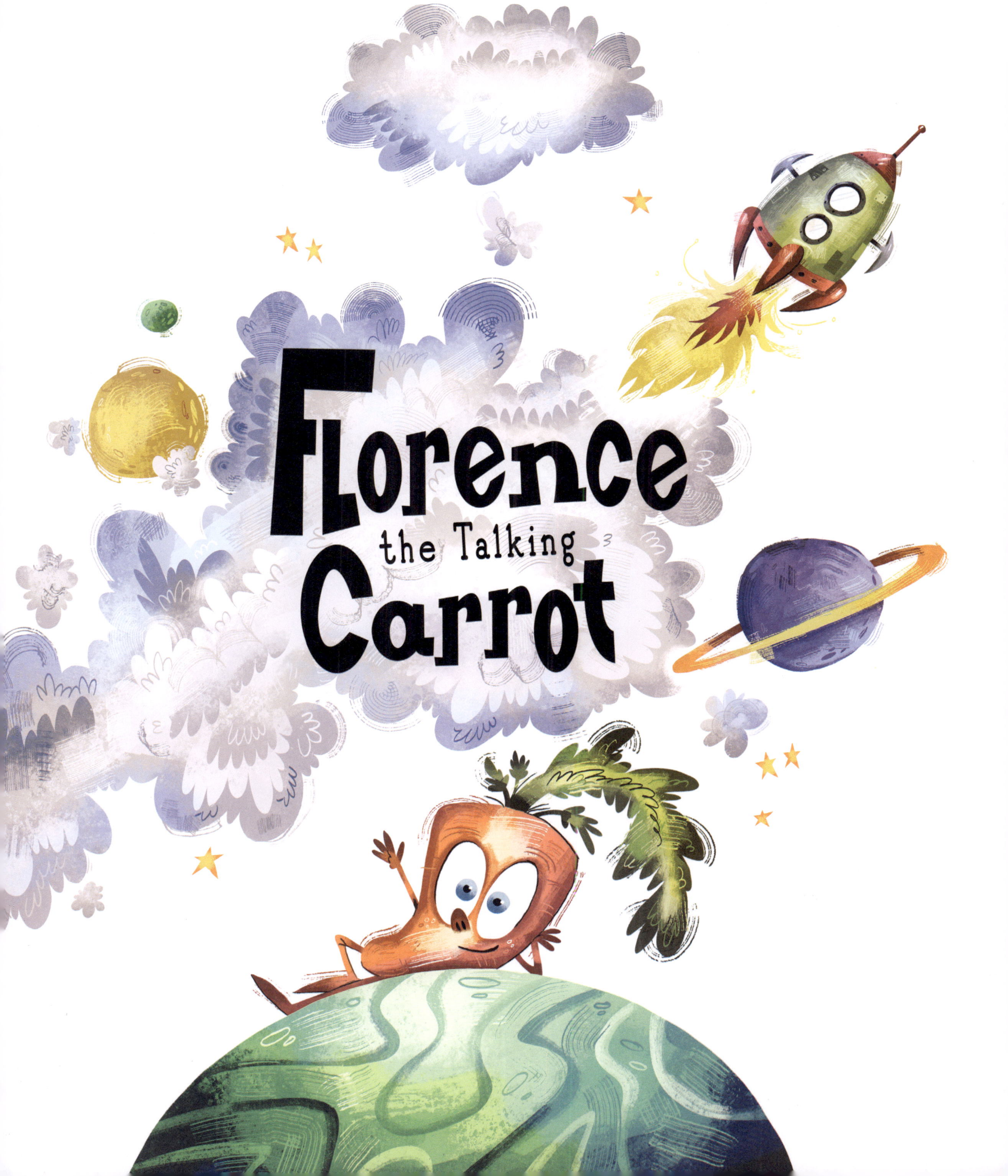
Florence
the Talking
Carrot

Here's Florence the Talking Carrot, a truly amazing thing.
A chattering carrot, a vocalizing veg, sometimes she even sings.

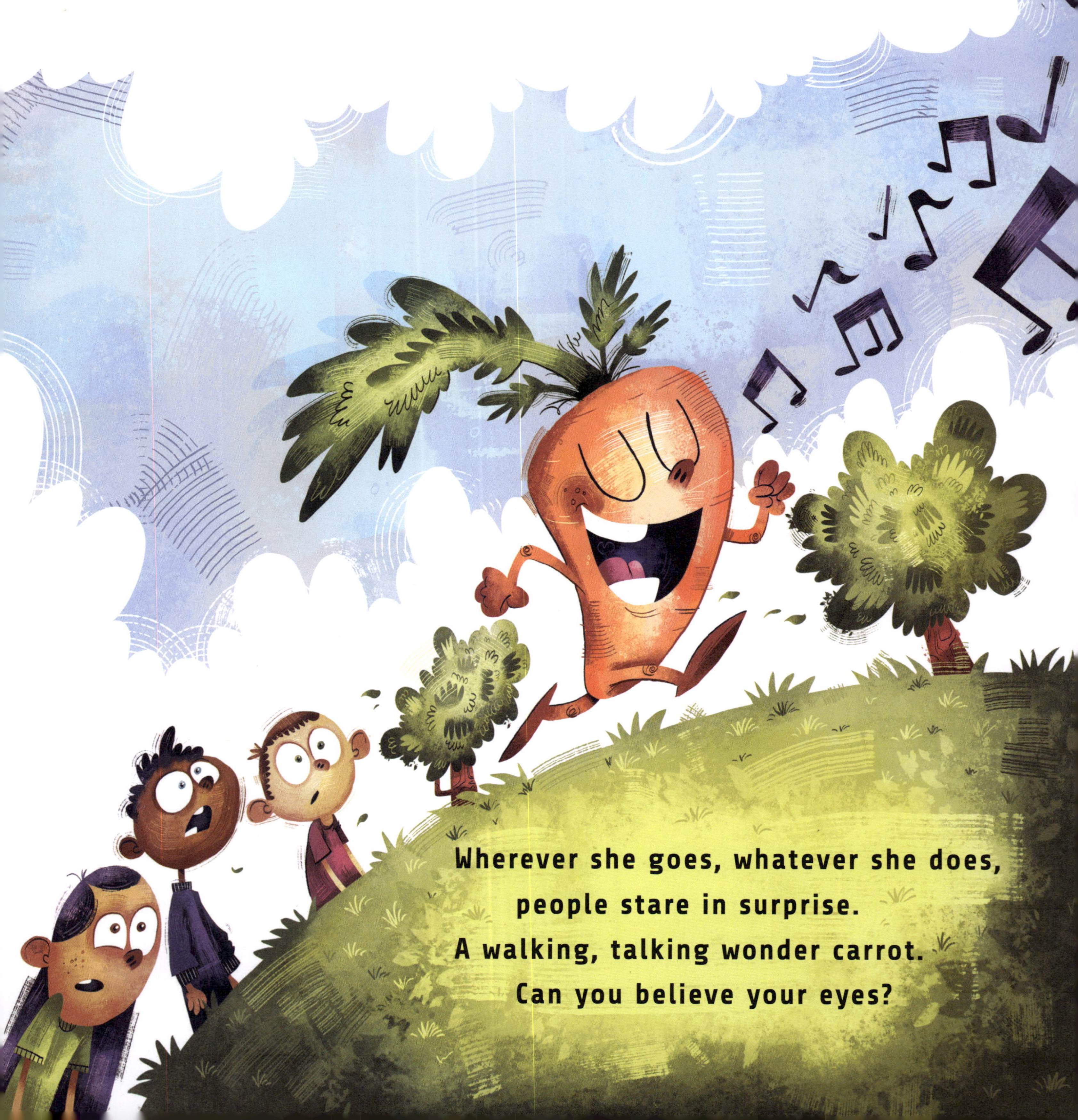

Wherever she goes, whatever she does,
people stare in surprise.
A walking, talking wonder carrot.
Can you believe your eyes?

"Yeah, OK, I'm a talking carrot, but I can't change who I am.
So I'm Florence the Talking Carrot, but I've got a secret plan.
What if there's another me, somewhere on this planet?
Maybe I can track them down! It can't be that hard, can it?

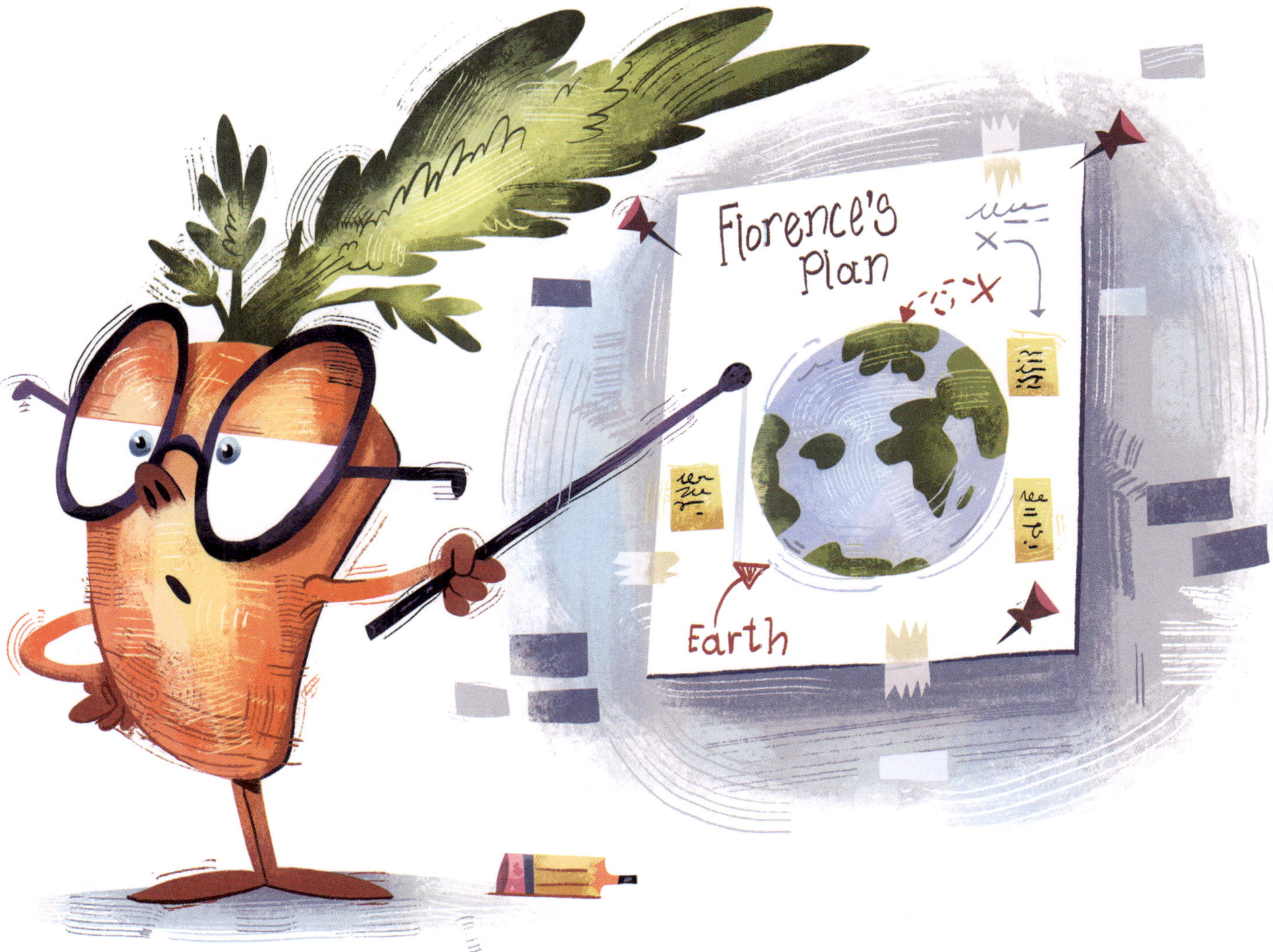


Then it won't just be me, the talking carrot, the amazing one and only.
If there's two, I won't stand out. And perhaps I won't feel so lonely."

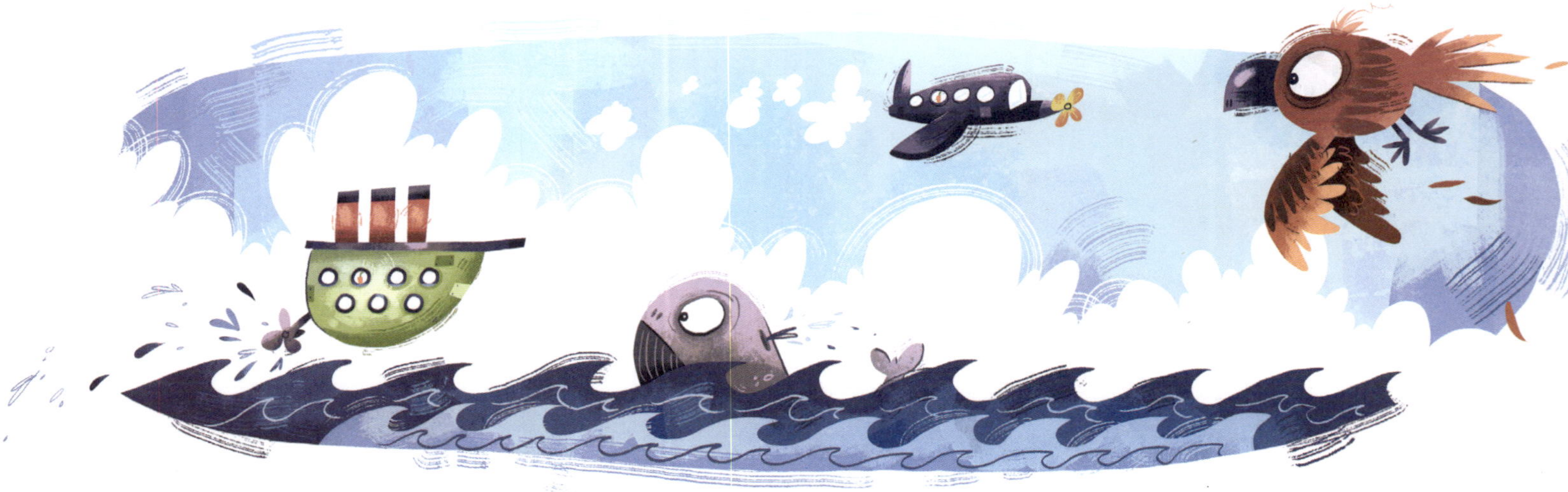

Off goes Florence on her search, traveling by sea and air.
But everywhere she travels, people still stop and stare.

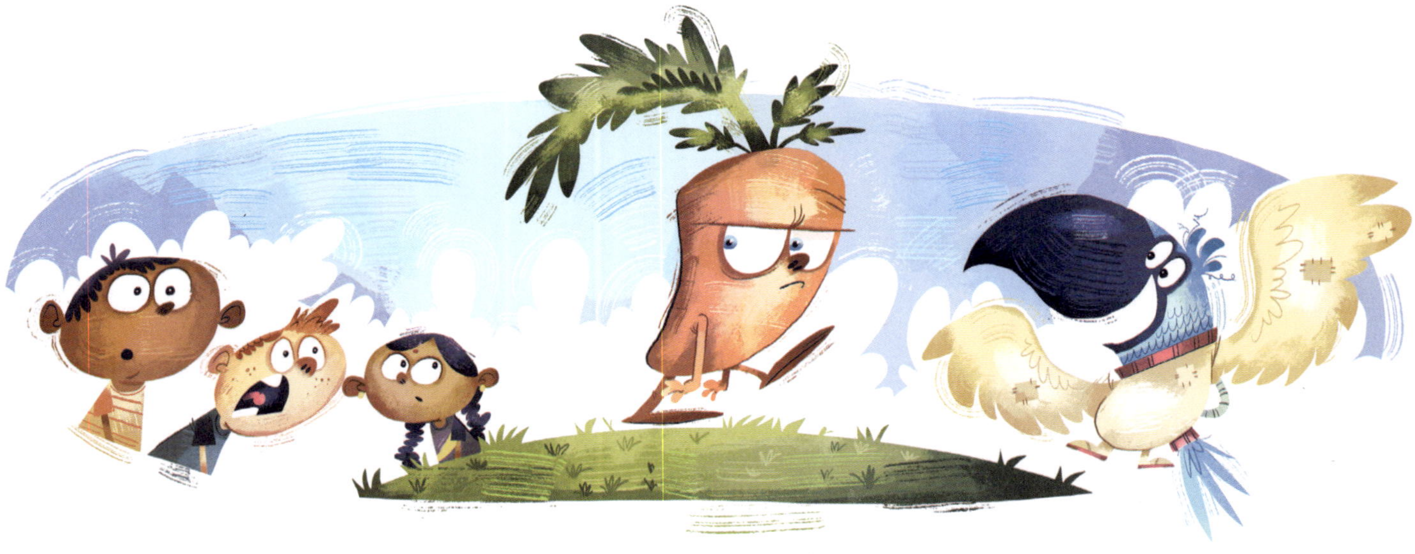

Still no luck, there's just no sign of another carrot.
But then Florence meets up with Meg, a space-exploring parrot.

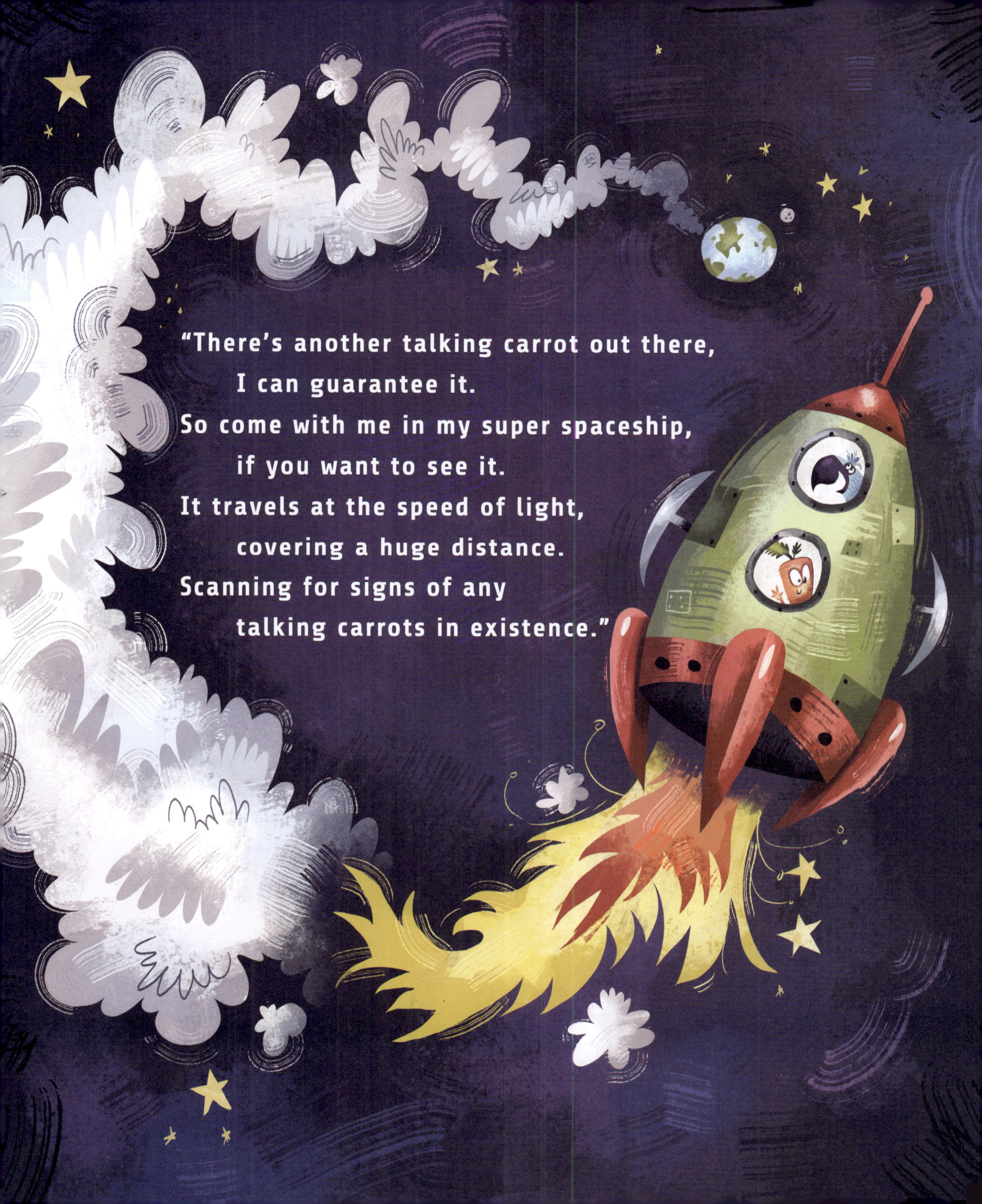

“There’s another talking carrot out there,
I can guarantee it.
So come with me in my super spaceship,
if you want to see it.
It travels at the speed of light,
covering a huge distance.
Scanning for signs of any
talking carrots in existence.”

Two galaxies along, the scanner beeps... Something is detected!
Another planet with life on it, just as Meg suspected.
As the spaceship comes in to land, Florence gets excited,
wondering if another carrot has finally been sighted.

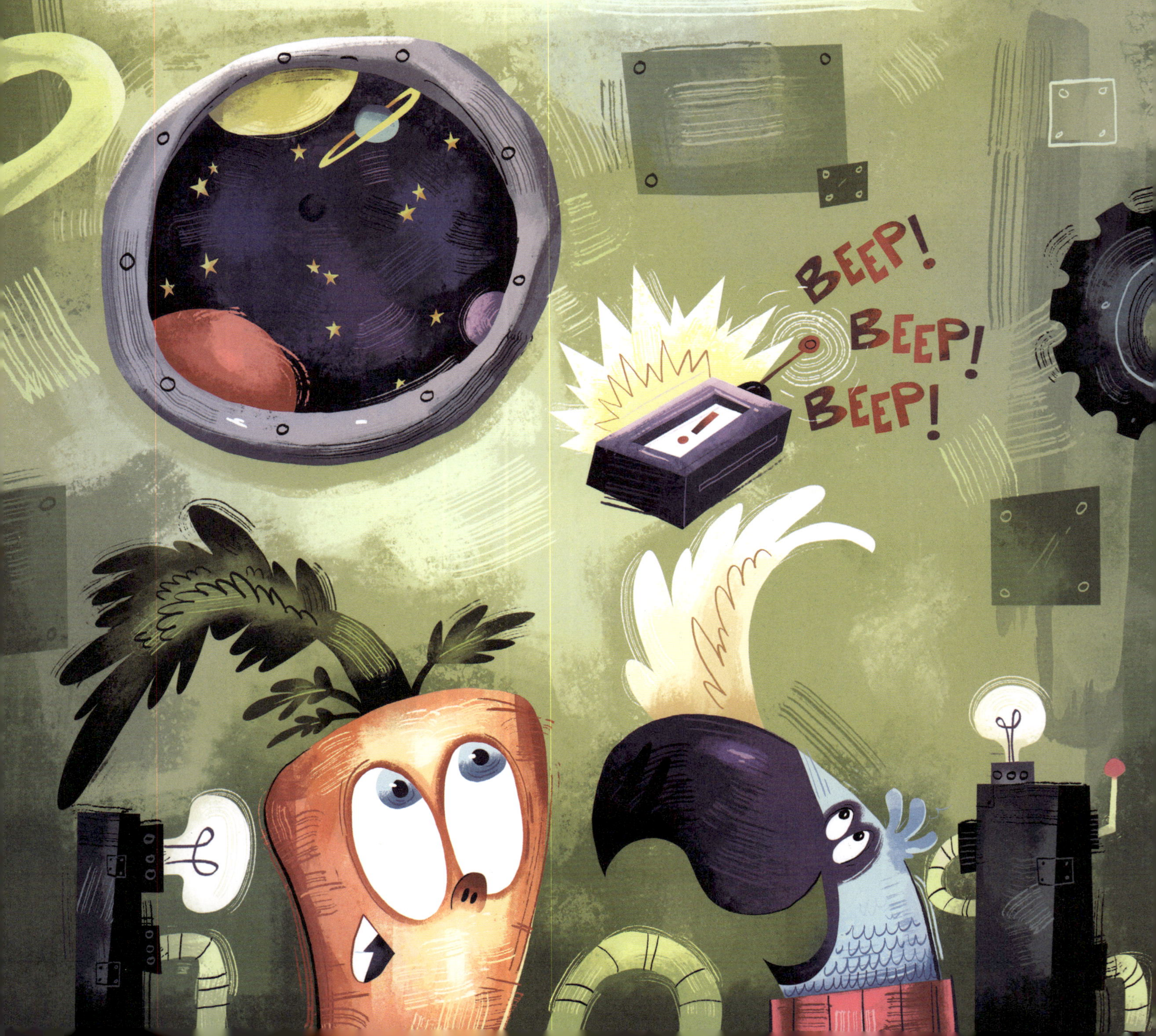

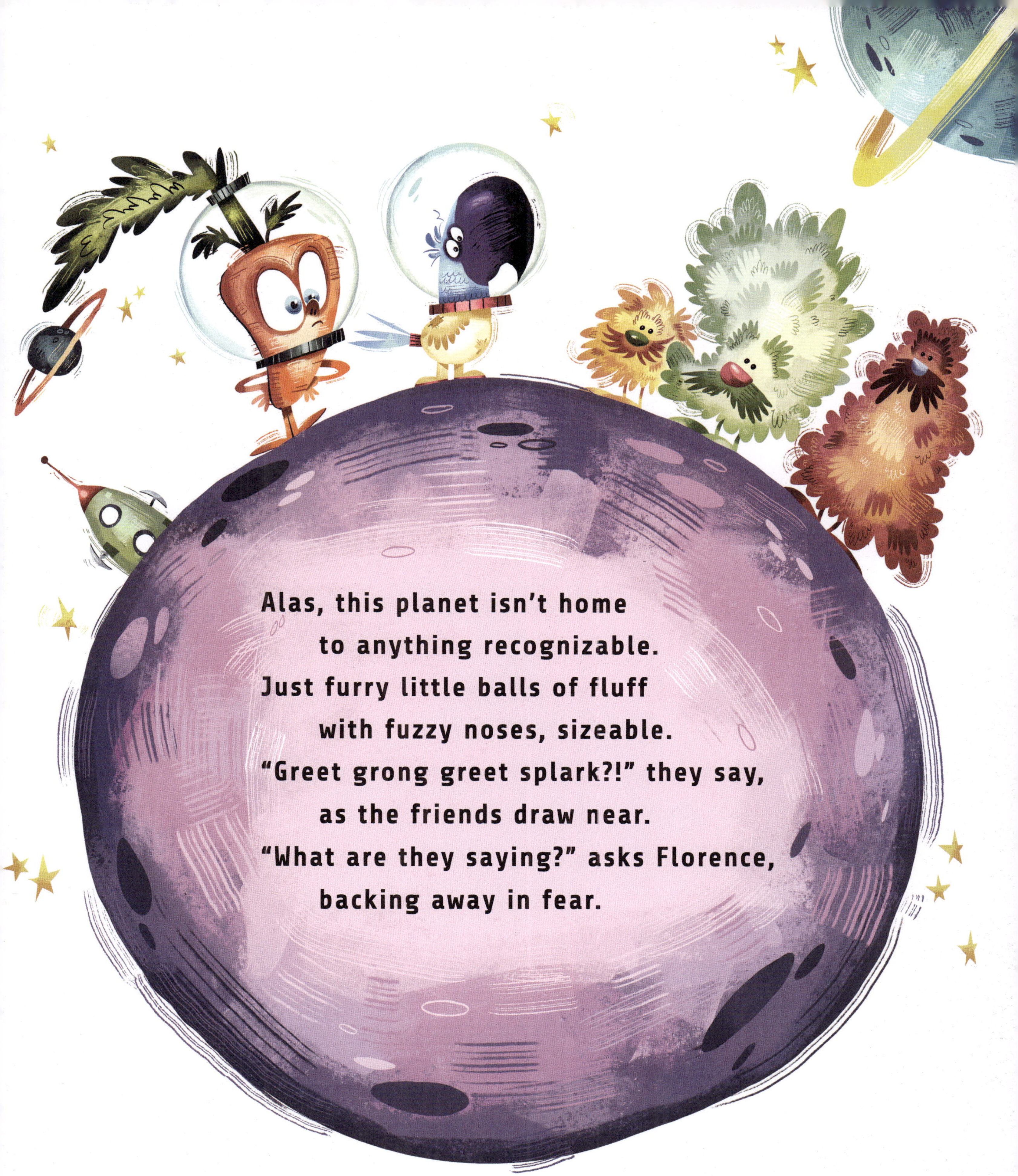

Alas, this planet isn't home
to anything recognizable.
Just furry little balls of fluff
with fuzzy noses, sizeable.
"Greet grong greet splark?!" they say,
as the friends draw near.
"What are they saying?" asks Florence,
backing away in fear.

Meg's machine searches for the language and retrieves it, then turns it into English – "A talking carrot, can you believe it?!"

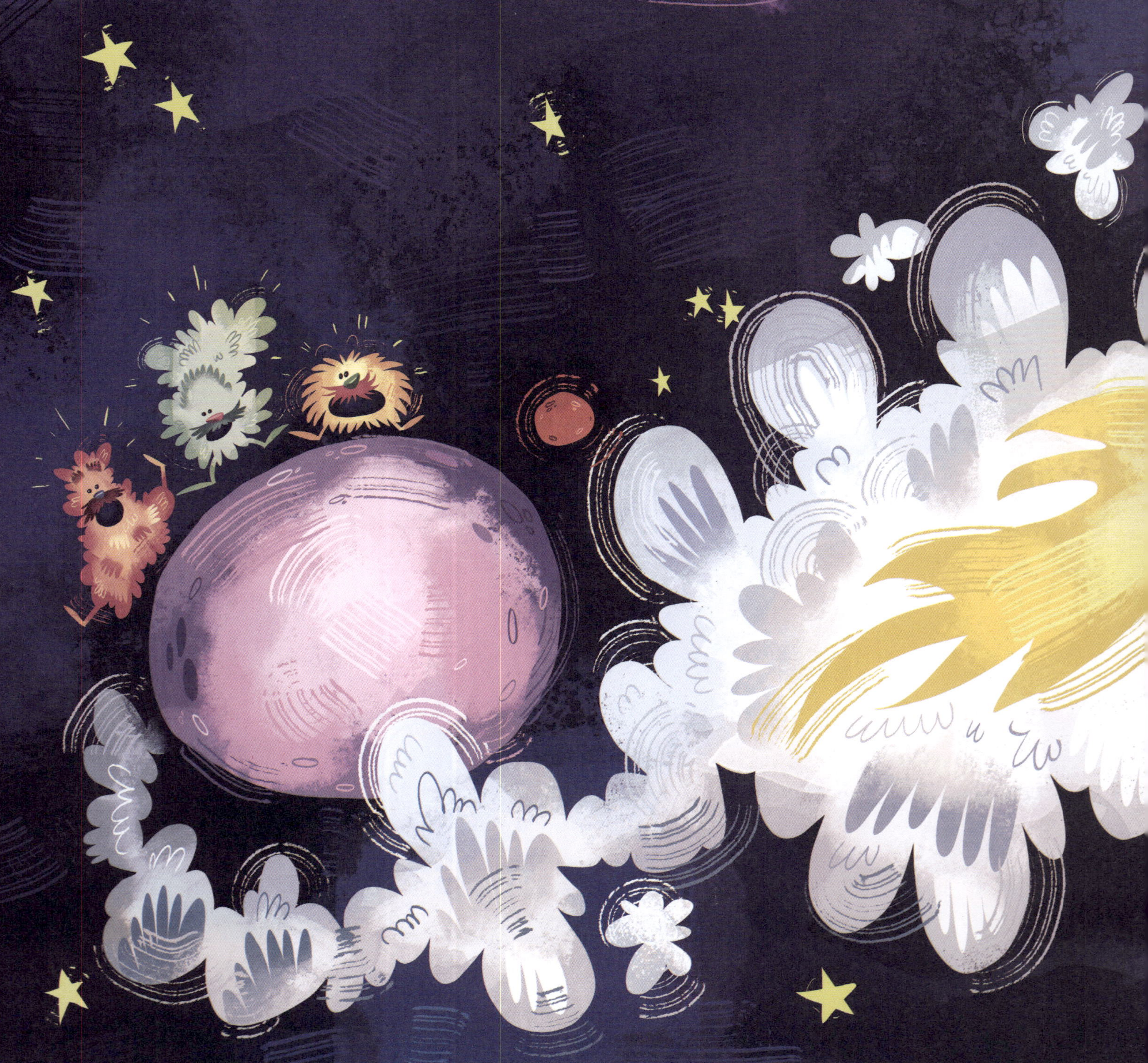

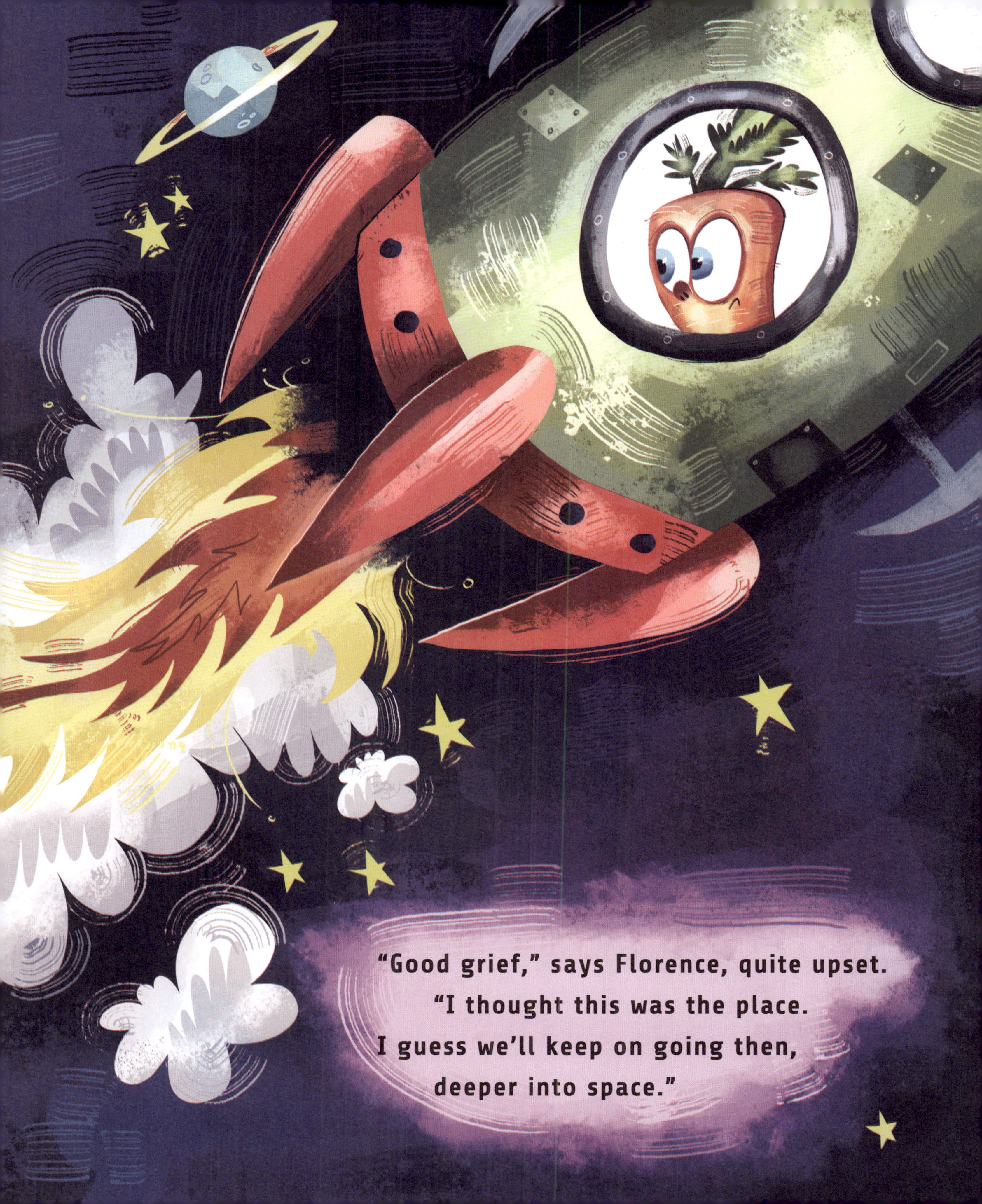

“Good grief,” says Florence, quite upset.
“I thought this was the place.
I guess we’ll keep on going then,
deeper into space.”

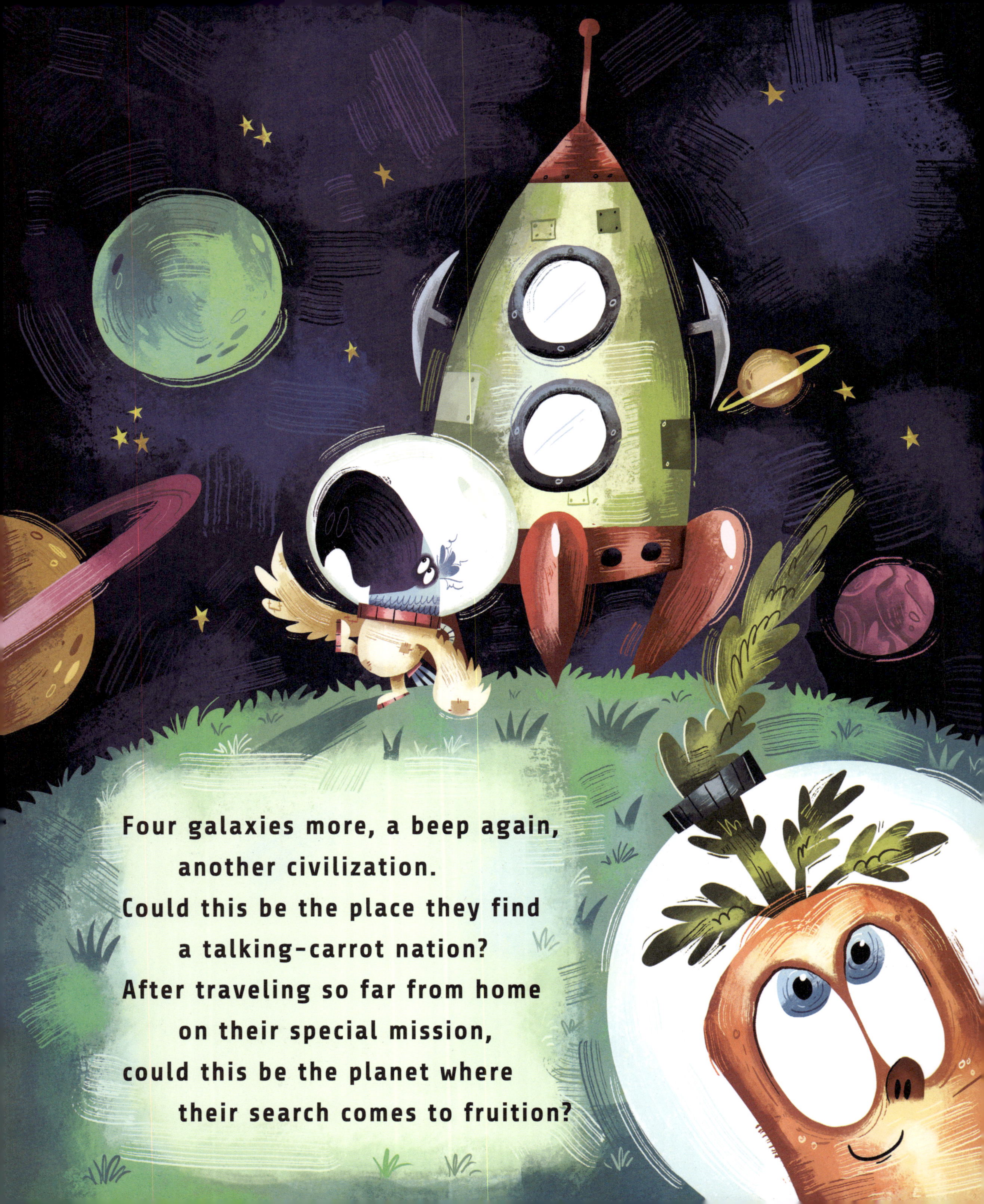

Four galaxies more, a beep again,
another civilization.
Could this be the place they find
a talking-carrot nation?
After traveling so far from home
on their special mission,
could this be the planet where
their search comes to fruition?

Alas, this planet isn't home
to any talking veg.
Just giant jelly creatures here,
to meet the friends instead.
"Wibble wobble wibble woo!" they say,
pointing and staring.
"What are they saying this time then?" asks Florence,
now despairing.

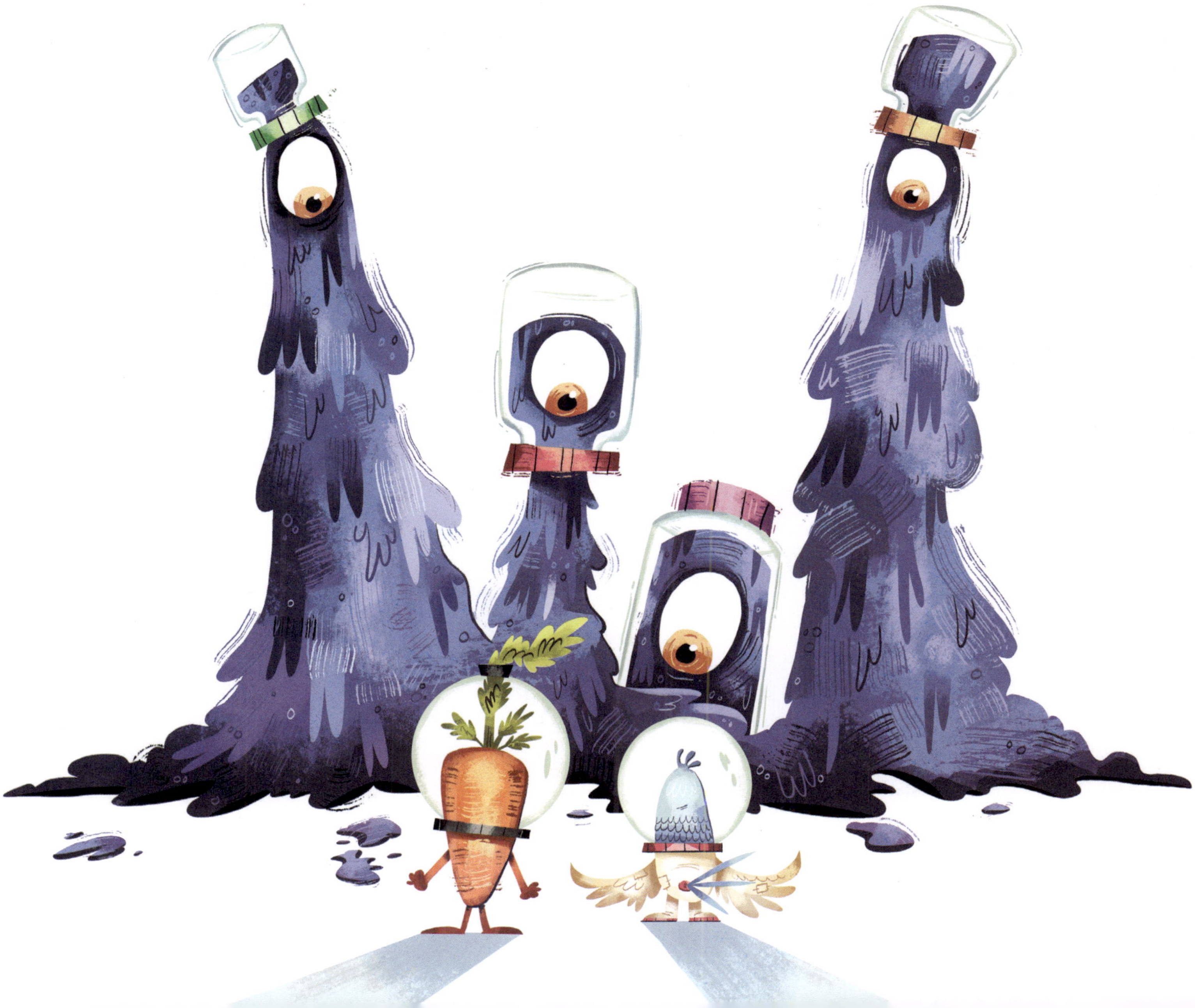

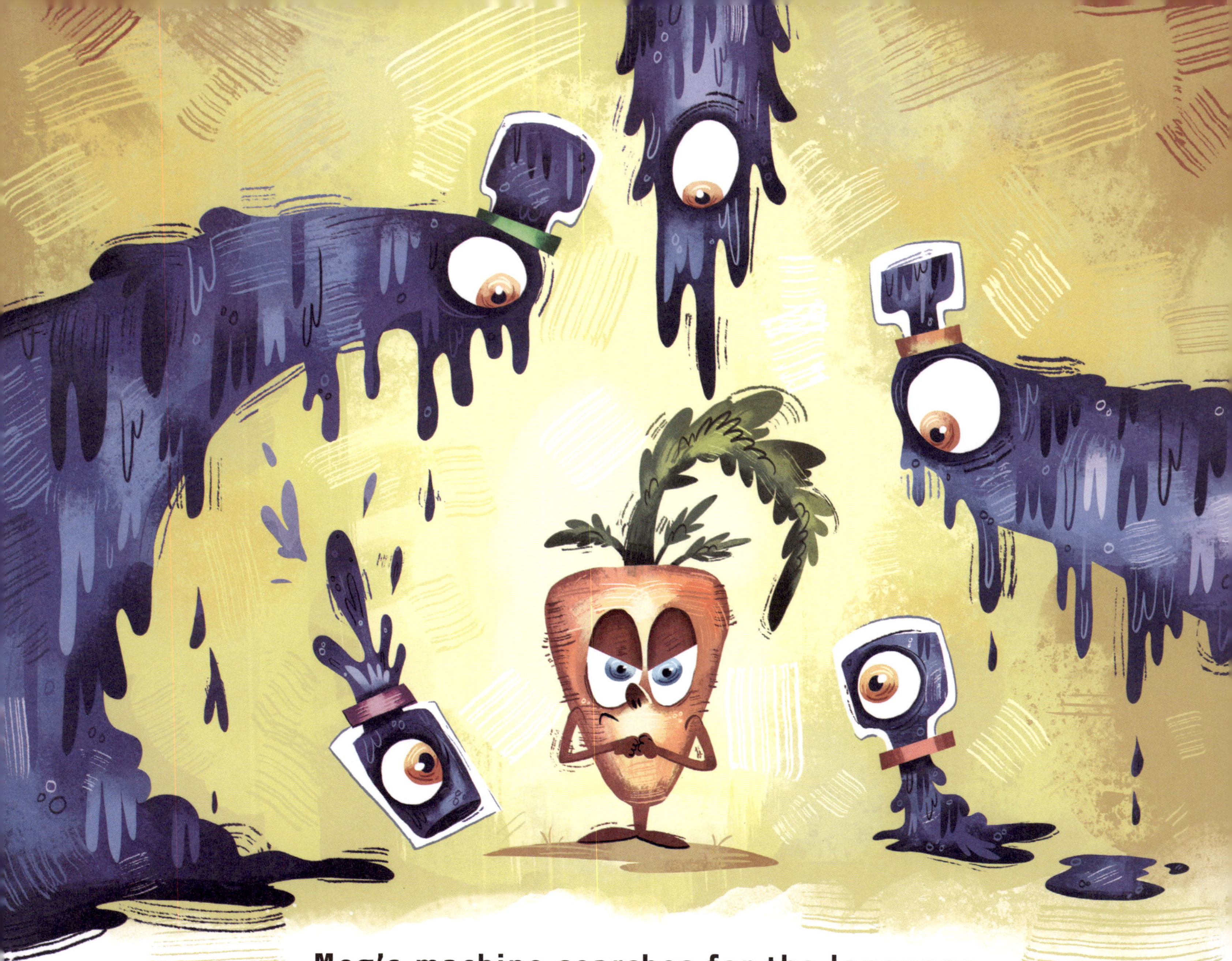

Meg's machine searches for the language
and translates it,
then turns it into English – "A talking carrot,
and I nearly ate it!"
"Good grief," says Florence, quite upset.
"They thought I was a snack!
I guess we'll keep on going then,
there's no point turning back."

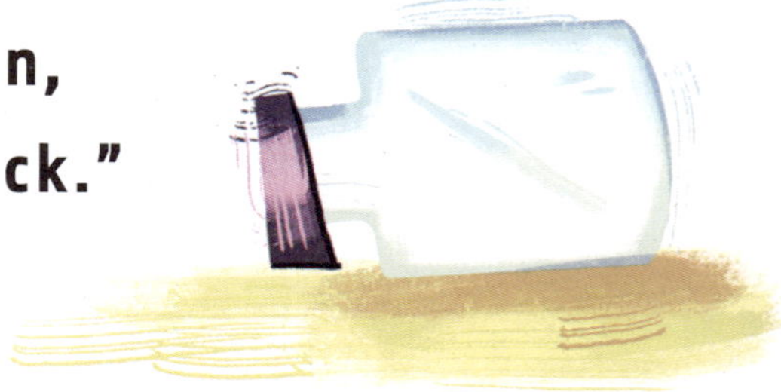

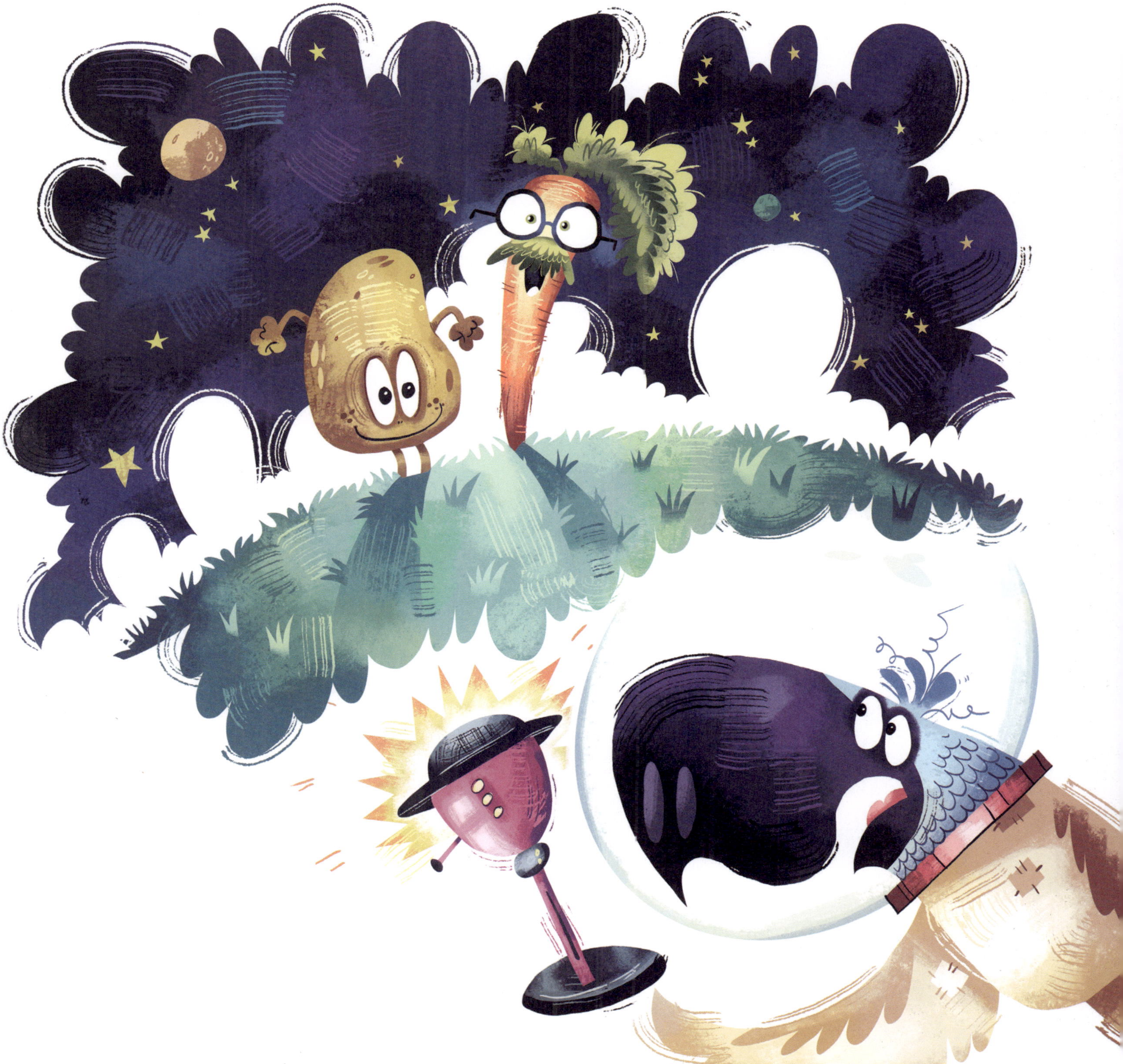

"Wait, there's more," says Meg,
holding out the flashing translator.
"We were visited by another carrot last year,
with his friend, a talking potato."

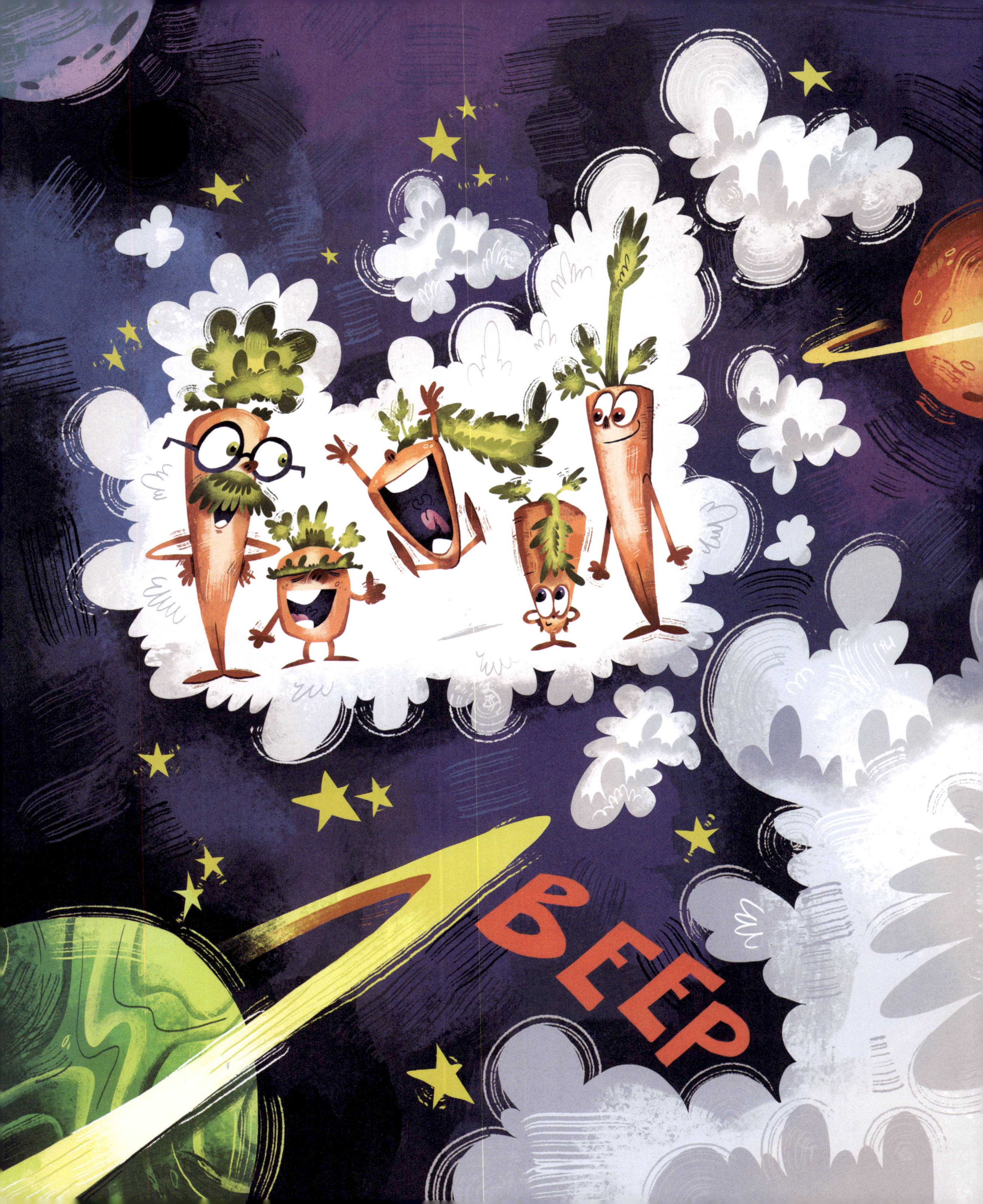
BEEP

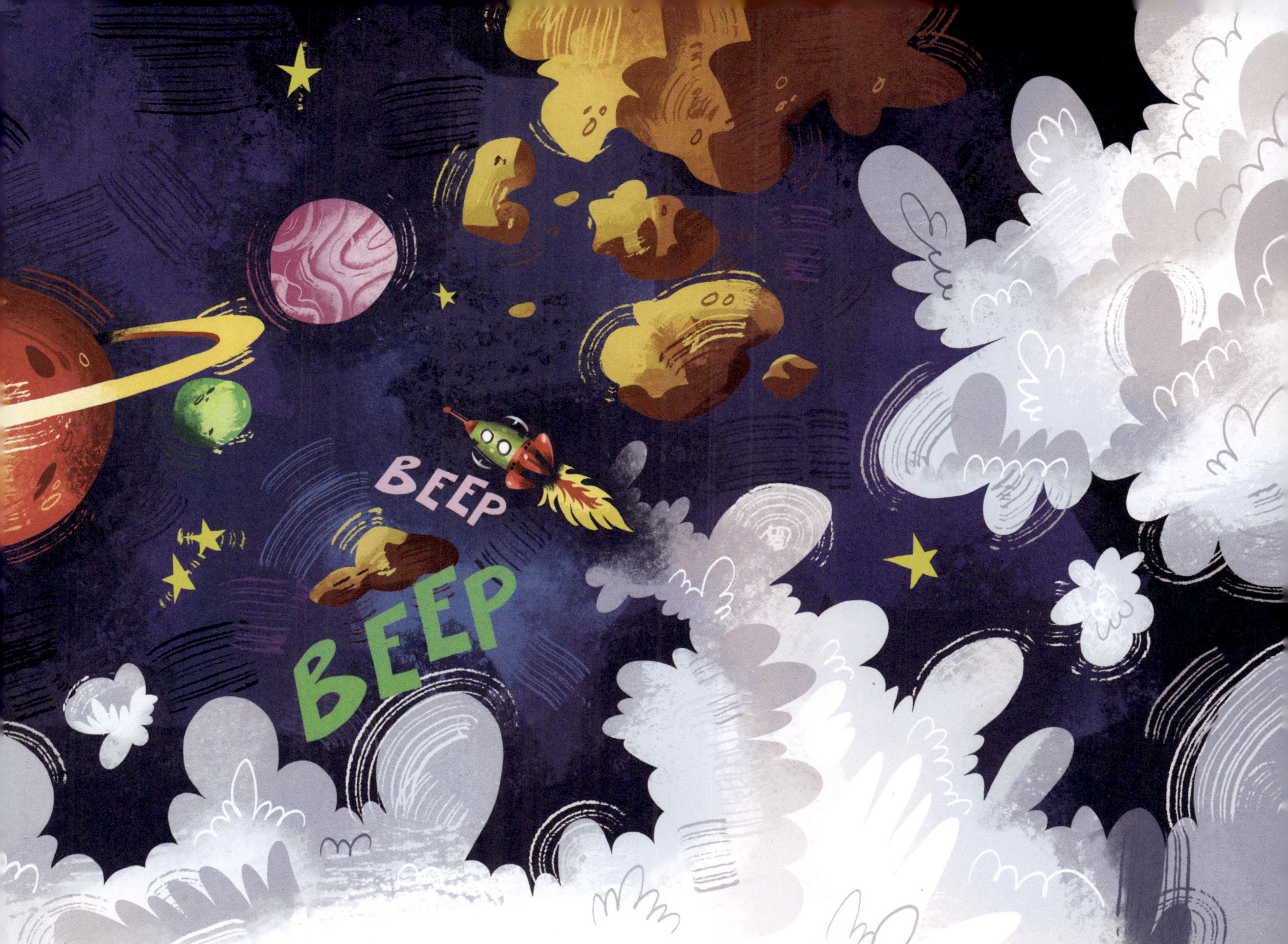


This is amazing, this is news,
another Florence has been found!
There are other talking veg out there,
traveling around.
"I hope we find them," Florence says.
"It would be great to see.
But at the moment, just knowing they exist
is enough for me."

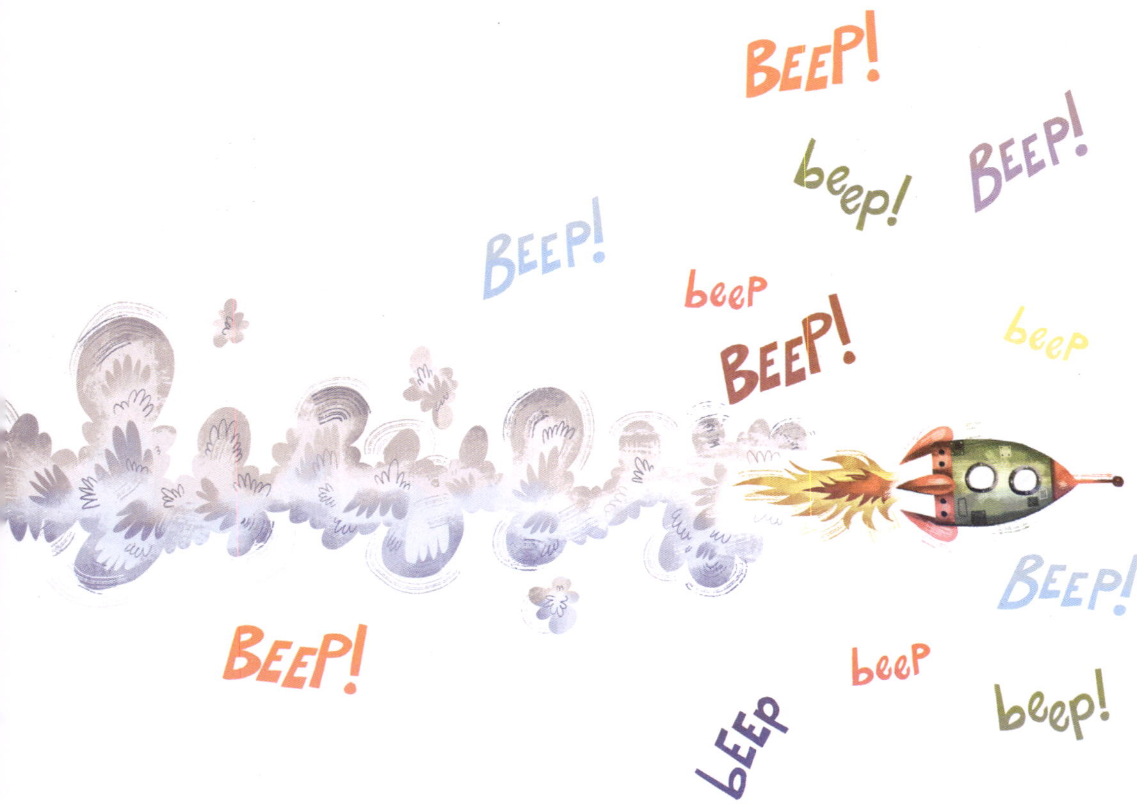


The End?

TURN THE PAGE FOR
INSIGHTS FROM THE ARTIST

# Florence the Talking Carrot

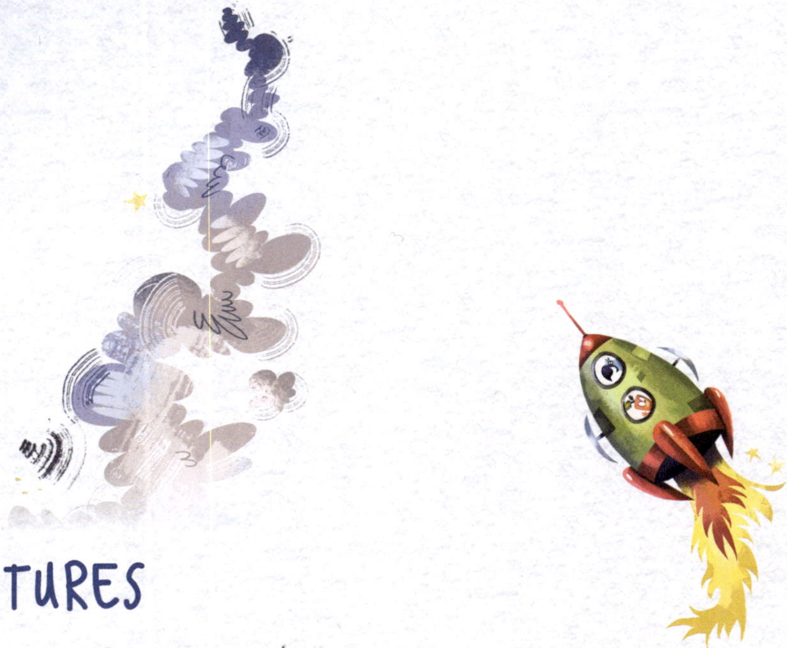

## DEVELOPING KEY FEATURES

### CHARACTER

When starting a new project, one of the first things to do is to draw the main character. The worst thing you can do at this stage is get stuck staring at a blank page. Creating some quick sketches will help get your brain working and give you a frame of reference when making changes later on. Even if you only get one sketch down, this will make the research stage a lot easier.

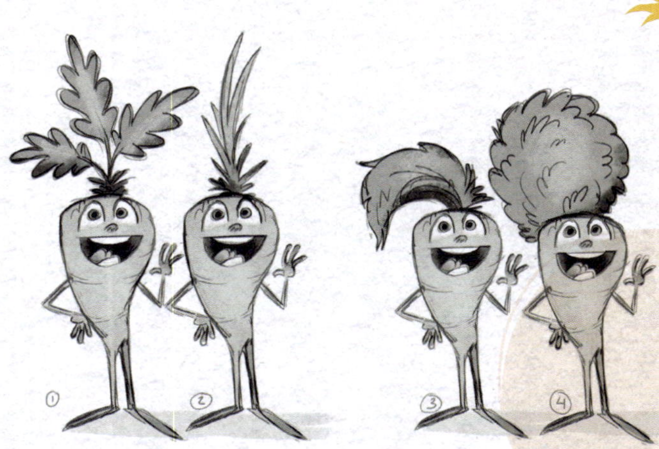

Rough design sketches exploring lots of different shapes and hairstyles. There are no wrong answers at this stage – have fun experimenting with their character.

With the character of Florence, the color looked great (you can't change the color of a carrot too much!) and the style was fun, but I didn't like how old she looked. The story felt like it needed a younger character who was more accessible to the audience (6–8 years). In my next few attempts I drew a much cuter design, still in the same style but changing her proportions: her eyes are bigger, her body is much smaller, and her legs are shorter.

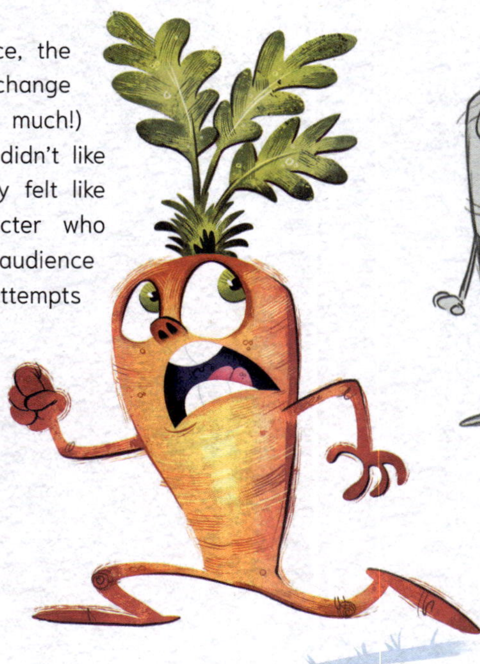

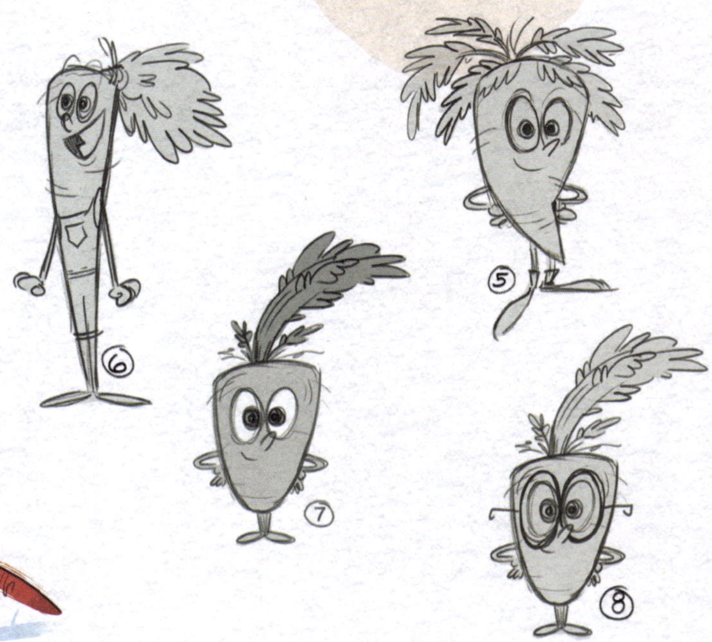

Once you have found a design you like that fits well with the story, it's time to create a final sketch of the character. Creating lots of character sketches from every angle, and with different poses and emotions, will make for a stronger design. The important thing to remember at this stage is there are no wrong answers. Every scribble and sketch could be just what's needed for the character. Remember, you won't really see it in your head until you put it down on the paper.

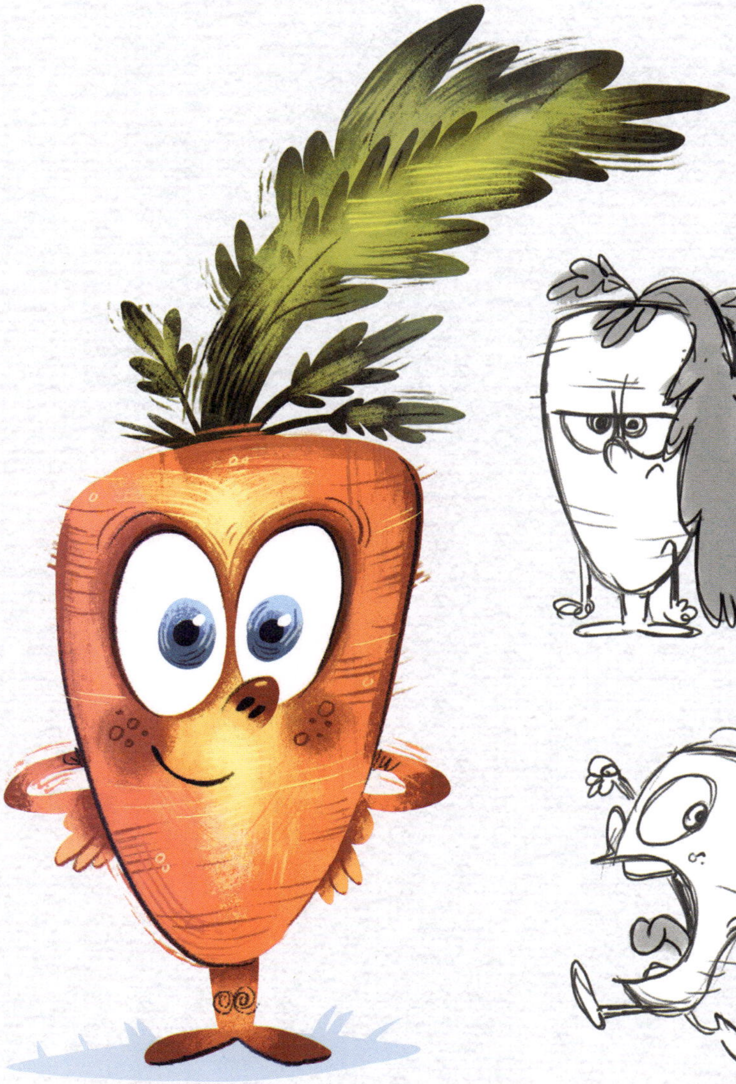

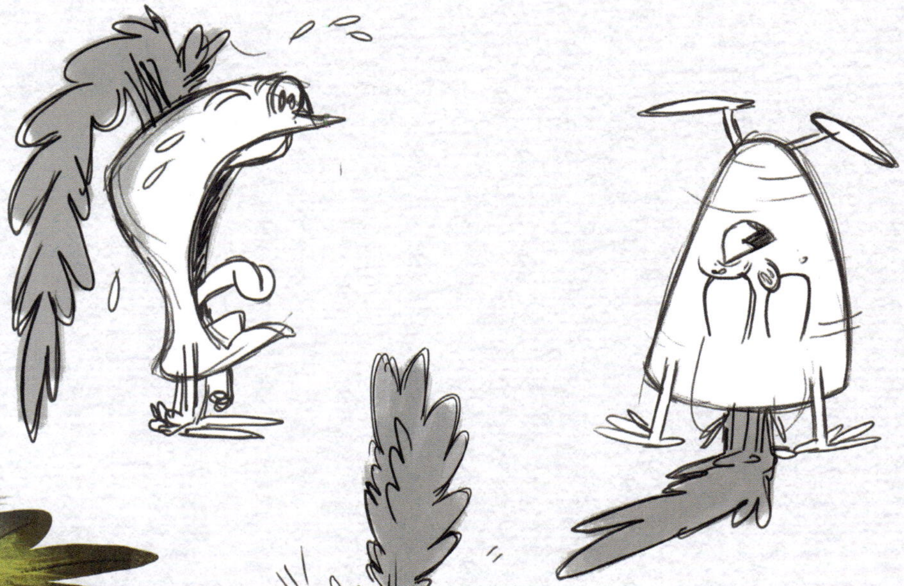

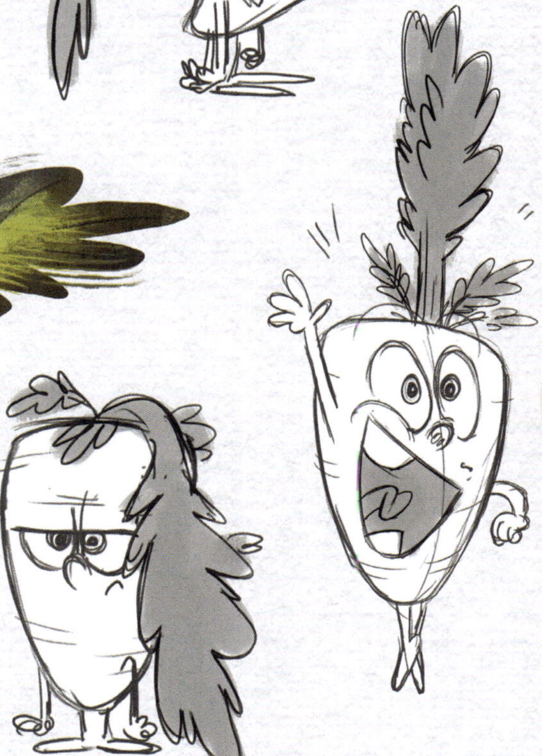

The final design for Florence, plus sketches of different emotions, poses, and gestures. I wanted her to feel very animated.

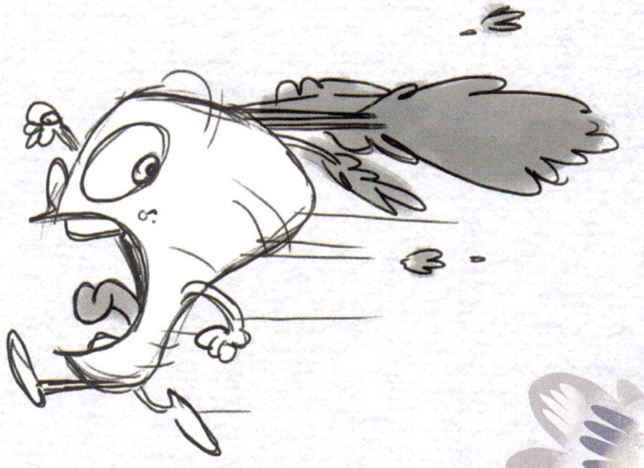

Final color palette

## MEG

Meg's design came very quickly. From time to time you will draw one sketch and immediately know it will work. Nevertheless, it's important that you still sketch out and explore a variety of other designs and color palettes. Never do just one sketch. Even if you end up going with the first design, it's nice to know you exhausted all other options.

After exploring alternate designs and making sure the style is consistent, the next step to designing a secondary character is to put them alongside the main character to make sure they work together. For these two characters, a carrot and a parrot, the hardest thing to work around was the color. Meg started out red, but seeing her next to Florence made it clear they couldn't be the same color temperature. Making Meg blue instead solved the problem and kept the two characters from blending together.

The same rules apply here: sketch and re-sketch your secondary character with different emotions and poses. Get to know your characters inside and out. Think of your sketches like a form of "interviewing" your characters to make sure they deserve the job you're giving them.

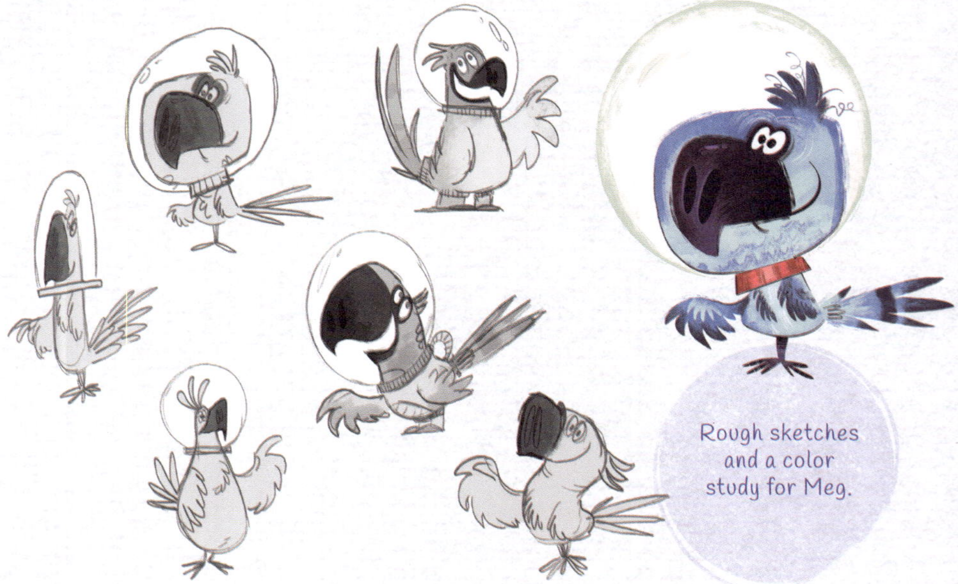

Rough sketches and a color study for Meg.

Possible color palettes for Meg. Here I attempted to work out what colors worked best, not only for Meg's design, but with Florence's design too.

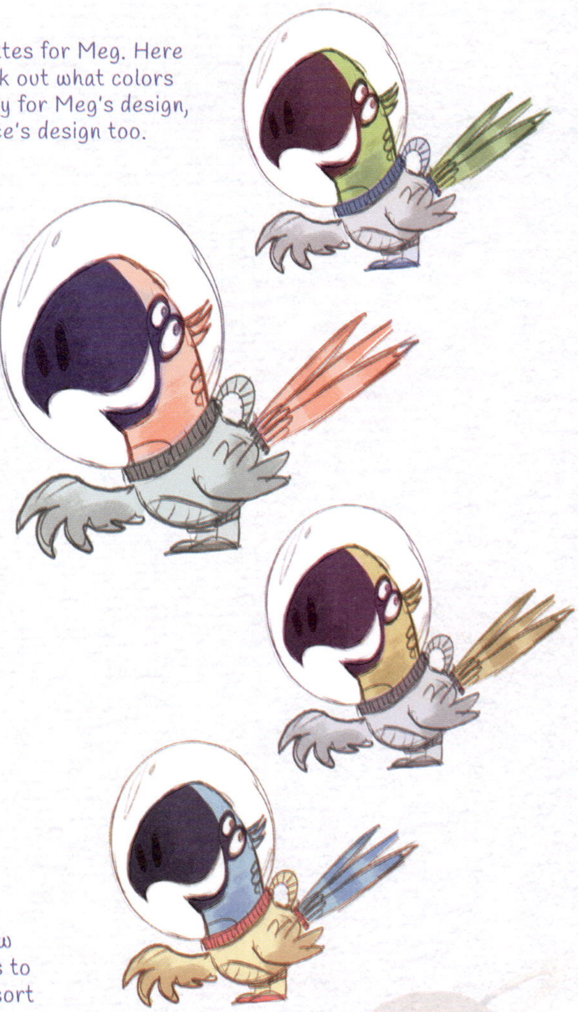

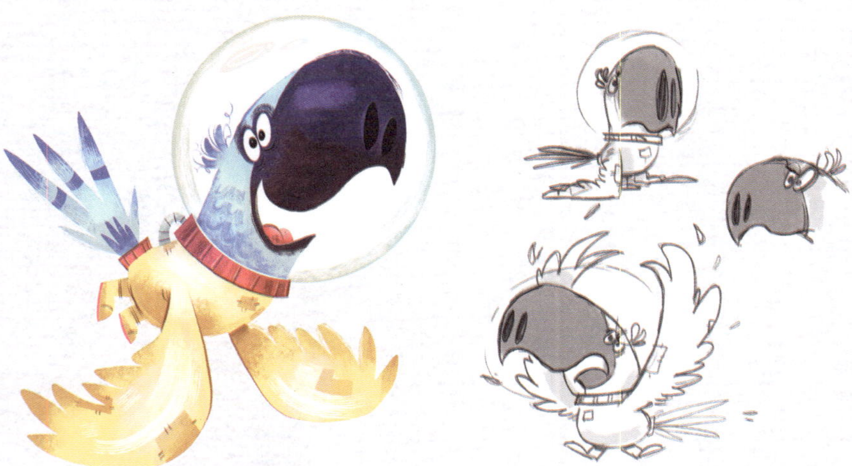

The final design for Meg, plus a few sketches showing different emotions to further explore her character. This sort of exploration will come in handy when you're sketching out the rest of a book.

Possible color palettes for Meg

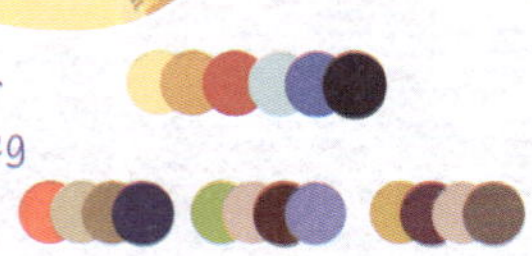

## SPACESHIP

Designing vehicles might seem like a whole different challenge, and in many ways it is. But if you think of your vehicles, props, and scenes as if they're characters all of their own, it will come a lot easier to you. Designing Meg's spaceship provided a means to further define her personality.

Another important factor to determine is how your vehicle works. We all know how parrots fly and what a carrot is, but no one has seen this particular vehicle before. Ask yourself questions like: What is this part of the vehicle used for? Does the vehicle shoot flames or smoke? Maybe both?!

## ALIENS

Seeing the word "alien" in the story text can set your mind reeling. Aliens can look like anything, which means it's possible to make many mistakes when designing them. Luckily, you have the rest of the story text to draw ideas from too.

In *Florence the Talking Carrot*, the story mentions two types of aliens: "fluffy" aliens and "jelly" aliens. Right away this helps to narrow down their designs. Since these are secondary characters, you can be as creative and absurd as you like when sketching ideas. These characters don't appear often in the story, so you want them to have an impact. For example, the jelly aliens ended up having jars on their heads so they looked like jelly/jam spilling out from its jar. This type of visual humor can add a lot of narrative interest to your world. Considering the story's intended age range while designing will also help with design elements like this. What would you have laughed at as a kid? Chances are other kids will laugh at that too.

The alien characters in this story always appear in groups, so there's no need to narrow it down to just one design. Keep all of your sketches and use multiple designs to make them into groups.

Exploring different types of spaceships, as well as the smoke and fire it w ll shoot out in the story. Vehicles can be challenging, but remember to give them character.

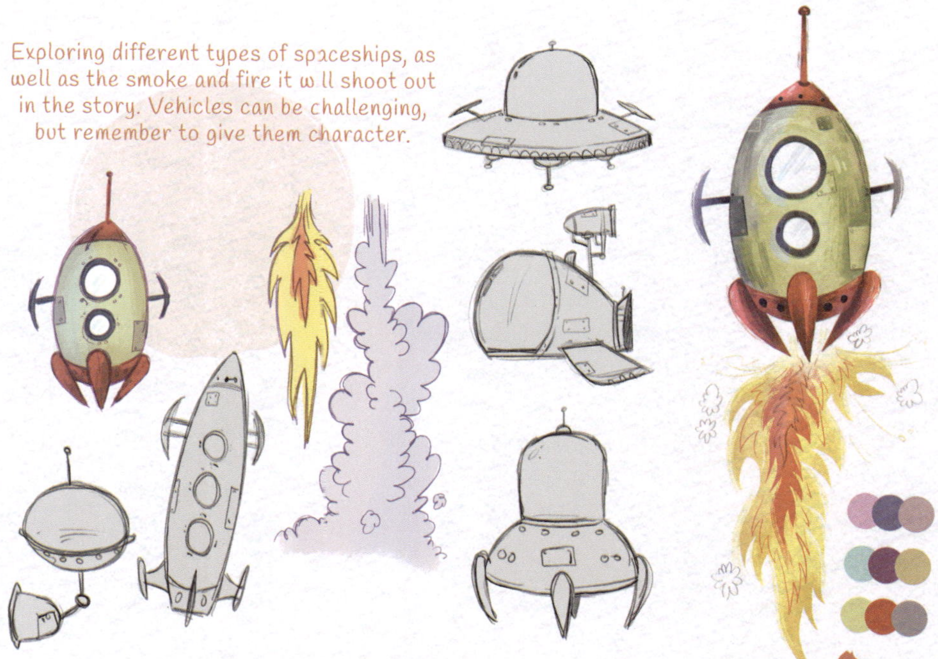

The final design for Meg's spaceship with possible color palettes. I wanted it to be a different color to the characters and settled on a soft green that would allow the characters' saturation to pop.

Sketches exploring the two different types of aliens, designed with the intention of looking like they belong together in a group.

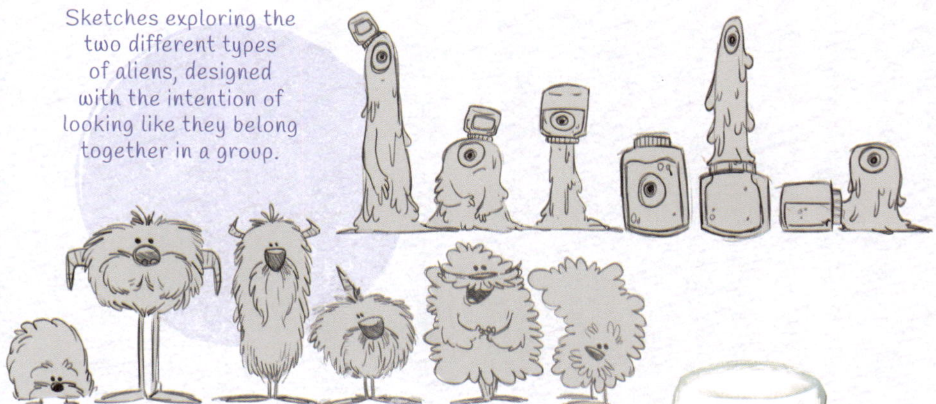

Two color versions of the aliens, one of each type. I wanted them to look completely different, almost opposite in terms of their design.

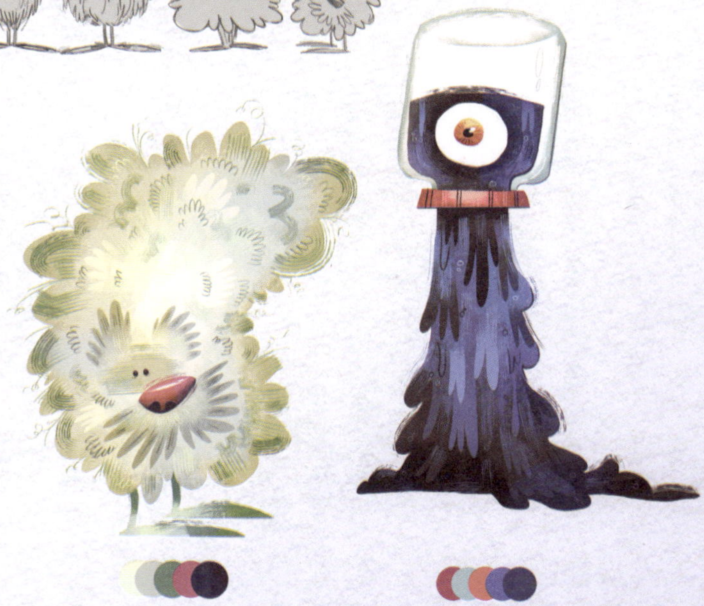

# ANALYSIS

When you start the process of designing the pages in a book, it's important to get the mood right. Before anything else, you need your illustrations to match the emotions you want the audience to feel. In *Florence the Talking Carrot*, the illustrations could have been dark, gritty, and scary, giving the book an entirely different feel. While this idea definitely came to mind, I quickly decided that this story, with its rhyming text and over-the-top style, needed to be light-hearted and funny. When considering the mood, many things can change when you start making decisions.

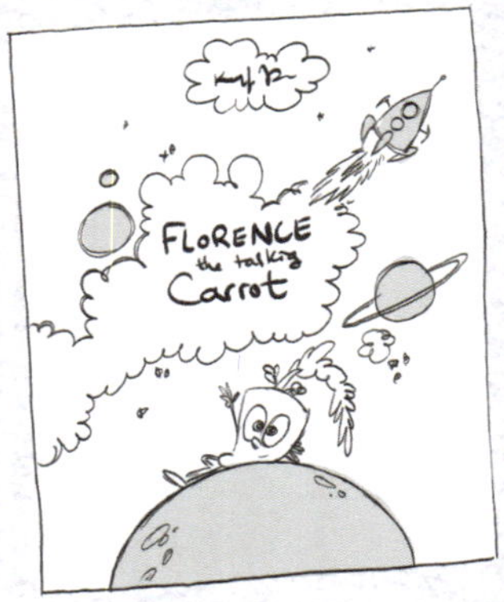


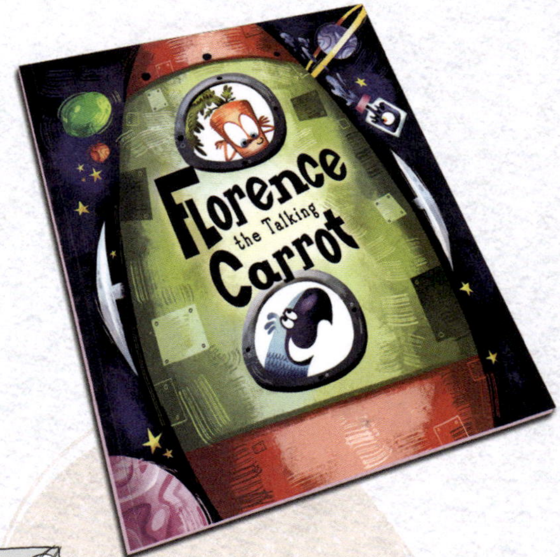


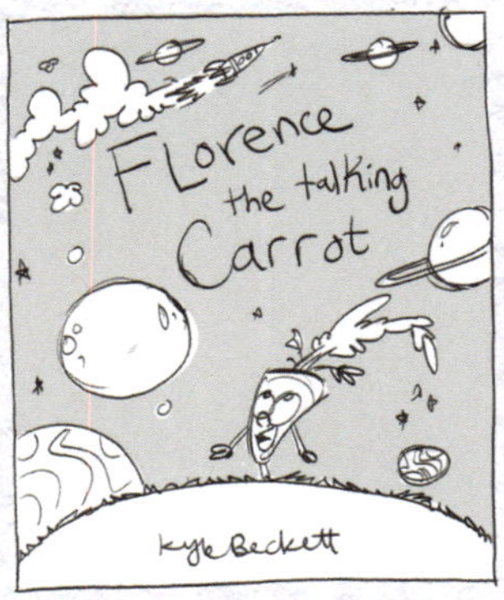


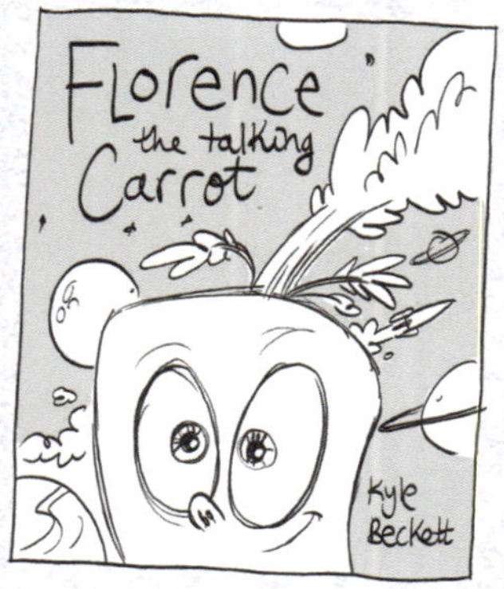


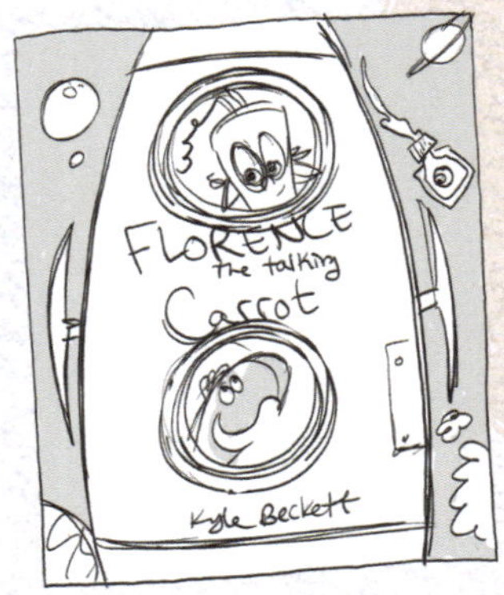


The first thing anyone buying your book will see is the cover, so be sure to spend time exploring to give yourself plenty of options to choose from. Make it stand out!

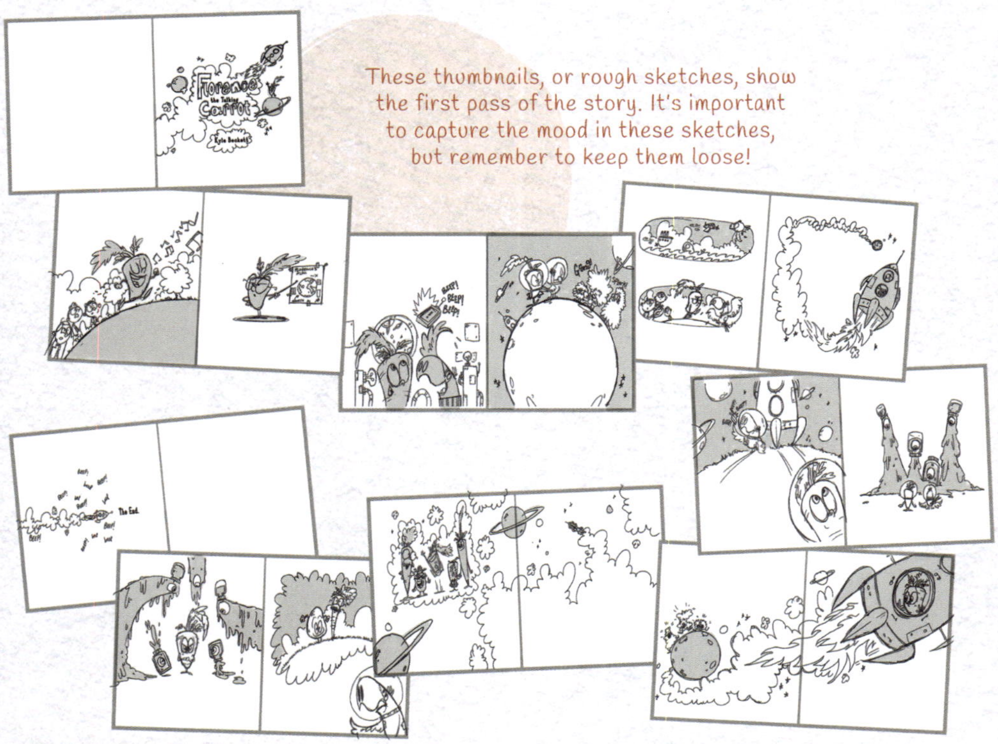

These thumbnails, or rough sketches, show the first pass of the story. It's important to capture the mood in these sketches, but remember to keep them loose!

While the mood and design came easily for this story, it was difficult to figure out what to show and what not to show on the pages. That's where thumbnailing is useful. I find the best part of the bookmaking process is seeing all of the story in one place for the first time. I group my thumbnails on one page, allowing me to view them together before I move on to the color stage. Creating thumbnails of each spread gives you the opportunity to look at the flow of the book. Are there too many pages where the characters are all the same size? Is everything full-page, or do you have vignettes and spot illustrations to break it up? Remember, it's not just about what you show on the page; it's about what happens between the pages too.

Here are two of the spreads shown in the three stages of the design process: the sketches, the color roughs, and the final artwork.

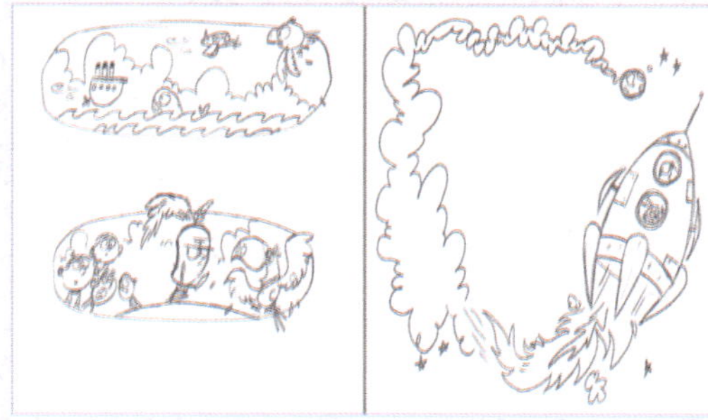

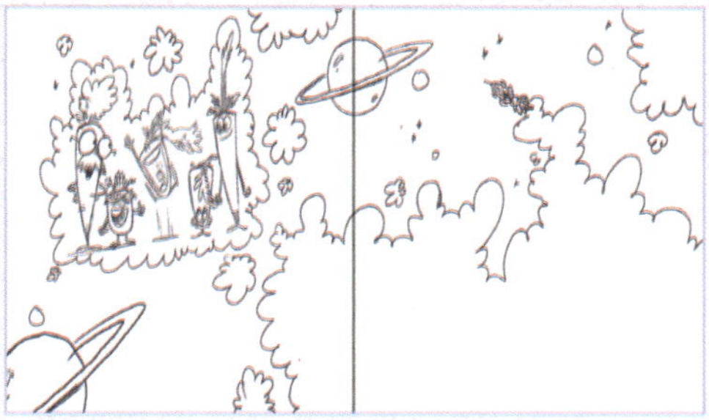

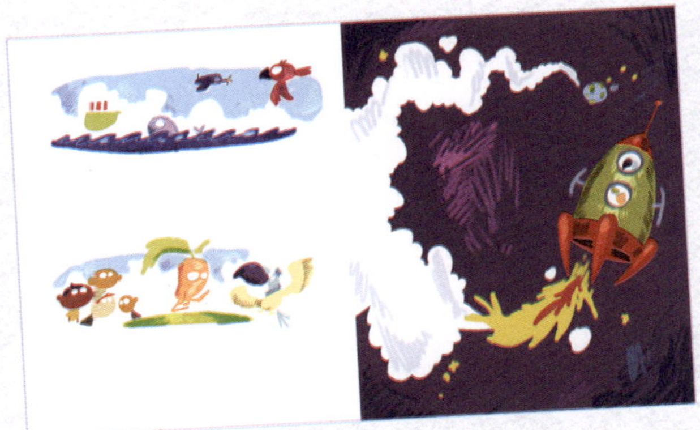

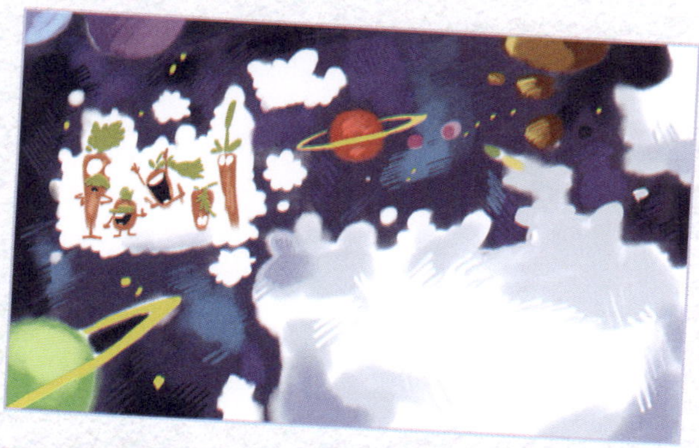

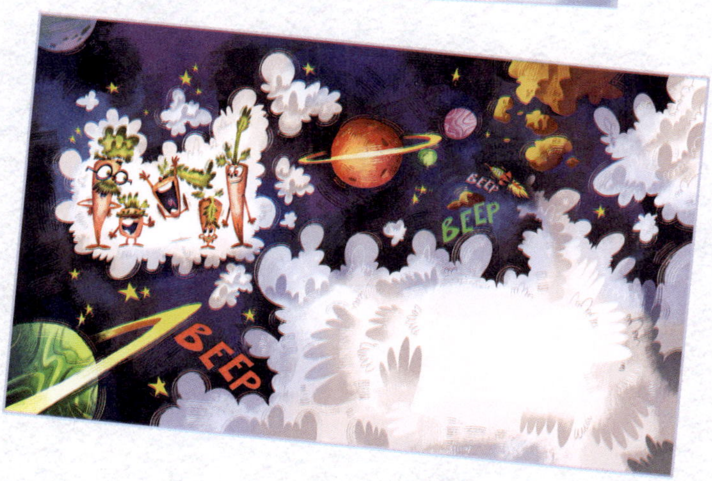


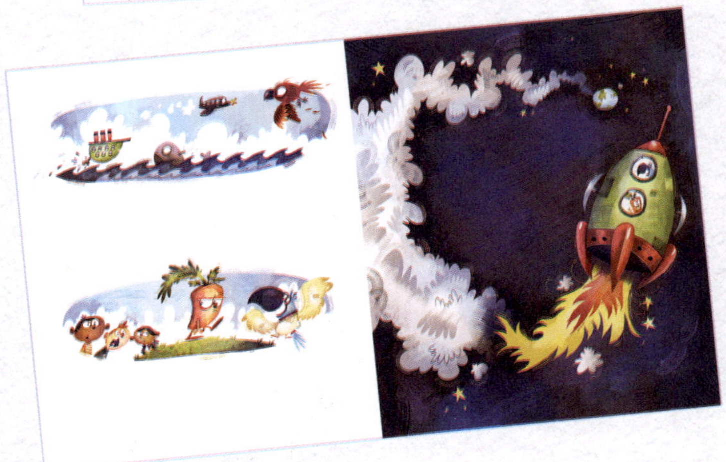

If I could give any advice to budding artists and storytellers, it would be to stay inspired and never lose sight of the book in your head. It's very easy to see another person's work and want to create something similar, but always remember that you are the only one who can make that book you're dreaming about.

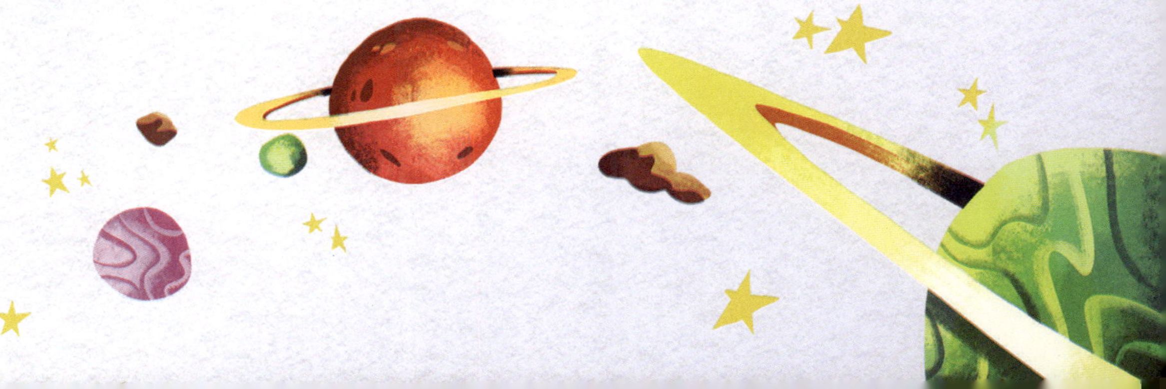

# I am not a Tree Climber

Written by

GREG DOBBINS

Illustrated by

KATE PELLERIN "POOPIKAT"

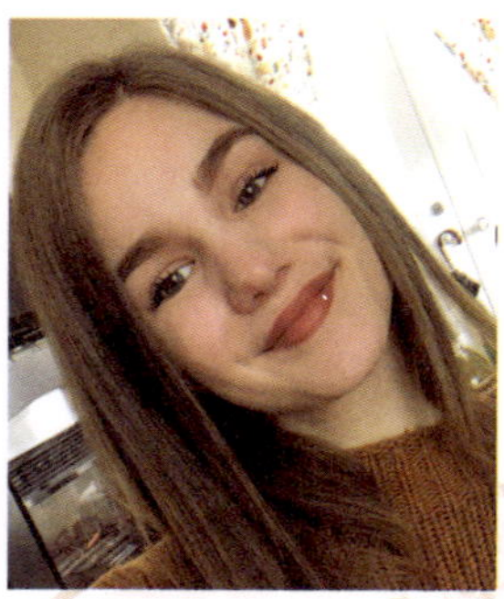

Freelance illustrator
**poopikat.com**

Kate is a Canadian-based artist currently living in Toronto. She specializes in children's book illustration and character design.

A STORY FOR AGES 6–8 YEARS

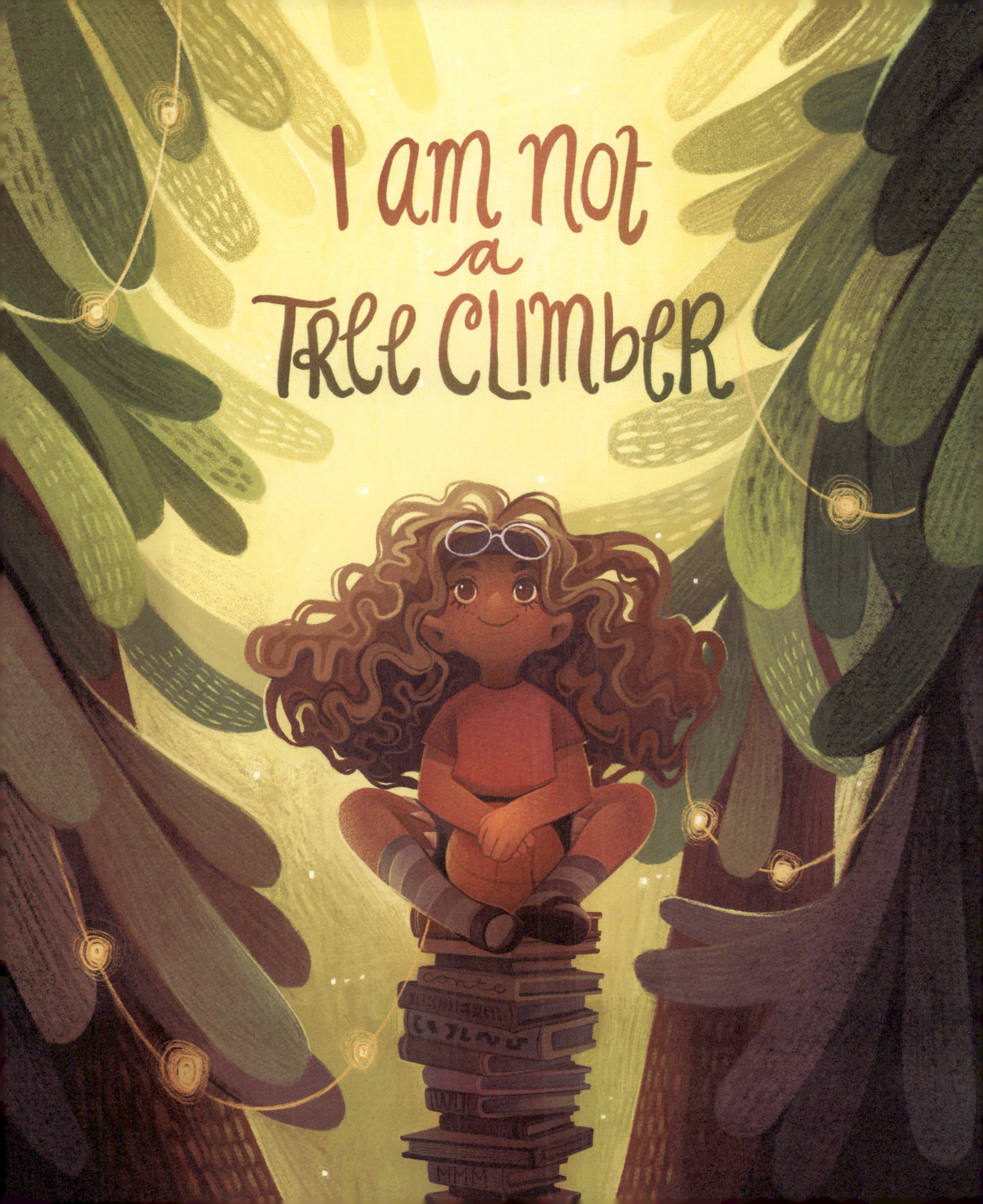
I am not a Tree Climber

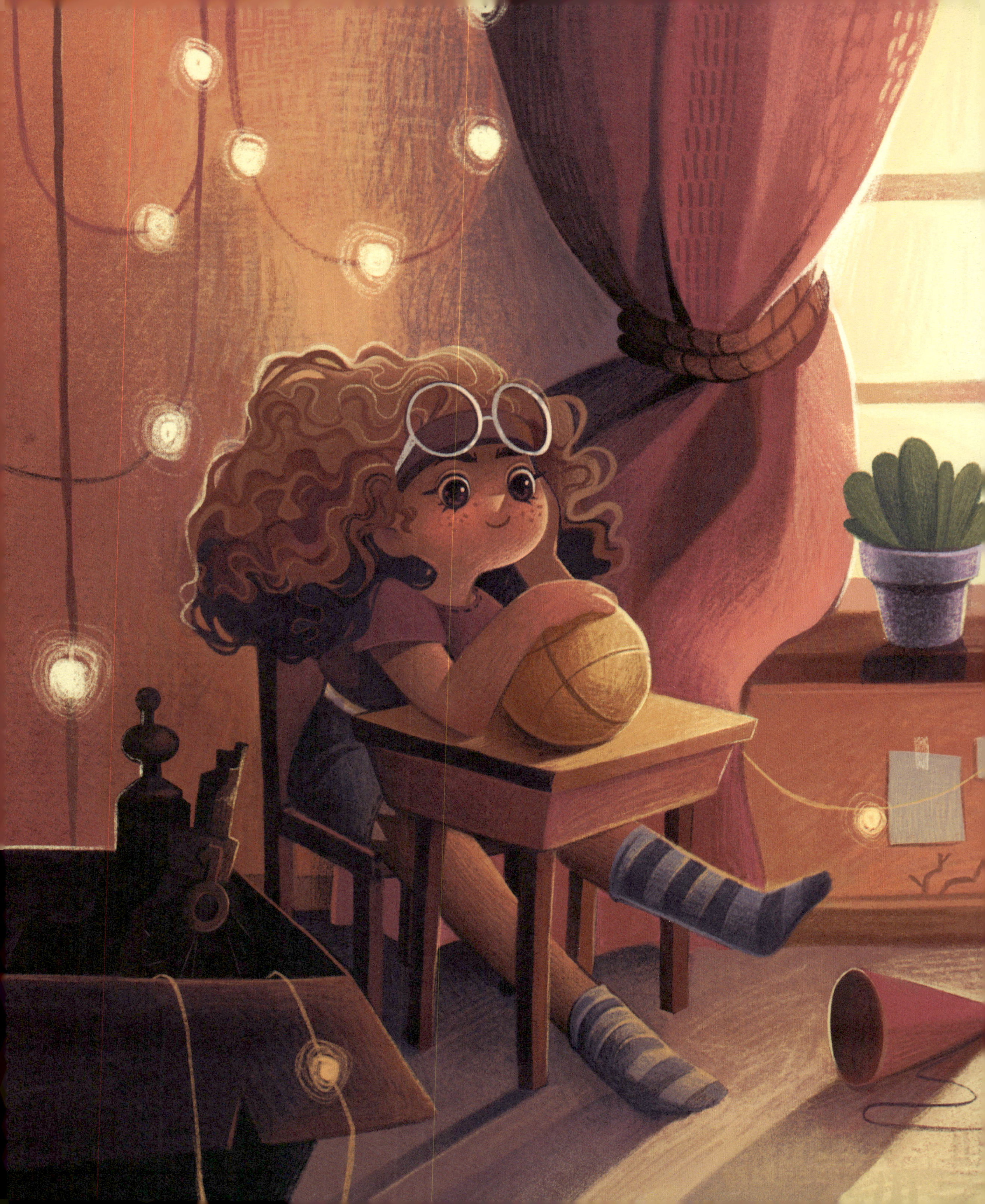

**Hi!** I'm Jasminder Cartwright, Jazz for short. You've probably never heard of me though. I'm quiet, you see. I fade into the background, and sometimes people hardly even notice that I'm there at all. But it would be nice to be noticed sometimes. To win something, or get an answer right at school, or be a social media star. To be cool.

But to be properly cool I'd need to be like some of my friends: good at football, or kickboxing, or juggling. I'm OK at football, I've never tried kickboxing, and when I attempted juggling, let's just say it took ages to clean up the broken eggs in the kitchen, and Dad was not happy!

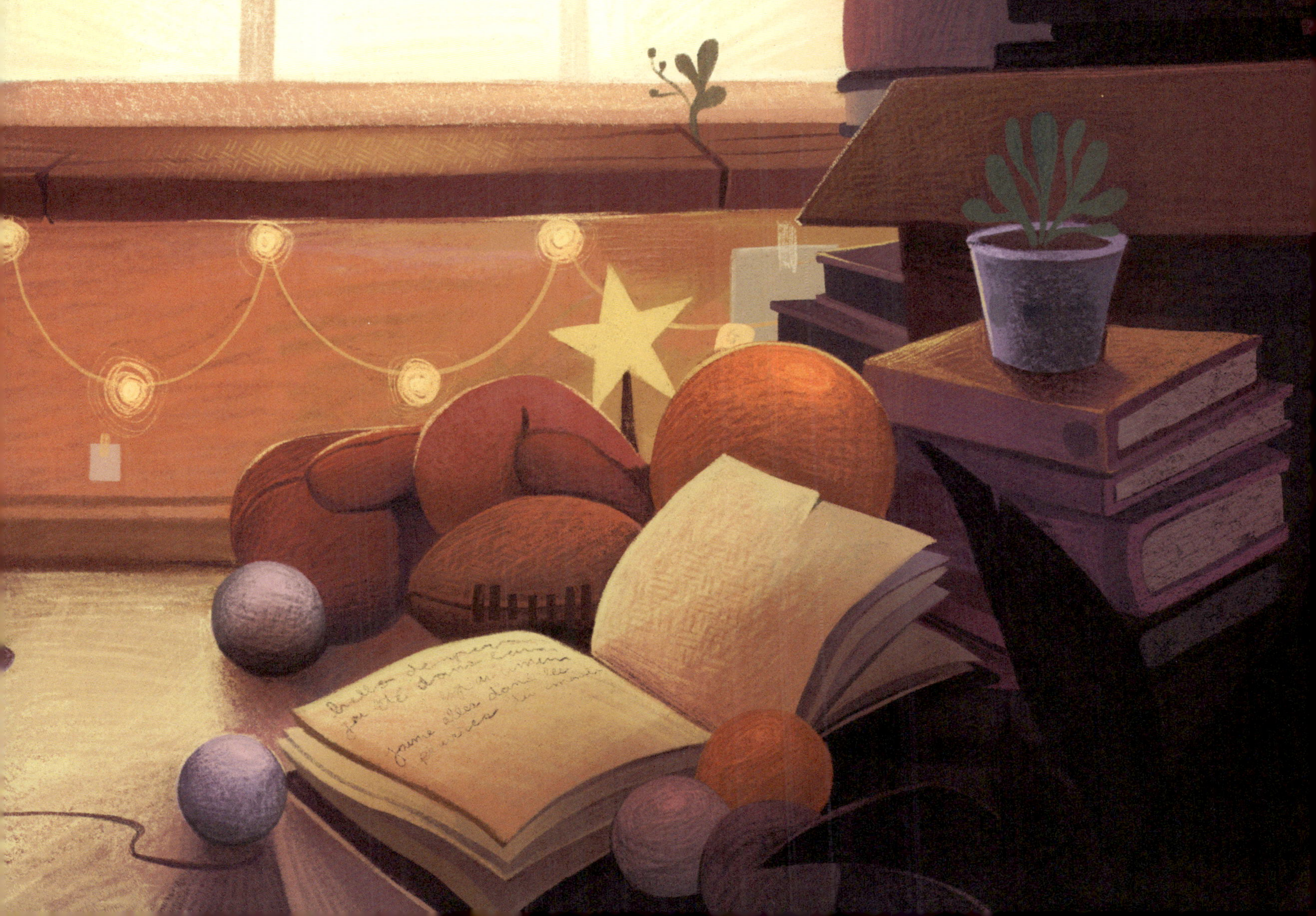

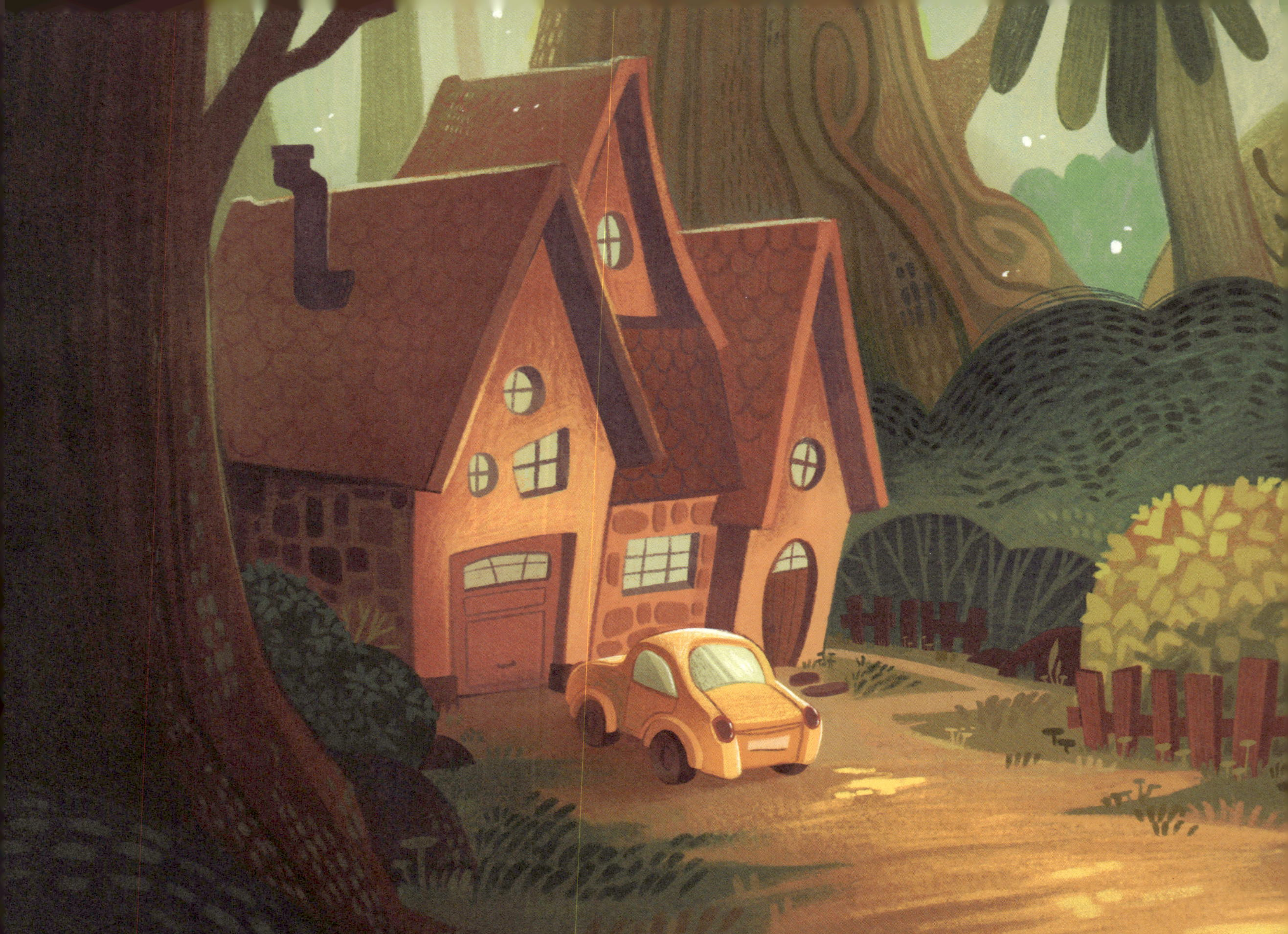

Which leaves me hidden in the middle. Not cool, not uncool. So I decided to do something about it. I had a plan… I was going to be a skateboarder! Not just any old skateboarder though – I was going to be a backwards, blindfolded skateboarder!

So, on the driveway, blindfold on, I stepped onto the skateboard and pushed off. Backwards! Don't forget that bit. And… I was doing it! I was skateboarding, backwards, while blindfolded. I was a backwards, blindfolded skateboarder. Going quite fast. Woahhh. Going really fast, actually. Going…

ARGHHHHH!

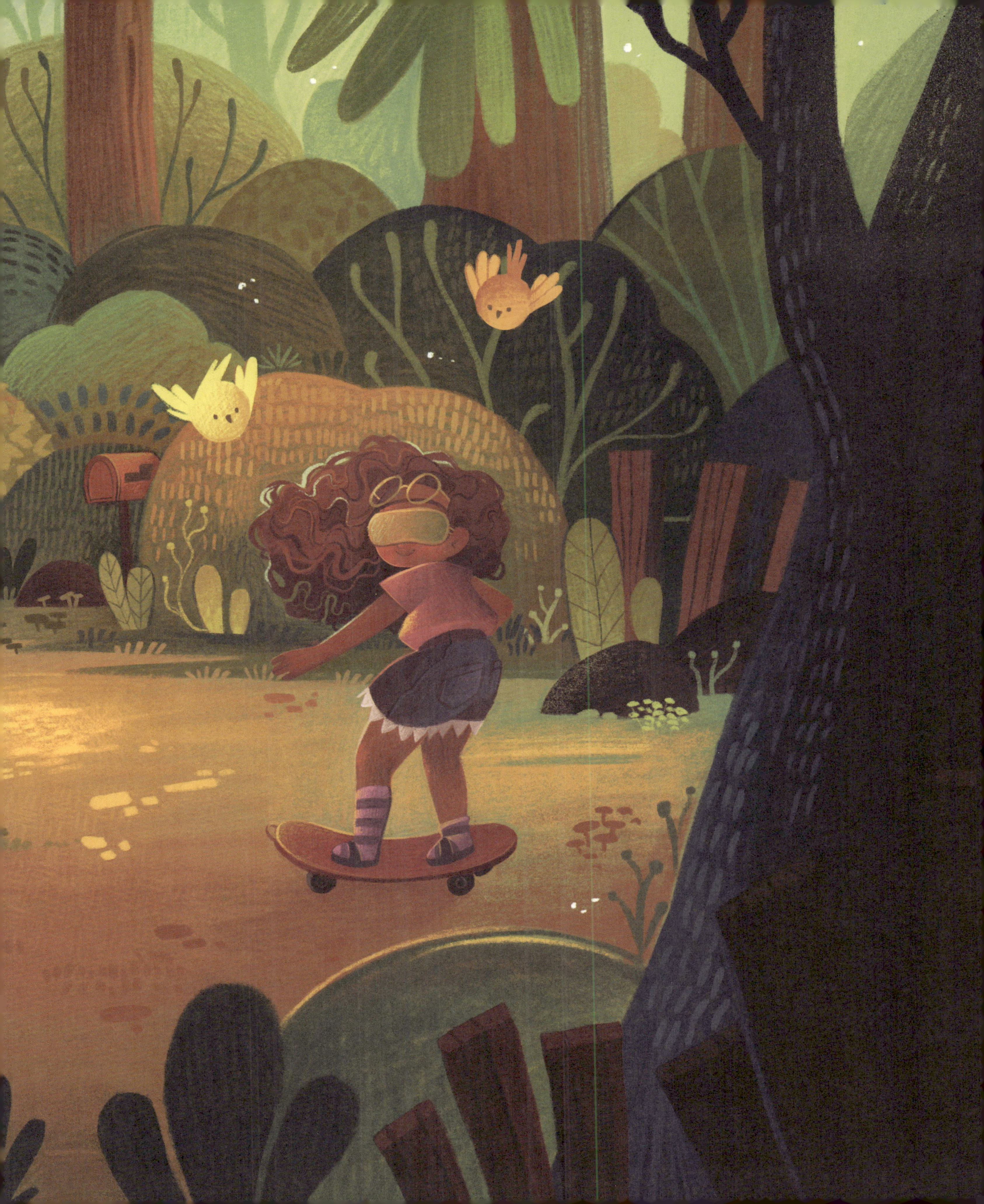

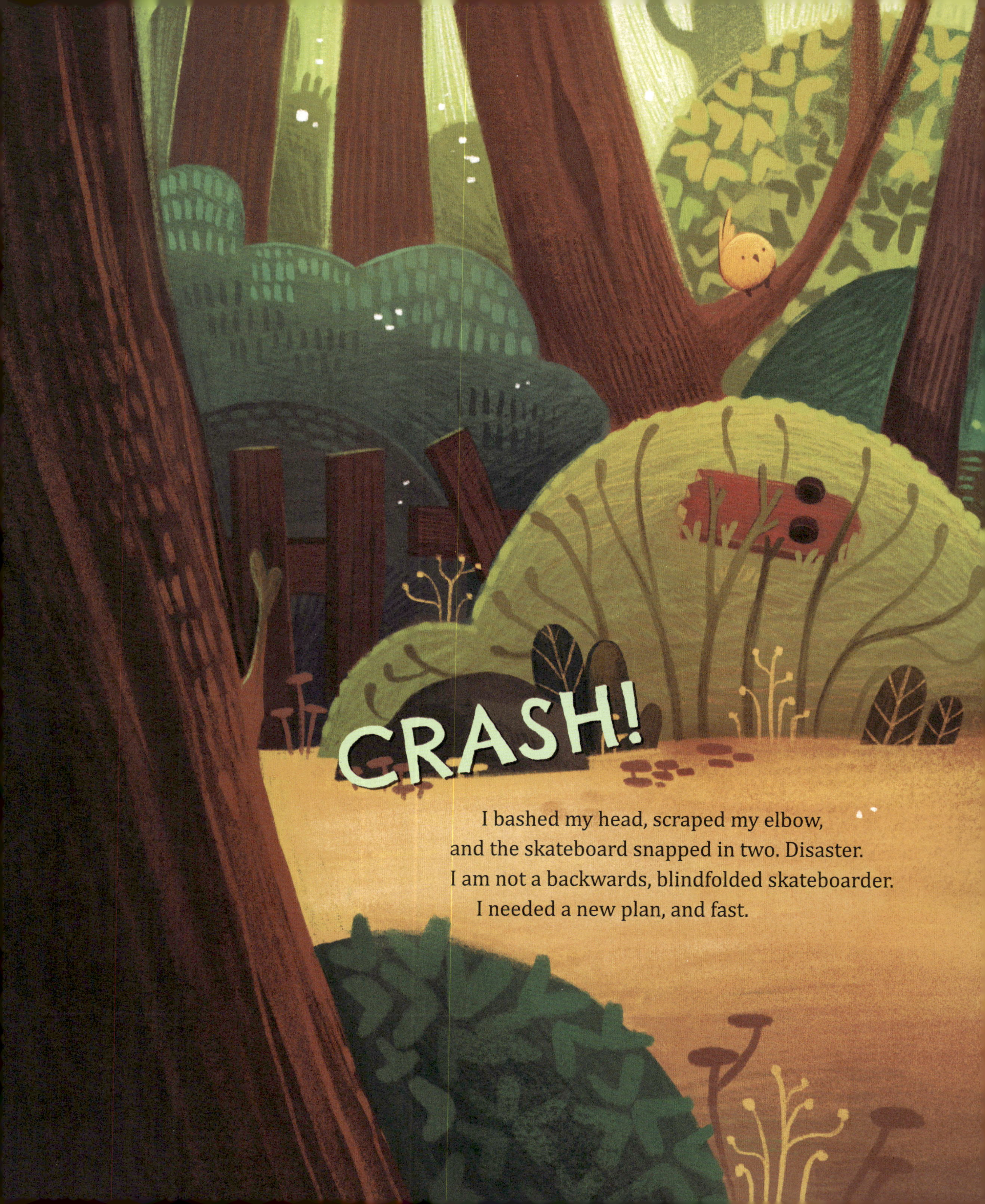


I bashed my head, scraped my elbow,
and the skateboard snapped in two. Disaster.
I am not a backwards, blindfolded skateboarder.
I needed a new plan, and fast.

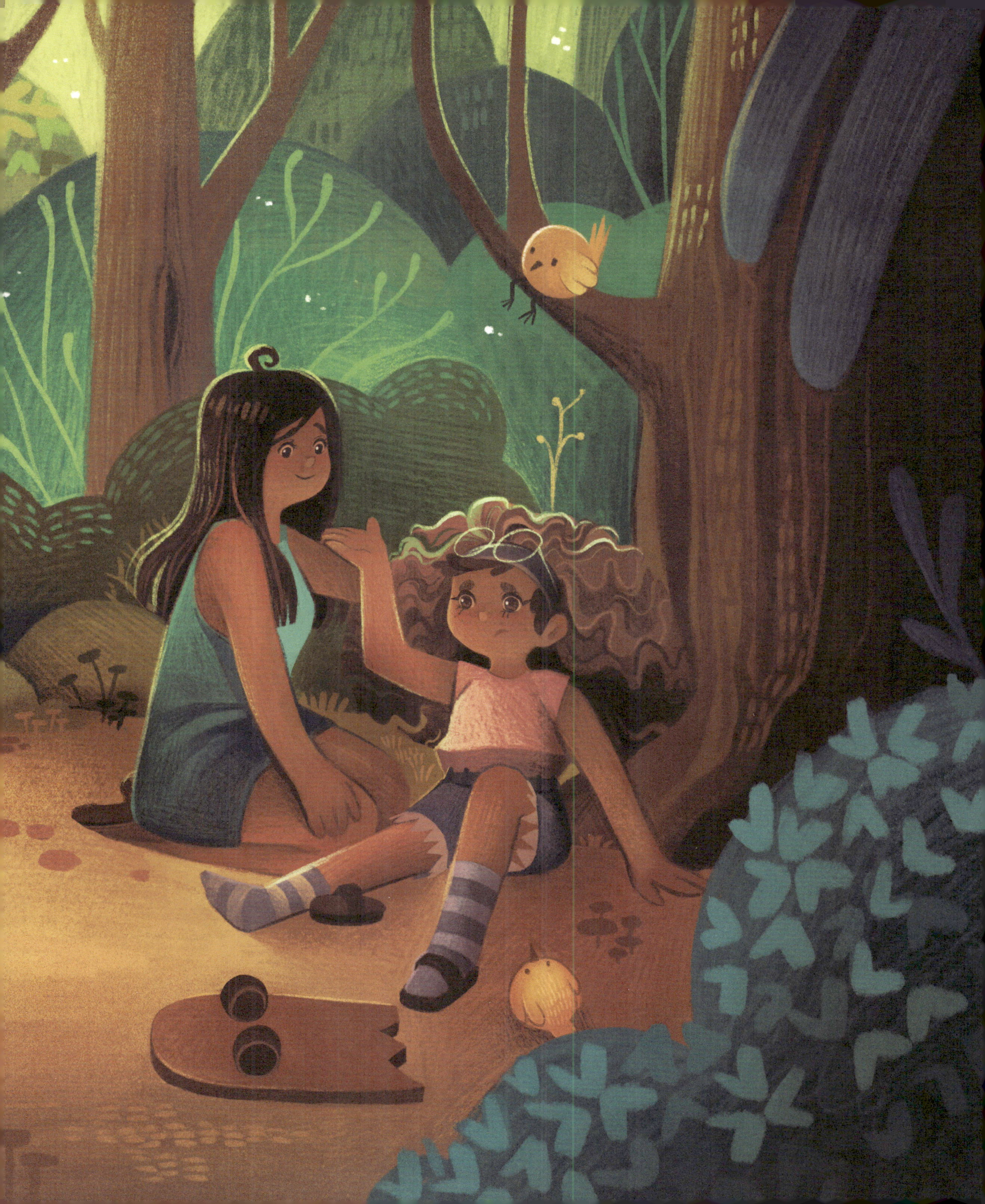

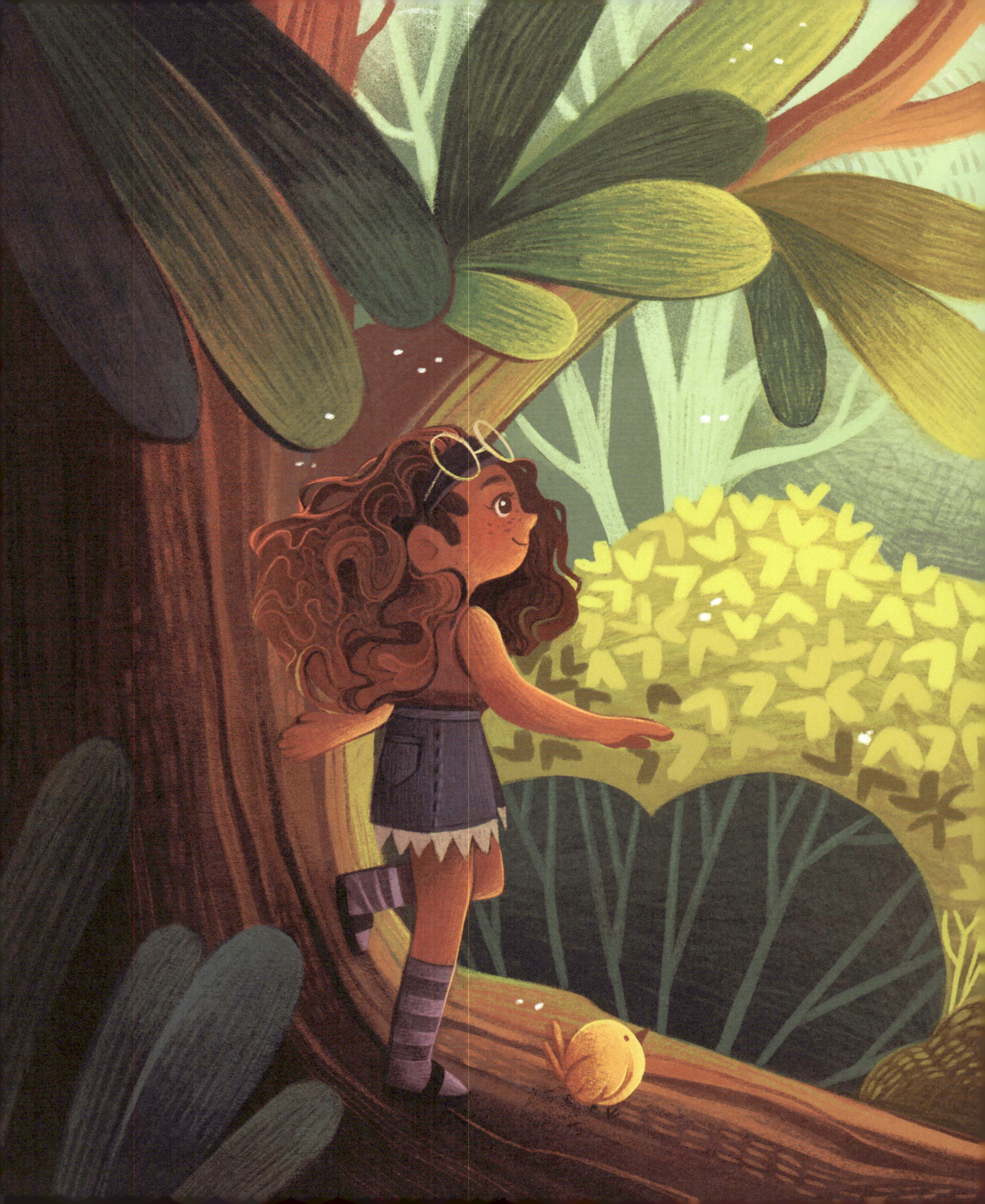

D'you know what's really cool? Climbing trees! And I'd worked out how to climb the tree at the bottom of our garden, something I'd wanted to do for ages. I had a plan. A proper diagram, actually. I'd used a ruler and one of those pop-up pencils, and it had mathematical symbols drawn on and everything.

And you know what? It worked! It was easy, just following the route I'd planned out – as simple as walking to school, and a lot more fun at the end, let me tell you. What a view from the top! I looked across the rooftops and wished I could fly. That gave me an idea! I folded the tree-climbing map up into a paper airplane and launched it into the sky!

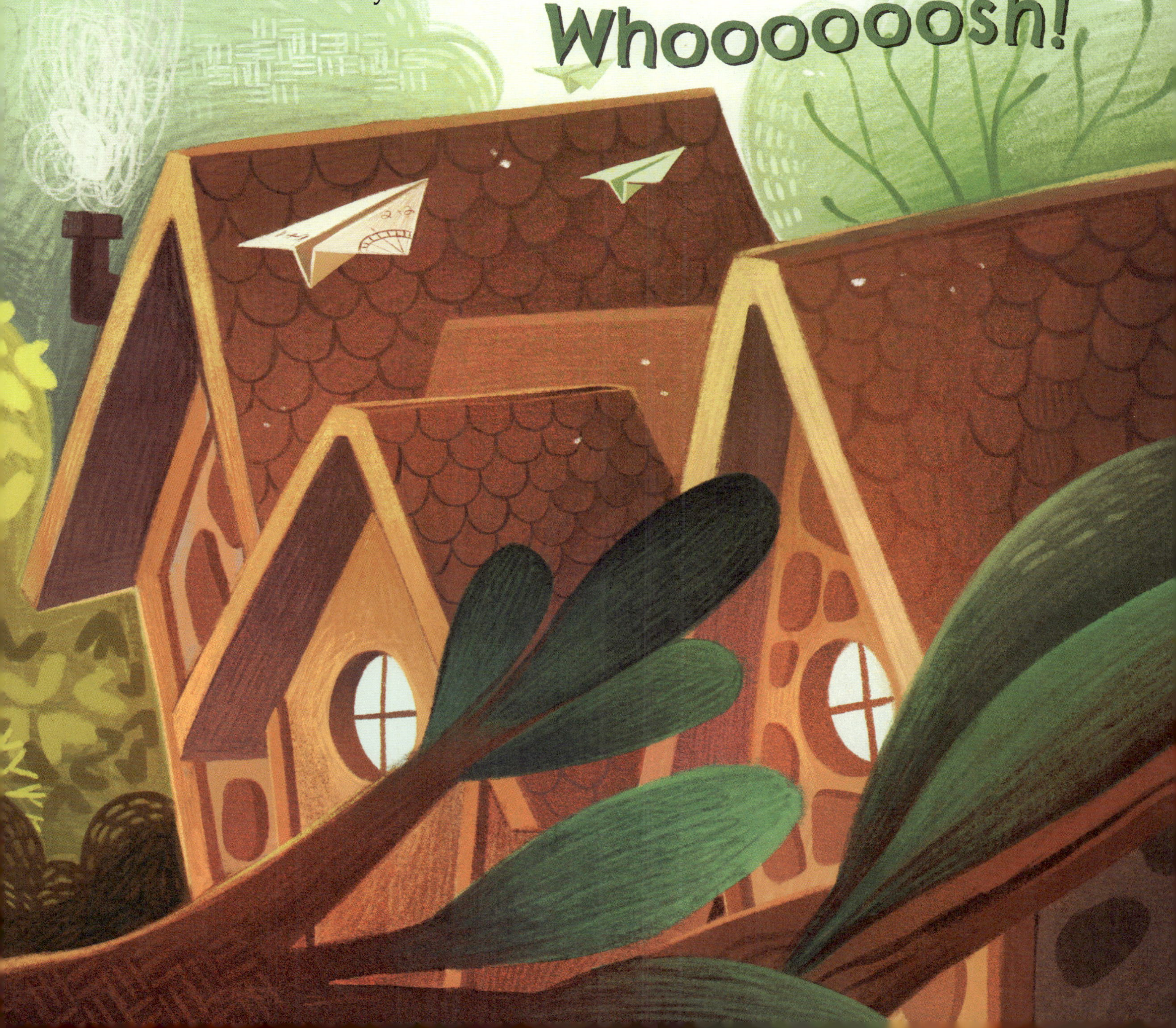

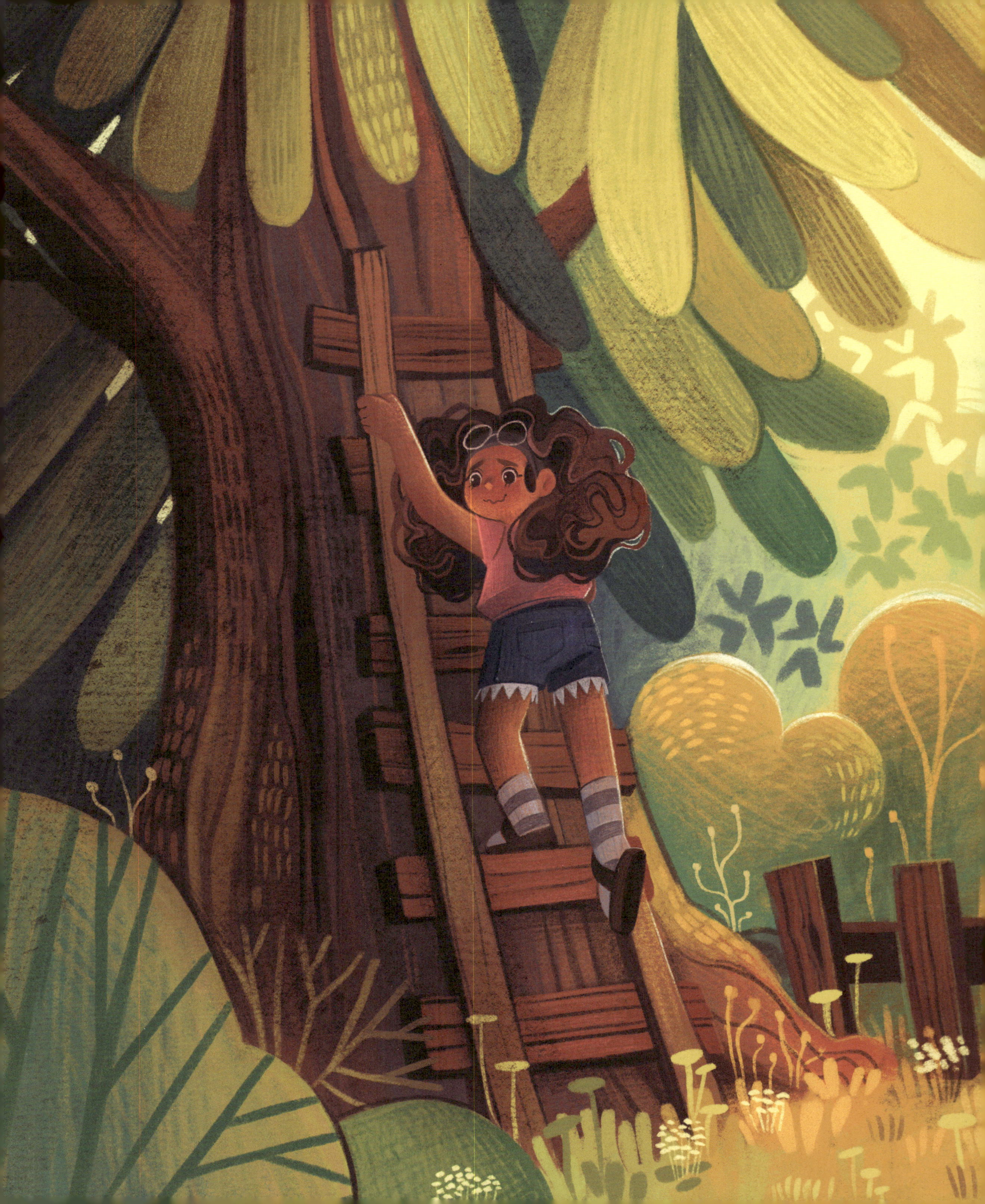

Oh. You know how I needed a map to climb up the tree? Well, as you may have worked out, I needed a map to climb down too. Oops.

I tried, I really did. At one point I was only three branches from the bottom, but I had to head back up again to get around a big branch, and I ended up two branches from the top again, and then I couldn't remember which way I'd come. Then Mum came home and she had to get a ladder to get me down. I am not a tree climber. I needed a new plan, and fast.

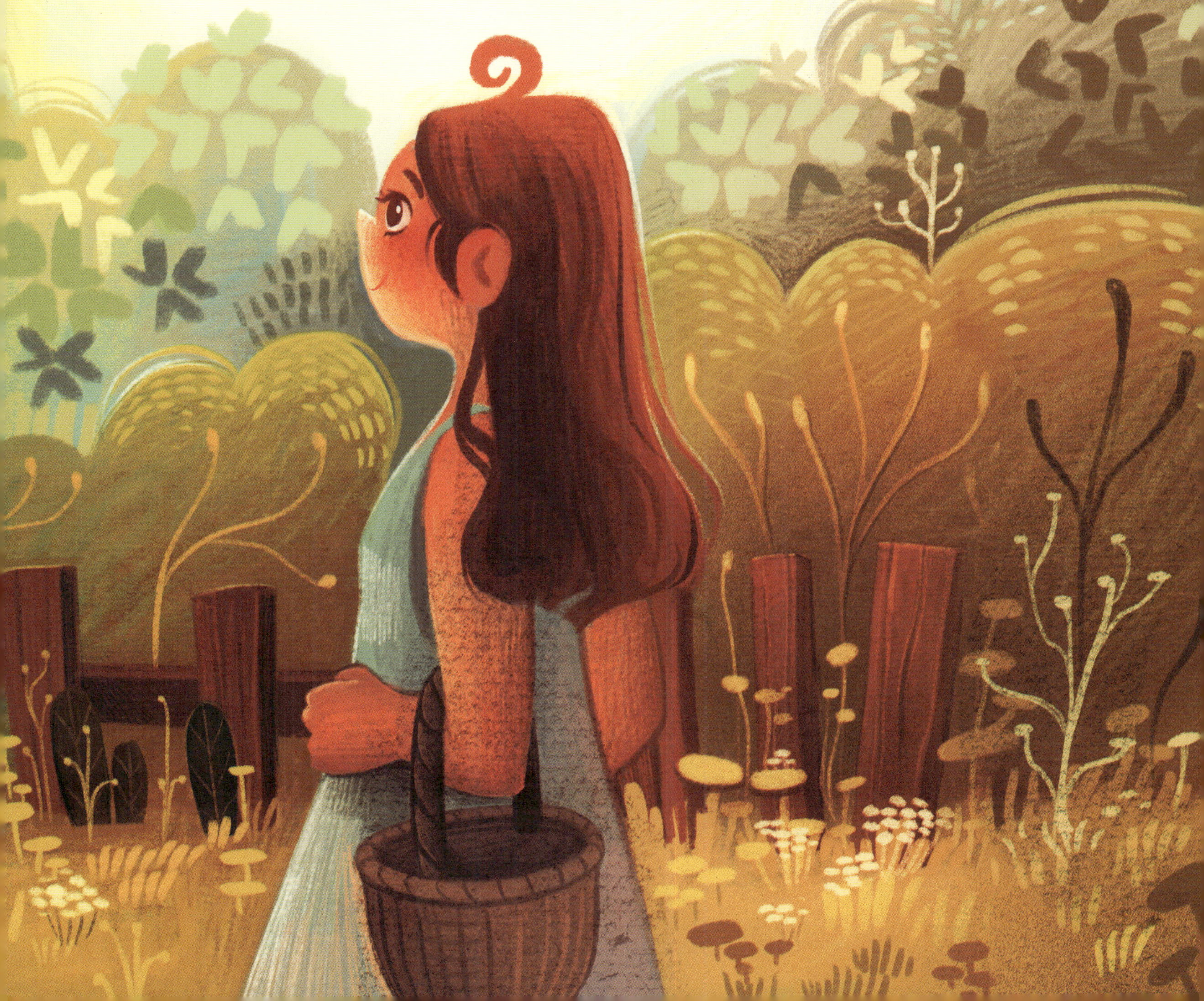

I decided I needed something less physical. Art! Painting is cool, right? And there's no chance of falling over or getting stuck in a tree, unless you do it really, really badly. So, I got the paints out and got painting. OK... my first go wasn't great. It was meant to be a self-portrait, but it looked like I had three eyes and two noses.

Like an alien! Hee hee! Yeah, I'll just change it into a painting of an alien. Slop some purple hair on... and big green tentacles... add a spaceship in the background... hmm, needs some lasers... yellow paint...

split splot splat!

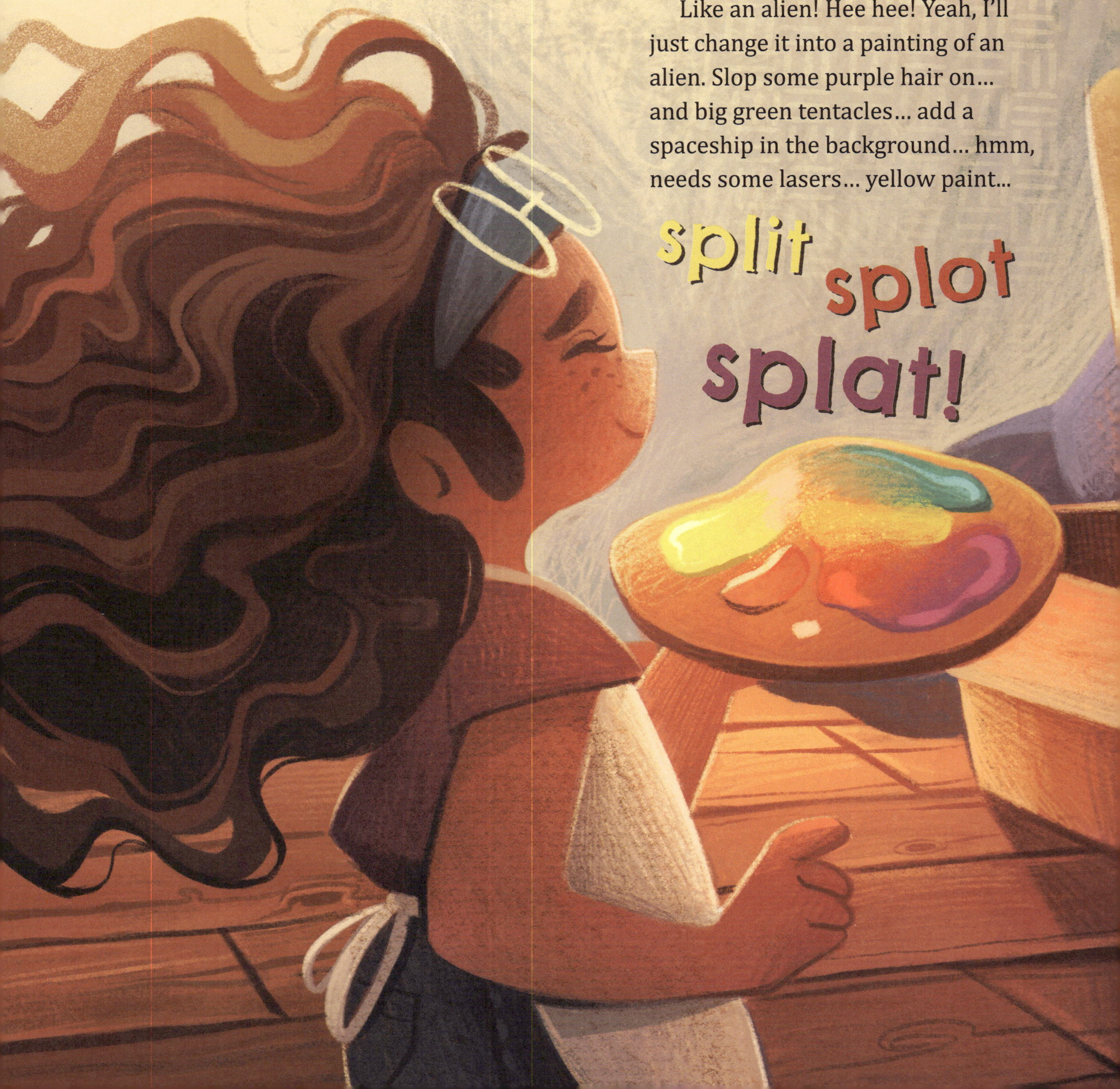

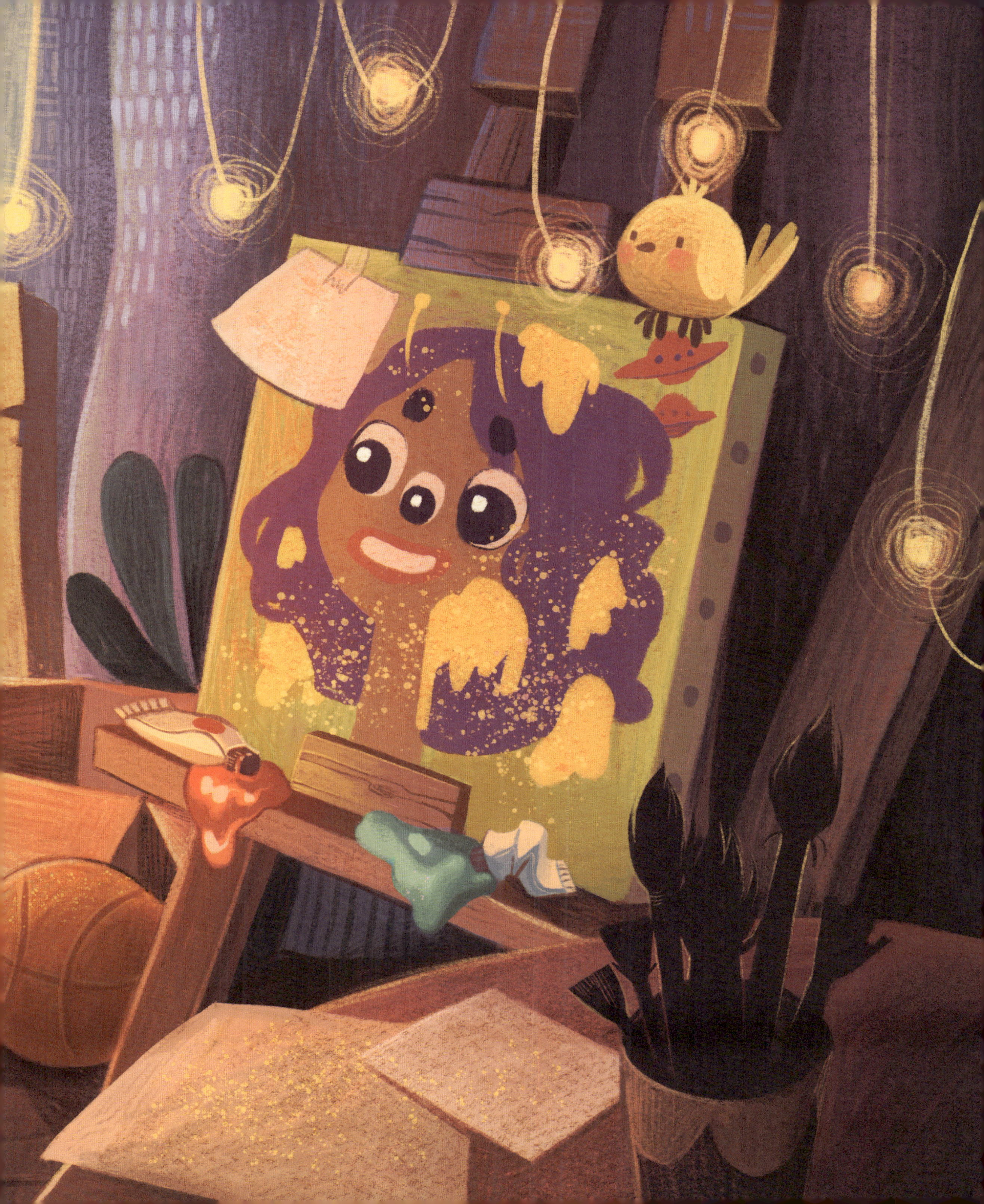

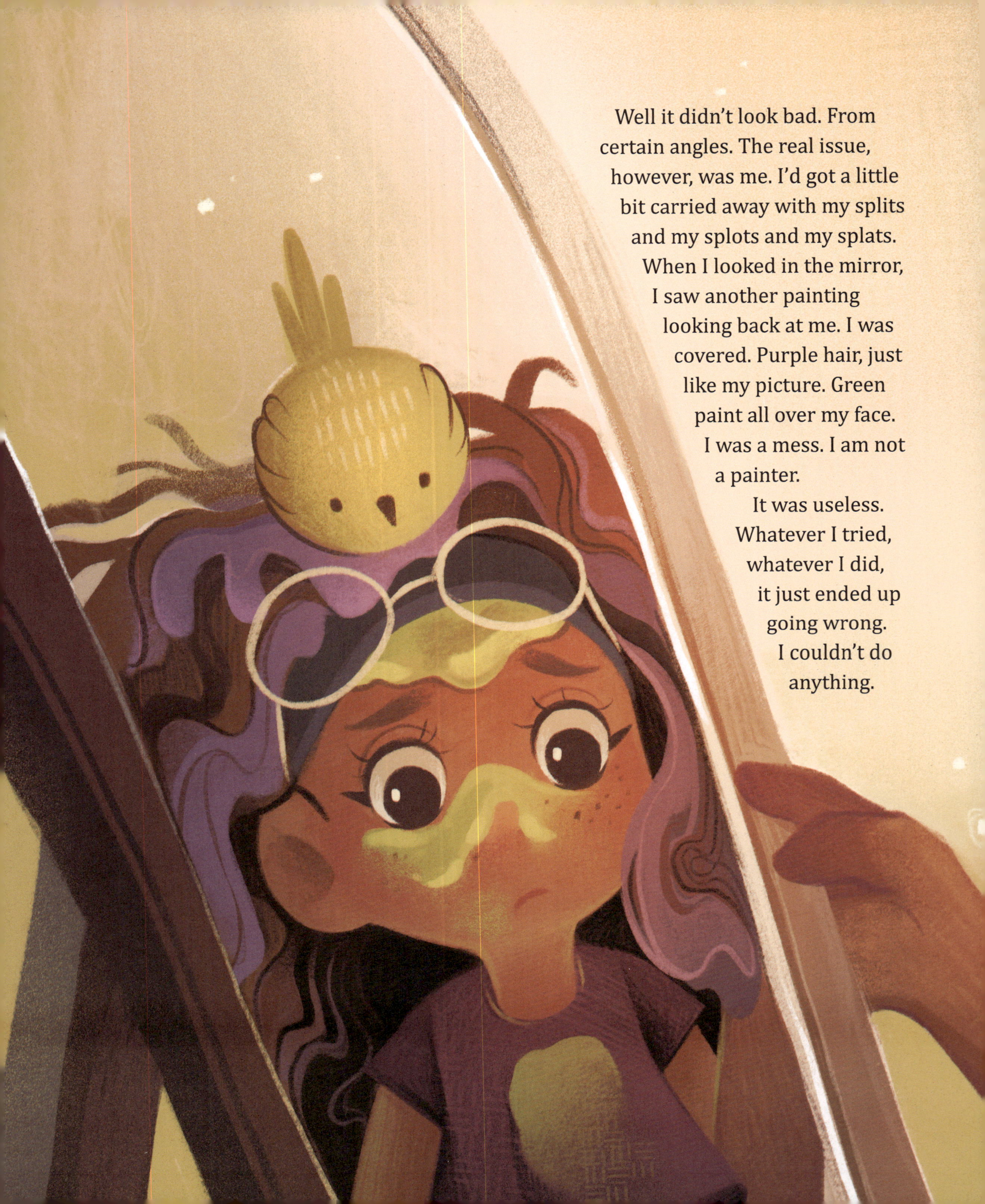

Well it didn't look bad. From certain angles. The real issue, however, was me. I'd got a little bit carried away with my splits and my splots and my splats. When I looked in the mirror, I saw another painting looking back at me. I was covered. Purple hair, just like my picture. Green paint all over my face. I was a mess. I am not a painter.

It was useless. Whatever I tried, whatever I did, it just ended up going wrong. I couldn't do anything.

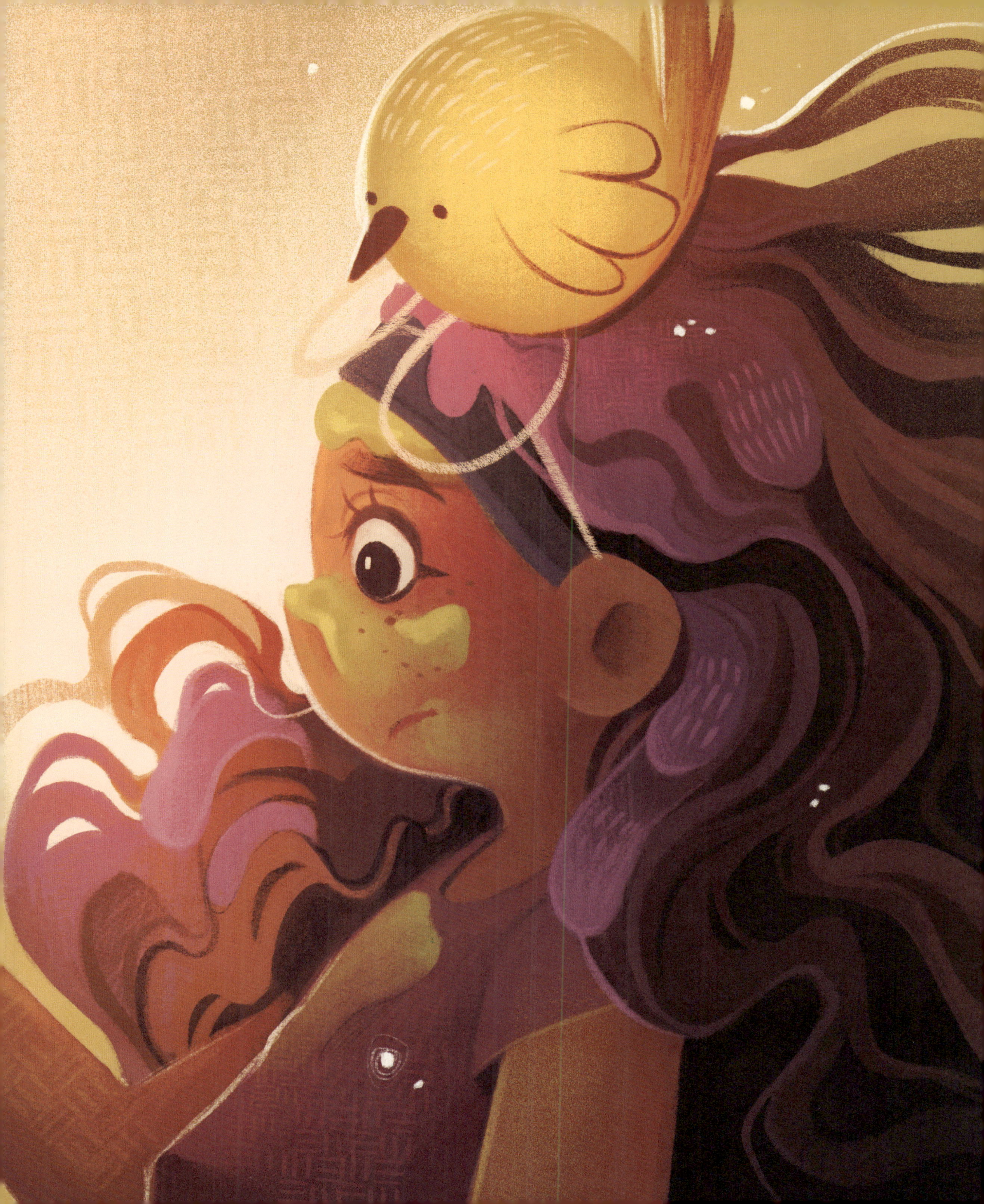

But then, something occurred to me. I've told you all about what happened to me, haven't I? It's kind of like a story really, isn't it? See? That's it! I know what I'm good at now. I know what I can do. It took me a while, but I've finally figured it out…

I'm a writer! I hope you liked my story.

**See ya!**

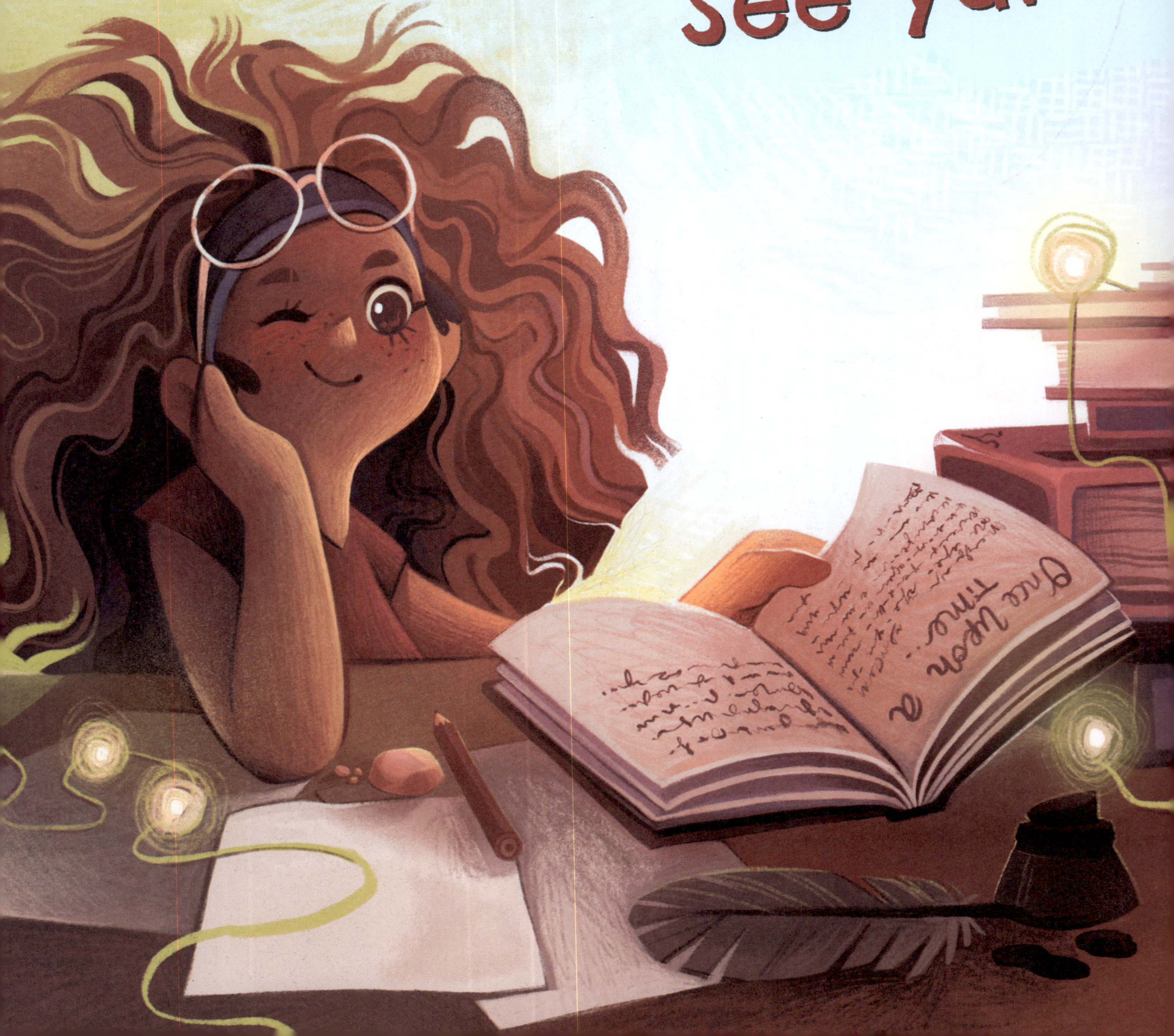

TURN THE PAGE FOR
INSIGHTS FROM THE ARTIST

# I am not a Tree Climber

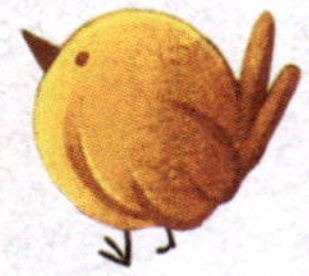

## DEVELOPING KEY FEATURES

### CHARACTER

Creating a character for a children's book with a target age range of 6–8 years can be quite complex, as this is a transitional age for children. While you want to make sure your character looks young, they should look slightly older than the target age range, as children often aspire to be older than they are. Jasminder, the protagonist of *I Am Not a Tree Climber*, is creative, enthusiastic, and a little bit clumsy, so creating a version of her that encapsulated all of her personality was key. I drew her with a wild, untamed hairstyle and uneven, striped socks to show her vibrant and playful character.

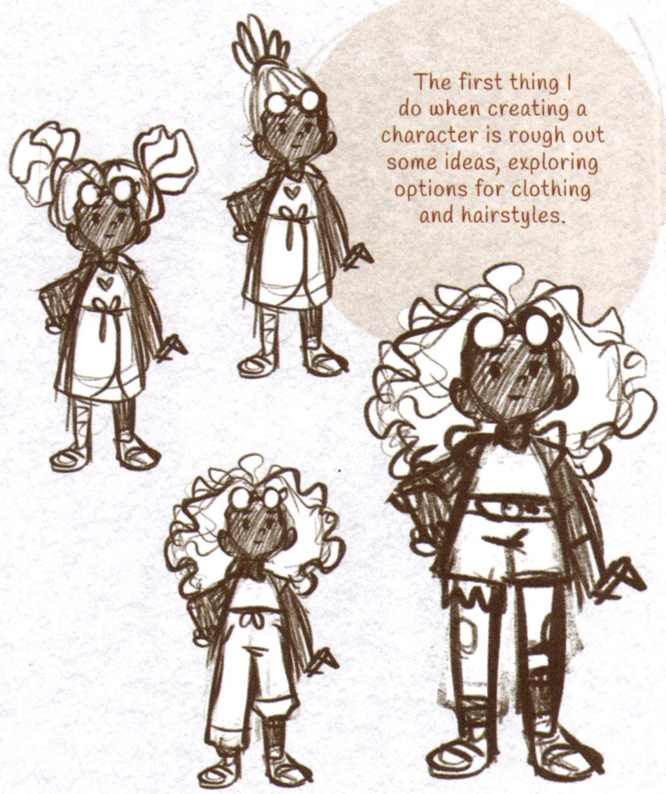

The first thing I do when creating a character is rough out some ideas, exploring options for clothing and hairstyles.

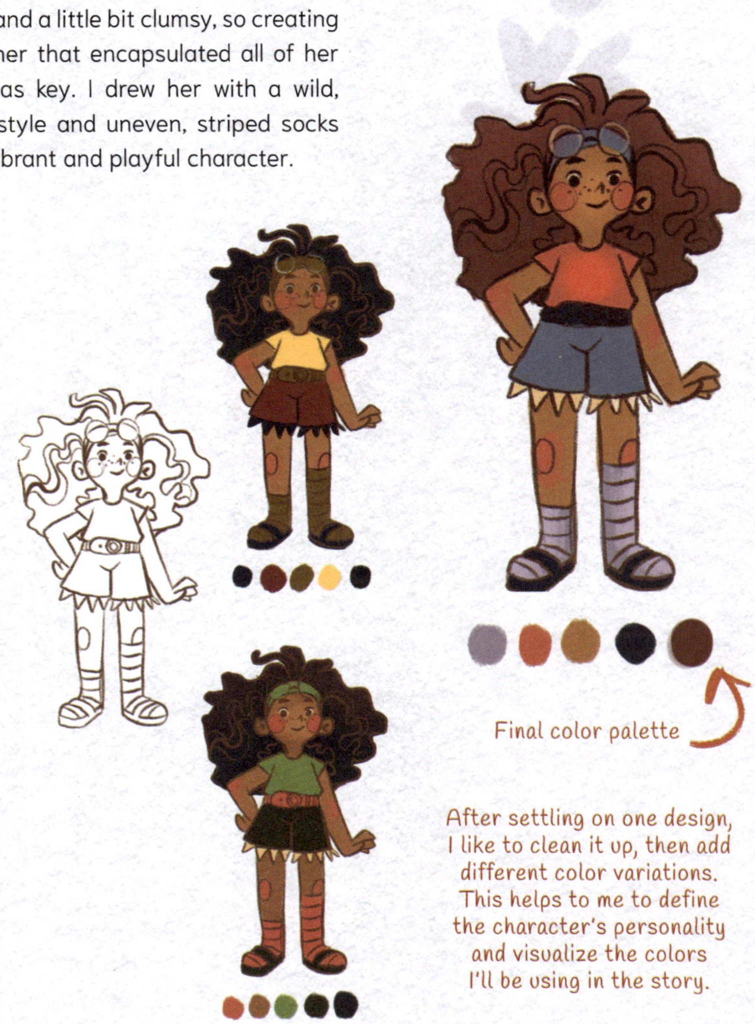

Final color palette

After settling on one design, I like to clean it up, then add different color variations. This helps to me to define the character's personality and visualize the colors I'll be using in the story.

I find it helpful to create an expression sheet for the character so you can refer to it throughout the story.

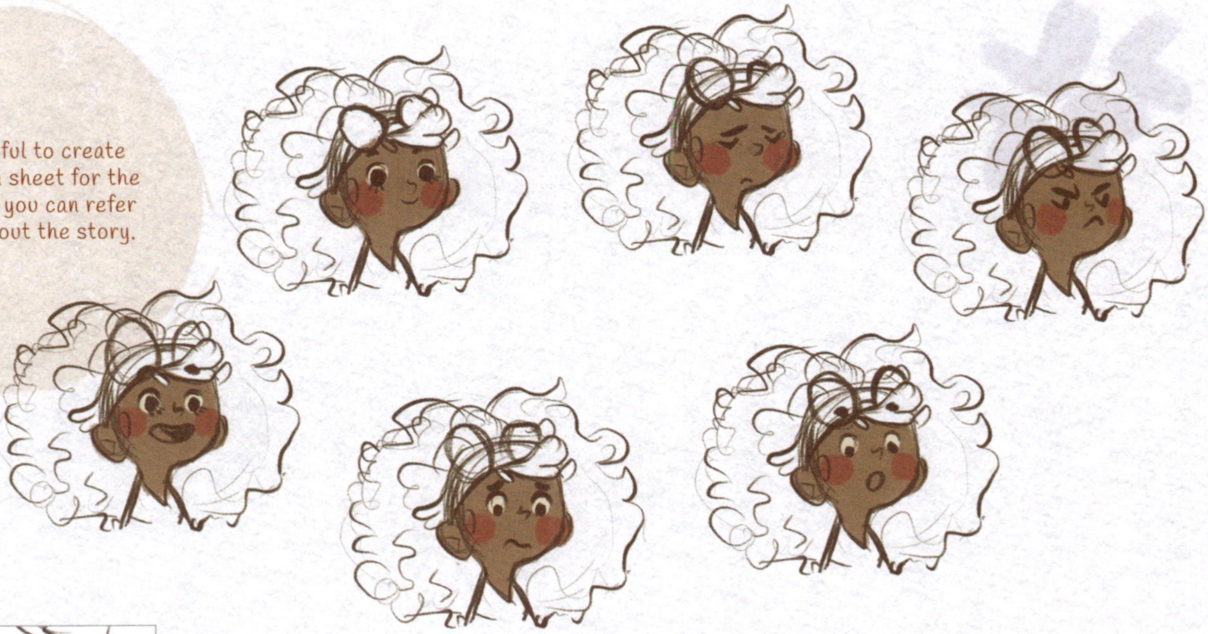

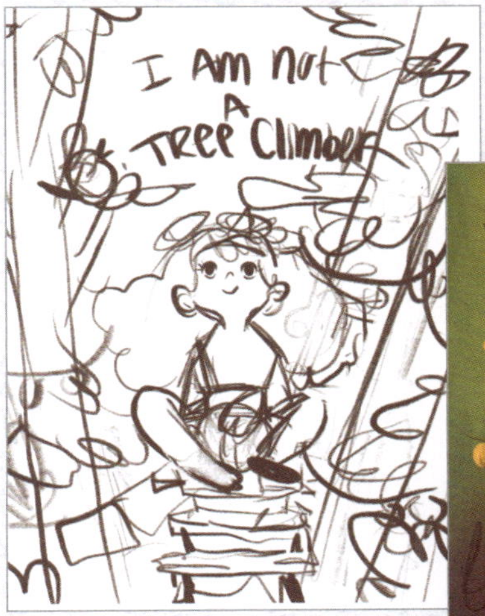


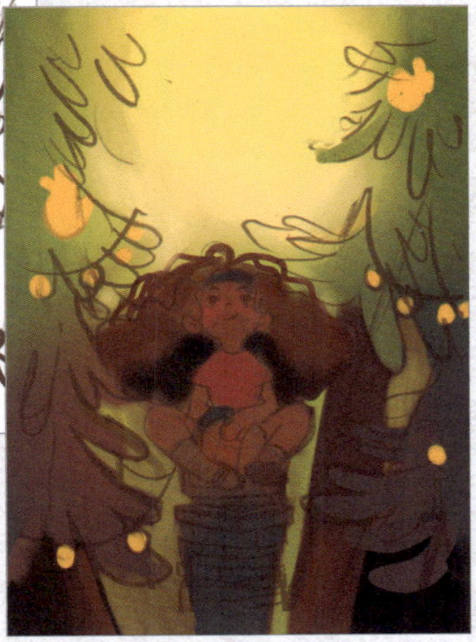

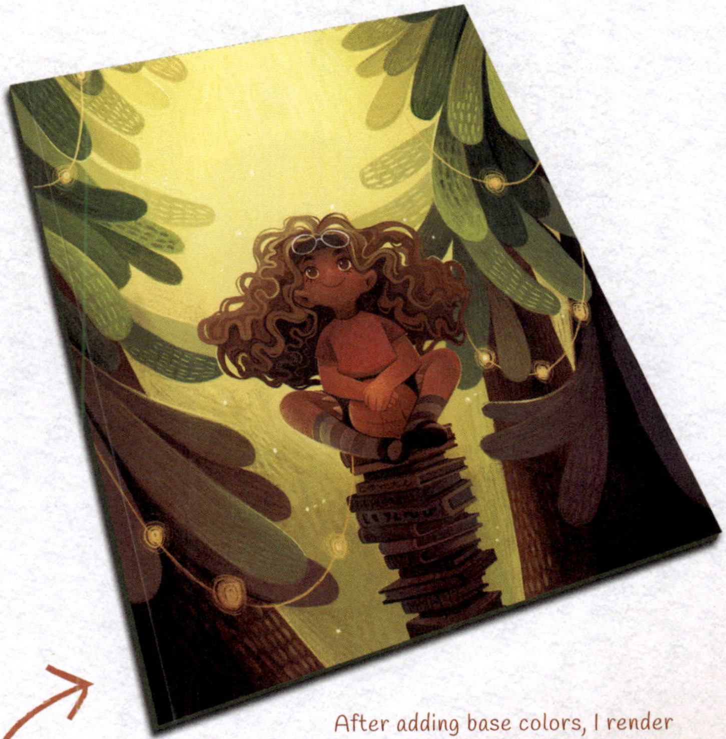

When I'm ready to start my spreads, I begin by roughing my character in very loosely. I don't rely on linework much when rendering, so leaving the sketch loose helps me to develop the pose for the character and their environment.

When a character has a strong personality, I make them stand out in their environment by creating a strong contrast around them.

After adding base colors, I render everything on one layer. Throughout the process I keep in mind that everything in the composition should lead the viewer's eyes to the character. This is why I chose to highlight some areas, while keeping the background slightly more toned down.

## ENVIRONMENT & MOOD

Environment and mood are very important in children's picture books as they create a world for your character to live in. For *I Am Not a Tree Climber* I drew environments that evoke happiness and wonder, rather than gloominess, as the protagonist has an optimistic outlook throughout the story. I tried to imagine what kind of world this little girl lived in, what her favorite colors were, and what ignited her curiosity in her surroundings.

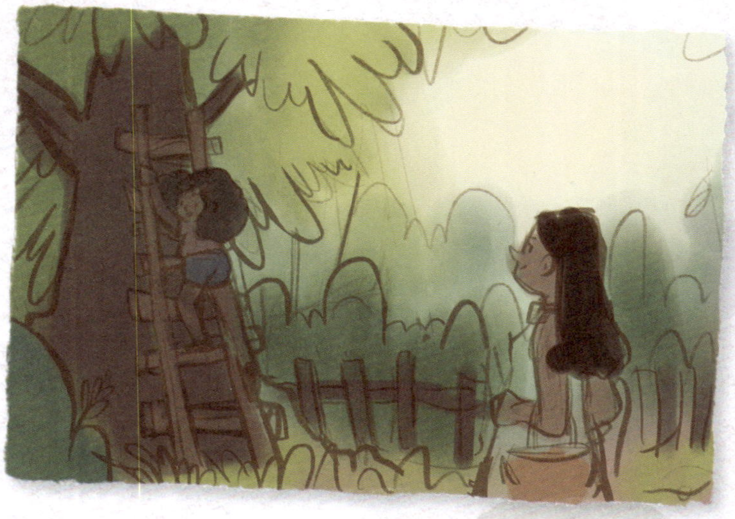

Colors can be tricky, which is why I started with a less saturated palette and created numerous different color schemes before arriving at a final base color.

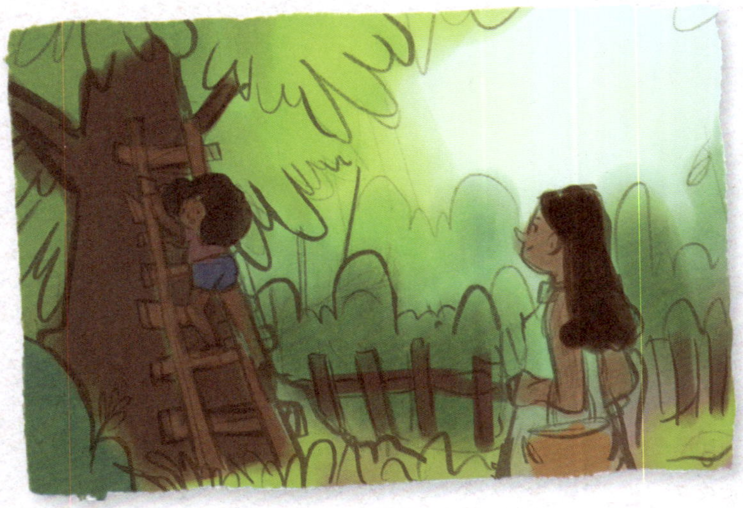

Time of day can influence the mood of an illustration. Setting this scene in the afternoon allowed for a warmer color palette.

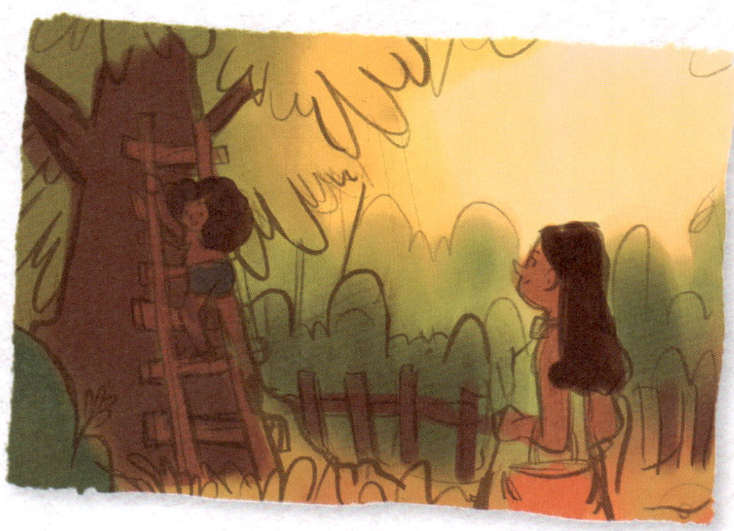

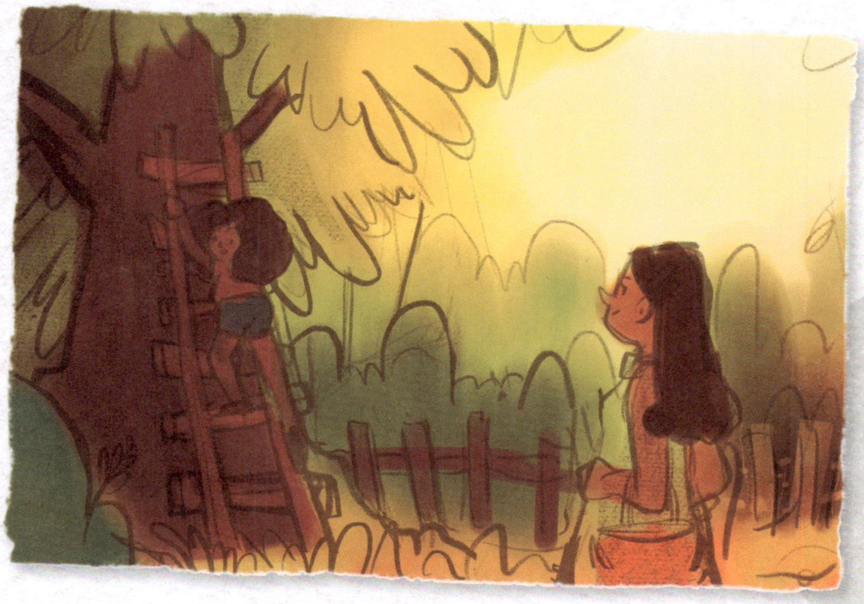

Deciding on the time of day and weather for each scene helps with understanding what colors to choose. For example, a sunny day would call for bright yellows, greens, and other warm, vibrant colors, whereas a rainy day would most likely need dull, unsaturated colors and would make the pages appear a lot darker.

Tonal values are vital as they really help with lighting. They also help to distinguish the importance of the different elements in the composition.

Taking all the steps mentioned on these two pages into consideration resulted in this final spread.

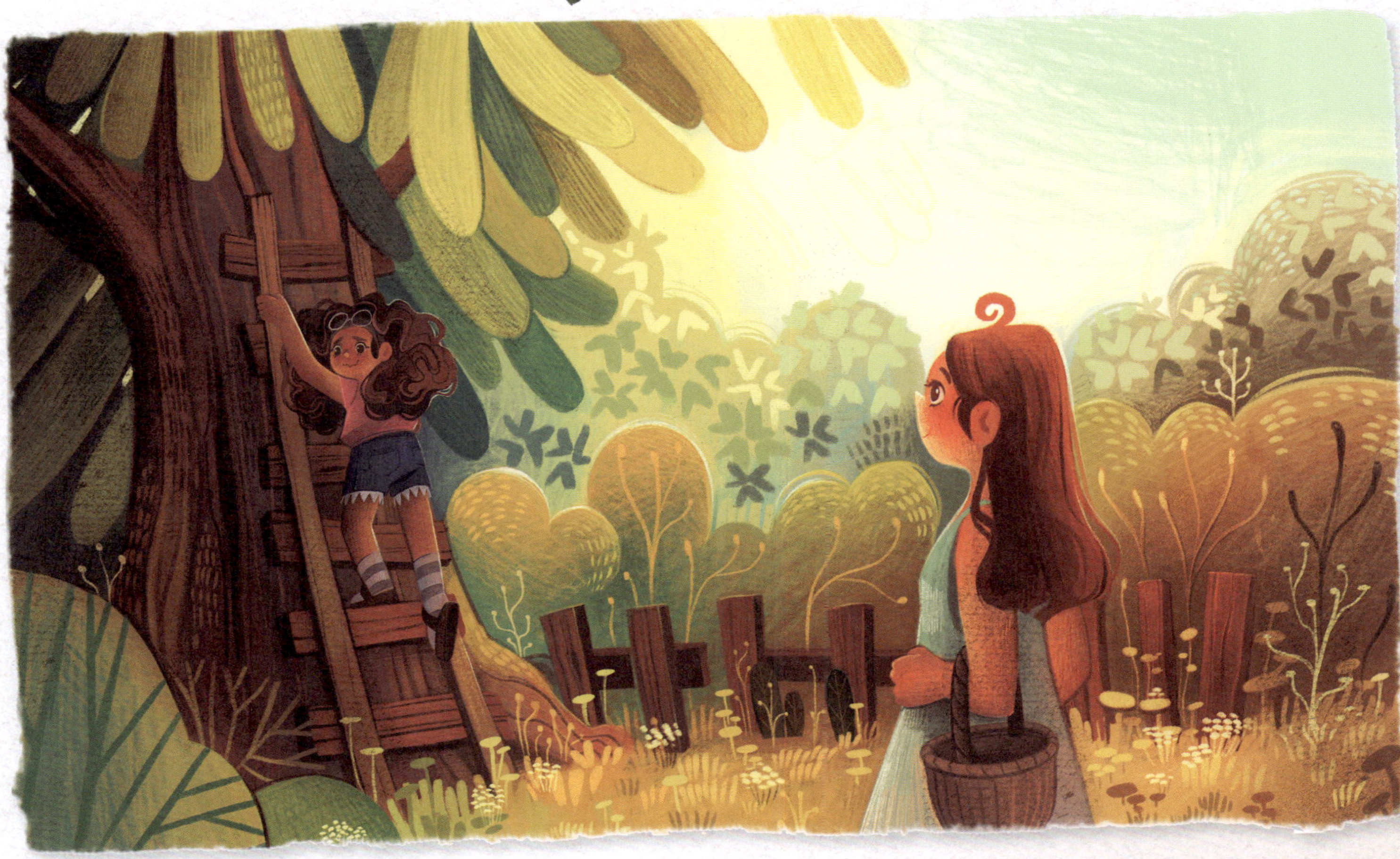

## STYLE

Another important factor in creating these spreads was keeping the same stylistic approach throughout each major part of the story. When the story takes place in the same environment (whether indoors or outdoors), it's important to ensure your details all link together in some way. I made sure the foliage and greenery were similar on each spread, as well as the house and other shapes and details. To make sure everything matches, a useful tip is to roughly sketch out each scene, then look at them together to see what works and what doesn't. Ensuring everything lines up and has the correct placement is also very important in making the setting and composition believable to the reader.

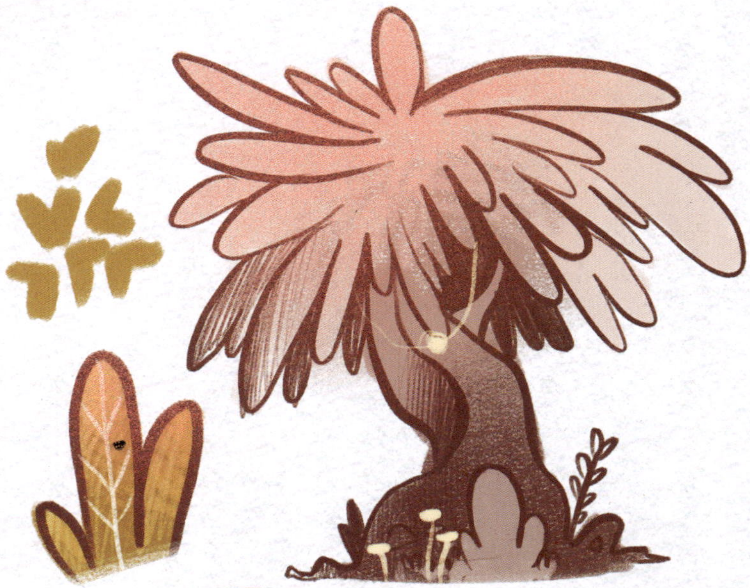

When designing a series of illustrations, taking a cohesive approach will ensure the illustrations work together as a set. I find it useful to create a reference sheet featuring prominent objects and details from the story to refer back to.

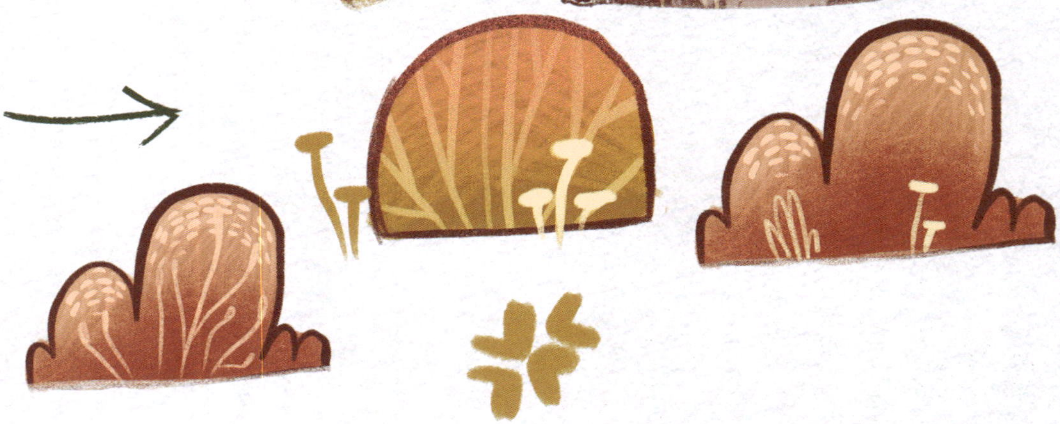

It can also be helpful to make a texture reference sheet. Referring back to your texture guide will prevent you from going overboard and allow you to maintain the same stylistic approach throughout your illustrations.

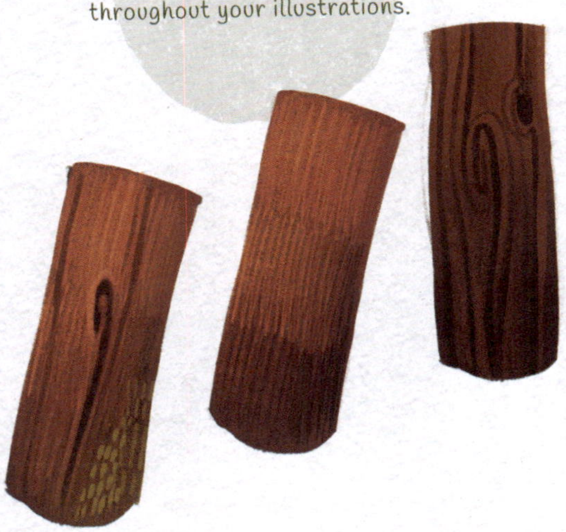

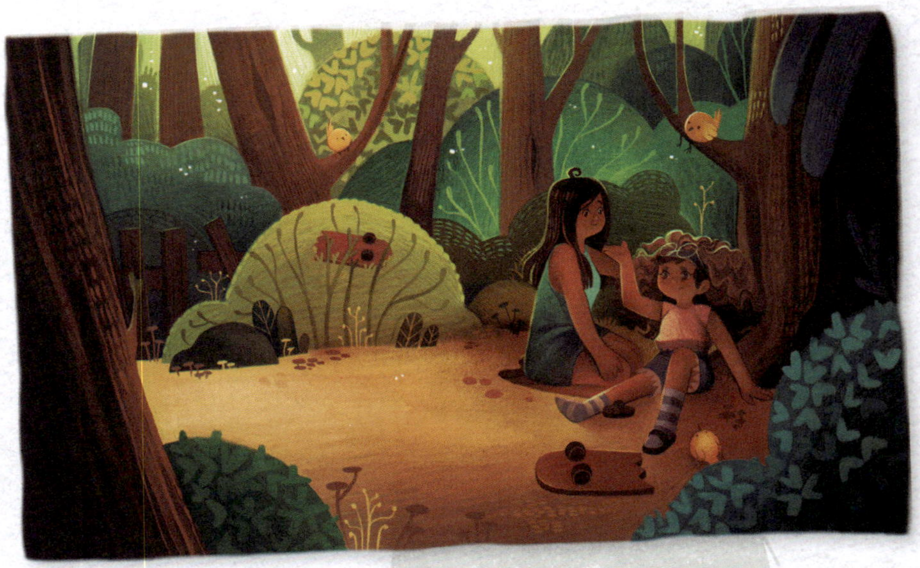

Here is an example of repetitive textures and shapes used throughout one illustration, created using the reference guides.

## SECONDARY ELEMENTS

The use of secondary elements is one of the most important things in a story. These can include objects such as toys or household items, as well as companions such as pets or minor characters. When reading a story manuscript, I like to consider whether my character seems like the messy type or prefers things neat and tidy. Jasminder reminded me of someone who was a bit disorganized, so I designed the indoor scenes with that in mind. When sketching the rough designs for some of the indoor spreads I challenged myself to try to include as many items as I could, arranging them in a disorganized way to portray her playful, slightly messy personality.

Another important aspect to consider is the type of objects that are already included in the story text. The challenge is to decide what to include and what to "mute." I chose what stood out the most to me and illustrated these with more contrast, in comparison to the elements that didn't stand out quite as much.

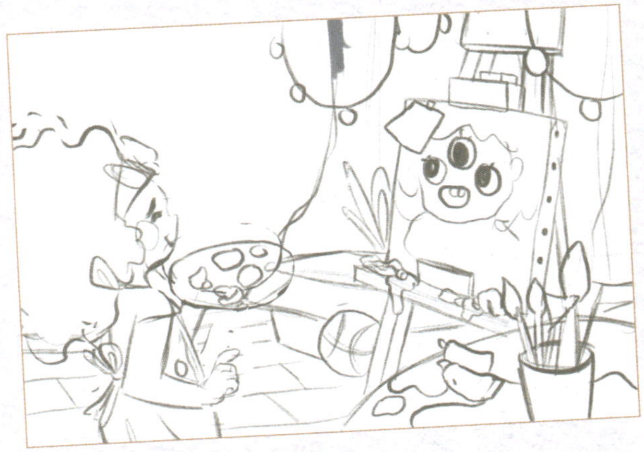

Use the objects in a room to reveal your character's personality. In this painting scene I clustered lots of art supplies together, making sure nothing looked too ordered or neatly lined up. This helped create the idea of disorganization and playfulness.

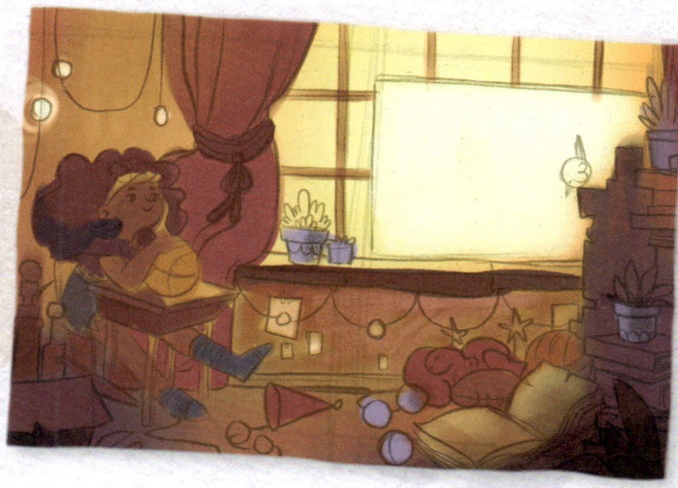

This rough spread shows Jasminder's messy bedroom, where each individual item mentioned in the text can be seen within the illustration.

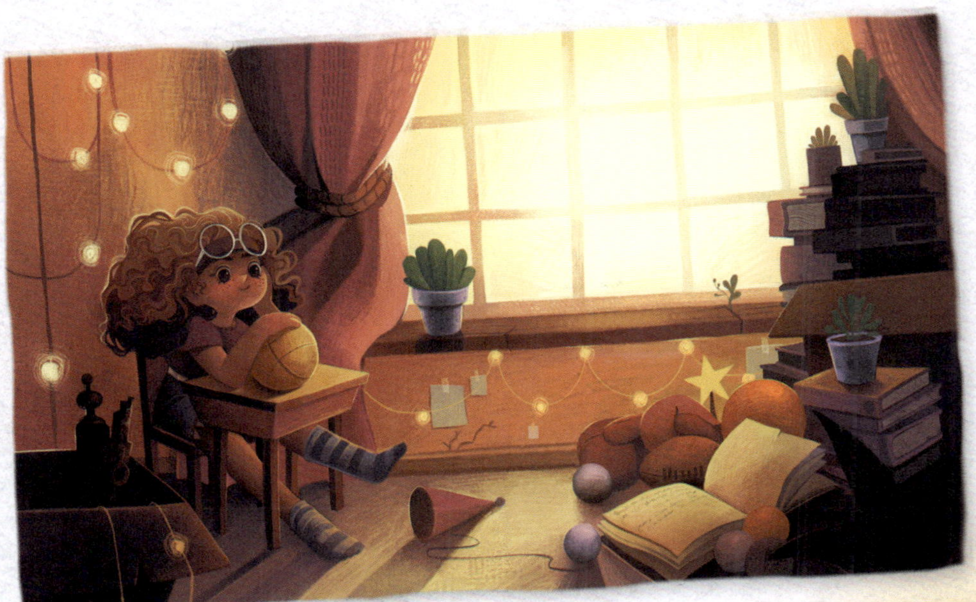

This final spread design shows the difference in tones and contrast of each item. The items I wanted the reader to spot first are more vibrant and make up a larger portion of the room, in comparison to some other less important items. I did this to keep a compositional balance and to divert the reader's focus to particular objects.

# ANALYSIS

Before starting work on the illustrations for *I Am Not a Tree Climber* I had a very different setting in mind, with a clear vision of how some scenes would be illustrated and which color combinations I would use. The placement of the story text and remembering the gutter area both played a part in the illustrations changing for the final spreads. It can be challenging to create an illustration when there is a lot of story text to be included, because I enjoy adding lots of details to my drawings. It can also prove a challenge when the text contains many different characteristics to illustrate. My biggest tip for illustrating a story with a lot of text is to plan out where the text will be placed from the start. Try to create a text box or rough shape to remind you to plan your illustration around it. Sometimes you can take an element of the composition and leave it a little less detailed than others parts, so it can potentially become an area for the text to sit.

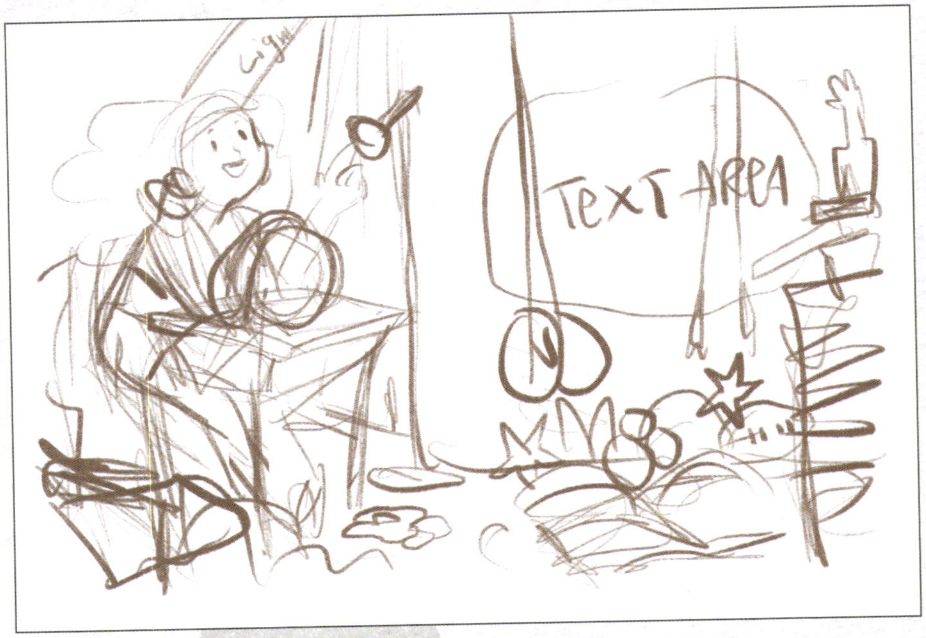


My initial idea sketches are always very rough. Drawing loosely allows me to get my ideas down as fast as I can; then once I'm happy I can start to tweak and adjust them.

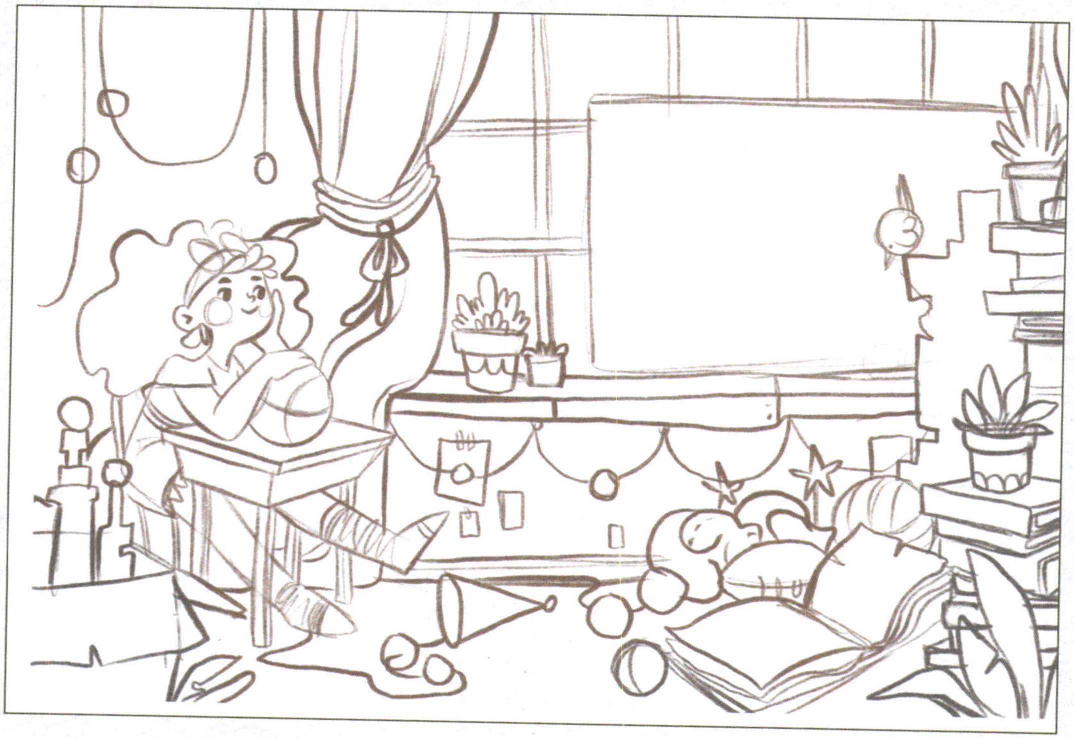

Here is the final line art with a text box. This was particularly challenging because the text had many elements to include and was quite long. After many attempts and adjustments, I finally got it to work. Keep working at it!

I love illustrating children's books – each one is different and I always learn something new each time. My final piece of advice to budding artists is to try to explore new possibilities in every story you create, stepping out of your comfort zone with each new illustration. This will develop your narrative skills as well as your illustrative style. Have fun with it and stay true to your art.

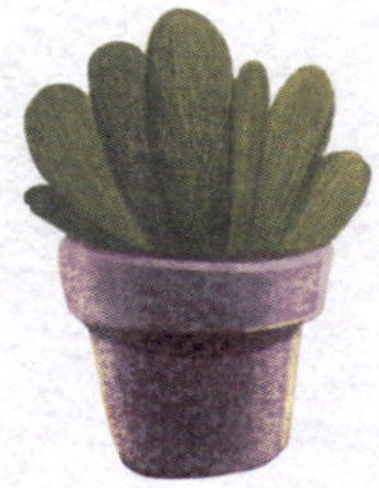

The final version of the opening spread.

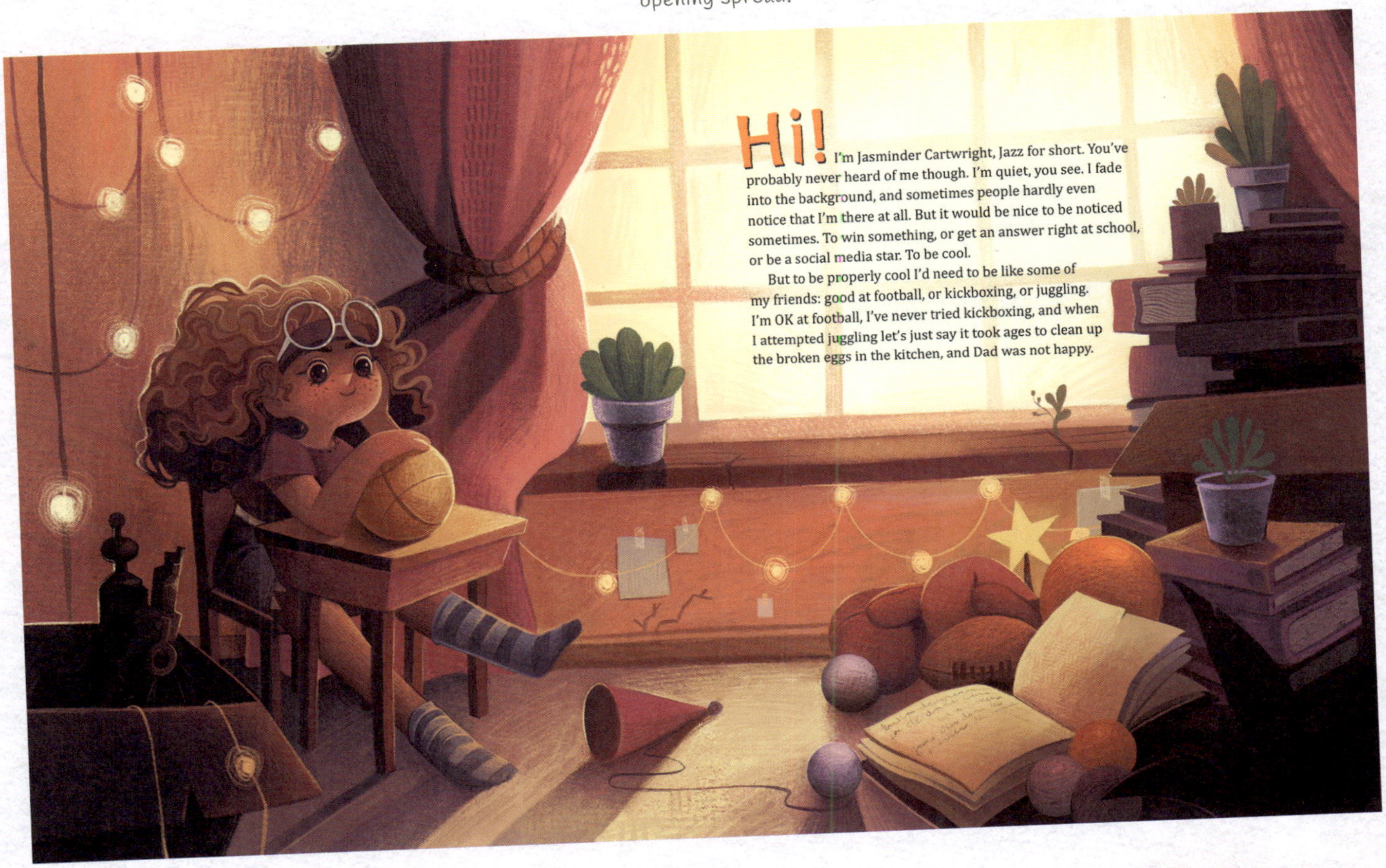


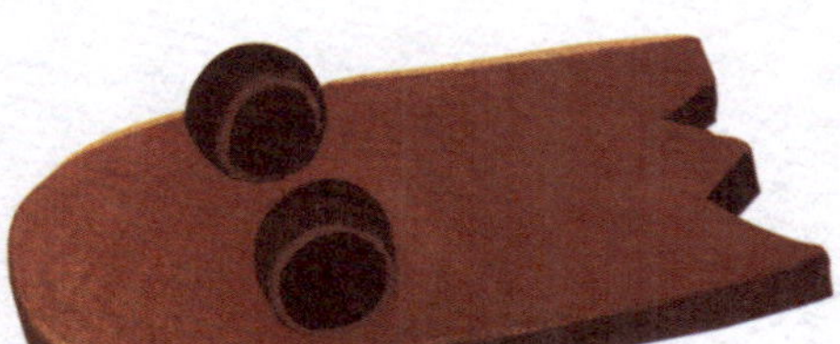

# GLOSSARY

## BY RUTH HAMMOND

**Artist's block**
When an artist struggles to access their creativity to create new work, feels like they have run out of things to draw, or that their work isn't turning out as well as intended.

**Bleed**
Measuring approximately 3-5mm, the bleed is the small border that extends beyond the edge of the page; the excess bit of page that gets cut off when the book is trimmed to size. Artists should ensure any full-page artwork extends to the very edge of the bleed to make sure no white is exposed if the cut is inaccurate.

**Book advance**
Most traditional publishers will give an author an advance against royalties, which is a sum of money based on what they think the book will earn. It covers the cost of the time it will take the illustrator to create the artwork for the book. Once this advance is paid off in sales, the author and illustrator will then receive royalties based on each additional sale.

**Color theory**
Theoretical guidance for mixing colors and creating a specific color combination/color palette to use in a piece of artwork.

**Continuity**
The consistency of the characters, plot, objects, and places over the course of the book. As an illustrator, it's important to convey continuity throughout all of these aspects in the artwork by using consistent character design, color palette, and environment.

**Contract**
A legally binding agreement between two parties. In book illustration, this is usually between the client (publisher or author) and the illustrator to ensure the work is supplied to the client's requirements and that the illustrator is paid for their work.

**Double-page spread**
Full bleed artwork which extends across two adjacent pages, bleeding to the edge of the paper with the gutter in the middle. Double-page spreads are often used to depict a large scene or environment.

**Dummy book**
A mock-up of the book containing draft spreads to show how the artwork and text looks once laid out together, and if anything has been lost down the gutter. It should be the correct size and number of pages.

**End pages**
Pages positioned at the very start and end of a hardcover book, typically consisting of an illustrated pattern. These attach the internal pages to the cover and hide the inside of the cover which is often gray-board. Sometimes the first and final page of the main book block are stuck to the inside covers to create the end pages (page 1 and page 32, for example) – in this case, p2–3 and p30–31 would be patterned or a plain color. Alternatively, sometimes extra sheets of paper are used as end pages, instead.

**Font**
A collection of typed characters with a similar design. These characters include both lowercase and uppercase letters, as well as numbers, punctuation marks, and symbols. Changing the font can alter the look and feel of the text, and can therefore help or hinder the readability of the text, as well as helping to emphasize important words.

**Full-bleed artwork**
Artwork that extends to the edges of the page and into the bleed.

**Gutter**
The central dip in a double-page spread that leads to the binding of perfect bound and hardcover books. Any artwork or text that falls in the gutter will be difficult to read.

**Imprint page**
A page at the start of a book which details the publisher's imprint and copyright information.

**Mood**
Set by the tone, mood is the overall feeling or atmosphere of a text or image, often created by the author's imagery and choice of words.

**Narrative devices**
Common techniques used by the author, and illustrator, to tell a story. These can include: action, conflict, page turns, humor, symbolism, character development, environment, and perspective.

**Pacing**
The pace at which the story is told. This is determined by the length of the scenes, how fast the action moves, and how quickly the reader is given information, all of which are reflected in the accompanying illustrations. Fast-paced scenes, such as action scenes, are better shown through vignette/spot illustrations, whereas slower paced scenes are best shown over a double-page spread.

**Perfect bound**
A type of soft cover (paperback) book binding where adhesive is used to hold the cover and pages together.

**Plagiarism**
When a writer or artist takes someone else's ideas or creative work and passes it off as their own.

**Portfolio**
A collection of work that showcases an artist's best pieces.

**Readability**
The clarity of the artwork and how legible the illustration is; whether the reader will be able to easily distinguish everything that is going on without the aid of the text or an explanation.

**Relatability**
How well the reader can relate to or sympathize with the characters, narrative, and world created on the pages.

**Royalties**
The sum paid to the illustrator and author for each copy of the book sold.

**Single page illustration**
Full bleed artwork that extends over the entirety of a single page.

**Spread**
Two adjacent pages in a book. They may contain separate bits of content, or one full bleed illustration.

**Target audience**
Who the story and/or illustrations are aimed at. This is typically a set age group, but could also include a specific gender or ethnic group. Children's books are usually targeted at different age brackets, such as 0–24 months, 2–4 years, 4–6 years, and 6–8 years.

**Theme**
The subject or main idea that runs through the story. Recurring themes in children's books often include friendship and relationships, belonging and identity, courage, growing up, and family, along with more challenging themes such as racial issues, gender identity, loss, and grief.

**Thumbnailing**
An early stage of visual development that allows artists to draw small, rough sketches (called thumbnails) to work out the initial composition of an illustration.

**Title page**
A single page at the start of the book that features the title of the story. In picture books, the title is usually accompanied by a small illustration.

**Tone**
The feeling, emotion, or atmosphere created by the author or artist through their writing style and choice of words or imagery, setting the mood for the book. It is also linked to theme; a story with challenging themes will have a more grown-up tone.

**Vignette/spot illustrations**
Typically smaller than full bleed artwork, spot illustrations are smaller images that work with and around the text on the page to help tell story moments or to quicken the story pace with action artwork. They can be any shape and don't bleed to the edge of the paper.

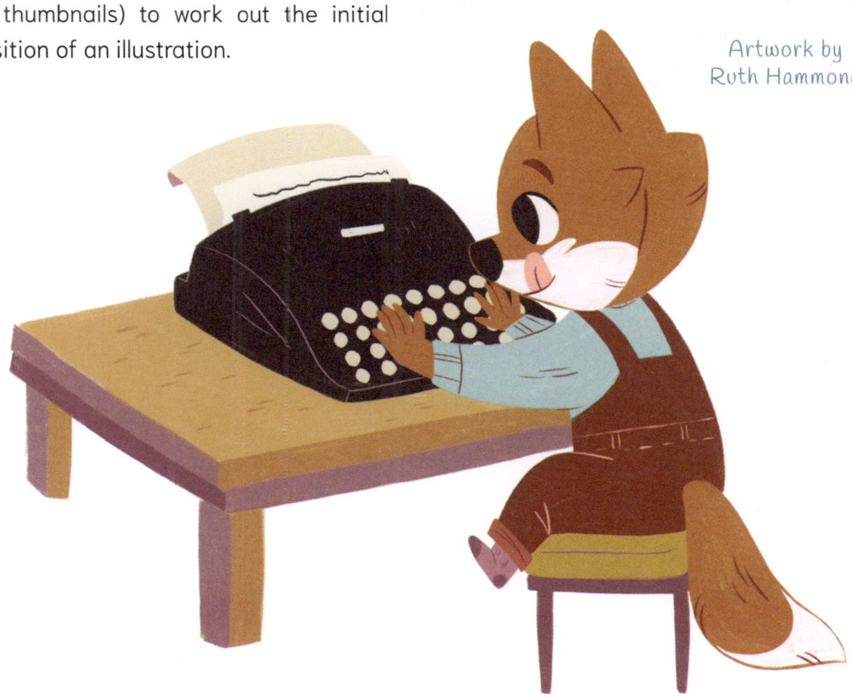

Artwork by Ruth Hammond

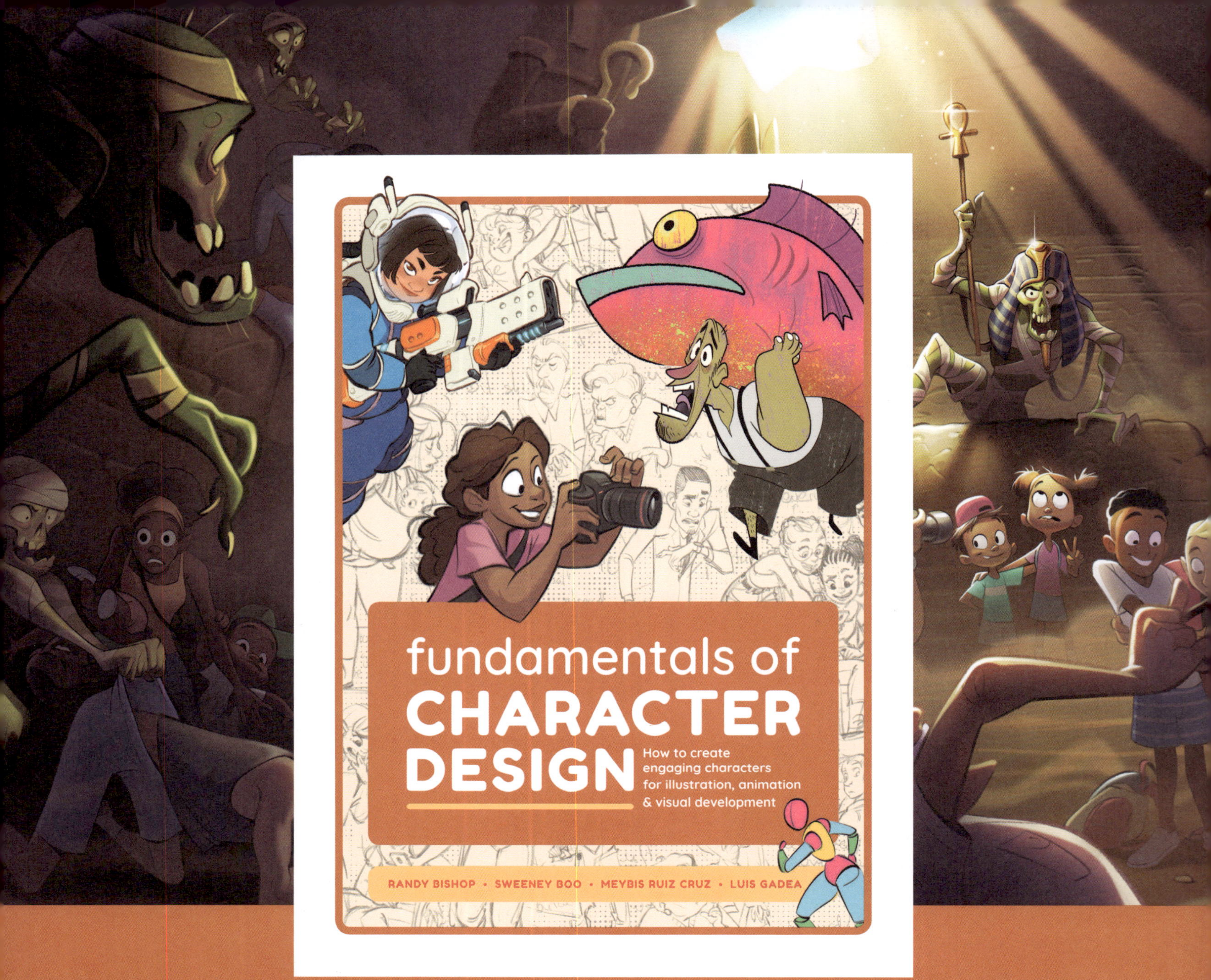
fundamentals of
CHARACTER DESIGN
How to create engaging characters for illustration, animation & visual development
RANDY BISHOP • SWEENEY BOO • MEYBIS RUIZ CRUZ • LUIS GADEA

# **3dtotal**Publishing

3dtotal Publishing is a trailblazing, creative publisher specializing in inspirational and educational resources for artists.

Our titles feature top industry professionals from around the globe who share their experience in skillfully written step-by-step tutorials and fascinating, detailed guides. Illustrated throughout with stunning artwork, these best-selling publications offer creative insight, expert advice, and essential motivation. Fans of digital art will enjoy our comprehensive volumes covering Adobe Photoshop, Procreate, and Blender, as well as our superb titles based around character design, including *Fundamentals of Character Design* and *Creating Characters for the Entertainment Industry*. The dedicated, high-quality blend of instruction and inspiration also extends to traditional art. Titles covering a range of techniques, genres, and abilities allow your creativity to flourish while building essential skills.

Well-established within the industry, we now offer over 100 titles and counting, many of which have been translated into multiple languages around the world. With something for every artist, we are proud to say that our books offer the 3dtotal package:

**LEARN • CREATE • SHARE**

---

**Visit us at 3dtotalpublishing.com**

3dtotal Publishing is part of 3dtotal.com, a leading website for CG artists founded by Tom Greenway in 1999.

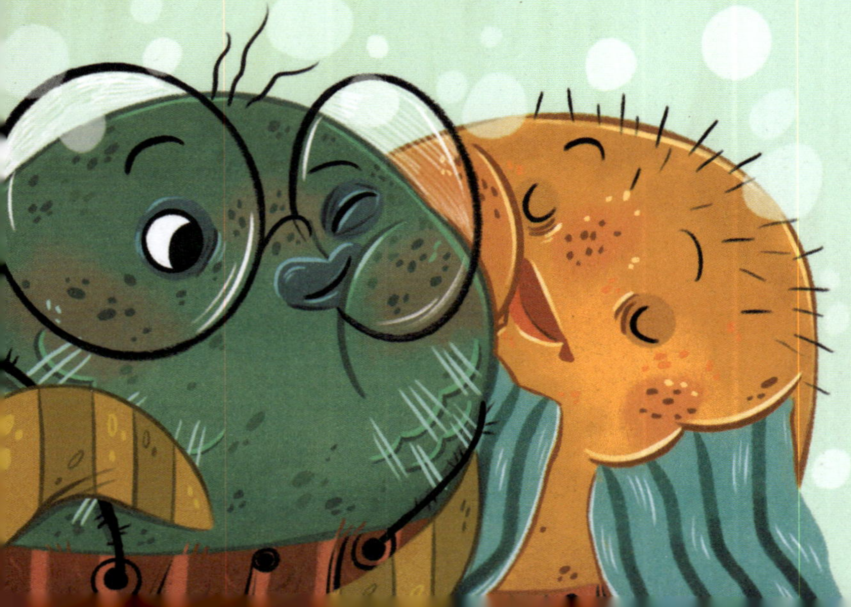

Artwork by Laura Proietti